Children's Literature Review

Guide to Gale Literary Criticism Series

For criticism on	Consult these Gale series
Authors now living or who died after December 31, 1959	*CONTEMPORARY LITERARY CRITICISM (CLC)*
Authors who died between 1900 and 1959	*TWENTIETH-CENTURY LITERARY CRITICISM (TCLC)*
Authors who died between 1800 and 1899	*NINETEENTH-CENTURY LITERATURE CRITICISM (NCLC)*
Authors who died between 1400 and 1799	*LITERATURE CRITICISM FROM 1400 TO 1800 (LC)* *SHAKESPEAREAN CRITICISM (SC)*
Authors who died before 1400	*CLASSICAL AND MEDIEVAL LITERATURE CRITICISM (CMLC)*
Black writers of the past two hundred years	*BLACK LITERATURE CRITICISM (BLC)*
Authors of books for children and young adults	*CHILDREN'S LITERATURE REVIEW (CLR)*
Dramatists	*DRAMA CRITICISM (DC)*
Hispanic writers of the late nineteenth and twentieth centuries	*HISPANIC LITERATURE CRITICISM (HLC)*
Native North American writers and orators of the eighteenth, nineteenth, and twentieth centuries	*NATIVE NORTH AMERICAN LITERATURE (NNAL)*
Poets	*POETRY CRITICISM (PC)*
Short story writers	*SHORT STORY CRITICISM (SSC)*
Major authors from the Renaissance to the present	*WORLD LITERATURE CRITICISM, 1500 TO THE PRESENT (WLC)*

ISSN 0362-4145

volume 45

Children's Literature Review

Excerpts from Reviews,
Criticism, and Commentary
on Books for Children
and Young People

Linda R. Andres
Editor

GALE

DETROIT • NEW YORK • TORONTO • LONDON

STAFF

Linda R. Andres, *Editor*

Charity Ann Dorgan, Mary Gillis, Alan Hedblad, Melissa Hill, Motoko Huthwaite, Paul Loeber,
Sean McCready, Zoran Minderovic, Diane Telgen, Crystal Towns, Debra Wells, *Contributing Editors*

Marilyn Allen, *Assistant Editor*

Joyce Nakamura, *Managing Editor*

Susan M. Trosky, *Permissions Manager*
Maria L. Franklin, *Permissions Specialist*
Michele M. Lonoconus, *Permissions Associate*
Andrea D. Grady, *Permissions Assistant*

Victoria B. Cariappa, *Research Manager*
Cheryl L. Warnock, *Project Coordinator*
Laura C. Bissey, Tamara C. Nott, Tracie Richardson, Norma Sawaya, Robert Whaley, *Research Associates*

Mary Beth Trimper, *Production Director*
Deborah Milliken, *Production Assistant*

Mikal Ansari, *Macintosh Artist*
Randy Bassett, *Image Database Supervisor*
Robert Duncan, Michael Logusz, *Imaging Specialists*
Pamela A. Reed, *Photography Coordinator*

∞™ This book is printed on acid-free paper that meets the minimum requirements of American National Standard for Information Sciences—Permanence Paper for Printed Library Materials, ANSI Z39.48-1984.

Library of Congress Catalog Card Number 76-643301
ISBN 0-7876-1139-5
ISSN 0362-4145
Printed in the United States of America

10 9 8 7 6 5 4 3 2 1

Contents

Preface   vii
Acknowledgments   xi

Preface

Literature for children and young adults has evolved into both a respected branch of creative writing and a successful industry. Currently, books for young readers are considered among the most popular segments of publishing. Criticism of juvenile literature is instrumental in recording the literary or artistic development of the creators of children's books as well as the trends and controversies that result from changing values or attitudes about young people and their literature. Designed to provide a permanent, accessible record of this ongoing scholarship, *Children's Literature Review (CLR)* presents parents, teachers, and librarians—those responsible for bringing children and books together—with the opportunity to make informed choices when selecting reading materials for the young. In addition, *CLR* provides researchers of children's literature with easy access to a wide variety of critical information from English-language sources in the field. Users will find balanced overviews of the careers of the authors and illustrators of the books that children and young adults are reading; these entries, which contain excerpts from published criticism in books and periodicals, assist users by sparking ideas for papers and assignments and suggesting supplementary and classroom reading. Ann L. Kalkhoff, president and editor of *Children's Book Review Service Inc.,* writes that "*CLR* has filled a gap in the field of children's books, and it is one series that will never lose its validity or importance."

Scope of the Series

Each volume of *CLR* profiles the careers of a selection of authors and illustrators of books for children and young adults from preschool through high school. Author lists in each volume reflect:

- an international scope.

- representation of authors of all eras.

- the variety of genres covered by children's and/or YA literature: picture books, fiction, nonfiction, poetry, folklore, and drama.

Although the focus of the series is on authors new to *CLR*, entries will be updated as the need arises.

Organization of This Book

An entry consists of the following elements: author heading, author portrait, author introduction, excerpts of criticism (each preceded by a bibliographical citation), and illustrations, when available.

- The **Author Heading** consists of the author's name followed by birth and death dates. The portion of the name outside the parentheses denotes the form under which the author is most frequently published. If the majority of the author's works for children were written under a pseudonym, the pseudonym will be listed in the author heading and the real name given on the first line of the author introduction. Also located at the beginning of the introduction are any other pseudonyms used by the author in writing for children and any name variations, including transliterated forms for authors whose languages use nonroman alphabets. Uncertainty as to a birth or death date is indicated by question marks.

- An **Author Portrait** is included when available.

- The **Author Introduction** contains information designed to introduce an author to *CLR* users by presenting an overview of the author's themes and styles, biographical facts that relate to the author's literary career or critical responses to the author's works, and information about major awards and prizes the author has received. The introduction begins by identifying the nationality of the author and by listing the genres in which s/he has written for children and young adults. Introductions also list a group of representative titles for which the author or illustrator being profiled is best known; this section, which begins with the words "major works include," follows the genre line of the introduction. For seminal figures, a listing of major works about the author follows when appropriate, highlighting important biographies about the author or illustrator that are not excerpted in the entry. The centered heading "Introduction" announces the body of the text.

- **Criticism** is located in three sections: **Author's Commentary** (when available), **General Commentary** (when available), and **Title Commentary** (commentary on specific titles).

  - The **Author's Commentary** presents background material written by the author or by an interviewer. This commentary may cover a specific work or several works. Author's commentary on more than one work appears after the author introduction, while commentary on an individual book follows the title entry heading.

  - The **General Commentary** consists of critical excerpts that consider more than one work by the author or illustrator being profiled. General commentary is preceded by the critic's name in boldface type or, in the case of unsigned criticism, by the title of the journal. *CLR* also features entries that emphasize general criticism on the oeuvre of an author or illustrator. When appropriate, a selection of reviews is included to supplement the general commentary.

  - The **Title Commentary** begins with the title entry headings, which precede the criticism on a title and cite publication information on the work being reviewed. Title headings list the title of the work as it appeared in its first English-language edition. The first English-language publication date of each work (unless otherwise noted) is listed in parentheses following the title. Differing U.S. and British titles follow the publication date within the parentheses. When a work is written by an individual other than the one being profiled, as is the case when illustrators are featured, the parenthetical material following the title cites the author of the work before listing its publication date.

    Entries in each title commentary section consist of critical excerpts on the author's individual works, arranged chronologically by publication date. The entries generally contain two to seven reviews per title, depending on the stature of the book and the amount of criticism it has generated. The editors select titles that reflect the entire scope of the author's literary contribution, covering each genre and subject. An effort is made to reprint criticism that represents the full range of each title's reception, from the year of its initial publication to current assessments. Thus, the reader is provided with a record of the author's critical history. Publication information (such as publisher names and book prices) and parenthetical numerical references (such as footnotes or page and line references to specific editions of works) have been deleted at the discretion of the editors to provide smoother reading of the text.

- Centered headings introduce each section, in which criticism is arranged chronologically; beginning with Volume 35, each excerpt is preceded by a boldface source heading for easier access by readers. Within the text, titles by authors being profiled are also highlighted in boldface type.

- Selected excerpts are preceded by **Explanatory Annotations,** which provide information on the critic or work of criticism to enhance the reader's understanding of the excerpt.

- A complete **Bibliographical Citation** designed to facilitate the location of the original book or article precedes each piece of criticism.

- Numerous **Illustrations** are featured in *CLR*. For entries on illustrators, an effort has been made to include illustrations that reflect the characteristics discussed in the criticism. Entries on authors who do not illustrate their own works may also include photographs and other illustrative material pertinent to their careers.

Special Features: Entries on Illustrators

Entries on authors who are also illustrators will occasionally feature commentary on selected works illustrated but not written by the author being profiled. These works are strongly associated with the illustrator and have received critical acclaim for their art. By including critical comment on works of this type, the editors wish to provide a more complete representation of the artist's career. Criticism on these works has been chosen to stress artistic, rather than literary, contributions. Title entry headings for works illustrated by the author being profiled are arranged chronologically within the entry by date of publication and include notes identifying the author of the illustrated work. In order to provide easier access for users, all titles illustrated by the subject of the entry are boldfaced.

CLR also includes entries on prominent illustrators who have contributed to the field of children's literature. These entries are designed to represent the development of the illustrator as an artist rather than as a literary stylist. The illustrator's section is organized like that of an author, with two exceptions: the introduction presents an overview of the illustrator's styles and techniques rather than outlining his or her literary background, and the commentary written by the illustrator on his or her works is called "illustrator's commentary" rather than "author's commentary." All titles of books containing illustrations by the artist being profiled are highlighted in boldface type.

Other Features: Acknowledgments, Indexes

- The **Acknowledgments** section, which immediately follows the preface, lists the sources from which material has been reprinted in the volume. It does not, however, list every book or periodical consulted for the volume.

- The **Cumulative Index to Authors** lists all of the authors who have appeared in *CLR* with cross-references to the biographical, autobiographical, and literary criticism series published by Gale Research. A full listing of the series titles appears before the first page of the indexes of this volume.

- The **Cumulative Index to Nationalities** lists authors alphabetically under their respective nationalities. Author names are followed by the volume number(s) in which they appear.

- The **Cumulative Index to Titles** lists titles covered in *CLR* followed by the volume and page number where criticism begins.

A Note to the Reader

CLR is one of several critical references sources in the Literature Criticism Series published by Gale Research. When writing papers, students who quote directly from any volume in the Literature Criticism

Series may use the following general forms to footnote reprinted criticism. The first example pertains to material drawn from periodicals, the second to material reprinted from books.

[1]T. S. Eliot, "John Donne," *The Nation and the Athenaeum,* 33 (9 June 1923), 321-32; excerpted and reprinted in *Literature Criticism from 1400 to 1800,* Vol. 10, ed. James E. Person, Jr. (Detroit: Gale Research, 1989), pp. 28-9.

[1]Henry Brooke, *Leslie Brooke and Johnny Crow* (Frederick Warne, 1982); excerpted and reprinted in *Children's Literature Review,* Vol. 20, ed. Gerard J. Senick (Detroit: Gale Research, 1990), p. 47.

Suggestions Are Welcome

In response to various suggestions, several features have been added to *CLR* since the beginning of the series, including author entries on retellers of traditional literature as well as those who have been the first to record oral tales and other folklore; entries on prominent illustrators featuring commentary on their styles and techniques; entries on authors whose works are considered controversial; occasional entries devoted to criticism on a single work or a series of works; sections in author introductions that list major works by and about the author or illustrator being profiled; explanatory notes that provide information on the critic or work of criticism to enhance the usefulness of the excerpt; more extensive illustrative material, such as holographs of manuscript pages and photographs of people and places pertinent to the careers of the authors and artists; a cumulative nationality index for easy access to authors by nationality; and occasional guest essays written specifically for *CLR* by prominent critics on subjects of their choice.

Readers who wish to suggest authors to appear in future volumes, or who have other suggestions, are cordially invited to contact the editor. By mail: Editor, *Children's Literature Review,* Gale Research, 835 Penobscot Bldg., 645 Griswold St., Detroit, MI 48226-4094; by telephone: (800) 347-GALE; by fax: (313) 961-6599; by E-mail: CYA@Gale.com.

Acknowledgments

The editors wish to thank the copyright holders of the excerpted criticism included in this volume and the permissions managers of many book and magazine publishing companies for assisting us in securing reproduction rights. We are also grateful to the staffs of the Detroit Public Library, the Library of Congress, the University of Detroit Mercy Library, Wayne State University Purdy/Kresge Library Complex, and the University of Michigan Libraries for making their resources available to us. Following is a list of the copyright holders who have granted us permission to reproduce material in this volume of *CLR*. Every effort has been made to trace copyright, but if omissions have been made, please let us know.

COPYRIGHTED EXCERPTS IN *CLR*, VOLUME 45, WERE REPRINTED FROM THE FOLLOWING PERIODICALS AND BOOKS:

The ALAN Review, v. 9, Fall, 1981; v. 13, Spring, 1986. Reproduced by permission.—*America,* v. 135, December 11, 1976. © 1976. All rights reserved. Reproduced with permission of America Press, Inc., 106 West 56th Street, New York, NY 10019.—*Appraisal: Science Books for Young People,* v. 7, Fall, 1974; v. 9, Winter, 1976; v. 19, Summer, 1986; v. 19, Fall, 1986; v. 24, Spring-Summer, 1991. Copyright © 1974, 1976, 1986, 1991 by the Children's Science Book Review Committee. All reproduced by permission.—*Best Sellers,* v. 37, February, 1978; v. 38, March, 1979; v. 41, May, 1981. Copyright 1978, 1979, 1981 by the University of Scranton. All reproduced by permission of the publisher.—*The Book Report,* v. 3, September-October, 1984; v. 8, May-June, 1989. © Copyright 1984, 1989 by Linworth Publishing, Inc., Worthington, Ohio. Both reproduced with permission.—*Book Window,* v. 8, Spring, 1981. © 1981 S.C.B.A. and contributors. Reproduced by permission of the publisher. —*Booklist,* v. 72, January 15, 1976; v. 72, February 15, 1976; v. 73, March 1, 1977; v. 73, June 1, 1977; v. 74, April 15, 1978; v. 74, June 15, 1978; v. 75, July 15, 1979; v. 76, January 1, 1980; v. 77, September 1, 1980; v. 76, December 15, 1979; v. 77, March 15, 1981; v. 77, July 1, 1981; v. 78, November 1, 1981; v. 78, May 1, 1982; v. 79, December 15, 1982; v. 79, April 15, 1983; v. 80, September 1, 1983; v. 80, October 1, 1983; v. 80, June 1, 1984; v. 80, June 15, 1984; v. 81, September 1, 1984; v. 81, April 1, 1985; v. 81, April 15, 1985; v. 81, July, 1985; v. 82, September 15, 1985; v. 82, October 15, 1985; v. 82, December 1, 1985; v. 82, December 15, 1985; v. 82, March 1, 1986; v. 82, June 15, 1986; v. 82, September 15, 1986; v. 83, March 15, 1987; v. 84, September 1, 1987; v. 84, October 15, 1987; v. 84, January 1, 1988; v. 84, March 15, 1988; v. 84, August, 1988; v. 85, September 1, 1988; v. 85, October 15, 1988; v. 85, February 15, 1989; v. 85, April 1, 1989; v. 85, April 15, 1989; v. 85, May 1, 1989; v. 85, July, 1989; v. 85, August, 1989; v. 86, November 1, 1989; v.86, February 15, 1990; v. 86, May 1, 1990; v. 86, August, 1990; v. 87, December 1, 1990; v. 87, December 15, 1990; v. 87, January 15, 1991; v. 87, February 11, 1991; v. 87, March 15, 1991; v. 87, May 15, 1991; v.87, July, 1991; v. 88, September 1, 1991; v. 88, January 1, 1992; v. 88, March 15, 1992; v. 88, April 15, 1992; v. 88, May 1, 1992; v. 88, June 15, 1992; v. 89, September 15, 1992; v. 89, November 1, 1992; v. 89, March 1, 1993; v. 89, July, 1993; v. 90, October 1, 1993; v. 90, December 1, 1993; v. 90, January 1, 1994; v. 90, February 15, 1994; v. 90, March 15, 1994; v. 91, September 15, 1994; v. 91, November 1, 1994; v. 91, January 15, 1995; v. 91, February 15, 1995; v. 91, April 15, 1995; v. 92, September 1, 1995; v. 92, October 1, 1995; v. 92, February 1, 1996; v. 92, April 1, 1996. Copyright © 1976, 1977, 1978, 1979, 1980, 1981, 1982, 1983, 1984, 1985, 1986,1987, 1988, 1989, 1990,1991, 1992, 1993, 1994, 1995, 1996 by the American Library Association. All reproduced by permission of the publisher.—*The Booklist,* v. 67, February 1, 1971; v. 69, July 1, 1973; v. 70, December 1, 1973; v. 70, April 1, 1974; v. 71, December 1, 1974; v. 72, September 1, 1975; v. 72, November 15, 1975. Copyright © 1971, 1973, 1974, 1975 by the American Library Association. All reproduced by permission.—*Books,* London, v. 3, October, 1989. Reproduced by permission. —*Books for Keeps,* n. 35, November, 1985; n. 41, January, 1986; n. 46, September, 1987; n. 71, November, 1991; n. 72, January, 1993; n. 73, March, 1993; n. 76, September, 1992; n. 80, May, 1993; n. 82, September, 1993; n. 83, November, 1993; n. 84, January, 1994; n. 86, May, 1994; n. 93, July, 1995; n. 97, March, 1996. Copyright © 1985, 1986, 1987, 1991, 1992, 1993, 1994, 1995, 1996 by School Bookshop Association. All reproduced by permission of the publisher.—*Books for Young People,* v. 1, October, 1987 for "Past and Present Merge in Painful, Haunting Tales" by Peter Carver./v. 3, February, 1989 for a review of "The Third Magic" by Joan McGrath. Reproduced by permission of the Literary Estate of Joan McGrath. Both reproduced by permission of the author.—*Books for Your*

ILLUSTRATIONS APPEARING IN *CLR*, VOLUME 45, WERE REPRODUCED FROM THE FOLLOWING SOURCES:

Children's
Literature
Review

Mirra Ginsburg

Russian-born American storyteller, editor, critic, and translator.

Major works include *The Sun's Asleep Behind the Hill* (1982), *Four Brave Sailors* (1987), *The Chinese Mirror* (1988), *Asleep, Asleep* (1992), and *The King Who Tried to Fry an Egg on His Head* (1994).

INTRODUCTION

Acclaimed as a storyteller, Ginsburg is widely recognized for her efforts to bring folktales from many cultures, including her native Russia, to the English-speaking world. In creating English-language versions of many known—and some lesser-known—folk stories, she combines her talents as a fluent and engaging storyteller, editor, translator, linguist, and folklorist. Ginsburg writes picture books for small children and often collaborates with noted artists such as Caldecott Honor winner Nancy Tafuri, creating work that appeals to children who are learning to read. Her best work has a timeless, universal quality that older children and even young adults easily respond to. For example, stories such *The Sun's Asleep Behind the Hill* speak to humankind's timeless fascination with celestial bodies. The sun, as Stith Thompson observed in his 1946 work *The Folktale*, may "not furnish a sufficiently broad scope for the folk imagination," but Ginsburg richly compensates for this somewhat restricted imaginative scope by tapping into fundamental mythological motifs, such as day and night, which inform many folk narratives, lending them immense emotional power. Indeed, the question "Where does the sun go?" may not inspire an intricate verbal tapestry of brilliantly varied images, but it contains a tremendous power that affects the reader on a pre-verbal level of consciousness. As Leonard S. Marcus has observed in his review of *The Sun's Asleep Behind the Hill*, the effect of the unusual arrangement of image and text in this story is "a rhythmic binding of image and emotions such as is always the nightsong or lullaby's secret subject." *Asleep, Asleep* exemplifies Ginsburg's mastery of language, in general, and her ability to transmute the hypnotic cadences of A. Vvedensky's Russian verse that inspired her work, in particular. Ginsburg's text, as Lauralyn Persson remarks, "is simple and repetitive, with just enough variation to avoid monotony." This prose lullaby draws on the power of language to create what a *Kirkus Review* critic described as "a lovely litany of . . . subtly modulated responses," which, in Meg Wolitzer's words, "brings us right into the still heart of the night."

Ginsburg's most distinctive works, critics assert, are her picture books, created in collaboration with artists. Indeed, these works, which exhibit a delicate, and suggestive, balance of image, poetic and visual, and verbal so-

nority, have received considerable critical acclaim. However, commentators have also praised her efforts to acquaint her readers with numerous folk traditions by creating English-language versions of stories from Siberia and Central Asia, as exemplified by such books as *The Master of the Winds and Other Tales from Siberia* (1970) and *The Kaha Bird: Tales from the Steppes of Central Asia* (1971). *The Kaha Bird*, which includes Tuvan, Tatar, Kazakh, Uygur, Tadzhik, Uzbek, Kirghiz, and Turkmenian stories, non-Russian tales from Russia and narratives from the Asian lands of the former Soviet Union, reveal a world that is still enigmatic and mysterious to Russians and Westerners alike. Incorporated into the Russian empire in the nineteenth century, the Central Asian lands, as Ginsburg explains in the introduction to her book, enjoy a rich cultural legacy, as evidenced by the Chinese, Indian, and Persian influences found in the regional folklore, as well as by the intersecting Christian, Moslem, and Buddhist communities.

In her retellings of traditional Russian tales, Ginsburg offers narratives presenting a variety of folk-motifs, including magic objects, animals with human traits, extraordinary events, heroes, fools, and deception. A passionate folklorist, she has found inspiration in a large variety of themes and narrative style, always willing, and able, to retell very old stories in a new and beguiling way. Yet Ginsburg, as commentators have noted, is an author who easily crosses the boundaries of genres. As a translator, she became interested in contemporary Russian children's literature, finding themes and ideas in the works of writers such as Kornei Chukovsky, the master of nonsense verse, and Daniil Kharms, who wrote for children and also produced absurdist stories for adults, which the Soviet rulers deemed insulting and subversive. In adapting her literary sources, Ginsburg displays her fascination with and mastery of language by focusing on poetic incantation, capturing a mythic dimension that folklore and literature share, and suspending the boundaries of genre and language.

Biographical Information

Born in Bobruisk, USSR (now Belarus), Ginsburg started writing as a child. Her education was interrupted when she left the USSR with her family. She lived in Latvia and Canada, finally settling in the United States. When she learned English, Ginsburg began writing again, trying a variety of genres. In order to earn a living, however, she turned to translation, eventually producing critically acclaimed translations of avant-garde writers and Russian classics, including Mikhail Bulgakov, Evgeny Zamyatin, Aleksei Remizov, and Andrei Platonov. The novels *Master and Margarita* (1967), by Bulgakov, and *We* (1972), by Zamyatin, both translated by Ginsburg, are numbered among the greatest accomplishments of twentieth-century Russian literature. She also provided introductory essays, explaining the genesis, structure, and themes of these works in the context of Soviet history. In addition, Ginsburg translated anthologies of Soviet science fiction, *The Diary of Nina Kosterina* (1968), a wartime diary for young adults, and *The White Ship* (1972), a novel by the Kirghiz writer Chingiz Aitmatov.

Major Works

In *Four Brave Sailors*, inspired by Daniil Kharms, Ginsburg describes a dream sequence: in a child's dream, four toy mice come to life, start on a perilous sea journey, brave a variety of calamities, then give up, turning back into toys, after spotting the young dreamer's cat. Ginsburg's text, which a *Kirkus Review* critic found "perfectly cadenced, with touches of both humor and mystery," explores the ambiguous realm between sleep and wakefulness, dreams and reality, striking a narrative balance which leads to an elegant ending but retains the story's magic. Reviewers also praised *The Chinese Mirror*, in which Ginsburg develops the magic object motif to weave a compelling narrative of illusion and misunderstanding. Seeing her reflection in a mirror that her husband had brought from China, a young wife becomes furious, because, not knowing what a mirror is, she sees the image of a stranger, perhaps a competitor. The mirror causes much distress, and a balance is re-established when it is broken into a hundred splinters. As a reviewer in *Publishers Weekly* noted, Ginsburg's "poetic and sparse retelling brings freshness and joy to this tale." Ginsburg relays another tale about jealousy in the Russian folktale *The King Who Tried to Fry an Egg on His Head*. A king marries off his daughters and then is envious because they are living better than he is. Heide Piehler described the tale as a "smooth and lively retelling." In *The Old Man and His Birds* (1994), which Ginsburg found in a collection of the nineteenth-century Russian folklorist Vladimir Dal, she constructs an elaborate riddle. As the old man's golden robes change colors, the landscape changes; birds fly out of his sleeves, presenting the reader with riddles within riddles and alerting him or her to the enigmatic nature of our world. Ginsburg's riddle, as Margaret Bush wrote, "superbly celebrat[es] the cycle of the seasons" and presents "symbol in a readily discernible guise." Indeed, Bush's observation summarizes Ginsburg's ability to illuminate the riddles that folk traditions have kept alive.

Awards

Ginsburg received the National Translation Grant in 1967, and the Lewis Carroll Shelf Award for her translation of *The Diary of Nina Kosterina* in 1972. She earned a Mildred L. Batchelder nomination for *The Kaha Bird: Tales from the Steppes of Central Asia* in 1973, and *The White Ship* was nominated the following year. *The Chick and the Duckling* was a Children's Book Showcase title, and Ginsburg was awarded a Guggenheim fellowship to translate the works of Alexey Remizov.

TITLE COMMENTARY

📖 *THE FOX AND THE HARE* (retold by Mirra Ginsburg, 1969)

Nell Miller

SOURCE: "Once Upon a Time, Etc.," in *The Christian Science Monitor*, November 6, 1969, p. B3.

Once upon a time in Russia a hare lived in a wooden house, and a fox lived in a house made of ice. When the warm weather came the fox's house melted, and he stole the hare's house by a low trick.

Then, says Mirra Ginsburg, who is telling all this about *The Fox and the Hare*, the hare asked different animals (a dog, a bear, a bull) to help him get his house back; and they all failed. But a certain brave rooster—aha!

Victor Nolden's pictures are washed in the freshest sunshine, almost jumping with joy even when they are sad. Probably they belong to the time when all the world was 3-6 years old.

Evelyn Stewart

SOURCE: A review of *The Fox and the Hare*, in *School Library Journal*, Vol. 17, No. 7, March, 1970, p. 128.

The large, bright, full-color pictures [by Victor Nolden] on every page carry this undistinguished and unconvincing story, a retelling of a Russian folktale. The Fox lives in a house of ice (not an igloo) and the Hare in a house of wood. When the coming of spring causes the Fox's house to melt, he takes over the Hare's. The cheated Hare seeks help from a dog, a bear, and a bull, all of whom are scared away simply by the Fox's threatening to scratch their eyes out. Then, the Rooster comes and stamps, pecks at the window, and flaps his wings, terrifying the Fox; and the Hare finally gets his home back. The illustrations, in pen-and-ink and watercolor, are fresh looking and just right for a folktale: the Hare wears a Russian-style fur hat; his cottage has a horse's head on the ridge pole; etc.

📖 *THE MASTER OF THE WINDS AND OTHER TALES FROM SIBERIA* (edited and translated by Mirra Ginsburg, 1970)

Kirkus Reviews

SOURCE: A review of *The Master of the Winds and Other Tales from Siberia*, in *Kirkus Reviews*, Vol. XXXVIII, No. 18, September 15, 1970, p. 1042.

Serious in intent, as the introduction and representation attest (fourteen stories from fourteen Siberian cultures,) and spirited in the fresh, agile translations. This is a motley collection of moods, ranging from the opening Mansi fable whose familiar title **"The Wise Owl"** belies its distinctive brand of sagacity, to the somber **"Mistress of Fire,"** of Seikup origin, in which the lesson of respect is learned the hard way. Most frivolous, perhaps, is the succinct, proverbial Ket legend of two men who take refuge in a bear cave and awaken the following spring after **"A Long Night's Sleep"** because "a guest does as his host does"; most intense, most convoluted are the Yakut and Dolgan entries—both quests whose final satisfactions contrast markedly with western archetypes. The Chukchi **"Maiden and the Moon"** enjoys a less literary rendering here than in the Morton *Harvest* version, and the majority of the remaining tales are altogether new—reworked from recent Russian compilations. They imply universals as much as they mirror regional similarities and differences, mythological and quotidien, and still they flow gently.

Lynda McConnell

SOURCE: A review of *The Master of the Winds and Other Tales from Siberia*, in *School Library Journal*, Vol. 17, No. 4, December, 1970, p. 48.

The first in a series of collections of regional tales of Russia, **The Master of the Winds** offers 14 folk stories of Siberia. They vividly portray the people of this harsh region and offer an interesting contrast to the more familiar folk tales in such collections as Daniels' *The Falcon, Under the Hat.* . . . A glimpse into the heritage of these native groups of Siberia, as well as a collection of good yarns, this should find a wide audience.

The Booklist

SOURCE: A review of *The Master of the Winds and Other Tales from Siberia*, in *The Booklist*, Vol. 67, No. 11, February 1, 1971, p. 450.

A selection of 14 tales drawn from the folk literature of the many small national groups that inhabit the northern and far eastern areas of Siberia. The daily life, customs, and beliefs of people who have successfully come to terms with a harsh environment form a background for stories of love and courage, of evil forces and evil creatures like the Ninwits, of men and animals, and of humor and mockery. An original and attractive collection appropriately illustrated [by Enrico Arno] with two-color pictures. The national origin of each story is indicated and an informative introduction is included.

Virginia Haviland

SOURCE: A review of *The Master of the Winds and Other Tales from Siberia*, in *The Horn Book Magazine*, Vol. XLVII, No. 2, April, 1971, p. 165.

Illustrated by Enrico Arno. A fresh, well-told compilation with some of its stories interestingly related to Eskimo lore. **"The Lost Song"** is actually labeled an Eskimo tale. And **"The Singing Man"** with its device of a ladder to the sky and **"The Ninwits"** with its universal motif of the throwing of things to create obstacles are akin to elements in William Sleator's retelling of the Tlingit tale *The Angry Moon*. The shaman or medicine man is frequently found in the stories and the sun, moon, and the stars often appear as characters. The background of mountains, rivers, tundra and taiga, with their yurt-dwelling hunters, gives a strong sense of place to the tales. A distinctive volume in every detail of bookmaking.

📖 *THREE ROLLS AND ONE DOUGHNUT: FABLES FROM RUSSIA* (retold by Mirra Ginsburg, 1970)

Kirkus Reviews

SOURCE: A review of *Three Rolls and One Doughnut: Fables from Russia*, in *Kirkus Reviews*, Vol. XXXVIII, No. 22, November 15, 1970, p. 1251.

Three rolls and one doughnut consumed in that order finally stave off a peasant's hunger and he reflects, "What a fool I was to have wasted all that good money on rolls! I should have bought a doughnut to begin with." And so go the nutshell fables, some proverbial and some predictable. "Steady, Old Gray," says the poor man to his horse while chauffering a boastful prevaricator, "we're coming to the bridge that breaks down under liars." Only a handful are widely familiar, deservedly, and just a few of the 28 fall (impishly, however) limp; there's a two-page spread of Riddles solvable by the attentive from the delicate drawings [of Anita Lobel], penned to perfection throughout in black-and-white and expressing triumph, dismay, consternation, complacence, the whole Russian repertory. Slyly. (Indeed the Fox is outfoxed by the Thrush, turning Aesop's tables like the Bubble who laughs last . . . and bursts.) Rapid reductions for restive listeners, not for self-readers, and a tastefully produced, piquant collaboration.

Clara Hulton

SOURCE: A review of *Three Rolls and One Doughnut*, in *School Library Journal*, Vol. 17, No. 6, February, 1971, p. 56.

A very attractive collection of 28 short fables and riddles from the many and varied cultures of the Soviet Union. Many have been translated for the first time by Miss Ginsburg, who is also the editor and translator of another 1970 collection, **The Master of the Winds and Other Tales from Siberia**. The fables are full of rollicking humor, which is heightened by Anita Lobel's lively, detailed line drawings. This is an excellent addition to the storyteller's shelf, to answer that inevitable request for "just one more."

Zena Sutherland

SOURCE: A review of *Three Rolls and One Doughnut*, in *Bulletin of the Center for Children's Books*, Vol. 25, No. 2, October, 1971, p. 25.

A compilation of riddles, tall tales, briefly told folk tales and some stories that are like fables, but lack the concluding moral although they point a moral. In "**Hatchet Gruel**" one recognizes "Stone Soup," and in "**How the Peasant Divided the Geese**," a variant of the pervasive folk tale in which a scoundrel tries to duplicate the good fortune of a worthy man and comes to no good. The illustrations [by Anita Lobel] have a cheery humor and interesting decorative details, and the stories—not retold with uniform success—are a good source of short, funny material for reading aloud.

Marcus Crouch

SOURCE: A review of *Three Rolls and One Doughnut*, in *The Junior Bookshelf*, Vol. 37, No. 5, October, 1973, p. 315.

Small children love the funny anecdote and retail the same traditional tales anew in each generation. Among those current in this country are variants of the tales of cunning and folly which Mirra Ginsburg has imported from Russia. Russia with its long peasant tradition is the ideal breeding-ground for them, and with exquisitely appropri-

ate line-drawings by Anita Lobel this book will give a great deal of pleasure. The tales are much shorter than fairy-stories, rarely extending beyond a single page. They might make excellent make-weights and encores in a story-telling session, where children should appreciate the oral quality as well as the ruthlessness.

THE KAHA BIRD: TALES FROM THE STEPPES OF CENTRAL ASIA (edited and translated by Mirra Ginsburg, 1971)

Kirkus Reviews

SOURCE: A review of *The Kaha Bird: Tales from the Steppes of Central Asia*, in *Kirkus Reviews*, Vol. XXXIX, No. 21, November 1, 1971, p. 1160.

A host of exotic peoples from Central Asia, Kazakhs, Kirghiz, Uzbeks and others less familiar, are represented by these recently collected tales, and this new cast of characters—wily khans, shaitans (evil spirits) and peris (fairies)—work some fresh variations on old folklore themes. The most notable character is the wise wife, whether old peasant woman or Golden Princess, who guides her helpless husband through a series of seemingly impossible tasks. Greed is the predominant motive, sometimes handled humorously, as in the tale of the tricksters who fake their own deaths (and end up "buried" side by side) in order to avoid sharing their gold with each other, or sometimes symbolically—the benevolent Kaha bird deserts mankind because it proves unworthy of her gifts. As a bonus, there is a sampling of Turkmenian riddles and one-liners, and, finally, the ultimate in tall tales, composed of one hundred successive lies. Mirra Ginsburg has provided a helpful introduction, but no anthropological background is necessary to appreciate these happy celebrations of wit and cunning.

Virginia Haviland

SOURCE: A review of *The Kaha Bird: Tales from the Steppes of Central Asia*, in *The Horn Book Magazine*, Vol. XLVII, December, 1971, pp. 607-08.

Illustrated by Richard Cuffari. "Second in a series of collections of non-Russian folk tales" out of old Russia, of which the first, **The Master of the Winds and Other Tales from Siberia**, brought together tales from northern Siberia. These nineteen stories come from twelve separate tribes or cultures of southern Siberia and Central Asia—lands of khans, beys, and yurt-dwellers. As in the previous book, the story patterns show influences from neighboring areas (Indian, Mongolian, Persian, European). The Turkmenian noodlehead tale, "**The Fool**," is a variant of the Epaminondas chain. Some tales from the old caravan routes have Eastern elements: The Kazakh story "**Two Tricksters**" has a distinct Middle Eastern flavor, as do the sayings in "**The Wise Nasreddin**." Great feats of magic characterize many of the selections—the long Uzbek story "**The Bear's Sons**" set in Tashkent and Chimkent has a hero of extravagant physical strength. Malevolent characters of "the endless steppe" include dragons, giants, shaitans (evil spirits), and the yalmauz (man-eating witches). The stories form a medley of backgrounds, styles, and lengths. A few of them have interest for the present-day storyteller's use. Especially tellable is the Tofalar tale "Living Water," which explains why the needles of pine, cedar, and fir are always green.

Lynda McConnell

SOURCE: A review of *The Kaha Bird: Tales from the Steppes of Central Asia,* in *School Library Journal,* Vol. 18, No. 5, January, 1972, p. 57.

The second in the series of collections of sectional stories from Russia which includes *The Master of the Winds: Tales from Siberia,* this offers 19 tales of southern Siberia and Central Asia. The folklore of 12 cultural groups of the area is represented. Included are stories involving magic and transformations, hero tales, and several short animal fables. The harshness of the region is depicted in some of the stories; others are variations of familiar European tales. The introduction states: "Many of these stories are new to Russian readers, and most will undoubtedly be new to the English-speaking reader"; however, no sources are cited. Both as an above-average collection of folk tales and as a view of the distinctive cultures of the "many non-Russian peoples who have been a part of Russia for centuries," this anthology will be useful in school and public libraries.

Zena Sutherland

SOURCE: A review of *The Kaha Bird: Tales from the Steppes of Central Asia,* in *Bulletin of the Center for Children's Books,* Vol. 25, No. 9, May, 1972, p. 139.

Endpaper maps show the areas from which the nineteen stories, non-Russian tales from Russia, in this collection came; their sources are a dozen cultures with mixed heritage. Some of the tales are heroic, some earthy, some explanatory ("Living Water," for example, is a "why" story) and many have a robust, sly peasant humor. The style of the retelling is smooth and flavorful, so that the book is as useful and enjoyable for reading aloud as it is for storytelling.

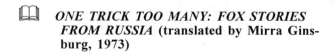 *ONE TRICK TOO MANY: FOX STORIES FROM RUSSIA* **(translated by Mirra Ginsburg, 1973)**

Kirkus Reviews

SOURCE: A review of *One Trick Too Many: Fox Stories from Russia,* in *Kirkus Reviews,* Vol. XLI, No. 8, April 15, 1973, p. 454.

Nine brief tales of trickery in which the fox outwits humans, lions, jackals, and even other foxes, sometimes carrying it off and sometimes playing one trick too many for his own good. The single theme can become monotonous when all nine stories are read at a sitting, but the author of *The Kaha Bird* and *Three Rolls and One Doughnut* tells them all with dispatch. Helen Siegl's full page red and gold woodcuts are a crafty combination of Eastern European folk art and her usual elegant, finely delineated animals.

The Booklist

SOURCE: A review of *One Trick Too Many: Fox Stories from Russia,* in *The Booklist,* Vol. 69, No. 21, July 1, 1973, p. 1021.

Nine lively fables to freshen up a storytellers repertoire, with beautifully bordered woodcuts in red, gold, and black making the picture book a visual treat. Although an introductory note explains the characteristics that each animal traditionally represents, these Russian tales—unlike some Western fables—do not seem stylized or didactic. The morals are well camouflaged in entertaining action, especially the deeds of the rapscallion fox.

Beryl Robinson

SOURCE: A review of *One Trick Too Many: Fox Stories from Russia,* in *The Horn Book Magazine,* Vol. XLIX, No. 4, August, 1973, p. 369.

Illustrated by Helen Siegl. The cunning of the fox has made him a favorite character in the folk tales of many nations. In this collection, the author has selected and translated nine Russian fox-tales, derived from both European and Asiatic sources. The style is bright and succinct, and the cunning of the fox is evident in all of the tales as he succeeds in outwitting the peasants and the other animals. Although sometimes, as in the stories of "The Red Fox and the Walking Stick" and "The Fox and the Quail," he attempts one trick too many and loses out altogether. Full-page woodcuts in handsome shades—predominately red and yellow—give lively expression to each tale.

Lynda McConnell

SOURCE: A review of *One Trick Too Many: Fox Stories from Russia,* in *School Library Journal,* Vol. 20, No. 1, September, 1973, p. 57.

A useful collection of nine Russian folk tales built around the wily fox, whose audacity and cunning have made him a favorite animal tale protagonist. The stories are skillfully told and lend themselves to reading aloud as a change of pace from the youngest-of-three-sons or poor-girl-marries-prince motifs. The rustic, four-color woodcuts [by Helen Siegl] with wide ornamental borders, portraying the fox in the midst of mischief, add greatly to the charm of the book.

📖 *THE LAZIES: TALES OF THE PEOPLES OF RUSSIA* (edited and translated by Mirra Ginsburg, 1973)

Kirkus Reviews

SOURCE: A review of *The Lazies: Tales of the Peoples of Russia,* in *Kirkus Reviews,* Vol. XLI, No. 18, September 15, 1973, p. 1040.

Fifteen short folk tales with laziness as the common theme are competently retold and accented with small, spare, playfully agile line drawings [by Marian Parry]. Some of the selections (such as **"The Three Knots"** and **"The Clever Thief"**) seem forced into the "lazies" category. Many are familiar but welcome—**"The Lazy Daughter"** is a lesser but passably diverting variant of Rumpelstiltskin, and the classic **"Who Will Wash the Pot"** could not be omitted. All told, the brevity and briskness of the tales should recommend the collection to uncommitted readers, who will be hard put to resist an opening like "In a certain village there lived a man who was so lazy that he would not even chew his food, but swallowed it in lumps."

Zena Sutherland

SOURCE: A review of *The Lazies: Tales of the Peoples of Russia,* in *Bulletin of the Center for Children's Books,* Vol. 27, No. 5, January, 1974, p. 78.

Fifteen humorous stories about lazy people or animals are illustrated with line drawings [by Marian Parry] that achieve a remarkably funny and effective strength for the economical use of line. The tales are typical of the genre; usually the lazy creature either learns a lesson and changes or there is a just—often harsh—punishment for indolence. The source of each tale is given, and the collection should be particularly useful as a storytelling source, since the selections vary in length.

Susan Stanton

SOURCE: A review of *The Lazies: Tales of the Peoples of Russia,* in *School Library Journal,* Vol. 20, No. 6, February, 1974, p. 63.

A collection of Russian folk tales, all on the theme of laziness and most not found in other anthologies. The selection of one little-known story with sexist overtones (similar in theme to "King Grisly-Beard") is questionable: **"The Princess Who Learned To Work"** is married to a peasant who had tamed the czar's wild bull by denying it food or water; the czar's lazy daughter is taught "to be a good wife" by the same starvation method. On the whole, however, the retellings are brisk, sprightly and complemented by amusing black-and-white line drawings [by Marian Parry], making this a passable supplementary title where easy-to-read folk tales are needed.

Mary M. Burns

SOURCE: A review of *The Lazies: Tales of the Peoples of Russia,* in *The Horn Book Magazine,* Vol. L, No. 2, April, 1974, p. 145.

Illustrated by Marian Parry. Fifteen variations on the theme of laziness have been culled from the folklore of the U.S.S.R. and gathered into an attractive, amusingly illustrated sampling of the folk wit and humor from such areas as Armenia, Avar, Azerbaidzhan, Evenk, Latvia, and Uygur. That indolence is not limited to the rich, to the poor, or to human beings is revealed in the selections, which include talking-beast tales, drolls, and fables as well as stories of princesses and peasants. And the universality of folk-tale situations—and of human behavior—is underscored by comparing the Russian **"Who Will Wash the Pot?"** with the English ballad, "Get Up and Bar the Door"; or **"The Lazy Daughter,"** a Karelian tale, with "Rumplestiltskin." Told in a pithy manner, the lively collection should delight both storytellers and listeners.

📖 *MUSHROOM IN THE RAIN* (adapted by Mirra Ginsburg, 1974)

Kirkus Reviews

SOURCE: A review of *Mushroom in the Rain,* in *Kirkus Reviews,* Vol. XLII, No. 1, January, 1974, p. 3.

"One day an ant was caught in the rain" and hid under a mushroom waiting for it to stop. Soon a butterfly comes along seeking shelter, and though "there is barely room for one," the ant moves over and lets him in. Then one by one a mouse, a sparrow and a rabbit (fleeing from a fox) squeeze in, each in a mobile series of six small pictures per page. When the rain stops and everyone comes out from under (all full of [Jose Aruego's and Ariane Dewey's] bouncy brightness) they all wonder how the five of them had managed to fit in, but as the last double-page closeup of not only greige but also orange, yellow, pink, violet, blue and green fungi happily reminds us, mushrooms grow when it rains. Sparkling, expansive fun, sure to be a runaway story hour success.

Sandra Paul

SOURCE: "Bedtime Tales," in *The Spectator,* No. 7641, December 7, 1974, pp. 739-40.

Mushroom in The Rain is colourful and funny, telling of how an ant and subsequently a butterfly, mouse, sparrow and rabbit all manage to squeeze under a mushroom to shelter from the rain. It progresses at an ideal pace for a very young child to follow the story and understand it.

The Junior Bookshelf

SOURCE: A review of *Mushroom in the Rain,* in

The Junior Bookshelf, Vol. 39, No. 1, February, 1975, p. 21.

A very simple tale of a number of animals sheltering from the rain under a mushroom. It seems impossible that there should be room for all but this is explained satisfactorily.

The illustrations are delightful, simple and splodgy, with just the right amount of detail to satisfy small children without confusing them, and building up at the end of the book into a fine display of colour.

THE PROUD MAIDEN, TUNGAK, AND THE SUN: A RUSSIAN ESKIMO TALE (retold by Mirra Ginsburg, 1974)

Kirkus Reviews

SOURCE: A review of *The Proud Maiden, Tungak, and the Sun: A Russian Eskimo Tale,* in *Kirkus Reviews,* Vol. XLII, No. 20, October 15, 1974, p. 1101.

Why the sun and the moon live in the sky, according to the Russian Eskimos who tell, charmingly, of Tungak, one time evil spirit of the tundra, and how an old couple saved the maiden he wanted to marry by causing him to melt into a puddle of oil, which their dogs then lapped up. Later the maiden marries the couple's radiantly handsome son and they go to live among the dwellers in the sky, annually removing the lard-burner from a hole in the floor of their tent and sliding down a leather strip to visit their parents—thereby bringing spring and brightness to the tundra. And when during the winter the wife becomes lonely, she removes the lard burner from the hole and peeks down—a full moon in the sky. Soviet artist Igor Galanin's blue and white illustrations borrow from folk art, Eskimo masks and post-nouveau decoration for a pleasing and surprisingly unified effect.

The Booklist

SOURCE: A review of *The Proud Maiden, Tungak, and the Sun: A Russian Eskimo Tale,* in *The Booklist,* Vol. 71, No. 7, December 1, 1974, p. 379.

From a relatively small cultural subgroup, the Eskimos of the Soviet Union, comes a fast-paced, enjoyable legend. When a beautiful but haughty maiden finds the evil spirit Tungak wishes to marry her, she flees from him through a blinding snowstorm. The maiden seeks shelter in an enormous, warm tent belonging to an old couple; Tungak follows but the heat melts him into a pool of fat. The maiden marries the sun and, thanks to this union, daylight now visits the north regularly, and the maiden sometimes bends her moon face toward the earth. The text sustains the story's importance and entertainment value. The framed, blue-and-white illustrations [by Igor Galanin] are highly stylized; human faces are annoyingly Anglo,

but the spirit Tungak's over-sized head is a cross between scary and comical, and the drawings generally contribute a dramatic effect.

Patricia McCue Marwell

SOURCE: A review of *The Proud Maiden, Tungak, and the Sun: A Russian Eskimo Tale,* in *School Library Journal,* Vol. 21, No. 5, January, 1975, p. 39.

A superb retelling of the Slavic-Eskimo folktale about the origins of the moon. In simple but dramatic prose, Ginsburg tells how Tungak, the evil spirit of the tundra, pursues a maiden whom he wishes to marry across the icy wastes until a clever old couple destroy the spirit by melting him. The maiden, now free to find happiness with a handsome hunter, the Sun, goes to live in the heavens as the moon. The story is well paced for reading aloud, and the blue cross-hatched drawings [by Igor Galanin] capture the harshness of the Arctic tundra.

Beryl Robinson

SOURCE: A review of *The Proud Maiden, Tungak, and the Sun: A Russian Eskimo Folk Tale,* in *The Horn Book Magazine,* Vol. LI, No. 2, April, 1975, pp. 144-45.

Illustrated by Igor Galanin. A myth of Russian Eskimo origin tells why extended periods of darkness alternate with periods of light and warmth in the Arctic. Long ago, the tundra was always dark and cold, for the greatly feared evil spirit Tungak was in control. But he was destroyed when he sought to marry a beautiful maiden who fled from him across the tundra until she found shelter in a brightly lighted tent. When Tungak followed her into the tent, he melted from the heat, for this was the home of the Sun's parents. The maiden became the Sun's bride and went to live with him in the sky, and if she looked down, people said that the moon was shining. When the two came to earth for a visit, they were accompanied by light and warmth. A sense of remoteness is vividly conveyed in full-page and doublespread illustrations, whose blues and whites suggest the arctic chill. Although a slightly stylized treatment is given to all the figures, only Tungak has a frightening mask for a face.

Philip Morrison and Phylis Morrison

SOURCE: A review of *The Proud Maiden, Tungak, and the Sun: A Russian Eskimo Tale,* in *Scientific American,* Vol. 233, No. 6, December, 1975, p. 142.

Once the tundra was always dark. In this fresh tale from the Russian Arctic we meet a new Persephone who brought the light and did not take it away. This lovely maiden is sought by a gross and harsh suitor, the evil spirit Tungak, all mask and sharp teeth. She flees to a strange tent, bright and warm from a great lard-burner. Fat Tungak is melted to nothing and the dogs chew up his bones. Her hosts turn out to be the family of the Sun; nowadays there is half a year of brightness because the Sun and his new wife come annually to visit her parents. The moon, too, is accounted for in this delightful myth from a dark and cold land. Fine drawings [by Igor Galanin]—perhaps etchings—reproduced in a clear blue monochrome complement the text very aptly.

HOW WILKA WENT TO SEA: AND OTHER TALES FROM WEST OF THE URALS (edited and translated by Mirra Ginsburg, 1975)

Kirkus Reviews

SOURCE: A review of *How Wilka Went to Sea: And Other Tales from West of the Urals*, in *Kirkus Reviews*, Vol. XLIII, No. 6, March 15, 1975, p. 312.

Cold air from north of the Arctic Circle adds crispness to some familiar folk themes, and Mongol and Buddhist influences from far west of the Urals contribute some exotic shamanist transformations and *shulmus* demons. In this eclectic collection of Finno-Ugric and Turkic tales, our favorites are the heroes from the far north—Wilka, who went to sea on an ice floe and returned to defeat a race of one-eyed, one-legged monsters and win a bride from the eerie moss-eaters, and the Saam who fell from heaven into a marsh where his head was used for a swan's nest until he escaped by biting and holding fast to a wolf's tail. Even the better known morals are dressed in fresh images—the old wife who nags her husband for more and better wishes from a benevolent talking birch tree gets both of them turned into bears at her own request, and Clever Durmian outwits a dumb giant Pyary with alacrity. A handsome presentation—and [Charles] Mikolaycak's illustrations which combine folk motifs and monumental figures—give the multi-ethnic selection a sense of continuity it might otherwise lack. Folklorists will welcome this third of Ginsburg's projected series of six volumes on non-Russian Soviet peoples and the stories' rich texture and foreign settings will be a treat for the more romantic segment of the fairytale audience.

Ruth M. McConnell

SOURCE: A review of *How Wilka Went to Sea and Other Tales from West of the Urals*, in *School Library Journal*, Vol. 21, No. 9, May, 1975, p. 55.

Ten vigorous folktales, a joy to read and useful for story hour, are masterfully told by the well-known translator. Third in a projected series of five volumes of regional tales of the U.S.S.R., this cuts a wide swath of European-Russian culture, from Lapp peoples in the northern area to Mongolic people in the northern area to Mongolic people in the south. There are tall tales; hero tales; tales of people with curious minds or greedy hearts; tales of wonder and sorcery. Though the cultures the tales represent are unfamiliar, their spirit and appeal are universal, e.g. **"The Beautiful Birch"** is a variant of "The Fisherman

and His Wife," and **"Syre-Varda"** is similar to parts of "The Seven Ravens" and "The Goose Girl." An exceptionally attractive item for folklore collections.

Ann A. Flowers

SOURCE: A review of *How Wilka Went to Sea and Other Tales from West of the Urals*, in *The Horn Book Magazine*, Vol. LI, No. 4, August, 1975, p. 377.

Illustrated by Charles Mikolaycak. The third in a series of collections of non-Russian folk tales from the Soviet Union following *The Master of the Winds* and *The Kaha Bird.* The varied collection contains tall tales, magic tales, and how-and-why tales. **"The Beautiful Birch"** is an unusual variant of "The Fisherman and His Wife." When the old man spares the birch from being chopped down, the tree grants wishes to him and his wife. As a result of their greed, they are turned into bears. The title story resembles an Eskimo tale in reflecting the harsh conditions of life in the far North. Short sentences and brisk action make these tales ideal for storytelling; the strong, bold, stylized illustrations complement the stories extremely well.

Zena Sutherland

SOURCE: A review of *How Wilka Went to Sea and Other Tales from West of the Urals*, in *Bulletin of the Center for Children's Books*, Vol. 29, No. 1, September, 1975, p. 9.

Nine Finno-Ugric and Turkic folktales are beautifully illustrated by soft, dramatic pictures with precise costume details. The tales abound with witches, giants, and wizards who are inevitably outwitted by the daring of youth or the wisdom of age; many of them attest to the close family relationships within the rural cultures from which they emanate. The title story is almost a situation comedy, a series of disasters from which stubborn, hapless Wilka emerges triumphant; the most dramatic story—although it has less action and violence than others—is **"The Beautiful Birch,"** a tale with a stunning ending.

HOW THE SUN WAS BROUGHT BACK TO THE SKY: ADAPTED FROM A SLOVENIAN FOLK TALE (1975)

Jane Abramson

SOURCE: A review of *How the Sun Was Brought Back to the Sky*, in *School Library Journal*, Vol. 21, No. 9, May, 1975, p. 46.

Ginsburg, an able and fluid translator, has dredged up a neglible Slovenian folktale for her latest retelling. Sick and tired of cloudy weather, a band of chicks decide to locate the missing sun. Traipsing through the countryside picking up fellow travellers (a snail, magpie, duck, etc.), the procession finally arrives at the sun's doorstep. There a cowering Old Sol confesses, "gray clouds (have) shut me out . . . I don't even know how to shine anymore," but after a little scrubbing and polishing, he is soon beaming again. Ginsburg has little to work with here, but her simple, unembroidered retelling only underscores the story's blandness. [Jose] Aruego and [Ariane] Dewey manage to weather through the tale by ignoring its point. The raison d'etre of this trek to the sun is bad weather, yet, from the first page, every spread in the book is bursting with color and light.

Kirkus Reviews

SOURCE: A review of *How the Sun Was Brought Back to the Sky,* in *Kirkus Reviews,* Vol. XLIII, No. 10, May 15, 1975 p. 562.

"One day gray clouds, huge as mountains, covered the sky." After three days, "the chicks got worried"—and so, equipped by the mother hen with a grain of rye and a poppy seed each, they set out to find the sun and bring it back into the sky. Their search leads them to a snail, a magpie, a rabbit, a duck and a hedgehog, each of whom leaves its separately enticing habitat to accompany the party to the sun's house in the sky. Taking the artists' glowing, blossomy pages as a clue, you'll expect the chicks to realize at last that the sun has been shining all along. But it turns out that Jose [Aruego] and Ariane [Dewey] are merely doing their own exuberant thing without any concessions to the text, where the scene becomes "clean, fresh and golden" only after the chicks have scrubbed and polished the sun at the end. The pictures are as delightful as usual and the tale has its charm, but preschoolers will be the first to point out that they don't tell the same story.

Mary M. Burns

SOURCE: A review of *How the Sun Was Brought Back to the Sky: Adapted from a Slovenian Folk Tale,* in *The Horn Book Magazine,* Vol. LI, No. 4, August, 1975, pp. 373-74.

Brilliant, full-color pictures outlined in pen and ink and executed in the artists' characteristically luxuriant color, are the compelling feature of a slight but appealing cumulative picture-story. The simple saga of the worried chicks who set out to find the sun which had "not come out for three whole days" is more universal than Slovenian. Repetitive rather than rhythmic, the text is understated—almost staid—in comparison with the flamboyant illustrations, which come to a climax in a golden-hued double-spread of the sun smiling benevolently on the chicks and their assorted small friends. "And if you don't believe . . . look out of the window and you'll see: the hen is there, the chicks are there, and the sun is there, and doesn't that prove that every word I said is true?"

Zena Sutherland

SOURCE: A review of *How the Sun Was Brought Back to*

the Sky, in *Bulletin of the Center for Children's Books,* Vol. 29, No. 3, November, 1975, p. 44.

Five plump yellow chicks, dismayed because for three days there has been no sun, only grey clouds, decide they will go off to find the sun and bring it back to the sky. They go to one animal after another, ride a mountain-top cloud to the moon, and are directed to the sun's house, accompanied by all the animals they've met. The sun sadly says the clouds have kept it out of the sky and it's forgotten how to shine; the animals clean and burnish the sun, and it fills the sky; the animals slide down the rays to earth. Silly, merry, and sunny, the story is matched by the artless insouciance of the vigorous, colorful pictures [by Jose Aruego and Ariane Dewey].

📖 *PAMPALCHE OF THE SILVER TEETH* (edited and translated by Mirra Ginsburg, 1976)

Kirkus Reviews

SOURCE: A review of *Pampalche of the Silver Teeth,* in *Kirkus Reviews,* Vol. XLIV, No. 2, January 15, 1976, p. 67.

An aptly handled Russian version of a common folklore motif—the beautiful young girl whose father is forced to promise her in marriage to some sort of monster. Here Pampalche escapes the huge Master of the Waters by fleeing through the woods to her sister's cliff-top home; she is aided by friendly animals and pursued toward the end by a witch allied with the would-be bridegroom. There are likely to be problems with the image of teeth "white as silver" and Rocco Negri doesn't especially help you visualize the heroine's beauty—but he does his job by making the forest perilous and the father's cottage homey, and his witch shows an ingenious application of the woodcut medium.

Ruth M. McConnell

SOURCE: A review of *Pampalche of the Silver Teeth,* in *School Library Journal,* Vol. 22, No. 7, March, 1976, p. 91.

Seized by the Master of the Waters while drinking from a lake, a hunter saves his own life by promising his beautiful daughter to his captor. The unwilling bride, however, disguises herself, eludes members of the wedding retinue, and finally, helped by animals, escapes from a witch. The tale should appeal to primary graders considering the attractive format and full-page woodcuts of strong design in bold colors [by Rocco Negri].

Zena Sutherland

SOURCE: A review of *Pampalche of the Silver Teeth,* in

Bulletin of the Center for Children's Books, Vol. 29, No. 9, May, 1976, p. 144.

A Russian folktale is adapted "for the picture-book audience," the jacket states, but the length, vocabulary, and complexity of the story indicate rather that it is appropriate for older, independent readers. It is illustrated [by Rocco Negri] with woodcuts that have strong composition and fittingly bucolic flavor but that are, on some pages, crowded with distracting details. The story: to escape marriage with the Master of the Waters who had threatened her father, beautiful young Pampalche disguises herself and runs off to her older sister's home. Pursued by her unwelcome suitor, she meets a series of peasant groups, each of them singing a song about hunting for the bride Pampalche; they do not recognize her, but an old crone does (she's a witch in disguise) and tries repeatedly to trap her. The girl outwits the witch, reaches her sister's mountaintop home, and rejoices that she is safe from that hateful monster, the Master of the Waters. While the security of the ending and the hunt-and-escape pattern of the story are satisfying, the ending seems oddly incomplete, since neither the father nor the Master of the Waters appears again—they have simply dropped out of the story.

Susan Meyers

SOURCE: A review of *Pampalche of the Silver Teeth,* in *The New York Times Book Review,* June 6, 1976, p. 55.

Sisterhood is powerful is the modern message of this old Russian tale. An innocent girl, Pampalche of the Silver Teeth, is literally sold down the river by her father. One day while the old man is drinking from the lake, the monstrous Master of the Waters grabs his beard and threatens to drown him unless he gives him his daughter in marriage. The monster cunningly throws fishing rights to all his lakes and rivers into the deal, and the bargain is struck.

Pampalche, however, will have none of this. Disguising herself, she sets off for her sister's house. She conducts herself prudently along the way, but when she meets the wicked witch Voover-Coove, who is intent on bringing her back to the Master of the Waters, Pampalche is tricked into revealing her identity. It is touch and go for a while, but with some help from her friends, the beasts of the forest, and from her resourceful sister, who sends her a magic silken ladder, Pampalche escapes and climbs to her sister's mountaintop home, safe at last from both lustful water monster and feckless father.

The strength of this vigorous story is matched by Rocco Negri's illustrations. His woodcuts, with their rough textures and earthy colors, successfully convey the atmosphere of the forest and the wickedness of Voover-Coove. But the mood of the tale is marred by the telling. Pampalche's song of victory, "I will not have to spend my life as the hateful monster's wife," sounds like the sing-song chant of a schoolgirl. Stock phrases such as, "she'd have her in her clutches," and sloppy construction, as in, "The old crone mumbled something toothlessly"—which brings to mind E. B. White's warning about adverbs being easy to make and better to avoid—don't help.

📖 ***THE AIR OF MARS AND OTHER STORIES OF TIME AND SPACE* (edited and translated by Mirra Ginsburg, 1976)**

Paul Heins

SOURCE: A review of *The Air of Mars and Other Stories of Time and Space,* in *The Horn Book Magazine,* Vol. LII, No. 4, August, 1976, pp. 410-11.

Translated from the Russian. Nine stories by different authors, published in the Soviet Union between 1964 and 1972. In a note the editor states: "There are no robots in the collection. Its characters are living beings, human and animal—residents of earth and of other planets, familiar and unfamiliar, present, past, and future." Space travel, however, is taken for granted, as is the power of shifting easily from the present to the past and from the future to the present. But most remarkable in these science fiction fantasies are the astonishing and unexpected situations which make them intriguing, powerful, and even occasionally humorous short stories. The translator has skillfully turned the original writing into excellently clear and flowing English. With notes about the versatile authors, some of whom are not professional writers.

📖 ***TWO GREEDY BEARS* (adapted by Mirra Ginsburg, 1976)**

Kirkus Reviews

SOURCE: A review of *Two Greedy Bears,* in *Kirkus Reviews,* Vol. XLIV, No. 18, September 15, 1976, p. 1034.

There's certainly a core of home truth in this fable about two bear cubs who find a big round cheese but are each so afraid that the other will get the bigger share that they are fair game for a fox, who eats the cheese herself while pretending to divide it for them. It's a good joke on the cubs, but it might have been a stronger one if [Jose Aruego and Ariane Dewey] had made the protagonists more substantial than a pair of soft bodied, button-eyed crib toys romping in a flowery fairyland.

Ruth M. McConnell

SOURCE: A review of *Two Greedy Bears,* in *School Library Journal,* Vol. 23, No. 4, December, 1976, p. 49.

Two bears frolic across these double-spreads of clear-toned, soft-hued meadow flowers and viny growth. When they find a cheese, they fight over who will get the larger piece. A fox offers to divide it for them, breaking it into uneven halves which she tries to "even" with successive bites until the bears are left with two equal crumbs and chagrined expressions. This mild, humorously illustrated version of a cautionary tale on greed should go down easy with pre-school and primary graders.

B. Clark

SOURCE: A review of *Two Greedy Bears,* in *The Junior Bookshelf,* Vol. 43, No. 1, February, 1979, p. 17.

Two little bear-cubs set out to see the world, and each tries to outdo the other: one is hungry, the other is hungrier; after they have fed, one has a stomach-ache, the other has a bigger one, and so forth. Then they find a piece of cheese, and have no means of dividing it, until along comes a wily fox who splits it for them in two unequal parts, and while he is nibbling to make the parts equal, he is eating it all except for two crumbs. I did not care very much for the drawings of the rather lumpy bears, or the wishy-washy pale blue fox, but the bears do learn a lesson from the fox in the very simple text which is based on an Hungarian folk-tale.

Elizabeth Weir

SOURCE: A review of *Two Greedy Bears,* in *The School Librarian,* Vol. 27, No. 1, March, 1979, p. 27.

A simple moral story adapted from a Hungarian folk tale showing how two bear cubs are made to look foolish because of their greed. A cunning fox offers to make sure they both receive equal shares of a large cheese, but of course he eats it all and they are left with only the crumbs. A story to amuse the very young, with bold lively illustrations which they will be able to follow with little difficulty.

Margery Fisher

SOURCE: A review of *Two Greedy Bears,* in *Growing Point,* Vol. 24, No. 2, July, 1985, p. 4475.

The immediate impact of this picture-book comes from the visual concept of young bears as bulbous, rollicking figures, giving point to the fanciful situation. These greedy animals quarrel over a hunk of cheese and are conned by a fox who offers to break it into two equal pieces; very little remains for them after his attentions. Idiosyncratic pictures catch the eye with oddities of shape and a considerable force of colour, in an amusing version of a Hungarian folk-tale.

📖 *THE STRONGEST ONE OF ALL: A CAUCA-SIAN FOLKTALE* **(adapted by Mirra Ginsburg, 1977)**

Amy Scholar

SOURCE: A review of *The Strongest One of All: A Cau-*

casian Folktale, in *School Library Journal,* Vol. 24, No. 3, November, 1977, p. 47.

Lamb, after slipping on the ice, wonders if the ice is "the strongest one of all?" No, for the sun melts the ice. Then, the sun must be the strongest one of all. Yet, the lamb reasons, the sun cannot be the strongest for the clouds can cover it over. The lamb keeps searching and wondering, until . . . he finds that each in turn is both the strongest and the weakest. Mirra Ginsburg skillfully retells the Russian version of this familiar tale with the added bonus of [Jose Aruego's and Ariane Dewey's] bright, cheerful illustrations. Small children will enjoy hearing and reading this light-hearted version.

Charlotte W. Draper

SOURCE: A review of *The Strongest One of All,* in *The Horn Book Magazine,* Vol. LIII, No. 6, December, 1977, pp. 658-59.

Based on a Caucasian folktale. Illustrated by Jose Aruego and Ariane Dewey. The simple story follows the pattern of many tales and legends. An endearingly woolly lamb slips on the ice and is convinced that ice must be the "'strongest one of all.'" But, says the ice, "'If I were the strongest, would the sun melt me?'"—and the lamb gambols off to ask the sun. The sun is covered by clouds, and clouds scatter into rain; so it goes until the earth explains that grass is the strongest because it pushes up through the ground. Then the grass asks, "'If I were the strongest, would a lamb pluck me, would a lamb eat me?'" The large print should be inviting to beginning readers. Soft but clear colors edged in black line conform to the subjects described—blue ice, orange-yellow sun, gray clouds—and convey to children a joy in their natural surroundings.

Elaine Moss

SOURCE: "Back to Basics," in *The Times Literary Supplement,* No. 3949, December 2, 1977, p. 1411.

The Strongest One of All by Mirra Ginsburg . . . has a basic text, about a lamb who discovers, in a circular quest, that the elements centre on himself, the consumer of the grass that pushes up through the earth watered by rain, descending from clouds that cover the sun that melts the ice that made him fall and ask "Ice, ice you made me fall. . . . Are you the strongest one of all?"

📖 *LITTLE RYSTU* **(adapted by Mirra Ginsburg, 1978)**

Kirkus Reviews

SOURCE: A review of *Little Rystu,* in *Kirkus Reviews,* Vol. XLVI, No. 3, February 1, 1978, p. 103.

Adapted from an Altai folktale of Soviet Central Asia, this

concerns a musical nature boy named Rystu ("My father is the blue mountain, and my mother is the milk lake") who is taken by the Khan to play a silver reed for his children. When Rystu refuses to play on command, he is sent to herd cows in the fields, and then to churn butter; but two magic words which he learns from the ants enable him to control not only the cows and other animals but also the Khan and his family—sending them dancing off and away, whereupon he runs off to freedom himself. In contrast to the harmonious natural surroundings, [Tony] Chen's elegant dancing figures have an amusing absurdity, and the words and pictures are altogether pleasant, polished, and of a piece. Still, there is an artificial, almost pious note in the description of Rystu's pristine bliss, and an arbitrary ring to the magic, which limit involvement.

Dorothea Scott

SOURCE: A review of *Little Rystu: An Altai Folktale,* in *School Library Journal,* Vol. 24, No. 7, March, 1978, p. 118.

An idyllic tale of a little orphan goatherd, Rystu, who lives in harmony with birds and animals in the Altai mountains of Central Asia. The innocent, trusting nature of Rystu is in sharp contrast to that of the selfish and overbearing local Khan who, riding by and hearing the sweet tones of Rystu's reed pipe, lures him away with false promises of a luxurious home where he will have the Khan's daughters as playmates. Rystu rides off with the Khan but, on reaching his magnificent white felt tent, he is offered as a slave to the daughters. Deeply hurt, Rystu refuses to play a note and is punished by being driven to work himself to death. He is finally rescued by ants who whisper a magic formula to him and all ends happily. Tony Chen's meticulously drawn illustrations . . . complement perfectly the appealing story.

Ann A. Flowers

SOURCE: A review of *Little Rystu: Adapted from an Altai Folktale,* in *The Horn Book Magazine,* Vol. LIV, No. 3, June, 1978, p. 269.

Little Rystu—whose name means happy—lived all by himself "at the foot of a blue mountain, on the shore of a milk lake." He could talk to animals and make beautiful music on a dry reed. When the deceitful Khan offered him a home, Rystu went cheerfully, only to find he would be a slave expected to amuse the Khan's children. His rebellion against the Khan and his eventual magical victory are pictured in clear, spacious illustrations showing Rystu and the Khan in Mongolian garb, beautiful beasts and birds, and on the end papers, the magnificent white felt tent of the Khan against the blue sky.

Elaine Moss

SOURCE: "Going to the Pictures," in *The Times Literary Supplement,* No. 3991, September 29, 1978, p. 1087.

Mirra Ginsburg's *Little Rystu* is a Central Asian folk tale about nature and the creative genius of a peasant boy: he can play a reed pipe to perfection in freedom but is incapable of making music on a silver pipe to entertain the Khan's children. Tony Chen's beige, sepia and blue paintings of children and animals have their own magic.

STRIDING SLIPPERS (adapted by Mirra Ginsburg, 1978)

Kirkus Reviews

SOURCE: A review of *Striding Slippers,* in *Kirkus Reviews,* Vol. XLVI, No. 7, April 1, 1978, p. 367.

To ease his work, a shepherd weaves himself a wonderful pair of striding slippers—a single step and he's across the field; and this traces the progress of the slippers from the time a passing stranger steals them from the shepherd. They are snitched again, then change hands twice more, and everyone who puts them on is sorry—for all the wearers are carried beyond their destinations and their slippered feet continue to thrash even after they fall. But finally the last of the hapless cheats is propelled back into the shepherd's field where the slippers' rightful owner takes them back—"and never in his life felt tired again." A simple, amusing Udmurt (Eastern Soviet) version of the dancing slippers motif, told with agility—though illustrated with a great deal of huffing and puffing.

Denise M. Wilms

SOURCE: A review of *Striding Slippers,* in *Booklist,* Vol. 74, No. 16, April 15, 1978, p. 1349.

A hardworking shepherd weaves striding slippers to make his herding chores more manageable, but they're stolen by an envious peasant. This new wearer finds himself carried away "fast as the wind" and unable to divest himself of his find, until village children remove them as he lies treading air on his back. The slippers then grace the feet of a covetous redbeard, who in turn gives them up to a greedy merchant: "With these marvelous slippers my workman will do the work of twenty men." That hapless laborer ends up thrashing wildly in the flour bin; the furious merchant dons them himself, only to be swept into the countryside where their maker retrieves them and drives the merchant from his field "like a straying cow." This Russian variant of a familiar folktale features [Sa Murdocca's] brisk navy lines with subdued clay-toned swatches of blue, tan, and salmon shades.

Jan Owens

SOURCE: A review of *Striding Slippers: An Udmurt Tale,* in *School Library Journal,* Vol. 24, No. 9, May, 1978, p. 54.

Crime does not pay in this humorous adaptation of a Russian morality tale. A poor shepherd weaves himself a pair of bark "striding slippers" that allow him to cross a field in a single bound, making herd-tending an easier job. A stranger, stealing the slippers, finds that his feet are out of control. After stumbling around the countryside, the slippers are finally removed, only to have them fall into the hands of another thief! A similar fate awaits all wearers until the footgear is returned to its original owner. Comical illustrations in muted colors include authentic Slavic details of costume and scenery.

THE FISHERMAN'S SON: ADAPTED FROM A GEORGIAN FOLKTALE (1979)

Patricia Dooley

SOURCE: A review of *The Fisherman's Son,* in *School Library Journal,* Vol. 26, No. 2, October, 1979, p. 139.

A variant of the familiar animal-helper tale, adapted from a Georgian original. The fisherman's son aids a fish, a deer, a stork, and a fox to escape from death, and in turn is given their help to win his heart's desire. The plot is not very complex, as there is only one test the lad must pass: to hide so that the maiden's magic mirror will not reveal him. The trick of the last animal, however, shows the tale's sly understanding of human nature. The fox conceals the young man under his true love's bed, and the mirror reflects "nothing but herself." The romantic but simple double-page spreads are alternately in full, luminous color and in brown line. Unfortunately, in a few places the illustrations are inconsistent with the text. The mirror's importance as a symbol is weakened by drawings in which it resembles a ping-pong paddle. The fish caught at the beginning were "silvery and gray and brown" says the text, "And shining bright among them was a little red one." But the picture shows a net full of blue and red fish, while the single magic one is shown on the following page—in brown line. Later on, this "little red fish" appears in shades of yellow, lavender, brown, and rust. The fish is gorgeous—but it's *not* red.

Virginia Haviland

SOURCE: A review of *The Fisherman's Son: Adapted from a Georgian Folktale,* in *The Horn Book Magazine,* Vol. LV, No. 6, December, 1979, p. 653.

Illustrated by Tony Chen. A maiden declares she will marry only a man clever enough to hide so that her magic mirror cannot find him. Four times the fisherman's son conceals himself to win her. The young hero succeeds because he has four charms, gifts from those he has helped—a scale from a little red fish, a hair from the hide of a deer saved from a hunter, a feather from the tail of a grateful stork, and a whisker from a fox's chin. In a proper fairy-tale climax the wedding feast lasts "a whole year." The artist has painted double-page spreads using rich, warm colors—red for the sail of a fishing boat, red-browns

for horse and deer, and turquoise for the onion domes of a great building. Line drawings alternating with the paintings are equally evocative in their portrayal of the lively action.

Roxanne Mackie

SOURCE: A review of *The Fisherman's Son,* in *The Christian Science Monitor,* December 3, 1979, p. B16.

Mirra Ginsburg has adapted [a] Georgian folk tale in *The Fisherman's Son.* It is a lesson in helping one another. In return for the kindness the fisherman's son does for each animal—a fish, a deer, a stork, and a fox—they promise to come to his aid when he needs them. In time, he does call on each of them to help him win the hand of the maiden he loves. It is a clever mirror the young man has to outwit, and the way he outwits it is even more so. The illustrations are handsomely done by Tony Chen, and the color is lush.

M. Hobbs

SOURCE: A review of *The Fisherman's Son,* in *The Junior Bookshelf,* Vol. 44, No. 4, August, 1980, pp. 167-68.

Mirra Ginsburg's good simple adaptation of an old Georgian folktale, *The Fisherman's Son,* is set on Tony Chen's soft wash backgrounds or against his sepia line-drawings which alternate with them. His beautiful muted or dark colours have vivid splashes of light. The elements of the tale are familiar: the grateful creatures who saved by the hero help him to his heart's desire. It is his princess herself who this time has set the impossible condition, to hide from her all-seeing magic mirror, but on the fourth try, the Fisherman's Son succeeds through the fox's slyness, and the creatures return to watch over the couple's happy married life.

THE TWELVE CLEVER BROTHERS AND OTHER FOOLS: FOLKTALES FROM RUSSIA (collected and adapted by Mirra Ginsburg, 1979)

Denise M. Wilms

SOURCE: A review of *The Twelve Clever Brothers and Other Fools: Folktales from Russia,* in *Booklist,* Vol. 76, No. 9, January 1, 1980, pp. 666-67.

This tidy assortment of Russian fool tales is thoroughly appealing. As Ginsburg tells them, they are punchy and pared down, with as much slapstick silliness as sly, quick humor. Once in a while the fool even wins out. [Charles] Mikolaycak's robust black-and-white scenes have a life of their own; they are rich in character and novel detail, with bold, close-up compositions that demand attention. The collection is a good entertainment package, rewarding when read either alone or aloud.

Kirkus Reviews

SOURCE: A review of *The Twelve Clever Brothers and Other Fools,* in *Kirkus Reviews,* Vol. XLVIII, No. 4, February 15, 1980, p. 218.

In the first of these 14 meager pickings from Russian folklore, twelve brothers on their way to town stop overnight at an inn and leave their sleds facing town so they will know which way to proceed in the morning. But the innkeeper tricks them by turning the sleds and they all end up back home. In the last story the twelve brothers return, this time sleeping outdoors in a circle, feet together in the center so that no one will be on the "outside," but then are unable to get up in the morning because no one can tell his own feet from the others. In some of the other entries a peasant raises a wolf cub with his goats; a poor man wins a golden hen, barters down, and ends up with a stick; and a foolish youngest brother sells his only possession, an ox, to a tree, then has the last laugh when he finds his "payment"—stolen treasure slashed in the hollow trunk. Some of the "tales" are only one-paragraph jokes; others draw out similar one-note japes for six or seven pages; none will add to the pool of fool stories. And as might be expected [Charles] Mikolaycak's turgid embellishments—one double-page prelude to each story—have nothing to do with folk humor and do nothing to draw viewers into the stories.

Zena Sutherland

SOURCE: A review of *The Twelve Clever Brothers and Other Fools,* in *Bulletin of the Center for Children's Books,* Vol. 33, No. 8, April, 1980, p. 152.

A frieze that looks like a band of red and white embroidery is a handsome contrast to the black and white of the print and the boldly designed but subtly executed pictures that introduce each story. Sources are identified: Russian, Latvian, Assyrian, Moldavian, etc. Many of the tales are variants of noodlehead stories from other cultures; the twelve clever brothers, for example, return to their own village by mistake, just as do the fools of Chelm, and the old familiar counting donkeys device is the base of another story. A very pleasant collection, adapted in sprightly style, and nice for reading aloud or alone, as well as for storytelling.

OOKIE-SPOOKY (retold by Mirra Ginsburg, 1979)

Publishers Weekly

SOURCE: A review of *Ookie-Spooky,* in *Publishers Weekly,* Vol. 217, No. 2, January 18, 1980, pp. 140-41.

Ginsburg's freewheeling verses turn [Korney] Chukovsky's original into gleeful nonsense, exuberantly illustrated by [Emily] McCully in dashing colors. Masha settles down in her room with a sketch-book and contentedly crayons portraits of family and friends. "This is a woolly sheep / And this is baby asleep." Then the child puzzles herself by drawing mysterious lines and curves that might be but are not a cat, a bull, a mule or a rat. The thing has six legs and great big teeth; it is a monster, in fact, Ookie-Spooky. The thing Masha conjures up is so horrible that she throws the book away and hides from Ookie-Spooky under her bed. Beginners should enjoy chanting the rhymes and will surely respond to Masha's pictures, inspired by those made by McCully's own small son.

THE NIGHT IT RAINED PANCAKES: ADAPTED FROM A RUSSIAN FOLKTALE (adapted by Mirra Ginsburg, 1979)

Roxanne Mackie

SOURCE: "Colorful Pictures, Lively Tales," in *The Christian Science Monitor,* April 14, 1980, p. B7.

Where does Mirra Ginsburg find the delightful folktales she is so good at adapting for young readers? Again, she gives us an amusing story, this time from a Russian lore. It concerns two brothers, Ivan and Stephan, and the pot of gold Ivan finds. Ivan, being more clever than his brother, must come up with a way to keep the gold from the lord of the manor. What does this have to do with it raining pancakes at night? That is part of the clever answer Ivan comes up with in this book for ages 6-9. Douglas Florian's illustrations add hilarity to this amusing tale.

Kirkus Reviews

SOURCE: A review of *The Night It Rained Pancakes,* in *Kirkus Reviews,* Vol. XLVIII, No. 8, April 15, 1980, p. 512.

If you can use more joke-type folk tales turned out in easy-reader form, you can probably amuse beginning readers with this version of a familiar ploy. Here farmer Ivan finds a pot of gold but fears his simple brother Stepan will blab and the landlord will demand the gold. So Ivan goes about hanging pancakes on trees, putting a fish in his rabbit trap and vice versa, just so when Stepan does tell of the gold it will be dismissed as one more pipe dream. Aside from the difference in dress (which puts Ivan in a most unlikely plowing outfit), [Douglas] Florian's crude cartoons make both brothers look equally simple.

Paul Heins

SOURCE: A review of *The Night It Rained Pancakes: Adapted from a Russian Folktale,* in *The Horn Book Magazine,* Vol. LVI, No. 4, August, 1980, p. 401.

When clever Ivan found a pot of gold while he was plowing, he knew he would have to prevent his simple brother Stepan from revealing the fact to the lord of the manor. Exchanging the contents of a rabbit trap and a fish net and hanging some of their supper pancakes on trees, Ivan was able to bamboozle Stepan into believing that the night they brought the gold home was full of incredible happenings. Despite his promise to remain silent, foolish Stepan could not keep the secret to himself, but his accounts of the events attending the haul served only to disgust the lord of the manor and to allay any suspicions concerning the concealed treasure. The easy-to-read book is illustrated with caricaturish colored line drawings—pictures which highlight the peasant humor and ingenuity of the story. No source is given for the tale.

📖 KITTEN FROM ONE TO TEN (1980)

Publishers Weekly

SOURCE: A review of *Kitten from One to Ten,* in *Publishers Weekly,* Vol. 217, No. 23, June 13, 1980, p. 74.

In verses as frisky as her little hero, Ginsburg entertains mightily while she introduces counting basics to toddlers. One kitten pussyfoots out of his basket and outdoors, looking for creatures smaller than he to play tricks on. He chases three squirrels, hisses four puppies, etc., having a high old time, until he stalks 10 yellow baby chicks. Then mama hen appears with a blasting "Cluck Clack!" and the cat's four paws hardly touch the ground as he races for the haven of his basket at home. The heaven-blue of each page creates a perfect background for the white-white of the prankster's fur and the spanking colors that gifted [Giulio] Maestro paints other creatures and objects in the miniature suspense story.

Barbara Elleman

SOURCE: A review of *Kitten from One to Ten,* in *Booklist,* Vol. 77, No. 1, September 1, 1980, p. 43.

One white, yellow-eyed kitten hops from its basket to explore the world. It curiously scampers across a blue, uncluttered backdrop to explore three squirrels, four puppies, five ducklings, six clowns, and so forth until it comes upon ten chicks, whereupon Mama Hen's "Cluck, clack" sends it home again. Children just learning their numbers will happily repeat the rhythmical lines ("To meow at seven stars in heaven, / To sniff at eight berries on a plate") and will find the familiar objects satisfying to count. There is just enough story to capture preschoolers' imaginations and enough substance to hold their attention.

📖 WHERE DOES THE SUN GO AT NIGHT? (adapted by Mirra Ginsburg, 1980)

Brenda Durrin Maloney

SOURCE: A review of *Where Does the Sun Go at Night?,* in *School Library Journal,* Vol. 27, No. 2, October, 1980, pp. 134-35.

[Jose] Aruego's and [Ariane] Dewey's familiar humorous animals watch the sun set and the first of a series of childlike questions is asked, "Where does the sun go at night?" The sun goes to his grandmother's house in the "deep blue sky" where it sleeps in a "woolly cloud." We see the animals burrowed into clouds, too, and their comic presence is a nice juxtaposition to the quiet rhythm of the words, much the same rhythm as in *Whose Mouse Are You?*. The most comic illustration shows the drowsy creatures being wakened by the morning's alarm clock. "Who is the clock? The village cock." A colorful flight of fancy produced by a winning author-illustrator team.

Kirkus Reviews

SOURCE: A review of *Where Does the Sun Go at Night?,* in *Kirkus Reviews,* Vol. XLIX, No. 1, January 1, 1981, pp. 1, 2.

A cheerful question-and-answer charmer, based on an Armenian song and played out (in a child's stead) by a passel of inquisitive barnyard animals. *Shrewdly* inquisitive, indeed, for the cow, sheep, pig, etc., follow up one query with the logical next: to the answer that the sun goes to his grandma's house at night, that he sleeps in his grandma's bed, they pose the question, "Who is his grandma?" And when they've learned that the sun sleeps under "a woolly cloud," they ask, naturally, "Who tucks him in?" But by this time, in the imaginative spirit of things, the cow, sheep, pig, etc., are each tucked into a woolly cloud themselves . . . until, come morning, they wake in a flowery meadow. But: "Who wakes the morning?" "The alarm clock." So: "Who is the clock?" We won't tell you the answer (a hint: it rhymes); we'll let you see the animals cringe—eyes closed, ears covered, even as you and me. A winning conceptualization—complete to each creature's cloud-borne dreams.

Mary M. Burns

SOURCE: A review of *Where Does the Sun Go at Night? Adapted from an Armenian Song,* in *The Horn Book Magazine,* Vol. LVII, No. 1, February, 1981, p. 41.

Illustrated by Jose Aruego and Ariane Dewey. The brief, childlike text, arranged as a series of questions and answers, resolves the mystery of the sun's nighttime whereabouts. It underscores the universality of the young child's perceptions—a notion extended in the brilliantly colored, anthropomorphic illustrations. Although executed in the artists' recognizable style, the pictures are by no means repetitions of previous work; they demonstrate subtle changes in placement, design, and control by synthesizing familiar techniques into a new statement. From the stylized, slightly cartooned animals wrapped in cloud blankets to the gorgeous cock hailing the dawn, the emphasis is on the characters as they act out the text—a clear perspective which results in a blithe-spirited book for the very young.

THE SUN'S ASLEEP BEHIND THE HILL (adapted by Mirra Ginsburg, 1982)

Patricia Dooley

SOURCE: A review of *The Sun's Asleep Behind the Hill,* in *School Library Journal,* Vol. 28, No. 7, March, 1982, p. 132.

The day winds to a close here in a wonderfully rhythmic and reassuringly orderly fashion. The sun grows tired and goes away "to sleep behind the hill": the breeze, the leaves, the bird, the squirrel and finally, inevitably, the child, also grow tired and seek their rest. The moon comes out, recapitulates the series, and takes possession of the nighttime world. This diurnal drama is set in a vast and rolling park: the artist first draws the scene from a great height, and the subsequent depth of field is interestingly varied throughout, right down to intimate close-ups of the bird and the squirrel in their nests. A kite flown by the small boy provides continuity, appearing on many pages, including the last, wordless image of the full moon shining on the sleeping child (the only indoor scene).

Kirkus Reviews

SOURCE: A review of *The Sun's Asleep Behind the Hill,* in *Kirkus Reviews,* Vol. L, No. 6, March 15, 1982, pp. 341-42.

"The sun shone / in the sky all day. / The sun grew tired / and went away." With those quiet, arresting lines begins an Armenian lullaby reconceived here in spacious, deep-toned pictures—with insets at alternate openings to illustrate the refrain ("The sun shone/ in the sky all day. / The sun grew tired / and went away / to sleep behind the hill"). As the twilight deepens, the leaves, the bird, and the squirrel each grows tired and seeks rest; and when the little boy (glimpsed from the first flying his kite) grows tired in turn, his mother carries him homeward—while the moon rises from behind the hill, sings its solitary song, and, on the last wordless page, shines into the little boy's room (where the kite hangs on the wall). That particular scene, potentially a children's-book cliché, has instead a wondering, timeless feel. Altogether a simple, reverberating entity.

Leonard S. Marcus

SOURCE: "Worlds without Words," in *The Washington Post Book Review,* Vol. XII, No. 19, May 9, 1982, pp. 17-18, 22.

The Sun's Asleep Behind the Hill, with text adapted from a traditional Armenian lyric by Mirra Ginsburg and with illustrations by Paul O. Zelinsky, is a poignantly affecting work, a picture book of exceptional unity and grace.

According to the hauntingly timbred vision of this night-song, sleep overtakes the natural world in little fits and starts, with word quietly passing from wind to leaf to bird that it is at last time to set aside the day's work for a night of rest.

The illustrator's atmospheric yet tautly observed paintings follow the progress of the sleepers, flashing backward, as the text does, to show them also at the height of day. In several paintings one image has been set within the borders of another, with the inset painting a variation, in time-of-day or of perspective, of the image on the page before. The effect of this unusual arrangement is much like that of the repetition of certain lines in the verse text: a rhythmic binding of image and emotions such as is always the nightsong or lullaby's secret subject, whatever the words set to its music happen to be.

Zena Sutherland

SOURCE: A review of *The Sun's Asleep Behind the Hill,* in *Bulletin of the Center for Children's Books,* Vol. 36, No. 1, September, 1982, p. 9.

Soft paintings of outdoor scenes grow more dark and quiet as the book progresses, a soothing visual accompaniment to Ginsburg's adaptation of an Armenian lullaby. The text has a pattern that gives it shape: the sun goes to sleep behind the hill, and the breeze comments on this and adds, "It's time that I was still," then the leaves comment on the retirement of the breeze (each comment is framed to set it apart from the linking text) and say, "Now we can also rest." A mother brings her child home as the park grows still and dark, the moon comes out, and the last picture shows the child sleeping in the moonlight. A gentle, peaceful book for bedtime reading-aloud.

ACROSS THE STREAM (1982)

Zena Sutherland

SOURCE: A review of *Across the Stream,* in *Bulletin of the Center for Children's Books,* Vol. 36, No. 6, February, 1983, p. 107.

A hen and her three chicks have a bad dream; they run to a stream, where an obliging duck and her three ducklings ferry them across, leaving the bad dream on the other side of the stream. This has some fallacies: the shared dream and also the "leaving" it as though it had a physical entity, but it's a story with a simple problem/solution structure, it's told in simple rhyme, and the large-scale pictures, colorful and cheerful, have the appeal of the animals, all of which make it a good picture book for reading aloud and showing, especially to a group.

Ethel L. Heins

SOURCE: A review of *Across the Stream,* in *The Horn Book Magazine,* Vol. LIX, No. 1, February, 1983, p. 37.

"A hen and three chicks / had a bad dream. / They ran and came / to a deep, wide stream. / The hen said, 'Cluck, / we are in luck. / I see three ducklings and a duck.'" The rhymed text serves as the briefest possible scenario for the simple tale; for only in the pictures does one see that the culprit of the nightmare is, in fact, a prowling fox. And although about fifty more words round out the verbal narrative, its visual representation actually conveys the full drama of the rescue. The full-page pictures, notable for composition; clean, unwavering line; and bright, cheery color, are perhaps the artist's finest work so far. They show the hen crossing the stream to safety on the back of the duck while the chicks astride the ducklings complete the procession—leaving a disappointed fox on the other side. Sharp-eyed observers will notice a tiny silhouetted figure of one of the characters placed at the bottom of most of the left-hand pages.

Margery Fisher

SOURCE: A review of *Across the Stream,* in *Growing Point,* Vol. 22, No. 1, May, 1983, p. 4081.

Like the classic 'Rosie's Walk', this nursery adventure from America has the simplest possible text, describing how after dreaming of a lurking enemy, a hen gets her family ferried over the stream by a friendly duck—'a chick on a duckling . . . the hen on the duck'. The enemy is seen only as a russet tail hanging outside the reeds on the bank just vacated. Bold, folksy illustrations in paint and ink line emphasise the contrasts of colour and shape in a gentle comedy of near-disaster right on the wave-length of a child of two and upwards.

Edward Blishen

SOURCE: "In Brief," in *The Times Literary Supplement,* No. 4190, July 22, 1983, p. 779.

Across the Stream . . . is a deceptively simple story aimed at the under-fives which is lifted above the ordinary by its minimal text and large fresh pictures. Mirra Ginsburg's words have enough drama in them to tell the tale of a hen and three chicks and their escape from a fox. They also have enough intrinsic interest to detain the reader over crisp rhymes ("The hen said Cluck, we are in luck") and intermittent rumba-like rhythms ("a chick on a duckling, a chick on a duckling, a chick on a duckling, and the hen on a duck"). The design is striking: the words are printed in a large clear black-letter script a few words to a page. The pictures are large and fill the frame. The whole thing has a clean calm feel about it: it is the sort of book that will stand up very well to the reading and rereading that this age group always demands.

THE MAGIC STOVE (adapted by Mirra Ginsburg, 1983)

Kirkus Reviews

SOURCE: A review of *The Magic Stove,* in *Kirkus Reviews,* Vol. LI, No. 9, May 1, 1983, pp. 519-20.

The old farm couple is poor and hungry, down to their last crust when the pecking of their rooster (their only animal) uncovers a little iron stove in the back yard. The stove, in true folk-tale form, proves an inexhaustible supplier of pies, with whatever filling the diner requests. But it is also, as the tale-type will have it, stolen by someone who doesn't need it: none other here than the king himself, who is passing by and invited in for a bite. How the stove is retrieved involves some business with the rooster, who follows the king and cries out an accusation in the midst of a feast. When the king's servants throw the rooster into a pond, the bird drinks up all the water; and when they then throw him into the fire, he spits the water out. The king slips, the rooster catches the stove and returns to his owners, "And there [man, woman, and rooster] are to this day, eating pie, and singing songs, and never troubled any more by thieving kings." Despite the rooster's clever survival tricks, a motif that might have been borrowed from another tale, this adaptation of a Russian "magic cooking pot" is flavorless and unremarkable. The pictures are inert, the figures fixed with stock, exaggerated expressions as if carved by an amateur without feeling.

Zena Sutherland

SOURCE: A review of *The Magic Stove,* in *Bulletin of the Center for Children's Books,* Vol. 37, No. 2, October, 1983, p. 27.

In a competent adaptation of a Russian folktale, a poor man's kindness is rewarded, a magic device is used, and justice triumphs over greed. All these traditional themes are combined in the story of a rooster who produces a magic stove (it makes any kind of pie one requests) and then retrieves it from the avaricious king who has stolen it from the peasant couple who had kindly shared their home and their bounty. The illustrations, pastel-tinted, have a spacious quality, a brisk use of line, and ornamental costume details; they are often naive in perspective or figure-drawing, but vigorous.

Barbara Peklo Serling

SOURCE: A review of *The Magic Stove,* in *School Library Journal,* Vol. 30, No. 2, October, 1983, pp. 148-49.

A poor little old man, a poor little old woman and a rooster share a hut. When the cupboard is bare, the rooster unearths a magic little stove which will bake any pie of one's choice. The man and woman are now secure until the king visits and steals the magic stove. The rooster sees all and follows the king to his palace, accusing him before his friends. The greedy king tries to drown, then burn the rooster, but the rooster survives and finally retrieves the magic stove from the thieving king. The little old man, the little old woman and the rooster live contentedly thereafter. The warmly colored illustrations by Linda Heller support the folk aspect of the tale with simple primitive but stylized drawings. The scenes are almost frozen on the page as if one stopped an old-time movie on a single frame. In this way the expressive action of the flowing story is accented. This pleasant rendering of a Russian folk tale deserves a moderate "crow" of praise.

FOUR BRAVE SAILORS (1987)

Kirkus Reviews

SOURCE: A review of *Four Brave Sailors,* in *Kirkus Reviews,* Vol. LV, No. 12, July 1, 1987, p. 991.

A delightful brief verse is amplified and embellished by some of Caldecott Honor winner [Nancy] Tafuri's most beautiful illustrations.

The sailors are toy mice in a ship on a small shelf above a sleeping child's bed; coming to life, they go out to a sea suggested by the wallpaper. "They do not fear / the storms, They do not fear / The whales, They do not fear / The pirates [seabirds] / With their scarlet sails. Their courage / Is a Legend / For all to marvel at. / They are afraid / Of nothing—/ EXCEPT / MY / TIGER / CAT"—and so come home to safety.

Perfectly cadenced, with touches of both humor and mystery, Ginsburg's text is well complemented by Tafuri's fantastical sea, intrepid adventurers, cozy toys and warm, sly cat. Bold, black outlining is invaded by large, stylized figures in black line and watercolor, combined with oversized boldface type in a striking, elegant design. Just right to share with the youngest.

Nancy A. Gifford

SOURCE: A review of *Four Brave Sailors,* in *School Library Journal,* Vol. 34, No. 2, October, 1987, p. 111.

Four toy mice come to life in a little boy's dream, pushing their sailboat off the shelf after the child and cat have gone to sleep. These four brave the waves as they pass penguins, a walrus, a polar bear, and pirates and they weather a fierce storm before returning to their shelf to face their one fear that becomes reality as the cat opens an eye. Large, clear, and colorful illustrations and short rhymed text should make this inviting to young children, both individually and in story programs. Children will be quick to notice that some of the animals the mice see on their voyage appear in stuffed form on a toy shelf when the mice return to the child's bedroom. There is a similar continuity with white seagulls on a blue background on the endpapers, gray gulls on the same blue on the child's bedroom wallpaper, and gulls flying around when the sailors are at sea. The art work is the dominant and stronger part of the book, and it's likely to attract numerous different "tellings" by children too young to appreciate the text but old enough to enjoy the illustrations.

Margery Fisher

SOURCE: A review of *Four Brave Sailors,* in *Growing Point,* Vol. 26, No. 5, January, 1988, p. 4924.

In a brief verse text a boy, who appears only at the end, recounts the adventures of four (presumably pet) mice in their middy costumes as they sail past whales, seal and walrus, fend off piratical seabirds, survive a storm, but shrink from the cat waiting for them at home. Mannered pictures lend a certain personality to the mice while the animals they encounter are posed more naturalistically on each facing page.

M. Hobbs

SOURCE: A review of *Four Brave Sailors,* in *The Junior Bookshelf,* Vol. 52, No. 1, February, 1988, pp. 19-20.

[Mirra] Ginsburg's seems a rather uncharacteristic fantasy, beautifully presented in her usual extra-large print and illustrated by Nancy Tafuri's enchanting soft colours, cool blues predominating, as befits the sailing theme. The reader can see that the puzzled narrator's four sailors are mice, whose voyages are dreamed by a small boy in bed, with a yellow cat sleeping at his feet, in a room with blue swallow-covered wallpaper which is also the endpapers. Fearlessly, the four face penguins, a walrus, polar bear, storms, whale, bird-pirates (though finally we are shown the creatures are toys), but the cat is another matter.

THE CHINESE MIRROR (adapted by Mirra Ginsburg, 1988)

Publishers Weekly

SOURCE: A review of *The Chinese Mirror,* in *Publishers Weekly,* Vol. 233, No. 4, February 12, 1988, p. 84.

In a setting of long ago Korea, a peasant who has traveled all the way to China brings back a small round mirror. Afraid its magic will be lost if everybody sees it, he hides it in a trunk. But he likes the mirror so much, he secretly looks at it and laughs about it to himself. His wife wonders what he is doing, and when she sneaks a look at it, sees a pretty young girl from China. She misunderstands the reflection, and believes it is her husband's mistress, and rushes to show her mother-in-law, who, of course, sees only a wrinkled old crone. Each person sees a different image in the mirror, and it is eventually smashed into 100 shiny splinters. A poetic and sparse retelling brings freshness and joy to this tale.

Kirkus Reviews

SOURCE: A review of *The Chinese Mirror,* in *Kirkus Reviews,* Vol. LVI, No. 5, March 1, 1988, p. 362.

In a Korean folktale, a traveler returns from China with an

unknown wonder: a small mirror. He thinks it's funny, the way it makes faces at him, but—not wanting to wear it out—hides it in a trunk. There his wife discovers it, and is horrified to think he has a picture of another, prettier woman. She wails to her mother-in-law that her faithless husband has brought a young wife from China—but the old woman, seeing a wrinkled crone, scoffs at her. So it goes till a final amusing error results in the mirror's destruction.

Although it does depend on an unlikely premise (surely even people who have never seen a mirror would have seen reflections in water), this is a delightful comedy, with all the appeal of such stories as "The Blind Men and the Elephant." Adopting a Korean genre style characterized by vigorous yet fluid brushwork in black augmented by watercolors in soft tints, Caldecott-winner [Margot] Zemach beautifully captures the story's humor and milieu. Perfect for sharing with a group.

Patricia Dooley

SOURCE: A review of *The Chinese Mirror,* in *School Library Journal,* Vol. 34, No. 8, April, 1988, p. 95.

When a traveller brings home the first mirror his Korean village has ever seen, it causes a chain of misperceptions. A lot of credulity is required here, both from the villagers and from readers. (Had no one ever seen a reflection in a puddle or a shiny pot?) Children might suspend their disbelief more readily if only there were a clear point to the confusion: but here the mistakes neither reveal character nor lead to a moral. Perhaps something has been lost in the retelling. [Margot] Zemach's pictures, inspired by two 18th-Century Korean genre painters, do what they can to provide interest. The appealing watercolors are Oriental in brushstrokes and details, Western in the cartoon-like exaggeration of expression and gesture. The art can't make up, however, for the kernal of wisdom missing from the heart of this folktale. Every culture has "Three Sillies" tales of naivete and foolishness. The more distant and exotic their origin, the harder it is for children to see themselves in them and the easier it is for them to laugh *at* those simpletons in foreign dress.

Zena Sutherland

SOURCE: A review of *The Chinese Mirror,* in *Bulletin of the Center for Children's Books,* Vol. 41, No. 9, May, 1988, p. 176.

Watercolor illustrations, more spare of line than is most of [Margot] Zemach's work, are "inspired by the paintings of two eighteenth-century Korean genre painters, Sin Yunbok and Kim Hong-do," an endpaper note states. The soft colors and sly humor of the pictures echo the quiet tone and humor of Ginsburg's retelling of a Korean folktale. When a villager returns from China with a strange object that mimics his actions (nobody knows what it is: a mirror) the members of his family take turns looking at the piece

of glass. The wife is jealous because she sees a picture of a pretty young woman, her mother-in-law is confused because the "picture" is that of an older woman, while the father-in-law is even more baffled, because the picture isn't that of a woman at all. No moral here, unless it is that things aren't what they seem, but the message to the reader is one children appreciate: you are smart enough to understand although the characters in the story are not. Nicely done.

Hanna B. Zeiger

SOURCE: A review of *The Chinese Mirror,* in *The Horn Book Magazine,* Vol. LXIV, No. 3, May-June, 1988, p. 365.

Illustrated by Margot Zemach. In a long, long ago time, a man leaves his village in Korea to travel all the way to China. While there, he buys a strange, round, shiny thing which makes funny faces back at him and gives him much pleasure. Bringing this mirror home, he hides it in a trunk and takes it out secretly from time to time to laugh. Overcome with curiosity, his wife spies on him, and, when he goes out, she looks into the shiny round thing, which sets off a comical chain of misperceptions. She wails because she thinks her husband has brought home a pretty, young woman whom he keeps in the trunk; her mother-in-law sees a wrinkled old crone, and her father-in-law sees the neighbor's grandpa in the mirror. When their son sees a little boy stealing his pebble, a passing neighbor looks into the mirror and shouts at the fat bully who looks back. Punching him in the nose, he shatters the mirror and gets rid of all the people in it. This elegantly simple little story is a seamless blend of folk-tale adaptation with illustrations that were inspired by Korean genre paintings of the eighteenth century.

ASLEEP, ASLEEP (1992)

Ilene Cooper

SOURCE: A review of *Asleep, Asleep,* in *Booklist,* Vol. 88, No. 17, May 1, 1992, p. 1608.

The number of good-night books continues to grow, but this special collaboration by Ginsburg and [Nancy] Tafuri should find a ready place on sleepy-time shelves. Handsome two-page spreads featuring large-scale paintings of animals contain the brief text: "Are the wolves asleep? Asleep." Dusky night colors come out of the forest and lake into the room where a mother holds her toddler. "Everything and everyone / Asleep, asleep. / Only you and the wind / are awake." But soon, mother, with the help of the breeze, puts child to sleep, too. The simple, hypnotic rhyme should have the same effect on listeners.

Elizabeth S. Watson

SOURCE: A review of *Asleep, Asleep,* in *The Horn*

Book Magazine, Vol. LXVIII, No. 3, May-June, 1992, p. 326.

Illustrated by Nancy Tafuri. The sleepy litany of a toddler fighting one more bedtime is softly answered by her mother in this mood poem perfectly illustrated with sleeping creatures, starlit meadows, and sheer curtains billowing in a summer evening's breeze. "Are the wolves asleep? Asleep. And the bees? Asleep. And the birds? Asleep, asleep." The size and shape of the book echo the solid comfort of the art and text. Each smooth, soft line reinforces the relaxed comfort of sleep. This spoken lullaby will help ease little ones into dreamland.

Meg Wolitzer

SOURCE: A review of *Asleep, Asleep,* in *The New York Times Book Review,* September 13, 1992, p. 36.

Asleep, Asleep, by Mirra Ginsburg, brings us right into the still heart of the night, when almost all the creatures of the earth are sleeping. "Are the wolves asleep?" the book begins, "Asleep. And the bees? Asleep. And the birds? Asleep, asleep. And the foxes? Fast asleep." It's not until the end of the book that we see the wakeful baby and her mother, whose questions and answers form a rhythmic lullaby. The prose, inspired by a Russian verse, is further enhanced by Nancy Tafuri's sweeping, colorful illustrations, each of which generously fills two facing pages, evoking a nocturnal, dreamy mood. The combination of text and pictures also creates a commendable parity among the animal kingdom in this book. Creatures that might seem fierce or just a little scary to children when awake are all made gentle and appealing through the great equalizer of sleep.

📖 THE KING WHO TRIED TO FRY AN EGG ON HIS HEAD (adapted by Mirra Ginsburg, 1994)

Deborah Stevenson

SOURCE: A review of *The King Who Tried to Fry an Egg on His Head,* in *Bulletin of the Center for Children's Books,* Vol. 47, No. 6, February, 1994, p. 187.

When an impoverished king gives his daughters in marriage to the Sun, the Moon, and the Raven in exchange for assistance in gathering the family's grain, the arrangement works out well and the girls are happy with their new spouses. Unfortunately the silly king tries to emulate the deeds of his new relations, but he can't cook an egg on his head like the Sun, light up the bathhouse with his fingers like the Moon, or sleep in a tree like the Raven; he eventually retires, bruised and dismayed after falling out of the tree, to the arms of his long-suffering wife. This story has an appealing blend of the noodlehead and the supernatural, with enough repetition to involve young listeners, who may themselves have encountered the pitfalls of imitation. [Will] Hillenbrand's pastel on rough paper illustrations have a pageant of hues and some intriguing

characters whose surreally enlarged heads cause their tiny features to appear humorous and slightly mournful, although the cheerful countenances of the magic sons-in-law are counterbalanced by some ethereal night scenes and a distinct—if genial—sense of power. There's no source note for the supposedly Russian tale, and the ending is a little flat, but the general happiness, loony slapstick, and hints of majesty in the tale will satisfy all manner of young eggheads.

Mary Harris Veeder

SOURCE: A review of *The King Who Tried to Fry an Egg on His Head,* in *Booklist,* Vol. 90, No. 12, February 15, 1994, p. 1084.

The first sentence of this story ("A long, long time ago, and far away, there lived a King") is fairy-tale boilerplate. The second ("This King was very poor, and he was not very clever") is not. The king makes marriages for his three beautiful daughters with the Sun, the Moon, and the Raven. When he goes to visit his children, he finds that all of them are living better than he is. From each son-in-law, the king learns a marvelous trick, but when he tries to practice the tricks for his wife, they don't work. The Sun can fry an egg on his head, but the king can't. The engaging simpleton of a monarch is more closely related to James Marshall's Stupids than to Prince Charming, and [Will] Hillenbrand's oil and oil pastel paintings, strong on golden reds, oranges, and golds, emphasize the gap. The king has patches on his sleeves, holes in his stockings, and the countenance of a cherubic Humpty-Dumpty Lenin. The humor is not directed at the king in a mean-spirited way. The monarch learns his limitations in the end, and readers—like the queen—will be happy.

Publishers Weekly

SOURCE: A review of *The King Who Tried to Fry an Egg on His Head,* in *Publishers Weekly,* Vol. 241, No. 12, March 21, 1994, p. 72.

This flat retelling of a Russian folktale may have lost something in the translation. An impoverished king marries off his three daughters to the Sun, the Moon and the Raven in return for the warmth, light and gathering skills that his prospective sons-in-law promise to provide. Not long after the princesses leave home, the king pays a visit to each newlywed couple, each time receiving gifts and special treatment from his hosts. But when the king subsequently attempts to duplicate the feats of the Sun, the Moon and the Raven for his wife back at home, he fails and is proven a fool. Ginsburg's simple sentences and chatty style set an appropriately light-hearted mood, but cannot overcome a lack of drama and a weak, abrupt denouement. Demonstrating a slightly different style here, [Will] Hillenbrand's richly hued oils offer a likable cast of egg-headed royalty and a wide range of perspectives. Unfortunately, even some inventive images—a spooky, gnarled tree; a bath house dissected by brilliant beams of moonlight—do little to elevate an unsatisfying story.

Nancy Vasilakis

SOURCE: A review of *The King Who Tried to Fry an Egg on His Head,* in *The Horn Book Magazine,* Vol. LXX, No. 2, March-April, 1994, p. 210.

Mirra Ginsburg is at the top of her form in this sprightly retelling of an old Russian folktale. A poor and foolish king offers to give his three daughters in marriage to the sun, the moon, and the raven, respectively, if they will in turn keep him warm, give him light, and help him pick up the grain he had dropped out of a mouse-eaten sack. The silly man's wishes come to pass as they might be expected to, and his daughters are taken away by their assigned mates. The king then goes to visit each one, with amusing results. When he imitates the sun, for example, who cooked an egg by breaking it over his fiery head, the egg that the king breaks over his own skull naturally just drips down his collar. The consequences of his visits to the other two princesses and their mates are equally disastrous. "I married a fool," repeats the long-suffering, even-tempered queen after each escapade. Following a final, painful fall from a tree, he vows never again, and the tale ends with a cleverly worded, tongue-in-cheek moral that the king and queen "lived peacefully and by their own wits forever after." Will Hillenbrand's chunky caricatures of bumbling royalty wearing rags are sure to evoke chuckles. The large figures and energetic compositions will show up well in group settings, although better attention might have been paid to the placement of the type on the pages. The nonsense, however, is bound to please.

Kirkus Reviews

SOURCE: A review of *The King Who Tried to Fry an Egg on His Head,* in *Kirkus Reviews,* Vol. LXII, No. 7, April 1, 1994, p. 479.

A Russian tale retold by a popular picture-book author (*Mushroom in the Rain; Two Greedy Bears*). Hoping to provide for his hungry family, a penniless king throws himself on the mercy of Sun, Moon, and Raven: If the Sun will warm him, if the Moon will give him light, and if the Raven will help him gather grain, he'll let them marry his three daughters. When the king goes to visit the happy couples, he comes home boasting of tricks learned from his sons-in-law—e.g., cooking an omelette on his head, like the Sun. Watching raw egg trickle down her husband's neck, his long-suffering wife remarks, "I married a fool" and cooks hers on the stove. After three such failures, he groans "Never again" and resolves to live by his own wits. [Will] Hillenbrand's illustrations for this comical head shaker employ royally rich colors and patterns, whimsical, skewed shapes, and wisps of line that deftly characterize the winsome daughters, put-upon queen, and feckless king. No source given.

Heide Piehler

SOURCE: A review of *The King Who Tried to Fry an Egg on His Head,* in *School Library Journal,* Vol. 40, No. 5, May, 1994, pp. 107-08.

Ginsburg continues the celebration of Russian folklore she began in *The Twelve Clever Brothers and Other Fools.* In this tale, a poor and foolish king lives in a "tumbledown palace" with his wife and daughters. Rather than starve to death, he makes a deal. If Sun will warm him, Moon give him light, and Raven gather grain, he will give each of them one of his daughters in marriage. The nontraditional sons-in-law all have unusual talents that the king tries to emulate—unsuccessfully, of course. Finally, after a fall from a tree, the foolish man decides that it's best to live by his own wits, however limited. Children will delight in the silly, often slapstick humor of the king's antics in this smooth and lively retelling. However, it is the illustrations that really bring the offbeat story to life. The folk-art paintings effectively combine regal blues and reds with rustic browns and yellows to create a sense of a royal fool. The characters' exaggerated proportions and flattened faces further add to the feeling of good-natured buffoonery. Libraries with a demand for funny books will want to consider this title.

THE OLD MAN AND HIS BIRDS (1994)

Kirkus Reviews

SOURCE: A review of *The Old Man and His Birds,* in *Kirkus Reviews,* Vol. LXII, No. 20, October 15, 1994, pp. 1407-08.

From Ginsburg (*The King Who Tried to Fry an Egg on His Head*) comes this folk riddle told in a spare, almost laconic, style. A mysterious old codger shakes three birds from his sleeve and thereby changes the seasons, an event reflected not only in the surrounding land but also in the color of the old man's voluminous robes. Shake a sleeve, and the birds bring a cold, white winter; another shake, and it is the prime of the year; shake it again, and the birds herald the good old summertime; once more, and the leaves begin to fall. The riddle lies in the birds, whose forms convey a message, and it brings a much needed sense of fun to the old man, who is not so much Olympian as just plain remote. The story projects little warmth and little to identify with, and [Donna] Ruff's pastel illustrations are too subdued to dazzle or charm the viewer. Something must have been lost in the adaptation.

What works here is the riddle; once that's solved there isn't much enticement to dip into these pages again.

Margaret Bush

SOURCE: A review of *The Old Man and His Birds,* in *The*

Horn Book Magazine, Vol. LXX, No. 6, November-December, 1996, pp. 718-19.

Illustrated by Donna Ruff. An old man in a golden robe that is itself part of a golden landscape is the central figure of a spare poetic tale warmly rendered in pastels. "He raised his right arm and shook it, and three birds flew out of his sleeve." As the golden robe turns white, animals hide inside bare trees, and a distant lighted house on a snowy hill is the hiding place of humans. Mirra Ginsburg credits the nineteenth-century Russian collector of folklore, Vladimir Dal, for the idea for this expressive view of the changing seasons. All scenes fill the beautifully developed double-page spreads, with the short text framed as an inset. Sometimes the white-bearded man in a golden, beribboned turban is only a small figure or even unseen. He then dominates in soft swirling splendor as he releases the birds. "The birds that fly out of the old man's sleeves aren't ordinary birds. Each has a name, and each has four wings. Each wing has seven feathers." In the end the parable is a mystical riddle, and the reader is posed a set of questions. "Why does each wing have seven feathers? Why is one half of every feather white, the other black? Can you guess? Can you tell?" Superbly celebrating the cycle of the seasons and presenting symbol in a readily discernible guise, this is a lovely story-hour choice.

Additional coverage of Ginsburg's life and career is contained in the following sources published by Gale Research: *Contemporary Authors New Revision Series,* Vols. 11, 28, 54; and *Something about the Author,* Vols. 6, 92.

Welwyn Wilton Katz

1948-

Canadian author of fiction for children and young adults.

Major works include *Witchery Hill* (1984), *False Face* (1987), *The Third Magic* (1988), *Whalesinger* (1990), *Out of the Dark* (1995).

INTRODUCTION

Katz is considered an outstanding writer of fantasy literature for young adults. Her award-winning novels feature elements of ancient legend and mythology and explore the intersection of ordinary reality with the realm of the supernatural. Among her varied sources are Arthurian legend, Viking history, Shakespearean drama, Iroquois shamanism, and stories of witchcraft. Motivated by a concern for nature and for the struggles of adolescents in the contemporary world, Katz's fiction is said to display an extraordinary inventiveness and sensitivity to the issues of youth. Within her often elaborate plots and exotic settings readers will find explorations of the more personal emotions of guilt, remorse, jealousy, and trust. Additionally, Katz's skillful characterizations are generally praised by critics, as is her seemingly effortless ability to blend the fantastic and the ordinary in her narratives for young people, most notably in the quasi-historical, imagined world of 13-year-old Ben Elliot in *Out of the Dark*.

Biographical Information

Katz was born on June 7, 1948, in London, Ontario, Canada, to parents of Cornish and Scottish ancestry. After receiving her bachelor of science degree in mathematics from the University of Western Ontario in 1970 she become a high school teacher, and, though unsatisfied with this profession, continued to teach for seven years. In the mid-1970s Katz discovered the works of J. R. R. Tolkien. Inspired by his writings, she began to compose a fantasy novel for adults. Writing during her summers and evenings, she eventually took a two-year leave of absence in order to finish the book. Katz submitted her resignation in 1979 and continued with revisions to her novel, but she failed to find a publisher for it. In the 1980s she adjusted the focus of her writing and began to compose a book for children. *The Prophecy of Tau Ridoo* was published in 1982, the first of her many successful novels for young readers. Her next published work, *Witchery Hill*, appeared in 1984. Inspired by a trip to the island of Guernsey in Britain, *Witchery Hill* elicited some negative reaction in Katz's native Canada due to its frank and explicit depiction of the evil acts associated with witchcraft. With a plot based upon ancient Iroquois myth and ritual, *False Face* also stirred controversy, this time among Native Americans, some of whom felt that their stories should not be told by members of other racial or ethnic groups. The work, however, earned critical accolades and has since been translated into five European languages. In the 1990s, Katz has continued to write well-received fiction for young adults and children. Her ecologically-minded *Whalesinger* and optimistic *Out of the Dark* are considered among her finest works.

Major Works

The Prophecy of Tau Ridoo, Katz's first novel, incorporates many of the fantastic themes that she was to exploit and develop in her later works. After being transported to the magical land of Tau Ridoo, the five Aubrey children encounter the evil forces of the Red General, whose power has kept the planet in darkness for centuries. With the aid of the good sorceress Cooky, the children restore light to this magical world. The conflict between good and evil is as pronounced in *Witchery Hill*. While visiting the island of Guernsey with his father, fourteen-year-old Mike discovers that the stepmother of his new friend Lisa is a witch with demonic powers. In *Sun God, Moon Witch* (1986) Katz complicates the struggle between good and evil by exploring the necessity of balance between order and chaos. Hawthorne (or "Thorny" as she is called), is a young Canadian girl vacationing in a small English town that lies near a circle of standing stones similar to those at Stonehenge. She encounters Mr. Belman, an unscrupulous industrialist who wants to destroy the stones. Thorny later learns that Belman is actually the evil Sun God and seeks to unleash destruction in the world by eliminating the magical rocks. *False Face* expands the focus of Katz's work to include non-European myth and legend. Its heroine, 13-year-old Laney McIntyre, discovers an Iroquois mask in a bog near her home in London, Ontario. Tom Walsh, her friend who is of partial Mohawk descent, warns Laney of the evil powers of the relic, to which her mother quickly succumbs. The novel was lauded by many critics, and Katz was praised for her deft handling of real-world issues, including strained parent-child relations and racial prejudice, within the contexts of a compelling fantasy plot. In *The Third Magic* Katz exploits Arthurian legend while creating her own magical world called Nwn. Mistaken for her ancestor, the legendary Morgan Le Fay, modern-day Morgan Lefevre finds herself transported to Nwn, where she must aid young Arddu in his battle against evil. Several commentators noted that *The Third Magic* suffers from undue complexity, though many admired its elaborate structure and unpredictability as well as its inventiveness as a recasting of the story of King Arthur.

The adventure story *Whalesinger* features Nick, a young Vancouverite, who learns that his summer working as a conservationist on the California coast will be under the direction of Ray Pembroke, a man he feels is responsible for his brother's death. Joined by Marty, a learning-disabled girl with an uncanny ability to communicate with a gray whale, Nick discovers the Pembroke's research mission is simply a cover for his plan to loot the lost treasures of a sunken ship from several centuries ago. Critics noted that *Whalesinger* exhibits superb characterization—especially in its detailed rendering of Marty and Nick—and an engaging plot as it explores themes of emotional vulnerability and the possibility of trust. *Come Like Shadows* (1993) follows a doomed production of *Macbeth* performed by Canada's Stratford Festival Company. Charged with locating a prop for the play, Kincardine "Kinney" O'Neil uncovers a magical mirror that contains the witches from William Shakespeare's drama. The evil contained in the mirror leads to several accidents on the set in this suspenseful and complex story that also examines important issues in contemporary Canadian politics and draws analogies between the histories of Scotland and Canada. *Time Ghost* (1994) represents Katz's tentative exploration of science fiction motifs. Set in 2044, the novel reveals an earth ravaged by pollution and overpopulation. Sara and Dani travel back in time fifty years to learn what greed and environmental exploitation have done to the planet. Set in Newfoundland near the site of the first Viking settlement in the New World, *Out of the Dark* reveals the fantasy world of Ben Elliot. New to the area, Ben is just beginning to deal with the recent murder of his mother. In order to escape reality, he imagines himself as Tor, a Viking shipbuilder. As Ben surmounts his feelings of anger, guilt, and loneliness, Katz blends

Ben's real and imagined stories into a final and compelling scene of hope for the future.

Awards

Katz's writings have frequently been cited by the Canadian Library Association; she received Book of the Year runner-up honors for her works *Witchery Hill* in 1985, *Sun God, Moon Witch* in 1987, *False Face* in 1988, and *The Third Magic* in 1989. *Out of the Dark* was also named a Canadian Library Association Young Adult Book Award Honor Book in 1996. In addition to numerous other awards, including the Max and Greta Ebel Award in 1987, *False Face* took the International Children's Fiction Prize in 1987.

AUTHOR'S COMMENTARY

Welwyn Wilton Katz

SOURCE: "My Own Story: Plain and Coloured," in *Canadian Children's Literature,* No. 54, 1989, pp. 31-6.

A week or so ago during one of many sleepless nights— there now, I've given you a bit of autobiography already!—anyway, there I was, lying in bed while the clock ticked on, worrying because I hadn't the faintest idea what I was going to say about my own story. Gracious! As someone once said to me, "You are an ordinary, middle-class lady who does ordinary, middle-class things and who just happens to write books that are banned in Rainy River!" With a background like that, where do I begin?

All the while I lay there worrying about the main event, so to speak, three bits of seemingly unrelated information were squirreling around in my brain. The first was very recent: an article in the Toronto Globe and Mail about a white woman who had written a story about a black, a story which had been removed from an anthology because, and I quote, the author had been "racist" to write a story about a culture not her own. The second was an anecdote told to me about a story-tellers' session held for professional librarians a few months ago. A native woman had spoken for an hour or so about the telling of native legends, and at the end of the session she shocked the entire room of predominantly white librarians by saying, "We don't want White people to tell *our* stories."

The third incident doing ugly polkas in my brain with these other two was something that had happened to me, personally. (No, not the banning in Rainy River. That was a rather predictable reaction of an overly-zealous library board to my book *Witchery Hill*—or rather, to its cover, for none of them had read the book itself. Though quite disgusting, their actions had more to do with preventing students from *reading* my books than with preventing me from *writing* what I chose. Though I suppose, of course, one could lead to the other. . . .)

No, the incident I'm referring to is one that happened to me after the publication of my book *False face. False face* is a novel for juveniles and young adults about Iroquois masks and traditions and their impact on a modern white girl and a half-Iroquois boy. The real villain of this book is prejudice in all its forms, whether racial or the much broader kind involving pre-judging someone by any kind of external characteristic at all. (For example, my heroine's resemblance to her father prevents her mother from seeing her as a person in her own right). Before I wrote *False face* I researched all the Iroquois lore very carefully. I took the greatest care in the actual writing to treat the Iroquois beliefs with respect. I deliberately made my hero only half-Iroquois, to avoid creating a character who could be seen in any way to speak for a minority group whose culture I do not intimately know. And yet, when *False face* was nominated for the Governor-General's Award for Children's Literature earlier this year, a local Iroquois group protested my nomination, on the basis that this was a story I had no right to tell, a story of someone else's beliefs.

When I first heard about this, I was horrified. *False face* tried to say that people are just people; that it doesn't matter whether someone is native or white; that the basic issues of life are the same for everyone. Those few Iroquois who protested my nomination were denying this. They were saying that a white person couldn't write about what matters to natives. They were saying that the theme of my entire book was in error.

Why? I kept asking. Why can't I write about what matters to natives? And what other stories can't I write, if I can't write this? *Are* there stories that are my stories, and stories that aren't?

I thought about the books I had written to date. Almost all of them involve things I have not experienced myself at first hand. *Sun God, Moon Witch* is based on the pre-Christian European religions of the Moon Goddess and the Sun God. Was I wrong to have invented a plot featuring two gods I have never myself worshipped? In *Witchery Hill,* my heroine, Lisa, is a diabetic. How dare I go into the mind of a girl with an incurable illness that I do not (thank God) have? In the same book Lisa and her friend Mike work against some nasty people who are practising witchcraft. I am not, I do assure you, a witch; I have never been to a sabbat. What right, then, did I have to write about witchcraft? My latest novel, *The Third Magic,* uses Welsh mythology and legend to invent a prehistory for King Arthur's sword Excalibur. Despite my Welsh name, I don't think I have any Welsh ancestors. Genetically I am as close to being pure Celt as is possible in the twentieth century, being Irish, Cornish and Highland Scot on both sides of my family. The Welsh of the time of King Arthur were Celts, too, but is that common bond enough for a modern Canadian writer to dare to take on what was originally a legend of Wales in the Dark Ages?

The ramifications began tumbling in, thick and dizzying. I do not hate my sister, or know a mother who could harm her child; how dare I then write (as I do in *False face*) about people who do? I am not a boy (another bit of autobiography, you see!); yet I use boys as main characters, and I go into their minds and speak their thoughts and feelings. I am no longer a child, and I have never been a child of the 1980's, yet I write about those children; they are my focus and my audience; I speak for them. Should I give it all up because I am telling stories that are not my own?

What then *is* my story? Am I stuck with writing things based on my own rather ordinary middle-class experiences? Or, may I—please!—be allowed to invent and imagine?

"My Story: Plain", or "My Story: Coloured"; it all comes down to that.

There is no creative art that can function without raw materials. The raw materials of fiction are people (or anthropomorphized animals), as well as all the things that matter to people: their strengths and weaknesses, their beliefs and their needs. A writer takes these things from the real world, because there is no other place to get them. A writer is an architect, using real-life building blocks to create an original construction of her own. It is an amazingly personal act, this picking and choosing and discarding and re-forming of real-life things. It is why no piece of writing, not even non-fiction, can be seen as completely independent of its author.

One of the dangers, of course, is that the real-life things the author chooses to mold may matter rather a lot to other people. To these people the author may seem presumptuous and egotistical in the extreme. After all, they reason, how can one person's self-invented plot and characters and theme be important enough to justify using as a *mere building block* a piece of an entire people's soul? One answer I can make to that is that if the author didn't use a piece of *somebody's* soul as a building block, the book wouldn't be worth reading. Another answer, an easier one, is that yes, of course it is presumptuous, and of course it is egotistical. But in a way it is presumptuous and egotistical to write a book at all.

When I think about it, really think about it, I quail at the thought that I have imagined myself as having had ten books' worth of things to say. But the truth is that most of the time I don't see myself as actively saying things or not saying things in my books at all, though of course I am. Even while I'm writing them my books seem to exist apart from me. They seem to want to be born in the same way that babies want to be born, conceived by me and yet independent of me, with their own needs and requirements that must be served. In *False Face,* for instance, when children ask me what parts of the Iroquois legends I mention are "real", I tell them that everything I wrote about the legends is accurate except for the way the masks change ownership. Then I tell them that I had to invent that part because of my plot. Had to. Not wanted to. *Had to.* That is the driving force behind all writers, I believe: that the book must be served. One does one's best to make everything as accurate and real as possible, but if in fiction some aspects of reality must be distorted for the sake of a larger and more sweeping truth, then the author has no choice in the matter: she must distort reality.

In an article in *CCL* last year, Jill Paton Walsh discussed this very point. Fiction is fiction. In fiction every fact, every bit of physical reality, must be suspect, because all of these facts are chosen and shaped by the author to fit her own—and the book's own—purposes. Everything we *see* in fiction is second-hand, seen through the author's eyes; and everything we *don't* see is invisible either because the author hasn't seen it herself or because she has chosen to keep it invisible. In fiction, therefore, the author is omnipresent.

Readers seem to know this, and as a result they are always trying to draw personal conclusions about an author based upon her stories. This process can be very unreliable. I gave a school talk last year in which the students had videotaped a debate for me: *Resolved, that Welwyn Wilton Katz doesn't like dogs.* Of course they were basing this idea on the puppy sacrifice in *Witchery Hill,* and on the way the family dog is beaten by the mother in *False face.* But two nasty things done to dogs by the authors' characters does not mean they are done, in a form of wishful thinking, by the author herself! In reality, I love dogs, and have a darling old Sheltie of my own. Even more important, any form of cruelty to animals nauseates me. It is for that very reason that I wrote those two horrific scenes. Something really terrible had to happen at those particular points in those two books, and I simply couldn't think of anything more terrible than hurting a helpless living creature. Those students were clever, in a way; for they picked out scenes in two of my books that *did* reveal something important about me as a person, even though what they thought it revealed was wrong.

Sometimes, readers will look at the characters of an author's books, and conclude that they are based on real people whom the author knows. In *False face,* for instance, my family went through a guessing game, trying to figure out who everyone "really" was. When my sister Robbie said who she thought was really Laney, my mother, who is a pretty smart lady, said, "Don't be silly, Robbie. *Welwyn's* Laney."

My mother was right—almost! There *was* a part of me that was Laney. But there was also a part of me that was chip-on-his-shoulder lonely Tom, and a part that was the revolting Rosemary, and one that was Laney's uptight, implacable mother and one that was her stubborn, self-defeating Dad. The germ of *all* these characters comes from my own character. It is the only way I have found to create characters that are "real". What I do is to look inside myself and find bits that are sad or angry or needy or arrogant or stubborn, and then I look at them for a long time, and imagine what would happen if those specific bits were faced with certain specific challenges. And then, somehow, those bits grow and change and become separate people with more characteristics than the ones I start-

ed them with. Myself, and not myself. My own story, plain and coloured.

Other personal conclusions can be made about an author by people who notice recurring themes or situations in her books. For instance, people often ask me if there is a personal reason why I write about troubled families. I can only answer that I have a very happy and fulfilling marriage myself, and that my own family life seemed quite normal all the years I was growing up, but it is a fact that my parents were divorced the year after I was married. Was their hidden unhappiness something I sensed and worried about while I was growing up, and is that why I write about kids in unhappy families now? I don't know. I do know that I *choose* to write about difficult family situations for a number of practical reasons. I do it to give my child protagonists the freedom I need them to have from "proper" parents who would send them to bed at eight o'clock and make sure they stayed there; I do it to force the child heroes to be self-reliant (instead of turning to their parents to solve the whole problem); I do it to provide some relevance for a large number of my readers who will also be members of broken families; and I do it to provide interesting conflicts. They are good reasons, but all the same, I wonder. Is my interest in broken families part of "My Story Plain", or "My Story Coloured"?

Or, maybe, is it both?

Which brings me to the true title of this essay:—not, My own story (plain or coloured), but, My own story: (plain *and* coloured). I think the latter has got it right, you know. There is authorial invention and there is authorial experience in every piece of writing there is. Mine is certainly no exception.

Lying there in bed, thinking about the people who had said to me and to other authors, "No, this story is ours, not yours; you cannot tell it," I woke up my husband by suddenly laughing out loud. How could *False face* be anything *but* my story? The plot of *False face* was of my own construction and imagination entirely: it was "my story coloured". The setting was real: places I knew, a city I'd lived in all my life. "My story plain", with only a few minor colourings. The theme was universal, neither Iroquois nor white, and my own choice: "story coloured", again. The characters were extensions of myself: "story plain *and* story coloured". What then was left? Some building blocks, merely; important, as are all building blocks, but chosen and coloured and shaped by me to fit the construction I was making. Some of the building blocks were Iroquois, and some were not; I used calculators and land developers and breakfast cereals as well as Iroquois masks. Does that make *False face* belong to Texas Instruments or to Sifton Construction or to Kellogg's? No, *False face* was *my* story, because no one but me could ever have told it the exact same way.

That's why I laughed, lying there in bed that sleepless night. I knew, suddenly, that *any* story I chose to tell would be my own story. Because the moment you begin to write a story you become a part of it, and it is changed forever more by your presence. You *are* the story, and the story is you.

I leapt out of bed, ran to my office, grabbed the first piece of paper I could find (which happened to be coloured, by the way), and wrote the heading: *My story, plain and coloured.*

GENERAL COMMENTARY

Marianne Micros

SOURCE: "When Is a Book Not a Book? The Novels of Welwyn Wilton Katz," in *Canadian Children's Literature,* No. 47, 1987, pp. 23-8.

On June 12, 1987, I talked with Welwyn Wilton Katz in her home in London, Ontario, amidst preparations for her daughter's birthday party. We discussed black magic, witchcraft, pure evil, jealousy, greed, and manipulation—all common elements in her novels. These elements have aroused mixed feelings in some of her readers, Katz told me. She was indeed surprised to be called a "pervert" by an irate bookstore patron who did not think anyone, especially writers of children's books, should write about evil, magic, and violence.

This is a familiar argument: children's books should not contain evil or violence, for the readers may be influenced to become violent themselves. Another argument is that because fantasies are "unrealistic", they are escapist literature and may cause children to hope for dream worlds or unrealistic solutions, instead of learning to cope with real problems. Both of these viewpoints are based on a consideration of fantasy and reality as separate entities.

It is difficult, however, to pin-point the dividing line between fantasy and reality, or—more to the point—to define what is "real." Katz and I discussed the nature of reality, its evasiveness and elusiveness, and the fact that people have different perceptions of reality. Katz believes, as is becoming more and more evident in her work, that fantasy and reality are not separate entities, but constantly blend or interact. "I like the interplay of fantasy and reality," Katz said, and readers delight in her subtle interweaving of the natural and the supernatural. In all Katz's books real children struggle with very human problems, some of these problems existing in the "real" world of adolescent awkwardness and difficult family relationships and others arising from a confrontation with unseen and/or supernatural forces.

Indeed, even in "real life," it is not a simple matter to isolate fantasy from reality, extraordinary from ordinary. For instance, in Katz's real life, it was a missing Indian mask that led to her writing *False face,* the book which would win the first International Children's Fiction Contest and hence a prize of $13,000, publication in six countries, and a trip to the International Children's Book Fair in Bologna, Italy. This mask had been withdrawn from exhibition at the Museum of Indian Archeology in London, Ontario, because the family that owned it feared that its public display would distort or destroy its religious significance and healing power. When Katz saw the empty display case, she imagined a dangerous mask discovered by a vulnerable young girl, and her book *False face* was conceived. To Katz the story of the real mask is as magical as the fantasy in a children's book. Likewise, her experience visiting various groups of standing stones in Britain and the sensations she experienced of a supernatural power emanating from those stones were as miraculous to her as the events in her book *Sun God, Moon Witch*. Katz and I agreed that supernatural elements pervade our real lives. We have both met, here in Ontario, people claiming to be witches and have heard of observations of the Black Mass.

If there is an interplay of fantasy with reality in ordinary life, it is just as likely that fantasy will be mixed with reality in the world of books. It is strange, then, that fantasy should be called a perversion. Since the beginnings of the literature we know, from fairy tales through the works of E. Nesbit, C. S. Lewis, Alan Garner, Madeleine L'Engle, Susan Cooper, and many others, fantasy has never been merely escapist literature, nor has it included senseless violence or meaningless depictions of evil. In Katz's books the young protagonists are learning to make moral choices, to recognize the reality of evil and human weakness so that they may become mature enough to cope with, and perhaps even change, their world. The supernatural elements guide the children to a recognition of realities that are invisible in the everyday, material world, realities that are universal, timeless, and spiritual. What might be called "fantasy" in Katz's books is actually an expression of a higher level of reality, one that is best grasped through intuition and perhaps best depicted through use of the supernatural. In *Sun God, Moon Witch,* for example, the god and the witch represent aspects of human nature, as well as cosmic energies. Katz's depiction of them as human-like is a way of making them visible and therefore comprehensible to readers. The fantasy elements in each book are real, as well as symbolical, and affect—even sometimes explain—the "real" events and relationships.

Still, fantasy books, and children's books in general, are not always taken seriously by adult readers. According to Katz, Janet Lunn was once asked, "When are you going to write a real book?" Are children's books not real? "When is a book not a book?", a riddle the protagonists of *Witchery Hill* must solve, is in some ways an unanswerable paradox: a book is more than a physical object, can exist without maintaining a physical presence, and always points beyond itself. Fiction and real life, like fantasy and reality, are inseparably intertwined.

As a writer, Katz has been growing increasingly more skillful at showing the inseparability of fantasy and reality, the interrelationships of the two levels as they play with and against each other. With each book her writing style and her development of structure have become more technically sophisticated and her themes more subtly presented. Recently, she has begun to focus more fully on the realistic aspects of the stories, while, paradoxically, developing more successfully the fantasy elements and their linkage with the real world. She is becoming more and more adept at combining the two lessons she learned as a public-school mathematics teacher: to listen to children (a lesson which helped her with the realism of her novels, especially in the creation of characters and the writing of dialogue); and to structure (a lesson she learned from planning her teaching day and from thinking about her discipline, mathematics, which she said "is magical . . . you can start with nothing and create a whole world").

Katz began creating worlds by writing a very long adult fantasy novel, then a very short children's book. Her first book, *The Prophecy of Tau Ridoo* (1982) was the first book of a trilogy, of which the other two were completed and contracted, but never published because of the publisher's financial difficulties. In this book Katz created a world that she referred to as "pure fantasy": the children, like the children in C. S. Lewis's Narnia series, enter another world through a passage in a house and undertake a journey to save a world from darkness and authoritarianism. The children are "real", but never three-dimensional, while Tau Ridoo is an obvious fantasy world replete with a witch-helper, a prince, and toys which have come to life. It is an allegorical world, in which light has been held captive in a hall of mirrors. The children, of course, triumph and return to their shadowy real world, in which their sick mother has now recovered. This book is certainly less realistic and less serious than Katz's later books, but the dialogue is lively and amusing and the relationships among the children playfully and colorfully described.

The next book Katz wrote was *Sun God, Moon Witch* (1986). This book did not at once find a publisher. It was set aside until after *Witchery Hill* came out; Katz then revised it, but in the end the early version was the one published. In *Sun God, Moon Witch,* the protagonists do not need to enter a fantasy world; rather, the supernatural level enters their world and affects their lives. Except for certain crossovers, however, the two worlds remain separate, even though the main character, Thorny McCall, must confront moral issues that bridge the gap between the two levels of reality. Thorny, in the realistic realm, is a young girl abandoned by her mother and raised by her manipulative, egotistical father. She is sent to stay with her Aunt Jenny and cousin Patrick in an English village near some ancient standing stones while her father and his new bride are on their honeymoon. On the supernatural level, Belman (who is really the sun god in human form) has come to the village to destroy the standing stones which are under the influence of his mother, the moon goddess, in order that he may overpower his mother and control the earth. The two worlds come together in Thorny's moral dilemma: in order to save the world from destruction, she must recognize Belman's similarity to her father and perceive and reject the manipulative charm both men hold over her.

Katz tackled some difficult technical problems in this book in her attempt to maintain the otherworldly quality of the supernatural level and introduce the moon goddess figure, who appears to Thorny in supernatural form. The fantasy-reality issue is further complicated by references to folklore about standing stones, scientific theories about earth forces, the magical effects of dowsing and charms, and the yin and the yang. Katz binds these elements together into an uneasy alliance in which the reality of a person's psychological make-up and the presence of such emotions as jealousy, possessiveness, and blind love have a direct effect on a human being's ability to bring under control the supernatural threats to the world. Patrick's jealousy of Thorny's attraction to Belman, and Thorny's need for security and unselfish parents almost prevent Thorny from saving the Stones, and thus the Earth, from destruction.

The book ends with a successful and spellbinding interplay between human and supernatural forces, as we, and the protagonists, realize that the sun god and moon witch, the yin and the yang, the male and female principles, do not constitute a simple opposition between good and evil: either has the potential for bad and good, death and life—it is the balance of those opposites that brings peace and harmony: "Each is worth nothing without the other, yet together they are everything. Let the halves struggle how they will, it is the union that triumphs." If that balance is achieved, the power of evil is neutralized, and life continues.

Witchery Hill (1984), published before but written after *Sun God, Moon Witch,* is also set in an English village and contains some similar themes and motifs—adolescent relationships, divorced parents, stepparents, confrontations with magic and evil, and the necessity of making moral choices. However, the fantasy world is not separate from the real world in this book, but has become an integral part of that world, existing even inside family members and villagers. For instance, when Mike and his divorced father visit family friends in England—Tony, his daughter Lisa, and his second wife Janine—Mike and Lisa discover the existence of a coven and witness black rites and violent power struggles. The children learn that the evil that exists within some human beings can harm, even kill others: Janine, a "real" wicked stepmother, will use violence and magic to gain control of the coven and to possess the secret book of magic, *Le vieux Albert.* To find *Le vieux Albert,* this key to dangerous magic, the children must solve the riddle, "When is a book not a book?" Katz does not hold back in *Witchery Hill:* there is violence (the sacrifice of a puppy, the death of Lisa's father, an attempt at human sacrifice, a terrifying duel between witches)—and there are realistic problems (Lisa's diabetes, Mike's father's inability to believe the truth, and the problems resulting from divorce). The events in *Witchery Hill* seem more horrifying than do those of *Sun God, Moon Witch* because in *Witchery Hill* the evil is hidden inside the real world. *Le vieux Albert* is not a book that is safely behind covers, but is a book that lives inside human minds and controls human lives. Although *Witchery Hill* ends with the triumph of good over evil and reconciliation of father and son, boy and girl, Katz has left the final outcome open to various possibilities. The potential for evil and violence is always present. The future for Lisa and Mike is uncertain. The reader does not close this book with a feeling that the story has ended, for the unfinished story enters our world and our lives, leaving us to wonder.

In writing her next book Katz says that she "took a giant leap." Her style becomes poetic and her structure complex, as she abandons traditional plot structure for an adventurous jumping about in time and in levels of reality. Though she makes use of the Arthurian material favored by so many writers of children's books, including Rosemary Sutcliffe, T. H. White, and Susan Cooper, her treatment of the material is not traditional. In *The third magic* (1988), the complex patterns of worlds and times shift and play with each other when a young girl is caught in the wrong time, having been accidentally transferred to another world in another century.

False face, the most recently completed novel, and the winner of the International Children's Fiction Contest, contains another innovation for Katz: it is set in her hometown of London, Ontario, a place she thought too boring to write about until she explored the underlayers of myth and human relationships revealed through the Indian mask mentioned earlier. Katz thinks she has "gone far" in this book, but in this case she means "gone far" in her depiction of the difficulties and cruelties in human interactions. This is a book in which the realism is more frightening than the fantasy, in which 13-year-old Laney's discovery of an evil Indian mask may be less frightening than are her interactions with her divorced parents. The powers unleashed affect the real world of the characters, in whom the potential for evil, hatred, and power are present.

It seems that the more Katz enhances the realism in her books, the stronger and more believable is the fantasy—and perhaps that is the paradox of the fantasy-reality relationship. The principle of magic, "As above . . . so below," referring to the correspondence of everything on earth to its cosmic or heavenly counterpart (planet, star, angel, etc.), is an important principle in all these novels, with their intimations of such relationships (e.g., sun and moon to stones and human interactions). To this we may add, "As out there . . . so in here": in Katz's novels objects, such as the mask and the stones, often symbolize human emotions, strengths, and weaknesses. In ancient times magic was not separated from human life (or from human psychology, as we would call it now). The two worlds were and are one. With each novel Katz is getting closer to showing the truth of that ancient view.

If there is not a clear dividing line between reality and fantasy, or between fiction and life, then how can we answer the question she poses in *Witchery Hill:* "When is a book not a book?" In *Witchery Hill* the "book" in question exists not as an external object, but as a mental construct. Katz's books, too, live on in the minds of the readers, who carry with them these blends of fantasy and reality, violence and love, until they coalesce into a richer new world.

Katz and I did not try to find answers to these perhaps unanswerable questions: we concluded our conversation of June 12th when we heard the sound of children arriving downstairs for a birthday party, oblivious to those dark forces unleashed in the fantasy worlds created in the upstairs study.

Dave Jenkinson

SOURCE: "Portraits: Welwyn Wilton Katz," in *Emergency Librarian,* Vol. 21, No. 2, November-December, 1993, pp. 61-5.

"In the process of my writing, setting began as a way of generating ideas, but it has become gradually more and more central to my writing, so that now it's really the core of the whole book and not just the idea for the book. It wasn't until I wrote *Whalesinger* that I realized how settings are the heart of my writing. There are certain places that just 'speak' out to you. Point Reyes, California, was like that. I researched it and found Point Reyes was a spot where Sir Francis Drake was believed to have stopped. That 'fact' sort of 'jiggled' a little. It wasn't enough for a book, but, when I love a place and when there's something neat about its history, and, if I can make that historical fact resonate with something modern, then I know I have a book. I just have to figure it out.

"I started researching *Whalesinger* seriously in August of 1988 and didn't write a word until January, 1989, which, for me, is a frighteningly long period. And then I started writing, and I was writing well. I had good solid characters and everything, but, for some reason, something in me was just not ready to go past chapter six. I kept rewriting the first six, getting them perfect. Because I couldn't get beyond chapter six, I was afraid that there wasn't a book there. I had a plot but didn't have that gut understanding of what the book was, and it addresses issues I've never addressed in my life before. At the end of July, I had figured out what the book was about and just sat down and poured it out. In two months, I wrote 158 manuscript pages."

In *Whalesinger,* a summer job with an ocean conservation project takes Vancouverite Nick Young, 17, to Point Reyes, where he meets Marty Griffiths, 16, and Dr. Ray Pembroke. Though Nick finds himself romantically attracted to Marty, he targets Pembroke for revenge, believing him responsible for his elder brother's death. Had Welwyn limited *Whalesinger* to just these two elements, the book would have remained just another competent adventure/romance; however, by intertwining three seemingly disparate facts about the book's setting—Sir Francis Drake landed at Point Reyes; gray whales pass the Point on their northward migration; and the San Andreas Fault runs next to the Point—Welwyn has created a multilayered novel wherein the present repeats the past, and the "songs" of land and ocean mammals intermingle.

"In writing *The third magic,* the book prior to *Whalesinger,* the setting was very important but in a more intellectual way. I constructed the fantasy world setting to mirror certain myths and legends from our own world. That was a more analytical process than the 'heart' process for *Whalesinger.* But the real world setting was there for me too. I had been to England several times and to Tintagel twice and to all of the places that were Arthurian. The other setting, Nwm, was invented, but I felt as if it were real.

"Of all my books, *The third magic* was *the* hardest book to write: the hardest structurally and the hardest, in a sense, emotionally, because I had something I was really happy with, but the editors thought it too complex. It was a tremendously difficult process of revision. If I hadn't been certain it was the best writing I had ever done, I might have ended up hating it. I end up hating a lot of my books for quite a period of time after I've finished writing them, simply because of the effort that was put into them and the number of times they were rewritten. Hate is perhaps not the right word; sheer, utter boredom is better. I never hated *The third magic,* even when I struggled with it, and I don't hate it now. I even sat down and read it about a month after it was published; an unheard-of act, for I have not reread any of my books after publication."

Winner of the 1988 Governor General's Literary Award in the juvenile fiction category, *The third magic* sees Morgan Lefevre, 15, being mistaken for one of her own ancestors and being summoned through time to the alien world of Nwm. With only the boy Arddu as her companion, Morgan is caught between the opposing cruelties of the Circle and the Line, the two magics of Nwm. When Morgan and Arddu gain possession of an ancient weapon of the mysterious Third Magic, the Earth of King Arthur is drawn into the struggle as well.

Welwyn's being copublished in the United States and Canada posed some difficulties, in that she experienced a surfeit of editors. For example, with *The third magic,* there were four editors, two from each publishing house, "all apparently working independently with me. They all seemed to want different things. I determined I could never go through that again, even though the editing of my earlier published book, *False face,* was relatively easy under similar circumstances. It has two different editions, even so. The American edition is quite different; the same plot and same characters, but scenes are different. The American edition, which came out after the Canadian, was more like my original manuscript. Things I liked in the Canadian edition I put in the American, and things I agreed to reluctantly in the Canadian edition, I cut out of the American edition.

"I'd just finished the first draft of *The third magic* the day before I found out about the International Fiction Contest. I decided to shelve revisions for *The third magic* and try to write a book for that contest. *False face* was a very deliberate book because I was writing to deadline." The idea for the book came "when I went to the Museum of Indian Archeology in London, Ontario. There was an empty space in a display case with a sign saying the mask that had occupied that spot had been removed at the request of the Indian community due to its sensitive nature."

False face won the first International Fiction Contest and its prize was $13,000, publication in six countries, plus a trip for Welwyn to the International Children's Book Fair in Bologna, Italy. In the book, Laney McIntyre, 13, discovers an Iroquois false face mask in a marsh near her home. When her mother, an antique dealer, takes the mask from Laney, she unleashes the mask's malevolent powers. With the help of another 13 year old, Tom Walsh, whose mother and father are white and Mohawk respectively, Laney struggles to contain the mask's potency for evil.

The book's contents did evoke some complaints from the native community. "There was no formal approach to me, but a letter was sent to the Canada Council protesting my Governor General's Award nomination. Rather than being prejudiced against me for being white, I believe it was more a sense of 'How can I understand a culture that isn't my own?' There's some validity to that question, and that's why I made Tom half, not fully, native. You can't step into somebody else's culture and presume to speak for them, but the details of the false face ceremonies are recorded in scholarly sources of information. I thought I was making a fascinating culture a little more accessible to non-natives. And I was writing a book about prejudice. I thought that showing prejudice as harmful would be something everyone who had experienced prejudice could applaud.

"No matter what I do, I seem to write something that offends somebody. I don't do it to be controversial. I write what interests me, and I take stands. Unfortunately, that gets me into trouble. Just the fact that my books are fantasy disturbs some people because fantasy's not 'real.' I really do truly believe that my books are moral books; they're about good more than they're about evil. Good, of course, can't exist without its counterpart. It's human strengths that I celebrate in my books. I have to present conflict for the children to resolve, and I have to make problems in order for there to be plot. I'm sorry for my 'critics' because they're missing something fundamental about my books, which is that I celebrate the strength of children. A lot of people think children are to be protected and that they haven't got strength. I believe in kids solving their own problems."

Witchery Hill has offended some individuals simply because the title contains 'witch.' A runner-up for the 1984 Canadian Library Association Book of the Year Award, the book tells of a summer visit by Mike Lewis, 14, from Madison, Wisconsin, to the island of Guernsey in the English Channel, where he and new friend Lisa St. George, 13, dangerously stumble into the middle of a coven of witches struggling over possession of a secret book of magic, "a powerful book that is not a book." A 1986 CLA Book of the Year runner-up, *Sun God, Moon Witch* finds

Hawthorne McCall, 12, being sent to stay with an aunt and uncle in an English village located near a circle of 12 standing stones while her father and his new bride honeymoon. When a local industrialist threatens to destroy the prehistoric circle to build a cement plant, "Thorny" and her cousin Patrick, 13, fight to save the circle whose "power" is much more significant than most recognize.

"*Sun God, Moon Witch* came out of a lot of different things, including the story my father told me of how his father's well had been dowsed, and my own love affair with standing stones and stone circles. I'd read some fascinating stuff by Arthur Watkins about ley lines too. The challenge was to take these different ideas and make a single structure out of it and still use the white goddess lore." . . .

Unlike many fantasy writers, Welwyn makes much use of the real contemporary world. "'Other-world' fantasies are hard to invent, but they can be made relatively easily believable by the author with some small amount of care. However, trying to make two worlds believable is hard. With a contemporary, 'real' setting, people don't put aside their disbelief in the same way they do when they're suddenly thrust into a new world. *The third magic* is as close as I've come to writing an 'other world' fantasy. I'm very interested in the way the past and the magic of the past brush up against the present and the reality of the present. Any time I deal with fantasy, it's always that, the old magic brushing up against the new modern life. It has tremendous potential for interesting conflict and can also reveal a lot about the real world. To do an entire book in the other world without having some link to what we are as a people can reduce its applicability and its thematic importance."

The idea for *Come like shadows,* Welwyn's most recent book, didn't come out of a particular setting. "After *Whalesinger,* there was a period of time when I couldn't write. My marriage had broken up, and I was going through that crazy emotional stuff. What I needed was a really strong idea, something that would grab my attention and my imagination. When Doug, my second husband and a theater critic, mentioned that the 'Scottish play,' *Macbeth,* was cursed and had been cursed for centuries, that attracted me. I started doing research on the play's background. The bad luck that has happened in the last three centuries to people who tried to put on this play was an eye-opener! It goes beyond coincidence and the usual superstition stuff. None of what I put in the book was invented, though I wrote an alternative history for the real Macbeth's last two days.

"The real Macbeth and the one Shakespeare wrote about are not the same at all. Shakespeare's was invented to suit the story he wanted to write. I felt sorry for the real Macbeth because he's been treated badly by history. It fascinated me how an artist like Shakespeare could manipulate history to make something work better for him and how then it becomes true, insofar as what most people believe. That's how I got the idea for Jeneva, the director of a modern production of the play in Stratford,

who decides to say something with the play that Shakespeare never intended. She chooses to make a political statement with her production. That led me to the political situation in my own country. There are plenty of parallels between Scotland within Great Britain and Quebec within Canada, so the French-Canadian link to the 'Scottish play' was a reasonable option. That's basically how the theme of the book developed, by deciding Jeneva would put on a French vs. English production and then trying to figure out how that might have universal implications.

"The research on play production was also extensive. I spent a lot of time at Stratford wandering around backstage, doing the 'map' route and figuring out where everybody could go. What was most beneficial to me was observing artistic director Martha Henry and her cast and crew working on the play she was staging. It was enormously helpful seeing how it's really done. It isn't just the details that end up in a book that matter to me. I get stymied if I feel I can't write something because I don't know the way people think. I don't feel free to use my own imagination for the things that are 'real' in this world. I feel I have to portray them accurately because I'm doing things that aren't real as well. If people are going to catch me out on the real stuff, they'll never believe the imaginary.

"The actual plot for *Come like shadows* was something that came to me over a long period of time. Months of just thinking and trying not to think. I remember where I got the fundamental concept of how the three sisters of Shakespeare's play were going to be the three sisters of the earlier goddess worship and were going to take part in my contemporary story and be the unifiers. I was on tour, having a grilled cheese sandwich in a greasy spoon. I don't know why, but, all of a sudden, I just said aloud— 'Three weird sisters.' After that, I combed Shakespeare's play for something to connect them to the contemporary world. That's when I found the mirror." The magical mirror becomes the object that enslaves 17 year old Kincardine "Kinney" O'Neil, who has joined the Stratford Festival Company as a summer assistant to the director, and Lucas, a young actor fascinated by the true historical Macbeth.

"I'm already working on another book, but it's totally different for me. Instead of doing tons of research, as I've done with the last five books, it came about when I was driving my daughter to school one day, and she said, 'Mom, if all the time zones of the world meet at the North Pole, then what time is it there?' I drove about three blocks before answering, 'I suppose, it's no time, or all time,' and that was it. I'm almost finished the second draft of that book. I knew the beginning and the ending before I started, but I didn't have a clue about the middle. Because I was discovering things as I wrote, I had a ball with it. I've called it *Time ghost*.

"I'm also writing a play about how people lose their belief in life. I see it as a family play. As well, I've been writing some short stories, but for adults. In them, I tried a bunch of new things I've never done before, like writing in the first person present tense. I've had some success with them and won the *Grain* short fiction contest (1993) with a story called **'You can take them back.'** I think it's really helped me with my kids' writing because, for a while, all my books were veering toward the adult. I think I was trying to write for adults without actually doing it. Now I feel free to go back to the age group I started with, the 11 to 14 year olds. *Time ghost* is for that age group, as is the one I've planned for next, which is going to take place in Newfoundland. I went to Newfoundland this summer to do the setting research for that book. I loved the way the place melded perfectly with my ideas for the plot. Now all I have to do is write the book!"

TITLE COMMENTARY

📖 *WITCHERY HILL* (1984)

Joan McGrath

SOURCE: A review of *Witchery Hill,* in *Quill and Quire,* Vol. 51, No. 2, February, 1985, p. 18.

Neither its innocent-looking cover nor its title, **Witchery Hill,** prepares young readers for this powerful dose of the occult. Trepied Hill, Guernsey is the legend-haunted site of a prehistoric tomb, which has become a favoured spot for the repulsive activities of a coven of witches.

An American youngster, 14-year-old Mike, goes on vacation to the Channel Islands with his father. Their host's daughter, teenage Lisa, does not get along with her glamorous stepmother, and it's therefore all too easy for Mike and his father to dismiss her warnings of evil and danger as mere symptoms of jealousy and spite. Then the sudden and suspicious death of the local witchmaster precipitates a struggle for power within the local coven, and one of the aspirants is Lisa's stepmother, Janine. Mike and Lisa find themselves endangered by demonic powers and the remorseless cruelty of the fanatical coven and without assistance or support from the sceptical adult world. The denouement, a sacrifice on a bloodied altar-stone, is quite shocking.

This is a genuine junior Gothic chiller, complete with lashings of gore, several deaths, and convincing suggestions that evil has a physical presence. It also shakes one's belief that good will always triumph in the battle between the forces of good and evil. A rather complex novel, **Witchery Hill** should be reserved for fairly sophisticated readers.

Margery Fisher

SOURCE: A review of *Witchery Hill,* in *Growing Point,* Vol. 27, No. 5, January, 1989, pp. 5089-90.

So far [in this review] we have been dealing with books which capable readers as young as ten could enjoy, both for action and in varying degrees for the implied ideas in them. **Witchery Hill** is another matter. Set in Guernsey, it describes in strong detail the operation of a coven which does not confine its activities to formal dances on a legendary hill, for the leaders of the group go as far as murder in their struggle for power. Teenage Mike, on a visit with his father and Lisa, daughter of their host, are involved in danger and are forced to witness unpleasant aspects of human frailty which impose a burden on their years. Seton Goch, a local landowner, is killed for the sake of certain ancient, sinister books of magic coveted by his son Enoch and also by Lisa's stepmother Janine; while the boy and girl realise the iniquity of this diabolical struggle, they almost go beyond their powers in trying to stop the harm that threatens Lisa's father. There is a nasty undercurrent to the story, an element of implied sexuality which makes it uncomfortable reading; the young, possibly hardened by indulgence in fantasy-games, should at least keep control of their imagination if they are tempted to look at the story as a comment on normal human behaviour.

📖 *SUN GOD, MOON WITCH* (1986)

Eva Martin

SOURCE: A review of *Sun God, Moon Witch,* in *Quill and Quire,* Vol. 52, No. 10, October, 1986, p. 24.

[Sun God, Moon Witch] is a traditional story of a fierce struggle between good and evil that has an unusual, complicated twist. The setting is a small village in England where there is an ancient circle of standing stones similar to those at Stonehenge. Hawthorne, Thorny for short, arrives from Canada to spend summer holidays with her cousins and finds a village controversy brewing. An industrial developer wants to remove the stones to gain access to the chalk he believes lies beneath them. Folklorists, scientists, and the local people are appalled at the idea, for there are many ancient myths attached to the stones, and they fear strong forces will be disturbed and violent destruction will occur. Unwittingly, Thorny becomes involved in a struggle between the moon goddess of the stones and her son the sun god, the evil force in the story. The struggle reaches a peak during a total eclipse of the moon by the sun.

The author has a deep understanding of Welsh and British folklore, which she has skilfully woven through the story. What makes this story different from most fantasy novels, is that good and evil are not simply white and black. The dark side of the moon goddess—her desire for ultimate power over her son—is well portrayed, while the sun god is not completely evil. Their struggle is mirrored within the adolescent Thorny. She is trying to free herself from the people who dominate her, especially her father, and to achieve some degree of independence, while controlling the darker side of her nature.

The main characters are developed thoroughly, the action is gripping, and the build-up of tension as all the pieces of the puzzle begin to fit together is breathtaking and not without violence. Unfortunately, the ending includes a long explanation of why things happened as they did, which lessens its total impact.

Michael Steig

SOURCE: "Grown-Up Children," in *Canadian Literature,* No. 116, Spring, 1988, pp. 236-38.

Resembling some of the fantasies of Alan Garner (in mirroring actual human relationships in legendary events which recur in the present) and of Susan Cooper (in presenting a universe in which the forces of good and evil are balanced evenly, and embodied in supernatural figures or in humans with special powers), Welwyn Katz's *Sun God, Moon Witch* does not match those authors' novels in quality of narrative or structure. I do not find the Manichean approach to fantasy very rewarding (even when done by such a talented writer as Cooper), but the greatest problem with Katz's book is that with all its trappings of myth and legend it lacks mystery. The uncanny—and implicitly sexual—power of the villain, Mr. Belman, is spelled out by chapter 3, so that the reader can easily deduce in succeeding chapters that he is the evil one (the "Sun god") of the two opposing forces.

By chapter 5, the "Moon witch" makes her appearance to Thorny, the child protagonist, telling her that she is destined by her name (Hawthorn) to save the world from chaos by saving the stone circle that Mr. Belman in his guise as a developer has been given permission to destroy. Although there is some interesting material about theories as to the original purpose of stone circles in Europe, the story itself is not, as the blurb has it, a "riveting tale of good and evil," but rather one of arbitrarily opposed forces that have little relation to the earthly experiences of the human characters, even though the author creates such connections—Mr. Belman's resemblance to Thorny's father is made clear, but too early and too mechanically. The problem is partly one of structure and emphasis: what could be effective as truly mysterious forces becomes banal when presented so baldly, and sometimes in language that is supposed to be dignified but is actually flat and awkward—as when the Moon witch tells Thorny, "Thou art hawthorn in more than name. Like it, thou are strongest when thou strugglest."

📖 *FALSE FACE* (1987)

Peter Carver

SOURCE: "Past and Present Merge in Painful, Haunting Tales," in *Books for Young People,* Vol. 1, No. 5, October, 1987, p. 10.

Welwyn Wilton Katz's reputation has been established on the strength of two young-adult novels published by Groundwood Books, *Witchery Hill* and *Sun God, Moon Witch,* both focusing on the ancient lore of European

civilization. *False Face,* winner of Groundwood's International Fiction Contest, is set in London, Ontario (the author's home turf) and confirms her growing talent as a compelling story-teller.

The story is, first of all, about 13-year-old Laney McIntyre, whose burdens in life include a revoltingly selfish older sister and a divorced mother who does not much care for her younger daughter. Since separating from Laney's father, Alicia McIntyre, a beautiful and industrious antique dealer, delights in heaping scorn on her former husband's overall lack of ambition. Laney's misfortune is her physical resemblance to her father.

The story is also about Tom Walsh, one of Laney's schoolmates, who is of mixed white and Indian blood. Alienated by culture and values he finds in the city, Tom is desperate to turn back to his dead father's people to find his place in the world. In fact, both youngsters, victims of a past beyond their control, are involved in a painful search for identity.

Laney and Tom are drawn together over the discovery of an Indian false-face mask in a bog near Laney's home. As soon as the mask is unearthed by the McIntyre family dog, a flood of difficulties sweeps through the youngsters' lives. Is the mask a trigger for some evil power? Has Alicia the capacity to use this power against Laney? How can Laney deal with her mother's growing animosity towards her? What about the ethical issue of who really owns the mask—a relic of the culture of which Tom is one legitimate inheritor? How can we handle the implications of our past, in order to create a sensible future? All these questions are brought together in one of the most terrifying and powerful climaxes of recent adolescent fiction.

Complex currents surge through Katz's story, but even though the final pages provide us with plenty of insight into Laney and Tom and their realization of the significance of their lives, *False Face* does not fade when the last line has been read. Katz is too good a writer to tie things up neatly, and the vibrations of this many-layered novel hum in the reader's mind for days after.

Kirkus Reviews

SOURCE: A review of *False Face,* in *Kirkus Reviews,* Vol. LVI, No. 15, August 1, 1988, p. 1151.

When 13-year-old Laney McIntyre finds a tiny wooden mask in a bog in London, Canada, Tom, a half-Indian boy in her class, warns her not to disturb Indian remains. He recognizes the larger companion mask that Laney's mother finds as an Iroquois false face, connected to a spirit whose power is both curative and destructive. As acts of supernatural vengeance begin to occur in the McIntyre home, Laney and Tom struggle to unlock the secrets of the masks.

Several conflicts here become intertwined: Laney receives

the brunt of her mother's anger against her divorced father, whom she resembles; her parents' fundamental differences (one is an antique dealer, the other an archaeologist) clash over the problem of what to do with the masks. Meanwhile, Tom learns a valuable lesson about prejudice when he seeks help from his tribal elders.

Katz's choppy prose, composed mostly of simple sentences and fragments, is not quite equal to the depth of the concepts she presents, and the jacket is dramatic but inaccurate in depicting of Laney. Still, an entertaining blend of the real and the super-natural. In an afterword, Katz gives references and tells how she got the idea for the book, providing a glimpse of the writing process to young readers.

Ilene Cooper

SOURCE: A review of *False Face,* in *Booklist,* Vol. 85, No. 4, October 15, 1988, p. 410.

Thirteen-year-old Laney McIntyre is the image of her archaeologist father, and her mother, an antique dealer, takes out her dislike of her ex-husband on Laney. The antipathy between mother and daughter grows when two Iroquois false-face masks come into their home exuding evil and power. Eventually Mrs. McIntyre must choose between what the mask can offer her, and the life of her daughter. Katz is juggling a full load here: child-parent relationships, Indian customs and heritage, and a subplot concerning a half-white, half-Indian boy who has serious conflicts about where he belongs. With all this to handle, including the supernatural ambience that pervades the story, Katz' plotting does get a little convoluted in places. Nevertheless, it is a tribute to her skills that readers will be involved enough to follow the story to its dramatic conclusion. Research is evident, and the Ontario setting of this Canadian import is a plus.

Sarah Ellis

SOURCE: "1987 Notable Canadian Young Adult Fiction," in *CM: A Reviewing Journal of Canadian Materials for Young People,* Vol. XVI, No. 6, November, 1988, pp. 206-07.

The much recognized novel *False Face* is an example of new fantasy. Katz wandered afar in her previous books but in this one she comes home. Young Laney McIntyre finds, in the bog close to her London, Ontario, home, an Iroquois false face mask. By unearthing this artifact she sparks a series of events whereby the ancient mythic power of Iroquois ritual and ceremony is unleashed in the everyday world.

This device of myth seeping or exploding into the rational world, using as an entrance our own duplicities and troubled relationships, is one that is a mark of contemporary fantasy writing for the young. Rare now is the wardrobe door or the rabbit hole. Instead, the supernatural co-exists with the real world.

Such an approach allows the writer a gritty, immediate creation of character. The conflicts of good and evil are simultaneously cosmic and domestic. In *False Face* Laney's alienation from her materialistic, judgemental mother, her conflicts with her sister, and her sorrow at her parents' divorce provide the weak place by which the power of the mask can emerge. Likewise, her schoolmate Tom's confusion about his dual Indian and European heritage allows a passage for ancient tragedy to be re-enacted. And it is entirely plausible. Katz is particularly effective in capturing the seriousness of family tension.

She is also powerful in her descriptions of the rituals of the Society of Faces that lie at the heart of the book. She writes in a strong clear style, avoiding pretension or melodrama. The words are simple and convincing:

> Laney leaned against the wall. Her heart was a drum, thudding, thudding. Her mind was hazy as longhouse smoke. Rattle. Rattle. Summon the people, summon the god, summon the hatred, let it all come to pass. Nothing could stop it, anyway. Nothing could change what was to be. Events to be played out, events she had started. And the Round Dance to come; and death on the longhouse floor.

In an author's note Katz tells of how an artifact in a museum of Indian archaeology gave her the idea for the book. The power of objects to evoke the cultures of the past is one that underlies much British juvenile fiction but has not been much explored by Canadian writers for young adults. *False Face* is a welcome book, not just for readers in Scandinavia and South America, who may see in it their first glimpse of Canada, but for our own young adults who may well see in it their first glimpse of the stories that live in our landscape.

*****

Readers should be aware that native people in southwestern Ontario have serious objections to the depiction of Iroquois ritual and belief (specifically the use of sacred masks) in *False Face*. The following is a quote from Joanna Bedard, executive director of the Woodland Cultural Centre in Brantford, Ont., which represents the Mississaugas of the New Credit, the Mohawks of the Bay of Quinte, the Mohawks of Gibson, the Delaware Nation, the Oneidas of the Thames, and the Six Nations of the Grand River:

> It is particularly important that young people have a positive appreciation for the values and traditions of Indian spirituality, its practices and customs. *False Face* by Welwyn Wilton Katz undermines this goal of understanding and appreciation of Indian, particularly Iroquoian, culture. Even though it is a work of fiction the book distorts and promotes as evil the use of masks by the Iroquois. Because the author specifically uses the Six Nations Reserve as a prop for the storyline and acknowledges the research undertaken at the

Museum of Indian Archeology in London, the book may appear to its intended audience of young readers to be an accurate portrayal of the use of masks. . . . .

False Face promotes misunderstanding and detracts from the respect due to the sacred symbols of the traditional beliefs of the Longhouse.

Naomi Caldwell-Wood and Lisa A. Mitten

SOURCE: A review of *False Face,* in *Multicultural Review,* Vol. 1, No. 2, April, 1992, p. 31.

An exciting and well-told story of a white female teen (Laney) and a mixed-blood male teen (Tom) who accidentally unearth an old Iroquois false face mask. The portrayal of the Iroquois and nonsense presented about the mask, however, are way off base and very insulting. The author is obviously familiar with the locale of the story, and places on the Six Nations Reserve in Ontario are accurately described. Katz conjures up a ridiculously evil power that is supposed to inhabit the false face mask and alter the personalities of characters who attempt to possess the mask. This goes beyond the wild fantasies of a creative author. False face masks are an integral part of traditional Iroquois religion practised today on the very reserve that Katz describes so well. Her description of the mask as an absolute evil amounts to religious intolerance and fosters the conception of Native, non-Christian religions as savage pagan rituals.

THE THIRD MAGIC (1988)

Joan McGrath

SOURCE: A review of *The Third Magic,* in *Books for Young People,* Vol. 3, No. 1, February, 1989, p. 10.

He calls himself Arddu, but his birth name is A'Casta, "the Abomination," an outcast belonging nowhere in the magic-ruled other-world of Nwm. Arddu's twin, Rigan, is a powerful Sister of the Circle. At age 15 she is transported to far distant Earth to carry out a mysterious mission, leaving Arddu bereft. Then the Linesmen, enemies of the Circle, try to use him as the crux of a plot to force Rigan's return to Nwm. Meanwhile, back on Earth, restless teenager Morgan Lefevre is strangely fascinated with the Arthurian legends and broods over them persistently. While on a visit to Arthur's birthplace, Tintagel, Morgan is magically transported to Arddu's world and thrown into his struggle for survival by her uncanny likeness to his sister Rigan.

The story's conception is elaborate, to say the least. Shifts in time and a well-realized alien world with a complex magical belief system are intertwined with the tale of Britain's warrior king. Unfortunately, Welwyn Wilton Katz fails to sustain the epic pitch she attempts to establish; for instance, there are frequent jarring lapses into colloquial speech patterns. Another difficulty is posed by the unpronounceable invented names lavishly sprinkled through-

out, which make an already complicated story still more difficult to follow.

This ambitious work is unlikely to find favour with any reader not already familiar with the tangled relationship of Arthur and his sister Morgan le Fay and with Merlin's supernatural interference in their lives. But *The Third Magic* will provide a challenging read for teens with a well-developed taste for the fantasy genre.

Robert Strang

SOURCE: A review of *The Third Magic,* in *Bulletin of the Center for Children's Books,* Vol. 42, No. 6, February, 1989, p. 150.

Ambitiously and extensively plotted, this science-fiction/fantasy saga takes Arthurian legend for its narrative core. 15-year-old Morgan LeFevre has come to Tintagel to help her father with a TV documentary on King Arthur. Morrigan, a Sister in a matriarchal society on the planet Nwm, has also been sent to Tintagel, but centuries before, where her ordained destiny is to become Morgan Le Fay, sister of Arthur and mother of Mordred. Arthur and Earth are pawns in a classic good-and-evil conflict between the Circle and the Line, its evil male counterpart. The story gets far more complicated than this (it eventually turns out that Morgan is her own ancestress) and readers not familiar with genre quirks will be quickly swamped. The first third of the book is convoluted even by genre standards, but once Morgan is kidnapped to Nwm and embarks on a quest for the Grail, most of the confusion is cleared up and the book gains excitement and direction. The plotting leaves little room for theme or character development, but fantasy fans who enjoy cleverly worked-out time-and-space-travel-fiction will find here a unique recasting of a legend.

Kieran Kealy

SOURCE: "The Circle, the Line and the Third Magic," in *Canadian Children's Literature,* No. 53, 1989, pp. 87-8.

The Third Magic, award-winner Welwyn Wilton Katz's most recent fantasy, combines the same elements that ensured the success of her earlier works: a deep interest in mythology, a careful attention to psychological characterization and a simple ability to tell a highly suspenseful and wonderfully unpredictable story.

Even to begin to sketch the extremely complex story that Katz provides would be virtually impossible. Her hero, Arddu, lives outside of time in the magical world of Nwm, while the heroine, Morgan Lefevre, is from modern-day Canada, mistakenly summoned to Nwm because of her psychic affinity to one of her own ancestors, Arddu's twin sister, Rigan. Ultimately the protagonists' adventures bring them to the magical world of Arthur and Merlin, where Katz provides an absolutely fascinating retelling of the legend of Arthur's claim to kingship.

There is much to praise in Katz's ambitious tale, but there are also problems. The major difficulty is that the story, particularly in its early stages, often becomes bogged down in creating tantalizingly complex mythologies. The primary antagonists in Arddu's world, for example, are the Circle and the Line, a conflict delineated by a series of evocative but often unresolved associations: Moon vs. Sun, Ice vs. Fire, Encircling vs. Alignment and most importantly, Male vs. Female. The Circle, possessors of the First Magic, and the Line, possessors of the Second Magic, are described as equally cruel, selfish and brutal, necessitating the rebirth of the Old Magic, the Third Magic, which comes to be associated with Morgan and Arddu. Though the ultimate need for harmony in the world is made quite clear, the full implications of this Nwmian battle of the sexes are somewhat ambiguous, particularly when it is related to the very sketchy account of the relationship between Morgan's earthly parents, a charismatic television producer and his stereotypically repressed wife.

I don't think it is coincidence that the story truly comes alive only when the ambiguities of the Nwmian mythology are left behind and the protagonists begin their final quest to return the sword of the Third Magic to its rightful place and, by doing so, rewrite the Arthurian legend. Here, especially in the final scenes, one realizes just how gifted a story-teller Katz can be and why she truly deserves her place as one of Canada's most renowned children's fantasists.

WHALESINGER (1990)

Margaret Mackey

SOURCE: A review of *Whalesinger,* in *CM: A Reviewing Journal of Canadian Materials for Young People,* Vol. XIX, No. 2, March, 1991, p. 105.

When Nick, aged seventeen, joins a conservation group working on the California coast, he discovers that his father has found him a job with the man he blames for his brother's death, Ray Pembroke, a highly respected conservationist and fund raiser.

Nick's rage is compounded as he begins to suspect that Pembroke is using the conservation project as a smoke screen while he hunts for a frigate sunk in Sir Francis Drake's day. Together with Marty, a babysitter accompanying a family working at the site, Nick looks for evidence to support an accusation that most people would find laughable.

Whalesinger is a lively and contemporary adventure story. The plot revolves around such up-to-date elements as conservation, computers, whale-saving, California earthquakes, modern underwater treasure-hunting—even a specific learning disability. Nick and Marty come to terms with problems that seemed suffocating in Vancouver, Nick by confronting his demon, and Marty by creating a relationship with two whales stranded in the shallow bay.

If anything, this book is too crowded with incident—too many sub-themes, too many accidents and emergencies. It hovers on the brink of clutter more than once. In the end, however, Katz ties up all her loose ends and achieves a coherent and attractive story.

Dorothy Furches

SOURCE: A review of *Whalesinger,* in *Voice of Youth Advocates,* Vol. 14, No. 1, April, 1991, p. 31.

A lonely gray whale sings her songs of the ages to her sick calf. She is summering in Drake's Bay, off the coast of California at Point Reyes, waiting for the calf to heal. She waits and sings.

Seventeen year old Nick has joined a conservation research project as Dr. Anderson's research assistant on Point Reyes. There he meets Marty, a shy 15 year old girl who is babysitting the children of two marine biologists. Together Nick and Marty learn that Dr. Pembroke, the project commander, is using the project as a cover to plunder the supposed treasure of a sunken frigate belonging to Sir Francis Drake. Marty also learns that she hears the whalesong. And what she hears from the waiting whale changes her life completely.

This multilevel novel is sure to please the older teen reader interested in marine studies and sunken treasures. It is made more realistic and appealing by the research acknowledgments which are as exciting to read as the text. A map of Point Reyes National Seashore is included. Highly recommended.

Patricia Manning

SOURCE: A review of *Whalesinger,* in *School Library Journal,* Vol. 37, No. 5, May, 1991, p. 111.

In a sturdy framework of the ecology and geology of Point Reyes and Drake's Bay, Katz threads an intricate warp that features a group of scientists engaged in research, a historical occurrence on Drake's ship, the migration pattern of the gray whale, and an impending earthquake and accompanying *tsunami.* Over and under this she weaves a complex pattern of science, personalities, a lost treasure, and a whale mother with an ailing baby. Nick, 17, is not yet over the death of his loved older brother. Marty, 16, has learning difficulties, but an innate empathy that appeals to Nick, and that allows her to communicate with the whale mother. Pembroke, the science-villain, seeks a treasure on a ship scuttled by Drake, indifferent to any ethical dilemmas involved. A lot goes on here, including a first-rate introduction to scientific methods. Clearly depicted are the strange behaviors often observed in animals just prior to a major earthquake, including the coupling of Nick and Marty (safe sex is practiced). Some readers might find Nick's response to Marty's confusion afterwards extremely simplistic (" . . . But with you . . . it was beautiful . . ."). Have we heard *that* line before? While strands of the plot go slightly awry, and the development of some of the characters is contrived, the book is substantial enough to keep readers going. The final apocalyptic scenes outweigh some of the more lurid ones of the sunken ship and its long-buried cargo. The major characters, although battered, come through alive, and perhaps more whole to face their future. Intriguing.

J. R. Wytenbroek

SOURCE: "*Whalesinger,* Powerful, Provocative," in *Canadian Children's Literature,* No. 64, 1991, pp. 95-6.

Katz has been a controversial writer from the start. Her first novel, *Witchery Hill,* created problems for the author because of its depiction of Satanism. In *False face* it was the use of the Iroquois False Face masks that caused trouble. In *Whalesinger* Katz has done it again, this time with sex. Apparently, there has been an outcry regarding the sex scene in the novel. However, what the outcry is about is rather obscure. Is it the scene itself? That seems unlikely, because Katz describes nothing more than a kiss, a rather intense kiss, but only a kiss. The rest of the scene is left entirely to the imagination of the reader. Is it because there is sex in a novel written for mid- to late-adolescents? There are a lot of books with much more explicit sex in them on the market for this age group, and most of them are far less tasteful in their presentation of the act. Therefore, the problem is difficult to pinpoint, possibly because there is no real problem here at all.

Despite the controversies, Katz has always been a very good writer. Her skills have developed over the years, so that each novel has been better than the last. Indeed, *Whalesinger* breaks through onto a new, higher plane. First, the characterization is superb. Both Marty and Nick, with all their fears, resentments, pain, and desires are clearly portrayed. Nick is bright but embittered and has vowed never to let himself care about another human being because it hurts too much, and Marty is unsure and learning-disabled, lacking support and love in her life through no choice of her own. Both develop consistently and convincingly throughout the novel. Nick faces and finally comes to terms with his hatred for the man he believes killed his idolized older brother, realizing that his hatred is more destructive for him than it is for his enemy. Marty, intuitive but inarticulate, develops a much stronger sense of self-worth, realizing that she has strengths and gifts of her own, a realization particularly augmented by her beautiful and deep relationship with the gray whale mother that has summered off the Californian coast, where the two young people and a group of academics are involved in a research project. Both Marty and Nick develop through love, love of each other as well as Marty's love of the whale, which heals them, opening them both to the possibility of a true, fulfilling relationship together.

Marty's growing relationship with whales, and her ability to communicate with the mother is finely and movingly portrayed, her deep need for affirmation and the mother whale's deep loneliness reach out to the other, creating a link between human and cetacean which is profound. Katz actually presents part of some perceptions of this relationship and the world through the whale's mind, an audacious step for any fiction writer. However, this technique works, partly because Katz has managed to make the whale's perceptions and ways of thinking alien enough that the animal does not become anthropomorphized, and partly because of the very human-seeming feelings of the whale—feelings of loneliness, isolation, concern for her calf, grief, love. Somehow the alienness of the perceptions and the humanness of the motions combine to create a powerful unity that become the whale, and could be nothing else.

The plot is also engaging. As Agatha Christie's continued popularity proves, we never grow out of our love of mysteries and adventure, no matter how mature we become. Katz uses a mystery format in this novel, centering the action of the plot on both a suspected murder and an illegal search for sunken treasure. Katz leaves the reader guessing about the murder until the last chapter of the novel. Thus the author is presenting three quite different lines of action in this novel. She is following the personal and interpersonal development of the two young people. Then Katz presents the plot concerning the whale, summered off shore, with her racial memory of another summer off this same shore, centuries before, and sees the past of that far-off time repeating itself in the present. Finally, there is the double mystery about Richard's death and the sunken treasure.

Katz's control over her material in this novel is masterly. The plot is continually fascinating. This novel should be too complex to work well in its 212 pages, yet it works extremely well, because of the author's skill in being succinct and yet penetrating in what she does present. The theme of the importance of emotional openness and love to heal many of the hurts even young people have already sustained informs this novel on every level. Tied in with this theme is the idea of trust, the need for vulnerability, and respect of the other, the damaging effects of hatred and bitterness, the need for forgiveness. And woven throughout all is the Song of the whale, tying places and times together in a unity that transcends all the individual elements of the novel, making it a spiritual *tour de force* as well. This is one novel not to be missed.

COME LIKE SHADOWS (1993)

Barbara L. Michasiw

SOURCE: A review of *Come Like Shadows,* in *Quill and Quire,* Vol. 59, No. 2, February, 1993, p. 36.

Come Like Shadows is a brew about witches and its cauldron bubbles with a complex mixture of ingredients: a Stratford production of *Macbeth* straitjacketed to dramatize the French-English conflict between Montcalm and Wolfe, a magic mirror that has trapped the real Macbeth in a 1,000-year time warp with a witch, two violent deaths, a "suicide," and an exploration of personal responsibility in two young lives.

Sixteen-year-old Kincardine O'Neil joins the Stratford Festival Company as an assistant to the director, Jeneva Strachan. Despite her love of theatre and admiration for Jeneva, Kinney quickly finds that she cannot agree with an interpretation of *Macbeth* that indulges Jeneva's personal vendetta against the Québécois. But when she sees an actor die during rehearsal, Kinney is drawn into the mysterious cycle of bad luck that surrounds the play. Soon a magic mirror enslaves Kinney and her actor friend Lucas, who is fascinated by the historical figure of the real Macbeth.

The narrative shifts between Kinney and Lucas, adding to the insight and texture of the novel. But, unlike in Katz's critically-acclaimed *False Face,* the fantasy she creates in *Come Like Shadows* is difficult to reconcile with reality. There is, nevertheless, much to enjoy in this novel: the Stratford setting, the drama in fact and fantasy, the intricate plot that profoundly tests her two young protagonists. But these diverse elements do not produce a seamless illusion. This is a challenging story that will probably not be comfortably accessible to readers below the grade 6 level.

Mary Jane Santos

SOURCE: A review of *Come Like Shadows,* in *Voice of Youth Advocates,* Vol. 16, No. 4, October, 1993, p. 228.

What happens when Shakespeare's *Macbeth,* the Stratford Theater Festival in Canada, a magical mirror, three witches and sixteen-year-old Kinny O'Neil meet? A fast-paced new suspense novel titled *Come Like Shadows* is born.

Kincardine (Kinny) O'Neil, named for the town where she was born, comes to Stratford, Ontario, to work for the summer with her mother's best friend, Jeneva Strachan, a director at the famous Stratford Theater Festival. Kinny's parents hope that by exposing her to the Shakespeare theater, Kinny will soon come to her senses and give up yet another of her whimsical career ideas. But Kinny arrives in Stratford full of hope and excitement, only to be given the most mundane jobs and to be completely ignored by most of the company, including Jeneva. When Kinny is finally given the somewhat challenging job of finding a needed prop, a mirror, she combs several secondhand and antique shops before finding the "perfect" prop. The mirror, however, instead of reflecting Kinny's face, shows her a glimpse of a hunchbacked, evil witch. When another actor, Lucas, peers into the mirror, he begins to see the true history of the Scottish king, Macbeth. Is the mirror haunted by the ghosts and witches of the real Macbeth?

When the mirror becomes part of the production, strange and deadly things begin to occur, and the long held belief that Shakespeare's play *Macbeth* is cursed becomes more and more believable as cast members die mysteriously and all of Kinny's wishes begin to come true. The mystery of the mirror eventually becomes evident to Kinny, and she realizes that only by sacrificing herself will other members of the company be saved. Will others understand the mystery in the mirror in time to save Kinny?

Set against the backdrop of the Shakespearean theater, *Come Like Shadows* is an intriguing mystery/fantasy with well developed characters and realistic dialogue. Katz manages to keep readers' interest while educating them to Shakespeare, Scottish history and even some contemporary political problems in Canada. Even the most avid young adult mystery reader will find solving this mystery a challenge, and the appearance of witches and a magical mirror will satisfy the fantasy reader. A good read, recommended for most public and school libraries.

Lucinda Snyder Whitehurst

SOURCE: A review of *Come Like Shadows,* in *School Library Journal,* Vol. 39, No. 12, December, 1993, p. 134.

Kincardine O'Neil, 16, passionately wants to be an actress. To expose her to the harsh realities of theater life, her mother persuades an old friend, now a famous director, to give Kinny a summer job as an assistant. *Macbeth* (or the Scottish play, as the superstitious actors call it) is said to be cursed, and this production lives up to its reputation. Before the run is over, the cast faces deaths, accidents, and a fire. The biggest threat of all, however, comes from three ancient witches who have been tied up with the play for centuries because of their involvement with the real Macbeth. The premise is promising. Katz advances the theory that Macbeth was actually a good man who has been wronged by history. Well-researched details add authentic texture to the theater setting. Nevertheless, at times the narrative drags. Alternating viewpoints from Kinny, a young actor, Macbeth himself, and the witches often make the story convoluted and difficult to follow, especially in the beginning. There is also a subplot about French Canadian politics. Although this book will not have wide appeal, it will be appreciated by drama and Shakespeare enthusiasts.

Jeanne Triner

SOURCE: A review of *Come Like Shadows,* in *Booklist,* Vol. 90, No. 7, December 1, 1993, p. 685.

Sixteen-year-old Kinny O'Neil is thrilled to have a summer job as an assistant on the production of *Macbeth* at Canada's Stratford Festival Theater. Soon, however, it appears there might be truth to the theater superstition that the play is cursed. The company experiences a host of grisly "accidents" that all seem to revolve around the ancient mirror Kinny has found for a prop. Both Kinny and Lucas, a young actor with whom she forms an uneasy friendship, see visions of the real Macbeth in the mirror and are slowly drawn into the sinister circle of power controlled by none other than Macbeth's witches. The author sets some wonderful mystical scenes, uses imagery well, and does an excellent job of maintaining suspense throughout. Her reiteration of the theme and message of Shakespeare's *Macbeth* in this modern tale is cleverly and subtly achieved. This is, however, a very complex story, and while careful reading reveals that all of the pieces do fit together, probably only good readers or those fascinated by theater or sorcery will stick with it to the end. The author's use of the heroine to mount the soapbox for the cause of French Canadians gets a bit tedious after a while, but, overall, the characters are well drawn, the plot is tight, and the historic information presented in such a way that the novel would be an effective supplement to units on Shakespeare, theater, and Canadian or Scottish history.

Gerald Rubio

SOURCE: "Will the Real Macbeth Please Step Forth?" in *Canadian Children's Literature,* No. 79, 1995, pp. 90-1.

This is a truly remarkable book. Katz's novel examines the many faces of Macbeth over a 900-year period: she presents the historical Scottish king who ruled well for ten years only to be defeated by the English in 1057; she offers reasons (accurate with one exception) for Shakespeare's characterization of him as murderer and tyrant; she creates two protagonists who are intimately involved in a modern Stratford, Ontario production of *Macbeth* which reinterprets and stages the play as a commentary on Quebec/English Canada politics. The novel is an exciting read and accessible to young adults on its own, but it could equally well serve educators as a vehicle for introducing students to the differences between fiction and fact, about the ways in which "facts" are interpreted for political or personal purposes, for illustration of how older literature can reveal truths about the present, for discussions of contemporary and non-traditional productions of the classic plays, even for consideration of what is involved in learning to act a role or direct a performance.

The title quotes the apparition scene in *Macbeth* (IV,1,111) as the Witches conjure visions of eight of Banquo's descendents, the last with a mirror revealing yet more shadowy successors. In Katz' fiction, the originals of Shakespeare's Witches actually existed in Macbeth's time and are responsible both for Shakespeare's view of Macbeth and for the inexplicable misfortunes and accidents which have plagued productions of the play through the ages. Katz's witches' coven consisted of Maiden, Mother, and Hag; because they worshipped and preserved memories of their "Goddess" they were rewarded with near—but *conditional*—immortality (Anne Rice's vampires take note!): each lived hundreds of years, but eventually the eldest (aided by her Sisters) was forced to seduce a young girl into permitting her body to be inhabited by her soul. The exchange of the novel was to take place in a sacred Stone Circle in Scotland; Hag and girl, after reciting the

appropriate incantation three times, are to be projected *into* a mirror, their souls exchanged: the girl's soul is then to remain in the mirror while the Hag's emerges in her body. Katz' Macbeth, however, interrupts the ceremony. He had been tempted by the Witches throughout his career, but he always rejected them. Finally, in hiding and knowing he will be captured the following morning, Macbeth seeks the witches, not for himself, but to prevent the English domination of his country. The witches ignore him, however, because they are in the process of tricking a young girl into permitting the Hag to inhabit her body. Macbeth realizes what they are doing and, to save the child, enters the mirror with the Hag himself. In doing so, he changes the incantation's word "past" to "future": he saves the child, but is trapped in the mirror with the vindictive Hag. The mirror, with them trapped within, disappears into the future; it has the power, however, to attract the Hag's sister witches, and they search for it over the next few hundred years.

The mirror first resurfaces in Renaissance England where the Hag emerges to discover Shakespeare writing his *Macbeth* truthfully: his central character has no faults. The vindictive Hag annotates his *Holinshed* so as to inspire him to depict Macbeth as the murderous tyrant we know; she also gives him an actual incantation to use to attract her sisters to performances of the play. She and the real Macbeth remain imprisoned in the mirror until it makes its way (by chance? by its inherent powers?) into a present day Stratford (Ontario) production of the play.

And here our young protagonists enter the picture. Sixteen-year-old Kinny (an apprentice assisting at rehearsals) purchases the mirror for use as a prop and is shocked to see the witches and the young girl they are tempting in it; she is later tempted by it and apparently granted unasked-for wishes. Twenty-year-old Lucas, by contrast, sees only the actual Macbeth in it, and learns the truth of his character from it. The two realize that somehow the mirror is connected with the disasters which overtake the production—two deaths and a fire—before the climax of the novel in Scotland (the production goes on tour) in the Goddess Circle where it all began 900-odd years earlier.

Katz has, however, created protagonists infinitely more three-dimensional and thematically relevant both to the Macbeth story and to contemporary Canadian politics than my outline of the fantasy plot suggests. Kinny is an English Montrealer who believes that Quebec is justified in its desire to preserve culture no matter at what cost to the nation as a whole. Lucas is from a French Canadian family which migrated to the U.S. before his birth; although he speaks only English and has tried to deny his heritage, he is discriminated against in America. The play's director was formerly a highly-acclaimed actress who has been denied work and grants in Quebec because she was English-speaking; in retaliation, her production of *Macbeth* is set in pre-Confederation Quebec with the villain Macbeth dressed as a foppish Montcalm and Malcolm as General Wolfe. Overriding the entire novel are explicit and implied parallels and contrasts between Macbeth's

Scotland (which lost its independence because of his defeat) and Canada.

📖 *TIME GHOST* (1994)

Joanne Findon

SOURCE: A review of *Time Ghost,* in *Quill and Quire,* Vol. 60, No. 11, November, 1994, p. 37.

It is 2044, and human "progress" has ravaged the Earth. But when Sara's activist grandmother insists on a trip to the North Pole, one of "the last pockets of real life left," Sara agrees to go only because her best friend, Dani, wants to join them. Complicating matters are the girls' science-struck brothers, who want to come along to conduct a time-travelling experiment. Meanwhile, Grandma is determined to stop a company, owned by a man named Mr. Duguay, from drilling for oil at the Pole. A tense confrontation over an old pendant transports Sara, Dani, and Mr. Duguay back into Grandma's past. There, Sara is trapped inside Grandma's 12-year-old body, Mr. Duguay inhabits her father's body, and an invisible Dani must find a way to bring them all back to 2044.

This is an intriguing novel that combines time-travel strategies with a near-future setting. The world of 2044 is similar enough to our own to be frighteningly real, and the story's environmental warnings are clear. Placing Sara inside the body and mind of her young grandmother is a bold stroke that allows author Welwyn Wilton Katz to explore the emotional core of the story in powerful ways.

Unfortunately, the novel has problems. More than one savvy young teen will spot the flaws in the scientific framework of this future world. Moreover, six full chapters go by before the girls travel back in time, and by then the reader is growing impatient. Most problematic is the time-travel technique itself; the excessive detailing of *how* the characters travel between past and present slows the story down and distracts attention from the novel's true concerns. The characters do grow emotionally through their experiences, and Sara and Mr. Duguay literally see life through another person's eyes. But the mechanisms of their growth and development are too obvious, and Mr. Duguay's rapid conversion at the end is barely believable.

Because of Katz's past successes in the fantasy genre, expectations will be high for this book. Unfortunately, *Time Ghost* fails to create either the wonder of *The Third Magic* or the emotional resonance of *Whalesinger*.

Virginia Davis

SOURCE: A review of *Time Ghost,* in *CM: A Reviewing Journal of Canadian Materials for Young People,* Vol. XXII, No. 6, December, 1994, p. 210.

Time Ghost by Welwyn Wilton Katz is fantasy, incorpo-

rates time travel, and can be called science fiction as well, since its essential premise is an extension of scientific thinking. The premise? Since all time zones meet at the North Pole, the Pole is a place of no real time—or it's all times at once. If one were at the North Pole when time travel was activated, one could theoretically travel through time to any moment in time.

The creator of the theory does not anticipate another possibility that occurs when the two young heroines are tossed back in time: one of them enters the body of a past-time host; the other, ghostlike, can observe. Being inside another person means being able to speak only if the host is asleep, being able to see only if the host's eyes are open, and being able to move only if the host can be willed to move. This time-traveller/host relationship, the rapidly moving plot, and the discovery of what one generation can teach another all make this novel compelling.

Roger Sutton

SOURCE: A review of *Time Ghost,* in *Bulletin of the Center for Children's Books,* Vol. 48, No. 9, May, 1995, p. 312.

An exceptionally well-executed time-travel matrix forms the structural heart of this novel about two girls, Sara and Dani, who, with their brothers and Sara's formidable grandmother, travel to the Arctic—what's left of it anyway. The setting is the mid-twenty-first century when much of earth's natural beauty and resources have been destroyed by pollution, overpopulation, and the "Greysuits" (Grandma's name for an ever-greedy corporate elite), who are intent upon taking the rest. In contrast to the nature-loving Dani, Sara has been whiny and scared the whole trip, but both girls are frightened when, along with one of the Greysuits, they find themselves back in the past, specifically Grandma's past, when she was a young girl living on a quiet lake in 1993. While there isn't enough room in this review to go into the details of how the time travel works, it in fact works very well indeed, and Katz brings the travelers back home (always a trick) with the same assurance. The ecological theme occasionally rears its head into preachiness, but it is generally kept in check by the slick turns of plot and the realism of the characters. Grandma may be right, but she is rather overbearing, and Sara's reliving of a crucial episode in Grandma's girlhood brings each to a more reasonable understanding of the other.

📖 *OUT OF THE DARK* (1995)

Ronald Jobe

SOURCE: A review of *Out of the Dark,* in *Journal of Adolescent and Adult Literacy,* Vol. 39, No. 6, March, 1996, p. 521.

Can there be a connection between the young seal dying

on the rocks today and those killed by Vikings at the same spot?

A young teen returns with his father and brother to a small village in Newfoundland. Still suffering after his mother's murder several years ago, Ben is in no mood to associate with the locals. He is constantly reminded of the Norse tales his mother told him and seeks solace in his wood carving, a skill they shared.

Living in a house across the bay from L'Anse aux Meadows, the historic site of the earliest Norse settlements in North America, Ben finds that the tales of the past take on new life as they merge with the present. Using his father's boat, Ben visits the Viking site often.

Katz uses italics to skillfully weave a double subplot, one relating the saga of Odin and the gods and the other relating the account of Tor, a master boat builder and hunter. Each account proves to be a parallel prediction of what is to come. As Ben reads passages from their Vinland accounts of the Viking settlement and the unfortunate relations with the Skraelings, or natives, he is unwittingly led to make discoveries about the Vikings.

Katz masterfully elicits the power of the landscape in this harsh section of Newfoundland. The characters, both ancient and modern, have to be constantly alert to the ever-changing weather patterns if they want to survive the sudden violent storms. Katz allows readers to experience the silence of the landscape, to be frozen in their reading as Ben follows the accounts of the Vinland settlers.

In this quiet story, YA readers will relate to the hurt Ben feels, his frustration at being in a small village instead of Ottawa, the annoyance at both father and brother pressuring him to accept friendships, and the dramatic power of the climax with its contrasting choice between violence or friendship. Individual readers will relate to how Ben feels and consider options in their own lives of which they had previously been unaware.

Publishers Weekly

SOURCE: A review of *Out of the Dark,* in *Publishers Weekly,* Vol. 243, No. 29, July 15, 1996, pp. 74-5.

A boy's coming to terms with the death of his mother is the crux of this slow-paced but thoughtful story [*Out of The Dark*]. Ben's father attempts to start a new life by moving from Ottawa to a small, coastal town in Newfoundland. To 13-year-old Ben, however, the move means a further loss of the familiar; furthermore, the townsfolk seem insular, suspicious and, in many ways, backward. A local historical Viking settlement, L'Anse aux Meadows, proves at first a worthy diversion but soon fuels an obsessive game that Ben plays out entirely in his imagination, casting himself as Tor, a Viking shipbuilder. Katz (*Time Ghost*) alternates Ben's real life with scenes from the Tor game, which are based on Ben's reading of the Vinland sagas and passages from Norse mythology. Unfortunate-

ly, the formality in language, the myriad Scandinavian names and uneven story lines make the Tor scenes difficult to follow. Ultimately they serve as little more than regular interruptions to Ben's "real" story, which is resolved in a powerful final scene—perhaps the book's finest moment, and one worth waiting for.

Laurence Steven

SOURCE: "The Search for a Shared Home," in *Canadian Children's Literature,* No. 82, 1996, pp. 81-2.

In *Out of the Dark,* Welwyn Wilton Katz successfully continues to explore the main concerns of her fiction for young adults: the search for emotional wholeness of teens with problems, the pervasive influence of history and myth on the present, and the interpenetration of fantasy and reality as the way by which the "real-world" present and historical-mythic past interact. Through this interpenetration she also wrestles, again, with the question of who rightfully belongs to a place.

Thirteen-year-old Ben Elliott and his nine-year-old brother Keith have moved to Ship Cove, Newfoundland, with their author father Lorne, who had grown up there. Their mother, Frances, has been killed in a parking lot shooting in Florida, and Lorne has taken the boys "home." The problem is that Ship Cove is not home to Ben, and he resents the move as an imposition. The one thing that saves the situation for him is that across the bay from their house is L'Anse aux Meadows, the restored site of one of the Viking landfalls. Lorne and Frances had met one summer while working on her father's archeological dig at the site, and Ben has inherited his mother's love of things Viking. He knows *The Vinland Sagas* thoroughly, and since being little has "played Viking" by imagining himself to be Tor, a young shipbuilder who accompanies Karsefnie and Gudrid to settle Vinland.

In *Whalesinger* (1990), Katz develops the historical/tourist site marking Sir Francis Drake's harbour at Point Reyes, California, by having the past episode penetrate into the present story. Similarly, in *Out of the Dark* Katz details the restored Viking settlement and Ben's imaginary recreation of its inhabitants in order to have the Viking clash with native people (Skraelings) increasingly mirror, and eventually come to shape, Ben's encounter with kids of Ship Cove. The question Katz explores is whether the outside can plant a "home" in inhospitable territory. For Ben the territory is not only Newfoundland, but also the uncharted emotional ground he finds himself on after his mother is murdered. The title, *Out of the Dark,* comes from the story Frances tells Ben about the aftermath of the Norse Apocalypse, Ragnarok, where when everything is dead, "only then, out of the dark, will life begin again." The climax of the story occurs when Ben/Tor has to make a choice of whether to throw the Viking axe away or to bury it in the head of Ross Colbourne/Skraeling. In the actual saga it is the native chief who throws the iron axe into the lake, in a gesture of rejection of all things European. The Vikings finally abandon Vinland, knowing they cannot win the land, and that they could never share it with the Skraelings. By adapting the saga to have Ben/Tor holding the axe, Katz enables the abandoning of it to be a gesture of acceptance, goodwill, and trust rather than rejection. It also allows the Skraelings/Ship Cove kids the opportunity to express the same. It enables the ground—the "home"—to be shared:

> Tor had gone away from here, but he, Ben, would stay. And this time, he would make Vinland work.

The search for a shared ground between Native and European was also central to Katz's *False Face* in which a mixed-race boy, Tom, and a white girl, Laney, tentatively enter a new, unstereotyped human territory while dealing with the havoc caused by Iroquois medicine masks of power which are irresponsibly possessed by Laney's mother. Upon the book's nomination for Trillium and Governor General's awards, Katz was charged with cultural appropriation by members of the Iroquois nation. Eight years later, by having Ben know he would "make Vinland work," Katz responds to those who accused her of treading where she has no business. The land is a shared home, and we must make it work. Katz's fiction is an impressive contribution to that task.

Judy Sasges

SOURCE: A review of *Out of the Dark,* in *Voice of Youth Advocates,* Vol. 19, No. 5, December, 1996, pp. 270-71.

Thirteen-year-old Ben blames himself for his mother's violent death in a Florida parking lot. Now living with his father and younger brother in a small Newfoundland town, he withdraws into a fantasy Viking world. As Tor, a ship-builder assigned to protecting the Lady Gudrid and her child, Ben has the opportunity to redeem himself. In the real world, redemption is not quite so easy. Ben's bitterness and inability to articulate his pain alienate his family and community. His only comfort is found in building a model ship, a project similar to ones he shared with his mother. Despite the shipbuilding and fantasy world, Ben's impotence and anger grow until a violent act is almost inevitable. Instead of violence, Ben faces his demons and acknowledges both his mother's death and her legacy.

Katz's masterful portrayal of Ben results in a fully-developed character. His guilt feelings and self-destructive tendencies are achingly real. The reader understands Ben's frustration as the rage builds and he is tempted to react with violence. Isolated and alone, he finally realizes that he must accept his mother's death, reach out to others, and continue his life. The fantasy Viking world is evocative but not intrusive and provides insight into Ben's state of mind. Fantasy and reality blend seamlessly into a well-crafted coming-of-age story.

Additional coverage of Katz's life and career is contained in the following sources published by Gale Research: *Authors and Artists for Young Adults,* Vol. 19; *Contemporary Authors,* Vol. 154; *Junior DISCovering Authors* (CD-ROM); *Something about the Author,* Vol. 62; and *Something about the Author Autobiography Series,* Vol. 25.

Holly Keller

1942-

American author and illustrator of picture books for young children.

Major works include *Too Big* (1983), *Ten Sleepy Sheep* (1983), *Geraldine's Blanket* (1984), *Goodbye Max* (1987), *The Best Present* (1989).

INTRODUCTION

Holly Keller writes and illustrates picture books for pre-school and early elementary school children. Her simple, perceptive stories reveal the reality of a youngster's world. She explores the difficult situations common to many small children, such as getting a new brother, going to school for the first time, or dealing with the death of a pet. Keller's universal appeal is that she is objective in her presentation of childhood situations and the accompanying emotions. Using animal characters, humorous prose, and simple artwork, Keller shows an uncanny knack for understanding how children actually feel as they confront the trials and tribulations of their early years.

Biographical Information

Keller was born on February 11, 1942, in New York City. In 1963, Keller married a pediatrician, and in that same year she received a bachelor's degree from Sarah Lawrence College. A year later she earned a master's degree from Columbia University. Keller also studied art at both Manhattanville College and the Parsons School of Design. However, it wasn't until the age of forty that, encouraged by a printmaking instructor to pursue book illustration, Keller started on her career as an author and illustrator of works for children. Her husband's young patients and her own children both inspired and provided Keller with many ideas for her stories.

Major Works

Keller frequently peoples her stories with animals. Perhaps two of her most engaging characters are a little opossum named Henry and the piglet Geraldine. Readers first met Henry in *Too Big*. In this story, the opossum wishes that he could do all of the things that his new brother can do: wear diapers, drink milk from a bottle, and captivate everyone's attention. But Henry cannot because he is just too big. Finally, when Henry tries to wear one of the baby's new outfits, he looks so ridiculous that everyone—Mom, Grandma, and Grandpa, even Henry himself—laughs.

Henry's next big event is Independence Day. In *Henry's*

Fourth of July (1985), the little opossum celebrates the holiday for the first time that he can recall. He picnics, runs a sack race, and sees fireworks. All in all, he has a great day—quite unlike the beginnings of his fifth birthday. In *Henry's Happy Birthday* (1990), the opossum fears his party will be disastrous, because his mother insists he wear a shirt and tie to the party, he loses at one of the games, the presents do not look like the gifts he was promised, and his cake is not chocolate. Henry finally wishes that it was someone else's birthday as he blows out the candles on his sorry vanilla cake. But then Henry's consternation turns to pleasure when the birthday cake tastes good, when he does indeed receive that inflatable crocodile, and when he has fun at his own party. Though Henry regrets that he wasted his birthday wish, he is encouraged to think all year of a better wish for his sixth birthday party.

Like Henry, Geraldine the pig struggles to make her way in the world. Keller first introduces her piglet heroine in *Geraldine's Blanket*. This little piggy's parents pressure her to abandon her baby blanket, but Geraldine just cannot give up the shredded rag yet. With the help of her aunt, Geraldine devises a way to keep her blanket and her dignity.

The next book about Geraldine finds her awaiting the first snowfall of the season. In this story, *Geraldine's Big Snow* (1988), the little pig embodies all the anticipation and excitement a youngster feels before the first sled ride of winter. *Geraldine's Baby Brother* (1994) chronicles the pig's reactions to a sibling whom she resents at first sight. When Willie is inconsolable and cries all night, Geraldine decides to tell him to be quiet in no uncertain terms. But when she goes in to speak with him, she finds Willie cooing and smiling at her. She thinks him sort of cute and reads Willie (and herself) to sleep. Geraldine and Willie are on friendlier terms in *Geraldine First* (1996). Nevertheless the big sister is exasperated with her little copycat brother. Willie apes all of Geraldine's activities until she tricks him into happily cleaning up after her.

Keller offers reluctant sleepers a humorous bedtime story in *Ten Sleepy Sheep.* Lewis tries counting sheep to cure his insomnia, but the sheep throw a party and keep him awake instead. Keller addressed a more sober issue in *Goodbye Max,* the story of a boy whose dog has died. The boy has to come to terms with Max's death before he can accept the new puppy his father has given him. Alice Miller Bregman applauded Keller's "realistic, sympathetic and appropriately understated treatment of a difficult subject." *The Best Present* is also of a more serious nature. Katie is upset because she is too young to visit her grandmother in the hospital. She tries to appear older but fails and has to leave her get-well bouquet with an elevator operator. When her grandmother returns home, Katie is happy to learn that not only did her grandmother get the flowers but that she felt they were the best present she had received.

Through stories such as these, Keller teaches children to cope with life's problems while giving them an enjoyable read. The gentle humor in her stories is generated by her characters' personalities or actions. Her prose style is honest and direct, but also touching. Marcus Crouch noted that Holly Keller "extract[s] the full quota of emotion out of the story but never laps[es] into sentimentality."

Keller's illustrations are simple yet fanciful. Her cartoon-style line-and-wash drawings feature bright colors and add a cheerfulness to the pages. Keller also adds clever details to her illustrations. For example, the page borders in *What Alvin Wanted* (1990) show a flower motif from a hat worn by Alvin's mother. And what did Alvin want throughout the story? His mom, who left absently on an errand without kissing him goodbye. Keller again incorporates an important symbol in the borders of *Island Baby* (1992). She decorates them with colorful, amusing birds in this story about sending a little one—whether bird or human—on its flight to independence. In *Furry* (1992)—the story of an allergic child's search for a hairless pet—she even decorates the armchair's legs with animal paws.

Keller's drawings and stories have been delighting children since the early 1980s. Known for what Judith Sharman termed her "sure touch with text and illustration,"

Keller continues to be a reliable source of enjoyable books that teach small ones how to handle some of life's big, difficult situations.

Awards

The Library of Congress named *Ten Sleepy Sheep* its Children's Book of the Year in 1983. The next year *School Library Journal* awarded *Geraldine's Blanket* its Best Book of the Year honor. In 1987 the Child Study Association named *Goodbye Max* as Book of the Year. *The Best Present* was cited as a Notable Children's Trade Book in the field of social studies in 1989.

TITLE COMMENTARY

CROMWELL'S GLASSES (1982)

Carolyn Noah

SOURCE: A review of *Cromwell's Glasses,* in *School Library Journal,* Vol. 28, No. 7, March, 1982, p. 136.

Winsome rabbit Cromwell is unlike other young rabbits from the start—he is terribly nearsighted. Until he's big enough for eyeglasses, he causes annoyances for his siblings and anguish for himself. New glasses, though giving Cromwell vision, make him the object of family ridicule until a playground buddy makes fun of him. Then the family closes ranks, and Cromwell begins to feel good about himself and his family. This brief tale thoughtfully treats the difficulties that glasses present to a young child, and with a positive resolution, everyone comes up smiling. . . . Two-color drawings of humorous people-like rabbits are a complement to this picture book. In treating a trying subject with effective lightness, *Cromwell's Glasses* will make a serviceable addition to storytime collections.

Ilene Cooper

SOURCE: A review of *Cromwell's Glasses,* in *Booklist,* Vol. 78, No. 17, May 1, 1982, p. 1161.

Little Cromwell Rabbit is near-sighted. He goes through an eye exam and gets glasses, which solves his vision problems; but now the kids in the playground laugh at his "goggles." His sister, who has had her own reservations about the glasses, leaps to his defense, and while they play Cromwell finds out how much nicer it is to see. Cromwell's cartooned face resembles a pear with ears, but this will only make readers more receptive to the bibliotherapeutic message. Done in tones of rose and brown, many of the pictures are set off in a frame, adding to the comic-strip effect. Slight story and simple message, but effectively intertwined.

Margery Fisher

SOURCE: A review of *Cromwell's Glasses*, in *Growing Point*, Vol. 24, No. 3, September, 1985, p. 4483.

Rabbits lend themselves readily to humanisation. The rounded faces and bulging eyes do not quite caricature innocent small children; the prominent incisors are a boon to artists of comic line; the body can be dressed without too much improbability; as for rabbit temperament, the choice of this animal as supreme trickster, alongside Spider and Coyote, must remain a mystery. With Peter Rabbit in mind as surely the type-specimen, let us examine a few recent examples of the way rabbits have been used to demonstrate the moods and activities of the young. The situation in **Cromwell's Glasses** is instructive; this American picture-book is in its offhand way a miniature psychological case-book. Youngest in his family, short-sighted Cromwell annoys his siblings with his blundering behaviour and things seem no better when he is fitted with spectacles, for the other rabbit children in the park laugh at his 'crazy goggles'. But conscience pricks his sisters after they have seen how well the little brother now comports himself in ball games and hopscotch and they cheerfully tow him home in a toy cart, reconciled to goggles and all. Brown and red wash and ink line decorate animated scenes, in light caricature, in which a human lifestyle is comically equated with certain natural movements of the rabbit's face and limbs.

📖 TOO BIG (1983)

Ilene Cooper

SOURCE: A review of *Too Big*, in *Booklist*, Vol. 79, No. 16, April 15, 1983, p. 1095.

Henry welcomes home his baby brother Jake, and while he is not overtly jealous, he does try to take part in activities such as sucking on a bottle and wearing a diaper. Everything he wants to do is quashed by the statement, "You're too big." When a package arrives for Jake, Henry opens it and puts on the outfit that has come as a gift. Seeing Henry stuffed into the outfit, the family understands that he's been upset, but even Henry has to laugh when he realizes he is just too big. Appeased with a bicycle and some hugs, Henry seems well on his way to assuming his status as older brother. Henry and his family are an appealing group of possums, and though the subject of sibling rivalry is treated simply, this could be effective with preschoolers experiencing jealousy pangs. The framed, minimally lined drawings, mostly done in shades of baby blue, spice an understanding text with graphic wit.

Cheryl Lynn Gage

SOURCE: A review of *Too Big*, in *School Library Journal*, Vol. 29, No. 10, August, 1983, p. 53.

Henry, a possum-like creature, attempts to draw attention

from his new baby brother to himself by regressing to an imitation of infancy. When he stuffs himself into his brother's new baby suit and all his relatives laugh, he realizes he is "too big." As a pacifier Grandpa gives him a tricycle and Mama gives him something "nobody is too big for," a hug. Children will relate to this humorous story of sibling jealousy. The facial expressions on the simple, softly colored drawings are particularly well done in presenting the mood of the story.

Sarah Wintle

SOURCE: "The Daily Round: Picture Books 2," in *Times Literary Supplement*, No. 4200, September 30, 1983, p. 1050.

Holly Keller's **Too Big** combines sympathy with comedy in both its story and its illustrations. It is a variation on the old theme of the awfulness of being joined by a new baby. Keller's characters are plump grey creatures with scaly pink mouse tails, vole-like faces and mops of stringy hair. Baby Jake has some of the unformed, hairless, and hideous aspects of most new-born creatures—a nice touch of realism—and young Henry behaves with obstreperous self-pity. The book manages to be both touching and funny.

Mary M. Burns

SOURCE: A review of *Too Big*, in *The Horn Book Magazine*, Vol. LX, No. 1, February, 1984, p. 43.

Opossums are the engaging characters in a fresh interpretation of a familiar situation—the jealousy of an older child for a new arrival. Disturbed by the attention lavished on baby Jake, young Henry tries a variety of methods to assert his territorial imperative—from climbing into the baby's bassinet to playing a lullaby on a drum. Each time, an adult remarks that he is too big for the particular act—a comment which Henry neither appreciates nor apprehends. Then he squeezes into an outfit scaled to Jake's size, not his. Initially embarrassed but soon triumphantly self-assured, he joins in the general laughter and takes his rightful place as the elder son. His newly accepted position is acknowledged with a bicycle from Grandpa and a warm hug from Mama with the comforting reminder that no one outgrows a little demonstration of affection. Conveyed in text and illustrations, the humor is gentle rather than condescending, developing naturally from the characters' personalities and actions. The book is comfortably sized for small hands, its square shape well suited to the ingenuous line drawings washed in soft pink, blue, and gray.

📖 TEN SLEEPY SHEEP (1983)

Kirkus Reviews

SOURCE: A review of *Ten Sleepy Sheep*, in *Kirkus Reviews*, Vol. LI, No. 17 September 1, 1983, p. J150.

How many ways to re-say good-night? It could be the test

of a picture-book author/illustrator's inventiveness—which Keller passes with modest aplomb. The night Lewis can't sleep, Papa brings him a glass of water, Mama reads him a story, and Grandma sings him a song. (That, pitched perfectly, is just the way it reads.) But, with Lewis still popping out of bed (sleepily rubbing his eyes), Grandpa tells him to "Count sheep." And—snugly abed: "The first sheep had a red balloon. The second had a drum. . . ." When the room is filled with dancing sheep, Lewis shouts (no Wild-Thing-like rhyme): "Please! I'm trying to sleep!" Unheeded, he picks the sheep up, puts them into bed, brings each a glass of water, reads them a story . . . and climbs into bed beside them, to fall asleep (with a balloon rising from the footboard). Perky (not pretty-pretty) pink and blue; lightly whimsical, slightly French (those fluffy sheep); in toto, neatly done—and nice.

Ilene Cooper

SOURCE: A review of *Ten Sleepy Sheep,* in *Booklist,* Vol. 80, No. 3, October 1, 1983, p. 296.

Counting sheep to fall asleep? That's what Lewis' grandfather tells him to try when glasses of water and songs don't work. So Lewis starts counting—but he hasn't counted on the sheep coming with balloons, cookies, streamers, and soap bubbles, leaving Lewis with a party on his hands instead of restful slumber. Lewis begins picking up the sheep, one by one, giving them water, and calming them down with a story until finally they're out for the count—as is Lewis. This delightful story moves from the everyday "I can't fall asleep" syndrome to fantastic fun, and readers should enjoy the trip. The spare pen drawings, dabbed with pinks and purples, are more likable than unusual. Still, Keller manages to turn her look-alike sheep into real party animals with just a few strokes of the pen.

Elizabeth M. Simmons

SOURCE: A review of *Ten Sleepy Sheep,* in *School Library Journal,* Vol. 30, No. 6, February, 1984, p. 59.

This simple story is ideal for those young children who follow a certain ritual each night at bedtime. When Lewis couldn't get to sleep one night, his father brought him a glass of water, his mother read him a story and his grandmother sang a song but nothing worked. Finally his grandfather suggested that he try counting sheep. Soon Lewis had a bedroom full of noisy sheep, and still he could not sleep. So he picked them up one by one and put them into bed, gave each of them a drink of water, read a story and sang a song. Soon all the sheep—but not Lewis—were asleep. Finally he decides to join them in bed and before you know it, he's asleep too. Pen-and-ink illustrations with soft washes of pink and blue provide a humorous addition to a bedtime story that even the most reluctant sleeper will enjoy.

Margery Fisher

SOURCE: A review of *Ten Sleepy Sheep,* in *Growing Point,* Vol. 22, No. 6, March, 1984, p. 4220.

A simple, irresistible joke is beautifully sustained in this elegantly produced picture-book from America. When Grandpa suggests that Lewis should count sheep and stop his nightly importunities, the boy is haunted by images of an eccentric flock whose members blow bubbles, eat biscuits and generally racket about—so much so that in despair he tricks them into bed, comforts them with a drink and a story, and falls asleep in their midst. Ink line and scantily applied pastel colours extend with cheerful humour the congenial paradox.

GERALDINE'S BLANKET (1984)

Kirkus Reviews

SOURCE: A review of *Geraldine's Blanket,* in *Kirkus Reviews,* Vol. LII, Nos. 1-5, March 1, 1984, pp. J5-6.

For [Geraldine], a piglet with aplomb, growing up doesn't mean giving up her baby blanket—and any child under similar parental pressure will savor her symbolic victory. There is, indeed, less trauma than pertinacity here. Past babyhood, we hear and see, "She took it with her everywhere . . . and she always found a use for it." It's a flying cape when she soars on the swing, a knapsack when she goes to the market. In time, from patching and trimming, it looks woebegone—and Daddy gets cross. "Geraldine covered her ears." Mama tries to hide it; Geraldine, quickly finding it, pins it to her dress in the daytime and tucks it under her pillow at night. Then, after Mama and Papa talk "in whispers," Aunt Bessie, who gave Geraldine the blanket when she was born, gives her "a new present": a doll named Rosa, whom Geraldine loves. No more blanket, as Mama and Papa insist? Not Geraldine: with scissors, the blanket is made over—"Now Rosa has the blanket," says she, "and I have Rosa." In deft, spare, pink-and-gold-tinged cartoons, it all looks as lovable as the blanket, as spiffy as Geraldine.

Ilene Cooper

SOURCE: A review of *Geraldine's Blanket,* in *Booklist,* Vol. 80, No. 20, June 15, 1984, p. 1484.

Geraldine, a little pig, loves the blanket Aunt Bessie sent her when she was born. Pink and covered with roses, it makes a comforting companion. No matter how worn and frayed it gets, and no matter how often her parents hide it or urge her to give it up, Geraldine continues to hang on. At Christmas she gets another present from Aunt Bessie, a doll she names Rosa. Her parents at first think and then insist that now is the time to say a permanent good-bye to the blanket, but Geraldine has a different idea. She makes a dress for Rosa out of the blanket; now she can carry her two favorite possessions around with her. Keller's simply drawn, pink Geraldine is a likable heroine (though her parents seem rather unfeeling), and preschoolers should respond to her predicament. The pink and green bordered artwork is filled with humorous nuances, many of which are in the expressive faces of the pig family. A novel look at a familiar problem, and one that may provide a solution for some families.

Annie L. Okie

SOURCE: A review of *Geraldine's Blanket,* in *School Library Journal,* Vol. 30, No. 10, August, 1984, p. 62.

Even the gift of a new doll is not enough to persuade Geraldine the pig to give up her beloved but bedraggled baby blanket. When her parents finally insist that she get rid of it, she outwits them by cutting the blanket up to make a dress for her doll. Simply but wonderfully expressive line drawings washed with pastel colors capture the gentleness and humor of the story. Children will enjoy Keller's portrayal of Geraldine's stubbornness and her parents' reaction to it. The text is short and the vocabulary easy, making this satisfying story appropriate both for very young children and beginning readers.

Margery Fisher

SOURCE: A review of *Geraldine's Blanket,* in *Growing Point,* Vol. 25, No. 3, September, 1986, p. 4689.

Pigs standing in, as so often, for human beings, exemplify one familiar aspect of nursery life, the comfortblanket. Small children (and even larger ones still clinging to a surviving few inches of rag) should appreciate the doleful result when father and mother try to get rid of the battered piece of wool which has consoled Geraldine for so long. The stubborn piglet finds a solution to the problem at once clever and amusing and the author has matched her brief, artless text with illustrations in a caricature style, basically pink and muted orange, which accommodate human feelings to a pig's face with unerring skill and spanking humour.

📖 *ROCK COLLECTING* (written by Roma Gans, 1984)

Joseph T. Hannibal

SOURCE: A review of *Rock Collecting,* in *Science Books & Films,* Vol. 20, No. 5, May-June, 1985, p. 307.

This book is an introduction to rocks and rock collecting for young people. It discusses and illustrates various igneous, sedimentary, and metamorphic rocks, describing some of their properties, uses, and methods of formation. It also gives some gentle advice on starting a rock collection. Although much of the explanatory material is adequate for an introduction to the topic, some of it is incomplete or misleading; for example, quartz and other minerals are identified as "rocks" (the word "mineral" is never mentioned in the text). Notably absent in a book on collecting is any mention of the need to keep locality information and other data with specimens; youngsters should be encouraged to label the rocks they collect. The book's brightly colored drawings are attractive and cheery (if not always informative; one illustration is of a group of cats!). The black-and-white photographs of rocks and minerals, although satisfactory, pale beside the drawings. This book is far from first rate, but it could serve to introduce the topic.

📖 *WILL IT RAIN?* (1984)

Marge Loch-Wouters

SOURCE: A review of *Will It Rain?,* in *School Library Journal,* Vol. 31, No. 4, December, 1984, p. 72.

Keller has produced a simple anatomy of a rainstorm that will appeal to preschoolers. Squirrel is the first to notice the change in the air. Soon other animals become aware of the chilly breeze and darkening skies, and they ask each other, "Will it rain?" And indeed it does! The rain begins with plenty of thunder and lightning, and the animals seek shelter in burrows, nests and under bushes. The quiet misty aftermath of the storm finds the animals beginning to reappear once more to greet the sun. Keller's watercolors of the storm are a wonderful counterpoint to her affable cartoon animals. In this story, she combines a description of an approaching storm with the reaction of the animals to it. The result is a book that is gently exciting and one that children can both learn from and enjoy.

Margery Fisher

SOURCE: A review of *Will It Rain?,* in *Growing Point,* Vol. 24, No. 2, July, 1985, p. 4476.

In a tree beside a pond, fancifully depicted in hatched wash and line, robin, chipmunk, squirrel, duck and other denizens are uneasy at a coming storm; they take shelter from the rain in their various ways (rabbit under a tree-root, mouse beneath a fern) until 'suddenly it was quiet' and 'the sun came out.' An elegantly simple text at the foot of the successive pages directs attention to pictures which dramatise the animals comically but still relate them positively to their environment. From America a book from an author/artist with an original graphic technique skilfully used.

📖 *HENRY'S FOURTH OF JULY* (1985; published in England as *Henry's Picnic*)

Ilene Cooper

SOURCE: A review of *Henry's Fourth of July,* in *Booklist,* Vol. 81, No. 15, April 1, 1985, p. 1120.

Henry, a young opossum, is excited by the prospect of

staying up for his first Fourth of July fireworks. The festivities include Papa's hearty picnic basket, a parade, potato-sack races, a cooling swim, and the pièce de résistance—colorful fireworks bursting across the night sky. Keller's simply told tale manages to convey all the fun and excitement of our nation's birthday. The softly colored drawings, many drawn on large expanses of white, are filled with humorous nuances. A happy introduction to Fourth of July celebrations for the very young.

Zena Sutherland

SOURCE: A review of *Henry's Fourth of July,* in *Bulletin of the Center for Children's Books,* Vol. 38, No. 9, May, 1985, p. 168.

Tinted line drawings that have little polish but quite a bit of animation show Henry and his family (the usual picture book representation of mice as being clothed and having hands and feet, but tails and whiskers) attending and enjoying a picnic. Henry enjoys all the activities, particularly eating, winning third prize in a sack race, and staying up late to watch fireworks. Mama assures him, as she tucks him into bed, that they can go again next year. This is written in a simple, pleasant style, and the lack of plot is compensated for by the roster of activities.

Lucy Young Clem

SOURCE: A review of *Henry's Fourth of July,* in *School Library Journal,* Vol. 32, No. 1, September, 1985, p. 120.

Possums Henry and his baby brother Jake are back, and now Henry is big enough to stay up and watch the Fourth of July fireworks. The family arrives just in time for the parade. Afterwards, Henry comes in third in the sack race and wins a little bear. At last it's time for the big event, and the fireworks appear. "It went too fast," says Henry, and then falls asleep with a smile. The softly colored illustrations give the pages a warm and cozy feeling that meshes perfectly with the comfortable story. There are some painless lessons about competition and growing up here. Picture books about this holiday are hard to find, and story hour groups will enjoy this one.

Jill Bennett

SOURCE: A review of *Henry's Picnic,* in *The School Librarian,* Vol. 34, No. 2, June, 1986, p. 144.

In *Henry's Picnic,* Henry and his family are celebrating the Fourth of July at a summer picnic complete with a parade, races and fireworks, but only by reading the calendar hanging on Henry's bedroom wall do we discover the reason for the festivities. Young audiences this side of the Atlantic could well miss the significance of the date and wonder why the whole town seems to be taking part. Even so, learner readers and listeners can enjoy the easy-

to-read story and delight in the amusing illustrations of the quaint rodents' revels.

WHEN FRANCIE WAS SICK (1985)

Publishers Weekly

SOURCE: A review of *When Francie Was Sick,* in *Publishers Weekly,* Vol. 228, No. 7, August 16, 1985, p. 70.

Like the charmers in *Cromwell's Glasses, Ten Sleepy Sheep,* etc., ailing Francie is sure to attract little readers. Keller tells simply and directly what happens when Francie wakes up with a scratchy throat and a stomach ache. Mom says, "No school today," tucks the child into bed and leaves her to rest with a kiss. Francie clutches her pink rabbit and wonders if her friend Emily will save her a cupcake from Emily's birthday party. She hears the subdued sounds in the house, dozes off. . . . Later Francie's aunt arrives with gifts that help her niece feel better: chicken soup and a book with jokes and puzzles. Sunny colors and ingenious items in Keller's pictures increase immeasurably the pleasure of Francie's company.

Zena Sutherland

SOURCE: A review of *When Francie Was Sick,* in *Bulletin of the Center for Children's Books,* Vol. 39, No. 4, December, 1985, p. 70.

A pleasant book, brief and bright, and not very substantial, describes a day of an illness so slight that by afternoon it's over. Francie has a scratchy throat and stomach pain. Part of a day in bed, with a long nap and a light meal, does the trick. This hasn't much of a story line, but it does capture the sense of being cozy, shut off, and coddled that makes many children enjoy being slightly ill. The illustrations are repetitive, all the faces having dots or lines for barely-established features in round pink faces.

A BEAR FOR CHRISTMAS (1986)

Pat Trigg

SOURCE: "A Season to Be Giving," in *Books for Keeps,* No. 41, January, 1986, pp. 4-5.

A Bear for Christmas deal[s] with the awful anxiety about what you are getting for Christmas and the dreadful temptation of hidden parcels. In *A Bear for Christmas* Joey tracks down a present he knows is for him. He opens it and finds a big bear he immediately names Fred. Trouble begins when he lets his friend Arnold into the secret and a squabble leads to Fred getting ripped. Joey's guilt and anxiety ruin the Christmas preparations for him but luckily he has a wise mum and everything is cleared up on Christmas morning. As usual Holly Keller has her finger on exactly how children feel.

Ilene Cooper

SOURCE: A review of *A Bear for Christmas*, in *Booklist*, Vol. 83, No. 2, September 15, 1986, p. 133.

A simple little story that deals with a common Christmas-time emotion—inquisitiveness. When a big box arrives from Grandma, Joey is dying to know what's inside. Finally he can't resist and goes up to the attic where he finds a big brown teddy bear inside the package. A visit from his friend, Arnold, prompts Joey to show off the bear, but when a tug-of-war ensues the newly named Fred Bear gets ripped. This almost ruins Joey's holiday—he's too upset to trim the tree or sing carols. On Christmas morning, however, he finds Fred in one piece. A miracle? No. His mother peeked, too, and repaired the damages. Keller illustrates this gentle fare with easy line drawings colored with a soft palette. A warm holiday piece.

Judith Gloyer

SOURCE: A review of *A Bear for Christmas*, in *School Library Journal*, Vol. 33, No. 2, October, 1986, pp. 110-11.

A package from Grandma arrives early, and Joey can't resist opening it. Then he can't resist taking out the wonderful Teddy bear inside, and the bear is accidently ripped. After this Joey can't eat or take part in the family's pre-Christmas activities. On Christmas he doesn't want to open the package. Mom lifts the bear out saying, "I think he's better now." To Joey's puzzled, "How did you know?" Mom replies, "I peeked too." Ah, that in the rush of Christmas preparations we could all be as sensitive as Joey's mother. The softly-toned simple pictures are a nice match to a family story at which both parents and children will nod knowingly and enjoy sharing.

📖 *GOODBYE MAX* (1987)

Denise M. Wilms

SOURCE: A review of *Goodbye, Max*, in *Booklist*, Vol. 83, No. 14, March 15, 1987, p. 1127.

Ben's dog Max has died, and Ben is too upset to welcome the replacement puppy his father has brought home: "He's ugly . . . and he can't do anything." Only after Ben properly mourns Max by thinking about him, talking over Max'[s] deeds with his friend Zach, and sitting down for a good cry can he find the emotional peace he needs to accept the new puppy. The story reflects a gentle sensitivity to which young children will respond. The pictures, however, are weak. Thin pen-line figures have a cartoon look that doesn't suit the story, and the soft pastel washes don't sufficiently soften the lines' brittle edges. Nevertheless, this story of mourning a pet is effective; its understated wisdom will stay with its young audience.

Alice Miller Bregman

SOURCE: "The Seven Ages of Dog," in *The New York Times Book Review*, May 17, 1987, pp. 40-1.

Holly Keller's young hero, Ben, doesn't know what to do to say "Goodbye, Max." . . . But before he can accept the new puppy his Papa brings home after his dog Max dies, he has to find a way to express his grief. For the first week, Ben spends most of his free time in his room, staring out the window at "the place where Papa had buried Max the week before," and remembering how Max got sick, taking him to the vet, wanting to stay home from school to take care of him, and the fact that Max died while he was at school.

"You shouldn't have made me go to school!" Ben yells at his mother. "There was nothing more to do," she replies gently. While that may have been true, there is something more Ben needs to do before he can think about a name for the new puppy—he needs to mourn. So does Ben's friend Zach, who was pretty fond of old Max himself. At first, Ben won't even come out of his room to talk to Zach. Then, one day on their paper route, the boys begin to talk about Max. They remember how he dropped Mr. Brown's paper in a puddle and how he ate Mrs. Murphy's television section and how bad his eyes had got and how old Max really was. And then Ben and Zach sit down on a curb and cry together for Max. When they stop crying, the boys wipe their eyes and go back to Ben's house and the new puppy. "Did you name him yet?" Zach asks. "No," Ben replies, "but we can now."

As I write this review with my new puppy (whose name, oddly enough, is Max) curled around my feet, I salute Holly Keller for her realistic, sympathetic and appropriately understated treatment of a difficult subject. No matter how old you are, it's hard to deal with the death of a pet, especially since there are no accepted rituals to be performed which would make it easier to cope with the feelings of loss. I'm not suggesting some version of *The Loved One*, but some informal memorial, like Zach and Ben's, is essential, and Ms. Keller has given both parents and children some guidance for when the inevitable happens. Her full-color illustrations are simple and subdued, reflecting Ben's sadness until the last pages where the naming of the new puppy takes place against a cheerful yellow background.

Elizabeth S. Watson

SOURCE: A review of *Goodbye, Max*, in *The Horn Book Magazine*, Vol. LXIII, No. 3, May-June, 1987, p. 332.

The death of a pet is never made easier because people keep saying, "He was old." In this simple story Ben is angry and sad because of his dog's death and wants neither to play with his friend, Zach, nor to accept the new puppy that Papa brings home. It takes Zach's understanding, fond memories, and shared tears to abate his friend's hurt. Holly Keller's drawings illustrate the story perfectly. Outlined in black ink, the pictures vary in color from soft pale yellows to bright reds. In some illustrations the figures stand alone against the white page, while in others the figures are set against a tinted background within a fine black border. Both text and pictures flow naturally throughout. Ben's adjustment and tentative healing will provide comfort to other youngsters who have had similar experiences. A sensitive treatment, beautifully handled.

Zena Sutherland

SOURCE: A review of *Goodbye, Max,* in *Bulletin of the Center for Children's Books,* Vol. 40, No. 10, June, 1987, pp. 190-91.

Watercolor paintings are light, clean, and spacious, with naivete in the drawing of human figures (round faces, eyes that are dots) and little animation. Still, the art is used deftly to help tell the story of a boy who mourns the death of an old, beloved dog and who resists the charms of a new puppy. Keller does a nice job of showing the anger Ben feels about Max's death, the guilt and grief. Mother is gentle and understanding, but it isn't until he can reminisce about Max with a friend, and laugh fondly at these memories, that Ben can accept the new puppy. Touching without being somber, this can serve to prepare or assuage children who have had or who face similar experience.

M. Crouch

SOURCE: A review of *Goodbye, Max,* in *The Junior Bookshelf,* Vol. 51, No. 5, October, 1987, p. 217.

In **Goodbye, Max,** the subject is the death of a pet. The old dog has died, and Ben is not to be consoled by the gift of a new puppy or by kind words or companionship. The normality of work helps, so Ben goes on his paper-round with his friend Zach. Zach is reminded of Max's exploits when he helped with the deliveries, and Ben finds himself matching anecdote with anecdote. A barrier has been broken, and Zach and Ben sit on the kerb and have a good healing cry. Now Ben can go home to pick up his life. Holly Keller's drawings are strongly formal and she is careful not to give distinctive features to her characters. Ben is Everyman in his grief and recovery. The text is masterly in its economy and restraint.

📖 *LIZZIE'S INVITATION* (1987)

Ilene Cooper

SOURCE: A review of *Lizzie's Invitation,* in *Booklist,* Vol. 84, No. 1, September 1, 1987, p. 65.

When Kate starts passing out invitations to her birthday party, Lizzie waits expectantly for hers. She doesn't get one, however, and feels terrible about it—in art class she draws nothing but angry faces, and she can barely choke

down her peanut butter sandwich. The day of the party dawns rainy, just right for Lizzie's dark mood. But a walk in the park provides some revelations. She meets Amanda, who was also not invited to the party; the girls hit it off and go back to Amanda's house where they play dolls, bake jelly cookies, and discover that surprises can be waiting just around the corner from the bad times. Keller is right on the mark with her realistic, sensitive portrayal of a child's emotions. Unlined watercolors project a hopeful brightness and warmth despite the dreary day and unhappy feelings. Bibliotherapy, yes, but a heartfelt story as well.

Bessie Egan

SOURCE: A review of *Lizzie's Invitation,* in *School Library Journal,* Vol. 34, No. 7, March, 1988, p. 168.

Keller makes a child's emotional dilemma the subject of a sensitive picture book. Lizzie is disappointed when she doesn't receive an invitation to a party even though many of her classmates are invited. On the day of the party she takes a walk and meets Amanda, a classmate who, like Lizzie, was not invited to the party, and together they spend a wonderful afternoon becoming friends. Whimsical watercolor drawings perfectly complement the simple story and capture Lizzie's varied emotions. A comforting picture book that will provide reassurance to preschoolers who are faced with a disappointing experience.

Maisie Roberts

SOURCE: A review of *Lizzie's Invitation,* in *The School Librarian,* Vol. 36, No. 2, May, 1988, p. 53.

The ability to see life through child-like eyes results in choosing subjects with which children identify. Here Kate is handing out party invitations at school, and Lizzie appears to have been left out. This sort of disappointment provokes different reactions in the very young for whom this book is intended. Outraged anger is the most common, but Lizzie keeps her hurt feelings to herself. The tale is told in two or three short sentences per page, accompanied by sensitive, brightly-coloured illustrations by the author. The general layout is attractive with instant appeal. The story also has a happy ending when Lizzie meets a classmate who has been left off the party list too. Provided the initiative comes from the listeners or readers, some worthwhile discussions might arise from this picture story book.

R. Baines

SOURCE: A review of *Lizzie's Invitation,* in *The Junior Bookshelf,* Vol. 52, No. 3, June, 1988, p. 130.

At lunchtime Kate gives party invitations to some of the other children at nursery school, but Lizzie doesn't get one. In consequence her lunch tastes funny, and when it

and ten came blowing bubbles.

From Ten Sleepy Sheep, *written and illustrated by Holly Keller.*

is time to paint all her pictures are of angry faces. She is no happier on Saturday, which is the day of Kate's party, but when she goes out for a walk in the rain she meets Amanda, who hasn't had an invitation either. Together the two little girls rediscover the joys of happy hours spent with a friend.

Holly Keller has illustrated her charming book with simple watercolours in clear shades, on which raindrops, park railings and facial features are indicated by minimal pencil lines.

📖 *GERALDINE'S BIG SNOW* (1988)

Ilene Cooper

SOURCE: A review of *Geraldine's Big Snow,* in *Booklist,* Vol. 84, No. 22, August, 1988, p. 1927.

Geraldine, a little pig child, is eagerly awaiting the first snow of the season and driving her mother slightly batty as she demands to know when, where, and how much of it will arrive. To Mother's relief, Geraldine goes outside and runs into three neighbors who are gathering food and books in preparation for the predicted snowfall. But even this evidence is not enough to convince Geraldine that the snow will actually come. Though she goes to sleep skeptically eyeing cloudy skies, by next morning the white has descended, and Geraldine and her neighbors enjoy the winter fun. Little ones who have awaited their own snowstorms will appreciate Geraldine's anticipation as well as the story's wry humor. The simply drawn figures, defined in ink, play out the action in squared watercolor scenes. The short text and the familiar subject matter will make this an enticing story hour choice as cold weather approaches.

Janet Hickman

SOURCE: A review of *Geraldine's Big Snow,* in *Language Arts,* Vol. 66, No. 1, January, 1989, pp. 65-6.

A foot of snow is predicted and Geraldine can't wait, indoors or out. She wears herself out with waiting, and "Then in the night it came." Of course Geraldine is ecstatic. The pared-down dialogue suggests more than it says, to wit: "'I'm going outside to wait' / 'Good,' Mama said." Simple illustrations are cheerful in spite of grayed colors that suggest a coming storm, with bright touches and patterned clothing for balance. Geraldine may be a pig (I like the two-toed boots that fit her hooflike feet), but her experience with waiting out a weather forecast will be familiar to young children wherever snow falls.

Trev Jones

SOURCE: A review of *Geraldine's Big Snow,* in *School Library Journal,* Vol. 35, No. 6, February, 1989, p. 72.

Like most young children, plump pig Geraldine waits with impatient anticipation for the first big snowstorm of the season. While the neighbors go about their preparations, stocking shelves and supplementing leisure reading supplies, Geraldine gazes longingly at the still-dry sky. Geraldine is a winning character, as are her animal neighbors. Readers will see and feel her frustration, impatience, and final satisfaction as the snow does indeed fall, and she gets her long-awaited sled ride. With its soft, clean colors and illustrations large enough for group sharing, this is the perfect choice to pair with [Ezra J.] Keats' *The Snowy Day* for a winter story session for toddlers. It's fresh, appealing, and perfectly delightful.

Margery Fisher

SOURCE: A review of *Geraldine's Big Snow,* in *Growing Point,* Vol. 28, No. 1, May, 1989, p. 5164.

Human dress and expressions signify that the little pig impatiently waiting for the forecasted snow is standing in for a child, encouraged when she sees Mrs. Wilson buying apples for pies, Mr. Peters laying in books for a possible siege and Mr. Harper filling his bird-feeder. Surely when Uncle Albert hitches a snow-plough to his tractor the snow will come any minute? But it doesn't and the pictures show in vivacious terms the growing restlessness of the piglet until the triumphant moment when her sledge at last comes into its own. Flamboyant wash and line are used for odd shapes of people and animals, alive with the fun and good cheer of a postcard winter.

Jill Paton Walsh

SOURCE: A review of *Geraldine's Big Snow,* in *Books* (London), Vol. 3, No. 7, October, 1989, p. 17.

Geraldine's Big Snow has it just right. Geraldine, a small pig, is waiting for the forecast snow; a cast of pleasantly animalised neighbours are making ready—getting in supplies, fetching library books, loading bird-feeders. All day it doesn't come, but in the night 'millions of snowflakes piled up on houses and trees . . .' A gentle, simple and shapely story matched with soft colours and clear lines in the pictures, and a little touch of wit to add savour.

📖 *THE BEST PRESENT* (1989)

Zena Sutherland

SOURCE: A review of *The Best Present,* in *Bulletin of the Center for Children's Books,* Vol. 42, No. 7, March, 1989, pp. 173-74.

Wash and line pictures that are effectively composed but awkwardly drawn illustrate a story that is simply told. Rosie is eight, two years too young to be allowed to visit her hospitalized grandmother. Hoping she will pass for ten, Rosie dons hat and gloves and invests her savings ($2.80) in flowers (3 carnations) and goes off secretly to the hospital. The ruse doesn't work, and Rosie sadly turns the flowers over to the elevator man, saying they were for her Grandma Alice on the 7th floor. This instruction seems to be adequate, because after Grandma is home, she shows Rosie the pressed flowers and tells her they were the best present she received during her convalescence. The story has a gentle quality, but it may be too static to appeal to some children.

Ilene Cooper

SOURCE: A review of *The Best Present,* in *Booklist,* Vol. 85, No. 15, April 1, 1989, pp. 1385-86

Rosie is sad. Not only is her grandmother having an operation, but Rosie can't visit because she's too young. Hoping to look the required 10 years of age, she puts on her friend Katie's dress-up clothes and unbraids her hair. But when she arrives at the hospital with her carnations, she is cowed by the elevator operator, who asks her how old she is. Leaving the flowers to be taken upstairs, a glum Rosie goes home. The story ends on a happier note when a recuperating Grandma arrives at Rosie's house and shows her the gifts and cards she's received while in the hospital—the present she loves most is Rosie's bouquet, which she has pressed to keep forever. This story has a warm, dear feeling that will touch young listeners. The uncluttered artwork, watercolors outlined in pen, captures the story's intrinsic compassion, concern, and, of course, love.

Kirkus Reviews

SOURCE: A review of *The Best Present,* in *Kirkus Reviews,* Vol. LVII, No. 9, May 1, 1989, p. 694.

There's enough genuine feeling in this realistic story to make a miniature novel. Rosie is sad and anxious because Grandma is in the hospital and Rosie, at eight, is too young to visit her. Friend Kate helps dress Rosie in hat and gloves in the hope that she will pass for ten; Rosie equips herself with flowers and braves the hospital. But when a hospital guard questions her age, her confidence is undone; quickly handing the elevator man the flowers ("for Grandma Alice on . . . seventh"), she flees. Happily, when Grandma finally does come home, it turns out that she did get Rosie's carnations, and still has them, neatly pressed—a message of love received, valued, and understood. Keller's simply drawn illustrations, their sparse details harmoniously arranged, are a nice complement to her warm, satisfying story.

M. Crouch

SOURCE: A review of *The Best Present,* in *The Junior Bookshelf,* Vol. 53, No. 6, December, 1989, p. 269.

Holly Keller deals tenderly with a real-life problem. Rosie longs to go with her mother to visit Grandma in hospital, but children under ten are not allowed and Rosie is only eight. Rosie's friend Kate has an idea. She dresses Rosie up with hat, gloves and handbag to make her look older, and, armed with a pound's worth of flowers, she faces the hospital authorities. Alas, she does not get farther than the lift door. The lift man takes the flowers, and Rosie goes home humiliated. There is a happy ending. Holly Keller uses the simplest of words to maximum effect, extracting the full quota of emotion out of the story but never lapsing into sentimentality. Her pictures have the same qualities of directness and honesty. How wise she is not to emphasize the features of her characters, leaving each reader to fill in the details with his own favourite child and grandma.

Lee Galda

SOURCE: "What a Character!" in *The Reading Teacher,* Vol. 43, No. 3, December, 1989, pp. 244-45.

When I read for my own pleasure, one of the nicest things that can happen as I read is that I discover a character that I love. Having found such a character, I'm always sorry to put the book down, and it's a struggle to get dinner on the table. I've been this way since I was a child. Many children read this way. Even young children, who often focus on plot, are captured by especially well-drawn characters. . . .

Holly Keller develops a very resourceful character in *The Best Present*. Only eight, Rosie is not allowed to visit her grandmother in the hospital. When she tries to look older and sneak up to see her grandmother, she is unable to lie about her age and sends her flowers up with the elevator man. Ashamed of what she tried to do, she tells no one. But when grandma comes home, there are her flowers, carefully pressed between the pages of a book. The relationship between Rosie and her grandmother is strong.

MAXINE IN THE MIDDLE (1989)

Kirkus Reviews

SOURCE: A review of *Maxine in the Middle,* in *Kirkus Reviews,* Vol. LVII, No. 13, July 1, 1989, p. 992.

A familiar problem with a nice twist in its resolution: Maxine's parents seem oblivious to the needs of their middle child, not only dressing her in older sister Rosalie's hand-me-downs but denying her her own box of crayons: Rosalie gets one for herself, but Maxine has to share with little Sammy. When she's the only one who doesn't get a drumstick on Christmas, it's the last straw: like [William] Steig's Spinky, she retires to the yard. Then it's Rosalie and Sammy who discover how much they miss her, cajole her back in, and make her feel treasured after all—while Mama serves "doughnut holes and peanut butter and jelly without bread" to prove how nice middle things can be. Keller's spare, stylized pictures of this rabbit family are as warmly satisfying as her simple text.

Ilene Cooper

SOURCE: A review of *Maxine in the Middle,* in *Booklist,* Vol. 85, No. 22, August, 1989, p. 1979.

Maxine is the bunny in the middle. She gets stuck wearing her big sister's hand-me-downs, and she has to share her crayons with her younger brother. It seems as if Maxine is always getting the short end of the stick, so one day she decides to leave. It doesn't take her siblings long to realize that they miss their sister. To lure her back, they plan a party in her honor with ice cream and a Monkey-in-the-Middle game—and Maxine never has to be the monkey. Mama gets into the act, too. She provides doughnut holes for a snack, proving that sometimes things in the middle are best. Keller's chronicle of Maxine's trials is overly long, but otherwise this is an entertaining look at family life. The bouncy pictures executed in crisp, clear colors are fun, while amply illustrating Maxine's unhappiness. Any middle child will easily identify with this—and there's a message for other siblings, too.

Publishers Weekly

SOURCE: A review of *Maxine in the Middle,* in *Publishers Weekly,* Vol. 236, No. 8, August 25, 1989, p. 63.

It isn't easy being in the middle. Hand-me-down clothing, last year's Halloween costume, and missing all the special privileges that seem to go with being oldest or youngest leaves middle-child Maxine feeling left out and unloved. Christmas dinner is the last straw. Rosalie, the oldest, gets a drumstick, and Sammy gets the other one because he is the youngest. Maxine is left out—again. When she takes up residence in the backyard tree house, it isn't long before Rosalie and Sammy begin to miss her. Games that were fun for three turn boring when there are only two. The two lonely siblings plan a party to entice Maxine back into the family. Sammy and Rosalie decorate Maxine's ice cream with a cherry and Mom serves doughnut holes with peanut butter and jelly to show that middle things are sometimes best. This tender tale dealing with the woes of the middle child is sensitively written in an unassuming, nonjudgmental manner.

Martha Rosen

SOURCE: A review of *Maxine in the Middle,* in *School Library Journal,* Vol. 35, No. 13, September, 1989, p. 228.

Maxine, the middle rabbit, is caught between her two siblings. She wears her older sister's hand-me down dresses, and has to share her crayons with little brother, Sammy. After a sequence of misadventures in which she is short-changed because of her middle-child status, Maxine disappears up a tree on a snowy winter's night. She thereby makes her point, and the family celebrates with a party, games, and "middle food"—doughnut holes and peanut butter and jelly without bread. This mildly entertaining picture book just misses the mark. Many children will be slightly baffled by what all the fuss is about, since Maxine's problems could be solved simply with a new school dress, a clever Halloween costume, and/or a new box of crayons. Although Keller's rabbit family is engaging in these energetic and colorful cartoon-like illustrations, the text is flat and predictable, lacking suspense and surprise. . . . Maxine's defection from her family seems an overreaction. This is only a "fair to middlin" middle-child story.

SHOOTING STARS (written by Franklyn M. Branley, 1989)

John Peters

SOURCE: A review of *Shooting Stars,* in *School Library Journal,* Vol. 35, No. 13, September, 1989, p. 238.

Keller's clean-lined color illustrations (supplemented by a pair of photos) provide pleasant, sometimes fanciful accompaniment to this simple essay on the origin and nature of meteors. Branley's suggestions that young readers "lie down and gaze at the sky for an hour or so" may not be generally taken, but, as usual, his discussion is full of clearly stated, easily grasped facts and ideas: the fact that "a shooting star is not a star," the chances of being hit (not unlikely, since some airborne dust is extraterrestrial) or hurt (astronomical), some famous close encounters, and the like. This fresh look at a popular subject will be equally at home in the astronomy section and on the picture-book shelves.

WHAT ALVIN WANTED (1990)

Kirkus Reviews

SOURCE: A review of *What Alvin Wanted,* in *Kir-

kus Reviews, Vol. LVIII, No. 3, February 1, 1990, p. 180.

When Mama leaves little Alvin with Libby and Sam, they try everything they can think of to comfort him, but to no avail. Alvin can't tell them what he *does* want, only what he *doesn't*—until Mama comes home and cures all with the kiss she forgot to give him on the way out. Keller's warm, ultra-simple, sweetly designed illustrations strike just the right gently humorous note; a decorative border, echoing Mama's hat, provides a clue for sharp-eyed young "readers." A nicely perceptive glimpse into two-year-old psychology and the affections of young children.

Ilene Cooper

SOURCE: A review of *What Alvin Wanted,* in *Booklist,* Vol. 86, No. 12, February 15, 1990, p. 1166.

What does Alvin want? Mama has gone out to do errands, leaving him with his brother and sister. Though Sam and Libby try endlessly to cheer him up, Alvin doesn't want to go to the playground nor does he want cookies and milk. However, the instant she comes home, Mama realizes why Alvin's upset—she forgot to give him a kiss goodbye. A kiss hello suffices. Keller's engaging, brightly colored mice people scamper across the pages in a clean, appealing layout. The text is attractively bordered with flowers that spruce up the white, bright spreads. A good selection for story hours.

Elizabeth S. Watson

SOURCE: A review of *What Alvin Wanted,* in *The Horn Book Magazine,* Vol. LXVI, No. 3, May-June, 1990, p. 326.

Mouse toddler Alvin is inconsolable despite the tender attention of his siblings; just what Alvin wants remains a mystery until Mom returns home with the satisfying solution. This insightful look at a common family problem—the youngest child who can't explain what's wrong—is handled with just enough sparkle and humor that it zips along to the logical conclusion without a hint of sentimentality. The mice children are simply drawn; a lot of meaning is expressed with careful but minimal detail—even the attitude of Alvin's tail expresses his dejected mood. The attractive fruit- and flower-filled borders on the pages of text echo the trim on Mom's hat, while the pages of illustration are framed by a simple black line. The book will appeal both to the youngest children and to their older siblings who have faced similarly trying times.

Zena Sutherland

SOURCE: A review of *What Alvin Wanted,* in *Bulletin of the Center for Children's Books,* Vol. 43, No. 11, July-August, 1990, p. 269.

The youngest of a mouse family, Alvin is disconsolate when Mama goes off on an errand, leaving him in the care of siblings Libby and Sam. They try to solace Alvin, they try to amuse Alvin, they take Alvin to the playground. Finally Mama comes home and guesses what the trouble is: she had neglected to kiss Alvin good-bye. The kiss is delivered, and Alvin (a real whiner) cheers up. Flat simple paintings on the recto pages face a few lines of text on each florally-bordered verso page. Pleasant and direct, but this is a picture of a situation rather than a story.

M. Crouch

SOURCE: A review of *What Alvin Wanted,* in *The Junior Bookshelf,* Vol. 54, No. 5, October, 1990, p. 217.

Alvin is, I suppose, a mouse, but the story of what he wanted has something to say to humans. In fact Mama and her family, apart from tails and ears, could well be people in a familiar situation. Libby and Sam are left to care for Alvin while Mama goes out. Alvin is distressed, and nothing that brother and sister do will comfort him. At last Mama returns and diagnoses Alvin's complaint. All is well. Words and pictures are of a simplicity appropriate to the small drama. The book is from America, the situation universal. The very youngest will like this one.

EARS ARE FOR HEARING (written by Paul Showers, 1990)

Denise L. Moll

SOURCE: A review of *Ears Are for Hearing,* in *School Library Journal,* Vol. 36, No. 8, August, 1990, pp. 143-44.

A delightful book that genuinely succeeds in being informative without being boring. In clear, highly readable text, the anatomy and function of the ear is explained, detailing the mechanics of hearing, the role of the inner ear in balance, and causes of hearing loss. Keller's lively illustrations are appealing, with large, simple diagrams that detail each component of the ear, coupled with scenes of active children. There is an even representation of male and female figures, although there is no diversity of ethnic groups pictured. While there are several books available on the senses in general, this is unique in its comprehensive presentation of the subject for this age group. School librarians will want to call it to the attention of teachers as well as students, while public libraries will want it to round out their collections.

AN OCTOPUS IS AMAZING (written by Patricia Lauber, 1990)

Eunice Weech

SOURCE: A review of *An Octopus Is Amazing,* in *School Library Journal,* Vol. 36, No. 9, September, 1990, p. 217.

An assortment of facts are presented in this charming introduction to the truly amazing octopus. Lauber's chatty, fact-filled text makes the book a good read-aloud, and Keller's amusing and colorful drawings enhance it by depicting exactly what is described on each page—a perfect match of text and illustration. . . .

HENRY'S HAPPY BIRTHDAY (1990)

Elizabeth S. Watson

SOURCE: A review of *Henry's Happy Birthday,* in *The Horn Book Magazine,* Vol. LXVI, No. 6, November-December, 1990, p. 729.

Henry is pretty sure that nothing will be right at his party: the cake isn't chocolate and appears too plain; Mark's present doesn't look like the "thing" Mark has promised him; and Henry isn't winning any games. When the time comes to make his birthday wish, Henry unhappily wishes that "this were someone else's birthday." Of course, the party does evolve properly, and Henry does have a fine time—ultimately regretting only his wasted wish. The illustrations catch the spirit, hopes, and fears of the birthday child and the other celebrants with warm, rich watercolors outlined in black ink. An appealing and refreshingly honest approach to the traditional birthday party story.

Jacqueline Elsner

SOURCE: A review of *Henry's Happy Birthday,* in *School Library Journal,* Vol. 36, No. 12, December, 1990, pp. 81-2.

Henry, who last celebrated **Henry's Fourth of July,** observes a frustrating birthday. His cake is vanilla, not the requested chocolate. The presents don't look promising; one kid even leaves his gift at home. Henry takes his disappointments with some grace, for as long as he can. Blowing out the candles he wishes "that this were someone else's birthday." But the day turns around. He loves his presents and the cake, he has to admit, is quite good. Later Mama comforts and assures him that he can spend a whole year thinking of a better wish. Even with the cozy ending, this story of clouds with silver linings seems awry. Unlike Shirley Hughes' *Alfie Gives a Hand,* in which the child acts out on the special day, here the family and friends heap too much turmoil on Henry. Full-color watercolor and black ink are used in Keller's familiar spare style. Pages have lots of white space and there is a deft use of line to bring humor and personality to the mice characters. The typeface is easy to read, large, and graceful. Solid first-grade readers can manage the text.

HORACE (1991)

Ilene Cooper

SOURCE: A review of *Horace,* in *Booklist,* Vol. 87, No. 11, February 11, 1991, p. 1130.

Horace is a little spotted leopard who lives with his tiger parents. He is with them because, as his mother tries to tell him, he lost his first family and needed a new one: "We liked your spots, and wanted you to be our child." However, Horace always falls asleep before he hears the whole story. His life with his family is sweet, but during his birthday party, Horace turns sad when he realizes all his cousins have stripes, and he begins to dream about going to a place where everyone looks like him. Keller's gentle story will, of course, have special significance for adopted children, but even those who are not adopted, who simply feel like the odd one out, are going to empathize with Horace. Illustrated with some of Keller's nicest work to date—boldly colored and more refined—these cartoons have a gentleness to them that draws from the text. That Horace returns home is no surprise, but readers will be glad when he finally listens to the end of his mother's story.

Anna Biagioni Hart

SOURCE: A review of *Horace,* in *School Library Journal,* Vol. 37, No. 4, April, 1991, p. 97.

An adoption fable that has attractive, simple drawings in pen and watercolor; humor; and a graceful incorporation of several complex themes. Leopard-spotted Horace has tiger-striped parents, and he experiences the normal feelings of adopted children who do not look like their parents. Once or twice he wishes for different parents, and he has trouble accepting his looks. He decides to find a family where he belongs, and runs off to the park. There Horace makes friends with a kind family who look just like him, and who invite him to come with them. He realizes he wants to return to his own home and his own parents. Adults should be prepared to explain the part of the story in which Horace is told that he "lost" his first family, a word open to interpretation by preschoolers. Most adoption stories for young children use photos or drawings in a documentary or didactic way. Keller's use of appealing animal characters in a fictional tale is a welcome approach.

Margery Fisher

SOURCE: A review of *Horace,* in *Growing Point,* Vol. 30, No. 3, September, 1991, pp. 5588-89.

Here is the idea of adoption as a child might see it but with animals for characters. When a childless couple of tigers adopt an orphaned jaguar cub the mother tries to explain about the small animal's position in the family but the jaguar is upset to observe that his spots are different from the stripes of his adoptive parents and tries to claim a place in a jaguar group, only to realise that he misses his 'Mum' and sees the point of her explanation—'If you chose me', he asks, 'Can I choose you too?' Dressed animals shown in mannered style in bright paint and thick line should carry the message easily to small children, especially to those who may find themselves in a perplexing domestic situation.

THE NEW BOY (1991)

Ilene Cooper

SOURCE: A review of *The New Boy,* in *Booklist,* Vol. 87, No. 21, July, 1991, p. 2050.

Milton is the new boy in class, and the kids immediately tag him as weird. Milton doesn't help his image when he puts a bug in a lunch box and knocks down the other kids' blocks. Rather surprisingly, then, when Henry calls Milton "bad!" Milton goes into full retreat and suddenly becomes the best kid in the class, helpful to the point of cleaning the turtle tank. The kids don't much like Milton in this guise either, but they're distracted when another new boy, Stanley, arrives. Now he's the one who's weird, and Milton settles into being just one of the gang. The message here, one supposes, is that if you wait long enough, the spotlight will focus on someone else. Still, it's disturbing that Milton, so recently new, is among the first to start the name-calling. On the plus side, Keller does peg classroom interaction, and her mice children, as usual, are instantly appealing.

Nancy Seiner

SOURCE: A review of *The New Boy,* in *School Library Journal,* Vol. 37, No. 11, November, 1991, p. 100.

A subtle lesson in human nature comes across in this bouncy story of Milton, the new boy in Miss Higgins's kindergarten class of mice, rabbits, and squirrels. At first he terrorizes everyone, putting a caterpillar into Mindy's lunchbox, eating all the cherries on Gregory's special cupcakes, and singing during rest period. Abruptly he becomes angelic. His constant volunteering to clean, pick up, and fix is more annoying than his naughty behavior. Only when Stanley, an even newer boy, arrives, does Milton relax. Young children will have no trouble seeing their own classes in this cheery setting. Plants, pets, toys, and art supplies scattered against a warm background of melon and tangerine or standing out on a white page make this classroom universal. At an early age, children know what it is to be the victim, the weird kid, the prankster. They will identify with the resilient animal classmates. The story is constructed expertly, with each of Milton's misdeeds building suspense. When Stanley arrives and Milton settles down, children will nod their heads, "Here it goes again." This is a delightful way to show, without preaching, how hard it is to be the new kid.

Judith Sharman

SOURCE: A review of *The New Boy,* in *Books for Keeps,* No. 86, May, 1994, p. 10.

Holly Keller has just the right touch in this book. She depicts Milton's struggle as a new boy trying to become accepted and sensitively shows the difficulties the rest of the group have in adapting to fit him in. No matter what he does, whether he is good or bad, he remains the odd one out until another child joins the class and becomes 'the new boy'. Holly Keller seems to specialise in books exploring areas that children find hard to deal with but her charm is that she never judges—just lays the situation before us and leaves us to come to our own conclusions.

FURRY (1992)

Kirkus Reviews

SOURCE: A review of *Furry,* in *Kirkus Reviews,* Vol. LX, No. 3, February 1, 1992, pp. 185-86.

The author of several simple but unusually perceptive stories about the dramas in the lives of small children addresses the disappointment of an allergic child who firmly believes that "Only pets with fur are fun." After some realistic encounters with the pets she *can't* have, Laura finally accepts one offered by her little brother Alfie, a sympathetic tot who has been working on her problem right along: an appealing chameleon. Alfie even comes up with the perfect name: "Furry." Nice family dynamics, cheery, straightforward illustrations, and believable, easily read dialogue—in another solid contribution from a reliable author.

Hazel Rochman

SOURCE: A review of *Furry,* in *Booklist,* Vol. 88, No. 4, March 15, 1992, p. 1388.

Laura wants a pet. But furry animals make her sneeze and wheeze and break out in a rash. When Bennie brings his gerbil to school for show and tell, Laura's face swells up like a balloon. Even birds make her head ache. Her small brother has the perfect solution—a chameleon—and though Laura's first response is "ugh," she's fascinated. Keller's bright, clear watercolor-and-pen pictures have immediate child appeal, with humor and drama and an occasional wry detail, like the armchair legs that resemble an animal's paws. Every kid will recognize the affectionate family dynamics: when your parents' "no" changes to "maybe," you don't have to nag anymore. And every itchy sniffler who yearns for a cuddly pet will sympathize with Laura's moping and her smiling compromise: "Maybe."

Lauralyn Persson

SOURCE: A review of *Furry,* in *School Library Journal,* Vol. 38, No. 4, April, 1992, p. 94.

Like most children, Laura wants a pet. Unfortunately, she's allergic to animals with fur or feathers. Finally, her brother Alfie suggests a chameleon. Although she resists the idea at first ("It looks like a dragon with measles"), watching it change colors fascinates her. All ends well with her carrying her new pet, "Furry," upstairs to her room. Keller has a knack for creating appealing picture books about real problems that real children encounter. Most of her past protagonists have been animals; here, they are people, simple characters with lots of personality. The story is smoothly told, with no extraneous words or incidents. The fresh watercolor cartoons are nicely balanced and varied, and suit the understated, straightforward tone of the story. Many children experience the frustration of being allergic to something they want, yet it is rarely discussed. Keller handles the topic very well.

📖 *ISLAND BABY* (1992)

Julie Corsaro

SOURCE: A review of *Island Baby,* in *Booklist,* Vol. 89, No. 2, September 15, 1992, p. 155.

Child-pleasing paintings in vibrant tropical hues illustrate an affectionate and reassuring story about a small black boy and an injured baby bird. After finishing his morning duties at his grandfather's bird hospital, Simon discovers a baby flamingo floundering in the Caribbean Sea. Loving Pops scoops "Baby" out of the water, and Simon spends the summer nursing it back to health. Then come the "dreaded" words: "It's about time to set Baby free." Sad at first, Simon is proud when he sees a flock of flamingos in flight, as proud as his mother promises him she will be when he starts school in the fall. Surrounded by decorative borders containing handsomely plumed birds, each full page of text faces a full-page illustration in watercolor and black pen that shows expressive characters amid the lovely island landscape.

Ruth Semrau

SOURCE: A review of *Island Baby,* in *School Library Journal,* Vol. 38, No. 11, November, 1992, p. 72.

Simon helps his grandfather run a hospital for sick and wounded birds. One day, with Pops' help, he rescues a baby flamingo with a broken leg. He cares for his patient all summer until, reluctantly, he releases Baby in a salt marsh with other flamingos. Readers will see the parallel relationship between Simon and the adults in his life. They are about to let him go off to school just as he is setting his friend free in the wild. Simon is proud of his protegeé's accomplishments even though he is sad to see him go. Keller's highly stylized paintings are lovelier than ever. The boy's face is depicted as a circle of one flat shade of brown topped with a black crescent of hair, two tiny squiggly lines for nose and mouth. But his eyes, in spite of the lack of detail, still show a dreamy contentment as parrots perch along his outstretched arms. Wide bands of bright colors decorated with rows of brilliant birds border text on the left and face full-page paintings

filled with hot sun, cool shade, and skies of polarized blue. A beautifully oblique tale of passages, Keller's pictures and story are pleasing to both the eye and the heart. Simon is destined to become a favorite with children who are just beginning to loosen their family ties and to form new ones with the larger world.

Valerie A. Canady

SOURCE: A review of *Island Baby,* in *Multicultural Review,* Vol. 2, No. 3, September, 1993, p. 83.

Colorful, tropical illustrations and a lush Caribbean setting provide the background for ***Island Baby,*** a simple, warm story about a small African-American boy who helps out in a bird hospital. Little Simon joins Pops in his bird hospital for a few hours every day where he enjoys helping the injured and sick tropical birds. The parrots, flamingos, and other island birds literally dot the pages throughout the text. Parents and children alike will enjoy this positive tale of Simon and his nurturing, caring abilities.

Although Simon's mother is present in only a few scenes and there is no mention of a father, you still get the sense he is from a loving, caring home. Even his relationship with Pops suggests a warm and nurturing friendship. The title of the story comes from a small bird that Simon befriends.

Island Baby depicts a positive message about independence and youthful ambitions. Simon hopes to one day own his own bird hospital. This story provides a nice opportunity for parents and young children to snuggle up and enjoy.

📖 *HARRY AND TUCK* (1993)

Kirkus Reviews

SOURCE: A review of *Harry and Tuck,* in *Kirkus Reviews,* Vol. LXI, No. 8, April 15, 1993, p. 531.

Though Harry and Tuck may not always want the same thing, each twin knows the other's preferences. When one is hurt, both need Band-Aids; and they take blame together or (realistically if less laudably) accuse each other of a deed no one can pin on either. When they start kindergarten in separate classes, it's a worrisome parting ("'Who will tickle me if I cry?' Tucker asked, wondering if he might be just about to"), but by day's end both have happy experiences to share. Deftly, Keller chooses incidents and concrete details that perfectly illustrate the boys' special friendship, gently suggesting that independent identities will enrich both without threatening their unity. In her simply drawn, cheerily colored illustrations, the identical boys echo each other on every carefully constructed page—until they choose to dress differently for the second day of school. Warmhearted and exceptionally attractive.

Publishers Weekly

SOURCE: A review of *Harry and Tuck,* in *Publishers Weekly,* Vol. 240, No. 17, April 26, 1993, p. 77.

Though not as distinctive as some of Keller's previous titles—*Island Baby, Horace, Ten Sleepy Sheep*—this is a pleasant if modest book about twin brothers who are identical in every way. These siblings look and dress alike; they communicate with each other without using words. When Harrison gets poison ivy, Tucker itches, too; and when Tucker falls off his bike, Harrison complains that *his* elbow hurts ("So Mama put Band-Aids on both of them"). On the first day of kindergarten, the boys are unhappy to learn they've been assigned to different classes. But each has a great time, and as school lets out they share the particulars of their busy day. And the next morning, in a declaration of individuality that may be lost on youngsters, the two dress in dissimilar clothes. Obviously, twins will be this book's most appreciative audience, and will best comprehend Keller's sometimes precious prose: as the two climb a tree, "Harrison sang a little song. Tucker hummed an answer. And they giggled, because they understood."

Carolyn Phelan

SOURCE: A review of *Harry and Tuck,* in *Booklist,* Vol. 89, No. 21, July, 1993, p. 1974.

Twins Harrison and Tucker are so in tune with each other that when Harrison steps in poison ivy, Tucker itches, and when Tucker falls off his bike, Harrison needs a bandage too. In kindergarten Harry and Tuck (as their teachers soon call them) go to different classrooms. As they take their first steps away from each other, the twins' initial uncertainty gives way to increasing confidence in their newfound independence. Illustrating the text with simplicity and directness, Keller uses line drawings with bright, watercolor washes. Varied in layout, the pages have a clean, spare look that's as quietly pleasing as the story. Prediction: this upbeat picture book will make many a young child wish for a twin.

GRANDFATHER'S DREAM (1994)

Elizabeth Bush

SOURCE: A review of *Grandfather's Dream,* in *Booklist,* Vol. 90, No. 4, March 15, 1994, pp. 1373-74.

Sarus cranes, long regarded as good luck, have disappeared from the Mekong Delta after canals drained the land during the Vietnam War. Now young Nam's village has an opportunity to lure the cranes back by building dikes to restore the wetlands feeding ground. The villagers are divided along generational lines. Nam's mother argues that drained fields are more useful for growing rice. But Grandfather values tradition and believes the cranes are entitled to their original home. The experiment

is allowed a year's trial. During the following dry season, Nam's dogs retrieve two baby birds, and when he and Papa visit the feeding ground, they discover the birds have indeed returned. Grandfather happily joins other Tam Nong villagers as they admire the beautiful flock in flight. But he cautions Nam that it is "up to you" whether the birds will stay. Keller's argument for wildlife restoration springs from her involvement in project "Saving Cranes in Vietnam." Understandably, she gives little attention to arguments in favor of retaining land for farming. Clear ink and watercolor illustrations capture the stilt village and surrounding terrain well. However, only a small section of dike, which is critical to the villagers' strategy, is depicted in a single frame. This volume will be useful in geography curricula and in exploring war's consequences, as well as in environmental studies.

Kirkus Reviews

SOURCE: A review of *Grandfather's Dream,* in *Kirkus Reviews,* Vol. LXI, No. 8, April 15, 1994, p. 558.

There's disagreement in Nam's Vietnamese village: His grandfather hopes that, now the war is over, cranes will return to the area set aside for them; but Mama and Papa (among others) want to plant rice there. As planned, the monsoon floods the cranes' reserve with water held by the new dikes; but after the dry season's return the village committee decides to wait for the cranes until the next rains, but no longer. Then Nam's dog finds a crane nestling and gives it to him, unhurt. Papa and Nam make sure that there's a whole flock of the birds before telling Grandfather, and, after all, everyone rejoices. Keller's narration, based on her experience with an Earthwatch project, is suffused with the affection between the boy and his grandfather and the warm security of their community, a strong setting for a debate that epitomizes the worldwide struggle between land use and conservation. Her simple, stylized art is both handsome as pure design and effective as narrative illustration with appeal for young children. A fine contribution.

Sue Norris

SOURCE: A review of *Grandfather's Dream,* in *School Library Journal,* Vol. 40, No. 6, June, 1994, p. 107.

Nam lives with his parents, his grandfather, two lively puppies, and assorted other animals in a small village in the Mekong delta. Before the Vietnam War, this area was home to the Sarus crane, considered to be a symbol of long life and happy families, but during the fighting, canals were dug to drain the wetlands and the cranes disappeared. These facts, necessary to understanding the story, are given in a prologue. In Keller's carefully crafted story, Nam's grandfather hopes that the building of new dikes will restore the wetlands and prompt the return of the birds that he remembers so fondly from his youth. The boy's parents think that the land would be better used for planting rice. The relationship between Nam and his grandfa-

From Grandfather's Dream, *written and illustrated by Holly Keller.*

ther is an affectionate one—they share a love for animals and stories. After the monsoons come, the wetlands are restored, and eventually the cranes return and their magnificence wins over even the most practical villagers. This is a beautiful book with many layers of meaning and an important message. The simple illustrations, done in flat washes of watercolor in earthy tones and outlined in black pen, are lovely and appealing. They add just the right amount of drama and charm for a story told in very simple prose.

📖 GERALDINE'S BABY BROTHER (1994)

Harriett Fargnoli

SOURCE: A review of *Geraldine's Baby Brother,* in *School Library Journal,* Vol. 40, No. 8, August, 1994, p. 133.

The porcine heroine of **Geraldine's Blanket** and **Geraldine's Big Snow** is back—with a new brother. Willie, swaddled in his very own blanket, is mostly mouth and trotters AND all noise. Geraldine doesn't warm up to him right

away—typically he gets all the attention—but patience and resourcefulness are her resident virtues. In the middle of the night, the siblings have a heart-to-heart and big sister reads them both to sleep. The text is simple, and the charmingly drawn watercolor illustrations have just the right detail. Aunt Bessie and Mrs. Wilson make cameo appearances and baby doll Rosa is spied as well—in her pink blanket dress, of course. This expressive pig's appeal remains timeless.

Kirkus Reviews

SOURCE: A review of *Geraldine's Baby Brother,* in *Kirkus Reviews,* Vol. LXII, No. 16, August 15, 1994, p. 1131.

From the author of **Geraldine's Blanket** and **Geraldine's Big Snow**, comes another story featuring the little piglet and her new baby brother. At first, Geraldine doesn't like baby Willie. But in the middle of the night, Geraldine confronts the baby and forbids him to cry. He makes some baby faces, and Geraldine actually laughs. Then she reads him some stories and falls asleep. In the morning, she has a slightly warmer feeling towards her new sibling and even asks if she can give him his bottle. The plight of the older child when faced with a new baby in the family is a common enough experience; here it is treated with wit and humor. Geraldine is allowed to have her feelings, and by the end of the book, they have altered somewhat, though not completely. Keller deftly avoids a sugar-coated ending in which Geraldine is wholly converted. Instead, readers are shown that the acceptance of a new family member takes time. The whimsical line drawings add to the overall charm.

A wise, funny, accepting little book.

Nancy Vasilakis

SOURCE: A review of *Geraldine's Baby Brother,* in *The Horn Book Magazine,* Vol. LXX, No. 6, November-December, 1994, pp. 720-21.

The popular heroine of **Geraldine's Blanket** and **Geraldine's Big Snow** is in a snit over the arrival of the new baby in the family. She had wanted a brother, but "not *that* one," she decides now that he is here. It's a story that older siblings will find depressingly familiar. Significant adults spend so much time catering to the squalling infant that they forget Geraldine's lunch or bathtime or bedtime. No matter. Geraldine occupies herself by tying the baby's diapers into knots or playing with Mother's make-up and dresses. Still feeling slighted, however, she turns down the offer of her favorite supper and in a huff goes to bed early. When Willie's crying awakens her in the middle of the night, she stalks into the nursery and confronts her new little brother on her own stern terms. He yawns, he gurgles, he sticks out his tongue. "You're weird," Geraldine pronounces. In the morning Mother finds Geraldine asleep in the chair next to Willie's cradle, where she had settled herself to read him a story. In her calm, low-key way, Keller offers her young audience the opportunity to see their frustrations reflected in Geraldine's travails, while at the same time reassuring them that things are never entirely out of her control. Geraldine's dignity remains intact to the very end. "Can I give you a hug?" asks Mother when she wakes Geraldine up for breakfast. Geraldine bestows the promise of reconciliation. "Soon," she answers. The solid rounded shapes, uncluttered compositions, and cheerful orange and green hues in the illustrations reinforce the reassuring tone of this familiar domestic drama, which is as old as time and yet frightfully new to each generation of youthful players who act it out afresh.

ROSATA (1995)

Kirkus Reviews

SOURCE: A review of *Rosata,* in *Kirkus Reviews,* Vol. LXIV, No. 14, July 15, 1995, pp. 1025-26.

Camilla comes into the possession of an old hat bedecked with a small bird made of real feathers. She names the bird Rosata and they become inseparable friends. They go to school together, have long talks, and when Camilla's brother Victor is rude to Rosata, stand firm as friends. Then a girl Camilla's age moves in next door; just like that, Camilla has a new inseparable friend.

Keller is so tentative with the double-edged nature of her story that some readers may find the ending abrupt. It's so subtle, and leaves so many things unsaid, that the sudden displacement of Rosata is bewildering, even if she is inanimate. She may be merely a transitional friend for Camilla, but she is plainly dumped when someone better comes along, and Camilla—portrayed as a sensitive, dreamy girl—shows no remorse. The delicate watercolors—soft washes with pen-and-ink edges—underscore the story's poignancy. Wistful, evocative—and perhaps best for sharing.

Annie Ayres

SOURCE: A review of *Rosata,* in *Booklist,* Vol. 92, No. 3, October 1, 1995, p. 326.

Entranced by an old hat "decorated with velvet flowers and a small bird made out of real feathers," Camilla names the bird Rosata and talks to her "gently every day." Even though her family and classmates find the unusual friendship peculiar, Camilla is happy and content to have a hat for a best friend and loyally takes Rosata everywhere. When a little girl just her age moves in next door, Camilla makes a new friend and eventually leaves Rosata safely atop her bedroom bookcase when she goes to play with her neighbor. Filled with bold and simplified shapes painted in velvet-soft watercolors, the illustrations are colored with the poignancy of growing up and making friends. Tenderly told, this picture book could be included in any story hour that features special friendships.

Mary M. Burns

SOURCE: A review of *Rosata,* in *The Horn Book Magazine,* Vol. LXXI, No. 6, November-December, 1995, p. 734-35.

This understated picture-story improves with each reading, for it evokes a variety of emotions with ease and style. The central character is Camilla, a child of about six, who one day retrieves a hatbox dropped by the garbage truck and, much to her delight, finds therein a magnificent hat adorned with velvet roses and a small feathered bird. Enchanted, Camilla names the bird Rosata and transforms her into a companion—much to the concern of her mother, the amusement of her brother, and the gibes of her schoolmates. Then, one day, a girl just Camilla's age moves in next door. Their friendship deepens, and Rosata is sometimes left behind as the two become engrossed in games, trips to the movies, or trick-or-treating on Halloween. Camilla begins manufacturing excuses for leaving Rosata at home, climaxing in Rosata's disappearance. When she is finally discovered on a chair in her small owner's room, languishing at the bottom of a pile of miscellany, it is Camilla's mother who finds the happy solution: put the hat on top of her daughter's bookcase, where Rosata is visible but not intrusive. An original variant on the security blanket or favorite-but-outgrown toy theme, the book blends a judiciously honed text with meticulously executed, full-color watercolor illustrations, subtly enhanced with fine pen lines. Full of depth and feeling, the book is remarkable for its restraint and light-handed approach.

📖 *GERALDINE FIRST* (1996)

Kirkus Reviews

SOURCE: A review of *Geraldine First,* in *Kirkus Reviews,* Vol. LXIV, No. 4, February 15, 1996, p. 296.

Geraldine is back and this time her little brother, Willie, trails after her, saying everything she says and doing everything she does. "Stop copying me, Willie," snaps Geraldine. But Willie just giggles, until Geraldine turns the tables and figures out how to get some useful mileage out of his mimicry. Young readers will recognize Geraldine's predicament and will laugh out loud as Willie falls unwittingly into her plan. Keller conveys through her cheerful illustrations not only the many moods of her young heroine, but also a subplot involving Mama and Papa's own reactions to the bickering siblings.

Virginia Opocensky

SOURCE: A review of *Geraldine First,* in *School Library Journal,* Vol. 42, No. 5, May, 1996, p. 93.

That feisty pig Geraldine is totally exasperated with her little brother, Willie, who copies everything she says and does. "Don't copy me" is her standard refrain until she

has to clean her room and shrewdly puts the copy cat to good use. Once again Keller captures a normal sibling dilemma with understated humor and a satisfying denouement. Expressive, marvelously minimalist pen-and-watercolor drawings delineate typical parents, fractious kids, and ordinary situations, extending the story beyond the words.

Maeve Visser Knoth

SOURCE: A review of *Geraldine First,* in *The Horn Book Magazine,* Vol. LXXII, No. 3, May-June, 1996, pp. 325-26.

Like many older sisters, Geraldine is frustrated that her younger brother, Willie, is forever copying her. Just as she loses what little patience she had, Geraldine has an epiphany and turns her brother's admiration to good use. At Geraldine's suggestion, Willie copies Geraldine until he has inadvertently cleaned up her room. Geraldine and Willie are well-drawn characters, and their actions and emotions are true to childhood and sibling relationships. Readers will empathize with Geraldine's feelings of frustration and then of pride and confidence that she is indeed first in her own, and sometimes in her brother's, eyes. Keller expertly captures shades of emotion in her watercolor-and-ink illustrations. In a particularly wonderful double-page spread, Geraldine watches her brother struggle with piles of her blocks. Geraldine's smug expression and Willie's toddlerlike happiness at being allowed to play with his sister are made apparent with subtle line and posture. Readers will be pleased to discover another story about the endearing and very human pig family.

Additional coverage of Keller's life and career is contained in the following sources published by Gale Research: *Contemporary Authors,* Vol. 118, and *Something about the Author,* Vols. 42, 76.

Betsy C(rippen) Maestro
1944-

Giulio Maestro
1942-

Betsy: American author of picture books.
Giulio: American author/illustrator of picture books.

Major works include *Harriet Goes to the Circus: A Number Concept Book* (1977), *The Story of the Statue of Liberty* (1986), *Ferryboat* (1986), *A More Perfect Union: The Story of Our Constitution* (1987), *The Discovery of the Americas* (1991), all written by Betsy and illustrated by her husband, Giulio.

INTRODUCTION

Betsy and Giulio Maestro have collaborated on over seventy picture books for children, including poetry, animal fantasy, scientific and historical nonfiction, and concept books on numbers and language. Praised for their understanding of young children, the Maestros have successfully taken complicated ideas and expressed them through simple words and clear, colorful illustrations that attract and instruct preschoolers and primary graders. From elementary introductions of haiku, prepositional opposites, or ordinal numbers, to ambitious undertakings on such topical subjects as the building of the Statue of Liberty or how American democracy works, the Maestros have made significant contributions to the education and entertainment of generations of young readers and listeners. Giulio Maestro has also illustrated for numerous other authors and for his own books, the latter known for their humorous wordplay. As a reviewer for *Publishers Weekly* stated, "Distilling the broad and complex nature of their subject to its essence" is the forte of the Maestro team.

Biographical Information

Born in New York, the daughter of a nursery school teacher mother, Betsy began her career as a kindergarten and first grade teacher in Connecticut. Although she was aware, during her eleven years of teaching, of the dearth of good nonfiction material for the very young, it was only after she met and married Giulio, an established writer and illustrator, in 1972, that she began writing for children herself. Giulio was likewise born and raised in New York, where he had worked in advertising before becoming a freelance artist. His works have been exhibited by the American Institute of Graphic Arts, the Art Directors Club of New York, and the New York Society of Illustrators. Betsy's first book, *A Wise Monkey Tale* (1975), was told in folktale style and illustrated by her husband. For her second book, the two created Harriet, the popular roller-skating white elephant who features in several of their concept books.

After twenty-five years and nearly three times that many books together, the two have expanded their range to include grade school students and science and history topics. They have two children and live in Connecticut.

Major Works

The award-winning *Harriet Goes to the Circus: A Number Concept Book* hinges on a plot where the last in line becomes first, an effective lesson on ordinal numbers. Hurt feelings are satisfactorily resolved by having all ten animals sit in a circle. First introduced in their book *Where Is My Friend? A Word Concept Book* (1976), Harriet is a snow-white elephant who stands out in Giulio's boldly colorful pictures and appeals to children as she roller-skates through city and country, home, school, and work places in the various succeeding concept books. Betsy's well-researched and lively *The Story of the Statue of Liberty* begins with the French sculptor, Frederic Bartholdi, and covers the fifteen years of his work in Paris and his supervision of the statue's journey to New York. In full-color double-page spreads, using unusual angles to show scale and dimension, Giulio's watercolor paintings depict the drama and development of the historic work of art.

Winner of a Social Studies Trade Book Award, *Ferryboat* was based on the Chester-Hadlyme Ferry that the Maestros ride in Connecticut. Pictures and words realistically describe how the ferry works and show how people, bicycles, and cars are transported from shore to shore on the boat whose front end is the same as its back. *A More Perfect Union: The Story of Our Constitution,* lauded as the best book for younger readers to celebrate the bicentennial of the Constitution, is an accurate, informative account of the creation of this important document. Giulio's watercolor double-page spreads and eighteenth-

century details of buildings and clothes bring the period of the Founding Fathers to life. In *The Discovery of the Americas,* the Maestros tackle not only the voyages of Columbus five hundred years ago, but also discuss migrations dating back to the Stone Age, including Phoenician, Chinese, and Japanese explorations as well as Leif Ericsson and other Viking expeditions. Giulio's large, colorful land- and seascapes are mixed with helpful maps and globes and further supported with informative appendices.

Awards

Fat Polka-Dot Cat and Other Haiku, in 1976, and *The Story of the Statue of Liberty,* in 1987, both written by Betsy, plus numerous other books by other authors, all illustrated by Giulio, were selected as Child Study Association of America's Children's Books of the Year; *Harriet Goes to the Circus,* in 1978, *Lambs for Dinner,* in 1979, and several others including Giulio's own *Halloween Howls,* in 1984, were selected as Children's Choices by the International Reading Association and the Children's Book Council. The Maestros received American Library Association Notable Book citations, in 1981, for their *Traffic: A Book of Opposites;* in 1987, for *A More Perfect Union;* and in 1991, for *The Discovery of the Americas. Ferryboat* was selected as a Notable Children's Trade Book in the Field of Social Studies by the National Council for Social Studies and the Children's Book Council in 1986. Giulio's *The Tortoise's Tug of War* was included in the American Institute of Graphic Arts Children's Book Show, 1971-72, as was *Three Kittens,* 1973-74; *Harriet Goes to the Circus* received a Merit Award from the Art Director's Club of New York in 1978.

TITLE COMMENTARY

📖   *THE TORTOISE'S TUG OF WAR* (retold and
       illustrated by Giulio Maestro, 1971)

Kirkus Reviews

SOURCE: A review of *The Tortoise's Tug of War,* in *Kirkus Reviews,* Vol. XL, No. 1, January 1, 1972, p. 2.

Based on a South American variant of the familiar African tale, this casual adaptation casts a tortoise as the playful trickster who separately challenges two large animals (here a whale and a tapir) to a tug-of-war, then surreptitiously sets them to pulling against each other until each concedes exhaustion. The writing, while agreeable enough, is neither here nor there, ranging instead from "Hey, Whale" and "O, come on" to the untranslated word "sipó" for the vine Tortoise uses as his rope. But it's the lush pictures that predominate, and in fact the backgrounds—especially a spectacular deep blue sea—quite subordinate Tortoise's cleverness to the artist's performance. It's all visually opulent—but verbally Peggy Appiah's version in *Ananse the Spider* pulls more weight.

Zena Sutherland

SOURCE: A review of *The Tortoise's Tug of War,* in *Bulletin of the Center for Children's Books,* Vol. 25, No. 8, April, 1972, p. 126.

Based on a South American folktale, "Which was Stronger, the Tortoise, the Tapir, or the Whale," a nicely told variant of the familiar story of the small animal who tricks two large ones, each of whom thinks he is struggling against the small challenger, since he cannot see the other contestant at the end of a long vine or rope. Here the wily tortoise fools the tapir and the whale, and the story ends when he has just found another victim—an anteater—and gone off to look for a jaguar. The illustrations have a verdant charm, and sly humor in the animal characters.

Virginia Haviland

SOURCE: A review of *The Tortoise's Tug of War,* in *The Horn Book Magazine,* Vol. XLVIII, No. 2, April, 1972, p. 137.

A pleasing South American variant of the animal fable in which two powerful animals engage in a tug of war arranged by a weak, but sly, creature. In this version, a whale and a tapir, unknowingly tied to each other, strain themselves to the point of exhaustion. In *The Extraordinary Tug-of-War,* colorfully illustrated by John Burningham, Letta Schatz presents an African version with an elephant, a hippopotamus, and a hare. The author's version is acceptable, but his retelling is less significant than his full-color paintings, which are lively and distinctive in composition and color.

Mary Lou McGrew

SOURCE: A review of *The Tortoise's Tug of War,* in *Library Journal,* Vol. 97, No. 9, May 15, 1972, p. 1904.

The wily tortoise pits two mighty protagonists against each other by challenging the whale and the tapir to tugs of war with him. He then secures a sipó or vine to each, and leaves both with the impression that he is at the other end. After watching gleefully from behind a bush while the two tug themselves into a state of exhaustion, the tortoise unties them and claims victory over each. The story ends amusingly with the tortoise preparing to work the same trick on two more victims. Maestro uses hues of blue, pink, and purple in the whale's habitat opposing the pungent yellows, browns, and greens of the tapir's and tortoise's to achieve an unusual gradation of color. While Letta Schatz' *The Extraordinary Tug of War,* in which the Hare hoodwinks the Elephant and the Hippopotamus, tells a similar tale, the distinctive illustrations recommend this variation.

 THE REMARKABLE PLANT IN APARTMENT 4 (written and illustrated by Giulio Maestro, 1973; British edition as *The Remarkable Plant in Flat No. 4,* 1974)

Kirkus Reviews

SOURCE: A review of *The Remarkable Plant in Apartment 4,* in *Kirkus Reviews,* Vol. XLI, No. 8, April 15, 1973, p. 453.

Maestro's story is just a frame for his luxuriant pictures of the plant that grows overnight in Michael's room, sending its roots through to the Zelnick's apartment downstairs so that Mr. and Mrs. Zelnick set up tent and campfire in their bedroom, and extending its branches over to Rotondo's next door, inspiring Mr. Rotondo to make all sorts of fantastic furniture from the twisted vines. Back at Michael's, he and his father run electric trains along the branches, his parents exult in the explosion of red and gold flowers, and a whole menagerie of brilliant tropical birds and insects fills out the scene. We have the feeling that Maestro's plant is rooted in precariously shallow ground, but his freewheeling foliage makes the greening of a city block an enticingly euphoric occasion.

Zena Sutherland

SOURCE: A review of *The Remarkable Plant in Apartment 4,* in *Bulletin of the Center for Children's Books,* Vol. 27, No. 1, September, 1973, p. 13.

A story that begins realistically keeps its ingenuous tone after branching out into fantasy: the illustrations, lusty and imaginative, extend the text and illustrate the peculiar advantage of the author-illustrator in achieving unity. Michael buys a small plant that the vendor claims will grow overnight, which proves to be an accurate prognostication. By morning, the roots have penetrated to the apartment below, where a distracted tenant complains—while her husband placidly decides to set up a tent. Next door, it is an irritated husband who complains that he can't get at his breakfast because of branches, while his wife happily feeds the birds. Oh, yes, birds—and worms—and earth—and flowers—and insects—the plant, now a tree, provides its own environment. The ludicrous exaggeration of text and the lively profusion of verdure in the illustrations are nicely set off by the matter-of-fact way in which the tenants all adapt to the burgeoning plant.

Virginia Lee Gleason

SOURCE: A review of *The Remarkable Plant in Apartment 4,* in *Library Journal,* Vol. 98, No. 16, September 15, 1973, p. 2642.

A zany modern fantasy in which a city child, Michael, buys a small plant guaranteed by the pushcart vender to grow overnight. By morning, the plant has filled Michael's room, pushed roots covered with insects into the apartment below, and sent branches filled with fanciful birds into the apartment next door. The people downstairs camp among the roots. The man next door forms furniture from the branches. Michael's family finds flowers growing faster than they can be picked. The tale is fairly humorous (though older children may reject it as silly), and the large, colorful, cartoon-style wash and pencil paintings make it suitable for pre-school story hour.

R. Baines

SOURCE: A review of *The Remarkable Plant in Flat No. 4*, in *The Junior Bookshelf,* Vol. 38, No. 3, June, 1974, pp. 149-50.

It is a superb salesman who can convince a small, roller-skating boy that he wants to buy a pot plant. By all the laws of logic Michael's parents, friends and neighbours should view his purchase with detestation, for overnight the plant grows to giant size, its roots in the flat below that of Michael's family, its branches—laden with singing birds—in the flat above. Most improbably they all embark enthusiastically on rural hobbies: camping, feeding the birds, and picking flowers.

The pages are filled by flat watercolour drawings, and the vivid flowers are so attractive that it is almost possible to believe in the enthusiasm shown by their involuntary cultivators. The creepy-crawlies walking on the leaves of the plant are creatures of character rather than beauty.

Margery Fisher

SOURCE: A review of *The Remarkable Plant in Flat No. 4*, in *Growing Point,* Vol. 13, No. 3, September, 1974, p. 2461.

From America, a fantasy in which we can see, first successively, then simultaneously on several levels, how Michael's plant, bought from a street barrow, invades Mrs. Selznick's bedroom and Mr. Rotondo's kitchen and proves useful as clothes line, garden and railway track. In watercolour and ink the details of the strange event are brilliantly shown; the personalisation of numerous birds and insects that choose this ecological niche is especially witty.

📖 *A WISE MONKEY TALE* (1975)

Kirkus Reviews

SOURCE: A review of *A Wise Monkey Tale,* in *Kirkus Reviews,* Vol. XLIII, No. 20, October 15, 1975, p. 1176.

Inconsiderable business, in the manner of a folk tale about how Monkey fools the other animals when he falls into a deep hole in the jungle. Pretending to find a message from Gorilla on a banana leaf, he "reads" out: "If very wise you wish to be / Come down here, wait and see"—and for some reason Lion, Snake, Zebra and Elephant all swallow the bait, enabling Monkey to climb up over them and get out. It's a synthetic trick tale with as much wit as some traditional ones, for what that's worth—but so slight that the entire project seems more overblown than enlarged by Maestro's big, blooming, mildly stylized jungle scenes.

Denise M. Wilms

SOURCE: A review of *A Wise Monkey Tale,* in *The Booklist,* Vol. 72, No. 6, November 15, 1975, p. 456.

Vibrant colors transform Maestro's chubby-lined drawings and offer a nice contrast to the more subdued pastels he employed in **Two Good Friends** and Pushkin's **Who Said Meow?** The rich greens and browns of the story's jungle setting intensify the sunny brightness of the various animal characters who unwittingly become a part of Monkey's sage plan to extricate herself from the deep hole she has fallen into. The story, an original, shows a folktale influence with its simple, patterned plot and repetitious jingle, both of which make it admirably suited to pre-schoolers, who can enjoy listening while they gaze at the artist's splashy display.

Carol Chatfield

SOURCE: A review of *A Wise Monkey Tale,* in *School Library Journal,* Vol. 22, No. 5, January, 1976, pp. 38-9.

Monkey falls into a huge hole and cannot get out. Ingenuity saves the day, however, as she tricks Lion, Snake, Zebra, and Elephant into joining her in her prison. As the hole fills up and becomes uncomfortably crowded, a second trick enables monkey to climb up over the others and go on her way. The age old problem of landing in a jam is treated inventively here with a minimum of description and plenty of colorful pictures. All elements of the simple story blend together well. Second graders should read it easily, and younger children will have no trouble following the action through the bouncy illustrations.

Zena Sutherland

SOURCE: A review of *A Wise Monkey Tale,* in *Bulletin of the Center for Children's Books,* Vol. 29, No. 6, February, 1976, p. 100.

A variant of one of Aesop's fables is used as the plot for a picture book with pages crowded with animals and fantastic plants. Monkey falls into a deep hole; cleverly she inveigles other animals into climbing down (claiming to have a message from Gorilla that this will make them wise) and then climbs on them to get out. And, since they have been duped by Monkey into believing that the last action was based on another instruction from Gorilla, the others are not angry, "You will all know very soon just how wise I am," Monkey says, and disappears. The humor of the situation is just right for the read-aloud audience, and Monkey's clever triumph (little creature over a big lion and a bigger elephant) is stressed by the bright, bold illustrations of a grinning monkey and her worried companions.

📖 *WHERE IS MY FRIEND? A WORD CONCEPT BOOK* (1976)

Publishers Weekly

SOURCE: A review of *Where Is My Friend?*, in *Publishers Weekly*, Vol. 209, No. 3, January 19, 1976, p. 102.

The book is a joyful combination of a story and an introduction to word usage. Harriet the elephant is looking for her friend and she demonstrates the meanings of words as she climbs *up* and *down* a tree, *between* two trees and *around* them. Her search (on roller skates) is absorbing as she looks *under, over,* and *into* various places and, at last, finds her friend—a mouse—right *in front of* her. The text is minimum, just right for conveying concepts. And what a pleasure it is to gaze at Giulio Maestro's huge, blazingly colored pictures of all the doings.

Kirkus Reviews

SOURCE: A review of *Where Is My Friend?*, in *Kirkus Reviews*, Vol. XLIV, No. 3, February 1, 1976, p. 131.

Up a tree and *down* again, *between* two trees and then *around* them, *through* a gate, *under* a rock and *over* a hill, *into* a cave and *out* again. . . . So Harriet, a mobile and well-balanced elephant in search of a nameless friend, makes her vervey way through simple, stylized arrangements of high-powered, solid colors. It's the sort of lesson that might turn up as a *Sesame Street* skit, and in their own medium the Maestros pack just as smart a punch. (Oh yes: The friend, a mouse, turns up at last right in *front* of Harriet's nose.)

Barbara Elleman

SOURCE: A review of *Where Is My Friend?*, in *Booklist*, Vol. 72, No. 12, February 15, 1976, p. 856.

Harriet, an enterprising white elephant with an orange umbrella, looks for her friend up, down, between, and around trees without success. Donning roller skates, she continues her search through a gate, under a rock, over a hill (clutching red balloons), and into and out of a cave. But not until she looks "right in front of her nose" does she find her friend, a mouse with whom she merrily cavorts on the last page. Large black letters and simple, bright objects positioned against multicolored backgrounds make this a visual delight as well as a useful word-concept book.

Zena Sutherland

SOURCE: A review of *Where Is My Friend?*, in *Bulletin of the Center for Children's Books,* Vol. 29, No. 9, May, 1976, pp. 148-49.

Although told in narrative form, this has but a miniscule plot: Harriet looks for her friend, finally finds her. Harriet's an elephant, the friend a mouse. The writing is simple enough to be read by beginning independent readers, with large print and one short sentence on each double-page spread: "Harriet was looking for her friend," "She climbed *up* a tree," "She came *down* again," "Harriet looked *between* two trees," and so on. The letters italicized here are in heavier type, not italicized, on the pages. The illustrations are bright, poster-simple, spacious, and stylized in elementary fashion, so that they do not take attention away from the print. This achieves nicely its purpose, stressing words that can give young children concepts of position and direction.

School Library Journal

SOURCE: A review of *Where Is My Friend?*, in *School Library Journal*, Vol. 22, No. 9, May, 1976, p. 76.

Harriet, a white elephant on roller skates, searches for her friend in, around, between, and under various objects. Both the location and the identity of her friend provide a mild surprise in the end, and the lesson in spatial concepts (the different prepositions appear in bold face) is well presented. With Giulio Maestro's dazzling drawings this is as attractive in its way as Tana Hoban's photographs in *Over, Under & Through & Other Spatial Concepts.*

📖 *FAT POLKA-DOT CAT AND OTHER HAIKU* (1976)

Kirkus Reviews

SOURCE: A review of *Fat Polka-Dot Cat and Other Haiku,* in *Kirkus Reviews,* Vol. XLIV, No. 8, April 15, 1976, p. 464.

Haiku seem to be regaining the popularity they enjoyed in the mid-60s, but today picture-book authors are writing their own. Betsy Maestro returns to the 17-syllable form which even the translations of [Richard] Lewis [and Ezra Jack] Keats' *In a Spring Garden* played free with. But otherwise she tries so hard to keep the subjects familiar and the statements simple that the flash and intensity which make haiku fun to begin with are smoothed over. Not all of the observations are as prosaic as "We ate a kumquat / Planted a seed and waited. / Now we have a tree"; elsewhere Maestro points out a "quiet cardinal / . . . like a bright red ribbon" and a "Brown furry rabbit, / Its nose wiggly as jelly." Yet the total impression, sustained in husband Giulio's chunky shapes overlaid in light yellow, brown and pink, is of a cheery and serviceable nursery blanket . . . fine in its place but potentially constricting for youngsters ready to move out on their own.

Helen Gregory

SOURCE: A review of *Fat Polka-Dot Cat and Other Haiku,* in *School Library Journal,* Vol. 23, No. 1, September, 1976, p. 103.

Best of the haiku here are the fat polka-dot cat of the title, the image of a cardinal on a snowy tree, and "Little ladybug, / Do you think our flowerpots / Are a real garden?" Occasionally there is sentimental stuff with no surprise, e.g., "Brown furry rabbit, / Its nose wiggly as jelly, / Is tasting clover." Jarring, too, in nature poems such as these, is commercial, artificial imagery: "These flat stones are coins / Left from another time—stone / Quarters, pennies, dimes." A diminishing image at best. Nonetheless, large soft washes in charcoal, lemon yellow, and brown with sparks of orange and red are appealing, and there is not enough haiku in picture book format outside of *In a Spring Garden,* the beautiful collection edited by Richard Lewis and illustrated by Ezra Jack Keats. Maestro's book does, however, bring the form down to earth, which, at its best, is where it belongs.

Ruth M. Stein

SOURCE: A review of *Fat Polka-Dot Cat and Other Haiku,* in *Language Arts,* Vol. 54, No. 1, January, 1977, pp. 77-8.

Feeling that the very young child misses the point of traditional haiku, the author wrote her own for the benefit of her kindergarten class. Fifteen verses reflect the familiar world of the very young—a funny cat, a busy baby, plants, and animals. Black/white pictures alternate with others in muted color, highlighted by splotches of scarlet. The author, too, misses the point of haiku by concentrating on the seventeen-syllable pattern. Some of her imagery is weak, as in "quiet cardinal / is like a bright red ribbon / in the snow tree." Why not wait until children mature enough to appreciate the real thing instead of using poor imitations?

IN MY BOAT (1976)

Publishers Weekly

SOURCE: A review of *In My Boat,* in *Publishers Weekly,* Vol. 210, No. 23, December 6, 1976, p. 62.

The husband and wife team continue to invent blithe entertainments as author and illustrator; their latest is a nod to a starchy little girl. She is aboard her boat when a pirate ship passes by; she waves and they return her salute but don't have time to stop for a visit. A mother and baby whale sail by next, also too busy to stop, as are the monkey crew of a banana barge. Other sailors in rushing craft are elephants manning a canoe, 22 frogs in a boot, a circus boat packed with clowns and others, all in too much of a hurry to pass the time of day. Finally a handsome fellow in a rowboat comes by and he has time to stop, to the joy of the child—and why not? He's daddy.

Rich colors in the illustrations invite the eye again and again.

Zena Sutherland

SOURCE: A review of *In My Boat,* in *Bulletin of the Center for Children's Books,* Vol. 30, No. 7, March, 1977, p. 109.

While this boils down to a gag situation and a punch line, the pictures of animals and the mild humor of the fanciful situations may appeal to young children. A small girl is in a boat, and each vehicle that passes her has riders that wave but haven't time to stop (a banana barge full of monkeys, a seaplane full of birds, a hat filled with turtles, etc.) until her father comes by in his rowboat and, in a clipped ending, " . . . *he* had time to stop!" The pictures have vitality, but the whole is slight.

HARRIET GOES TO THE CIRCUS: A NUMBER CONCEPT BOOK (1977)

Marjorie Lewis

SOURCE: A review of *Harriet Goes to the Circus,* in *School Library Journal,* Vol. 23, No. 6, February, 1977, p. 57.

The familiar hard lines and brilliant flat colors of Maestro's drawings frame a lively story that teaches ordinal numbers. Harriet the elephant is thrilled to be first in line to see the circus. As the other animals, numbered second through tenth, queue up behind her, a door opens behind last place owl and positions are reversed—owl becomes first and Harriet last in line. All is solved to everyone's satisfaction when the guests find themselves seated in a circle to enjoy the clowns. The simple story teaches the number concept nicely and it might also be used to talk about the "me first" problem.

Barbara Elleman

SOURCE: A review of *Harriet Goes to the Circus,* in *Booklist,* Vol. 73, No. 13, March 1, 1977, p. 1016.

"Harriet was going to the circus, and she wanted to be the FIRST one there . . . Soon the others started to arrive. Her friend Mouse was SECOND. Duck was THIRD." And on down the line, ending with Owl in TENTH place. But when the door opens unexpectedly next to Owl, Harriet is chagrined to find Owl first and herself tenth until she sees a circle of chairs. With this simple story line, the Maestros introduce ordinal numbers and show their relationships to each other. Harriet, the white elephant whom preschoolers will remember from *Where Is My Friend?,* again captivates—this time with a pink balloon and green-and-white roller skates. Thick black lines restrain the vibrant purples, yellows, oranges, and greens from leaping off the page, making this a happy number awareness session.

Publishers Weekly

SOURCE: A review of *Harriet Goes to the Circus,* in *Publishers Weekly,* Vol. 211, No. 11, March 7, 1977, p. 99.

Bold, strong colors and a simple text in large print distinguish the Maestros' charming number concept book. Harriet, the frolicky elephant familiar to readers of *Where Is my Friend?,* wants to be first in line at the circus. Off she goes on her roller skates, smugly joyous when nine other perky animals turn up and cavort behind her. But a disaster ensues: the line reverses and Harriet is last. The happy ending bursts with activity and makes number learning an amusing experience.

Madge M. Dhus

SOURCE: A review of *Harriet Goes to the Circus,* in *Children's Book Review Service,* Vol. 5, No. 9, April, 1977, pp. 84-5.

This number concept book is designed to introduce ordinal numbers to pre-schoolers. Harriet the elephant is determined to be first in line for the circus. The story unfolds with the arrival of Harriet's friends and their specific positions in line. The authors upset Harriet's plans and she becomes last in line. All ends happily once the animals are inside the circus tent. This book would not be one you could read again and again to the same children. However, it accomplishes its purpose nicely by clearly defining ordinal numbers in a graphic way. The large print and superb illustrations make the book irresistible for "picture readers."

Zena Sutherland

SOURCE: A review of *Harriet Goes to the Circus,* in *Bulletin of the Center for Children's Books,* Vol. 30, No. 10, June, 1977, p. 163.

Harriet, an elephant, makes an effort to be early and is first in line, anxious to have a good seat at a circus performance. Mouse is second, Duck is third, et cetera. Owl is tenth and last, but somebody opens a door near Owl—so Owl is first and Harriet is tenth in line. But all is well: ten chairs are arranged in a circle around the ring, so everybody has a front seat. The text is minimally useful in reinforcing number concepts; the story is slight but adequately told. The illustrations are simple in composition, with large areas of solid color; the background details are few and slightly stylized, while the figures of the animals have more details and provide a note of action against the static background.

Mary M. Burns

SOURCE: A review of *Harriet Goes to the Circus,* in *The Horn Book Magazine,* Vol. LIII, No. 4, August, 1977, pp. 430-31.

Determined to be first in line for the best circus seat, Harriet, a pachyderm with persistence, rises early, dons roller skates, and zips to the entrance. The line grows behind her as second through tenth places are gradually filled with an assemblage of her acrobatic friends. But when another door unexpectedly opens and the order of entry is reversed, Harriet's elephantine composure suffers a setback. Fortunately, the solution—a circle of seats surrounding the center ring—happily insures equality for all. The combination of a simple story line with large, uncluttered poster-like illustrations executed in brilliant flat colors provides an effective and joyous introduction to ordinal numbers for preschoolers.

BUSY DAY: A BOOK OF ACTION WORDS (1978)

Publishers Weekly

SOURCE: A review of *Busy Day: A Book of Action Words,* in *Publishers Weekly,* Vol. 213, No. 10, March 6, 1978, p. 101.

The Maestros' new book is uncommonly imaginative and a source of fun for toddlers as well as an artful introduction to verbs. An amiable elephant stretches luxuriously after a good night's sleep in the first of many amusing color pictures. The kicker is that the elephant is in the top half of a pair of bunk beds. In the lower is his coworker, a mustachioed human. This page illustrates "waking," and the next shows the pals "washing," and so on with most of the action involving their jobs with a traveling circus, the performers and audience. The last picture, "sleeping," shows the friends snuggled in their bunks after an honest day's work.

Kirkus Reviews

SOURCE: A review of *Busy Day: A Book of Action Words,* in *Kirkus Reviews,* Vol. XLVI, No. 6, March 15, 1978, p. 300.

Waking (elephant in top bunk, mustached man in lower), washing (man at sink with washcloth, elephant outdoors with trunk), dressing (in gaudy costumes), eating (stacks of pancakes), working (putting up a circus tent): so begins the Maestros' latest concept book, which takes the two circus performers through a busy day in comfortably unsophisticated cartoons and (the only text) a series of lower case "action words." Effectively simple, with just enough of a visual story to keep things moving without distracting from the exercise.

R. J. DeSanti

SOURCE: A review of *Busy Day: A Book of Action Words,* in *School Library Journal,* Vol. 25, No. 1, September, 1978, p. 120.

This portrays activities which might be performed during

a day at the circus. Each page contains an action word with an "ing" ending (29 in all) and an accompanying illustration which depicts circus characters or animals engaged in waking, washing, dressing, eating, working, resting, playing, sleeping, etc. The setting of a circus lends continuity; the full-color illustrations are sprightly and humorous; and the text will serve admirably for the development of sight vocabulary reading skills.

LAMBS FOR DINNER (1978)

Caroline S. Parr

SOURCE: A review of *Lambs for Dinner,* in *School Library Journal,* Vol. 25, No. 5, January, 1979, p. 44.

A variation on "The Wolf and the Seven Little Kids," diluted for beginning readers. In this version Mr. Wolf tries to trick four sheep into coming with him so he can "have them for dinner." Warned by their working mother (pants-suited in the mostly pastel illustrations), the lambs refuse Mr. Wolf entry despite his disguising his voice with honey. But when Mr. Wolf dusts his fur with white flour, the lambs are fooled, and Mr. Wolf takes three of them away in his bag. Mama and the remaining lamb go to Mr. Wolf's house and find the three captives just sitting down to dinner. "I like to have my friends for dinner, but I would never eat them!" says Mr. Wolf. The play on words is just right for beginning readers, but Maestro's tampering with the traditional folk tale leaves it much weakened; if Mr. Wolf is friendly, his attempts to catch the lambs become pointless.

Kirkus Reviews

SOURCE: A review of *Lambs for Dinner,* in *Kirkus Reviews,* Vol. XLVII, No. 2, January 15, 1979, pp. 61-2.

The much-storied wolf who tries to get the little lambs to open the door, and finally succeeds by disguising himself as their mother (honey for his voice, flour for white fur), becomes a sort of shaggy dog in Maestro's let-down ending. As feared all along, the wolf does have the lambs for dinner—as guests; and he passes them bread and soup as politely as you please. The Maestros' change the Grimms' seven kids into prim little lamb girls to begin with, but the wolf lives up to the stereotype—popping the children into his sack, grinning lecherously with butcher knife in hand, etc.—simply for the sake of surprise. Children will get the joke, but it's a groaner.

Zena Sutherland

SOURCE: A review of *Lambs for Dinner,* in *Bulletin of the Center for Children's Books,* Vol. 32, No. 7, March, 1979, p. 122.

Every day as she left for work, Mama Sheep warned her four children not to open the door, for "Mr. Wolf told me

that he wants to have you for dinner." The first time he knocked, Mr. Wolf was told to go away; the next time, he said he was Mama, but they knew Mama's voice was sweeter. He ate some honey, but they spotted his grey fur; Mama's fur was white. He covered himself with flour, and the ruse worked. They opened the door and Mr. Wolf caught and bagged three of the four. Sounds familiar? No, there's a twist: Mama comes home, rushes to Mr. Wolf's house, and finds her happy progeny sitting at the table waiting to be served. The story is simply told and is illustrated with rather static but nicely composed pictures. Nicely constructed, the tale's operative phrase opens opportunities for discussion of the alternative meanings words may have. However, it may be hard for young children to understand why anyone who is so anxious to be hospitable goes through the flour and honey deceptions and then carries his guests off in a large bag.

ON THE GO: A BOOK OF ADJECTIVES (1979)

Publishers Weekly

SOURCE: A review of *On the Go: A Book of Adjectives,* in *Publishers Weekly,* Vol. 215, No. 19, May 7, 1979, p. 83.

The Maestros score again with their followup to *Busy Day: A Book of Action Words,* a treat for beginners who laughed through its pages and learned about verbs. Here, Betsy uses only captions to tell a spirited story featuring adjectives. Giulio's expert cartoons, in bold primary colors, begin with a skinny clown and his fat elephant friend reporting to the circus. Finding it closed, they are "sad," but get a "happy" idea. One is "neat," one "messy" as they pack for a vacation at the seashore. From this point on, all the pictures and adjectives reveal their various adventures. At last, the "tired" travelers get back home to discover the "happy" news that the circus is opening again.

Kirkus Reviews

SOURCE: A review of *On the Go: A Book of Adjectives,* in *Kirkus Reviews,* Vol. XLVII, No. 12, June 15, 1979, p. 683.

The elephant and clown who demonstrated "action words" in the Maestros' *Busy Day* now act out a string of adjectives, which are the only words accompanying their visual story. When their circus closes ("sad"), the two go off on a beach holiday, get "lost" (at a crossroads) and "tired" (driving into the hotel), are "afraid" of a seeming shark fin when they're swimming, then "surprised" when it turns out to be a human swimmer's water wing. They act "silly" at the crazy mirrors and get "dizzy" on a carnival ride, and after a few more reversals end up "happy" at the reopened circus. Like *Busy Day,* this is essentially a learning tool, but snappier than many wordless adventures that lack its pedagogical intent.

Now Owl was FIRST, Turtle was SECOND,
Dog was THIRD, Lizard was FOURTH,
Cat was FIFTH, Snake was SIXTH,
Monkey was SEVENTH, Duck was EIGHTH,
Mouse was NINTH, and Harriet was TENTH.

From Harriet Goes to the Circus: A Number Concept Book, *written by Betsy Maestro. Illustrated by Giulio Maestro.*

Barbara Elleman

SOURCE: A review of *On the Go: A Book of Adjectives,* in *Booklist,* Vol. 75, No. 22, July 15, 1979, p. 1628.

With the circus closed, an elephant and his clown friend decide to vacation at the beach. They pack, stop for lunch, get lost, find a motel, go sunning and swimming, enjoy the boardwalk amusements, change a tire on the way home, and happily find a sign announcing Circus Opens Tomorrow. This simple plot line provides background for the introduction and lively visualization of 29 adjectives such as *messy, full, lost, noisy, brave, wet, dizzy, dirty, happy.* In some places, though not consistently, the words are juxtaposed with their opposites (*hot/cold*). The Maestros' caricature of the adjectives gives emphasis while injecting humor, and reading teachers will find that the cartoon drawings, buoyant with shades of blue and orange, make this also usable with older children needing vocabulary practice.

Daisy Kouzel

SOURCE: A review of *On the Go: A Book of Adjectives,* in *School Library Journal,* Vol. 26, No. 1, September, 1979, p. 117.

This attractive, diminutive (6" x 6½" book, presenting 29 common adjectives, will be useful to parents and teachers of slow or recalcitrant learners, thanks to the lively illustrations in bright blue, red, and terra cotta, which elucidate the concepts via the humor-laden activities of a man and his pet elephant. A must-have complement to the Maestros' intelligently conceived ***Busy Day: A Book of Action Words***.

📖 *HARRIET READS SIGNS AND MORE SIGNS: A WORD CONCEPT BOOK* (1981)

Publishers Weekly

SOURCE: A review of *Harriet Reads Signs and More Signs,* in *Publishers Weekly,* Vol. 219, No. 8, February 20, 1981, p. 95.

The Maestros have created popular concept books on numbers, words, adjectives and nouns. Their new effort stars the likable elephant girl Harriet as she roller-skates through her town and pays close attention to signs. She waits on the sidewalk while a sign warns DON'T WALK and crosses when it switches to WALK. She obeys the command DETOUR where a fallen tree blocks the street, the STOP sign at the railroad crossing and she certainly does KEEP OFF THE GRASS. BAKERY OPEN and ICE CREAM are a joy to encounter, and Harriet buys treats that she takes to where the best sign of all hangs: GRANDMA'S HOUSE. The text is most accessible and the big illustrations are in dazzling colors.

Denise M. Wilms

SOURCE: A review of *Harriet Reads Signs and More Signs,* in *Booklist,* Vol. 77, No. 14, March 15, 1981, p. 1030.

Harriet the elephant, last seen in **Harriet Goes to the Circus,** here visits her grandmother. But the main focus is on her roller-skating jaunt through town to get there: Harriet follows the sign that says To Town, waits at the Don't Walk sign, detours at the Detour sign, skates right by the Bus Stop sign, etc. The lesson in learning common signs is bolstered by sure touches of child appeal in Harriet's breezing right on by the school, getting a cake at the bakery, and buying herself an ice-cream treat. Bright, flat, candy shades of turquoise, green, purple, yellow, salmon, and hot pink completely fill the pages. The rounded cars, chunky buildings, and various other town vistas take their slightly stylized shape from thick, black lines; animal figures that people Harriet's path sport amusing, amiable expressions. This is very well conceived and deftly executed.

Kirkus Reviews

SOURCE: A review of *Harriet Reads Signs and More Signs,* in *Kirkus Reviews,* Vol. XLIX, No. 9, May 1, 1981, p. 568.

Against the series' usual flat, simple designs and poster-paper colors, elephant Harriet roller skates across town (but often looks like she's just walking), diligently observing all the traffic and other signs along the way. She sees DON'T WALK and waits for the green WALK before crossing, she goes "another way" on encountering a DETOUR sign, stops on the sidewalk when passing a big house with a KEEP OFF THE GRASS sign, and so on. There are stops at a BAKERY, U.S. MAIL, and ICE CREAM truck before Harriet arrives at her destination, an odd little structure cutely and unrealistically equipped with the sign GRANDMA'S HOUSE. It might serve as a preparation for straight reading or street- and town-crossing, but this has less story, less learning-content, and less style than other Maestro word-concept books.

TRAFFIC: A BOOK OF OPPOSITES (1981)

Publishers Weekly

SOURCE: A review of *Traffic: A Book of Opposites,* in *Publishers Weekly,* Vol. 220, No. 12, September, 1981, p. 154.

The latest addition to the Maestros' primers afford little

boys and girls happy playtime while instilling conceptions of directly opposite word meanings. In vivid colors, the illustrations feature simplified shapes that children will recognize readily as they follow the long journey of a compact car. On its way home, the car goes *over* one bridge and *under* another, *right* at one corner and *left* at the next; it *stops* at red lights and *goes* at the green. The traveler passes and is passed by trucks *empty* and *full*; it shares the road with other cars, *big* and *small* until finally, it fetches up in the driveway at home at the end of the *day*: "Good *night!*"

Denise M. Wilms

SOURCE: A review of *Traffic: A Book of Opposites,* in *Booklist,* Vol. 78, No. 5, November 1, 1981, p. 392.

A little rounded magenta car is the focal point for this exploration of opposites. "Go home, little car. Go *over* the bridge. Go *under* the bridge. Take a *left* turn. Take a *right* turn. *Stop* at the red light. *Go* at the green light." All this occurs against bold strokes of pure, flat color. Depending on landscape, deep purple or green predominates, with yellow, red, and royal blue the most common accents. Although shapes are reduced to simple blocks of unlined color, compositions can be crowded, with bright hues in sharp, busy contrast. The effect is both cheerful and absorbing: complex enough for scrutiny, clean enough for easy enjoyment.

Christina Olson

SOURCE: A review of *Traffic: A Book of Opposites,* in *School Library Journal,* Vol. 28, No. 5, January, 1982, p. 68.

The raison d'être here is to impart the concept of antonymy. But the text is entirely secondary to this stunning example of graphic design. The pages chart the progress of a "little car" as it goes *over* a bridge and *under* a bridge; on a *narrow* road and a *wide* road. The stylized design uses halftone overlays for rich quality of color and spotlighted detail. Using surrounding white space for further contrast, each page delivers a razzle-dazzle impact of purple-green-orange-gold-pink-yellow-blue-red. Granted, the book is designed rather than illustrated, but the effect is so startlingly inviting that a child might provide a narration for the car's exercise in traffic and ignore the text altogether.

Zena Sutherland

SOURCE: A review of *Traffic: A Book of Opposites,* in *Bulletin of the Center for Children's Books,* Vol. 35, No. 8, April, 1982, p. 154.

Brightly colored pages, with vehicles and background stripped of details, so that the solid masses of color have a poster-like simplicity, are almost distractingly vivid. Each page has one brief sentence, and the facing pages are paired to give contrast: "That house is *far* away," "This house is *near*," and "Take a *left* turn," "Take a *right* turn." (The book uses boldface rather than italics.) Eye-catching rather than appealing, the book can be used for reading aloud as well as for independent reading by beginners; although it comprises opposites of different kinds (size, position, direction, etc.) it can encourage observation and comparison, and vehicles usually appeal to children.

ON THE TOWN: A BOOK OF CLOTHING WORDS (1983)

Publishers Weekly

SOURCE: A review of *On the Town: A Book of Clothing Words,* in *Publishers Weekly,* Vol. 224, No. 7, August 12, 1983, p. 67.

Among the many characters that have amused and taught boys and girls too young to read are the urbane man and his buddy, the amiable elephant, who play a return engagement in the Maestros' latest. Coming after their hectic **Busy Day** and **On the Go,** the friends' leisure time is heartily appreciated, as we see in the color-splashed drawings. The only words are captions identifying the partners' bathing suits and sandals as they frolic in a pool, sports clothes they don for a fast game of tennis, etc. As the hours progress, the man and the elephant meet various people who give the Maestros the opportunity to write large about skirts, blouses, raincoats, and evening clothes as the recreation seekers end the day with their dates (in dresses) attending a concert.

Kirkus Reviews

SOURCE: A review of *On the Town: A Book of Clothing Words,* in *Kirkus Reviews,* Vol. LI, No. 17, September 1, 1983, p. J-153.

The elephant and the mustachioed man who demonstrated "action words" in the Maestros' **Busy Day** and acted out adjectives in **On the Go** now show off "clothing words." With the circus connection broken (the man is no longer a clown), it's all the funnier to see the two step out—still with a certain razzmatazz—in bathing suits and sandals, starting a day that will take them, with appropriate changes of attire, from the swimming pool to the tennis court to the lake and lunch (with a lady friend for each), through a rainstorm to a fancy evening concert: shirts, ties, belts, suits, shoes, coats, hats, gloves (hand-in-hand with their also-gloved lady friends) . . . and then to bed (plain slip-ons for the man, rabbit slippers for the elephant). Debonair and delightful—with a big-and-little tinge and that disarming, Babar-like incongruity.

Liza Bliss

SOURCE: A review of *On the Town: A Book of Clothing Words,* in *School Library Journal,* Vol. 30, No. 3, November, 1983, p. 66.

Readers familiar with the Maestro style will recognize the fresh, good-natured approach and the resourcefulness which make **On the Town** click. Two well-dressed friends—a man and an elephant—are enjoying a day on the town together. As they move from swimming pool to tennis court to restaurant to the opera, a change of clothing reflects each new activity. In the otherwise gray and while illustrations, one item of clothing receives color highlight in each picture. The word for the highlighted item appears in lowercase letters in the same position on each page; the book is otherwise wordless. The sight of an elephant wearing, with such endearing nonchalance, the designed-for-human clothing (even managing to pull on his gigantic socks with his trunk) will hold young readers' interest while they look and think twice about the highlighted clothes. Words like *sneakers, T-shirts, bathing suits* and *sandals* are introduced with never an intrusion into the readers' enjoyment or a shadow of didacticism. Although the book can serve as a great vocabulary builder, its uncluttered, lighthearted illustrations are a joy in themselves.

Kate M. Flanagan

SOURCE: A review of *On the Town: A Book of Clothing Words,* in *The Horn Book Magazine,* Vol. LX, No. 2, February, 1984, p. 44.

A man and an elephant go from morning swim to bedtime, spending an eventful day—which includes a tennis game and various outings with their dates. They don appropriate outfits, similar in style but amusingly different in size. By the day's end twenty-nine articles of clothing have been featured—among them, bathing suits, underpants, sweaters, dresses (on the lady friends), pajamas, slippers. Each highlighted item is identified in boldface type in the corner of the page and is shown in color, contrasting with the gray wash of the rest of the illustration. The uncluttered, cartoonlike pictures have an understated humor that should be obvious even to the very young.

HALLOWEEN HOWLS: RIDDLES THAT ARE A SCREAM (written and illustrated by Giulio Maestro, 1983)

Publishers Weekly

SOURCE: A review of *Halloween Howls,* in *Publishers Weekly,* Vol. 224, No. 8, August 19, 1983, p. 78.

"How does a vampire make a sandwich?" "With a loaf of dread." "What is a chilling Halloween dessert?" "Blood-curdling cream." "What do you call a skeleton when he's not working?" "Lazybones." Maestro's cornucopia of riddles stars ghosts, monsters, skeletons, ghouls and witches all cavorting in funny, violently colored pictures. Since kids dearly love this brand of humor, the book should be very popular among boys and girls planning Halloween festivities during the coming months and for years afterward.

Karen Stang Hanley

SOURCE: A review of *Halloween Howls: Riddles That Are a Scream,* in *Booklist,* Vol. 80, No. 3, October 1, 1983, p. 299.

There are puns galore ("Why did the ghost's car stop dead? It ran out of gasps") in this newest collection of Halloween humor, which features enough vampires, mummies, and other creepy favorites to satiate even the most exacting fanciers of ghastly riddles. While the nearly 60 conundrums are standard stuff, Maestro's lively full-color scenes on every page accentuate the silliness and make this an eye-catching Halloween item.

📖 *BIG CITY PORT* **(with Ellen DelVecchio, 1983)**

Denise M. Wilms

SOURCE: A review of *Big City Port,* in *Booklist,* Vol. 80, No. 1, September 1, 1983, p. 88.

"A big city port is a busy place. Boats and ships come into the port to load and unload. It is a safe place for them to dock." So begins this picture-book rendition of how all kinds of ships and boats come into port and dock at the piers to unload their cargo. Expansive double-page spreads lay out panoramas of liners, cargo ships, tugs, and freighters that are maneuvering in and out of the harbor. Crisp lines with industrial-looking blues, reds, and yellows for color create vivid expanses that make the introduction crystal clear to young audiences.

Kirkus Reviews

SOURCE: A review of *Big City Port,* in *Kirkus Reviews,* Vol. LI, No. 17, September 1, 1983, p. J-152.

A little, platitudinous information about ports—combined with dry but detailed illustrations that do at least convey a sense of loading-and-unloading activity. The text is of the sort that says almost nothing in a nondescript way: "A big city port is a busy place"; "Tugboats push and pull each big ship through the harbor to the docks"; "The ocean liner has docked, and the passengers are getting off." The pictures have no zest either, and as maritime illustrations no particular skill (none of the ships, for one thing, seem to be actually in the water); but Maestro's ability to delineate tiny objects and depict minuscule scenes provides us with effective views of cargoholds, cargo-handling operations, and docks. OK, then, as a pictorial panorama supplementing Donald Crews' *Harbor* and complementing, to a degree, Gail Gibbons' *Boats.*

Lauralyn Levesque

SOURCE: A review of *Big City Port,* in *School Library Journal,* Vol. 30, No. 3, November, 1983, p. 66.

This picture book shows everyday activity in a busy city port. The simple text briefly describes the different types of ships that come into a large harbor; the attractive color illustrations provide plenty of pertinent detail, and are done in a realistic style. Taken as a whole, the book is a successful example of a clear and interesting nonfiction book for preschoolers.

Margery Fisher

SOURCE: A review of *Big City Port,* in *Growing Point,* Vol. 23, No. 2, July, 1984, p. 4289.

General and particular merge in **Big City Port,** for the mannered, blandly bright pictures and the carefully planned sequence of activities show that this is an idealised example, designed to demonstrate, again to children around seven or eight, the way a great port works—in theory, that is, for here are no labour disputes, no dirt or untidiness or wasted space. Toylike ships of many kinds and buildings of lego-like symmetry indicate how tugs, cranes, trucks and trains play their part in loading and unloading passengers and goods, how the traffic in and out of the port is controlled. The balance between text and pictures tilts towards the decorative visualisation, for which simple, unqualified statements provide a link and point to an order.

📖 *AROUND THE CLOCK WITH HARRIET: A BOOK ABOUT TELLING TIME* **(1984)**

Publishers Weekly

SOURCE: A review of *Around the Clock with Harriet,* in *Publishers Weekly,* Vol. 225, No. 15, April 13, 1984, p. 72.

The Maestros specialize in picture books with tips on communications—words, signs, numbers—encapsulated in airy stories. The elephant girl Harriet is familiar to readers of her three previous adventures in learning. Here she returns to display the benefits of a gift from Grandma, a watch. At 8 A.M., Harriet knows it's time to get up. By 9 A.M., she's dressed, ready for breakfast. At 10 A.M., having cleaned the kitchen, Harriet is out playing a fast game of ball with her pals. At 11 A.M., we see her choosing a book at the library. So it goes until 8 P.M. when Harriet snuggles into bed. Gala pictures in poster-bold hues are a cinch to captivate the toddler set. The Maestros' hints on Harriet's housework, conversely, may tempt parents to dwell on the elephant girl's dutiful nature as much as on the lessons in telling time.

Denise M. Wilms

SOURCE: A review of *Around the Clock with Harriet: A*

Book about Telling Time, in *Booklist,* Vol. 80, No. 19, June 1, 1984, p. 1400.

A practical lesson in telling time, this has the Maestros' characteristically bright, bold pictures and a "story" that contributes a lot toward making sense of what the hours on a clock stand for. Youngsters will watch Harriet the elephant wake up at eight, breakfast at nine, play outside at ten, go to the library at eleven, etc. Minutes and other subtleties of time telling aren't the province here. Rather the story and accompanying clock inset on each page provide the first steps in understanding both what the hours mean and how they measure the day. A jolly place to begin time-telling work with younger children.

Susan D. Denniston

SOURCE: A review of *Around the Clock with Harriet: A Book about Telling Time,* in *School Library Journal,* Vol. 31, No. 1, September, 1984, p. 106.

Harriet the elephant returns, this time to demonstrate her ability to tell time. Pre-readers, as well as beginning readers, will enjoy accompanying Harriet through various events in her day as they learn to distinguish among the hours on the clock and the activities that occur at specific times. Vividly colored illustrations are cheerful and large. . . .

HARRIET AT PLAY; HARRIET AT SCHOOL; HARRIET AT HOME; HARRIET AT WORK (1984)

Carrie Carmichael

SOURCE: "Designed for the Smallest," in *The New York Times Book Review,* November 11, 1984, p. 57.

Betsy and Giulio Maestro have developed a series on Harriet; their Babar-reminiscent elephant—*Harriet at Play,* also at home, at school and at work. This elephant runs through a child's day in simple line drawings and bright colors. But when we see Harriet at work, she never gets off her property. She cleans, she cooks, she paints and she gardens. She never ventures far afield, delivering groceries or washing cars, and she never gets paid for her industry!

Tom S. Hurlburt

SOURCE: A review of *Harriet at Home,* in *School Library Journal,* Vol. 31, No. 4, December, 1984, pp. 73-4.

Short factual sentences serve as captions to the brightly colored glossy illustrations in this board book series. Harriet, an elephant, with the help of a number of her animal friends, depicts activities familiar to most youngsters, thus clarifying common words associated with these activities. The key words in each sentence (13 to 19 per book) are printed in bold-face type. Items of furniture are

introduced in **Harriet at Home; Harriet at Play** includes the words *puzzle, crayons* and *blocks;* in **Harriet at School,** the elephant *paints, marches* and has *juice;* in **Harriet at Work** she *fixes, paints* and *bakes.* The illustrations are clear enough to illuminate the concept the sentence is advancing, although Harriet's expression never changes whether working, playing or studying. These books will catch the eye and hold the interest of most young children as well as beginning readers.

CAMPING OUT: A BOOK OF ACTION WORDS (1984)

Publishers Weekly

SOURCE: A review of *Camping Out: A Book of Action Words,* in *Publishers Weekly,* Vol. 227, No. 20, May 17, 1985, p. 118.

The mustachioed man and his pal the elephant return, in the Maestros' new little book, to tell and show beginning communicators the meanings of more basic words. As in **Busy Day, On the Go,** etc., a single-word caption appears on each color-bright page depicting the friends "planning" an outing first, studying a map of campsites. On the succeeding pages, they are "packing" their gear, "loading" the van and "driving" to the woodland haven with a lake where they pitch a tent and get ready for a good time. Swimming, building a fire, cooking in the outdoors, singing around the campfire, sharing the work and snuggling down in their sleeping bags at night, the man and elephant make the most of their vacation before they pack up and head for home. The lessons in verb usage are easy to learn in this vivacious primer.

Anita Silvey

SOURCE: A review of *Camping Out: A Book of Action Words,* in *The Horn Book Magazine,* Vol. LXI, No. 3, May-June, 1985, p. 328.

Books that seek to entertain the young while teaching them concepts are generally quite dreary, but Betsy and Giulio Maestro are masters at combining these two factors to create delightful and enjoyable books. Their most recent collaboration features the elephant and man of **On the Town** involved in action—or more accurately, in action words. The cover alone—which shows them roasting hot dogs over an open fire, with the elephant holding the fork in his knotted trunk—sets the stage for a volume of funny and beguiling illustrations. Their activities include planning, packing, loading, driving, unloading, and all kinds of antics on the campground until they leave. The book not only celebrates the joy of camping, it also celebrates the joy of verbs.

Ilene Cooper

SOURCE: A review of *Camping Out: A Book of Ac-*

tion Words, in *Booklist,* Vol. 81, No. 21, July, 1985, p. 1558.

The Maestros' popular man and elephant duo, who appeared in **On the Go** and several others, take their act to the campground. Using one verb per page, and a sprightly picture to illustrate it, this conjures up a story kids will like, featuring the planning, packing, driving, carrying, diving, fishing, cooking, and hiking that make up a camping trip. The soft, pastel water-colors have a cartoon look, deftly injecting humor into the scenes. Teachers can make ample use of this as it is or as a starting point for students who want to make up their own story using action words.

Margaret Gross

SOURCE: A review of *Camping Out: A Book of Action Words,* in *School Library Journal,* Vol. 32, No. 1, September, 1985, p. 121.

The curly-haired mustached man and the large elephant from **Busy Day** demonstrate 30 action verbs as they relax on an overnight camp-out. From planning to driving to folding (the tent) and leaving again, each scene is carefully portrayed in finely drawn watercolors. Shaded pastels and one verb per page depict the friends enjoying typical outdoor pastimes—diving, fishing, cooking, singing. Children who have camped or enjoyed a cookout will pour over these pictures and relive their own experiences. Another hit from this well-known author/illustrator team.

📖 ***TRAIN WHISTLES: A LANGUAGE IN CODE***
(written by Helen Roney Sattler and illustrated by Giulio Maestro, 1985)

Zena Sutherland

SOURCE: A review of *Train Whistles: A Language in Code,* in *Bulletin of the Center for Children's Books,* Vol. 38, No. 9, May, 1985, p. 175.

Precisely drawn trains set against verdant landscapes or busy railroad yards are softly colored and are nicely integrated with the informative, simply written text. Sattler discusses the fact that most train personnel today use diverse methods of communication and that train whistles, once used heavily, are used less today but are still used and still important. As she describes the journey of a freight train, the author explains the kind of whistle signal (number of toots and their length) that is a code for a different situation. This is the kind of book that could easily stimulate a search for further knowledge on the subject or on trains in general.

Jeffrey A. French

SOURCE: A review of *Train Whistles,* in *School Library Journal,* Vol. 32, No. 1, September, 1985, p. 125.

Featuring a text that has been updated to reflect the railroad's increasing reliance on electronics, this revision reads somewhat more clearly than the original due to some subtle reorganization and smoother transitional passages. Sattler describes the meaning of several audible train signals and demonstrates their use in the course of a typical freight train journey. An addendum lists the signals covered in the book as well as a few additional signals. Maestro's clear and colorful illustrations for **Train Whistles**—replacing Tom Funk's—are similar to, but more subdued than, his work in **Big City Port** and complement the text very well. Its attractive illustrative material, more contemporary typeface and cover graphics coupled with preschoolers' chronic interest in trains should make **Train Whistles** an essential purchase for most libraries.

Beverly A. Maffei

SOURCE: A review of *Train Whistles,* in *Appraisal: Science Books for Young People,* Vol. 19, No. 4, Fall, 1986, pp. 80-1.

Although train whistles are not heard as often today (having been replaced by radios, telephones, lights and electronic signals), their distinctive sounds and sound patterns can be fascinating. In their simply presented and easily read picture book, Sattler and Maestro have decoded the special language of train whistles, allowing the reader to "listen" to the messages. Train whistles are a necessary form of communication for train crews in sending messages to crews who cannot be reached in any other way. The various combinations of long and short blasts have specific meanings. For example: "two long blasts, a short blast and another long mean—"'Stop, cars and people. Wait until the train has passed.'" The text defines the most common whistle patterns and their meaning. Each two-page, color illustration focuses on a different type of train, or a detail of a train, car or engine. Seasons, weather and locales change in the pictures. A glossary of how these most common train whistles sound, and their respective meanings, is expanded at the end of the book.

📖 ***THROUGH THE YEAR WITH HARRIET***
(1985)

Denise M. Wilms

SOURCE: A review of *Through the Year with Harriet,* in *Booklist,* Vol. 82, No. 4, October 15, 1985, p. 339.

Poor Harriet. Her birthday was great fun, but it will be a whole year before the next one rolls around. How does she pass the time? In a story designed to teach the months of the year and coordinate them with the changes in seasons, youngsters see Harriet engaged in activities such as making a snowman in January, ice-skating in February, scooping up the last of the snow in March, starting a garden in April, etc., until it's time for her birthday again. The book is bold and bright with Harriet's portly white figure standing out against an array of intense, flat candy colors. The effect is a stand-out cartoon display. The story's concepts are effectively presented, and it's likely to become an oft-used classroom resource as well as an eye-catching independent reading choice.

Lucy Young Clem

SOURCE: A review of *Through the Year with Harriet,* in *School Library Journal,* Vol. 32, No. 5, January, 1986, p. 58.

The Maestros have produced another excellent concept book, this one teaching the months of the year. Simple, flat illustrations in appealing bright colors show Harriet the elephant child in activities to which any child can relate. Events marking each month are those a child would notice and observe. There's a nice continuity provided by Harriet's garden, planted in April and producing tomatoes in August and pumpkins in October. Holidays are not mentioned in the text, but the illustrations hold clues about them. There's much to talk about here. . . .

📖 *SPACE TELESCOPE: A VOYAGE INTO SPACE BOOK* **(written by Franklyn Mansfield Branley and illustrated by Giulio Maestro, 1985)**

R. William Shaw

SOURCE: A review of *Space Telescope,* in *Science Books & Films,* Vol. 21, No. 2, November-December, 1985, p. 85.

Space Telescope describes the large optical telescope scheduled to be launched into orbit in 1986. Nearly as large as the famous Mt. Wilson instrument, this telescope will play a role in a new, integrated attack on the frontiers of astrophysics. Since the space telescope will be able to peer farther into space than earth-bound telescopes and will also utilize a wide spectral range, scientists expect to greatly extend their knowledge. The majority of the book offers a detailed description of the instrument, illustrated by a number of superb cutaway drawings [by Maestro] that permit insights impossible with photographs alone. These drawings give the book lasting value. The introductory chapter is an interesting historical sketch of telescopes and a discussion of their power, which could be more detailed since many readers have an inadequate understanding of how a telescope works. . . . The book will appeal to young readers as well as those who prefer science without too much technical detail.

Lavinia C. Demos

SOURCE: A review of *Space Telescope,* in *Appraisal: Science Books for Young People,* Vol. 19, No. 2, Summer, 1986, pp. 18-19.

The most interesting aspect of Space Telescope is the environment in which it operates. Otherwise it's much like

large telescopes now in use here and in the Soviet Union. The sections of this book which describe Space Telescope's placement in orbit, its potential for repair and even redesign in situ, and the information it will collect are all clearly and concisely written. The rest lacks focus. Is this a book about telescopes or a book about space technology? The facts, although generally accurate, are oddly scrambled. Several terms are inadequately defined, and the information is difficult to absorb, yet often incomplete.

Nevertheless, there will be plenty of customers eager for this timely and up-to-date offering. It's an attractive book, with good black and white diagrams [by Maestro] and photographs that are absolutely essential to the text. The reading and comprehension level is definitely above the lower limit of third grade indicated by the publisher.

📖 *RAZZLE-DAZZLE RIDDLES* **(written and illustrated by Giulio Maestro, 1985)**

Linda Callaghan

SOURCE: A review of *Razzle-Dazzle Riddles,* in *Booklist,* Vol. 82, No. 8, December 15, 1985, p. 629.

Using riddles to introduce readers to new vocabulary, Maestro presents a varied mix of words, puns, phrases, and slang expressions. Each page contains a single riddle printed at the top of the page with the answer below a large cartoon illustration. Although the green and blue washes only brighten the pages a little, Maestro's line drawings do affect a jovial mood. Young riddlers seeking new material to stump their friends will enjoy this slim collection.

Eva Elisabeth Von Ancken

SOURCE: A review of *Razzle-Dazzle Riddles,* in *School Library Journal,* Vol. 32, No. 9, May, 1986, p. 82.

Razzle-dazzle this is not. Standard riddles, one to a page with dark, uninspired illustrations are a disappointment after Maestro's more cheerful works. The ostensible aim of this book is vocabulary enrichment, but riddles such as "What is a ghostly police officer? A Detective Inspector" goes beyond the age level indicated by the format. The more simple jokes such as "What is a puppy on a mountain peak? Top dog" are weak even for the most ardent riddlers. Riddle and joke books are always popular fare and are invaluable in encouraging beginning or slower readers to find fun in books, but there are many better choices than this one.

📖 *HURRICANE WATCH* **(written by Franklyn Mansfield Branley, illustrated by Giulio Maestro, 1986)**

Zena Sutherland

SOURCE: A review of *Hurricane Watch,* in *Bulletin of the*

Center for Children's Books, Vol. 39, No. 5, January, 1986, p. 82.

One of the more specifically focused topics in this series opens with a few pages explaining the weather conditions that can build into a hurricane and then launches into descriptions of effects and damages to populated coastal areas. Weather watch, preparation, and evacuation procedures round out the information. Both the diagrams and the watercolor storm scenes are effective, the text straightforward.

Jonathan R. Betz-Zall

SOURCE: A review of *Hurricane Watch,* in *School Library Journal,* Vol. 32, No. 5, January, 1986, p. 54.

Basic information about hurricanes in a brief, heavily illustrated format well-suited to early elementary school children. Branley describes hurricane formation, paths and destructive power using short sentences and colorful vocabulary. The descriptions don't include the real-life stories found in books on hurricanes for grades four and up, but this is more than made up for in the illustrations, which clearly convey the pounding force of the hurricane winds and water. The illustrations are also well-keyed to the text and employ such effective devices as comic strip-style sequencing. Branley and Maestro are to be lauded for effectively portraying the inherent drama of a hurricane as they explain the science behind such a storm and provide common-sense safety advice.

THE STORY OF THE STATUE OF LIBERTY (1986)

Barbara Elleman

SOURCE: A review of *The Story of the Statue of Liberty,* in *Booklist,* Vol. 82, No. 13, March 1, 1986, p. 1020.

In contrast to the other books about the Lady in the Harbor that feature photographs or black-and-white drawings, the Maestros' presentation is in full color. Information has been pared to the bare facts, without loss of flavor, and is given in an intriguing and lively manner. The full thrust, however, is in the drawings. Pictures of Bartholdi sketching Bedloe's Island on an early visit to New York, sculpting models in his Paris studio, and overseeing the erection of the skeleton provide an intimate, you-are-there approach. The statue's grandeur is keenly realized with numerous views of her construction as well as when she is seen in full glory on her island setting. Children who are fascinated by dimension will enjoy contrasting the size of the men working on the structure with the Lady herself. A spectacular two-page spread, with the statue surrounded by fireworks, makes a fitting conclusion. Appended are several pages of statistics and statements about size, restoration, and chronology, which parents and teachers will find useful when expanding upon the subject.

Zena Sutherland

SOURCE: A review of *The Story of the Statue of Liberty,* in *Bulletin of the Center for Children's Books,* Vol. 39, No. 8, April, 1986, p. 153.

Far and away the most attractive of the spate of books celebrating the centennial of the Statue of Liberty, this unfolds the story in a simple, read-aloud text set into panoramic watercolor spreads that are striking enough for use with classes or groups of children. The opening aerial view of Liberty Island encircled with sea and ships makes a breathtaking introduction, and the monumental scale of the statue is clearly conveyed in oversize drawings as the building history progresses, climaxing in a night scene in which the lady is lit up with fireworks. Several concluding pages give additional information: a table of dates, dimensions of the statue, important people in its construction, and notes on repairs. From one flag-centered endpaper to another, this is a well-designed book.

Deborah Vose

SOURCE: A review of *The Story of the Statue of Liberty,* in *School Library Journal,* Vol. 32, No. 8, April, 1986, p. 76.

At last, an outstanding picture book on the Statue of Liberty. Although Maestro simplifies the story—including only the most important people's names, for example—she still presents an accurate account of what happened. The exceptional drawings are visually delightful—primarily in the blue-green range, although they are in full color—and cover most of every page. Human figures—workers, tourists—are included in many drawings, indicating the statue's tremendous scale. Further, the drawings involve viewers through the use of unusual perspectives and angles and by placing the statue in scenes of city life. One depicts Bartholdi sketching the statue in the foreground as he gazes at its future site on Bedloe's Island. Another is of cranes and cables supporting laborers as they put Lady Liberty's immense cloak in place over her steel frame. This title totally eclipses the previous picture book on the same subject, [Thelma] Nason's *Our Statue of Liberty.* A section, "Additional Information about the Statue . . . ," includes excellent lists of dimensions, important people who helped with construction, repairs from 1980-86, a table of dates and Emma Lazarus' poem as well as other interesting facts. There is no index, but the facts section makes this book nearly as useful to middle-grade readers doing research as many of the other new titles on this topic. . . . A striking book.

Publishers Weekly

SOURCE: A review of *The Story of the Statue of Liberty,* in *Publishers Weekly,* Vol. 229, No. 22, May 30, 1986, p. 62.

The Maestros have once again produced a winner. Unlike

most of the season's Statue of Liberty offerings, this one's a picture book, and it's a fascinating look at America's most famous statue. Lively, informational text and detailed, watercolor paintings provide a clear introduction to the history of the statue and its meaning to France, America and to America's immigrants. The book can be read to younger children, while new readers can easily tackle the simple text on their own. For the child who might have more questions, a well-organized appendix full of information is included. *The Story of the Statue of Liberty* is among the best of a bumper crop.

Elizabeth S. Watson

SOURCE: A review of *The Story of the Statue of Liberty*, in *The Horn Book Magazine,* Vol. LXII, No. 3, May-June, 1986, pp. 339-40.

Nearly twenty titles have been published recently about the Statue of Liberty. . . . The Maestros' full-color picture book is written for the youngest audience of any of the recent publications. The text is very simple yet manages to convey all the major events in Liberty's creation. Although the text is slightly choppy, perhaps due to an attempt to simplify, the illustrations transcend any possible argument with the text. The full-color water colors, which show amazing detail and are extremely rich, vary from delicate renderings of the armatures to a precise depiction of the tablet held in Liberty's left hand, and they become almost robust as fireworks explode around Liberty on the final pages. The book features six pages of additional information about the statue, including summaries of important events and people plus details of the restoration work not found elsewhere. Careful attention has been paid to type size and style and to the appealing layout of the additional information section. Tying together the entire book are end-papers featuring the French and American flags. . . .

▢ *FERRYBOAT* (1986)

Publishers Weekly

SOURCE: A review of *Ferryboat,* in *Publishers Weekly,* Vol. 229, No. 17, April 25, 1986, p. 93.

Many children in this country have never seen a ferryboat, much less experienced the thrill of riding one. Wife-and-husband team Betsy and Giulio Maestro ride the Chester-Hadlyme Ferry near their home in Connecticut. This book is fashioned after that ferry, and their words and pictures are so completely involving that it's almost like being on the real thing. The author carefully explains the workings of the ferry and takes readers from shore to shore, lovingly describing the sights and sounds of the ride. "The ferry doesn't have to turn around. Its front is the same as its back!" The double-page spreads, with a deep blue river and lush tree-lined shores, are colorful and appealing.

Margaret A. Bush

SOURCE: A review of *Ferryboat,* in *The Horn Book Magazine,* Vol. LXII, No. 3, May-June, 1986, p. 341.

"If you want to cross the river at Chester, you have to take the ferry." Sunny water colors, beginning with a nice low aerial view of the river with a small ferry approaching its slip, follow a family through a day's outing on a country ferry. Plentiful realistic details fill the full-page pictures, and a simple text states the various stages of the trip including the waiting line, driving the cars on board, leaving the slip, views of the river while crossing, the approach to the other side, disembarking, and finally waiting at evening for the return trip on the day's last crossing. A historical note on the last page summarizes the history of the Chester-Hadlyme Ferry in Connecticut and the pictured vessel, Selden III. The information about the specific boat adds to the realism, but the scenes will be equally familiar to readers in many states who enjoy crossing bays, lakes, and rivers on the homely, hard working ferries. Some will miss the sea gulls—for this river is inland—but young and old will thoroughly enjoy this warm, lingering reliving of a favorite mode of travel.

Denise M. Wilms

SOURCE: A review of *Ferryboat,* in *Booklist,* Vol. 82, No. 20, June 15, 1986, p. 1542.

"If you want to cross the river at Chester, you have to take the ferry." That's the forthright beginning to an introduction to ferry boats that depicts cars crossing from one pleasant countryside shore to the other. Readers see that people on foot and on bicycles also ride the ferry and that automobiles are squeezed tight to fit aboard. They'll find it interesting too that the ferry doesn't have to turn around. "Its front is the same as its back!" The facts are supported by gentle watercolor paintings with neat lines and quiet shadings. A thoroughly pleasant introduction to a fascinating journey—especially for children who have never experienced such a ride.

Connie Tyrrell Burns

SOURCE: A review of *Ferryboat,* in *School Library Journal,* Vol. 33, No. 1, September, 1986, p. 124.

A charming treat, *Ferryboat* describes, in simple text and with bright watercolor illustrations, a family's crossing of the Connecticut River from Chester to Hadlyme. How the ferry operates (it never needs to turn around since the front is the same as the back!) is sure to fascinate young armchair mariners. The use of the first-person plural and the perspective used in the illustrations allow children to feel a part of this journey. The lovely blues and greens evoke the summer season, and the magnificent sunset is breathtaking. An appended map and historical note about the ferry enhance the amount of information conveyed so effortlessly and appropriately for the age group addressed.

📖 *A MORE PERFECT UNION: THE STORY OF OUR CONSTITUTION* (1987)

Publishers Weekly

SOURCE: A review of *A More Perfect Union: The Story of Our Constitution,* in *Publishers Weekly,* Vol. 231, No. 25, June 26, 1987, p. 74.

The bicentennial of the Constitution has spawned numerous books but perhaps none so perfectly designed to explore with younger readers the serious message behind the celebration. As with the Maestros's *The Story of the Statue of Liberty,* they have collaborated on a simple, straightforward account using an oversize format with full-color illustration throughout. There is an excellent, fact-filled addenda that also includes the Preamble, chronologies and summaries of the Articles of the Constitution, the Bill of Rights, the Amendments and the Connecticut Compromise. This fine book places important events in historical context; it deserves to be read not only during the year-long celebration, but anytime.

Kirkus Reviews

SOURCE: A review of *A More Perfect Union: The Story of Our Constitution,* in *Kirkus Reviews,* Vol. LV, No. 12, July 1, 1987, p. 996.

For the youngest children able to understand the concepts involved, a lavishly illustrated summary of the events surrounding the writing and adoption of the Constitution.

Covering more briefly the same ground as [Jean] Fritz's *Shh! We're Writing the Constitution,* Maestro mentions the delegates' travel problems and living arrangements as well as the major proposals and compromises concerning the composition of Congress. Appended information includes summaries of the content of the seven Articles and the Bill of Rights, a list of the signers, and a table of dates. As in last year's *Story of the Statue of Liberty,* colorful panoramic illustrations give a sense of having been there, in spite of the rather clumsy drawing of figures and faces.

This should be invaluable as explanation to younger children of the year's bicentennial celebrations of the Constitution.

Elizabeth S. Watson

SOURCE: A review of *A More Perfect Union: The Story of Our Constitution,* in *The Horn Book Magazine,* Vol. LXIII, No. 4, July-August, 1987, pp. 487-88.

Our nation is getting ready for a second bicentennial celebration. Parades, fireworks, speeches, lectures, and discussions are all being planned. What happened to good old 1976? As a nation, we are only two hundred years old

this year. Prior to the Constitutional Convention in 1787 we existed only as a confederation of individual states; without the creation and adoption of this essential document our country would certainly not have maintained its independence. So bring on the flags and bands and nearly a dozen children's books about the Constitution to celebrate. For the youngest students of the Constitution, the Maestros have created a companion volume to their *Story of the Statue of Liberty.* The charming illustrations depict the Founding Fathers and Old Philadelphia with a wealth of detail in architecture, furnishings, and dress. The simple text is fleshed out by an appended five-page information section that includes summaries of the articles and amendments, a list of the signers, and a table of dates. . . .

Christine Behrmann

SOURCE: A review of *A More Perfect Union: The Story of Our Constitution,* in *School Library Journal,* Vol. 34, No. 1, September, 1987, pp. 175-76.

Once again, the Maestros have produced a simple, attractive, and informative book about a milestone in American history. Here they cover the birth of the Constitution from the initial decision to hold the convention, through the summer meetings in Philadelphia, the ratification struggle, the first election, and the adoption of the Bill of Rights. The facts are put forward clearly, but in no way is this a detailed account. Left out, for example, are the events leading to the Convention and the debates on the slavery issue which occured during its course. Instead, the focus is on the most basic issue—the decisions on the organization of the government which resulted in the Great Compromise. The book does get to the core of the achievement of the Constitution—the establishment of a governmental structure which has been adaptable to change for 200 years—but some of the significance is lost in this pared-down description. The pastel-colored paintings are most effective when they present panoramas and least effective when depicting the members of the convention, most of whom look alike except for hair color. A final section includes lists of the signers as well as of all those who attended; chronologies of events and the dates of ratification; and simple summaries of the Articles of the Constitution and amendments to it. The simplest and most accessible history of the Constitution to date.

Ilene Cooper

SOURCE: A review of *A More Perfect Union: The Story of Our Constitution,* in *Booklist,* Vol. 84, No. 1, September 1, 1987, p. 68.

The bicentennial of the Constitution has brought forth a spate of books; here is one for young children that explains how this extraordinary document came about. The book describes how in the summer of 1787 the nation's leaders saw that America would fall apart unless something was done to fortify the government. They decided to hold a convention in Philadelphia to hammer out the direction of the country. In clear, simple sentences the authors explain the various points of view of the representatives and how compromises were made. The book then moves through the ratification process and the adoption of the Bill of Rights four years later. Handsome pastel watercolors re-create the events, though the evocative two-page spreads of eighteenth-century life may appeal more than the scenes of the intense debates inside the State House on Chestnut Street. Appended are a chronology, summaries of the Constitution and its amendments, notes on the Connecticut compromise, and interesting facts about the signers of the document. This book may need to be introduced to children, but it will be well worth the effort.

Betsy Hearne

SOURCE: A review of *A More Perfect Union: The Story of Our Constitution,* in *Bulletin of the Center for Children's Books,* Vol. 41, No. 2, October, 1987, p. 34.

In undertaking the difficult task of simplifying the Constitutional Convention of 1787 into picture-book format, the Maestros have succeeded in producing a smooth, informationally balanced text and some impressive double-page spreads, though the closeup figures are stiff and awkward. Beginning with a map and description of the states' disunity, they focus on the delegates' arrival in Philadelphia, the ensuing debates, the compromises made and principles agreed on, and the finalizing of the document that was ratified the following year. A five-page appendix summarizes the articles of the constitution, names the signers, gives a table of important dates, offers some interesting notes, and lists the amendments. Since Jean Fritz' *Shh! We're Writing the Constitution* is for a slightly older audience, this will be most useful as the earliest introduction available to the Constitution.

📖 *TORNADO ALERT!* **(written by Franklyn Mansfield Branley and illustrated by Giulio Maestro, 1988)**

Roger Sutton

SOURCE: A review of *Tornado Alert!,* in *Bulletin of the Center for Children's Books,* Vol. 42, No. 1, September, 1988, p. 4.

Since Dorothy Gale's tornado is a primal scene for many television-age children, this early science book will probably find a wider than usual audience. While both text and pictures clearly show the hows and wheres of tornadoes, they don't skimp on the drama, with almost every double-page spread dominated by a ferocious twister in an eerie blue/green/purple sky. The text is brief and simple: "Tornadoes can pick up branches and boards, stones and bricks, cars, and sometimes even people." A concluding section of safety instructions offers a reassuring close.

Todd Morning

SOURCE: A review of *Tornado Alert!,* in *School Library Journal,* Vol. 35, No. 3, November, 1988, p. 100.

Another excellent addition to this science series that has opened up a host of subjects to young readers. This book tells what tornadoes look like, why they occur, when they occur, and what to do when one strikes. A few incidents of disastrous tornadoes are mentioned, such as the time when a tornado in Minnesota lifted a passenger train from its tracks and carried it 80 feet through the air. The writing is clear, concise, and rhythmic. Maestro's color drawings are also clear and understandable, and fit well with the book's design. . . . It should be just the thing for young readers interested in the subject.

📖 *DOLLARS AND CENTS FOR HARRIET* **(1988)**

Denise M. Wilms

SOURCE: A review of *Dollars and Cents for Harriet,* in *Booklist,* Vol. 85, No. 1, September 1, 1988, p. 81.

Harriet, the cheerful child elephant star of other concept books by the Maestros, here learns to manage money. A brief storyline is provided: Harriet wants to buy a toy but only has one dollar, and she must find a way to earn four more. Each job she undertakes pays her a dollar, but it always comes in a different form. By the time Harriet has her five dollars, youngsters will clearly see how 100 pennies, 20 nickels, 10 dimes, and 4 quarters all add up to one dollar. They'll also see how five one-dollar bills equal one five-dollar bill. The illustrations are bold, the palette bright. This adds up to a painless introduction to the mathematics of money.

Martha Rosen

SOURCE: A review of *Dollars and Cents for Harriet,* in *School Library Journal,* Vol. 35, No. 5, January, 1989, p. 65.

Harriet is one "white elephant" who will not end up just sitting on a shelf. Once again this author/illustrator team has created an attractive and appealing concept book that should be popular with the preschool and primary grade audience. In this offering, Harriet learns the value of a dollar—five dollars, actually—because she needs to earn enough to buy herself a gift. There is even a slight element of surprise, as the identity of the desired item, a large kite, is not revealed until the last page. With their usual flair for color and clarity, the Maestros here enumerate the ways that coins can add up to a dollar. With each successive job, Harriet collects the needed change in a variety of combinations. In addition to counting her pennies, nickels, and dimes, Harriet cheerfully shoulders the responsibilities necessary for making a dollar. Although this picture book does not rival the ingenuity of design displayed in Tana Hoban's *26 Letters and 99 Cents,* the bold primary colors and Harriet's engaging perseverance ensure that you'll get your money's worth.

📖 TAXI: A BOOK OF CITY WORDS (with Giulio Maestro, 1989)

Kirkus Reviews

SOURCE: A review of *Taxi: A Book of City Words,* in *Kirkus Reviews,* Vol LVII, No. 4, February 15, 1989, p. 296.

In another of the Maestro's colorful concept picture books, a taxi takes young readers through a city full of experiences and provides the terms to go with them. Morning and the taxi's work begin together as the taxi and its unnamed driver pick up passengers going to different urban destinations: office buildings, zoo, theater, apartment house, coffee shop, airport, etc. Each one- or two-word term is printed in boldface in a brief, simple text accompanying a large, full-color illustration. By the time the taxi returns to its garage at the day's end, 29 scenes have been introduced.

The instructive text here is well complemented by the panoramic illustrations, full of crisply delineated details. Despite the distant point of view (like a wide-angle effect), the focus on detail preserves interest; the reader is informed without being overwhelmed. An attractive introduction to urban variety.

Anna Biagioni Hart

SOURCE: A review of *Taxi: A Book of City Words,* in *School Library Journal,* Vol. 35, No. 8, April, 1989, p. 86.

Here's a day's tour of a large city by taxi recounted with a kind of textbook plainness. The yellow taxi is an unremarkable machine with an anonymous driver, but it provides the dramatic link that holds this list of city words together. The urban landscape is the real protagonist of the book, and its rhythms are shown very well. Full-color drawings illustrate the taxi's work day and its many stops—theater, department store, hospital, and so on. An entire page is devoted to each concept. These city words are helpfully printed in bold face type in the context of a sentence, but they are not defined. However, almost all of the words will be familiar to young readers, and one or two subtleties such as the difference between *street* and *avenue* are not terribly important. Young city kids and their country cousins will sense the movement and bustle of a metropolis on these pages. One can almost hear the noisy honking of horns. Beginning readers whose native language is not English will like it, also, for its two lines of text on each page and its directness and simplicity.

Denise Wilms

SOURCE: A review of *Taxi: A Book of City Words,* in *Booklist,* Vol. 85, No. 16, April 15, 1989, p. 1468.

A taxi picking up and dropping off people all over a large metropolis is the thread of continuity in a text designed to introduce words common to a big city. Included are *apartment house, office building, railroad station, pier, tunnel, bridge, airport,* and *coffee shop.* Obviously, these words don't necessarily apply only to big cities, though many are placed in the context of one; for example, a large ocean liner is docked at a *pier,* and *street* is shown as a narrow passageway between two high rises. That bit of bias aside, this book amiably surveys the sights and scenes found about a city's landscape, and nonurban dwellers, with a bit of adult interpretation, will find this an enjoyable way to get a sense of a New York type of hustle bustle. Watercolor drawings, many with novel perspectives, depict the shifting cityscape.

📖 SNOW DAY (1989)

Robert Strang

SOURCE: A review of *Snow Day,* in *Bulletin of the Center for Children's Books,* Vol. 43, No. 2, October, 1989, p. 37.

"For the children, it's a holiday," but for the adults there remains the task of clearing all that snow away. The Maestros clearly describe and illustrate the different ways snow is removed after a blizzard: from driveways, roads, airports, harbors, and city streets. The tone is rather catalogish and the pictures only serviceable, but snowbound kids (okay, parents) may appreciate the sense of proportion this provides on a no-school day.

Denise Wilms

SOURCE: A review of *Snow Day,* in *Booklist,* Vol. 86, No. 5, November 1, 1989, p. 554.

Snow days are special days; for a brief time the world seems to stand still—at least from a child's point of view. Though school is closed and Mom and Dad are at home, others are working hard to see that business as usual will once again prevail. The Maestros capture the duality of these days, showing families at home instead of at school or work and city and state employees toiling night and day with their big trucks and machines to clear the snow away. The view extends beyond the small town to encompass snow removal at airports, rail lines, and river ports; the expanded perspective adds substance, leading young children to consider what's going on beyond their doorstep the next snowbound day. The charcoal-and-wash drawings, which nicely carry forth the mood, are realistic in style, in contrast to the bright, slick colors and cartoon-like drawings seen in much of Maestro's other work.

Leda Schubert

SOURCE: A review of *Snow Day,* in *School Library Journal,* Vol. 36, No. 1, January, 1990, p. 97.

After a major snowstorm, it's a snow day for all, and a

town digs out. Kids go sledding and throw snowballs, grownups endure, and many work crews and their vehicles begin the difficult day-long job of clearing snow. The story moves from town to highway to the nearby airport and harbor, and then back to the town again. By evening, life has returned to normal. In a visual ode to snow movers, pages are filled with shovels, snowblowers, power company trucks, plows, tow trucks, state police cars, and even icebreakers. Orange trucks contrast with blue-white snow in the cheerful illustrations. Double-page spreads with perspective shifts provide panoramic views; skies clear in time for a brilliant sunset. With its short text, this should be accessible to vehicle-loving young children, and is a natural to lead readers to related material.

📖 *TEMPERATURE AND YOU* (1989)

Robert Strang

SOURCE: A review of *Temperature and You,* in *Bulletin of the Center for Children's Books,* Vol. 43, No. 8, April, 1990, p. 192.

A basic introduction to temperature begins with the weather (and an illustration of melting icicles) and makes a logical progression to heating and air-conditioning, cooking and refrigeration, and, finally, body temperature. While not making a clear distinction between temperature (a measured degree of heat) and heat itself, the book is generally characterized by an age-appropriate use of examples (snowman, oven), concepts (skin is "a little like a blanket"), and advice ("You cannot control the temperature outside. Inside your house, you can change the temperature to make it more comfortable"). Color illustrations are stiff but large, clear, and sensible. An end note expands on some of the concepts mentioned in the text, useful for parents who wonder why shivering makes you warmer.

Denise Wilms

SOURCE: A review of *Temperature and You,* in *Booklist,* Vol. 86, No. 17, May 1, 1990, p. 1708.

"Temperature is how hot or cold something is"—a simple enough concept but one young children don't think about in terms of their everyday lives. The Maestros cultivate this awareness by showing how a thermometer's red line indicates relative warmth or cold, how sunlight affects seasonal air temperatures, and how heat and cold are harnessed to make our lives more comfortable. A little biology is provided as well in portions that describe body temperature, fever, and steps taken to keep a body warm or cool. Friendly pictures in perky colors show specifically what the authors are talking about; the book's open, cheerful appearance makes this suitable as a nonfiction read-aloud.

Sylvia S. Marantz

SOURCE: A review of *Temperature and You,* in *School*

Library Journal, Vol. 37, No. 1, January, 1991, pp. 86-7.

An extremely elementary summary of what temperature is and how it is measured on thermometers, without mentioning numbers—only high and low. Maestro explains the concept of temperature in terms children can understand: snow and ice versus lots of sunshine and the warmth of summer; the usefulness of cold to preserve food in refrigerators in contrast to that of heat for ironing wrinkles out. Giulio Maestro's flat, realistic watercolors fill every page, reinforcing and supplementing the text. His characters are middle-class, interracial, nonsexist, family oriented housedwellers in Pleasantville, USA who enact scenes from everyday life on well-designed pages. For curious readers, the final page of notes gives a few more detailed explanations of such terms as boiling points, shivering and sweating, and Fahrenheit and Celsius scales. However, science teachers will find this limited beyond simply introducing the concepts of hot and cold.

Louise L. Sherman

SOURCE: A review of *Temperature and You,* in *Appraisal: Science Books for Young People,* Vol. 24, Nos. 2-3, Spring-Summer, 1991, p. 29.

This very simple, straightforward presentation of the concept of temperature for the youngest readers is given some added interest through the Maestro's appealing illustrations. Measurement of temperature is introduced and all thermometers (except fever) are shown in both Celsius and Fahrenheit scales, though those terms are not mentioned in the text. Sunshine as the source of warmth is discussed but, though the text tells readers, "Your body has its own temperature," there is no explanation of how bodies attain warmth. The control of temperature indoors, through heating and air conditioning, is mentioned, as well as other ways in which heat and cold are used by people, such as: refrigeration, cooking, and ironing. The ways people keep their bodies warm and cool through clothing, food and drink, and exercise are mentioned. A section called, "Notes About Temperature" is appended, which introduces the terms Celsius and Fahrenheit, as well as explaining other terms previously introduced in the text. This presentation is adequate and possibly useful for small children who are curious about temperature. It does not have enough appeal to entice general readers, however. . . .

📖 *DELIVERY VAN: WORDS FOR TOWN AND COUNTRY* (1990)

Lori A. Janick

SOURCE: A review of *Delivery Van: Words for Town and Country,* in *School Library Journal,* Vol. 36, No. 9, September, 1990, pp. 217-18.

In this companion book to *Taxi: A Book of City Words* a delivery van leaves the city early in the morning to distribute packages. Readers follow Pat, the deliverywoman, into town where she makes stops at a hardware store, a pharmacy, and a library. As the van progresses to the country, Pat visits an antique shop, a dairy farm, and a general store. Maestro's watercolor illustrations are colorful and detailed, with white space skillfully used to give the book a fresh, uncluttered look. Key words are emphasized in bold print. Pat greets friends and customers along the way, adding a personal touch that is often lacking in concept books. A visually appealing and useful introduction to town and country.

Carolyn Phelan

SOURCE: A review of *Delivery Van: Words for Town and Country,* in *Booklist,* Vol. 87, No. 8, December 15, 1990, pp. 857-58.

Subtitled **Words for Town and Country,** this is the second picture book in the series that began with **Taxi: A Book of City Words**. Pat drives her van through the village and surrounding countryside, delivering packages to a *shopping center, bank, garden center, library, farm, service station, country inn,* and so forth. Key words are targeted in boldface type. Each oversize page carries a line-and-watercolor illustration of life in an affluent rural community. While the overall setting may be an idealized view of American town and country life, a picture of a pretty shopping center—any shopping center, for that matter—is a novelty in children's book publishing. Teachers may use the book to teach word recognition, but its main audience will be preschoolers old enough to delight in the familiar.

A SEA FULL OF SHARKS (1990)

Frances E. Millhouser

SOURCE: A review of *A Sea Full of Sharks,* in *School Library Journal,* Vol. 36, No. 10, October, 1990, p. 111.

Brightly illustrated with full-color drawings on almost every page, this overview provides enough specific details on sharks to be a useful addition to any collection. Several interesting tidbits highlight some of the unique characteristics of sharks. Maestro also provides a brief but effective description of the range and power of the sharks' senses. In addition to drawings of over 20 kinds of sharks, Giulio Maestro has included an excellent double-page map of the world showing broad differences in water temperatures and the types of sharks that inhabit those specific areas. Drawings of sharks' teeth are done life size, including a fossilized shark tooth. Even without chapters, index, or glossary, this is a good browsing book. . . .

Kirkus Reviews

SOURCE: A review of *A Sea Full of Sharks,* in *Kir-*

kus Reviews, Vol. LXIII, No. 20, October 15, 1990, p. 1458.

"When something is awesome, you feel respect, fear, and wonder . . . Most of us feel this way about sharks—a little scared, but very curious" begins this sensible book that does exactly what it sets out to do: to satisfy that curiosity with fascinating, well-organized facts and allay unreasonable fears while pointing out which sharks really *can* present a danger, and under what circumstances. The illustrations are simple and clear, and without falling into the sensationalism that often mars books on this popular topic, they maintain interest with their choice of subjects: a diver-scientist in a sharkproof cage; another hitching a ride on the fin of the harmless whale shark; comparisons of the teeth of some of the 350 species, many of which are also illustrated. An excellent introduction that packs in a lot of information.

Hazel Rochman

SOURCE: A review of *A Sea Full of Sharks,* in *Booklist,* Vol. 87, No. 10, January 15, 1991, p. 1058.

Fearful fascination draws us to a book about sharks, and the Maestros feed that excitement with lots of astonishing facts. Clear and dramatic, their combination of text and double-page illustrations in pencil and watercolor reveals how a great diversity of sharks feed, breathe, swim, breed, etc. The art is a little garish, with a bright turquoise background, and the text overuses the exclamation point. The "awesome" information needs no such histrionics. For example, in its lifetime, a shark can go through thousands of teeth. A large part of the shark's brain is used for the sense of smell. Some sharks cover immense distances and may travel all over the world; some live at the very bottom of the sea and hardly move at all. Most aren't dangerous unless disturbed; however, the tiger, blue, bull, hammerhead, and great white sharks are very dangerous to people. This is great for reading aloud and is sure to generate enthusiastic group discussion.

THE DISCOVERY OF THE AMERICAS (1991)

Robert Strang

SOURCE: A review of *The Discovery of the Americas,* in *Bulletin of the Center for Children's Books,* Vol. 44, No. 8, April, 1991, pp. 199-200.

Beginning quite properly with the Stone Age migration across the land bridge from Asia, the Maestros remind us of possible Japanese, Chinese, and Phoenician expeditions, along with St. Brendan and Leif Ericsson before getting around to the voyages of Columbus. It's a welcome context, as are the parallel descriptions of highly advanced cultures that were flourishing in America all the while Europeans were busy "discovering" it. "The Europeans brought diseases that killed many of the natives, and a strange new way of life they did not understand or accept. Many lost their lives, and most lost their freedom, their customs, and their pride." The continuous text is forthright and well organized. Pencil-and-watercolor illustrations in this large-format book are more variously successful: the land- and sea-scapes are dramatic, the maps are clear and well-placed, the portraits and human figures are crude and sometimes garishly colored. Appended "additional information" includes a chronology, an annotated list of early American inhabitants, more information on the "age of discovery" and "other interesting voyages." A useful review for Columbus Day.

Ruth Semrau

SOURCE: A review of *The Discovery of the Americas*, in *School Library Journal,* Vol. 37, No. 4, April, 1991, p. 114.

While this title is self-explanatory, it barely conveys the depth of the book's grand scope. The Maestros begin at the beginning as far as we know it, with the crossing of the Bering Land Bridge over 20,000 years ago. They carefully trace what is known of those Stone Age people, and include little-known points such as the possible visits of Phoenician explorers, Irish monks, Japanese fishermen, as well as the fairly well-documented Viking settlements. Illustrations show striking visual comparisons of ancient artifacts from both the Old and New Worlds, which reveal strong similarities. An appropriate emphasis is given to the thousands of years of human civilizations before Europeans established permanent settlements. The arrival of Columbus takes place almost halfway through the book. Conflicts between explorers who were fiercely ethnocentric and the native people who were often just as fierce in their own defense are treated with trenchant objectivity. Attractive, easy-to-use appendixes give tables of dates, pre-Columbian cultures, European explorers, and other facts. Giulio Maestro has achieved a happy mingling of artistic maps that include clear, descriptive diagrams of voyages and land routes, balanced with beautiful interpretations of broad landscapes in luscious colors of sky, cloud, sea, mountain, and forest. The dazzlingly clean and accurate prose and the exhilarating beauty of the pictures combine for an extraordinary achievement in both history and art.

Carolyn Phelan

SOURCE: A review of *The Discovery of the Americas*, in *Booklist,* Vol. 87, No. 18, May 15, 1991, p. 1801.

In a book published just in time for the 1992 Columbus celebrations, the Maestros put the celebrated explorer's achievements into a broader historical context by chronicling the discovery and rediscovery of America throughout the centuries. Beginning with the passage of nomadic Asian tribes to North America during the Ice Age, the book covers climatic changes, the rise and fall of civilizations, and the possibility of early overseas visits from the Japanese, the Phoenicians, and the Chinese before looking at the more familiar history of European voyages of exploration, from St. Brendan to Magellan. Expansive, full-color artwork dominates the large pages, picturing maps, globes, and artifacts as well as landscapes, seascapes, and dramatic events. Apart from displaying awkwardly drawn human figures on occasion, the handsome illustrations confidently portray historical and hypothetical happenings. Appendixes include a detailed chronology, a summary of ancient and early American peoples, and background discussions of the Age of Discovery and the naming of America. An attractive book with a good balance between text and illustration.

Kirkus Reviews

SOURCE: A review of *The Discovery of the Americas*, in *Kirkus Reviews,* Vol. LIX, No. 10, May 15, 1991, pp. 673-74.

The Maestros do a real service here in presenting the more familiar explorers in the context of *all* the migrations that have populated the Western Hemisphere, beginning with the Ice Age journeys across the land bridge from Siberia to Alaska. Though the information is simply stated, it is lucid, well balanced, and scrupulous in distinguishing conjectures from documented facts and in pointing out the tragic effects of the Europeans' arrival on the Native Americans. The large, profusely illustrated format is handsome; and while Giulio Maestro's depictions of people are merely serviceable, he mixes his media to splendid effect to evoke sweeping landscapes in Newfoundland, the Caribbean, or even a brooding Gobi Desert. Maps; five pages of "Additional Information" include a table of dates and a list of early American groups. An outstanding introduction.

Publishers Weekly

SOURCE: A review of *The Discovery of the Americas*, in *Publishers Weekly,* Vol. 238, No. 23, May 24, 1991, p. 59.

The talented creators of such nonfiction books as *The Story of the Statue of Liberty* and *A More Perfect Union* offer a lively picture-book introduction to new world exploration that successfully avoids the traditional Eurocentric approach. Beginning with a brisk explanation of population theories (including early migration from Asia to the Americas over a land bridge), the authors present information on both hunter-gatherer and agrarian societies, and the development and decline of great civilizations such as the Maya, Hopewell and Inca. Readers are introduced to such diverse explorers of the Americas as St. Brendan, Eric the Red, Leif Ericsson, Cabot, Vespucci, Balboa, Magellan and, of course, Columbus. All this is accomplished via the Maestros' characteristic mix of accessible prose complemented by maps and striking watercolor paintings. Also included are useful tables and explanatory notes. As the 500th anniversary of Columbus's famed discovery approaches, this attractive work is an essential resource.

HOW DO APPLES GROW? (1992)

Kirkus Reviews

SOURCE: A review of *How Do Apples Grow?*, in *Kirkus Reviews,* Vol. LIX, No. 24, December 15, 1991, p. 1600.

A straightforward, carefully detailed presentation of how "fruit comes from flowers," from winter's snow-covered buds through pollination and growth to ripening and harvest. Like the text, the illustrations are admirably clear and attractive, including the larger-than-life depiction of the parts of the flower at different stages. An excellent contribution to the solidly useful "Let's-Read-and-Find-Out-Science" series.

Carolyn K. Jenks

SOURCE: A review of *How Do Apples Grow?,* in *The Horn Book Magazine,* Vol. LXVIII, No. 2, January-February, 1992, p. 94.

Among the large number of information books about apples, this entry in the Let's-Read-and-Find-Out-Science series deserves notice as one of the better ones. Its focus is the development of an apple, from a spring bud to a ripe fruit. The text is simple and clear, and the pencil-and-watercolor illustrations range from scenes through the seasons to labeled close-ups of the apple bud, blossom, and fruit. The information is given in an atmosphere of wonder and appreciation of nature, while describing with great clarity the parts of the blossoms, the way bees help to fertilize them, and the feeding of the fruit by sugar made in the leaves. A child will come away from the book with an appreciation of both the scientific facts about and the natural beauty of this common fruit.

Herbert Grossman

SOURCE: A review of *How Do Apples Grow?*, in *Science Books & Films,* Vol. 28, No. 3, April, 1992, p. 83.

This book is one of a series of Let's-Read-and-Find-Out-Science books written for early elementary school children. Information on the dust cover suggests that the level of difficulty is between five and nine years, but seven to nine years may be more accurate. Certainly, the illustrations and amount of information on each page appear to be more suitable for the latter age range. Young readers will be neither overwhelmed nor bored by the amount of material. The overall coverage is brief enough for 2nd and 3rd graders to cope with, but long enough to cover the topic well. The book is scientifically accurate; however, there are a couple of items that the authors should have included. Most young students probably would like to know what forms the fleshy, edible part of the apple. This could be presented in a short paragraph without illustrations. They might also like to see how a pollen grain germinates and helps fertilize the female cell. Both sexes are pictured, as are dark- and light-skinned children. A

rural setting, including an apple orchard and a pond, is depicted. Most of the illustrations are of apple flowers and apples. This book is recommended highly as a clear and interesting introduction to the science of fruits.

ALL ABOARD OVERNIGHT: A BOOK OF COMPOUNDS (1992)

Carolyn Phelan

SOURCE: A review of *All Aboard Overnight: A Book of Compound Words,* in *Booklist,* Vol. 88, No. 16, April 15, 1992, p. 1533.

A little girl describes an overnight train trip with her mother, and a line-and-watercolor picture on each page illustrates her experiences. The simple text, which includes a liberal sprinkling of the compound words promised in the subtitle, explains what's happening. Drawn to the book by the dramatic sweep of an oncoming train on the jacket, preschool choo-choo lovers will find plenty to entertain them in this child's-eye view of train travel. Year after year, primary grade teachers will come back to the book as an introduction to compound words: "Mom and I grab our *suitcases.* We're off to the *railroad* station." While the story itself is bland and the drawings of people are sometimes awkward, these problems diminish when compared with the overall usefulness of the book.

Cheryl Cufari

SOURCE: A review of *All Aboard Overnight: A Book of Compound Words,* in *School Library Journal,* Vol. 38, No. 5, May, 1992, p. 106.

A concept book with a story that blends perfectly into the language arts and social studies curricula. Concentrating on the use of compound words, it tells of the train ride a young girl and her mother take to visit the child's grandparents, from the time they leave for the railroad station until they greet the elderly couple at the top of the station stairway. The text, one or two sentences per page with the compound words in bold, is easy enough for beginning readers. The pen-and-ink and watercolor illustrations further the story, partly because of Maestro's attention to detail both within the train and the passing scenery of city and countryside. Fellow passengers of diverse ethnic backgrounds enjoy the trip as well. A good introduction to compound words, and a likely choice for transportation units.

BIKE TRIP (1992)

Sheilamae O'Hara

SOURCE: A review of *Bike Trip,* in *Booklist,* Vol. 88, No. 9, January 1, 1992, p. 832.

Joshua, who appears to be about nine, tells a simple story of a bike trip he takes with his parents and younger sister from their rural home into town. The book has the look of a favorite childhood experience that remains in the memory, not because it is spectacular or exciting but because it is so perfect. There is nothing to mar the bike trip: no litter along the roadside; no graffiti on the buildings. Even the cows in the field and the passing cars and trucks look freshly washed. The Maestros stress bicycle safety without belaboring the point, and the text and pictures make an unremarkable bike trip seem so inviting that it may actually lure some children (and parents) away from the television to try it themselves.

Kirkus Reviews

SOURCE: A review of *Bike Trip*, in *Kirkus Reviews*, Vol. LX, No. 1, January 1, 1992, p. 60.

Josh, who looks about eight, recounts a pleasant family outing incorporating safe biking practices (e.g., riding on the right, "single file, and not too close together, in case we have to stop suddenly"). Sights along the way and a small-town street fair at the destination make this seem like a story.... Sunny, evocative watercolors of the Connecticut countryside make this unusually appealing, though Maestro's people are less adroitly rendered. Safety rules are summarized more explicitly on the last page. Useful and attractive.

Mary Lou Budd

SOURCE: A review of *Bike Trip*, in *School Library Journal*, Vol. 38, No. 3, March, 1992, p. 232.

From the first sentence, "Today's the day!," readers are drawn into the joy of a family outing that takes them on a pleasant, leisurely bike trip into town and back home again. The story never lags and the ending, too, is exuberant. This set of parents and their two young children not only know how to have fun, but also how to do it safely. Masterfully slipped into the smooth text are tips for making such an excursion successful (wearing helmets, traveling with the traffic in single file, walking the bikes across busy intersections, etc.). The realistic watercolor illustrations span double pages and include just enough softly hued detail to add interest and present information for a picture-book lesson in safety. The warmth of a family enjoying one another's company is certain to give feelings of satisfaction and well being from beginning to end. . . .

📖 *TAKE A LOOK AT SNAKES* (1992)

Ruth S. Vose

SOURCE: A review of *Take a Look at Snakes*, in *School Library Journal*, Vol. 38, No. 9, September, 1992, p. 249.

This colorfully illustrated introduction avoids most of the pitfalls common to such simplified nonfiction. Maestro introduces her readers to the snake's body, behavior, and life cycle in clear, concise statements, aptly expanded by the detailed pictures of over 30 types of snakes. There are diagrams of the different ways in which they move, cutaway pictures showing the skeleton and internal organs, and, of course, the requisite closeup of poisonous fangs. Readers will be intrigued by the world map color-coded to show their "Chance of meeting a dangerous snake," and will be surprised at how rare these opportunities are in most locations. This, in fact, is Maestro's basic point; she succeeds admirably in showing how fascinating snakes are, and how, in most cases, they are beneficial to humankind. The one flaw is her dismissal of hibernation as "very deep sleep"; surely a better explanation is possible even at this level. Similar material for this age group appears in [Patricia] Lauber's *Snakes Are Hunters*, but Maestro's superior illustrations and clarity of presentation make this book a worthwhile purchase.

Kay Weisman

SOURCE: A review of *Take a Look at Snakes*, in *Booklist*, Vol. 89, No. 5, November 1, 1992, p. 516.

In this companion to *A Sea Full of Sharks*, the Maestros offer information about the varieties, habitats, behaviors, and physical characteristics of snakes. Although they present general facts about the reptiles, the authors also convey many specific details. Watercolor-and-pencil illustrations, appearing on every page, identify individual species and show the traits described in the text. A balanced presentation that downplays the sensational, this will make an excellent choice for reading aloud or report writing. . . .

Elizabeth S. Watson

SOURCE: A review of *Take a Look at Snakes*, in *The Horn Book Magazine*, Vol. LXVIII, No. 6, November-December, 1992, p. 736.

An introductory book on snakes provides a great deal of information that is clearly detailed in the watercolor and pencil drawings and in the fine diagrams. Different varieties of snakes are used to detail the various functions and actions described, and in each case the type of snake is clearly labeled. The information includes historical perspective, physical characteristics, differences between varieties, and even geographic locations. Those who are not snake lovers will be delighted to learn that not only Ireland but also Iceland and New Zealand are snake free. Text and illustrations work perfectly together to extend the child's understanding.

Joseph Patrick Kennedy

SOURCE: A review of *Take a Look at Snakes*, in *Science Books & Films*, Vol. 29, No. 1, January-February, 1993, p. 20.

"Snakes are not really strange—they are just very different from most other animals, including humans." There seems to be a natural curiosity about snakes, and in this book one will find some aspects of the biology of these maligned reptiles. The range of material presented is broad and includes information on the number of different kinds of snakes there are, the range of sizes they appear in, and their anatomy, locomotion, shedding of the skin, prey, and venom, as well as a final page of facts entitled "Did you know that. . . ???" The book could have been improved in a number of particulars. For example, descriptions of the threatening and death-feigning behaviors of hognose snakes would have been justified. Those who have not seen a hognose snake elevate the anterior part of its body and spread it somewhat hoodlike, while hissing, might have difficulty understanding such behavior, as well as what is going on when "the Hognose falls down and pretends to be ill." Also, a consistent usage of the term "venomous" would have been preferable to the intermingling of "poisonous" and "venomous." In a similar vein, it is long past the time to abandon the term "cold-blooded" in discussions of temperature regulation in reptiles, and *absorb* what is left of the yolk" is preferable to *"eat* what is left of the yolk" in reference to the nourishment of recently hatched snakes. Finally, the illustration of a spitting cobra might suggest that venom is ejected from oral structures other than the specialized fangs. Notwithstanding these examples and others, this is a good presentation. The bright jacket, pictorial cover, and color illustrations on every page of this book make it an attractive look at snakes for young readers.

📖 THE STORY OF MONEY (1993)

Robert Strang

SOURCE: A review of *The Story of Money,* in *Bulletin of the Center for Children's Books,* Vol. 46, No. 7, March, 1993, p. 219.

The Maestros prove rather decisively here that while money changes everything, it's more to the point that everything changes money. Their concise history goes all the way back to hunters-and-gatherers, who had no need for money ("There was no place to spend it"), through bartering cultures and on to the use of products such as salt, shells, blankets, and barley as currency. The Sumerians were the first to invent metal money (out of silver—"Everybody wanted it"), and various countries went on to further refine the process by which humans could trade, up to and including credit cards and ATMs: "In the future, there will be other kinds of electronic cashless money." Explanations are clear and seamless in the way they explain how changing societal needs affect what kind of money people use and how it is transacted. In depicting human figures and landscapes the illustrations are somewhat generic, but the pictures of various currencies are detailed and usually life-sized, and the format is large and spacious. Appended material includes various anecdotes about money, but there is neither an index nor a bibliography.

Stephanie Zvirin

SOURCE: A review of *The Story of Money,* in *Booklist,* Vol. 89, No. 13, March 1, 1993, p. 1233.

The ancient Sumerians invented the idea of making money from precious metal; Ethiopians accepted salt as money; and Yap islanders used round stones, some as large as 12 feet across. These are but a few of the intriguing facts in this nicely orchestrated balance of art and information. Clear, direct text outlines global economic development, zeroing in briefly on the evolution of America's monetary system. Sweeping double-page spreads and smaller paintings add a sense of story to the facts, and there are plenty of finely detailed pictures of money to inspect—a Spanish piece of eight, an English 10-pound note, a Chinese coin with a square hole in its center. The book's final roundup of curious facts will be fun to browse. As it has good potential for classroom use, this is well worth attention.

Dot Minzer

SOURCE: A review of *The Story of Money,* in *School Library Journal,* Vol. 39, No. 4, April, 1993, p. 137.

A successful, readable presentation of a complicated subject. Using a historical perspective, Maestro traces the development of trade from its earliest beginnings among wandering tribes, through the arrival of the marketplace and barter system, to the adoption of various mediums of exchange. She notes the origin of paper money and its lack of early success, followed by the early years of our country and the establishment of the U.S. Mint and the Federal Bureau of Engraving and Printing. An explanation is given as to how coins are minted and paper currency is printed, cut, starched, and circulated. Cashless money (checks and credit cards) is explained as well as the advent of the automated teller machines. Additional information, including a description of the most common U.S. coins and bills and some units of exchange for other countries, is appended. Giulio Maestro's meticulously drawn watercolor illustrations brighten each page. His sketched versions of early coins are clear and well detailed. Written in narrative form, this title does not provide as much information as [Neale S.] Godfrey's *The Kids' Money Book,* which uses a question-and-answer format; however, it is a windfall for whole-language classrooms and for nonfiction pleasure readers.

📖 IT FIGURES!: FUN FIGURES OF SPEECH (written by Marvin Terban and illustrated by Giulio Maestro, 1993)

Molly Godley

SOURCE: A review of *It Figures!: Fun Figures of Speech,* in *School Library Journal,* Vol. 39, No. 11, November, 1993, p. 121.

An enjoyable and informative title. Terban introduces

metaphors, similies, onomatopeia, alliteration, hyperbole, and personification. Maestro's cartoons reinforce the material and help readers to understand the concepts fully. Like the pair's other collaborative efforts on the English language, such as **Superdupers! Mad as a Wet Hen, I Think I Thought,** this one makes working with words play. Upon using this humorously presented book, children will truly improve their styles of writing.

Julie Corsaro

SOURCE: A review of *It Figures!: Fun Figures of Speech,* in *Booklist,* Vol. 90, No. 7, December 1, 1993, pp. 689-90.

Emphasizing ways in which readers can improve their writing, a master of children's wordplay tackles six of the most frequently used figures of speech—similes, metaphors, onomatopoeia, alliteration, hyperbole, and personification. In each of the well-organized chapters, Terban includes a clear definition of the figure of speech, familiar and lesser-known examples from folklore and literature, writing exercises, and ways to avoid pitfalls such as clichés and mixed metaphors. As in the author and illustrator's other lively books about language, Maestro's small, comic-style drawings are interspersed throughout the lucid text. A good choice for whole-language classrooms.

RIDDLE CITY, USA: A BOOK OF GEOGRAPHY RIDDLES (written by son, Marco, and Giulio Maestro, and illustrated by Giulio Maestro, 1994)

Hazel Rochman

SOURCE: A review of *Riddle City, USA: A Book of Geography Riddles,* in *Booklist,* Vol. 90, Nos. 19 & 20, June 1 & June 15, 1994, pp. 1827-28.

Puns on place-names are funny, even those you've heard before. What city hatched in Illinois? Chick-ago. What was the river called after the wedding? Mrs. Sippi. On each page, there's a riddle about a city, state, river, or famous place, with a garishly colorful cartoon that picks up the literal images of the wordplay. The answer to each riddle includes a snippet of information or an anecdote, sometimes serious, sometimes silly. After the groans and giggles, kids may go to the clear double-page-spread map of the U.S. at the front of the book. Playing with nonsense in names is a way to discover the fascination of geography facts and the fun of language.

Linda Greengrass

SOURCE: A review of *Riddle City, USA: A Book of Geography Riddles,* in *School Library Journal,* Vol. 40, No. 7, July, 1994, pp. 111-12.

An ambitious enterprise that has uneven results. The Maestros (father and son) present 60 original riddles in-

volving geographical references to the 50 states. Bright, colorful cartoons provide clues to the answers, and a U.S. map offers even more help. Some of the puns that form the basis for the riddles are amusing and understandable, while others require much more of a stretch. It is unlikely that even the most geography-conversant child will be able to solve many of the entries without extensive poring over the map. Even when the "answers" have been figured out, some of the place names won't make sense or the humor will be too obscure for average youngsters. This is by no means an essential purchase, but most collections can always use a new riddle book, and one that throws in a little geography can't hurt.

EXPLORATION AND CONQUEST: THE AMERICAS AFTER COLUMBUS: 1500–1620 (1994)

Cyrisse Jaffee

SOURCE: A review of *Exploration and Conquest: The Americas After Columbus: 1500–1620,* in *School Library Journal,* Vol. 40, No. 9, September, 1994, pp. 232-33.

This companion to **The Discovery of the Americas** provides an interesting discussion of the European exploration and conquest of the "New World." The author carefully explains that, "The great gain of one people was the great loss of another" and traces the disastrous effects that the Portuguese, Spanish, English, French, and Dutch had on the native peoples of the Americas, while acknowledging the benefits the Europeans enjoyed—gold, land, rich natural resources, and power. North, Central, and South America are discussed, as are the beginnings of the African slave trade. Detailed descriptions of the different native cultures are not provided—the focus is on European politics and rivalry—and there are no chapter divisions, which makes the information somewhat difficult to digest. Although the text is occasionally blunt and dry, this is still a good introduction to a complex topic from a multicultural perspective, beautifully illustrated with lush watercolor and colored-pencil drawings.

Carolyn Phelan

SOURCE: A review of *Exploration and Conquest: The Americas after Columbus: 1500–1620,* in *Booklist,* Vol. 91, No. 5, November 1, 1994, pp. 503-04.

A sequel to **The Discovery of the Americas**, this oversize book discusses the exploration of the Americas from 1492 to 1625. The book's most outstanding feature is its full-color artwork. Large, double-page spreads give scope to dramatic landscapes, while smaller pictures on every page show events, places, and maps pertinent to the text. The text forms one long story introducing explorers such as Cortés, Pizarro, de Soto, Cabot, Verrazano, Cartier, Champlain, and Hudson as well as the founding of the Lost Colony and the Jamestown settlement. Throughout the book, the Maestros make clear that European exploration

From The Discovery of the Americas, *written by Betsy Maestro. Illustrated by Giulio Maestro.*

and colonization had disastrous consequences for Native Americans, who were destroyed by war, treachery, and disease. While it may not provide sufficient information for middle-grade students writing reports on individual explorers, this book provides a useful overview of the period in a format accessible to a wide age range.

📖 *MACHO NACHO AND OTHER RHYMING RIDDLES* (written and illustrated by Giulio Maestro, 1994)

Amy Adler

SOURCE: A review of *Macho Nacho and Other Rhyming Riddles,* in *School Library Journal,* Vol. 40, No. 11, November, 1994, p. 100.

"What do you call a he-man tortilla chip? A *macho nacho,*" of course. Although some of the more than 50 riddles with rhyming punchlines in this colorful volume are a bit of a stretch ("Which athlete has a hard serve? A *tennis menace*"), most of them are fun. In fact, the book's greatest asset is the author's final invitation to readers and listeners to write their own riddles, with a game that will draw out their creativity. While not an essential purchase, this slim volume, with its whimsical, full-page watercolor illustrations, has enough charm to entice children to open it and discover the fun inside.

April Judge

SOURCE: A review of *Macho Nacho and Other Rhyming Riddles,* in *Booklist,* Vol. 91, No. 10, January 15, 1995, p. 932.

A witty collection of riddles based on the traditional word game known as Inky Pinky, Stinky Pinky, or Hinky Pinky, in which the two-word answers rhyme. Although each riddle and its answer appear in close proximity on the same page, beginning readers will chuckle as they put on their thinking caps and guess the answer to such questions as "What did the egg laugh at?" ("A yolk joke.") Full-color, humorous, and brightly colored illustrations complement each riddle and give visual clues to help answer them. Directions for playing a game of Hinky Pinky are included.

📖 *BATS: NIGHT FLIERS* (1994)

Lisa Wu Stowe

SOURCE: A review of *Bat: Night Fliers,* in *School Library Journal,* Vol. 40, No. 12, December, 1994, p. 100.

Dispelling common myths and misconceptions about these amazing creatures, and replacing them with facts, is the primary goal of this attractive picture book. Basic information is given in language that will prove both interesting and readily understandable to young children. An effort is made to stress the wonder, beauty, and usefulness of the animals while downplaying the idea that they are weird or ugly. Pencil and watercolor illustrations are informative and appealing even though the colors are occasionally too vibrant. . . . All in all, the Maestros' book provides an accurate and appealing look at bats that is on a par with Millicent Selsam and Joyce Hunt's *A First Look at Bats.* Young readers will be fascinated by its straightforward presentation.

Kirkus Reviews

SOURCE: A review of *Bats: Night Fliers,* in *Kirkus Reviews,* Vol. LXII, No. 24, December 15, 1994, p. 1570.

Bat's aren't evil, just strange, and the bum rap they have received since day one is undeserved. To clear up some misconceptions: Bats do not attack humans, nor drink their blood; they are not filthy little creatures—on the contrary, they are quite clean; and they don't carry rabies any more than any other animal. The Maestros get up close and personal with these nocturnal ramblers, cover their physiology and life cycle, explain their living and eating habits, unravel echolocation, and give a glimpse of a few of the more than 1,000 different bat species. What emerges is a, well, not exactly cute, but at least a fascinating, intelligent beast, sweetly mammalian, and more effective than DDT in controlling the insect population. The watercolor-and-pencil illustrations are smartly dramatic without getting sensational.

An excellent introduction, told with warmth and care by Maestro. Bats couldn't have asked for a better public relations effort. Have you hugged a bat today?

THE VOICE OF THE PEOPLE: AMERICAN DEMOCRACY IN ACTION (1996)

Stephanie Zvirin

SOURCE: A review of *The Voice of the People: American Democracy in Action,* in *Booklist,* Vol. 92, No. 15, April 1, 1996, pp. 1358, 1360.

Colorful, amply detailed scenes will lure readers into this fact-filled book, which makes a good companion to the author/illustrator's **A More Perfect Union: The Story of Our Constitution**. In fact, this book starts with information about the Constitution as the backbone of our government. The text, straightforward without being stiff, does a masterful job of distilling a complicated subject. Coverage ranges widely—from the campaign and election process to distribution of power among the three government branches—and the eye-catching paintings, sometimes full page, convey the tradition and the dignity as well as the occasional hoopla. Several maps are included, as is a follow-up section of quick facts and related information. Not only a good source for information, this is also an energetic overview that may instill civic pride.

Publishers Weekly

SOURCE: A review of *The Voice of the People: American Democracy in Action,* in *Publishers Weekly,* Vol. 243, No. 15, April 8, 1996, pp. 69-70.

With election time drawing near, curious readers can turn to this handy primer for a better understanding of the electoral process, and of the origins and workings of American democracy. Distilling the broad and complex nature of their subject to its essence, this proficient author-illustrator team shows how the government has had to "grow and change to keep up with both the population and modern thinking." Among the topics explored in the detailed, anecdote-studded narrative are the responsibilities of the three branches of the federal government and the function of political parties. Versatile watercolor and colored-pencil illustrations capture a measure of the theatrics involved in a contemporary election. They also offer a balanced range of images from across the political and historical spectrum: impressive likenesses of a number of past and present political figures; postcard-like images of key government buildings; dramatic renderings of the aftermath of the Supreme Court's 1954 decision to integrate public schools; facsimiles of government documents; even whimsical campaign memorabilia (the Carter peanut coin bank) and a snowy scene on primary day in New Hampshire. Elementary teachers will find this an engaging supplement to American history textbooks.

Lucinda Snyder Whitehurst

SOURCE: A review of *The Voice of the People: American Democracy in Action,* in *School Library Journal,* Vol. 42, No. 6, June, 1996, p. 144.

In describing "American democracy in action," the Maestros first explain how our system of government differs from those of other nations. Next there is a history of the Constitution and the amendments, a description of the three branches of government, and then a detailed section on how a presidential election works. The book is in narrative form, not separated into sections. Although one topic flows smoothly into the next, the arrangement makes it a little difficult to find information on a specific topic. However, as everyone scrambles for sources in this election year, it is nice to find a full explanation of the process here. Each step is covered, including political parties, primaries, conventions, voting, and the Electoral College. There is, however, a factual error concerning the House of Representatives. The text states, "The size of the House of Representatives changes with the population. As the population increases, so does the number of Representatives." Although that is the way the House was originally organized, the membership is now set at 435. The number of representatives a state has may increase or decrease according to population changes in that state, but the total number remains the same. The vivid, exquisitely detailed watercolor-and-colored pencil illustrations have a great deal of appeal. They have the realistic detail of photographs, but are warmer and more inviting. It is unfortunate that a small mistake mars this otherwise well-done, handsome presentation.

THE STORY OF RELIGION (1996)

Kirkus Reviews

SOURCE: A review of *The Story of Religion,* in *Kirkus Reviews,* Vol. LXIV, No. 12, June 15, 1996, p. 902.

An illustrated synopsis of the genesis and basic ideas of each of the world's major religions, as well as of some minor ones. Among the back matter is a list of sacred books, another of major festivals, and an interesting compilation of the various renderings of the Golden Rule, a form of which exists in almost all systems of belief. Betsy Maestro (with Giulio Maestro) begins carefully, earnestly preaching the importance of diversity and balance, and taking for granted that religions are not handed down by deities but evolve from a people's own need to find meaning in life. She gallops through primitive religions, and hits her stride when she begins telling about the actual beliefs and histories of various cultures, beginning with the Chinese. Given the space limitations of the picture-book format, these are elegant and precise pieces. Giulio Maestro's beautiful illustrations are done in an array of styles, often reflecting the motifs and palettes of the culture under discussion. Most children will want to know more, but there is no bibliography nor list of further reading. Still, this is, in many ways, a revelatory work and a provocative introduction to a complicated subject.

Publishers Weekly

SOURCE: A review of *The Story of Religion,* in *Publishers Weekly,* Vol. 243, No. 31, July 29, 1996, p. 86.

By beginning with humankind's earliest religious beliefs and ending with humanity's organization of these beliefs, the Maestros lead children on a whirlwind tour of the world's great religious traditions. They begin by pointing out that, despite the diversity of religious traditions, human questions about the creation of the world and the meaning of death are universal. They move from animistic beliefs of early tribal religions to the mythic religious structures of ancient Egyptian, Greek and Roman religions to the monotheism of Judaism, Christianity and Islam and the polytheism of Hinduism and Buddhism. The authors weave the beliefs, myths and practices of each religion into a narrative tapestry that, they believe, demonstrates the unity lying beneath the diversity of all religions as well as the dynamic character of these religious traditions in today's world. Included in the book are brief sections describing the sacred texts, festivals and holidays. There is also a short description of other religions, such as Zoroastrianism, that are not included in the book itself, and the Maestros list the various ways in which different religions express their own versions of the maxim "All things you want people to do to you, do so to them." Color drawings of the gods, founders and important practices of each religion, like a Hindu family offering a sacrifice at their home shrine, bring these religions to life.

Elizabeth Bush

SOURCE: A review of *The Story of Religion,* in *Bulletin of the Center for Children's Books,* Vol. 50, No. 1, September, 1996, pp. 23-4.

It's no wonder that, at only forty-eight pages from title to index, this ambitious work hardly fulfills its promise. Following some obvious opening comments on the human condition ("Humans spend a good deal of time thinking. All people have ideas and beliefs, but they do not always share the same ideas and beliefs"), Maestro breezes over "early" or "primal" religions from Asia to the Americas. Remarks such as "All early religions were polytheistic" call for fine-tuning, while summaries of specific religious cultures are too broad to be informative ("Civilizations in the Americas, such as the ancient Maya, also believed in many gods and goddesses. The deities of sun and moon were greatly revered, and calendars and rituals were based on their activities"). Each of the "great world faiths" receives slightly more detailed treatment, with a brief history, a cursory look at rituals, and an honest effort to set it within a chronological and philosophical framework of world beliefs. Mixed-media art offers a visual introduction to important religious landmarks and images, but too often

the captions fail to point out their significance (e.g., "Athena," "a tripod jug and goblet," "a heavenly dragon disk"). The author's staunch defense of religious plurality ("The fact that in this world there are so many people following so many different paths to God shows that there is no one right way") is bound to raise hackles in some faith communities but will appeal to others. Undemanding readers looking for a few basic facts and a lot of browsable, if unconnected, art may find what they want here.

Jane Gardner Connor

SOURCE: A review of *The Story of Religion,* in *School Library Journal,* Vol. 42, No. 9, September, 1996, p. 218.

Using the same large format as the Maestros' ***The Discovery of the Americas,*** Betsy Maestro has written a fine basic introduction to religion. It is quite an ambitious effort to look at the development of various beliefs in a way that can be understood by fairly young children, but she succeeds admirably. Beginning with early polytheistic beliefs in multiple spirits or gods and goddesses, and their usual strong link to nature, the author moves on to introduce Taoism and teachings of Confucius, Hinduism and Buddhism, Judaism, Christianity, and Islam. Even though the coverage of each is only a few pages, the author clearly explains the development of the religion and its major tenets. She takes the viewpoint that all religions are equally valid, and tries to show ideas and customs that are found in most faiths, thus showing children the diversity of beliefs in the world and encouraging tolerance and understanding. The text is written as a long essay rather than being broken into chapters, but there is an index at the front of the book. Giulio Maestro's art tries to capture the artistic tradition of the dominant culture of each religion discussed while showing major symbols or important events. This means that the book may have less artistic unity than most of his books, but it meshes very well with the text. The different styles reinforce the uniqueness of each tradition. An attractive, interesting, and informative title.

📖 OUR PATCHWORK PLANET: THE STORY OF PLATE TECTONICS (written by Helen Roney Sattler and illustrated by Giulio Maestro, 1995)

Mary Harris Veeder

SOURCE: A review of *Our Patchwork Planet: The Story of Plate Tectonics,* in *Booklist,* Vol. 91, No. 12, February 15, 1995, p. 1081.

The best nonfiction takes a topic that could be dull and makes it fascinating. Here, as appropriate for a book on plate tectonics, readers will almost be able to feel the ground move under their feet. After a slightly slow beginning, the book takes off, with a combination of illustrations and text making it possible for readers to see the planet in an entirely new way—by the motion that is constantly going on. Photographs taken by satellite and enhanced by computer technology help make the global perspective visible. Instead of fixing on particular volcanoes, mountains, or earthquakes, Sattler conveys the movement of the whole, showing plates that resemble "vanilla wafers on top of chocolate pudding." A list of further readings is appended.

Elizabeth Bush

SOURCE: A review of *Our Patchwork Planet: The Story of Plate Tectonics,* in *Bulletin of the Center for Children's Books,* Vol. 48, No. 8, April, 1995, p. 286.

In this brief but thorough discussion of plate tectonics, Sattler covers collision and subduction, rifting, faulting, and related earth-building processes. The text moves smoothly from description of plates, to plate movement and resultant geomorphology, to consideration of the impact of plate movement on future human activities. Eschewing overworn accounts of earthquake and volcanic devastation, Sattler enlivens the hard science with subtler suggestions for Earth's distant future: "New York City may be sitting on . . . a fault" that could split Long Island in two; "either the Great Basin area or the Rio Grande Rift will someday separate enough to open a new ocean." Report writers and students seeking material to supplement textbook lessons will particularly appreciate Maestro's comprehensible diagrams and maps, as well as the index and reading list which features a host of readily accessible periodical articles. This title will claim a place even in basic science collections and will be useful to readers well into junior high.

Additional coverage of the Maestros' lives and careers is contained in the following sources published by Gale Research: *Contemporary Authors New Revision Series,* Vol. 37; *Major Authors and Illustrators for Children and Young Adults;* and *Something about the Author,* Vol. 59.

Robert Newton Peck
1928-

American author of stories and poetry for young adults.

Major works include *A Day No Pigs Would Die* (1972), *Millie's Boy* (1973), *Hang for Treason* (1976), *Clunie* (1979), the *Soup* series.

INTRODUCTION

Robert Newton Peck is an exceptionally prolific writer for young adults and middle graders whose works include moving coming-of-age stories set in realistically depicted rural surroundings and lighthearted comical works often recommended for reluctant readers. In such works as *Millie's Boy, Justice Lion* (1981), *Spanish Hoop* (1985), and particularly in the work for which Peck is best known, *A Day No Pigs Would Die,* the author is praised for his sensitive portrayal of the struggles that often attend the movement from childhood to adulthood, for his poetic yet realistic portrayal of both the beauty and the harshness of the natural world which is so integral to his characters' lives, and for his effective use of colloquial speech. In works such as *Soup* (1974) and its many sequels, on the other hand, Peck is known for producing simplistic stories based on broad, often slapstick humor. Many of Peck's works draw, explicitly or implicitly, on his own childhood in rural Vermont, and he has stated that his greatest fear for young people today is that they seem ignorant of nature and the ways of animals.

Biographical Information

The youngest of seven children born to illiterate farmers in rural Vermont, Robert Newton Peck was the first in his family to attend school. There he met Miss Kelly, his teacher, as well as Luther Wesley Vinson, nicknamed Soup, the boy who would become his best friend; like Peck himself, Miss Kelly and Soup appear as themselves in Peck's *Soup* books. Peck's father slaughtered pigs to earn the family's living during the harsh years of the Depression; both his father and his father's profession would be featured in *A Day No Pigs Would Die,* a book some consider a classic among coming-of-age novels. Like many of his characters, Peck believes in hard work and staying close to nature. He is also a music lover, and plays "self-taught ragtime piano, by ear, sometimes by fingers." It is this love of music to which he attributes the frequent appearance of songs in his books for young adults. Peck enjoys going to schools to talk to the children who read his books, and he encourages kids to write to him, promising a response. "Life is fun. It's a hoot and a holler," Peck has said. "If you can't revel in America and enjoy all the wonderful Americans you meet, you wouldn't be happy in Heaven or even in Florida."

Major Works

Peck's reputation was established with his first publication for young adults, a novel called *A Day No Pigs Would Die.* In this book, a character named Rob Peck makes the difficult journey from age twelve to thirteen, a year during which he loses much of what means the most to him and learns how to be a man in the terms demanded by his family's Shaker beliefs. Much has been made of the novel's graphic opening scene, in which young Rob helps a cow give birth, and nearly gets killed himself in the process. The unsentimental portrayal of life on a farm in the 1930s, symbolized by this scene, stands against what critics found to be heart-rending scenes of emotion when, for example, Rob must help his father kill the pet pig he was given as a reward for helping the cow give birth. *A Day No Pigs Would Die* is considered "an honest, unpretentious book" by Jonathan Yardley, and its worth continues to be defended on the grounds of its literary merit.

Indeed, *A Day No Pigs Would Die* has become the standard against which most of Peck's works for young adults are measured. And since the early 1970s, when *A Day No Pigs Would Die* was first published, the author has produced another fifty books. Among the most popular are *Soup* and its dozen or so sequels. Like *A Day No Pigs Would Die* only in that it centers on a character who shares the author's name, *Soup* and those that followed—including *Soup and Me* (1975), *Soup for President* (1978), *Soup in the Saddle* (1983), and *Soup on Ice* (1985), among others—chronicle the idyllic side of life among poor, rural people in the Vermont of the 1930s, and have earned comparisons to Mark Twain's *Adventures of Tom Sawyer*. Fans of the series praise its nostalgic portrait of old-time childhood hijinks and note that these books are ideal for reluctant readers, particularly boys, while *Soup*'s detractors sometimes find its down-home humor a little too coy, its episodic plots nonsensical.

Awards

Many of Peck's books have won awards, most notably *A Day No Pigs Would Die,* which received *a Book World*'s Children's Spring Festival Award Honor Book citation, 1973, and the *Media & Methods* Award (paperback), 1975, was named one of American Library Association's Best Books for Young Adults, 1975, won the Colorado Children's Book Award from the University of Colorado, 1977, and was named one of New York Public Library Books for the Teen Age, 1980, 1981; *Millie's Boy* was chosen as one of *New York Times* Outstanding Books, 1973, and a Child Study Association of America's Children's Book of the Year, 1973; *Hang for Treason* was chosen as one of New York Public Library's Books for the Teen Age, 1980, 1981, 1982; *Soup for President* garnered the Mark Twain Award, 1981; *Clunie* was named one of New York Public Library's Books for the Teen Age, 1980, 1982; and *Soup on Ice* was chosen as one of Child Study Association of America's Children's Books of the Year, 1987.

GENERAL COMMENTARY

Paul Janeczko

SOURCE: "Confessions of an Ex-Kid: Robert Newton Peck," in *English Journal,* Vol. 68, No. 5, May, 1979, pp. 18-19.

For a moment I thought I was in Hollywood. I rubbed my eyes and looked out the window at the russet and gold leaves of Maine's dwindling autumn, then back at the six-foot-four man standing in front of me wearing jeans and a matching jacket, and sporting a slightly soiled white cowboy hat. I quickly checked his feet. Sure enough: mule-ear boots! "Hi, Paul," he said, smiling broadly. "I'm Peck." He pumped my hand as if he were trying to raise water from an ancient Vermont well. "Nice to meet you," I mumbled. The man has an uncanny resemblance to Henry Fonda in *The Ox-Bow Incident.* And his speech! He even *sounded* like Fonda (a Fonda who had taken elocution lessons from James Stewart, no less!).

When I asked him if we could go somewhere quiet to do the interview, he scowled. "There's no need for that. Let's just walk around and swap lies. You can write whatever you want." So we did walk. Peck waved to all the teachers and librarians participating in the Festival of Children's Literature sponsored by the University of Maine at Farmington. I cursed myself for not having a photographic memory.

When I asked him where biography ended and fiction began in *A Day No Pigs Would Die* and the "Soup" books, he stopped and rested a big hand on my shoulder. "Much of those books are autobiography." He winked at me and added, "With a garnish or two of fiction thrown in."

"What about Miss Kelly?"

"Oh, she's real. Still alive in Vermont. She's ninety-four now, you know." He had a faraway look in his eyes. "Good old Miss Kelly . . . I can't imagine anyone meeting her on the street and saying, 'Good day, Winifred.'" He laughed. "No sir. In fact, when that dear woman dies and goes to heaven, Saint Peter's going to say, 'Miss Kelly, nice to see you. We were expecting you.' And she's going to say, 'Peter, you may be seated. I'll take over now.'" Again he laughed, this time thumping my shoulder.

After we had walked on a little while, I asked him how Soup got his name.

"Well, his real name was Luther, but you know how kids go through a phase when they hate their names? Well, that was Soup. Whenever his mom stepped onto the back porch and called, 'Looother,' why he never answered. He was that embarrassed. So his mom started shouting, 'Soup's on,' when she wanted him in a hurry. Then she shortened that and just called, 'Sooop.'"

Peck stopped to autograph some books, returned to find me scribbling notes I was sure I was going to forget. "Look, I'm going to talk to some kids at a grammar school around here. Want to come along? Good," he added before I had a chance to accept his invitation. Fifteen minutes later we were at Wilton Academy.

He shambled into the small auditorium with the shiny smooth floor. A hundred sixth graders, on squeaky folding chairs, waited in ambush. When they heard the rear door open, they turned and broke into applause and cheering. Peck flashed a wide grin then pushed back his white hat. Kids love the good guys.

For the next sixty minutes, he entertained those kids with tales of Vermont, jokes, and questions. Even did his famous bandana trick. He made a fist, extending his index finger toward the ceiling. Covering his fist with a red bandana, he told the kids, "You're going to have to help me on this one with some counting." "One . . . two . . ." they shouted, and on "Three!" he whipped off the bandana to reveal . . . two fingers! The kids groaned, then cheered madly.

He surely ruffled a few feathers when he suggested that the kids not be rude if the library didn't have any of his books. He simply told the kids to set fire to the wastebaskets! And I could see the English teachers wince when he told the kids to raise their right hands and promise never to write an outline. "A good piece of fiction is rarely based on an outline," he assured his audience. "People who write outlines are people who never learned to write English."

Before leaving the auditorium, he gave his audience some advice about writing: "Don't *tell* a story. That's *boring!* Your teachers don't want words. They want pictures. They want you to *show* them a story. That's what you've got to do." As he walked to the car, he told me, "I love turning kids on to books and writing. What a treat."

Over coffee in the university snack bar, Peck talked a little about writing. He feels he owes his readers "a clean, strong book. I am not Walter Matthau who would say any four-letter word in a kid's movie just to make a buck." As a writer of books of local color and local history, Peck faces a problem that a writer of books with contemporary settings doesn't face. "The key is to keep the talk, scenery, gear, and activities in the period. That's the tough part. But," he added with a smile, "it's also the fun." He told me that a great many Pecks were born and raised within hearing of Fort Ticonderoga's cannons. "In my early exposure to history," he recalled, "the fort was Miss Kelly's central topic." Peck feels that his best book is *The King's Iron,* but he claims *Eagle Fur* as his favorite. "I'm Benet," he confided to me.

We parted company: Peck to socialize and autograph more books, me to deliver my afternoon conference. When I saw him again several hours later, he was standing at the front of a packed dining hall ready to deliver his after-dinner "speech." But anyone who came expecting an organized, polished speech must have been surprised because Peck bounced around and covered a lot of ground. He shared jokes (one listener later likened him to a "stand-up comedian in a night club"), stories, and insights. Yet all were moved by his sensitivity.

For openers, he gave a little of his background. He claimed to be an "expert skier, a dismal dancer. During World War II I was a machine gunner. When that madness was over, I worked as a lumberjack, in a paper mill, and as a hog killer. It's not easy writing four books a year, but it sure beats killing hogs. I love playing ragtime piano. I've written and published twenty-two songs, and written a whole mess of TV commercials and advertising jingles."

The author recalled that his writing career really got started years ago when he had to write a poem for Miss Kelly. The poem, about his barn cat, was called "Sarah's Wondrous Thing."

He said that the planet Earth has "only one problem: human population. If human life is sacred, *all* life is sacred. To me, morality is how life acts. Nothing more. As a male, I was created to breed, hunt, and wage war. I am probably a bad parent, as parenthood is the hardest job in the world. So many of us perform it so badly."

Bits of New England wisdom punctuated his remarks. "Success is built out of failure," he reminded us, "like making saddles." Later, he said, "Every day of your life you have to do something you're afraid of or you'll turn to jelly."

The quietest moments came when he made an offer and a promise to his audience. "*You* find the student who's a misfit. The kid who doesn't know where he's going. The one no one cares about. You get that kid to write me a letter. *Don't* do it for him. Let *him* do it or it won't work. And I promise you that I will answer that kid's letter. And maybe, just maybe, for one day he'll be somebody. He'll be able to hold his head high. Will you do that for me? I promise I'll write back. And you know what a promise means to a Vermonter, and to the son of Haven Peck."

Following the banquet, after he had signed more copies of his books, we sneaked off to Fiddleheads, a local pub. There I asked him what he enjoys in life besides writing and turning kids on to books. "Well," he said, taking a swallow of his dark beer, "I am a lucky man because there are a lot of things I enjoy. I've been damned lucky, Paul. I enjoy my wealth and my fame, and being Director of the Rollins College Writers' Conference. I enjoy my family, my land, my animals, and my new Florida home. But there are other things that I enjoy, like a nip from my horse or a kiss from my daughter. I like to watch my linebacker son cream a halfback, to see my wife brush her hair, to remember Rollins College, to weep as I finish writing a novel . . . to sing barbershop and play ragtime piano." He paused for another swallow of beer, then continued. "And to look west at a sundown sky and be aware of what Mama told me: that gratitude is the sweetest prayer."

He was staring at his hands spread out on the oak table, when a woman approached. "Oh, Mr. Peck," she gushed, "I just love the way you write for kids. Are you an ex-teacher?" Peck looked up at her. "No," he said softly, "just an ex-kid."

TITLE COMMENTARY

📖   *A DAY NO PIGS WOULD DIE* (1972)

Christopher Lehmann-Haupt

SOURCE: "City Life and Country Life," in *The New York Times Book Review,* January 4, 1973, p. 35.

Robert Newton Peck's charming and simple *A Day No Pigs Would Die,* [is] a memoir in the form of a novel about the author's upbringing in the Shaker tradition on a Vermont farm in the 1920's. Indeed so perfectly fused are the understated rhetoric and action of Mr. Peck's story that if it achieves the popularity it probably deserves, it will seem ripe for the kind of parodies that Richard Bach's *Jonathan Livingston Seagull* has lately been getting.

For so determined has Mr. Peck been to dramatize in both his story and his dialogue the lack of "frills" of the Shaker Way that he often flirts with making his characters seem ludicrously stolid and simple. And were one not caught up in the emotion of his story, one might well give over to giggling. (Boy: "Papa, is that the mission they preach on at the meeting?" Papa: "It is. And every man must face his own mission. Mine is pigs.")

But you need have no fear of giggling, because on a first reading at least you'll find yourself caught up in the novel's emotion from the very opening scene, which I will somewhat hesitantly describe here as the young narrator's account of how he almost gets killed helping a cow to give birth to two bull calves, but which I can guarantee nevertheless will grab and not let you go. And though at times Mr. Peck seems on the verge of sentimentalizing the relationship of young Bob and the pig he receives as a reward for helping that cow to calve, there is really not an ounce of sentimentality in the entire book. (Coyness, yes; sentimentality, no.)

Quite the contrary: it is a stunning little dramatization of the brutality of life on a Vermont farm, of the necessary cruelty of nature, and of one family's attempt to transcend the hardness of life by accepting it. And while . . . there is no rhetoric about love—in fact nobody in *A Day No Pigs Would Die* ever mentions the word love, or any other emotion, for that matter—love nevertheless suffuses every page.

Jonathan Yardley

SOURCE: A review of *A Day No Pigs Would Die,* in *The New York Times Book Review,* May 13, 1973, p. 37.

What can you say about an 8-month-old pig that died? Not a great deal, as it happens, and fortunately Robert Newton Peck has wasted few words in this modest and affecting little book (it seems more a reminiscence than a novel) about a 12-year-old boy who learns some hard but useful lessons.

The boy, like the author, is named Robert Peck, and like the author he is a member of Vermont's Shaker community. In the spring of his 13th year he does a neighbor a favor, and is rewarded with a newborn pig, a female, which he names Pinky and comes to love greatly. Not much happens until the end, when Pinky proves barren and—barren female pigs being of little use to poor, thrifty people—is slaughtered. But in a quiet way Rob Peck learns about such matters as the dignity of his father, an unlettered but hardworking and loyal man, the value of neighbors and the importance of the fences that separate his

land from theirs, the preciousness of possessions that are honestly earned, and the permanence of the simple but honorable Shaker tradition—"Shaker Law"—to which his family adheres.

A Day No Pigs Would Die has been promoted in the style of *True Grit* and *Addie Pray,* and probably it will appeal to readers who are hooked on easy nostalgia. But there is more to it than that. It is sentiment without sentimentality—no easy feat—and it is an honest, unpretentious book. Doubtless many adults will like it, but it would be good reading for older children, even though (or perhaps, these days, *because*) it gets faintly gamy in a passage or two.

The Times Literary Supplement

SOURCE: "Swine Fever," in *The Times Literary Supplement,* No. 3728, August 17, 1973, p. 945.

The elegant narrow format, and the charming vignette by Faith Jacques at each chapter's head, are a fit tingly old-fashioned dress for Robert Newton Peck's little tale—or a camouflage for an extended and treacly short story, depending on your degree of cynicism.

As a reward for saving a neighbour's cow, a boy on a Vermont farm is given a pig which eventually proves to be barren. The Shaker-sect family, who live by the direct work of their own hands, can not afford to feed a useless animal, and the pig has to be killed. Accepting this is depicted as the boy's first step towards manhood; at the close of the book, his father has died and the boy is about to take charge of the family and farm.

A Day No Pigs Would Die is told in a first-person vernacular which, though it saltily conveys Shaker turns of speech, poses an insoluble problem to the author. The "I" who begins "I should of been in school that April day" (which is fair enough), goes on to identify himself in sympathy and in fact with the immediate, unrelenting, farming grind. That first-person *could* not also write "Most of the land lay open to the sun; and it was soft and brown, ready to be mated with seed", which is strictly poetry farming, and deeply sloppy at that.

M. Kip Hartvigsen and Christen Brog Hartvigsen

SOURCE: "Haven Peck's Legacy in *A Day No Pigs Would Die,*" in *English Journal,* Vol. 74, No. 4, April, 1985, pp. 41-5.

Robert Newton Peck's *A Day No Pigs Would Die* was generally acclaimed when it was published in 1972. Unlike one reviewer who cautioned readers that the novel was "heartwarmy," most other critics recognized the power of the spare, episodic story of a hard-working Shaker father, Haven Peck, bringing his young son, Rob, to manhood. Since its publication, the novel has appeared on nearly every "best" list of young adult fiction. In addition, according to two recent surveys, *A Day No Pigs*

Would Die is a frequently taught novel in college-level young adult literature courses. For a number of reasons, the novel deserves its acclaim and popularity: the sincere, evocative reminiscences; the Twain-like humor arising from a twelve-year-old narrator's naiveté; the complex characterizations; the gritty depiction of farm life; the stripped-down, yet rich style. These achievements, which establish Peck as a gifted storyteller, combine with a theme of substance—a boy's carefully guided passage into manhood and his acceptance of adult responsibility.

Rob Peck's initiation into adulthood is markedly unlike many in contemporary young adult fiction. While many other novels show young people groping for direction and answers and finding little but confusion and alienation from adults, *A Day No Pigs Would Die* portrays a loving, loyal family, who prepare a son for the harshness *and* beauty of life, instilling in him the values to cope with and appreciate that life. In fact, Peck's novel may achieve the status of a contemporary young adult classic, an accolade deserved in large measure because of Peck's moving portrait of a father's quiet ways teaching his son about the necessities of duty and of living in harmony with nature, one's family, and neighbors.

The structure of the novel seems deceptively simple. At first Peck may appear to have done no more than relate— albeit vividly—incidents about a Shaker youth growing up on a Vermont farm. A closer look, however, reveals a careful framing of incidents underscoring the cycle of life. Peck's story begins on an April day with a ripping tale of young Rob singlehandedly helping a neighbor's cow, Apron, give difficult birth to her calf. Peck describes vividly Rob's efforts to pull a partially delivered calf from its mother's womb. Before Rob is finished, the cow twice drags him, bare-bottomed, through dirt and stickers, once by a pant leg he has tied to the unborn calf's neck and a second time by his arm, which ends up being chomped to the bone. With birth at the center of the first chapter, Peck's novel is underway. At novel's end, the story will complete the cycle begun here, passing from this incident of birth to death, and from death to rebirth. In the interim, Rob's critical thirteenth year is one of learning, and his teacher is his father.

If there is one thing young Rob Peck knows, it is hard work. After a few days' recovery from his ordeal with Apron, Rob hobbles rather deliberately to the kitchen where his father welcomes him back with a "Good. . . . I can use a hand, and you look ready as rain." Even though Rob "limped a bit more than need be . . . it didn't do a lick of good"—he is shortly out resetting a post in the fence. He works side by side with his father, never evading hard work. Indeed, as he walks past the Widow Bascom's one day and finds her needing help toting some flower pots, Rob responds, "It wasn't chore time yet, and I could spare the work."

Being a hard worker is a virtue for a Shaker boy. But Haven Peck knows that Rob must be more than that to be a man; a man who manages a farm and himself must feel a responsibility toward the work he does, a dedication Haven Peck exemplifies unwaveringly. When Rob tells him that it seems "what we have most is dirt and work," his father explains,

> True enough. But it be *our* dirt, Rob. This land will be all ours, in just a few more years. As to the work, what matters is that we have the back to do it. Some days I get the notion that I can't knife even one more of Clay Sander's pigs. Yet I always do, 'cause it's got to be done. It's my mission.

In the course of the novel, Haven not only teaches Rob the hows of farm life—how to build a pig pen, how to yoke an ox, how to plow a field, how to smoke an apple orchard, how to slaughter hogs—he also clarifies for Rob the "earthy reasons" behind their work, the practical, deeply rooted cause for carrying out their tasks. For instance, after Rob receives Pinky, a piglet, from his neighbor Mr. Tanner as a reward for saving Apron and her calves, he can hardly see past the excitement of possessing something of his very own. But his father reminds him that he'll have to take care of Pinky and that she must have a pen away from Daisy, the family cow, and the ox, Solomon.

"Why that?" [Rob asks.]

"Close pork will curdle milk, boy. That's plain common."

"I wonder why that is."

"It's just a law."

"Shaker law?"

"Yes, but deeper than that."

Haven explains to Rob that the law allows for the instincts of a cow and pig: "It goes back when Daisy and Pinky were wild. Daisy knows that Pinky and her kind have teeth. Tusk. And pigs are meat eaters, cows ain't. . . . It's like Shaker law. It all goes way back."

Rob begins to stand up proud under his share of the responsibility, explaining carefully to Pinky at one point, "If'n I'm not to home come chore time, Hell won't have it. Papa gets mighty stirred up over that. Right he should. Chores are my mission, not his." By the time Rob goes to Rutland Fair, he is not only a good worker, he is a responsible one. Accompanying the Tanners, he sees what work needs to be done and vigorously ties into it. Mr. Tanner even reports to Haven that he deserves a ribbon for "best-behaved boy." Upon arriving home, Rob realizes on his own that his father has assumed some extra responsibility in chores while he's been gone, and Rob solemnly tells him, "I'm beholding." Finally, when Pinky must be killed, Rob never questions the earthy reason behind the tormenting job. Once again his father stands beside him as they work to show him "what being a man is all about, boy. It's just doing what's got to be done."

By the end of *A Day No Pigs Would Die,* young Rob is yoked well to his work. He completes his chores on the day his father dies because they have to be done and because, too, the rhythm of the work lets him know that life goes on. He notices how his father's tools are almost golden where his father held them, as if they were "gilded by work." Work has become for him, as Haven Peck taught him, a mission, something to be grateful for because as a person sees and does "what's got to be done," he also sees purpose to his existence.

A second accomplishment of Haven Peck is teaching Rob to understand nature and people. Rob learns to accept nature's laws, which encompass predatory violence as well as soul-stirring beauty. And he learns the higher laws of love and tolerance, which enable him to live in harmony with other people.

A Shaker farm boy has many occasions to observe the predatory instincts in animals: a weasel preying upon chickens, a crow preying upon a frog, stronger chickens beating weaker chickens out of squirrel meat. Through his observations, Rob comes to understand what might seem cruel and senseless. He watches a hawk prey upon a field rabbit and listens to the rabbit's death cry, a sound that "don't forget very easy. Like a newborn baby . . . even a call for help, for somebody to come and end its hurting." But as he watches this scene, Rob imagines the hawk afterwards landing at his nest with his kill, his hungry brood waiting for warm rabbit, and he understands something of the predatory laws of nature.

In a natural way, Rob comes to understand his own position in the predator chain, never questioning the honor of his father's occupation as a hog killer, his father's hopes of killing a deer to sustain the family through a New England winter, or his own liking for tanned rabbit from his mama's oven and nutmeats taken from a hunted squirrel's stomach to spread on a chocolate cake. Never in Peck's novel do readers glimpse waste or wanton killing. Rather, farm people like the Pecks take from nature what is necessary for their survival and regard themselves as having a high calling in animal husbandry and crops. "'We farmers,' says Mr. Tanner, 'are stewards. Our lot is to tend all of God's good living things, and I say there's nothing finer.'"

Peck the novelist has expressed his concern [in *Twentieth-Century Children's Writers*] that young people understand their relationship with nature, that they know "pork chops are not made by Dupont out of soybeans. Pigs are killed because man is a predator; all of Nature is predatory." But there is more to learn about nature than the violence of the predator chain: his simple Shaker ways allow Rob a transcendental appreciation of nature as well. For example, some images that linger in Rob's mind are the goldenrod color of a late summer valley—"like somebody broke eggs all over the hillside"; a flower that seems to smile at the sun; the music of wind blowing through trees; and Rob's favorite sight, the "pink and peaches" color of a sunset that makes him feel clean all over even if he had worked all day. For every harshness in nature,

Rob learns there is a compensation—a scene of beauty, a renewal.

Rob's learning about nature's ways parallels his education about what he should do to get along with others. Haven Peck's subtle example is of principal importance in his son's education about people, some of which, again, finds its basis in the natural world. A conversation about fences early in the novel defines Haven's code of conduct toward others. One spring day as Rob and his papa reset a post in the fence separating the Tanner and Peck farms, Rob comments,

> "Fences sure are funny, aren't they, Papa? . . . I guess that humans are the only things on earth that take everything they own and fence it off."

> "Not true," Papa said. . . . "A female robin won't fly to a male until he owns a piece of the woods. He's got to fence it off. . . . Lots of times when you hear that old robin sing, what he's singing about is . . . keep off my tree. That whistle you hear is his fence."

Haven continues that making fences is "a peaceable war," and fences prevent misunderstandings—a fence sets men together, not apart." Haven Peck's seemingly simple observation provides a profound basis for his own code of social conduct: do what needs to be done to set men together, not apart. In fact, several episodes have a divisive conflict at heart, providing Rob with ample opportunity to see his father's code tested against the realities of life.

On one occasion, one of the most dramatic, Rob is awakened in the middle of a blustery night and asked to accompany his father to a nearby church. May Hillman has come to the Peck home for help, reporting that her husband, Sebring, has gone to a nearby churchyard to dig up the graves of his illegitimate daughter and the child's mother, wanting to make claim on what is rightfully his. Tragedy and sin had shrouded their deaths. The child's mother, Letty Phelps, had drowned her baby and afterwards hanged herself. In addition, Haven Peck's involvement in the events goes beyond neighborly concern—Letty is Haven's kin. Thus the episode provides Haven with a worthy test of his code. Such conflicts often provide in life as well as in literature the motivation for vengeance.

The Pecks, once at the churchyard, are caught up in an emotional scene. Encountering Seeb Hillman, Haven announces his intentions to take him home. Hillman responds, "Not 'til this work is done. And the sin and trouble is ended for all to see and all to know." Haven's first response is in his own interest: "She's my kin . . . and I don't aim to see kin dug up in the cover of nightfall. Best you drop your shovel." Haven learns, however, that Hillman's intention is to recover only the box of the child and decides to help Hillman after all: "Let's get our young ones home and rested proper." Later, on the way home, Hillman expresses to Haven his sorrow about Letty. Haven responds, willing to forgive and forget, "It's over and done."

In other episodes, Haven's sensitivity to others—as well as Rob's mother's sensitivity—abounds, for instance when Haven brings his injured son a whistle and some gum; when he cautions Rob not ever to speak of being barren in front of his Aunt Matty, a woman never able to bear children; when Rob's mother chides Aunt Carrie for having her nose where it shouldn't be—a prurient interest in the Widow Bascom's relationship with her new hired hand: "What goes on under a neighbor's quilt is naught to me," Mrs. Peck says; and when, in the novel's climactic scene, Haven Peck can hardly bear the pain he brings his son when circumstances make the slaughter of Pinky necessary.

Rob's test of how well he has learned the values of hard work, responsibility, and harmony with nature's laws and mankind comes in the climactic scene of the book, the slaughter of Pinky. He is called upon to share the responsibility for a piece of distasteful work that must, nevertheless, be done. He must accept the inevitable conclusion that a barren pig must be used for meat by a poor Shaker family. Thus, he must accept his own mission and the way animals, even a beloved pet, fit into that mission. Perhaps most significantly, Rob must forgive his father for insisting on the killing, showing that he is as sensitive to his father's heartbreak as his father is to Rob's.

The slaughter of Pinky is surely one of the most riveting scenes in young adult fiction and one that has not gone uncriticized. Jean Kelty in "The Cult of Kill in Adolescent Fiction" [in *English Journal*] condemns *A Day No Pigs Would Die* because a boy must kill to become a man and because the characters take lightly brutal birth and death scenes on a farm. To dismiss the novel because of its violence, however, is to interpret the novel's scope too narrowly and to misread the characters' reactions to violence. Violence in *A Day No Pigs Would Die* is not for its own sake; it is never gratuitous. On the contrary, the novel's climax is infused with meaning and emotion, not the least bit hackneyed or sentimental. Peck carefully prepares his readers for this scene, making it a dramatic representation of all that is not fair about life, those hateful parts of experience that cannot be altered but must be faced.

Throughout his year with Pinky, Rob's hope is to rear her as a brood sow; in that way she will have a very long life. But Rob's father has taught him that there is little if any relationship between what people want and need and what they get. "Need is a weak word," he has told Rob. "Ain't what you need that matters. It's what you do." By late fall, Rob knows that Pinky is barren and she must be slaughtered; she has become a frill, and there's no room for a frill in a Shaker family. He accepts that. At one point he calmly observes to his father, "It isn't fair, is it, Papa?" to which his father replies, "It isn't a fair world." Rob's recognition of this injustice does not save Pinky, but Rob by this time is mature enough to see the harsh realities of life and stand up to them.

Throughout the slaughter sequence, rendered with enough detail to accord the scene the stature necessary to make it

stand for Rob's passage into manhood, perhaps it is the image of Haven Peck that finally haunts the reader as much as Rob's broken heart. He gives his son one last intense lesson on responsibility and love. By this point in the story, readers can imagine Haven Peck's heavy heart as he sharpens his butchering tools. Death is his living, and yet he is not insensitive to it. Especially when he is called upon to slaughter his son's pet pig, he must summon courage to carry out what needs to be done. Finally, all he can say to Rob is, "Help me, boy . . . it's time."

Understandably, Rob wavers. "Papa . . . I don't think I can." Haven Peck's answer may seem callous—"That ain't the issue, Rob. We have to." But of course it is not. The father, sensing his own imminent death, knows his son will have many tasks to do by himself that will be unbearable, that will be unfair, but that must be done. Rob must help kill the pig to show that he can do what life asks of him, but in the way Haven Peck performs his task, he also shows a sensitivity to his boy's hurt. Rob has never seen his father work so fast. "Papa was breathing the way no man or beast should breathe. . . . I knew his hands must of been just about froze off; but he kept working, with no gloves." It is as if he cannot pause or he himself will not be able to go through with the killing and butchering.

Rob passes part of his test; he helps his father kill Pinky. But at first he hates his father for it: "I hated him for killing her, and hated him for every pig he ever killed in his lifetime." He is bitter that the only thing he could ever look at and say "mine" was now only a "sopping wet lake of red slush." He weeps and admits to his father, "Oh, Papa. My heart's broke." And in his father's reply readers see what he had been trying to teach Rob all along—to love and cherish people and help them to carry out the tasks in life that have to be done: "'So is mine,' said Papa. 'But I'm thankful you're a man.'"

After moments of silence, Rob passes the crucial test of doing what should be done to set men together, not apart. He realizes his papa killed Pinky "because he had to. Hated to and had to. And he knew that he'd never have to say to me that he was sorry." The scene closes with a mutual love and understanding between father and son. Haven Peck tries to brush away his son's tears with his big, rough, cold hand, still dripping with Pinky's blood. Rob takes the hand, holds it, and kisses it again and again, "so he'd understand that I'd forgive him even if he killed me." The closing image of the chapter, Haven Peck "rak[ing] the sleeve of his work shirt across his eyes," shows a man shedding tears of hurt, of love, and of gratitude for a mature son.

By the end of the novel, a year from its beginning, the seasons are starting the cycle anew. On the third day of May, Rob finds his father dead in the barn. By that time, the life cycle continues in a new generation because Rob is ready to assume responsibility for the farm. In Rob's actions on the day of his father's death, readers see that he has learned his lessons well and is ready to carry on his father's work. "Papa. . . . it's all right. You can sleep this morning. . . . I'll do the chores. There's no need to work any more. You just rest." Now Rob is the one to feed all the animals, to do the morning work that always must be taken care of on a farm. He is the one to make sure his mother is comforted, to be the example of sensitivity. He is far away from the boy of chapter one who ran from school because his Shaker ways were ridiculed. He is selfless, doing what has to be done, and trying to make it easier for those around him.

As Haven Peck is laid to rest and the novel ends, the impression that holds the readers' minds and hearts is not so much the boy who has reached manhood but the father who lived in such a way that the boy has grown so well. Rob's pride in his father and love for him shine in every encounter in the book ("I want to be like you, Papa. . . . And I will. I'll be just like you.") and are most noticeable when Rob names the people who came to pay his father tribute at his funeral. "They'd come because they respected him and honored him. . . . He always said he wasn't poor, but I figured he was just having fun with himself. But he was sober. He had a lot, Papa did." Before his death, Haven Peck prepared his son for the life he would need to lead and left him a legacy of wealth, as shown in this speech:

> We have one another to tend to, and this land to tend. And one day we'll own it outright. We have Solomon here to wind up a capstan and help us haul our burdens. . . . We have Daisy's hot milk. We got rain to wash up with, to get the grime off us. We can look at sundown and see it all, so that it wets the eye and hastens the heart. We hear all the music that's in the wind, so much music that it itches my foot to start tapping. Just like a fiddle.

The enduring, unshakable values are those of a courageous display of duty to others and to tasks at hand and a vision that appreciates the natural order of life, be it fair or unfair, beautiful or ugly. Haven Peck taught his son that life is not always fair, that work is often dirty business, that often things have to be done regardless of conflicting need or desire. And yet, by showing Rob the love, beauty, humor, and joy mixed into daily tasks, the harsh lessons are not overwhelming. Nature gives as much as it takes, and the same hard work that wearies the body invigorates the soul as people work together to build a life.

PATH OF HUNTERS: ANIMAL STRUGGLE IN A MEADOW (1973)

Kirkus Reviews

SOURCE: A review of *Path of Hunters: Animal Struggle in a Meadow,* in *Kirkus Reviews,* Vol. XLI, No. 4, February 15, 1973, p. 199.

Close up views of various small animals, most seen in the process of catching and eating each other or avoiding being caught. A shrew who is "constantly plagued by his own ruthless appetite" and would starve after five or six hours without food slaughters a snapping turtle, tears off the head and eats the "deliciously warm, soft internal organs." An owl swoops up a mother rabbit who emits a "futile death cry . . . the only noise she had ever made in her lifetime—one agonized note." A terrier chases a blacksnake who disgorges in his flight a still live fieldmouse he has just swallowed. A muskrat dies after chewing off his own foot to escape a trap—and is found by a boy who feels "a slight tremble in his gut, as he knew the rapture and the regret of his first kill." This last might evoke in readers a slight tremor of protest, and Peck can be a bit annoying in his tendency to anthropomorphize (referring to an ant who "could not have lowered herself into the position of a worker" which would be "beneath her dignity") and editorialize (when a mouse kills half the litter she can't feed, "it was the only thing to do and she did it . . . the sacrifice of half her litter was a sign of her responsibility to life"). But his observations are acute and subtly charged, he conveys the tension in the air and the rapidity of heartbeat with unobtrusive precision, and [illustrator Betty] Fraser's fine line black and white drawings are similarly low-keyed, exact and respectful.

Beryl Robinson

SOURCE: A review of *Path of Hunters: Animal Struggle in a Meadow,* in *The Horn Book Magazine,* Vol. XLIX, No. 4, August, 1973, p. 393.

Many a neophyte naturalist has begun his career with an intensive study of a small area, observing closely the life cycles and interactions of plant and animal species. Designed to stimulate interest in animal life in one small meadow, the author has described a considerable number of life cycles to be observed from one spring to the next. A black bat, a brown beetle, a flicker, a marmot, a skunk, a blacksnake, a mouse, a snowshoe rabbit, a great horned owl—and because there is a pond in the meadow—a turtle, a muskrat, a frog, an opossum are some of the animals—large and easily observed, or small and furtive—that live out their lives in the meadow. At the time that their activities are being recorded, they are all involved in some aspect of their life cycle: mating, birth, survival, death. Details are explicit and often poetic as mates are found, homes are built, and the young are born. The struggle is continuous, the hunt for food fierce; and death stalks life in a never-ending pattern. Free from sentimentality, objective although sensitive, a coherent narrative despite the many lives described, this is first-rate nature writing. The black-and-white sketches imaginatively placed interpret the text visually.

Beryl B. Beatley

SOURCE: A review of *Path of Hunters: Animal Struggle in a Meadow,* in *Appraisal: Science Books for Young People,* Vol. 7, No. 3, Fall, 1974, pp. 33-4.

This small book contains a remarkable saga of wildlife in a meadow, a wood, a pond, a toolshed, all around a house and near men and dogs. It is told by a master storyteller (see *A Day No Pigs Would Die*) in such a vivid style and using such choice language that the reader is held captive and believes himself right there, watching, experiencing, feeling as a snapping turtle pursues a bat for his dinner, a love-sick marmot searches for a mate, and a skunk experiences surprise as he peeks out of his overturned elm tree following a storm. We are afforded a glimpse of the field mouse's precarious life. The black snake disgorges his live prey before our very eyes as he turns on his adversary. The account is an incessant struggle for survival. It seems obvious to me that these tales of a cycle of seasons in the life of many of the animals found in northeastern United States, both large and small come from careful personal observation. The story, although fictionalized and humanized, contains for each animal such a wealth of information, interwoven in so a gripping tale that the reader is compelled to read every word. The line drawings which appear on almost every page add greatly to the pleasing format and give distinction to the book.

D. A. Young

SOURCE: A review of *Path of Hunters: Animal Struggle in a Meadow*, in *The Junior Bookshelf*, Vol. 39, No. 2, April, 1975, pp. 126-27.

Children accustomed to the charm of puppies and kittens and with the general concept of animals as furry, if not cuddly, friends going gently about their quaint business in the calm and peace of the country landscape will be jolted into another world if they read *Path of Hunters*. Here, in all its savage violence, is the bloodstained tapestry of life and death as the hunter in turn becomes the hunted. Driven by the needs of insatiable hunger the fieldmouse eats its young, to be swallowed in turn by the blacksnake. The possum kills the rabbit, and is attacked by the tawny owl. The muskrat bites through the bone of his own leg to free himself from the steel trap set by the greatest predator of them all, man.

Birth, hunger and death are the main threads woven inexorably into that pattern called, euphemistically, the balance of nature. The writing is direct and compelling. The visit to the pet shop will never be quite the same again, and the awareness of the harsh reality beneath the quiet of the meadow will not easily be lost.

📖 *MILLIE'S BOY* (1973)

The Booklist

SOURCE: A review of *Millie's Boy*, in *The Booklist*, Vol. 70, No. 7, December 1, 1973, pp. 382-83.

In the gripping opening scene sixteen-year-old Tit (for Titmouse) Smith is wounded and his prostitute mother is killed by a scattergun blast in the dark. To avoid the County Farm Tit leaves town before he is fully recovered to find his unknown father and true identity. Tracked by wild dogs on his way to his mother's home town Tit is rescued by Fern Bodeen, a strapping woman doctor who patches his reopened gun wound and takes him into her home. Romantic interest is provided by Fern's lovely niece and suspense is sustained through Tit's suspicions about his mother's murder and his final violent run-in with the man who fathered him. The weak ending and few graphically violent scenes are balanced by well-done characterizations, dialog, and pre-turn-of-the-century New England background, and although this lacks the depth and impact of *A Day No Pigs Would Die* it is a holding story laced with adventure and humor.

Tom Heffernan

SOURCE: A review of *Millie's Boy*, in *Children's Literature: Annual of The Modern Language Association Seminar on Children's Literature and The Children's Literature Association*, Vol. 4, 1975, pp. 207-08.

Millie's Boy continues the use of the turn of the century southern Vermont setting that Robert Newton Peck introduced in *A Day No Pigs Would Die*. The earlier book was a bit of family history; it described isolated rural life in a residually Shaker community, and delivered a heavy dose of ruralism somewhat on the order of descriptions that Homer Croy might have written years ago, but colored by an overly sentimental examination of the boy narrator's psychology. Even worse was the effort to turn the boy into another Huck Finn by giving him cute ways of expressing his incomprehension of the world. Colorfulness via naiveté has its limits and they are as readily detected by young as by old readers.

Millie's Boy, however, is something else. Time and setting are more or less the same as in *A Day No Pigs Would Die,* but the protagonist is the son of the village whore and the book opens with him being shot and injured by the unseen figure who has just murdered his mother. Definitely a stronger cup of tea.

There is plenty of adventure in the book that is well calculated for young readers: quest [for] the mother's murderer, escape from ravenous coydogs, near death in a hole in the ice of Lake Champlain, and life with a female country doctor of a Marjorie Main cut.

The main quest of the young hero, however, is not for his mother's murderer, but for his own father. He finds him and learns that he is the most vicious man in the countryside, well known to be an unprosecuted murderer. When the father announces his intention of raping a girl with whom, unknown to him, the son is in love, the father's words do justice to the deed: ". . . it'll draw enough loving out of me to make do all winter. I won't be able to walk without help until the four of March. Neither will she. Because if there is one way I aim to do this Christmas, it's to split that little vix into two even pieces. One in each hand." Two impulses strike the boy—one to knife his father to death, the other to castrate him with telegraph wire.

For whom is this book intended? Is it written on the assumption that innocence ends earlier than we usually think? Or that it ought to? If the book could pass as an adult novel, it could simply be called one. But it isn't. The point of view and the framing of the story clearly indicate that it is a children's book.

There is something else in the book that raises a question about its suitability for young audiences. The raw treatment of sex and the extreme violence in the book may not make it unfit for every young reader. But there are scenes between the hero and Amy, the ward of the country doctor he is living with, which have that peculiar teasing quality of the prurient movie. For example, she sits down on his bed in her nightgown; they have a pillow fight; she gets a feather down the back of her nightgown; he gets it out. Facing sex is mature, but playing with titillation is neither mature nor useful. It is no more commendable in a book for adolescents than in a book that capitalizes on the adolescent fantasies of adults.

James T. Henke

SOURCE: "The Death of the Mother, the Rebirth of the Son: *Millie's Boy* and *Father Figure*," in *Children's literature in education,* Vol. 14, No. 1, Spring, 1983, pp. 21-34.

Millie's Boy opens with the murder of 16-year-old Tit Smith's mother. Illegitimate Tit enters their darkened apartment only to be felled by the shotgun blast that kills Millie. Sheriff Gus Tobin discovers the severely wounded boy and nurses him back to some semblance of health, intending eventually to deposit him in the "County Farm," a home for paupers and orphans. Tit, however, discovers that his mother had come to Cornwall, Vermont, from Ticonderoga, "her rightful home," and learns her real name, Millicent Sabbathday. He slips out of Cornwall and heads across the backcountry for "Ti," where he intends to find the rest of his identity.

On a backwoods road, the hero is saved from a pack of vicious coydogs by Dr. Fern Bodeen. She packs the boy into her wagon and heads for Ticonderoga, where she lives with her orphaned niece Amy. But Tit is not out of the woods yet, either literally or figuratively. During the journey, he manages to fall into the icy December waters of Lake Champlain and has to be rescued a second time by Dr. Bodeen.

Tit does arrive in Ticonderoga, but Robert Newton Peck does not allow his hero nor his reader much of a breather. Shortly after the youth's arrival, he and Amy accompany Fern to the Adirondacks, where she has been summoned to treat accident victims in a logging camp bossed by George Washington Ostrander. At the Ironville camp, the boy's quest draws to a close. He learns his full name, discovers that Ostrander is his father, and quickly finds out that the man has become little more than an "animal in pants." After Millie had left Ticonderoga, pregnant with Tit, the logger had married. A few years later, his wife

and daughter had been butchered by drunken Indians, and grief and rage has turned Ostrander into a human brute. Intuitively, Tit distrusts and fears his father, and his intuition proves correct. The logging boss tries to rape Amy. In a violent fight, the hero attempts to protect the girl, only to be beaten to the ground by Ostrander. About to be choked to death by the stronger man, who may be unaware that the boy is his son, Tit is rescued for the final time. Turk, the dog that the crazed logger has brutalized and has trained to kill Indians, flashes from out of nowhere to seize its hated master by the neck. George Washington Ostrander dies in the jaws of the living embodiment of his own sick bestiality.

Obviously, young readers will not find *Millie's Boy* boring fare. Robert Newton Peck has given them a fast-paced adventure/detective thriller. It is this last feature of the novel, its detective-story trappings, that the teacher can turn to advantage in the classroom. When I discussed *Millie's Boy* with several groups of junior high readers, I began by talking about Tit Smith as a detective whose chore is to piece together a number of clues that will reveal his identity. Just so, Peck invites his reader to play sleuth by providing him with a number of "clues" that, if carefully deciphered, will reveal a "hidden" significance to Smith's story. I asked the students to find the answers to four questions: when was the hero born, when does he discover his full name, at what time of year does the story end, and in what year does it end? Then I asked the students if they could detect a pattern to these chronological clues and, if so, could the pattern hint at an imaginative way to interpret the literal details of Millie's murder and Tit's wounding?

The "mystery" was easily solved. Gus Tobin tells the hero that he was born on the "twenty-two of April," the Easter of 1882. Amy tells Tit his full name, Timothy Sabbathday, on Christmas Eve. (She discovers the name recorded on the flyleaf of the Sabbathday family Bible.) The boy writes a letter to Gus dated "7 April," and "a week or two later"—on or about the hero's 17th birthday—the former sheriff arrives in Ticonderoga, bringing the story to a close. The year is 1899. The pattern, readily perceived by the students, is one of rebirth and rejuvenation marked by the celebration of Christ's resurrection, his nativity, spring, and the death of one century and the imminent birth of a new.

Cued by the novel's chronology, many of my young investigators detected the rebirth theme operating in the book's explosive first chapter. Searching for Millie, Tit enters the total darkness of their apartment. simultaneously, there is a blinding flash of light and a deafening roar. Suddenly, he finds himself "curled up" on the floor in a fetal position, dazed, confused, and in pain. The boy wallows in "the warm slime" of his own and his mother's blood, unable to tell where "mine began or hers quit." Literally, of course, the author is describing a brutal murder and assault. Figuratively, however, the description also suggests the process of birth seen first from the viewpoint of the newborn infant thrust from the dark, quiet security of its mother's womb into a world of glare, noise, pain, fear, and confusion.

That this reading is the product of Robert Newton Peck's imagination and not the fancy of his reader is made evident by other details in the work. After Gus Tobin discovers the wounded Tit, he rushes the boy to his office, swabs down the naked youth as one would a newborn, and then removes the buckshot pellet from his stomach. Then, the sheriff cradles the wounded hero in his arms and offers strange solace: "let this pain remind you, boy. Your ma took worse pain than this when she bore you. . . . Remember her hurt, just like your gut hurts now." Later in the novel, Peck again links the murder and assault to Tit's actual birth. Fern is telling the boy about "the time that Millie got herself in trouble . . . in a family way." Young Smith tells us, "My stomach hurt. A slow pain started somewhere in my gut (near the bullet hole)." Finally, twice in the novel, the wound in the boy's stomach is described as a second navel.

Symbolically, then, the mother's death occasions the rebirth of the son. Or perhaps it would be more accurate to say that Millie's death begins Tit's rebirth; for apparently, Peck sees that rebirth not as a single event, but as a protracted process, the hero's quest "to find out who I really was." This seems evident from the continuing references to birth and rebirth—both literal and figurative—that mark various milestones in the boy's search. For instance, when he discovers his mother's real name (and thus his own family name) on the county farm admissions slip filled out by Gus, Tit tells us that he feels "all naked and fresh-born." Later on the way to Ticonderoga, Fern pulls him from a hole in the ice of Lake Champlain. His hands are so numb that he must clamp the team's reins, which she has thrown him, between his teeth. With this "umbilical cord," Dr. Bodeen, who has helped birth her share of babies, pulls the helpless youth back into life. Expertly, she cuts the frozen clothes from his body, and as Tit says, "in less than a minute, I was naked as birth." In the brief romantic interlude in the middle of Peck's novel, he may give his reader yet another provocatively allusive episode. Amy slips into Tit's room late one night. The two giggle and joke, awkwardly exploring their attraction for one another. Amy has brought the hero a gift—an apple! To be sure, one balks at the Adam and Eve parallel, especially when this apple episode culminates in a coltish pillow fight. Nonetheless, the Adam and Eve story is relevant here. Just before this scene, Fern had warned Tit against his obsessive need to find his father: "Maybe you shouldn't try to fly from one busted nest [Millie] into another [his father]. Because when a young bird leaves the nest, he leaves it permanent. The only nest he has after that is the one he helps build for the next clutch of eggs." Peck appropriately follows this sage admonition on the necessity for a new beginning with the allusion to Adam and Eve, the archetypal parents who were cast out from the security of the Garden and begot the human race. Even a rough parallel to the significance of Eve's apple may be at work here. She gave Adam to eat of the fruit from the tree of the knowledge of good and evil. At the Ironville camp, Amy gives Tit the knowledge of good, his full name. She also inadvertently causes him to see the face of evil, the vicious lust that she unwittingly inspires in his father.

In the Ironville camp, the process of the hero's rebirth is completed. Tit's hair is "orange-carrot-red." When he sees that Ostrander's hair is the same color, he suddenly realizes that the logging boss is his father. The boy tells us that "I felt a funny feeling. It was like getting born." But Tit does not take off his hat and reveal himself. Something about Ostrander makes him feel uneasy. So, this momentous discovery is still only a part of the process of rebirth, not the completed act.

Later that Christmas Eve, Tit stands with Amy and Fern around a huge yule log, singing of "the long-ago birth of a child on a cold and snowy evening." He is struck by his feelings of love and kinship for the two women. Now, he is able to sever any last vestiges of emotional dependence on Ostrander. He says, "As we stood there singing, I forgot all else. I wasn't even Tit Smith anymore, but the new me didn't need no father or no name." The hero has shed the false identity that has stunted him and the even falser notion that a father and a "real" name can provide him with a genuine identity. He comes to recognize that that which makes one a person is one's own humanity, the self within. Later, he will describe his new awareness this way: "what I was looking to hitch myself to is right inside me, so I found the only man that matters." With this hard-won knowledge as midwife, Tit is finally reborn, a fact symbolically underscored by Peck when he has Amy present the youth with her discovery of the young man's name, Timothy Sabbathday: "Sabbath" for the beginning, the first day of the week; "Timothy," which means convert, one "born again.". . .

Robert Newton Peck has given his readers a protagonist who is "heroic." In the frontier mode, young Smith is tough, shrewd, and gutsy. He is a doer, not a doubter. And in spite of the scoffs directed at the late John Wayne, the type is ingrained in our cultural imagination. Not surprisingly, then, Peck focuses not on the psychology of his hero's quest, but on its physicality. In addition, he sets that action against the backdrop of the familiar ritual celebrations of birth, hope, and rejuvenation: Christmas and Easter. These celebrations, of course, are in one sense a reflection of that more primal cycle of nature in whose inevitability and regularity mankind takes comfort. Tit ends his narrative: "The hard of winter was over. Deep in the earth, the April corn was almost green." So, much more than a story of an individual's rite of passage, Robert Newton Peck's novel is the symbolic celebration of all boys, of all adolescents, and their relationship to the inexorable rhythms of life that insure that one day the child will blossom into an adult and the hard winter will be over.

📖 *SOUP* (1974)

Kirkus Reviews

SOURCE: A review of *Soup,* in *Kirkus Reviews,* Vol. XLII, No. 5, March 1, 1974, pp. 244-45.

Rob's friend Soup can talk him into just about anything—

rolling downhill in a barrel, smoking cornsilk in an acorn pipe, and even cheating old Mr. Diskin by hiding a stone inside a tinfoil ball they're selling him for movie money. But at the end when Rob cries because "I only get hurt" while Soup gets new orange shoes which squeak "just like you have birds between your toes," it's Soup who insists on swapping shoes on the first day the new pair is worn to school. Peck starts the ten separate homespun reminiscences of his Vermont childhood with crafty attention getters such as "I don't think we ought to do it, Soup" or "'You're afraid.' 'No I'm not.' 'Then what are you standing there for?'" The mood ranges from rapture over the dewy September taste of a silver football valve to more earthbound reactions to Janice Riker, a twelve-year-old with "the body of a hunchedback, bowlegged ape and the brainpower of a bean," who would tie you to a tree, gag you with one of her smelly old stockings, and then stuff a bug up your nose. These nostalgic sketches all seem somehow closer to Tom Sawyer's time than to our own, but Peck clearly remembers how it was.

The Booklist

SOURCE: A review of *Soup,* in *The Booklist,* Vol. 70, No. 15, April 1, 1974, p. 878.

Peck strings together a series of entertaining, autobiographical recollections centered around boyhood good times with his friend Soup. Soup's real name is Luther Wesley Vinson, but as Peck recalls, "I called him Luther just once, which prompted Soup to break me of a very bad habit before it really got formed." Each incident reawakens familiar images of the past as Peck tells of their throwing apples from sticks and inevitably breaking a window, rolling down a hill inside a barrel, or sneaking a smoke from cornsilk "tobacco" in an acorn pipe. Neighborhood characters add color to the tellings. Janice Riker, the only person Soup is afraid of, is expert at captive and torture games; Aunt Carrie constantly wishes thrashings on Peck, but we are treated to her comic downfall as a trussed-up captive in a downpour. Charles Gehm's freshly evocative pencil sketches perfectly capture, and even intensify the moods of the vignettes. Adults will relish this look at a misty past; hopefully children will do the same, especially those who liked *A Day No Pigs Would Die.*

Marilyn Sachs

SOURCE: "Mementos from the Past," in *The New York Times Book Review,* May 5, 1974, p. 40.

Reminiscing is pretty much an adult pleasure. Watch out! If you find yourself harking back fondly to the Beatles or The Days When the City Streets Were Safe or even the Vietnam war, you're probably beyond the pale and on your way toward middle age. The older you get, the more you like to talk about your own childhood. This can create problems in a room full of adults where everybody wants to talk about his own childhood and nobody wants to listen to yours.

But it's not so bad for a writer—especially of children's books. Kids aren't generally going to talk about their childhood (except for my nephew Arthur, who can tell you what happened to him during his late fours), and they will put up good-naturedly with your reminiscing if you'll wrap a story around it.

Robert Peck proved himself a master of the genre with his moving and engaging book, *A Day No Pigs Would Die,* based on his own boyhood in rural Vermont during the twenties. With *Soup* he is back again for another go-round, but this time it doesn't work nearly so well. Soup is the name of Peck's best friend when he was a boy. Between them, one or the other is consistently drawn into mischief. There are 10 vignettes which deal with broken windows, rolling barrels, fistfights with bullies and other assorted pranks that fall under the heading of boyhood adventures. Several of the stories are funny, and one or two are touching but by and large there is a strained quality to the writing and a hearty wholesomeness to the book that is disappointing.

Zena Sutherland

SOURCE: A review of *Soup,* in *Bulletin of the Center for Children's Books,* Vol. 28, No. 2, October, 1974, p. 35.

Soup was Robert Peck's best friend during his boyhood, and this is an episodic account of some of the ploys and scrapes the two shared when they were in elementary school. There's a homespun humor and an aura of nostalgia about these rural anecdotes, but the first try at smoking, the confrontation with an irritated neighbor, or the contretemps with a school nurse all seem just a little too hayseed-cute, and the book lacks the variety of mood or tempo it needs to compensate for the omission of a story line.

FAWN (1975)

Kirkus Reviews

SOURCE: A review of *Fawn,* in *Kirkus Reviews,* Vol. XLII, No. 23, December 1, 1974, p. 1271.

Aside from the dappled title, this deceptively sleek small novel does manage to convey not only the pristine wilderness surrounding Fort Carillon (Fort Ticonderoga) in 1758, but also the despoilation of war. When the British march on the French-held fort (the distant bagpipes buzzing like insects), Fawn, son of a Mohawk outcast mother and an ex-Jesuit Frenchman, ponders the two ways of life: that of his father ("He is clever with thought, clumsy with things") and his deceased grandfather Old Foot from whom he learned a nerveless, watchful stoicism. Fawn steals in and around the gathering conflict, observes the doomed French and British, some Yankees, some hated Hurons, and even makes a friend (surprisingly—and unnecessarily—the young Benedict Arnold). His French father elects to fight or die with his countrymen but Fawn is somehow driven to rescue him. At the close father and son meet and part from the ruins of their home, both freshly secure in their hitherto unrevealed love for one another. Peck manages to avoid for the most part the spavined speech usually set forth as early Indian, and in spite of the sentimental overlay, the story moves with ease toward a predictable (young adult) audience.

Henry M. Yaple

SOURCE: A review of *Fawn*, in *Library Journal*, Vol. 100, No. 6, March 15, 1975, p. 603.

This novel, set during the Anglo-French battle for Fort Ticonderoga in 1758, concerns the plight of a French/Mohawk boy. Fawn Charbon fears that the superior British forces will annihilate his father and the other French defenders, but his Mohawk heritage makes it impossible for him to fight with the French and their Huron allies. As the result of some farfetched circumstances, Fawn enlists the young Benedict Arnold in a plan to save his father. However, the British fail to defeat the French, and Fawn's father is saved. The historical details of this novel, including young Arnold's presence, are accurate, but though the narrative is vivid, plot and characterization are weak. Light fiction that will entertain teenage and adult readers.

Sue Ann Jargstorf

SOURCE: A review of *Fawn*, in *School Library Journal*, Vol. 21, No. 9, May, 1975, p. 66.

Fawn is the son of the scholarly Jesuit Henri Charbon and grandson of the Mohawk Old Foot. When English soldiers try to wrest control of Fort Carillon from the French, Charbon enters the fort to share the fate of his outnumbered countrymen. Fawn, caught between two heritages, proclaims, "I am Mohawk," and, for three danger-filled July days in 1758, slips through the forest observing the battle preparations and savagery of the French, English, and Indians. Fawn kills to save a newly acquired friend from Huron torture; wraps and buries his father's books; and crawls through a drainage ditch to persuade Charbon to leave the doomed fort. Montcalm's French are the unexpected victors and Father and son meet, each changed by events. Lyrical prose, vivid descriptions, convincing characterization, and fast pacing make this a first-rate historical novel.

WILD CAT (1975)

Kirkus Reviews

SOURCE: A review of *Wild Cat*, in *Kirkus Reviews*, Vol. XLIII, No. 8, April 15, 1975, p. 457.

Wild Cat is the accurate, exciting and very bloody saga of a big city stray. The story of the little calico female, from the time she plops out of her mother's body "like an egg yolk" up through her own first litter, is superficially the same as any other life cycle story. But Peck doesn't leave the usual discreet distance between us and the visceral reality of an animal's life in the wild. You can actually smell the wet paper bag and garbage-filled alley that are the calico kitten's first homes and, when the kitten plays with an old golf ball that's lodged in a circular drain, the experience is dizzying for the reader as well as her. Nor does Peck spare us the violent details as the kitten's two brothers are eaten by a stray dog ("the tiny bones cracked into warm digestible fragments") or as she fights a death battle with a canny old rat or the rat's fate when it's eaten by a big white tom who happens along ("his fangs crunched into the spine of the rat . . . next he ate the rat's stomach and kidneys; and after that the rubbery yellow-white layer of body fat beneath the white belly fur"). Even those who accept all this on the grounds of realism may be disturbed by the Lawrentian treatment of the calico's subsequent love affair with the macho white tom ("his odor was strange, yet it was strong and comforting, the smell of a warrior and hunter" . . . "she relaxed to accept him, until his body flooded her with the hot rush of his seed"). Artistically *Wild Cat* is far superior to the usual tame, washed-out nature lesson; however the vivid specifics are added for dramatic as well as strictly documentary purposes, and readers who lack the stomach for this sort of thing needn't feel they're closing their eyes to reality. With excellent (and undisturbing) drawings by Hal Frenck, this is powerful, well done stuff, but not for the more tender-hearted youngster.

Eden Ross Lipson

SOURCE: "Here Kitty, Kitty," in *The New York Times Book Review*, May 4, 1975, pp. 37-8.

The saga of *Wild Cat* begins in the womb and birth canal of a mother cat who is wedged in an alley somewhere, and moves briskly from one trauma (trucks, siblings being eaten, crunch, crunch, by dogs) to another (sex, rats, loss of mate, plunge into river, birth.) The line drawings by Hal Frenck are tense and convincing. The text has a sensual enthusiasm sometimes reminiscent of old-style pornography: "Her body felt the pain and shock of her first touch of a male. But then she relaxed to accept him until his body flooded her with the hot rush of his seed."

These are not the usual itsypoo kitty-cat books for 8-year-olds who daydream of their pets in a pastel fantasy world and watch cat food commercials for reality therapy. And that's fine. Unfortunately these book-books have a relentless socialist-realist quality of didactic naturalism that is utterly humorless and unappealing. . . .

The Booklist

SOURCE: A review of *Wild Cat*, in *The Booklist*, Vol. 72, No. 1, September 1, 1975, pp. 44-5.

A sharply graphic narrative describes the harsh city existence of a wild calico cat. As a kitten she has a harrowing brush with the wheels of a diesel truck; other near-fatal encounters involve a scrounging dog and an attacking rat. More pleasant moments occur during the calico's partnership with a wild tom, the father of kittens whose birth brings the story full cycle. Peck's careful prose is vivid. His word choices effectively maximize a reader's sensory perception of events, resulting in a calculatedly realistic, sometimes gruesome, but unsensationalized animal biography.

John R. Pancella

SOURCE: A review of *Wild Cat,* in *Appraisal: Science Books for Young People,* Vol. 9, No. 1, Winter, 1976, p. 34.

The title of this book can be misleading. It is **Wild Cat,** not *Wildcat.* The publisher's note says this is a "sensitive, realistic, powerful story about a 'wild cat' who never knows the gentle touch of a loving hand." This may be understated. The opening paragraphs describe a birth, with the mother licking and eating the membranes, followed by another birth, on dirty rags, of a kitten that is deformed and defective. The mother eats this kitten along with the extra birth substance. This may be questionable fare for many children. It is realism, all right. A little later a kitten is trapped between the dual tires of a truck, dragged a complete circle and nearly crushed. More realism includes a hungry, one-eyed dog who eats one kitten whole. There are details about a first mouse kill and a fight to the death with a rat. The sensuous encounter with a big white tom, with the young female "hot with the sudden flush of maturity," and other vivid descriptions, leads the story full circle to another birth of kittens. This is wildlife in Manhattan, and teachers and parents should carefully consider whether to use the book with their children.

📖 *SOUP AND ME* (1975)

Kirkus Reviews

SOURCE: A review of *Soup and Me,* in *Kirkus Reviews,* Vol. XLIII, No. 20, October 15, 1975, p. 1186.

Peck obviously remembers the younger Robert Newton and his more daring buddy **Soup** with relish. They got into so much gol-durned trouble: shucking off their clothes for an early spring swim and having them stolen by old Janice Riker (she's the one with "hair like a Brillo pad, muscles like Tarzan . . . when she'd blow in your face, you'd swear she ate a toad for lunch"); building a manned torpedo out of an old "gallonized" iron tank to ram Janice's soap box racer. Later, Soup cuts Robert's hair and then patches up the mistakes by pasting locks back on with Pink Awful bubble gum. You can't completely resist these cow-licked rustics, and the holiday reminiscences—when the boys get stuck in the bell tower trying to ring Miss Kelly a Christmas salute, or nearly let an old turkey get the best of them before giving it to a poor family—work best because we expect a certain amount of sentimental indulgence at that time of year. If only Peck weren't

quite so taken with himself . . . he keeps *telling* us how cute these bratty boys are and you can't help wondering whether, like Soup, he's come to believe that he can sucker his friends into going along with anything.

Denise M. Wilms

SOURCE: A review of *Soup and Me,* in *Booklist,* Vol. 72, No. 10, January 15, 1976, p. 687.

These further episodes recollected from Peck's childhood lack the spontaneity and genuineness of the previous **Soup** collection. Here some of the earlier-met characters recede to the sidelines, and Mother and Aunt Carrie are generally one-dimensional enforcers of discipline; but the formidable Janice Riker reappears with a vengeance as she sinks the boys' clothing while they're stealing a forbidden swim in an icy spring pond. Later she gets her due when a neighbor mistakenly blames Janice for damage the boys have done to her garden while trying to wreck Janice's soapbox racer. A botched haircut, courtesy of Soup, and stolen pumpkins cause trouble for Rob, while Thanksgiving and Christmas are occasions for healthy sentiment. Overall, however, the humor is too obviously calculated to elicit a laugh; and Peck's indulgence in vivid, articulate description results in several overdrawn scenes and sometimes renders his homespun "so's" and "what says" out of place. The laughs—and there are a few—come almost in spite of the author's plans; readers hooked on his earlier memoirs will go along with this, though not as wholeheartedly.

Sister Avila

SOURCE: A review of *Soup and Me,* in *School Library Journal,* Vol. 22, No. 6, February, 1976, p. 48.

Fans of **Soup** will welcome further activities of the two mischievous country boys, Robert Peck and Soup. Written in the author's characteristic spare, humorous, and graphic style, the narrative moves from disastrous plots to get even with Janice Riker, the toughest kid in school, and an encounter with an enormous pumpkin on Hallowe'en, to a nearly catastrophic, aborted effort to give Miss Kelly, their beloved teacher, a unique Christmas present. The lively black-and-white illustrations enhance these fun-filled episodes.

📖 *BEE TREE AND OTHER STUFF* (1975)

Sister Avila

SOURCE: A review of *Bee Tree and Other Stuff,* in *School Library Journal,* Vol. 22, No. 3, November, 1975, pp. 81-2.

The author of **Soup** again reaches into his rural Vermont boyhood for its wealth of homey wisdom: "And what is my life worth? I know / It's just a rabbit track in snow.

/ At least a poet and a hare / Made tracks to say they went somewhere." The poems and their introductions relate the feelings of a boy brought up by plain people to have love for the simple life, the earth, and all living creatures. Covering a wide range of subjects, from Sarah's yearly litter of kittens to dust, tools, death, and rabbit trails, the poems are all enhanced by the rich vernacular of the poet's birthplace. A delight for readers of all ages and a treasure for teachers trying to inspire young poets to find beauty in ordinary things and events.

Arlene Stolzer Sandner

SOURCE: A review of *Bee Tree and Other Stuff*, in *Children's Book Review Service*, Vol. 4, No. 7, February, 1976, p. 63.

There is a rare combination of colloquial prose and refined poetry in this story about the author's experiences growing up in rural Vermont. The poems paint warm pastoral images, but some of the narrative in between poems is a bit too unpolished and crude for this reviewer's taste. The book is successful in its attempt to bring the reader close to the author's spirit of creativity and his sense of the simple joys of country life.

Beryl Robinson

SOURCE: A review of *Bee Tree and Other Stuff*, in *The Horn Book Magazine*, Vol. LII, No. 2, April, 1976, pp. 168-69.

The author celebrates his boyhood on a Vermont farm in a book that explores childhood memories of school, family and friends, hard work, the seasons, and death. A way of life and a philosophy of being are set forth clearly in a series of highly personal prose pieces, each followed by a related poem. The brief, informal comments are conversational in style and reflect the rural vernacular. Nostalgic, but not sentimental, they engender vivid, strong, sometimes earthy, often sensitive impressions of the land and the people who lived on it. Particularly moving are references to the author's father whose strength of character and capacity for hard work were first described in *A Day No Pigs Would Die*. One can experience the smells and sounds of barns, the feel of winter, the beauty of autumn; death is met by both man and beast. Respect for discipline and hard work is given frequent expression, but there is also fun. In the elegantly designed book, prose sections printed in black type alternate with poetry in sepia, and interspersed are many black line drawings that catch the various moods.

Curriculum Review

SOURCE: A review of *Bee Tree and Other Stuff*, in *Curriculum Review*, Vol. 16, No. 1, February, 1977, p. 17.

On a cold windy night a farm boy sleeps with his pig in the barn. The boy is Robert Newton Peck, author of *Bee Tree and Other Stuff*. Mr. Peck mixes prose and poetry in this book about his early life on a Vermont farm. The roots of his memory are the rhythms of his work and of the earth bound closely by a boy's will and strength. The chapter titles indicate the directions and concerns of this farmboy's life: "School," "Chores," "Hay," "Winter," "Death," "Hard Work," "Sun Dance," "Critters," and "Final Stone." Full page illustrations by Laura Lydecker introduce the chapters, and smaller drawings are placed between some of the poems and prose comments.

The subject matter of the poetry is reminiscent of that of Frost's poems. However, this poetry is unpolished; its message is simple: "A certain hallowed happiness I find / Inside my barn and silo, like a kirk. / There is solemnity and peace for me. / My chapel is a barn. My prayer is work." The various experiences employed to convey this message are Peck's "very property," built from the stones of his childhood. Like his stone fence, in the poems **"North Fence"** and **"Final Stone,"** these poems are mortarless and personal, set to the rhythm of a Vermonter's hands and back. Surrounding the circumference of his childhood, this book, like Peck's north fence, "sets men together, not apart."

HANG FOR TREASON (1976)

Kirkus Reviews

SOURCE: A review of *Hang for Treason*, in *Kirkus Reviews*, Vol. XLIV, No. 2, January 15, 1976, pp. 78-9.

The most arresting characterization here is surely fusty Ethan Allen, "good old boy" and land-grabber, whose rough and ready patriotism inspires Able Booker's short-lived interest in the art of soldiering. Able is the son of Tory farmer Noah Booker, who loses his own parents to marauding Indians in the eye-popping first scene here and who is finally killed along with Able's mother and sister when renegade Yankees come to burn his barn. In spite of the violent, and ironic, clashes between generations, Able most often has his mind—and when he can manage it, his hands—on the nubile and eager Miss Comfort Starr. Right up until Comfort and Able finally get themselves hitched, her presence runs like a bawdy joke through the homespun morality of Booker family life and the hayseed anti-heroics that culminate when the Green Mountain Boys bumble their way into a sleeping Fort Ticonderoga. One can't help picturing this as a blockbuster John Wayne movie (he's too old for Able, but might make it as Noah) and that sums up both the best and worst of Peck's characteristically boisterous saga of '76.

Sue Ann Jargstorf

SOURCE: A review of *Hang for Treason*, in *School Library Journal*, Vol. 22, No. 7, March, 1976, p. 117.

Reminiscent of Peck's *Fawn,* this is another story of alienation between father and son with possession of Fort Ticonderoga again a focal point. The time, however, is 1775, and the rift is between American patriots and Tories, not England and France. An Indian attack in 1745, chillingly described, left Noah Booker without a family and, since British soldiers finally freed "Verdmont," Noah is loyal to King George. His 17-year-old son Able slips away to join Ethan Allen's Green Mountain Boys, spies on the British, and participates in Fort Ticonderoga's capture by the joint forces of Allen and Benedict Arnold. Observing the resulting pillage and the rapaciousness of Allen's followers, Able realizes his dream might differ from his father's but his ways must be as honorable. Returning to the family farm, he finds it the scene of another massacre. Noah's first-person narration often seems larger than life, with bawdy scenes (as when he dreams of and courts his libidinous girl friend, Comfort) and a bundle of action guaranteed to hold readers spellbound.

Martin Levin

SOURCE: A review of *Hang for Treason,* in *The New York Times Book Review,* April 4, 1976, p. 32.

Being a colonial Vermonter could mean that you might lose your scalp to a French and Indian raiding party. Or your land in the Vermont-New York boundary dispute. Or your neck as the redcoats became edgy about rebellion. Or everything if your friends and neighbors thought you a Tory.

A smattering of these tragedies twice decimates the family of 17-year-old Able Booker, settlers on the Vermont shore of Lake Champlain. After Able sees one of his young neighbors hanged by the British garrison at Fort Ticonderoga, he joins the Green Mountain Boys and helps change the fort's ownership.

Robert Newton Peck (author of *A Day No Pigs Would Die*) approaches Revolutionary history with a lively, ebullient style that nonetheless suggests some of the pain and confusion of divided loyalties.

Curriculum Review

SOURCE: A review of *Hang for Treason,* in *Curriculum Review,* Vol. 17, No. 1, February, 1978, pp. 75-6.

Robert Newton Peck, soldier, lumberman, hog killer, and piano player, has also written a novel about the American Revolution for young readers, *Hang for Treason.* Centered around Lake Champlain and Fort Ticonderoga, the action tells the story of Able Booker whose philosophy is, "It ain't how much life, it's how much laughter." Able is at one time a happy, carefree 17-year-old. Then the war comes; one of Able's friends is hanged by the British, another is killed by an angry mob. With divided loyalties, the bitterness of civil strife, and the sorrow of tragic loss, Able is no longer a boy. The novel is well plotted and

maintains a rapid, engrossing pace. The use of vernacular dialog is especially effective.

RABBITS AND REDCOATS (1976)

Barbara F. Miles

SOURCE: A review of *Rabbits and Redcoats,* in *School Library Journal,* Vol. 22, No. 8, April, 1976, p. 77.

Interest Wheelock and Chapter Harrow, two young Vermont lads, get in on some of the early Revolutionary War action by following Ethan Allen's Green Mountain Boys across Lake Champlain to attack Fort Ticonderoga. Having made friends trading with some of the young British soldiers stationed at the Fort, the boys help one of the enemy escape after the attack, and are relieved to see their friends safe. The short episode, narrated by Chapter Harrow, employs jargon authentic to the time. While the market will be inundated with Bicentennial fiction, this will sustain reader interest due to the realistic portrayals of the feelings of the young teenage boys, their conflicts and lack of understanding of the larger issues involved in war.

Willard M. Wallace

SOURCE: A review of *Rabbits and Redcoats,* in *The New York Times Book Review,* May 2, 1976, p. 26.

Rabbits and Redcoats is Chapter Harrow's account of the part he and his friend Interest Wheelock play in Ethan Allen's capture of Fort Ticonderoga. Chapter, 16 years old, wants to be a journalist like Sam Adams, whom his father detests. Certainly he doesn't care to be a soldier. But neither does he, or, for that matter, Interest, want to be left out of Ethan's attack on the Fort.

Once in the Fort, they save a British soldier, Peter Geer, from a half-cracked patriot. They know Geer from having traded with the soldiers before the war. Geer would like to farm instead of soldier, so all three slip away to Vermont, where Geer eventually marries the girl for whom the other two are rivals.

It is a simple, reasonably plausible tale, though only a fragment. The dialogue among the three boys rings true. Less convincing is the benign portrayal of Ethan Allen and quite unconvincing is that of Benedict Arnold, who, in some sort of clairvoyant mood, is already looking forward to defeating General John Burgoyne two years later. It is regrettable that though writing for a younger group, Mr. Peck did not retain the more valid conception of these two characters as portrayed in his recent ***Hang for Treason.***

Mary M. Burns

SOURCE: A review of *Rabbits and Redcoats,* in *The Horn*

Book Magazine, Vol. LII, No. 6, December, 1976, pp. 626-27.

The idea that romantic notions of war disappear in battle is the unifying theme of an attractively produced historical vignette based on the capture of Fort Ticonderoga in May 1775 by Ethan Allen and his Green Mountain Boys. Viewed from the perspective of two teenaged boys, the story is set within a twenty-four-hour time span. It is narrated by Chapter Harrow who, with his friend Interest Wheelock, sneaks into the ranks of the Vermont revolutionaries so that they "can brag on how we nightrode with Ethan the time he took Ti." Although the ragged army is victorious over the British defenders, the two learn that defeat is not always dishonor nor victory a guarantee of dignity. They also realize that war, far from being a glorious adventure, is a blend of mundane discomforts with imminent danger. Remarkable for its spare, taut style which reflects the temper and cadence of rural colonial America, the book is one of those rarities—a well-researched, brief, eminently readable historical tale. Illustrated [by Laura Lydecker] with effective cross-hatched, pen-and-ink drawings.

📖 *HAMILTON* (1976)

Kirkus Reviews

SOURCE: A review of *Hamilton,* in *Kirkus Reviews,* Vol. XLIV, No. 7, April 1, 1976, p. 387.

"Fat was his future. Fat was his fate. This was no problem for Hamilton Pig, For a pig is just downright SUPPOSED to be big." Exactly. But the reiterated truth doesn't stop Peck from particularizing overalled Hamilton's sole attribute, his appetite, as both his personal problem—Hamilton can't win races and "a juvenile goat even kidded him some"—and his vindication—when, dreaming of food, he chomps the tail of a prowling wolf. [Illustrator Laura] Lydecker's pastel barnyard and skinny, dog-like wolf look appropriately, nostalgically old-fashioned, but Peck's attempt to find a new wrinkle in the type A standard picture book plot is just too mechanical. Featherweight.

Helen Gregory

SOURCE: A review of *Hamilton,* in *School Library Journal,* Vol. 23, No. 1, September, 1976, pp. 103-04.

From the time he's born, Hamilton the pig does nothing but eat. He becomes the laughing stock of the farm until a hungry wolf comes to visit and Hamilton routs the villain unawares and becomes the barnyard hero. Illustrated humorously with pleasant pastel drawings which should carry very well to story hour audiences and classes, the verse is lively but strains for cleverness: "The kitten and puppy both thought he was dumb. / A juvenile goat even kidded him some."

Ethna Sheehan

SOURCE: "Pile These Around the Christmas Tree," in *America,* Vol. 135, No. 19, December 11, 1976, p. 427.

Hamilton was a pig, and what a pig. He ate and ate, and when he was asleep he dreamed about eating. If you can believe it, that was why the hungry wolf who came marauding went away not only still hungry, but so humiliated that he never returned. The overjoyed farmyard animals gave Hamilton—what? A feast, of course. Hilarious verses plus equally funny pictures in pastel colors by Laura Lydecker show a likable pig and his friends and all the details of a big farm. Note: we are spared a glimpse into Hamilton's future.

📖 *KING OF KAZOO* (1976)

Helen Gregory

SOURCE: A review of *King of Kazoo,* in *School Library Journal,* Vol. 23, No. 2, October, 1976, p. 110.

An old cowpuncher, whose purple cow, Cow, walks out on him because he's always punching her, meets a pretty plumber who has no sink to fix and a young drummer with no drum. They solve the problem of an embarrassed ghost who must wear flowered sheets. In gratitude, the ghost sends them in quest of the King of Kazoo, equipped with three magic kazoos. This is solid silly stuff. Although unlikely to displace *The Wizard of Oz,* it's good for laughs and, as the author recommends, it would make a delightfully absurd play for young actors. Written as a quick-moving story with lots of corny/funny dialogue and songs, the book includes an appendix with melodies and pointers on adapting it to stage.

Publishers Weekly

SOURCE: A review of *King of Kazoo,* in *Publishers Weekly,* Vol. 210, No. 23, December 6, 1976, p. 63.

Peck took all the fetters off his imagination to produce this book of hilarious nonsense. It's really a tour de force of impossible happenings, impossible to resist laughing at. The fun starts when the Cowpuncher's lone Cow, a purple one, gets tired of being punched and runs away. The Cowpuncher follows her and meets a weepy girl, a Plumber with no sink to fix. As the story continues, others join the two and wind up at the court of the King of Kazoo who, of course, loves to play the kazoo. Peck includes words and music for the silly songs his characters sing. Many readers will deem [illustrator W. B.] Park's pictures, brilliant color cartoons and black-and-white jollities, even more attractive than the tall tales here.

Zena Sutherland

SOURCE: A review of *King of Kazoo,* in *Bulletin of the*

Center for Children's Books, Vol. 30, No. 9, May, 1977, p. 148.

This is identified on the dust jacket as a "musical comedy-fantasy" that can be adapted for performance. A cowpuncher has a purple cow that runs away because it is tired of being punched; a sweet young thing is discovered in a pool of her own tears because she is a plumber who cannot find a sink; the two join forces with a drummer who's lost his drum. A ghost who has been helped by them gives them a magic kazoo, a tiny knight takes them to the Peppermint Palace; the King of Kazoo shows them his collections of kazoos and purple animals. All ends with the King and his touchy Queen on good terms, the cowpuncher and cow reunited, and the plumber and drummer having found not only a drum to drum and a leak to fix, but each other. The writing is heavily slangy, often in western style, and sprinkled with word play: the King points out that he really ought to call his guests' chambers their "thirds" rather than their "quarters" since there are only three of them. The musical notation for the songs, melodic line only, is given at the back of the book, the lyrics being included there and also in the text. The illustrations are pedestrian, the text a contrived patchwork, barely redeemed by heavy-handed humor.

TRIG (1977)

Gale K. Shonkwiler

SOURCE: A review of *Trig,* in *School Library Journal,* Vol. 23, No. 6, February, 1977, p. 68.

Peck's mastery of the crisp vernacular of Depression era rural Vermont is evident in this clever narrative. Elizabeth Trigman, a pig-tailed, bespectacled little tomboy who owns a genuine Junior G-man gun, tells how she tricked Bud Griffin and Skip Warner and had a little fun with stuffy Aunt Augusta in the bargain. Everybody, except Aunt Augusta, has a good laugh. Although the story is hardly long enough to justify calling it a novel, it's certainly fun while it lasts.

Denise M. Wilms

SOURCE: A review of *Trig,* in *Booklist,* Vol. 73, No. 19, June 1, 1977, p. 1501.

Elizabeth Trigman, a spunky, straight-thinking Vermont farm girl, gets tidy revenge on two neighborhood boys who refuse to play with her because she's a girl. The idea is born when Trig gets a toy machine gun from understanding Uncle Fred; she wins the boys' allegiance with it, and they don't blink an eye when she prompts them to take a shot at Fred's crabby, fat wife Augusta, whose napping body fills the hammock "like a breeze to a frigate." The clattering "BBBRRAAATAT-TAT-TAT-TAT-TAT" flips Augusta "like a flapjack." She falls on Bud and Skip and knocks their heads together; but then she gets her finger stuck in the gun's trigger; the commotion

brings Trig's mom, who tries to help the blustering woman, but that's a loss when Augusta steps on a hornet which crawls into a hole in her stocking and proceeds up her leg, stinging all the while. Peck plays the scene for all it's worth just as he does the prior buildup. This is slapstick with a classic victim and an untraditional female leading rascal. The heavy doses of country talk and canny observations (" . . . he sure said a few things. Not what you'd call Sunday words either. More like Saturday night") are sometimes forced but overall funny.

LAST SUNDAY (1977)

Kirkus Reviews

SOURCE: A review of *Last Sunday,* in *Kirkus Reviews,* Vol. XLV, No. 13, July 1, 1977, p. 669.

In a style combining folksy colloquialisms and a sort of mock formality common to amateur attempts at humor, this is mascot Ruth Babson's account of a Sunday, July fourth, ball game between the Canby (Vermont) Catfish and the visiting team from nearby Wiggin. The day starts with Canby pitcher Sober McGinty out cold in a worse than usual Sunday morning hangover, but Ruth (or Babe, as she's called in honor of her talent for the game) and her six-foot aunt get him dressed and over to the field for what turns out to be his last game. The event, which Ruth views from the dugout beside manager Hawg Hogarth, is interrupted, in turn, by appearances on the diamond of Harv Winpenny's goat Butler, the neighboring town of Hoover's new hook-and-ladder truck, the Sons of Italy impromptu marching band, and at last the Jehovah Bible and Revival Tent and Organ Show. Helped and encouraged by Ruth, Sober stumbles through all this intended hilarity and then, danged if he don't, just stretches out right there by the dugout and breathes his last. A nervy ninth inning play on Peck's part, but it would take an umpire as partial as Canby's faithful Murph to allow it.

Ruth M. Stein

SOURCE: A review of *Last Sunday,* in *Language Arts,* Vol. 54, No. 7, October, 1977, p. 808.

A prolific author treats us to "the biggest baseball game of the season," when the Canby Catfish play the Wiggin Warriors on the Fourth of July in the days of Deanna Durbin, Shirley Temple, and the ten-cent hotdog. The main question is whether Sober McGinty will sober up long enough to finish the game for Canby. As twelve-year-old Ruth Babson narrates, we follow her from helping the drunken pitcher to fidgeting through Sunday church and dinner, eager to be with the team for which she is mascot and bat-girl. A goat, the volunteer fire company in full regalia, the Sons of Italy Marching band, and an assortment of memorable spectators, officials, and participants convert the lot into ". . . Vermont's biggest open-air insane asylum." When the fickle fans turn on McGinty, our gutsy heroine learns there are more important things than winning a ball game. In picturesque Vermont vernacular and with baseball savvy, Peck makes one hysterical afternoon a metaphorical comic/tragedy of the human condition.

Zena Sutherland

SOURCE: A review of *Last Sunday,* in *Bulletin of the Center for Children's Books,* Vol. 31, No. 5, January, 1978, p. 84.

Twelve year old Ruth ("Babe") Babson, mascot and ball girl for the Canby, Vermont baseball team, tells the story of the game of the year, when the team was playing their arch rivals from a neighboring town. Babe helps get Sober McGinty, the pitcher and her friend, on his feet and over to the diamond. The play-by-play is interrupted by a wandering goat, and a fire truck, and a Sons of Italy march, and a revivalist group. In other words, Peck reaches hard for humor and overdoes it; he also overdoes the homespun dialogue and occasionally lapses into weak construction ("His underwear were soiled . . .") or ornate writing (" . . . to partake further of those irresistible morsels so meticulously prepared by the culinary genius of Riley Shattuck,") or dialogue that seems out of the place in the (vaguely) 1930's setting: the coach asks Babe to get him a drink with, "Hit me again on the grape. You want another? I'll spring." The story ends with Sober's death: "As his tired lungs worked in and out, I closed my eyes to inhale part of his breathing. Holding his last breath inside me until it was sweet again."

Journal of Reading

SOURCE: A review of *Last Sunday,* in *Journal of Reading,* Vol. 22, No. 5, February, 1979, p. 474.

Those who read the Alfred Slote, Matt Christopher, Marion Renick, and Billy Libby sports books will find **Last Sunday,** by Robert Newton Peck, an appealing work, touching and witty. It focuses on Ruth "Babe" Babson, mascot and Catfish ball-girl, and her friendship with Dan McGinty, the star pitcher of the Canby Warriors and the town drunk. A high point for them and everyone in town is the baseball game on Sunday when Canby goes against their biggest rival of the year. Complicating the game plan are the numerous comic interruptions. With so much crazy action, even reluctant readers willingly read this book. Additionally, because of the author's sensitive treatment of friendship, it could generate discussion concerning characteristics of enduring friendship.

📖 *SOUP FOR PRESIDENT* (1978)

Kirkus Reviews

SOURCE: A review of *Soup for President,* in *Kirkus Reviews,* Vol. XLVI, No. 6, March 15, 1978, p. 307.

It's 1936; Alf Landon is sure to be the next President; Robert eyes the teacher's laundry soap (for cleansing foul mouths) uneasily when he inadvertently lets slip the word "Democrat"; and best buddy Soup is running for president of the class. Despite his tender feelings for the opposing candidate, Norma Jean Bissell, Robert does a bang-up job as Soup's campaign manager, outfitting his candidate with a mustache from the barber shop floor so he can rearrange the letters on county tax collector Kapuso's poster and use it as his own, and painting huge red letters on the side of Cyrus McCormick's barn. (What in tarnation is a SOUF, asks McCormick, as Robert hasn't left quite enough room to complete the P.) The ending, with Norma Jean herself casting the decisive vote for Soup, exposes even the fair-minded Mr. Peck to charges of unconscious sexism; and throughout—right up to the romantic fadeout—he lays on the hayseed innocence just as thick as ever. But it's hard not to laugh at some of the corny complications.

Zena Sutherland

SOURCE: A review of *Soup for President,* in *Bulletin of the Center for Children's Books,* Vol. 31, No. 10, June, 1978, p. 165.

Like the first two books about Soup and Rob (who tells the story) this is filled with corn-fed nostalgia. Peck's stories are based on his own boyhood in a small Vermont town, and his characters are all reminiscent of Rockwell's *Saturday Evening Post* covers: just a bit too jolly, or stupid, or surly. This volume has more cohesion than **Soup** or **Soup and Me;** although the chapters are still self-contained, they are less episodic, since the class election contest between Soup and Norma Jean Bissell provides continuity. The writing has humor and affection in describing the boys' pranks: painting Soup's name on a barn, tricking tough Janice, outfoxing the town curmudgeon. Yet for some readers the fact that most of the humor depends on tricks like the above or on someone's stupidity (Rob's idea of gallantry is singing the national anthem under Norma Jean's window; Rob thinks "Democrat" is a dirty word; Soup's father believes that "deportment" has to do with a store) may prove wearing.

Mary M. Burns

SOURCE: A review of *Soup for President,* in *The Horn Book Magazine,* Vol. LIV, No. 3, June, 1978, pp. 279-80.

References to the presidential race between Roosevelt and Landon in 1936 help to establish the setting for a nostalgic view of an era when youthful high jinks were interpreted as boyish pranks rather than as juvenile delinquency. Engaged in a project devised by their perceptive teacher, Robert's best friend Soup competes against the enchanting Norma Jean Bissell for the school presidency. The campaign strategy not only involves the two boys in a series of comic confrontations with a belligerent goat, a disgruntled school committeeman, and the class bully but also requires young Robert—who tells the story—to choose between his loyalty to Soup and his affection for the girl, "a blend of grace and scholarship." The conclusion, by today's standards, may disappoint those who would prefer Norma Jean to be more militant and less romantic, but in the context of the time and place, her attitude is believable. In contrast to John Fitzgerald's stories of the Great Brain, the book's style and tone suggest adult recollection. Thus, the story succeeds primarily as a humorous reminiscence of small-town attitudes and customs in the pre-World War II era.

Denise M. Wilms

SOURCE: A review of *Soup for President,* in *Booklist,* Vol. 74, No. 20, June 15, 1978, p. 1619.

Soup's running for class president against Rob's heart-throb Norma Jean Bissell is the focus of Peck's third evocation of boyhood days with best friend Soup. The premiere scrape involves surreptitiously painting Soup's name on the side of Mr. McGinley's barn—the school board member most pivotal in efforts to secure the class a $5 football and goalposts for the playing field. Adults enjoy a largely sympathetic casting. School nurse Miss Boland ably coaches the class' freewheeling football matches; Miss Kelly is the stern but fair and beloved school teacher who pushes Rob and Soup to restore Mr. McGinley's barn side and counsels Rob on how he might resolve the dilemma of wooing Norma Jean and voting for Soup. Peck has a knack for dialogue and scene building, and when his efforts are controlled the results are soundly entertaining. Here the effects are mixed with some scenes played too hard for their humor and with sentimentality spilling over (particularly in the talk Rob has with Miss Kelly). But the all-around affability is catchy and makes Peck's indulgences easier to disregard.

📖 EAGLE FUR (1978)

Kirkus Reviews

SOURCE: A review of *Eagle Fur,* in *Kirkus Reviews,* Vol. XLVI, No. 7, April 1, 1978, p. 391.

Another Peck coming-of-ager—this one set among voyageur fur traders in Canada and somewhat less macho-mindless and native-stomping than earlier versions. In 1754, 16-year-old Abbott Coe of England is sold to trader Skinner Benet of the Hudson's Bay Company for five years service as an indentured servant in return for passage paid to America. Skinner Benet is a terror even among thick-skinned French Canadians. He keeps his own bison to ride like a bucking bronco, he works his hired voyageurs to the bone, he cuffs Coe constantly to teach him a woodsman's alertness, and he has him steel-collared. Benet also has a 14-year-old Cree wife who is a growing boy's wet dream of a woodnymph, and who has more than an eye for the virgin hero. The bulk of the short novel is the record of a disastrous (but financially suc-

cessful) portage into Lake Ticonderoga where Benet trades for "eagle fur"—the furs where only the eagle flies (the Great Lakes country). Accompanied by a likable Coldstream Guardsman in full red regalia, the crew trek into the wilderness with two huge canoes, make their trades, then for the most part lose their lives to greedy Indians. Lively, to be sure, but still that old equation of maturity with brutality—it goes with the RNP territory.

Robert L. Burr

SOURCE: A review of *Eagle Fur,* in *Library Journal,* Vol. 103, No. 10, May 15, 1978, p. 1083.

In return for his passage to America, young Abbot Coe is bound with an iron collar and five years' servitude to S. Binet, chief factor of the Hudson Bay Company post at Ft. Albany on James Bay. The colorful and fast-paced novel traces the complex love-hate relationship between bondsman and master, and with it the growth of Abbot Coe to manhood in the rough Canadian wilderness of the 1750's. An expedition to the interior to trade for precious beaver pelts, the "eagle fur" of the title, provides plenty of action and accurately conveys the hardship, danger, mystery, and excitement of the voyageur's life. This entertaining and well-written novel should have wide appeal.

JoAnne Posch

SOURCE: A review of *Eagle Fur,* in *School Library Journal,* Vol. 25, No. 2, October, 1978, p. 164.

In 1754, 16-year-old Abbott Coe signs on as a bonded servant to the notoriously mean Skinner Benet, a trader for the Hudson's Bay Company, in order to book free passage from England to Canada. Along with a young ensign and several voyageurs, Coe and Benet head down the Albany River in search of the *Eagle Fur* (found in the area of "the five great lakes . . . where only the eagle can fly"). Encountering fatigue, rough waters, strenuous labor, and unfriendly Indians, the entourage eventually meets up with Sick Bear and his Cree braves to trade goods for the furs. The way home is a series of attacks by renegades (both French and Indian) who covet the valuable cargo. Benet and several voyageurs lose their lives and Coe returns to take over both Benet's job and his young common-law Indian wife. The anti-Indian sentiment of the 18th Century is pervasive albeit authentic. A useful, fictional account of an exciting period of North American history from the white-trader perspective.

Jenny L. Amy

SOURCE: A review of *Eagle Fur,* in *In Review: Canadian Books for Children,* Vol. 14, No. 1, February, 1980, pp. 53-4.

In his usual fashion, Robert Peck has produced a book

which will appeal to young adults. Peck presents the story of a 16 year old English orphan, Abbott Coe, who has come to Canada as an indentured servant to M. Benet, a factor of the Hudson's Bay Company. The plot is well structured, the story fast moving and the characters well developed. The story gives a good representation of life on the frontier and of the bleak and savage atmosphere of the times. The description of the fur trade business and the expeditions of the traders is skillfully woven into the story.

The character of Ensign Owen McKee, a young Scottish soldier and map-maker introduces the rising conflict between Britain and France in 1754. Romantic interest is provided by Doe, an Indian girl who belongs to Benet yet is loved and worshipped by Abbott. This powerfully written story gives us vivid descriptions of the life of Abbott Coe and his contemporaries in good times and during a savage encounter with an Indian band who want more for their beaver pelts or, Eagle Fur, by stealing it back to sell again to the French. The life and death struggles and the pitting of rough men against the rough environment is striking.

CLUNIE (1979)

Karen Ritter

SOURCE: A review of *Clunie,* in *School Library Journal,* Vol. 26, No. 3, November, 1979, p. 92.

The high school kids make fun of Clunie Finn for being "simple," but Braddy Macon appreciates her love of things like daisies and baby ducks. He risks his popularity and his growing relationship with Sally, the most sought-after girl in school, to defend Clunie from taunters led by chief bully Leo. Alternating chapters portray events from the different viewpoints of kind-hearted, level-headed Braddy, frustrated and increasingly violent Leo, Clunie's overprotective and guilt-tortured father, and Clunie herself, struggling with the frustrations of a heavy, awkward body and a slow mind. Driven by inner demons, Leo tries to rape Clunie who, husky and strong for her age, beats him to death with only a dim awareness of what she is doing. Later, she drowns in a river with Braddy trying desperately to save her; when he realizes that she would only end up locked in an institution, he lets her slip away. For a slightly younger reading audience, *Between Friends* by Sheila Garrigue treats a retarded girl's friendship in a gentler manner, with less violence and brutality.

Karen Bossard

SOURCE: A review of *Clunie,* in *Voice of Youth Advocates,* Vol. 2, No. 6, February, 1980, p. 32.

Braddy, busy with baseball, his girl friend Sally, and delivering the wash his mother takes in, makes time to protect Clunie Finn, a retarded girl being harassed by the town bully, Leo Bannon. Clunie has been warned by her father not to hit anyone because of her strength, but when Leo tries to rape her she beats him to death. Knowing she will be punished, she will not allow Braddy to save her after she has fallen into the deep pool above the dam. Well written and sensitive, Peck has recaptured some of the style and feeling of *A Day No Pigs Would Die.* The interest is YA, although the format makes it look as though it were for younger readers.

Kirkus Reviews

SOURCE: A review of *Clunie,* in *Kirkus Reviews,* Vol. XLVIII, No. 3, February 1, 1980, p. 135.

A moving story, though not altogether free of sentimentality or the heavy hand of Fate. Clunie Finn is 16, large and strong for her age, mentally retarded but with a simple awareness of her own feelings and others'. At school she is often ridiculed, to her misery. Clunie's chief tormentor is the swaggering, insecure Leo Bannon who has sexual designs on her; but Braddy Macon, another classmate, keeps an eye on Clunie, sometimes walking her safely home, and a gentle communion grows between these two. One day Leo's bludgeoned body is discovered in a field. It was Clunie who killed him, protecting herself from his assault. Braddy searches for the missing Clunie and finds her, but he cannot save her from drowning—in the very pond where, earlier, she had watched a turtle devour a duckling. Still, the reader feels a wrenching sadness, so successfully has Peck portrayed Clunie's vulnerability.

Patricia Lee Gauch

SOURCE: A review of *Clunie,* in *The New York Times Book Review,* February 24, 1980, p. 33.

Robert Newton Peck has never been more the consummate storyteller than in this book about Clunie Finn, a retarded farm girl caught in a web of adolescent cruelty.

Using a breathless present-tense narrative, he puts into play four very different teenagers who want something strangely similar out of the spring season: the simple, daisy-loving Clunie; Leo, a town bully boiling for attention; Braddy, a "white hat"; and Sally, the school tease.

Then he lets them loose in a series of alternately gentle and startling chapters, each putting a block on the scale that inevitably tips toward a rainy May afternoon tragedy.

One can occasionally fault the folksy rural dialect, wonder at Clunie's almost-perfect wisdom, and be infuriated with the one-sided treatment of Sally; nonetheless, *Clunie* is a sensitive, compelling story.

But for whom? There's the problem. Mr. Peck makes us care most about outsiders Leo and Clunie. Thus the chapter in which a hot, frustrated Leo is determined to stalk and have the gentle Clunie because "she'd never be able to squeal on ya" causes emotional mayhem.

The editors have neatly placed the book in the Young

Adult category; but that doesn't solve the problem. The book's vocabulary and appearance are more appealing to a younger (10 to 13) or less proficient reader—exactly the reader for whom the book is of questionable value. It is too late for should-haves. The dilemma will be how to do justice to a good book and the young or immature reader as well.

📖 *MR. LITTLE* (1979)

Anne Hanst Parker

SOURCE: A review of *Mr. Little,* in *School Library Journal,* Vol. 26, No. 3, November, 1979, p. 80.

Set in a small town in rural Vermont during what seems to be the 1930s, **Mr. Little** is the story of the relationship between two mischievous boys and their teacher. The tone is nostalgic and sentimental, similar in theme to Peck's **Soup** series although aimed at a slightly older audience. Finley Streeter and Stanley Dragavich are perturbed when they find their favorite instructor, Miss Kellogg, replaced by the self-possessed Lester Little, who does not take children in his brother's airplane or kiss them on the forehead and who does not seem at all dismayed at having to follow in the footsteps of so perfect a predecessor. Finley and Drag stuff dirty magazines in his umbrella, steal some of his underwear to display on a statue during a town pageant, but, in the end, are rescued by the butt of their jokes who also saves Miss Kellogg from drowning. Well written and pleasant, the story does impart some small message. However, its flip humor and superficiality rob it of emotional depth or impact.

Barbara Elleman

SOURCE: A review of *Mr. Little,* in *Booklist,* Vol. 76, No. 8, December 15, 1979, p. 615.

Drag and Finley, two young pranksters, are well known around town for their mischief. Expecting pretty Miss Kellogg to be their teacher, they are chagrined to discover a man—Lester Little—in charge of their classroom. Delighted with someone new to torment, they plant a copy of the magazine *Hotsy Harem* in his umbrella, but the trick fizzles out. Still determined to make the teacher the laughingstock of the village, the boys steal a pair of his undershorts off a clothesline and plan a whopper of a prank; it backfires, making Mr. Little a hero instead. The slight story is well paced and told almost entirely through dialogue and short sentences, which makes this accessible to reluctant and slow readers.

Kirkus Reviews

SOURCE: A review of *Mr. Little,* in *Kirkus Reviews,* Vol. XLVII, No. 24, December 15, 1979, p. 1431.

The small man in the dark suit is a great disappointment to the Siberia Central School class that's been looking forward to having pretty Miss Kellogg for a whole year—Miss K. who bestows kisses and rides in her brother's plane. But class cutups Finley Streeter and Stanley Dragavich discover that Lester Little, for all his mild appearance, is no slouch either. He can take a joke (a copy of *Hotsy Harem* tucked into his furled umbrella) and turn the tables. *And* he's not a tattle-tale: when the boys pull off their biggest, most embarrassing prank—decking the statue of the town heroine in his name-taped lavender (a case of the colors running) undershorts—he's the one who gets them out of the ensuing fix without giving them away. It's all pretty corny but not cruel or cheap—ending in a bit of wisdom that's worth reading for itself. Mr. L. has rescued Miss K.—returned to play that town heroine in a pageant—and become a hero himself. "But," he reminds the boys, "it takes so much *more* courage . . . to be a gentleman."

📖 *JUSTICE LION* (1981)

Wendy Dellett

SOURCE: A review of *Justice Lion,* in *School Library Journal,* Vol. 27, No. 7, March, 1981, pp. 158-59.

In 1923, the small town of Liberty, Vermont deals philosophically with Prohibition, and even Sheriff Tatum looks the other way as the "uproaders" on Kipp's Mountain distill home brew. But when an investigator from Washington arrives to force the issue and Justice Lion—patriarch of the Lion clan and respected Grand Old Mountaineer—is arrested for operating a still, the citizens of the town must make a choice between loyalty to their lifelong friends or fealty to the laws of their country. Muncie Bolt is particularly torn by his love for his father (the newly appointed District Attorney who must prosecute Justice Lion) and his intimacy with the kind and worthy Lion family. Muncie learns about the legal and moral meanings of right and wrong and about the importance of love and a sense of belonging in a story with a well-constructed plot and strong characterizations in the outspoken judge, Henry Gleason, and the warm and generous neighbor, Mrs. Bly. There are a few jarring anachronistic lapses, as when an old-timer misuses that modern grammatical horror, "hopefully," or when a 15-year-old says, "That would be neat." But most of the time the cadence of the Vermont idiom makes **Justice Lion** a pleasure to read.

Russell H. Goodyear

SOURCE: A review of *Justice Lion,* in *Best Sellers,* Vol. 41, No. 2, May, 1981, p. 80.

Muncie Bolt, 15, is the son of a rural Vermont lawyer. His best friend, Hem Lion, is a member of a clan of mountain people who have inhabited Kipp's Mountain since George II awarded it to them in a grant dated 1731. The Lions pride themselves on their independence and self-reliance.

The novel is set in 1923 during Prohibition. Most of the conflict stems from the arrival of a federal prohibition agent and the subsequent arrest of the Lion family patriarch, Justice Lion, for moonshining. As the newly-appointed District Attorney, Munice's father must prosecute Justice Lion. Consequently, Muncie must deal with conflicting loyalties: his love for Hem's sister, Blessing; his friendship with Hem, and his love for his father.

The story is gripping and the plot well-developed. The trial scenes give one a good understanding of the legal issues involved. There are several violent scenes which include a shooting and a gory description of an accident which results in death. However, the issues leading up to these violent scenes are treated honestly so that one does understand the why of them. There is a rather arousing sexual scene, yet it is treated with tenderness and sensitivity.

The most controversial aspect of the book is the author's espousal of the idea that people in isolated, rural areas would be better off it they were left alone by government. Nearly all adult authority figures in the novel advocate this attitude: Muncie's father, the sheriff, the county judge, and of course, the Lions. Nowhere does the novel give one the understanding that his attitude toward government reflects an American romantic myth, that of the rugged individualist, living just beyond the frontier, self-reliant, making his own laws and basing his morals on his personal interpretation of the Bible. The frontier has vanished, and government is a necessity for all men. One of the hard parts about growing up is learning to distinguish between myth and reality, and here the author betrays his readers; they deserve to see both sides of this issue.

This is a strong book, and I believe that young people should read books of this type, but with close adult supervision to ensure that they see all sides of the issues involved. I recommend *Justice Lion* for readers ages 14 and up.

Kirkus Reviews

SOURCE: A review of *Justice Lion,* in *Kirkus Reviews,* Vol. XLIX, No. 14, July 15, 1981, p. 876.

Town dweller Muncie Bolt, 15 in 1923, admires his "up-road" (backwoods) friend Hem Lion and feels honored to know Hem's rough father Justice, proud owner of the Vermont mountain land deeded to his family by George Rex himself. Justice and Muncie's lawyer father Jess respect each other. Muncie and Hem's sister Blessing Lion have longing eyes for each other—and, on one heady occasion in the woods, Muncie gets an eyeful. Then Jess Bolt is appointed district attorney, a job he's wanted, just when a federal agent comes to town and has Justice arrested for moonshining—an activity the local law enforcers have chosen to overlook. Muncie is torn between fondness for the Lions and loyalty to his father, who reluctantly prosecutes Justice in the trial that takes up the last half of the novel. Except that the moral issues are insufficiently compelling, it's a tolerable imitation of the popular courtroom drama, with much "countrysome" el-

oquence from the new judge and general obeisance to red-white-and-blue abstractions, along with corny chuckles from the folks on and off the jury. (We are spared Peck's usual low-grade slapstick in this more serious serving of nostalgic Americana.) In between sessions, Muncie engages in mushy conversations celebrating young love or simple living, while his grave father spouts such nuggets of wisdom as "our human condition is not a recipe of absolutes." Like the speeches at a 4th-of-July town picnic, it's likely to be taken for the real thing by a goodly portion of the audience.

William G. McBride

SOURCE: A review of *Justice Lion,* in *Voice of Youth Advocates,* Vol. 4, No. 3, August, 1981, p. 27.

In *Justice Lion* Peck brings us another tale of Vermont and its people and of a boy's approaching manhood. The circumstances, however, are different. The inhabitants of Liberty have ambivalent feelings about the hill people, most of whom are members of the Lion clan, headed by patriarch Justice. The feelings of ambivalence are mutual.

Muncie Bolt and his lawyer father, Jesse, however, have a sense of comradeship with the Lions because some years earlier Jesse successfully defended one of Justice's sons against a murder charge; and now Muncie and Justice's youngest son, Hem, have developed a strong friendship. But trouble is brewing. Most of the Lions make moonshine, the prohibition law has been recently passed, and federal agents have moved into the territory. Justice is arrested and held for trial, and Jesse must serve as the prosecuting attorney.

Much of the story centers around the trial and its aftermath. Questions of obedience—even to a law with which one disagrees—loyalty, friendship, justice, courage, and love concern all of the characters, especially Muncie through whose eyes the story is told. Some of the story is tragic; some of it is comic; all of it is real.

While *Justice Lion* is not as good as *A Day No Pigs Would Die,* it comes close and ranks easily with *Fawn* and *Hang for Treason.* Peck is a masterful storyteller and again has created a story that will have very broad appeal. It would be useful in any setting, classroom or library, with individuals, small groups, or an entire class. It would be as appropriate in a history class as in a literature class. After all, making a law is one thing; enforcing it is quite something else.

SOUP ON WHEELS (1981)

Don Lesson

SOURCE: A review of *Soup on Wheels,* in *The New York Times Book Review,* March 1, 1981, p. 24.

"Soup" Vinson and Rob Peck are in trouble again. This

time the stew the boys have cooked for themselves concerns their entry in the town's first annual "Vermont Mardy Grah."

Fans of the Soup series (this is the fifth volume) will no doubt welcome the return of the mischievous boys and their supporting cast: kindly Miss Kelly, the teacher, and Norma Jean, Rob's crush, capable of provoking his "entire body and soul to digress into an almost critical glandular condition."

There are new put-downs for the other regulars: fat Miss Boland, "who, dressed in white, looked less like a nurse and more like an iceberg"; mean Eddy Tacker, with "a fist near twice as hard as a wrecking ball"; and meaner Janice Riker, "with at least forty-three knuckles on each fist." We do meet, briefly, one new boy in town. His hands are also weapons, as is needed for a monicker like his, Beverly Bean.

For characterization and relationships we must make do with these wisecracks, for Mr. Peck is quick to get about the business of high jinks. The boys' misadventures ring as hollow as ever. But, as the stories are purportedly grounded in Mr. Peck's own upbringing, one can only conclude that truth can be more artificial than fiction.

Robert Newton Peck has written more than a score of books, and by now combines his ingredients with professional ease. Still, there is a cloying aftertaste to Soup's good-natured pranks. And it is reinforced by Charles Robinson's wholesome illustrations, which attempt leading us back to a never-existent past that one Soup cover blurb called, "a time when the days seemed a bit longer"—and the books more substantial, one might add.

David Fiday

SOURCE: A review of *Soup on Wheels,* in *School Library Journal,* Vol. 27, No. 8, April, 1981, p. 130.

Impeccably Peck! Quick action and continuing shenanigans abound as Rob, Soup's friend, narrates adventures, in school and out, of "Terror on Hoofs" Janice, beautiful Norma Jean Bissell, bully Eddy and the new boy in town with a different name, Beverly Bean. Rob and Soup compete for the first place prize in the small town "Mardy Grah." They are sure their zebra costume will win, based on their entrance; that entrance is the climax of the story, but the true surprise is who wins first place. Soup lovers and new admirers will enjoy the wit and humor of the highly entertaining book; hilarious subplot action moves the story to a too-soon ending.

Barbara Elleman

SOURCE: A review of *Soup on Wheels,* in *Booklist,* Vol. 77, No. 21, July 1, 1981, p. 1395.

In a loosely strung series of episodes, Soup and his friends

once more set the town upside down. A Vermont "Mardy Grah" for the entire village sparks the boys to devise a zebra costume, and when Rob hurts his foot Soup decides to put "the animal" on roller skates. Near disaster results as the two come zooming out of control through the parade in one of Peck's funnier scenes. Elsewhere, he introduces a new character—a southern boy named Beverly—in a development that has no connection to the rest of the plot. Incidents are related through the author's sparse style and funny dialogue, featuring Janice Riker in her usual nasty role.

📖 *KIRK'S LAW* (1981)

Kevin Kenny

SOURCE: A review of *Kirk's Law,* in *Voice of Youth Advocates,* Vol. 4, No. 6, February, 1992, p. 36.

Collin Pepper has a lot to learn. Pampered by his monied parents and the Greenwich, Connecticut lifestyle in which he has grown up (at least physically), Collin is not so self-indulgent that he can't recognize himself as a "candy-ass." A failure in public school, thrown out of boarding school, Collin is placed in the grizzled but sage hands of one Wishbone Kirk. Their isolated, agitated, and tempestuous cohabitation in a remote Vermont cabin forms the backdrop against which we learn of *Kirk's Law.*

Peck's latest endeavor is an altogether winning story of an adolescent who is bright enough to be disgusted by his own listless character, and his aged mentor, a Vermonter whose "law" is little more than a solid work ethic coupled with a respect for and understanding of the life forms which envelop his world. Readers familiar with Peck's *A Day No Pigs Would Die* will find a relatively familiar setting and wit, but the touching relationship developed in *Kirk's Law* make it an entity to be cherished and lauded on its own. Realistic dialogue, a fascinating setting, and fluid text make this a must. A joy.

Zena Sutherland

SOURCE: A review of *Kirk's Law,* in *Bulletin of the Center for Children's Books,* Vol. 35, No. 9, May, 1982, p. 176.

Collin's father, tired of having a lazy teenage son who is thrown out of one school after another, drives Collin up to the Vermont mountains to stay with Sabbath Kirk, an old codger who is going to make a man of the boy. How? By teaching him to shoot, hunt, fend for himself in the woods, et cetera. Collin, the narrator, conforms almost immediately, and by the time three weeks have passed and his parents pay a surprise visit, he has learned to cope with everything and has even performed an emergency appendectomy on old Kirk. By candlelight. The whole thing is so preposterous it's almost funny; it's hackneyed in conception and trite in characterization, and the writing style is marred by a persistent intrusion of irrelevant details.

📖 *BANJO* (1982)

Karen Jameyson

SOURCE: A review of *Banjo,* in *The Horn Book Magazine,* Vol. LVIII, No. 6, December, 1982, p. 653.

The author of the "Soup" books has spun yet another amusing small-town yarn, this one narrated by young Alvin Dickinson. To the shock of everyone in the one-room schoolhouse Alvin, for some reason, chooses "one original mess"—the grubby and unpopular Banjo Byler—as his partner in completing a homework assignment: to research a "'famous character.'" Unfortunately, Banjo insists that the two investigate the town's legendary hermit, Old Jake Horse, who lives near a deserted spar mine—territory forbidden to Alvin. At the mine the boys tumble deep into a silo bin, and only through Banjo's musical ingenuity—he carries his instrument with him everywhere—and through help from none other than Jake Horse himself do they escape. Brief and more predictable than some of the author's other stories, the book is still satisfying. Old Jake Horse makes a fairly standard crotchety hermit-with-a-soft-heart; but Banjo, with his layers of dirt, his trusty banjo, and his grin "that cracked open fresher than a raw egg," is a truly original character. He and Alvin are an entertaining team.

Ilene Cooper

SOURCE: A review of *Banjo,* in *Booklist,* Vol. 79, No. 8, December 15, 1982, p. 567.

Banjo is a dirty little country boy whose only friend is the banjo he always carries on his back. Alvin Dickinson doesn't want to pick him as his partner in a class project, but feels so sorry for him that he does. They are to write about a famous character, and Banjo knows just the one: Jake Horse, an old miner who is a hermit—or some say a ghost. The boys go looking for Horse in the dangerous, deserted spar mine and find trouble instead when they fall and are trapped in a hole. Not unexpectedly, they are saved by Jake Horse, and this experience has a life-affirming effect on both Banjo and Jake. Recounted in a sassy country accent and deadpan detail, this is predictable yet effortlessly told. It will go down as easily as hot grits on a cold morning. Peppered with rather surrealistic pencil sketches.

Anne L. McKeithen

SOURCE: A review of *Banjo,* in *The New York Times Book Review,* January 16, 1983, p. 22.

Relying on the rustic flavors of rural American life Robert Newton Peck gives us the story of Banjo Byler, the middle of 11 children who live with their mother in a "beat-up tarpaper shack with no glass in the windows." Banjo, who had never been chosen for anything, gets picked by classmate Alvin Dickinson as his partner to write a theme about a famous person. Banjo himself is famous at school for being smelly, unkempt and playing a mean banjo he carries everywhere.

The boys choose local hermit Jake Horse as the subject of their report, and, in pursuit of Jake, venture into an old mine that all the local children are warned to avoid. Disaster strikes when the two boys fall into an abandoned mine shaft and Banjo breaks his leg. Who should discover the boys' plight but mean Jake Horse?

Not tall enough to be a tale but still hard to believe, this slim volume presents an overdrawn variety of country bumpkins, strained language and forced plot elements. Black-and-white pencil drawings [by Andrew Glass] reinforce the stilted image of dumb-but-hopeful country folks. This story is difficult to place in time. It seems decades old in the descriptions of a one-room school, children named Agnes, Marybell and Alvin and a doctor who makes house calls. But a remark that someone "is bananas" seems more current. Though well-paced and suspenseful, *Banjo* cannot touch Peck's clean, homely evocation of Americana in *A Day No Pigs Would Die* or the fun of his "Soup" books.

Jane E. Gardner

SOURCE: A review of *Banjo,* in *School Library Journal,* Vol. 30, No. 3, November, 1983, p. 81.

Alvin's choice of Banjo Byler, a dirty, poor and unpopular boy, as his partner for a school assignment leads him into unexpected adventure. Banjo wants to write about a local hermit, Jake Horse, and on their journey to find him they stop to climb abandoned spar mine silos. Banjo falls in, but his shirt catches on a hook, breaking his fall but choking him. Peck's description of Alvin's dangerous rescue attempt and their fall to the silo bottom will rivet readers to the page. Alive, hurt and frightened, Banjo plays his ever-present (and unbroken) banjo to attract attention. Rescued by Jake Horse, for whom the experience renews interest in life, the boys return as heroes. Banjo is a changed boy making the story a testament to the power of friendship. Peck has written an exciting adventure tale with enough action to hold reluctant readers who will also be drawn by its short length. His typical countrified writing style helps bring the boys' personalities alive and gives the story humor; [Andrew] Glass' soft pencil drawings, with their cross-hatched backgrounds and exaggerated features, have a slightly eerie and yet humorous quality which suit well the story's tone.

📖 *SOUP IN THE SADDLE* (1983)

Kathleen Beach

SOURCE: A review of *Soup in the Saddle,* in *School Library Journal,* Vol. 29, No. 9, May, 1983, p. 75.

Set once again in the rural Vermont of some 40 to 50

years ago, Robert Newton Peck's latest in the "Soup" series strains unmercifully for laughs and mistakes an overworked plot for a well-developed one. Soup and Rob conspire with the county nurse to save their teacher, Miss Kelly, from the governor's cousin, an outspoken foe of one room schools and older teachers. Through a coincidence, this woman is scheduled to speak at the festivities honoring Miss Kelly's long service to the town of Learning. Perceiving this to be a major threat to their teacher, the boys hatch a harebrained scheme to keep her away. This involves an implausible masquerade, the use of a "borrowed" horse and saddle and more obvious slapstick than can be comfortably swallowed. The nonstop action is neither entertaining nor understandable. Characterization is negligible and depends upon such obvious devices as Soup's continual manipulation of Rob so that he escapes the dangerous jobs with no corresponding insight as to why Rob allows this to happen. The other characters are stick figures, good for one recurring joke each.

Randy Shipp

SOURCE: "More Adventures with Soup and Rob," in *The Christian Science Monitor,* May 13, 1983, p. B5.

Robert Newton Peck's 33rd volume is wonderful fun. It is also the sixth book to feature the inimitable heroes Soup and Rob—a twosome with whom any kid (or former kid) who's ever had a *best* best friend can identify.

In this volume, the discovery of an old saddle in the loft of a neighbor's barn is only the beginning of a series of adventures in the town of Learning, Vt. For even this discovery pales beside the news that their beloved Miss Kelly, who has taught in the one-room schoolhouse for 30 years, is to be honored with a parade, complete with a brass band and "Vermont's favorite singing cowboy, Hoot Holler."

Then comes the horrifying news that the tribute to Miss Kelly may be ruined by Dr. Elsa Pinkerton Uppit, "an extremely large woman, with flaming red hair and a very unpleasant face." This educational bureaucrat is the sworn enemy of all of Vermont's one-room schools and also dislikes older teachers. It remains for Soup and Rob to help save the day in a way that only they can.

The key to the book's appeal is author Robert Peck's deft characterization. The cast may seem somewhat stock. But it calls up instant images of a similar bunch at the Number Nine School in Salem, N.H., some 25 years ago—although our school had been converted from a two-roomer about four years before I arrived.

Fairly simple reading, *Soup in the Saddle* nonetheless has a lot to offer. It's the kind of book that may even tempt nonreaders. Even though most young readers won't have experienced a one-room school, they'll have no difficulty in identifying with the engaging heroes and sharing in their good-natured exploits.

Sam Leaton Sebesta

SOURCE: A review of *Soup in the Saddle,* in *The Reading Teacher,* Vol. 37, No. 2, November, 1983, p. 193.

Robert Newton Peck's comic nostalgic stories about Soup and Rob are reminiscent of Booth Tarkington's Penrod books but easier and more accessible to today's reader. ***Soup in the Saddle*** carries on the tradition, this time with the aid of a "borrowed" saddle and horse. The best help, though, is a mighty nice teacher who helps the boys thwart the plan of a classic do-badder named Dr. Elsa Pinkerton Uppit. It's tall-tale farce tempered with idyllic warmth.

DUKES (1984)

Kirkus Reviews

SOURCE: A review of *Dukes,* in *Kirkus Reviews,* Vol. LII, No. 4, February 15, 1984, p. 165.

Though presented as fiction for "both young and old," this tiny tale of turn-of-the-century Florida is very much in the manner of Peck's folksy-Americana juveniles. The narrator is twelve-ish orphan Lucky, adopted as an abandoned girl-babe by old alcoholic Nose McColgan ("my geezer") and his deaf-mute black boxer, "Big Baptist." Together, then, this odd, loving threesome travels by wagon from town to town—drumming up a crowd with music (Lucky on harmonica), then charging $1 a head for the locals to watch Big Baptist take on all comers. But Lucky knows that gentle, aging Baptist really hates to fight; on the other hand she dreams of saving enough money "to purchase our dirt, for a home place." And then, in the town of Caloosa, after a profitable two-night stint (made unusual by an impromptu lady mud-wrestle and a near-knockdown for Baptist), Lucky gets her home place—but only after tragedy: nasty doings by some local extortionists lead to a violent end for brave Baptist. Despite the overbearing sentimentality, the phony-happy endings, and Lucky's cutesy-dialect narration: a distinctive anecdote with flickers of grit and charm.

Anne H. Ross

SOURCE: A review of *Dukes,* in *Library Journal,* Vol. 109, No. 8, May 1, 1984, p. 916.

Peck is well known for his vivid and masterful portrayals of small-town life for juveniles and young adults. His latest YA novel will also be of interest to adult readers. A battered trio bound together by love and mutual need make their way through the Florida backwater towns. Lucky—who was found in the back of their "Dukes" wagon as an infant—narrates the story of their visit to cracker Caloosa around a dozen years later. With her are Eugene "Nose" McColgan, mid-seventies, and the black and deaf Big Baptist who fights all comers for a fee in their makeshift ring. The happy ending for Nose and Lucky jars a bit, coming right after the tragic and wrongful death of Big Baptist, but that is the novel's only fault.

Dana McDougald

SOURCE: A review of *Dukes,* in *The Book Report,* Vol. 3, No. 2, September-October, 1984, p. 35.

As a baby, Lucky was dumped in the back of Nose Mc-Colgan's wagon. Since then, she has been with the old Irishman and an aging and deaf black boxer named Big Baptist. They take their music and boxing show on the road, and despite their poverty, the trio shares dreams of settling down in a real home. This dream is threatened in Caloosa, where a sheriff forces them to give most of their savings for a business license. Tragedy follows as Baptist is shot and killed. But things work out well for Lucky when she is adopted by a kind couple, who later take in Nose.

Peck has written a story rich in characterization and emotion, which should appeal to boys and girls. The boxing sequences provide action, and the relationship of Lucky, Nose, and Baptist is truly heartwarming.

📖 *SOUP'S GOAT* (1984)

Cathryn Male

SOURCE: A review of *Soup's Goat,* in *School Library Journal,* Vol. 30, No. 7, March, 1984, p. 164.

Soup's up to his old tricks in still another account of Rob Peck's childhood escapades in rural Vermont. This time Rob and Soup attempt to win the class goat cart race proposed by Miss Boland, the school nurse. Soup devises a secret plan, utilizing his cousin's talent to swear like Donald Duck and the goat's fear of Miss Boland's favorite song as impetus to spur the goats on to victory. Unfortunately, much of what seemed fresh in the first Soup books now seems overworked. Readers figure out Soup's scheme long before Rob does. Peck stretches his plot rather thin, a fault only partially redeemed by Peck's occasional sparks of wit. Rob's teacher, Miss Kelly, his rival, Janice Riker, and his sweetheart, Norma Jean Bissell, are all adequately portrayed, but Rob's rhapsodizing over Norma Jean becomes a bit tiresome, as does his inability to keep up with Soup's antics. Soup fans may welcome his return, but they will find this book, like its predecessor *Soup in the Saddle,* to be more repetitive than original.

Zena Sutherland

SOURCE: A review of *Soup's Goat,* in *Bulletin of the Center for Children's Books,* Vol. 37, No. 8, April, 1984, p. 153.

Rob, the narrator of all the stories about himself and his pal, Soup, tells the story of the great goat-cart race orga-nized by the county nurse, a tuba-playing woman depict-ed as fatuous and foolish. Indeed, most of the depiction of characters is the same sort of superficial derogation. The writing style is self-consciously cutesy-Yankee, and the plot, which is tedious and equally cute, is contrived. Despite the weaknesses of the book, the sometimes-frantic action and the corny humor may appeal to some readers.

Nancy C. Hammond

SOURCE: A review of *Soup's Goat,* in *The Horn Book Magazine,* Vol. LX, No. 2, April, 1984, p. 198.

More spirited high jinks from Soup and Rob in the small Vermont town. When Soup's fastidious cousin Sexton Dilly—his parents' "perfect little precious"—arrives for a two-week visit and declines to participate in the two friends' usual pursuits, the pair suspects he is going to be "about as much fun as an all-night dentist." They are flabbergasted when Sexton divulges an incongruous tal-ent for swearing "for one entire minute without repeating one single word" and audaciously charges a fee for his impressive performance. But Soup, a tireless schemer, blackmails Sexton into using his talent to help himself and Rob win a goat-cart race on Goat Day. At the finish the three boys land with Dirty Laundry (the name of their cart constructed from a discarded hospital laundry cart) in a heap at the feet of the honorary guest, the famous South Sea explorer Dr. Frank Sumatra. Less sentimental and less episodic than the first volumes but still bursting with slapstick and puns, the narrative occasionally sacrifices verisimilitude for humor. Yet the boys' friendship, equal-ly dependent on loyalty and rivalry, is as true as ever. And female readers, peeved at previous portrayals of the class bully Janice Riker and of the dimpled, passive Nor-ma Jean, will be encouraged when the latter reveals her intelligence and gives the male chauvinist Soup a fitting comeuppance.

📖 *SPANISH HOOF* (1985)

Kirkus Reviews

SOURCE: A review of *Spanish Hoof,* in *Kirkus Reviews,* Vol. LIII, Nos. 1-5, March 1, 1985, p. J13.

Save that ranch and sell that pony: an utterly predictable yet endearingly sweet-'n'-earthy tale of cattle-ranching in Depression-era Florida—narrated by Harry (Harriet) Beecher, an eleven-year-old tomboy on the verge of all sorts of growing-up. The Beechers' ranch is Spanish Hoof; long-widowed Mama runs things, with dedicated help from 16-year-old Dab (a teasing/loving big brother to Harry), from ancient hired hand Poke (who doubles as cook), and from young hired hand Lightning (who works "at about one step ahead of whoa"). And, though times are hard, Spanish Hoof is getting along well enough for Harry to be given her very own pony—while Dab has enough spare time to start a-courtin' neighbor gal Trudy Sue (about which Harry has decidedly mixed feelings). Then, however, the Hoof is hit with one unlucky mishap after another: a brood-cow gets mud-stuck—and slaughtered by an alligator—while birthing a calf; Lightning gets beat up after a night of shady gambling in town; the whole new crop of calves has to be destroyed after an outbreak of contagious black leg; and Mama's doctor orders her to give up ranch-work forever—on account of her perilously weak heart. Can the Hoof be saved from bankruptcy and foreclosure by the Otookee Bank? Of course it can—but only after the hired hands volunteer their life-savings . . . and after Harry (now starting to like the idea of "Harriet") swallows her tears and allows Dabney to sell beloved pony Noble. Plain, sturdy work in Peck's tried-and-true manner—with just enough ranch-work grit and flinty humor to keep the sentimentality under control.

Karen Stang Hanley

SOURCE: A review of *Spanish Hoof*, in *Booklist*, Vol. 81, No. 16, April 15, 1985, p. 1198.

Times are hard on the Spanish Hoof cattle ranch in Florida in the midst of the Depression, but eleven-year-old Harry Beecher, absorbed in caring for her new horse, Noble, and avoiding her older brother Dabney's teasing, pays little heed. Then black leg disease strikes the ranch's calves, eliminating the Beecher's sole source of income. Newly aware of their serious money problems, Harry watches her widowed mother succumb to exhaustion, causing Dab to quit school in order to shoulder responsibility for the ranch's day-to-day operation. Steeling herself to do her share, Harry sells her horse, but her pain is tempered with pride in the awareness that her sacrifice makes her an equal partner, with her family and two hired hands, in securing the future of Spanish Hoof. Briefly described, this heartwarming story sounds more sentimental than it is. Peck's dialogue is shaped in crisp, homespun speech patterns that are both funny and expressive, making this an effective read-aloud for those comfortable with the colloquialisms. This rewarding story about a girl's departure from childhood and a loving extended family is also a natural for independent reading.

📖 *SOUP ON ICE* (1985)

Susan Roman

SOURCE: A review of *Soup on Ice,* in *Booklist*, Vol. 82, No. 2, September 15, 1985, p. 138.

Anticipation of Santa Claus' arrival on Christmas Eve in Learning, Vermont, gets Rob and Soup into a pack of trouble as they try to help in the behind-the-scene staging of the event. Joe Sutter, who usually dresses up in a Santa costume each year, is in the hospital with a broken leg. After all of the other possibilities for a substitute Santa are eliminated, Soup suggests that the local pool parlor owner, Slosh Dubinsky, the meanest guy in town, play

the role. What follows is fairly predictable—the meanest guy has the warmest heart, the poorest child gets the best gift (the one Soup and Rob covet), restoring the child's faith in Christmas; and the townspeople get a flashy and spectacular visit from Santa when his sleigh crashes into the town's huge Christmas tree with Soup and Rob aboard (as the attractive jacket illustration reveals). With all its humor, this Christmas story, the seventh adventure of Soup and his friends, will be in demand where the other escapades are popular.

Peggy Forehand

SOURCE: A review of *Soup on Ice,* in *School Library Journal,* Vol. 32, No. 2, October, 1985, p. 192.

There is no doubt that Peck has a flare for combining sentiment, humor and adventure in this seventh in the series. Soup and Rob are high-spirited friends whose good-natured pranks and old-fashioned trouble keep the pace light. These comical friends strive (with typical youthful rationale) to stay out of trouble in hope of great rewards on Christmas morn. With the best of intentions they assist their teacher and school nurse in arranging the town's celebrations, only to have their plan backfire and create a hilarious finale to the tree-lighting ceremony. More important than the humor of the tale is Peck's portrayal of Soup and Rob's compassion for a less fortunate friend and a misunderstood adult. Peck tells a story that portends the real Christmas spirit in subtle style.

📖 *SOUP ON FIRE* (1987)

Kirkus Reviews

SOURCE: A review of *Soup on Fire,* in *Kirkus Reviews,* Vol. LVI, No. 22, November 15, 1987, p. 1632.

In the ninth Soup and Rob adventure, Peck continues his nostalgic and gentle recounting of life in a small Vermont town during the 1930's.

As usual, Soup and Rob are finding it difficult to stay out of trouble. But this time their antics aren't witnessed by just their fellow townspeople; the bright lights of Hollywood are on them, too! The residents of Learning are ecstatic when they hear that the Hollywood Heartburn Talent Show is sending Fearless Ferguson to scout for new talent, and Soup is convinced that his newest plan is a sure-fire way for Rob and him to become Hollywood's newest stuntmen. But when Soup's plan backfires, the town finds itself knee-deep in strawberry-scented Bathsheba Bubble Bath.

With deceptive simplicity, Peck has written a lively, adventure-filled novel that perpetuates the idea that life used to be more staid and secure; but at the same time, he shatters the myth that all children were well-behaved and polite. Enjoyable fare for middle readers.

Ilene Cooper

SOURCE: A review of *Soup on Fire,* in *Booklist,* Vol. 84, No. 9, January 1, 1988, p. 787.

Hold your horses, Soup's back with his friend Rob Peck, a willing accomplice and chronicler of their deeds. It's a big day in Learning, Vermont, as two competing groups vie for the town's attention. There's Hollywood Heartburn's Talent Show, featuring the hero of the Saturday movie serials, Fearless Ferguson; coming to save the town's souls are Bishop Zion Zeal and his revival company, the Golden Prophets of Eternal Glory. Soup and Rob's only interest in the glory group is avoiding them, but Fearless Ferguson and company are another matter entirely. Whoever wins their talent-show search will get a free trip to Hollywood, and Soup is confident he knows the way to do it. Rob is sure Soup will get them in deep trouble, but as usually happens with these two rambunctious characters, after mistakes, mishaps, and madcap antics, things work out for the best. Peck's high humor is in evidence again as he ties wild action and jokes into a fine surprise package. As the series grows, so do its fans—libraries can expect more of both.

📖 *HALLAPOOSA* (1988)

Publishers Weekly

SOURCE: A review of *Hallapoosa,* in *Publishers Weekly,* Vol. 233, No. 13, April 1, 1988, p. 75.

Hallapoosa is an impoverished southern Florida town where 12-year-old Thane MacHugh and his sister Alma Lee, seven, newly orphaned, are sent in 1931 to live with their father's elderly brother Hiram, a gentlemanly bachelor who is also the town's justice of the peace. Peck (*The Day No Pigs Would Die*) saves his new novel from unbridled sweetness with a series of ingenious plot twists and a number of razor-sharp characters. One of these is Vestavia, the aging but still authoritarian black housekeeper who is determined to raise the bereft children in the same strict manner she brought up their father and uncle. Vestavia's close friend (a well-guarded secret in the strictly segregated community) is Miss Sellie Fulsom, the elderly, keen-eyed next-door neighbor whose memory holds most of the town's deepest secrets. Charlie Moon Sky, a canny half-breed Seminole, keeps a necessary watch on the newly arrived children, since a clan of brutal and meanspirited bootleggers plan to kidnap Alma Lee and sell her into white slavery as part of their scheme to avenge themselves on the MacHugh family for past wrongs. Alma Lee's eventual rescue involves most of the townspeople and some mysterious prisoners from the Hallapoosa jail, a combination that solves a group of knotty problems and ties up all loose strands in an agreeably surprising way.

Kirkus Reviews

SOURCE: A review of *Hallapoosa,* in *Kirkus Reviews,* Vol. LVI, No. 8, April 15, 1988, p. 567.

Peck takes another excursion into the rural past, this time to a small town in Depression-era Florida.

Told from the points of view of several of the town's residents, this is mostly about Hiram MacHugh, justice of the peace of Hallapoosa, who has spent his uneventful life in the shadow of his younger brother Bobby, a star athlete in high school. As middle age advances, Hiram's life is full of small pleasures, including the Saturday night visits of Glory, a young girl half his age. But these visits, and other habits, abruptly come to an end with the notification that Bobby and his wife have been killed in an automobile accident, leaving their twelve-year-old son and seven-year-old daughter in his care. The arrival of these children, like stones dropped into a still pool of water, has ever widening effects . . . until the entire town is involved in a climax that includes a murder, a kidnapping, and the return—from the dead—of Bobby.

A routine, predictable story in the familiar southern, rural slice-of-life vein—with characters who walk a thin line between archetype and stereotype—but Peck's language is a pungent, evocative pleasure here, and the book's a satisfying—if not particularly original—one.

Beth E. Andersen

SOURCE: A review of *Hallapoosa,* in *Voice of Youth Advocates,* Vol. 11, No. 5, December, 1988, p. 241.

Nothing is as it seems in Depression-plagued Hallapoosa, Florida, in 1931. A suspicious car/train wreck in northern Florida brings two young orphans to Hallapoosa to live with uncle Hiram McHugh, Justice of the Peace. Hiram takes his new child-rearing responsibilities seriously and gives up his bachelor vices (moonshine and Saturday night visits from the lovely but fallen Glory, a young "Cricker" struggling to provide for her son Lot while protecting them both from her father's incestuous rages). Soon there is a white slavery plot, a murder, a disappearing body, a kidnaping and the unveiling of secret drifters. Peck builds a delicious tension as he carefully unravels a fabric of deceit, woven to protect three innocent children. An all-night search for the missing child culminates in a deadly confrontation in the nearby swamp.

Peck, author of *A Day No Pigs Would Die,* has written a tale rich in beautifully-drawn characters coping with brutal times. Highly recommended.

📖 *THE HORSE HUNTERS* (1988)

Kirkus Reviews

SOURCE: A review of *The Horse Hunters,* in *Kirkus Reviews,* Vol. LVI, No. 18, September 15, 1988, p. 1352.

Like the author's *Hallapoosa, Dukes,* and his many other juvenile and adult novels, this tale about a Depression-era, rural Florida rancher's son who proves his manhood via a wild mustang roundup (a kind of trial-by-horse) is another blend of old-chestnut plotting and corn-fed sentiment—but the narrative lopes along easy and there's plenty of peppery talk and rugged action.

Fifteen-year-old Ladd Bodeen has gotten no respect from tough older brother Tate—now manager of the Buckle Tee ranch—ever since their father became a blank-eyed invalid after the accidental death of Ladd's mother. Then comes the chance for Ladd to set off by himself to capture a herd of wild mustangs in the South. Along the danger-packed way (Ladd's cherished mule is horribly eaten by a gator), Ladd will meet Cora, a spunky 20-year-old with a fatherless baby who lives in fierce isolation; and Mr. Dodge Yardell, another loner and former chum of Bodeen, Sr. Yardell, a thorny type who carves carousel horses, spouts wisdom about horses and life-as-she-should-be-lived, accompanies Ladd on the roundup, and aims to shoot the great white stallion ("Entirely male"! by golly)—which even in his golden years has been stealing mares. Ladd not only asks for the stallion's life, but insists that he should be the first to ride the animal. At the close, there's a hero's return in a procession that includes Cora and baby (Ladd offers them "protection") and Yardell, who reawakens Bodeen, Sr. And of course there's a new sense of brotherly love and Ladd's own proud sense of Being a Man.

A rite of passage, thundering-hoofbeats division. Old stuff in familiar and amiable sacking.

Hazel Rochman

SOURCE: A review of *Horse Hunters,* in *Booklist,* Vol. 85, No. 12, February 15, 1989, p. 995.

With little of the simplicity and restraint of his classic rite-of-passage novel, *A Day No Pigs Would Die,* Peck tells of 15-year-old Ladd Bodeen who finds his manhood when he captures a herd of wild horses, including a white stallion, in Florida in the 1930s. Readers who can get past the portentous messages ("Freedom isn't given, boy. It's taken. Grabbed") and the overdone folksiness (just about every sentence includes a downhome simile) will enjoy the adventure story. They will be moved by Ladd's struggle to prove himself to his macho older brother, by the action in the wilderness with everything from alligators to rattlesnakes, and by the contrast between Ladd's ignominious fall from a rodeo bull at the start of the book and his triumphant return with the captured horses at the end.

Jim Walz

SOURCE: A review of *The Horse Hunters,* in *The Book Report,* Vol. 8, No. 1, May-June, 1989, p. 46.

Pardner, if you're fed up with trendy teen novels of drugs and moody introspection, corral this yarn for a welcome change. Ladd's first-person account of turning 16 in Florida's outback during the summer of 1932 is another Peck

success. There's an exciting hunt for the state's last herd of wild mustangs, but the plot really hinges on Ladd's proving his manhood to himself, "the only measure that counted," and coming to terms with his family and their world. Colorful characters abound, from his stern older brother, guilt-ridden father, and long-dead mother to wise old Dodge (who "gentles" wild horses rather than "breaks" them), and Cora, the unwed teen mother who "sure had a shiny way to say things." Part and parcel of the whole shebang are the language and philosophy, reminiscent of another coming-of-age novel set in Florida, *The Yearling.* "Freedom isn't given, boy. It's taken." "Easy never comes first. What comes first is sweat." Both Jody Baxter and Ladd might have been cut from the same herd. So, if this is your brand of young'un, make this a first purchase.

Allan A. Cuseo

SOURCE: A review of *The Horse Hunters,* in *Voice of Youth Advocates,* Vol. 12, No. 2, June, 1989, p. 105.

The Bodeen family is a hurting family, tortured by past guilts and secrets which have caused father Sam to be semi-comatose; brother Tate, belligerent and taciturn; and 15 year old protagonist Ladd to search for the love and acceptance he has been denied. Peck's novel is a coming-of-age epic, similar to his *A Day No Pigs Would Die,* but more violent in story and, unfortunately, more lethargic in style. Peck's style, a combination of folk idiom in dialogue and legendary heroic characters, trespasses on the story. The reader is too mindful of the metaphors and similes which pop up in virtually every sentence more often than a jack rabbit in the moonlight. Violence, another Peck element, underlies the activities of the Bodeen daily life and Ladd's quest to capture the legendary heroic white wild stallion and the band of mares necessary to acquire property and profit for the family's Buckle Tee Ranch. Set in the Florida wilderness in the 1930s, Peck's tale is of Ladd's search for manhood, his search for his father's and brother's love, all paralleled with his search for the wild horses.

Peck's usual themes of endurance, freedom of choice, and humankind's basic goodness are affirmed. An underlying sexual tension, hinted at in previous Peck novels, surfaces as Ladd meets and is attracted to a young single woman, Cora. The earthy tone aids this tension but the graphically explicit, although not unwarranted violence will create an unpleasant read for some YAs. Booktalking possibilities abound but the ponderous pace will hinder some readers from finishing the novel.

ARLY (1989)

Jennifer Brown

SOURCE: A review of *Arly,* in *Children's Book Review Service,* Vol. 17, No. 11, June, 1989, p. 126.

Ten-year-old Arly Poole is growing up in 1927 in rural

Jailtown, Florida and it is a jail. His vegetable picking father and he live on Shack Row and can never erase their debt to the "company store." In two years Arly will be a full-time picker too, and there seems to be no hope until the steamer brings a schoolteacher. Arly's father is determined that this will be his son's ticket out, but it isn't easy. The bosses fight the school and Arly must make the emotional break from Jailtown. This is a powerful book which any caring adult should read, for as the author says, we still have this problem today, only their names are Marita and Pasco. Younger children will enjoy the book as an exciting and sometimes cruel adventure of a boy growing up.

Katharine Bruner

SOURCE: A review of *Arly,* in *School Library Journal,* Vol. 35, No. 10, June, 1989, p. 108.

Jailtown, Fla., in 1927 is a mean blight on the edge of Lake Okeechobee, controlled as tightly as a slave ship by field boss Roscoe Broda. In compelling, expressive dialect, Arly Poole tells how he and his friend Huff spy on the painted ladies at the Lucky Leg Social Palace; how his Papa is worn old from a lifetime of picking vegetables in the dusty shadeless fields; how deeply he feels for Huff's older sister, Essie May, whose developing womanhood has caught Broda's lecherous attention. But most of all he recounts the arrival of feisty Miss Binnie Hoe to be the town's first school teacher. Arly's Papa shoves him forward to be one of her pupils because he desperately wants for his son not to be trapped in the life of a picker. Miss Hoe recognizes the sparkling star within Arly and, because of her efforts and those of Brother Smith, an old black fisherman, his life will be salvaged. It is Arly himself, though, who imbues the story with special dimension. Peck has given his readers a true hero, compassionate and self-effacing, yet blazing with determination and courage. Arly's adventures at school, his encounters with evil, his moments of grief and despair, remain vivid long after the last page has been turned.

Phillis Wilson

SOURCE: A review of *Arly,* in *Booklist,* Vol. 85, No. 21, July, 1989, p. 1906.

Peck's message—the triumph of the human spirit over indomitable odds is not only possible, but a goal to relentlessly fight for—is admirably stated. Set in 1927 in a migrant camp in Jailtown, Florida, the story features 11-year-old Arly Poole, who lives with his father in Shack Row. Arly would live and die illiterate if not for the stranger who arrives one Sunday on the *Caloosahatchee Queen.* The delicate and restrained demeanor of Miss Binnie Hoe belie the underlying feistiness, good humor, and invincible will of this teacher who has come to start a school. Vivid descriptions evoke the beauty and the horror of the Okeechobee Swamp, which Captain Tant's whip and rope have turned into a virtual prison for the produce pickers

who live there. Peck balances action with characterization; readers will come to know Arly and his courageous but dying daddy and realize that Arly's greatest gift to his father is his ability to learn and get out. A memorable work and a beautiful tribute to teachers.

Doris Losey

SOURCE: A review of *Arly,* in *Voice of Youth Advocates,* Vol. 12, No. 3, August, 1989, p. 160.

Arly Poole, 12, lives on Shack Row in the picker town of Jailtown somewhere on the banks of Lake Okeechobee. Until the town's first school teacher arrives, he has no future except working in the sugar cane mill. Through the kindness of Miss Hoe, the teacher, Arly learns to read and eventually escapes his bleak future in Jailtown. Although the events occur in the 1920s, the author's postscript tries to draw a parallel with today's migrant children (who definitely experience hardships). However, if Peck hopes this novel will inspire readers to take action, I fear he will be disappointed. The book, which will appeal only to adults who like to read nostalgia, is poorly written, with an abundance of "purple prose," stereotypical characters, and a cliched plot. Difficult to read because of dialect and poor writing, this novel is definitely not recommended.

HIGBEE'S HALLOWEEN (1990)

Cindy Darling Codell

SOURCE: A review of *Higbee's Halloween,* in *School Library Journal,* Vol. 36, No. 10, October, 1990, p. 118.

Using familiar *Soup* patterns, Peck creates likable Quincy Cobb, who is frequently led astray by his friend Higbee Higginbottom. In rural Clod's Corner around the 1930s, Quince and Hig basically reflect the solid values of their community. They love their teacher for her devotion to them and admire the librarian's ability to organize civic activities. Placing a snake in a bully's lunch box, planning to liberate a pumpkin, and looking forward to a Halloween party are all part of a normal day until the Striker family arrives. Strongly reminiscent of the Herdmans in Barbara Robinson's *Best Christmas Pageant Ever*—but not quite as funny—the Strikers are the worst disciplined children imaginable. When they put a homemade "torture chamber" to use, Hig decides it is time for action. Peck's tendency to saddle nearly all characters with alliterative and strongly descriptive nomenclature can be irritating—a bully named Bruto Bigfister, a librarian called Miss Booky—but unsophisticated readers may find this quite comedic. The characters are interesting and true enough, and the well-paced plot and splashes of humor will urge even reluctant readers to race to the finish.

Kirkus Reviews

SOURCE: A review of *Higbee's Halloween,* in *Kir-*

kus Reviews, Vol. LVIII, No. 19, October 1, 1990, p. 1397.

Striker family members (Bubonico, Convulsia, and their children: Canker, Fester, Hernia, Jaundice, Scurvy, Typhus, and Zitt) have terrorized the small town of Clod's Corner long enough; it's time for Higbee Higginbottom and his all-too-obedient buddy, Quincy Cobb, to spring (or, more accurately, slide) into action. A Halloween party organized by Miss Booky, town librarian, provides the perfect opportunity—while a few odds and ends, a giant pumpkin, and Big Mouth (the town cannon) are the means, and Higbee's fevered brain provides the plan. Peck herds his predictable cast into line, slaps the humor on with a broad brush, unabashedly strokes teachers and librarians, and concludes with a literally explosive climax. Soup fans won't be disappointed in these new characters.

Nina VandeWater

SOURCE: A review of *Higbee's Halloween,* in *Voice of Youth Advocates,* Vol. 13, No. 5, December, 1990, pp. 287-88.

Higbee Higginbottom and Quincy Cobb (ages unspecified) team up in this tall tale of Halloween mischief. Higbee and Quincy are not just reminiscent of Peck's series starring Soup Vinson and Rob Peck—they *are* Soup and Rob. Miss Kelly, Miss Boland, Norma Jean Bissell, and Janice Riker, though renamed, are present as well. Presumably there is some publishing/marketing/legal impetus for this cloning. Of course, readers won't know what it is, and librarians will have to decide if they need another Soup series, which is already extensive.

The tale itself is adequate and revolves around Higbee's plot to annihilate the town troublemakers during Clod's Corners' annual Halloween bash. As usual, Higbee is the leader as Quincy resigns himself to the fate of those who must follow. "Just say no" to peer pressure hasn't reached Clod's Corners yet. Justice, Truth, and the Higginbottom Way triumph in the rip-roarin' conclusion.

📖 *ARLY'S RUN* (1991)

Kirkus Reviews

SOURCE: A review of *Arly's Run,* in *Kirkus Reviews,* Vol. LIX, No. 22, November 15, 1991, p. 1474.

In a sequel to *Arly,* the spirited young picker's quest for a new home and family takes him along a rocky road.

After his boat overturns on Lake Okeechobee and his companion, Brother Smith, is lost, Arly Poole finds himself branded and forced into a work gang, where he makes a friend in old Coo Coo. After months of hard, unpaid field labor, the two escape and take up with a wandering evangelist. Then a hurricane howls past, and Arly and a

few other stunned survivors are left wandering a devastated landscape.

Peck dedicates this book to Florida's migrant workers, with many of whom he worked and spoke, and his picture of their life (as it was in 1928) is a vivid one; even more compelling is his account of the hurricane and its aftermath. Eventually, Arly hooks up with an older woman, Mrs. Day, and a young orphan, Tar; Coo Coo reappears (then dies in a gun battle that, compared to the storm, seems anticlimactic), as do Brother Smith and several people from the previous book, including Liddy Tant and even Binnie Hoe, Arly's beloved teacher. By the end, Arly has his family. A well-told story.

Randy Meyer

SOURCE: A review of *Arly's Run,* in *Booklist,* Vol. 88, No. 8, December 15, 1991, p. 759.

Also set in the early part of the nineteenth century, Peck's sequel to *Arly* begins with the orphaned hero on the run from the Florida work farm where he had lived and worked with his father. Aided by Brother Smith, Arly escapes and sets off across Florida for Moore Haven, where his teacher, Miss Hoe, has arranged for a family to shelter him. After a violent storm separates Arly and Brother Smith, Arly continues his trek alone. Along the way, he's befriended by an alcoholic field hand and meets up with slave catchers and evangelists. When he finally reaches his destination, he is caught in the midst of a hurricane that wipes the town of Moore Haven off the map. Peck's writing is uneven. Some story elements are powerful—the lyrical southern dialect, the terrifying hurricane that nearly costs Arly his life. But the plotting of the journey is flawed. Trip episodes seem foreshortened to the point of artificiality, and the equally abrupt ending, which brings Miss Hoe back into the story, cheats readers who've put their faith in Arly's ability to find his own solutions. But structural flaws aside, teens will find the novel worth reading, if only for Arly's indomitable spirit and the exciting hurricane scene.

Elaine Fort Weischedel

SOURCE: A review of *Arly's Run,* in *School Library Journal,* Vol. 38, No. 2, February, 1992, p. 108.

Peck picks up the action just minutes from where it ended in *Arly* as Brother Smith is rowing the boy across Lake Okeechobee to a new life in Moore Haven. The boat capsizes, and Arly is left hanging onto an oar while Brother Smith supposedly drowns. He struggles ashore, only to be captured, branded, and forced into a work gang of migrant pickers. He befriends an old man called Coo Coo, and the two are hauled across the Florida produce fields for the best part of a year before Arly convinces his friend to escape. Things are looking up until the hurricane of 1928 hits; again the hero manages to survive. After more disasters, the book ends as he is once more poised for a better life. The pickers have only numbers, not names, and regularly lie down in the fields and die. The boy clings to the belief that if he can just reach Moore Haven everything will come out right, even though he knows it has been wiped out by the storm. Arly is the only character with any depth; the rest are so lightly sketched in as to be more caricatures than characters. And ultimately, he seems more like a pawn in some master's chess game, totally controlled by forces outside himself and content to have it so. Peck writes powerfully, but one wonders how many readers will hang on through the catalog of catastrophe that is Arly's life.

Kathy Elmore

SOURCE: A review of *Arly's Run,* in *Voice of Youth Advocates,* Vol. 15, No. 1, April, 1992, p. 34.

Arly's Run is the sequel to Peck's *Arly* published in 1989. Arly is a 12 year old white boy living in Florida during the late 1920s. As the story opens, Arly is being paddled across Lake Okeechobee to escape Jailtown for a new life. Due to bad weather, the boat capsizes and when Arly makes his way to shore, he's captured by company men who put him to work as a picker. The cruel treatment of the pickers is realistically portrayed as Arly is forced to work the fields without proper food, rest, and protection. He teams up with an elderly picker named Coo Coo, and it's their friendship that keeps them both going. The two manage to escape and join up with a traveling revival troupe where just as Arly begins to experience his first love a hurricane hits and devastates the area.

This historical adventure grabs the reader from the first chapter. The main characters are sympathetic and memorable. They show a nontraditional family, one made by love and caring. The treatment of the pickers is eye-opening. Although the intended audience is middle school/junior high, this title can be used with all age groups to start discussion on the plight of migrant workers. *Arly's Run* is highly recommended as an addition to all historical fiction collections.

📖 *A PART OF THE SKY* (1994)

Kirkus Reviews

SOURCE: A review of *A Part of the Sky,* in *Kirkus Reviews,* Vol. LXII, No. 14, July 15, 1994, p. 943.

The sequel to *A Day No Pigs Would Die* once again follows the young Robert Peck on his path to adulthood, but the strengths of the first novel—plain people, simple language, and old-fashioned Shaker values—are virtually parodied in this latest.

The hero bears the author's name, and the action takes place in a small town in Peck's native Vermont. Told from 13-year-old Rob's perspective, the narrative begins with his father's death, which leaves him in charge of the

land, his mother, his aunt, and $12-a-month mortgage payments that are almost impossible to scrape together even this early in the Depression. Next, their faithful, old cow goes dry and gets sold for dog meat. Then, their hard-working ox keels over. Finally, the worst drought to hit the area in years kicks in, and even the family's blister-raising efforts to haul water by hand from the creek can't save the crops. In addition to working his own land and going to school as often as he can, Rob helps out on a neighbor's farm and in a feed store until neither can afford to pay him any longer. When winter sets in and Rob is reduced to doing odd jobs for food and making a meal out of cracked corn intended for chickens, he remembers that "manhood is doing what has to be done" and sells the farm. In the three plumbing-less rooms above the feed store that the owner offers in exchange for work, Rob and his family are, of course, happy.

Rob comes of age *again*. We haven't waited long enough for this book.

Hazel Rochman

SOURCE: A review of *A Part of the Sky,* in *Booklist,* Vol. 91, No. 2, September 15, 1994, p. 137.

Peck's stirring autobiographical novel, *A Day No Pigs Would Die,* is a classic story of the bond between a Shaker boy and his father during hard times in Vermont. Unfortunately, this sequel reads like a sermon. Now that Rob's father is dead, the 13-year-old boy must take on the working of the small farm and the protection of his mother and elderly aunt. He must become "a man," as he often says. Lots of people agree ("To grow up is to stand up. Manly"). His kindly neighbors tell him that "manhood is doing what has to be done"; so do his wise teacher, his friend, and his saucy sweetheart. The Shaker idiom, so restrained in the first book, is self-consciously indulged here, more sentimental than strong. Everything is reverential and uplifting. Every character is noble, except for the villainous banker, of course, who's the opposite. Avi's *The Barn* is a far stronger historical novel about an uncertain farm boy thrust into early adulthood. However, Peck does create some fine poetic moments when the universals are rooted in the particulars of daily work. The book ends with a plainspoken account of how the mortgage is foreclosed and Rob and his family must leave the place they have worked and loved.

Joanne Schott

SOURCE: A review of *A Part of the Sky,* in *Quill & Quire,* Vol. 60, No. 11, November, 1994, p. 39.

The hard routine of farm work leaves Rob little time to mourn his father's death. His mother and Aunt Carrie help beyond their strength, even irrigating crops plant by plant with water carried from the creek. If they can continue to make payments for four more years, the small, poor Vermont farm will be their own. Death of aging stock, a drought that spoils the hope of even a small cash crop, and the approaching Depression soon change the family's priorities from planning to keep the farm to staving off starvation. Inevitably, the farm is lost.

Rob has absorbed his father's values of hard work, integrity, and a direct and simple relationship to life—it's a legacy that's part Shaker faith, part pure Vermont. When help comes, Rob and his family are able to accept it without shame.

This is an engrossing portrait of an adolescent boy and of a particular time and place. Author/illustrator Robert Newton Peck balances hardships with hope, Rob's extraordinary efforts with the flashes of humour that characterize his common experiences of mischief at school and the delight and dread of first love. The accents of New England speech ring through the prose, giving it individuality and richness. Sequel to *A Day No Pigs Would Die,* this has the same enduring themes and reality of characterization that will appeal to all ages, from older children to adults.

SOUP 1776 (1995)

Chris Sherman

SOURCE: A review of *Soup 1776,* in *Booklist,* Vol. 92, No. 1, September 1, 1995, p. 78.

In his fourteenth story about Soup and sidekick Rob, Peck resorts to nonstop one-liners, double entendres, and slapstick humor involving dropped drawers, pigeon droppings and curvaceous "patootsies," while he lambastes political correctness and historical revisionists. This time the duo are writing the script for Learning's Fourth of July pageant, a task that necessitates discovering what really happened in 1776, then rewriting history, manipulating a cast of befuddled townspeople, professional wrestlers, and loutish lumberjacks. Adults may find Peck's humor is heavy-handed and sophomoric ("My soul throbbed like a happy hemorrhoid"), with Soup portrayed as a bombastic, hyperactive hellion, and Rob a dithering, compliant companion. Preteens, however, may not be quite so critical and will probably find the silly characters and predictable mayhem hilarious.

Connie Pierce

SOURCE: A review of *Soup 1776,* in *School Library Journal,* Vol. 41, No. 10, October, 1995, p. 139.

Soup is back and causing more trouble for the good folks of Learning, VT. Here, he volunteers his sidekick, Rob Peck, to write a Fourth of July play that is historically accurate. Unfortunately, no one in the town can seem to agree on what actually happened back in 1776. Rob remains the level-headed character that readers love and with whom they can identify, but as usual, Soup is the one who steals the show. The action is fast paced as readers try to unravel the mystery of the secret ingredient Soup has in mind to make this play a blast. And a blast it is! Well written and fun to read.

Michael (Wayne) Rosen

1946-

English poet, playwright, editor, and author of fiction for children and young adults.

Major works include *You Can't Catch Me!* (1981), *Hairy Tales and Nursery Crimes* (1985), *We're Going on a Bear Hunt* (1989), *The Deadman Tapes* (1991), *Sonsense Nongs* (1992).

INTRODUCTION

Michael Rosen is a prolific poet and author of fiction whose collections of humorous and nonsense verse such as *Mind Your Own Business* (1974) and *Sonsense Nongs* have made him an extremely popular figure in contemporary children's literature. Noted for his exploitation of the possibilities of writing from and for the child's perspective, Rosen is credited with expanding the boundaries of poetry as a medium of childhood exploration. He observed in *Language Matters* that "while plenty of people have written about their childhood, they haven't written about it in the kind of speaking voice that is totally accessible to a child, so that they can read it out loud." Rosen's virtuosity with the child's voice is not limited, however, to the often playful verse of *Mind Your Own Business* and the like. He has also made successful use of a variety of cultural tales and retold them to new generations. The song-story *We're Going on a Bear Hunt* and the witty *How the Animals Got Their Colours: Animal Myths from Around the World* (1991) represent a few of Rosen's successful retellings. In addition, many of his writings, especially *The Deadman Tapes* and *Mind the Gap* (1992), aimed at older children and teens, confront disturbing modern social issues of particular importance to young people. Overall, however, Rosen's appeal for critics and children lies in his inventiveness with language and ability to invest everyday activities with charm and humor. Rosen summarized his attitude about the nature of his poetry as follows: "Mostly I write about myself. This is potentially very boring, but I try to make sure it isn't by meeting children in schools and libraries, and informally. I try to discover where my experiences overlap with theirs. Some people are worried about whether what I write is 'poetry.' If they are worried, let them call it something else, for example, 'stuff.'"

Biographical Information

Rosen was born on May 7, 1946, in Harrow, Middlesex, England. He was educated at the Middlesex Hospital Medical School and received his B.A. in English from Wadham College, Oxford, in 1969. His writing began while he was still in school and was influenced particularly in his mid-teens by James Joyce's novel *A Portrait of the Artist as a Young Man*. The work introduced Rosen

to the technique of autobiographical reminiscence using a child's—rather than an adult's—voice. While at Oxford, Rosen also became interested in theater and wrote a comic play that was performed at the Royal Court Theatre, and continued to pursue interests in drama and broadcasting. During this time he became inspired to write poetry by his mother's use of verse for several "Living Language" BBC Radio programs. Composing his poems from the point of view of the child, Rosen created the collection *Mind Your Own Business*. The successful poems of *Mind Your Own Business* and the volumes that followed earned Rosen the reputation as a gifted and original children's poet. Later he began to contribute his poetry to British television as part of the children's program "Talk Write Read" and in the early 1980s created the series *Everybody Here!* for the BBC. Meanwhile he continued to publish poetry, write stories for children, and edit collections of tales and verse for young people. Throughout the 1980s and into the 1990s Rosen produced a wide variety of children's books, collaborating with illustrators, including Quentin Blake, on such works as *Don't Put Mustard in the Custard* (1985), the clever retellings of *How Giraffe Got Such a Long Neck . . . And Why Rhino Is So Grumpy* (1993), and the humorous verse of *Sonsense Nongs* and *Nuts about Nuts* (1993).

Major Works

Most of Rosen's poetry reflects his playful enthusiasm for words, inventiveness, and eclectic gathering of rhymes, anecdotes, fairy tales, and childlike nonsense humor. The verse of *Wouldn't You Like to Know* (1977) and the award-winning *You Can't Catch Me!* reflects the poet's interest in exploring everyday activities and ordinary events from a child's extraordinary perspective. Thus, despite their relatively mundane topics—playing games, eating, anxiously awaiting the return of a lost dog, playfully provoking grown-ups—these poems are, as M. Hobbs writing for *Junior Bookshelf* noted, "deceptively simple" and display a skilled use of rhyme scheme and language. The poems of *Quick, Let's Get Out of Here* (1983) follow the same path. Existing as Rosen's "fantasies of everyday life," they relate incidents from childhood such as relations with siblings, birthday parties, and remembered visits with grandparents. *Freckly Feet and Itchy Knees* (1990) is a light-hearted rhythmic catalogue of human body parts from noses and eyes to knees and feet. *Mind the Gap*, poetic anecdotes and humor directed at teenagers, touches such topics as sexuality, racial inequality, and death. *Sonsense Nongs* is comprised of Rosen's own creations and parodies of songs, as well as the humorous contributions of children, while *Nuts about Nuts* is a celebration of food in quick-moving verse seen through the eyes of a young child. *Pilly Soems* (1995) continues in the tradition of *Sonsense Nongs*.

Among Rosen's stories and anecdotes for children, *Nasty!* (1982) includes four unabashedly creepy London tales related by a Cockney cleaning lady involving such subjects as a giant flea in the Underground and urban infestations of mice and wasps. Told in a simple colloquial style, these stories are designed to appeal to young children in form as well as subject matter. *Hairy Tales and Nursery Crimes* represents Rosen's dabbling with the fractured fairy tale and are surreal retellings of well-known stories, like the Pied Piper of Hamelin, full of jokes and nonsense. Likewise the lively story of *We're Going on a Bear Hunt* should be recognizable to many children as they follow a family on its onomatopoeic, "swishy swashy" trudge through mud, water, and snow in search of a bear. Rosen's other retellings include *How the Animals Got Their Colours: Animal Myths from Around the World*, a series of nine *pourqoui* tales from animal folklore, and *How Giraffe Got Such a Long Neck . . . And Why Rhino Is So Grumpy* of the same genre. Rosen's somewhat longer works of fiction include *You're Thinking about Doughnuts* (1987), a short novel devoted to the stories of little Frank. Frank joins his mother every Friday night as she cleans a museum, but this particular evening he watches all the exhibits come to life and relate their tales. Unlike his usually playful books, Rosen's novel *The Deadman Tapes* contains a series of bitter stories related by teenagers. Assembled as eight tapes found by young Paul Deadman when he moves into a new house, these tales docu-

ment the personal and social problems of modern adolescence.

Awards

Rosen's honors include a Signal Poetry Award in 1982 for *You Can't Catch Me!*, an Other Award from *Children's Book Bulletin* in 1983 for his book of miscellany, *Everybody Here!*, and Smarties Best Children's Book of the Year in 1989 for *We're Going on a Bear Hunt*. Additionally, his play *Backbone* was named Best Original Full-Length Play by the *Sunday Times* National Union of Students Drama Festival in 1968.

TITLE COMMENTARY

📖 *MIND YOUR OWN BUSINESS* (1974)

The Times Literary Supplement

SOURCE: "New Poet," in *The Times Literary Supplement*, No. 3760, March 29, 1974, p. 333.

Mind Your Own Business is, in fact, most kids' business. It is a book by a new young poet, which is mostly funny, but often more than that. There are no titles (except for **"The Sleepy Baby Sitter's Curse"**) which is, on the whole, fair enough as the book reads straight through, as if these were fragments of a verse autobiography rather than individual poems. There's a lot about Dad, who has a thumb which is "quite simply the world's fastest envelope burster" (and which, "if it dressed up, could easily pass as a broad bean or a big toe"). There's a bit about Mum and a good deal about a room-sharing brother. There's a memorable family wedding reception in a Wimpy Bar. It is a world of ABC cinemas, chips, dustbins, dyed hair.

If any one, around ten or eleven, still thinks poetry is soppy and mostly concerned with daffodils and moonlight, let him read this. Do not be put off by the whimsy of the author's note on the back jacket flap; Quentin Blake's drawings are a surer guide to the tone and zest of this attractive and original book.

Margaret Meek

SOURCE: A review of *Mind Your Own Business*, in *The School Librarian*, Vol. 22, No. 2, June, 1974, p. 184.

Poems specially written for children seem, even now, to be poised between the hymnody of Isaac Watts and the humorous versifying of the Victorians like Belloc and Carroll. Imbued with a strong sense of original sin, these authors and their modern successors exorcise it by direct attack or comic deprecation. The result is that our expectations are overlaid by these memories, or the echoes of rare voices, such as Walter de la Mare.

If, however, we have first-hand experience of children writing poetry to please themselves, we know that it can be strong, very funny, moving, idiosyncratic, with an immediacy that comes from the fusion of language and experience. Except in books like *Voices* children are rarely offered collections which match their pre-causal preoccupations.

Here, at last, is a real book of real poems for modern children, especially boys, exploiting language for the rumbustiousness of it, experience for its affective depth. The book is a combined operation. The illustrations exist in their own right, not simply to throw light on the poems which have their own visual imagery. Directness, clarity, economy and an eye for the incident the young select for contemplation: dogs, Dad's thumb, street scenes, all combine perception, imagination, reverie, memory, so that the reader discovers the modalities of experience in a way that makes him understand that poems and pictures are both ways of looking. Then he can go and make a book of his own.

Margery Fisher

SOURCE: A review of *Mind Your Own Business,* in *Growing Point,* Vol. 13, No. 3, September, 1974, pp. 2446-47.

In Michael Rosen's verse we have by contrast the apparently formless forms that characterise the kind of verse children are encouraged to write themselves. Given the subjects of *Mind your own business,* you could almost call this a book of telescoped narrative. These are anecdotal pieces, mainly concerned with family life and human relationships, making wry, deprecatingly humorous comments on an old shirt, children playing in a polluted river, two brothers in dispute. The impression is one of youthful haste, quick definition, dispersed thought. The seemingly casual form of the verse suits some subjects extremely well—for example, **"The sleepy baby-sitter's curse,"** where words and content are wittily matched. In other poems, like the one that begins "My brother got married in a wimpy bar", the looseness of form seems merely self-indulgent and throws one back in admiration to the succinct comedy of:

> Down behind the dustbin
> I met a dog called Jim.
> He didn't know me
> And I didn't know him.

It must be admitted that this miniature is greatly helped by Quentin Blake's drawing of the confrontation and indeed this artist has never been in better form than in his glosses on these shrewd, trendy jottings on life. Putting aside one's doubt about some of the poems, let me say that they had to be poems; prose would not have served in the same way for the overtones of this, for instance:

> My dad's thumb
> can stick pins in wood
> without flinching—
> it can crush family-sized match boxes
> in one stroke
> and lever off jam-jar lids without piercing
> at the pierce-here sign.

Children attracted by the bright, straightforward verbal images in this book might try to use it as a pattern; to the poet's credit, they will not find it easy.

Kirkus Reviews

SOURCE: A review of *Mind Your Own Business,* in *Kirkus Reviews,* Vol. XLIII, No. 1, January 1, 1975, p. 23.

As close to home as **"My Dad's thumb"** and as manic as the fantasy of how **"My brother got married in a wimpy bar,"** these verses are reeled off in an uninflected English accent so pronounced that some of the brash humor might pass American kids right by. Read aloud there'd be no problem ("It's not 'shield and sheaf' / it's 'bubble and squeak' round here"), and most of these bits sound like they must have been made for radio. On paper they tend to be garrulous and rambling—but studded with enough silly lines to inspire those juvenile wits who can penetrate the small-print giddiness and ha'penny jokes.

WOULDN'T YOU LIKE TO KNOW (1977)

John Fuller

SOURCE: "Poetry with Panache," in *The Times Literary Supplement,* No. 3944, October 28, 1977, p. 1275.

Yes, Michael Rosen's trick title really works. "What's that book you've got for review?" they ask. *"Wouldn't You Like to Know",* I reply. *"Go on, tell us!"* "Wouldn't You Like To Know." And so on. Eventually: "Is it any good?" "Well, yes, it is", I admit.

Chirpy, relaxed and good-humoured, Rosen satisfies most of the demands that children make of poems, playing for family sentiment, inventing silly phrases, insulting authority. There are poems about food, games, a lost dog. There is a letter from a lamp-post and an account of the phoenix. Is there too much variety? Some of the pieces fail to live up to the standard of panache he sets. The poem about the boy who fills in advertisers coupons in order to get sent letters really might have been better as a short story, for instance. The verse element has to fight for a hearing. I would have preferred instead a few more pages of dotty incantation along the lines of:

> The train now standing
> at Flatworm's heaven
> will not stop or start
> at Oldham, Newham
> You bring 'em, We buy 'em,

and all stations to
Kahalacahoo, Hawaii.

There's a long, slightly heartless poem about fishing which non-fishermen like myself may grind to a halt in. On the other hand, Rosen can sympathize with wasps ("The ragged cut edge of tin. / And who am I to dare to drag this weak waist / across that edge?") and may therefore appease sensitive children who have not yet sorted out their priorities in Animal Rights.

Quentin Blake's familiar deft scribbles underline Rosen's descriptive shorthand, while leaving the vein of controlled surrealism to work on its own—which is just right. The illustrations in places actually help to explain the poems (in terms of personae, for instance), which is also well conceived. All in all, this is an extremely likeable book, well designed and printed.

M. Hobbs

SOURCE: A review of *Wouldn't You Like to Know,* in *The Junior Bookshelf,* Vol. 42, No. 1, February, 1978, p. 48.

Michael Rosen's poems are deceptively simple, for even at their most proselike, they are shaped by a discipline of rhyme-schemes and language, and varied, often complicated rhythms. They cover much of the essence of a modern townboy's living, his relations with brothers and sisters, with parents, the elderly and toddlers, his anxieties, his love of nonsense, his imaginative moments (often taking wing from water, from the sound of names, or chance incidents). Three poems seem to me to stand out: the thoughts of a wasp during his long struggle in a jam-jar trap, meditations on a tower block, and the day when a lost pet returned. The funny jingles are delicious, and matched, as are all the changes of mood, most sensitively by Quentin Blake's wonderfully expressive illustrations.

John Gough

SOURCE: "Poems in a Context: Breaking the Anthology Trap," in *Children's literature in education,* Vol. 15, No. 4, Winter, 1984, pp. 204-10.

Michael Rosen's *Wouldn't You Like to Know?* presents a collection of poems in no particular order, most of which appear to have been written by one particular child about 10 years old, in one particular family, as these lines reflect:

> I'm the youngest in our house
>
> My brother gets letters—not many, but some,
> I don't know why—but I get none.
>
> Mum'll be coming home today.
> It's three weeks she's been away.
> When dad's alone
> all we eat
> is cold meat.

There is a coherence here which makes collective sense of the separate pieces. Because the poems relate to each other, through the personality of the poet, one poem leads in to others. And what we understand in one poem will help us understand others. We know the poet, and his family, and we can clearly infer that it is the same "I" who has also written the "non-I" poems.

YOU TELL ME (with Roger McGough, 1979)

Book Window

SOURCE: A review of *You Tell Me,* in *Book Window,* Vol. 8, No. 2, Spring, 1981, p. 25.

The poetry is rooted in the rueful and hilarious experiences of the early teens. Its great merit is that the readers will like it, before they have figured out that it is that dreaded school subject "poetry", and that can't be bad. Parents, teachers, friends (sometimes rather intimidating) appear in these poems often accompanied by that fine surprise or illumination which is the stuff of poetry.

YOU CAN'T CATCH ME! (1981)

M. Crouch

SOURCE: A review of *You Can't Catch Me!,* in *The Junior Bookshelf,* Vol. 46, No. 1, February, 1982, p. 22.

Michael Rosen and Quentin Blake have collaborated most successfully before, but this book represents a new departure for them. Word and image are very closely related, as if they came from a single creative experience. If anything there may be some loss of poetic quality, but the total impact of the book is infinitely greater. Both partners, besides being complete masters of their media, know just what makes a child tick. Witness the delicious terror of the poem in which junior taunts grandpa with "You can't catch me, GRUMBLE BELLY." As the child grows more daring and insulting, so Grandpa turns from an amiable old gentleman trying to read, to a Hyde-like monster, and back again. Each opening shows similar situations, of reality or fantasy, and a similar enjoyment of truth married to fun. A gorgeous book.

Ann G. Hay

SOURCE: A review of *You Can't Catch Me!,* in *British Book News,* Children's Supplement, Spring, 1982, p. 8.

This is a book of poems and pictures which belong together. That is not to say that without Quentin Blake's splendidly zany illustrations the poems would be nothing, but they need each other like fish needs chips or rhubarb needs custard. Any child from four upwards will recognize himself here; we have all had fluff under our beds, had problems with our shoe laces, and we have all found that: 'From the light switch / to my bed, / It's the Longest

Journey in the World.' Together they remind us of the joys of the home-made boat, of looking at peculiar grown-ups, of provoking an adult until you're not quite sure if he really *is* angry and of the irritation of having your hair and nails cut. The book is a real delight, and my thirteen-year-old reader fell about with laughter and pointed to his younger brothers, saying 'The people who did this book must have met us!'

Holly Sanhuber

SOURCE: A review of *You Can't Catch Me!*, in *School Library Journal*, Vol. 28, No. 9, May, 1982, p. 56.

Humorous verses filled with delicious nonsense are teamed with cartoon-like illustrations in Blake's well-known casual style. Untitled, unpaged, these poems vary in length but are consistent in appeal. Familiar situations (e.g., fear of the dark; taking pleasure in a sailboat) are amplified and extended by the artist's familiar scraggly line drawings with watercolor wash. Stylized faces with large noses suit the odd humor of the poems. One dialogue, between a father and his recalcitrant son, would be of interest to storytellers. Ciardi and Silverstein fans will greet this collection with chuckles and chortles.

📖 *I SEE A VOICE* (1981)

Roy Blatchford

SOURCE: "Coming up Rosen," in *The Times Educational Supplement*, No. 3418, January 1, 1982, p. 17.

In recent years Michael Rosen has probably contributed more than most contemporary poets to popularizing—in the real sense—poetry amongst school-children. His collections **Mind Your Own Business** and **You Tell Me** (written with Roger McGough) can be found dotted around most classrooms up and down the country, while Rosen himself regularly tours schools reading, reciting and writing poetry with youngsters. His latest volume takes the form of both an anthology and a commentary, five chapters corresponding with five television programmes transmitted last term in *The English Programme*. In the preface he writes: "After reading it, I hope that you'll feel able to do two things more confidently—write poems about things that interest you and write *about* poems that interest you".

Rosen presses the claim in his introduction for a "wide" definition of poetry: "Poems are jokes, lessons, games, speeches, complaints, boasts, hopes, dreams, rumours, insults, gossip, memories, lists". His anthology, not surprisingly, ranges from Tom Paxton, John Lennon and Peggy Seeger to Edward Brathwaite, Keith Douglas and a handful of simply stunning love-poems from a group of sixth form students.

In a first chapter titled "Responding To Poems" Rosen's commentary on Roger McGough's "Nooligan" and on

poetic techniques more generally offers a very personal view, chatty and direct in style, and reminiscent of his own idiomatic, jaunty verse. Similarly, the activities he has devised to extend pupils' response to the anthology are nicely open-ended and a welcome reminder to teenagers that poetry need not be a miserable, frustrating encounter with empty word-patterns. If a love for poetry is something caught rather than taught, Rosen's slim book is a model of its kind. . . .

Hilary Minns

SOURCE: A review of *I See a Voice*, in *The School Librarian*, Vol. 30, No. 1, March, 1982, p. 68.

A splendid book, intended I think for secondary pupils, though there are things in it I'd want ten-year-olds to know and feel. Michael Rosen presents poems by different authors and comments on them directly and personally. His task is that of 'arranging a meeting' between poet and reader. He accepts that the readers may be new to poetry, perhaps afraid of it, but he takes them on as equals and invites them to write poems themselves. He guides them through the process and takes time to explain the terminology: alliteration, metaphor, and so on. Issues of war, oppression, inequality and protest are dealt with through the poetry together with feelings of love, loneliness and hatred, so the book itself makes a powerful political statement and readers are made aware of their responsibility to themselves and others in society.

📖 *NASTY!* (1982)

Books for Your Children

SOURCE: A review of *Nasty!*, in *Books for Your Children*, Vol. 17, No. 2, Summer, 1982, p. 10.

Six very entertaining unashamedly 'nasty' stories by one of the most original talents working for children. Michael Rosen is a Londoner and a poet whose work for children is usually in the 'safer' form of funny poems. This collection of stories includes **"Once there was a King who promised he would never chop anyone's head off"** first published, very courageously, as a picture book by Andre Deutsch. All these stories have a very acceptable friendly conversational style though quite deliberate anarchical tone.

Margery Fisher

SOURCE: A review of *Nasty!*, in *Growing Point*, Vol. 21, No. 3, September, 1982, p. 3958.

This rather uneven collection of prose anecdotes at first seems to have a firm plan, with four ingenious horror-stories related by an impressionable Cockney cleaner. Her descriptions of the giant Bakerloo flea, the murderous swarm of winter wasps and the plague of mice, with a slightly less horrific enterprise to rescue a street for children to play in, are terse, racy and compact, and so redolent of her casual personality that the addition of two whimsical spoof fairy-tales seems a piece of bad judgement. In content and style they simply don't mix with the black humour of the four London tales and their shuddersome illustrations.

Steve Bowles

SOURCE: A review of *Nasty!,* in *The School Librarian,* Vol. 31, No. 1, March, 1983, p. 63.

This useful volume comprises three short stories and a couple of modern fables thrown in for good measure. Its usefulness depends on knowing an earlier story, **The Bakerloo flea,** which gives its name to another Rosen 'Knockout', and which can also be found in the hardback version of *Nasty!*

Following this tried and tested tale of a giant flea on the Underground, the Bakerloo Flea Woman tells stories about a winter when wasps were a serious menace in London's East End, local direct action to provide a zebra crossing on a dangerous road, and a witch-y way of dealing with mice. The first two are baggier than *Flea* and could have stood cutting, but they still have that simple, colloquial style which gives them a start over most of the more formally literary stories around. They offer lots of opportunities for classroom talk, if used as read-alouds by the teacher, as well as affording obvious jumping-off points for children's own writing. (Children mimic the style of the stories very well, for example.)

The two fables are less easily placed, though the longer **"Happy king"** picks up the political points of **"Wasps"** and **"Lollipop lady"** and might provoke discussion if properly handled.

INKY PINKY PONKY: CHILDREN'S PLAYGROUND RHYMES (edited by Michael Rosen, with Susanna Steele, 1982)

Margaret Meek

SOURCE: A review of *Inky Pinky Ponky: Children's Playground Rhymes,* in *The School Librarian,* Vol. 31, No. 3, September, 1983, p. 235.

A whole year late, this book has come back to me after being sent for trial with a group of juniors who wouldn't let it go. (They've got their own now.) So, given that the illustrations are Dan Jones at his best, and the verses collected by two experts at listening to children's verse, this is surely the children's favourite. Most interesting is the 'updating'. Many of the rhymes here are post-Opie. The habit and skill of playground rhyming neither dies nor fades away. The vigour of the send-up of adults ('Our teacher is a funny one'); the political satire ('Don't go to Granny's any more' is outside No. 10), the social ('My

old man's a dustman') and the literary ('Humpty Dumpty sat on a chair') all suggest that literature is alive and well and safe in the hands of children. Dan Jones brings London to life on the page: look at the graffiti (Rabelais to the last tooth on page 13) and the station advertisements. No better street scenes appear in any book.

QUICK, LET'S GET OUT OF HERE (1983)

George Szirtes

SOURCE: "Party-Fare," in *The Times Literary Supplement,* No. 4208, November 25, 1983, p. 1310.

Michael Rosen understands perfectly one area of childhood experience, though he is less a poet than a traditional Jewish story-teller of the homely and populist kind. His stories are performances before a congregation of children. He himself is the party-fare. He feeds his sheep.

However an unadulterated diet of Rosen would be like trying to survive on endless helpings of such stuff: crisps, sausages on sticks, jelly, ice-creams, fairy cakes and Pepsi. Of course children love it, and it would be a foolish parent who tried to exclude these elements of a child's diet by insisting on the virtues of wholefood. Highmindedness does not go down well with children, though adults heartily endorse it. The poems in **Quick, Let's Get Out of Here** are illustrated by the ubiquitous Quentin Blake, who gives lively and tangible form to the extrovert happy-go-luckies catered for by Rosen. There are no party-poopers to cast a blight on the proceedings, to get locked in cupboards, to cling unhealthily to their more confident peers, to be excluded from games. Everybody is terribly gregarious. The two or three moments of introversion are no more than one must humanly allow for, but the kids get over it.

Let us be quite unfair for a minute. This book has all the thin warmth of one of those post-war, open-plan primary schools. No corridors and few corners. Ideal for an absolutely enormous party with lashings and lashings. The children will have fun. And of course they do. Why should anyone be so old fashioned as to ask for anything else?

Margery Fisher

SOURCE: A review of *Quick, Let's Get Out of Here,* in *Growing Point,* Vol. 22, No. 6, March, 1984, p. 4227.

Family matters in the recurring father's-eye-view of the nappie-hating infant Eddie and a ten-year-old's attitude to food, school, girls and grown-ups, reflected in relaxed but precise lines. The versifier strikes a deeper note in an anecdote told by a paterfamilias about the sight, in war-devastated Berlin, of a dinosaur reconstruction thrown out of a museum into the street. Briskly appropriate drawings add mood and space to poems in an entirely popular, jaunty style which never becomes slick.

M. Hobbs

SOURCE: A review of *Quick, Let's Get Out of Here,* in *The Junior Bookshelf,* Vol. 48, No. 2, April, 1984, p. 89.

Michael Rosen has a remarkable gift for noticing poetry in the rhythms of everyday speech. At the same time, he can remember or think himself into the universal sensations of childhood with such immediacy that adults will be startled to recall experiences they thought they had forgotten, while children will appreciate his ability to put into words what they think and feel. The language—with nice meditative "yeah"s and "anyway"s—is nearer their own than A. A. Milne's, yet there is something of the quality that endeared *him* to so many generations in short rhythmical jingles like "We're bonking / we're bonking / we're bonking all the drains". Some are everyday earthy happenings, some come from daydreams, at the hour of waking or in the primeval world of the bath. There is nonsense—riddles and mad menus ("ping pong ball and chips . . . fillet of calculator"). The poems based on Michael Rosen's own child Eddie capture exactly for older brothers and sisters the charm as well as the infuriating nature of small toddlers "with these little fat rubbery legs / that go round like wheels". Other poems stem from the poet's childhood, the love-hate relationship with his brother, remembered incidents like visits to the old Jewish grandparents, the pathos of age and poverty, speech rhythms and phrases. And of course, it is almost impossible to imagine these poems without Quentin Blake's sketches everywhere which catch and fix characters even more firmly and underline the humour.

Gabrielle Maunder

SOURCE: A review of *Quick, Let's Get Out of Here,* in *The School Librarian,* Vol. 32, No. 2, June, 1984, p. 147.

In her book *Teaching English,* Tricia Evans has a nice image for the teaching of poetry—she discusses the 'shallow' and the 'deep' end. This pleases me, as it gives the impression of an activity which you have to discover through participation. You begin with your toe on the bottom and then find you can swim without it.

Michael Rosen's new book (or more properly, Michael Rosen and Quentin Blake's new book for never were poet and artist more essential to each other) is a perfect example of a book which beguiles you into believing it is your toe which is keeping you safe, then lifts you off the bottom until you are floating. Rosen's great gift, of course, is to take the commonplace events of childhood—in this case distinctly urban childhood—and find them significant enough to make poems from. Sometimes the result is an inconsequential poem, like the one about Christine Elkins who has two and a half boyfriends; sometimes a more powerful theme will spring from the pages, such as **'Skeletons'**—a memory at second hand of dinosaur skeletons in the bombed ruins of the Berlin Natural History Museum in 1946. The last produces a resonance in the

head and the words on the page make the image with irreducible economy.

Is it all as good as this? Inevitably, no—how could it be? Rosen works best when he disciplines himself to brevity. Many of the poems spread themselves over several large pages and it's here that the longueurs show, and one becomes aware of much made of little. But when they work, they work triumphantly. I long to take this book into a classroom long bound with poetry as problem, to show what can be done with poetry as pleasure.

HOW TO GET OUT OF THE BATH AND OTHER PROBLEMS (1984)

Anne Wood

SOURCE: A review of *How to Get Out of the Bath and Other Problems,* in *Books for Your Children,* Vol. 19, No. 2, Summer, 1984, p. 18.

One of the few books that faces the problem of reluctant readers and at the same time encourages idiosyncratic thinking among all children. A book that like its author refuses to be pigeonholed that will provide entertainment for solitary children to lots of family fun if some of the questions it poses are answered at home.

HAIRY TALES AND NURSERY CRIMES (1985)

Colin Walter

SOURCE: A review of *Hairy Tales and Nursery Crimes,* in *The School Librarian,* Vol. 33, No. 1, March, 1985, p. 40.

The eleven-year-old to whom I showed this collection of Rosen verse versions of five fairy tales and Browning's 'The Pied Piper', interspersed with some 'got-at' nursery rhymes, went away and returned smiling. 'Yes', she said, 'I like most of it. You have to read them very carefully.' I know what she meant; she meant what she said.

Children's liking for parody will assure their enjoyment of this book. It is not for hearing, and therein lies its secret and its appeal. It offers its fun by demanding close reading, and that, in turn, becomes fun. Further, re-reading, which is the stuff of reading poetry anyway, is necessary here as the reader fits the extravagances and the vagrant extras of Michael Rosen's pieces to the stories and rhymes we all know.

To get the point children have to attend to the language, and that *is* the point. If that appeal is to the child's secondary imagination, another appeal is to the child's primary imagination: to the play of words and the words of play; to the forbidden and the scurrilous. When it really is fun to read carefully, that's all right.

George Szirtes

SOURCE: "Wordslips," in *The Times Literary Supplement,* No. 4275, March 8, 1985, p. 270.

Mike Rosen's *Hairy Tales and Nursery Crimes* introduces children to the pleasures of Surrealism by rewriting some standard stories and rhymes in a mutated form. There are crowded passages, such as this paragraph from near the end of Rosen's version of the Pied Piper of Hamelin:

> This town's boring ever since my mates have gone. I can never forget the things Pepper promised me. We were going to a really hippy place where there were mushing streams, trees laden with brut, blunderful flowers, sparrows more frightly coloured than the teacocks, peas with no strings, and horses born with eagles' pings. I even believed my foot would get butter—then suddenly everything slopped and I was standing outsize on the hill.

One could sort the mutations into Spoonerisms, Malapropisms and other such categories but these would go for nothing were it not for the relatively uneventful passages which maintain our sense of expectation. And still they would fall rather flat if Rosen did not persist with each mutation in a literal fashion. That is, once the Hamelin rats have been transformed to hats they remain hats. Alan Baker's straight-faced drawings are a help here—their painstaking, pedestrian use of rapidograph dots and letraset textures add body to Rosen's slight jokes. But the jokes are improved in the telling aloud. Hansel's pocketful of stones, having become a rocket full of phones, suddenly appear in a spoonlit forest in the illustration overleaf. There is then further satisfaction in finding the children "a long way, bleep into the forest".

Some jokes are continued and elaborated, others are immediately dropped. Sometimes we are invited to step out of the pattern of mutations and admire their silliness: "It was about this time that Gristle told Handsel that the itch couldn't see. (Which Handsel knew all along because all the itches he knew just itched and nothing much else.)" While the fairy tales can be very funny the nursery rhymes are a bit of a flop, chiefly because all the jokes are one-off and seem arbitrary. There is not sufficient space to develop the cumulative effects that succeed so well in the stories. We are more amused when we can see the methane in the madness.

Books for Keeps

SOURCE: A review of *Hairy Tales and Nursery Crimes,* in *Books for Keeps,* No. 35, November, 1985, p. 6.

'What does Jack find at the top of the Tinstalk?' When you can appreciate the in-jokes of any group you really belong. Young readers and listeners with a rich background of tales and rhymes can claim their place in the literate community as they enjoy the word play and jokes arising from the outrageous liberties Mike Rosen takes with our traditional story heritage.

📖 *DON'T PUT MUSTARD IN THE CUSTARD* (1985)

Margery Fisher

SOURCE: A review of *Don't Put Mustard in the Custard,* in *Growing Point,* Vol. 24, No. 5, January, 1986, p. 4564.

The combination of Rosen and Blake means fun with an edge—shrewd, electrically lively, casually teasing, pyrotechnic—offering a picture of life as it is lived with toothbrush and baked beans, reproving parents and fraternal alliances, projects and peccadilloes. The coloured pictures mark the stages in each triumph or disaster, as always brilliantly expressive, as the lines are gloriously recitable. 'Digital Fidgetal Botch, a fly got into my watch. The digit digitted, the fly fidgeted. Digital Fidgetal Botch.' It looks easy enough—but don't you believe it!

Marcus Crouch

SOURCE: A review of *Don't Put Mustard in the Custard,* in *The School Librarian,* Vol. 34, No. 1, March, 1986, p. 53.

They've been together now, not for forty years but since 1974, long enough to establish Rosen and Blake as one of the really successful partnerships. They both like the ordinary dramas of everyday life and, while their reactions are similar, each gives his own personal emphasis so that verse and picture are genuinely complementary. Michael Rosen commands many different rhythmic and rhyming patterns and uses them to evoke the wry humour of his situations. In his many pictures—sometimes as many as four to a page—Quentin Blake explores the background as well as the central action of each poem, making it instantly and hilariously recognisable. Then, in the one excursion into the child's fantasy world, poet and artist join forces to present a vivid and by no means funny image of a boy's night fears. Children and parents—and perhaps even teachers!—will see the essential truth behind this farcical picture.

Colin Mills

SOURCE: A review of *Don't Put Mustard in the Custard,* in *Books for Keeps,* No. 46, September, 1987, p. 23.

Rosen at his near best, almost back to the tip-top form of collections like *Mind Your Own Business.* Here, he is at his very sharpest when the voice is a child's, often in conflict with over-parental adults. Sixes and sevens are close enough to '**Nursery**' to feel the vividness of it:—

> 'What's the Matter?'

> 'I had to sit on the naughty chair.'

He's a master at the extended word play which links breakfast table banter, playground lore and literacy. Read together **'Bathroom Fiddler',** and tell me which contemporary child won't warm to:—

'Oh video Oh video

The video the diddy oh'

Blake's pictures are a *part* of each poem: see what he does with perspective to convey the feel of the poem called **'Gone'.** Lots of the poems need action and gesture, so let the children read them and play with them. Then, they'll write their own.

📖 THE KINGFISHER BOOK OF CHILDREN'S POETRY (edited by Michael Rosen, 1985)

Charles Causley

SOURCE: "The Best Is the Best," in *The Times Educational Supplement*, No. 3622, February 14, 1986, p. R13.

Michael Rosen's **Kingfisher Book of Children's Poetry** has the chunky appearance and feel of a children's annual of the 1920s, with cheerful illustrations to match. The choice of 250 poems is catholic, spirited, often highly original, and includes Dekker's "The Curse", an Ibsen speech from *Peer Gynt,* a Day-Lewis version of Virgil on an eruption of Mount Etna, and a splendid Norman Nicholson ("The road is having / Its appendix out"). In all, it is an offering of work known and not-so-well known as solid, sustaining and digestible as a well-cooked meal of roast beef and Yorkshire pudding, and a bargain at the price. On the evidence of these five collections the anthologist's art is certainly alive and well, with Q's celebrated dictum (when faced with no alternative to a much-anthologized piece) strongly in evidence: "The best is the best, though a hundred judges have declared it so."

Anne Wood

SOURCE: A review of *The Kingfisher Book of Children's Poetry,* in *Books for Your Children,* Vol. 21, No. 1, Spring, 1986, p. 21.

This is the kind of volume that will be bought by well meaning friends and relatives as a gift, so thank goodness the publishers had the wit to invite Rosen to make the selection. Excellent value in every way, it fully justifies Rosen's ambition to encourage children to see poetry as something lively and entertaining which everybody can enjoy.

📖 THAT'D BE TELLING (edited by Michael Rosen, with Joan Griffiths, 1985)

Gill Weaver

SOURCE: A review of *That'd Be Telling,* in *Books*

for Your Children, Vol. 23, No. 2, Summer, 1988, p. 13.

This book is one of the best reads I've had for a long time and is a must for all families and classrooms. Michael Rosen has put together a collection filled with life and interest: here are tales of mystery, fun and trickery which will have children crying out for more. There is not one story which fails, yet the range is very wide, from cockney rhyming slang to Indian folk tales. The storytellers each introduce their story with an interesting and sympathetic description of its background culture and people and their presence in Britain, proving the richness of our multicultural country. But it is the stories which the children will remember and the music and colour of the different dialects.

Ann Wright

SOURCE: A review of *That'd Be Telling,* in *The School Librarian,* Vol. 36, No. 3, August, 1988, p. 100.

This lively and attractive collection of stories, rhymes and songs is united by its oral idiom and range of multicultural sources from Hongkong to the West Indies via the British Isles and Bangladesh. Traditional stories include three each about Anansi and Goha mixed in with Charles Causley's tale about his mother seeing a dancing bear, followed by his poem about the event. The selection is informal and often humorous, provoking thought and inviting participation. The eight sections reflect different kinds of interests, and encourage dipping-in as well as sustained reading; a variety of situations, behaviour and general topics are likely to stimulate the young reader and please different audiences.

The section on ghosts has four different stories from Ireland, Wales, the Dutch West Indies and Scotland. In none of these does a terrifying sheeted figure appear. Instead a profound sense of unease is communicated in A. L. Lloyd's story about the rats; and Seamus Heaney's retelling of a traditional tale ends, by contrast, on a note of tenderness. The stories, riddles and songs about weddings include cockney rhyming slang and funny accounts of various mishaps on the day. In another context, Miles Wootton's 'Instant food' and the rhyme about Lord Jim's tomatoes add contemporary humour likely to strike most junior readers as very entertaining. This anthology belongs in the not-to-be missed category for adults as well as children.

📖 WHEN DID YOU LAST WASH YOUR FEET? (1986)

C. E. J. Smith

SOURCE: A review of *When Did You Last Wash Your Feet?,* in *The School Librarian,* Vol. 34, No. 2, June, 1986, p. 185.

He did it with Roger McGough; he did it with Quentin

Blake; and now he has done it with Tony Pinchuck. Michael Rosen examines—irreverently, irrepressibly—the occupations and preoccupations of adolescence: spots, parental pressure, teachers' double standards, nuclear dumping, racial tension, sex, class, commerce, life and death. Pinchuck's pictures are as spiky, as shrewd, and as accurate as Rosen's verse: both could be encapsulated for their comments on the manners and mores of the eighties. There is more of the human condition here for today's teenagers than they'll find in any ten Active Tutorial lessons. Buy it.

George English

SOURCE: A review of *When Did You Last Wash Your Feet?*, in *Books for Your Children,* Vol. 22, No. 1, Spring, 1987, p. 17.

Over the last ten years Mike Rosen has emerged as one of the funniest poets we have. However his new collection is a move away from immediate laughter into more critical areas and explores racism, terminal illness, relationships and other serious issues. The humour remains, but in this book it has a cutting edge.

At first I have to say I didn't like it. It looked horrible; it was difficult to read. Then as I began to share it with family and friends and discussed the impact it had when my wife used it in school I saw the book's importance. And gradually as I probed the material I saw how moving and personal some of it was. Tony Pinchuck's illustrations add an edge to the book and should be popular with all 'Young Ones' fans.

📖 *A SPIDER BOUGHT A BICYCLE AND OTHER POEMS FOR YOUNG CHILDREN* (edited by Michael Rosen, 1986)

Shirley Toulson

SOURCE: "Travelling Companions," in *The Times Educational Supplement,* No. 3736, February 5, 1988, p. 55.

On the whole Michael Rosen's choice of poems will appeal to somewhat younger readers. He's brave enough to find an appealing wit, emphasized by Inga Moore's gentle, tongue-in-cheek drawings, in A A Milne's "Good Little Girl"; and he draws readily on some of the more cherished works of Anon from both sides of the Atlantic. It's good to find the cherry without a stone beside the gay baboon of the animal fair, as well as the skipping rhyme that teaches you how to spell "difficulty". These old favourites are somewhat uneasy companions to the extracts from "The Ancient Mariner" and "The Tempest"; they fit much better with a sharp quatrain from Günter Grass. I was glad to find that.

Donald Fry

SOURCE: A review of *A Spider Bought a Bicycle and*

Other Poems for Young Children, in *The School Librarian,* Vol. 36, No. 3, August, 1988, p. 104.

Ninety-four poems, by all sorts of people, past and present, from all over the world, in many different forms—and by some magic of compilation not at all a jumble but a delight from beginning to end, or wherever you decide to dip in. Beginners will find rhymes they know off by heart but have never seen in print before; they will find others they thought they knew but which take unexpected turns. Adults will find old favourites which they thought they would never see again, but which are here, dusted down and looking fresh. It's a book to read by yourself, and a book to share; for listening intently, joining in, laughing at, going back to for favourite pages.

Tagore is here, and Shakespeare; lots of Anon (including one of many discoveries—'We're broken-hearted gardeners, scarce got a bit of shoe'—from the nineteenth century); Reeves, Farjeon, but also Langston Hughes, Whitman, Gunter Grass. There's work by children and from community presses; and, most striking of all, work by people just going about their lives in their own part of the world and taking pleasure in capturing a moment of that in poetry.

Every poem has a page to itself, even if it's only two or three lines long, and every poem is illustrated by Inga Moore in small pastel drawings which complement the poems ingeniously and with much charm and a sense of humour. The drawings, and the collection as a whole, stress that poems, including those in the first person, are as much about girls as boys, about black children as well as white, which will come as no surprise to some children. Once borrowed, this book will be hard to return, and many families will want their own copies, to grow up with.

Ronald Jobe

SOURCE: A review of *A Spider Bought a Bicycle and Other Poems for Young Children,* in *School Library Journal,* Vol. 41, No. 6, June, 1995, p. 104.

A joyous collection of over 90 poems in which Rosen's love of language, life, and nonsense comes through. The volume is impressively wide-ranging in scope, from nursery rhymes to songs ("My Bonnie Lies Over the Ocean") to nature poems (Karla Kuskin's "When I Went Out"), and the selector does not underestimate the minds of the young; works by Shakespeare and Günter Grass are included. Poems such as Issa's "One Bath," "Burp" (anon.), and Jay Reed's "When I Was Small" reflect children's experiences. A strength of the collection is the undercurrent of humor and unexpected happenings, as well as the selections' terseness and elements of repetition. Pencil sketches extend the poems, adding great appeal and charm to the book. While some of the selections may be too British for American children, there is a rich abundance of verse for a variety of ages.

D. A. Young

SOURCE: A review of *A Spider Bought a Bicycle,* in *The Junior Bookshelf,* Vol. 59, No. 4, August, 1995, p. 137.

Michael Rosen keeps a toe in the traditional poetic stream of school anthologies. He relies heavily upon that overworked writer Anon but has slipped in Christina Rossetti, A. A. Milne, James Reeves, Coleridge, Shakespeare and a handful of his own adaptions. There are playground jingles, singing rhymes, music hall ditties and pithy aphorisms. The pencil illustrations are scattered generously over the quality-paper pages and nicely catch the mood of the text. It is more of a book to savour than a script for performance.

☐ *YOU'RE THINKING ABOUT DOUGHNUTS* (1987)

Bill Boyle

SOURCE: A review of *You're Thinking about Doughnuts,* in *British Book News Children's Books,* June, 1987, p. 27.

In this short novel Michael Rosen has managed to write a work that in retrospect may well be seen as a landmark in children's fiction, a standard bearer for a new style of 'social' writing.

Taking its starting point from the seemingly innocuous situation of little Frank accompanying his mother to her cleaning job at the museum, the tale soon hints at its dual purpose. On the surface of the story, Frank loses his mum and is led on a tour of the museum's exhibits in an attempt to track her down. This ploy is merely the author's clever vehicle for exposing a multitude of society's *malaises* and problems, ranging from anti-social group behaviour, through the wanton killing of wild animals for 'sport', to exploitation of cheap labour.

There are some brilliant cameos *en route,* of which the disembodied, programmed-to-spout-propaganda Space Suit ('I was nearly the space suit worn by John McKinley'), and the army of Stone statues all chanting 'oh, when the stones come marching in' in best football-crowd style, spring readily to mind.

There is so much, that is both thoughtful and funny, packed into the pages, that the only suitable comment is to say, get it and read it, it's brilliant!

Tom Lewis

SOURCE: A review of *You're Thinking about Doughnuts,* in *The School Librarian,* Vol. 36, No. 2, May, 1988, p. 59.

Every Friday night eight-year-old Frank reluctantly accompanies his mum to the museum where she works as a cleaner. He sits alone in the dark empty building with only the echoes of the past for company. Alone, that is, until this particular Friday night when museum exhibits come to life and take Frank, and the plastic skeleton, on a strange quest through the museum. As the tale unfolds we meet Greek statues that come to life and fight; a talking, empty space-suit that 'nearly' went to the moon; a stuffed tiger telling a moving story of her slaughter; the sinister statue of Joseph Bryman who provided the money to build the museum. The book operates at many levels. There is the enjoyable story itself, as one encounter gives way to another. Underlying this is the thought provoking, social and economic questioning of the honesty and integrity of an institutional building like a museum. At the same time the story operates at an informative level, providing the motivation to refer to non-fiction books for more insights. Such is the value of the informative within fiction.

☐ *THE HYPNOTISER* (1988)

D. A. Young

SOURCE: A review of *The Hypnotiser,* in *The Junior Bookshelf,* Vol. 52, No. 4, August, 1988, p. 191.

Michael Rosen writes engagingly about the inconsequential world of childhood and the strange madness of grown-ups. His verses don't rhyme but they lurch jaggedly from line to line making a thin easy-to-read column on each page. A mixture of the absurd, ridiculous and fanciful with a gritty grain of truth here and there will tickle the fancy of the young reader with an awakening sense of humour.

John Mole

SOURCE: "Rap, Pap and Poetry," in *The Times Educational Supplement,* No. 3776, November 11, 1988, p. 51.

With a six-pack of poetry books, it's hard to know where to place Michael Rosen. First, though, after consideration, because his act is that of a warm-up comedian. Garrulously up-front with a lean and nervy patter, he has made a name for himself as the Ben Elton of kid-verse, bringing a junior *Friday Night Live* into the Monday morning classrooms. His new collection, **The Hypnotiser,** is mainly loud and anecdotal, full of knowingly timed jokes calculated to register high on the Groanometer, and Andrew Tiffen's line and wash cartoons keep up with the pace, adding plenty of gags of their own.

Fun while they last, most of Rosen's pieces are variations on one of his titles **"The Michael Rosen Rap"** with a busy cast of mums, dads, teachers, assorted kids and pets working overtime, though tucked away in a few quiet corners are small, shy poems like **"George"**—touchingly observant, painfully true and built to survive the poet's otherwise rather insistent presence.

NORMA AND THE WASHING MACHINE (1988)

Chris Stephenson

SOURCE: A review of *Norma and the Washing Machine,* in *The School Librarian,* Vol. 37, No. 2, May, 1989, p. 62.

Norma and the washing machine invites a [clear] alliance with one character, and has proved [popular] with my young testers. Michael Rosen is well-attuned to the wavelengths of the classroom, and is particularly funny when pointing up the mismatch between the preoccupations of children and adults. A prime example of this occurs during the opening 'show and tell' session:

'Yes, that's very nice, Sameena,' said Miss Davis, 'but it's not really very interesting, is it?'

Sameena didn't hear Miss Davis say that because she was showing the game to three other children.

But the biggest joke of the story is when Norma wakes up next morning to find that she has grown a beard during the night. She is due to read out an 'interesting' story (about fairies in a washing machine) in assembly at school, and is very worried about reaction to her appearance. Her mother is very matter-of-fact about her beard, her little sister pulls it, the lollipop lady admires it, and as she is about to stand up in assembly . . . she wakes up—genuinely, this time. The impromptu story that she eventually tells in assembly, to the teacher's annoyance, is about a beard, rather than a fairy, in a washing machine. There are interesting psychological undertones to this tale—there is no mention of any adult males in it at all, which throws up all kinds of (adult) speculations about the root cause of Norma's strange nightmare. Children, who are more familiar with the stuff of nightmares, accepted the beard without question. The book's humour is reflected in the illustrations and the artist also shows a sensitivity to multicultural issues. For once, black people are portrayed in roles of authority.

WE'RE GOING ON A BEAR HUNT (retold by Michael Rosen, 1989; U.S. edition, 1992)

Denise Wilms

SOURCE: A review of *We're Going on a Bear Hunt,* in *Booklist,* Vol. 85, No. 22, August, 1989, pp. 1981-82.

A hearty chorus of "We're going on a bear hunt. / We're going to catch a big one. / What a beautiful day! / We're not scared" sets the blustery tone for this picture-book adventure that celebrates a family that is heading to the great outdoors. "Oh-oh! Grass! / Long, wavy grass. / We can't go over it. / We can't go under it. / Oh, no! / We've got to go through it! / Swishy swashy! / Swishy swashy! / Swishy swashy!" Each new challenge is bracketed by the choruses plus an onomatopoeic sound that captures the experience. The intrepid hikers take on a river, a mud flat, a forest, a snowstorm, a cave, and, of course, a bear, before racing home to the safety of their beds. There's plenty of fun to be had, resulting from the nearly irresistible invitation to shout the familiar refrains from this long-loved storytelling favorite. Expansive pictures, alternating color with black and white (for the refrains), provide sweeping landscapes that incorporate drama, jocularity, and interesting perspectives, while allowing children to get caught up in the enthusiasm.

Susan Perren

SOURCE: A review of *We're Going on a Bear Hunt,* in *Quill and Quire,* Vol. 55, No. 9, September, 1989, p. 25.

We're Going on a Bear Hunt is a retelling of an old action rhyme for children, well sprinkled with the repetition and chanting that young children love. In this version the collaboration of writer Michael Rosen and illustrator Helen Oxenbury has produced an exceptional picture book.

The bear hunters are a father and four children, the youngest of whom is carried astride dad's back. In their search for bear they must overcome many obstacles: long, wavy grass; a deep, cold river; thick, oozy mud; a big, dark forest; and so on. Each obstacle is presented to the reader by Oxenbury's double-spread, black-and-white drawings, which show the five hunters cowering in dismay. "Oh no!" they exclaim, aghast. But then they gather themselves together and chant this rallying cry:

We can't go over it.
We can't go under it.
Oh no!
We've got to go through it!

Oxenbury rewards us with luminous watercolour paintings of the family going through the obstacles—the thick, oozy mud, for instance ("Squelch squerch!"). When the bear hunters finally meet a bear they beat a hasty retreat, hilariously recorded. Our last sighting is of five heads peeking timidly out of a thick pink eiderdown.

We're Going on a Bear Hunt is as close to a perfect marriage of text and illustration as one can imagine. It invites audience participation and will give much pleasure to all.

M. Crouch

SOURCE: A review of *We're Going on a Bear Hunt,* in *The Junior Bookshelf,* Vol. 53, No. 5, October, 1989, p. 217.

The first adult reaction to *We're Going on a Bear Hunt* must be that here is a book for collectors. The second is that it is a book for the whole family to keep and pass on to the next generation or two. Michael Rosen shows great restraint in playing with a familiar popular rhyme, putting in just enough variations to give it 'body'. His partner is Helen Oxenbury who has a keen eye for the nice oddities of human behaviour. In alternate colour and monochrome (on the whole I prefer the latter) she follows the jolly family as they splash, squelch or stumble through natural obstacles on the way to an appointment with their ursine prey. Their retreat is much quicker, no less messy. The big page suits Ms Oxenbury very well, and her strong drawings are full of sharply observed detail. Fine printing, excellent colour, a large format, all ensure that the price will be high, but it is fully justified. Here is a book to keep.

Moira Small

SOURCE: A review of *We're Going on a Bear Hunt,* in *Books for Keeps,* No. 84, January, 1994, p. 6.

This large picture book recounts the action song many of us learned in Cubs and Brownies long ago. It's great fun to *do* all the actions, *say* all the words and then *look* at the delightful pictures. Because it's a little scary, it would probably be wise to make this a book to share. Definitely recommended for families with active Dads like the one in the pictures.

TELL TALES (1989)

Eve Gregory

SOURCE: A review of "Alice in Wonderland: Goldilocks and the Three Bears; The Three Little Pigs," in *The School Librarian,* Vol. 38, No. 1, February, 1990, p. 16.

Michael Rosen gives a chatty presentation of these classic fairy tales. Questions open up the story, invite the listener to converse with the characters and participate in the narrating: 'The middle-sized pig went off to the woods . . . And what did he find? Mushrooms? No. Bird's eggs? No . . . Wood.' The results give the stories a humour quite different from their original versions. The mere thought of the 'biggest little pig' telling the smallest to 'keep your hair on . . . it's going to be alright' is enough to have most classes in stitches. The illustrations, too, match this catchy and casual style; they are lively, detailed and attractive. The stories are ideal for story time, but the texts are repetitive and memorable enough to be read by most top infant or early junior children. Only **"Alice in Wonderland"** loses some impact from being shortened. The whole series (nine stories, 'Tell Tales') will be an asset to any infant of junior collection. Older children will gain much from comparing this 'untraditional' way of writing with more usual fairy tales and using the books as a model to extend their own repertoire of writing styles.

THE WICKED TRICKS OF TILL OWLY-GLASS (retold by Michael Rosen, 1989)

Neil Philip

SOURCE: "Till's Tricks," in *The Times Educational Supplement,* No. 3848, March 30, 1990, p. B11.

Michael Rosen has clearly had a good deal of fun in adapting the often coarse and sometimes cruel medieval jests about the peasant trickster Till Eulenspiegel into this elegant children's book. The resulting stories are pointed and amusing, occasionally earthy, but generally light in tone and easy in manner. They are encased in a frame tale about two English boys, on holiday in Germany, who are told stories of Till getting into mischief in order to keep them out of it. This is an ingenious way of bringing these old-fashioned jokes into a modern context though one might wish that the boys and Horst the storyteller had been given more vivid personalities.

The theme of the stories is pomposity punctured by low cunning. Typically, the wily Till plays upon the greed, self-importance or gullibility of some shopkeeper or merchant, inviting them, for instance, to pay to see a horse with its tail where its head should be (tied to a post). Occasionally, the social comedy rises beyond the simple rivalry between peasant and bourgeois, as when Till in a story which will remind readers of the folktale origin of Andersen's "Emperor's New Clothes" paints a nonexistent picture in honour of a snobbish landgrave, claiming that his masterpiece cannot be seen by a liar. The inclusion of this episode does show the limitations of Rosen's source material. For where Andersen's story is an imperishable masterpiece of human psychology, the tale of Till's painting is just a clever joke. But simple as they are, this and Till's other "wicked tricks" will probably go down well in playground and classroom today, as they have in the bar-room for centuries.

The main joy of the book, though, is not Rosen's capable storytelling, but Fritz Wegner's magnificently rumbustious and colourful illustrations, which bring almost every spread alive. These are really cheeky, good-humoured drawings which cannot fail to raise a smile.

M. Crouch

SOURCE: A review of *The Wicked Tricks of Till Owlyglass,* in *The Junior Bookshelf,* Vol. 54, No. 2, April, 1990, p. 89.

Till is the archetypal rogue, the man who acts the fool and so tricks the gullible into greater folly. We know him best from Strauss' tone-poem. He is a universal figure who crops up in one guise or another in many countries. I remember a picture-book by Erich Kastner with drawings by his compatriot Walter Trier in which he appeared as pure Czech in his earthiness. On the other hand Coster made him the hero of his great novel about the struggle of the Low Countries against the tyranny of Spain. In other words you can make anything of Till.

Michael Rosen, I feel, makes rather a meal of him. He uses the simplest of the folk-tales and strings them out to cover fourteen days, which is the extent of me and my brother's stay in Germany. Irritable and troublesome, the boys are taken to see old Horst who will cure them of their badness. This he does by telling them about

Till, who was more wicked than they could hope to be. He cures them, if not of badness, at least of boredom. Michael Rosen of course is as skillful and persuasive as ever, but not altogether at ease with the material. His book, very handsomely presented by the publisher, has the enormous advantage of many illustrations in colour by Fritz Wegner, whose work I do not seem to have seen for too long. He is at home with this European theme, and he sets the tales in their proper period and places, with loving pictures of medieval German towns and villages, exquisite in every detail.

FRECKLY FEET AND ITCHY KNEES (1990)

Publishers Weekly

SOURCE: A review of *Freckly Feet and Itchy Knees,* in *Publishers Weekly,* Vol. 237, No. 23, June 8, 1990, p. 54.

"I'm talking about noses / wet noses / warty noses / sleepy noses / when someone dozes," writes Rosen (*We're Going on a Bear Hunt*) in the opening lines of this spirited celebration of children's noses, hands, feet, eyes, knees and bellies. In verses featuring an informal rhyming scheme and a pleasantly irregular rhythm, the author elaborates on (among other things) what these body parts can do and where they can be found. Finally, he involves readers in the tongue-twisting text, entreating youngsters to give those hands a wave, those feet a tickle, those knees a scratch, etc. Sweeten fills each page with kids, grownups and animals involved in colorful, zany antics. Sometimes nonsensical, sometimes silly and always lighthearted, this paper-over-board book is ideal for reading aloud. Its verbal and visual action is nonstop.

Angela Redfern

SOURCE: A review of *Freckly Feet and Itchy Knees,* in *The School Librarian,* Vol. 38, No. 3, August, 1990, p. 104.

You will love **Freckly feet and itchy knees**. It is Michael Rosen at his best—with zany, zestful, rhythmic, rhyming word-play. There is nothing coy here as Rosen revels in the body as a joyous thing. It cannot fail to be a winner in the classroom—I bet '**Bellies**' will be the all-time favourite. Children will be joining in the text and will have the whole book off by heart in no time. Do pay careful attention to each whole page as the superb illustrations are quite hilarious. I will not forget in a hurry the dog at the vet's with shaking knees, or the prim pets pointing accusing paws.

CULTURE SHOCK (edited by Michael Rosen, 1990)

Fred D'Aguiar

SOURCE: "Culture Clubs," in *The Times Educational Supplement,* No. 3868, August 17, 1990, p. 18.

Culture Shock is by just about everyone and intended for schools and anyone besides. It reads less like a culture shock and more like a culture club, since graffiti is now an art form; rap an institution; dialect poetry a cause, several causes at that. . . . *Culture Shock* takes as its subtitle Adrian Mitchell's words:

> Most people ignore most poetry because
> most poetry ignores most people

The poem is balanced with the accuracy of a spirit level: the two halves of its sense divided equally. It belongs to worlds other than the poetic: the epigrammatic, the rhetorical, the tautological almost. . . .

Michael Rosen draws on every conceivable source for material from more than 95 contributors: graffiti, jokes, advertisements, gravestones, football songs, prose pieces, extracts from political speeches, diaries, allegory, fable. The few recognisable poems, and good ones too, must survive alongside the rest; by either passing for allegory or fable or by seeming more "poetic" than they might otherwise as a result of the juxtaposition of such diverse material. This serves a dual and sometimes antithetic function: it may reveal the poetry in the everyday, but mostly confirms why the material that is not poetry remains simply jokes, ads, graffiti and so on. There is an absence of the lyrical, not necessarily a bad thing, but the book does tend towards a functional view of poetry. Refreshing contributions from the Caribbean poets James Berry (recently OBE), Grace Nichols and John Agard, and a Black British appearance from the comical Millie Murray widen the scope of the language and introduce issues that should be treated more often in poetry. Since the poems are arranged alphabetically by author, John Agard's "Stereotype" is a punchy opening:

> Isn't there one thing
> you forgot to ask
> go on man ask ask
> This native will answer anything
> How about cricket?
> I suppose you're good at it?
> Hear this man
> good at it!
> Put the willow
> in me hand
> and watch me stripe
> de boundary

The poem exploits the stereotype of the West Indian in Britain (good at sport, happy-go-lucky, etc) in order to explode the myth. Humour is a major part of the poem's effect and typical of the anthology as a whole. Form and content gel in a similar fashion in Attila the Stockbroker's "Radio Rap". In this instance the repetitive rhythm and rhyme add to the poem's theme of the vacuous nature of much pop programming on the radio. Surprising choices are excellent poems by Bertolt Brecht, Raymond Carver, Miroslav Holub, Langston Hughes, Nilene Foxworth, D. H. Lawrence and Alice Walker. Some powerful illustrations by Andrzej Krauze extrapolate meanings from the poems, deepening the overall effect of the anthology. He deserves a mention on the front cover alongside the editor. But then the subtitle is on the back, just as a lot of the poetry is in the prose.

Mary Steele

SOURCE: A review of *Culture Shock,* in *The School Librarian,* Vol. 38, No. 4, November, 1990, p. 157.

Michael Rosen's intention in this collection is to surprise people into enjoying poetry. He has chosen mainly from the work of contemporary poets, excluding, incidentally, any of his own work. But there are also poems from Robert Herrick, D. H. Lawrence and Siegfried Sassoon, epigrams from Mahatma Gandhi, Abraham Lincoln, Dorothy Parker, and John Wilmot, Earl of Rochester, and a number of epitaphs, verses and graffiti gems from Anon. The great pleasure of this book is the way the selection and arrangement allow the reader to discover the associations between one poem and those on either side. There are no section headings giving heavy editorial direction: the shorter pieces act as mental sorbets to refresh and stimulate between the more substantial poems. The whole can be read through from cover to cover as a conversation with an editor who clearly likes very much talking to his teenage readership.

Judith Nicholls

SOURCE: A review of *Culture Shock,* in *Books for Your Children,* Vol. 26, No. 1, Spring, 1991, p. 16.

John Agard's lively, hard-hitting "Stereotype" sets the scene perfectly for this collection. He is a particularly appropriate poet to start an anthology which, like his own *Life Doesn't Frighten Me At All* would make an ideal gift for any teenager who thinks poetry is nothing to do with him.

This is a collection for the 90s, and, in parts at least, is as likely to shock traditionalists as it is to delight young readers. There are pithy poems from Dorothy Parker, Stevie Smith, Fiona Pitt-Kethley (no shortage of women poets here) and from two Rogers (Mcgough and Woddis).

Fran Landesman offers a few amusing thoughts in "Family Planning" and Liz Loxley an accusatory "Poem to Help Unemployment" whilst that earlier rebel, D. H. Lawrence, comments on the middle-class Englishman's hatred of his children.

As the blurb suggests, love and hate, racism, sexism, poverty and peer pressure: they are all included, and all highly readable. Michael Rosen knows how to grab his teenage audience by the throat and make it listen—but it will do so willingly.

Adrian Jackson

SOURCE: A review of *Culture Shock,* in *Books for Keeps,* No. 73, March, 1993, p. 11.

A superb collection; witty, iconoclastic, intelligent and determined not to be dull. The alphabetic arrangement is refreshing after so many theme collections. Attila the stockbroker rubs shoulders with Auden, Fiona Pitt-Kethley with Pope. There's graffiti and quotations, lines to laugh at, lines to ponder over. What a range of writers, ages and styles is woven together—and at this price! It's a pleasure to be able to teach with this, to have it in the classroom or just to have it in your pocket. There are gems throughout.

LITTLE RABBIT FOO FOO (1990)

JoAnn Rees

SOURCE: A review of *Little Rabbit Foo Foo,* in *School Library Journal,* Vol. 37, No. 2, February, 1991, p. 74.

Little Rabbit Foo Foo hops through the forest, picking up various creatures—field mice, wriggly worms, tigers, and goblins—and bopping them on the head with his red mallet. The Good Fairy warns him to stop, but finally turns him into a goon. This slightly retold version of a popular children's song has a lot of energy; unfortunately, Rosen includes neither music nor even a preface to let readers know that the tune is the same as "Down by the Railroad." The illustrations are bright, cheerful, and clearly detailed, if somewhat reminiscent of Saturday morning cartoons. Amusing, but not an essential purchase—acting out the song is still more fun than reading it aloud.

Jan Mark

SOURCE: A review of *Little Rabbit Foo Foo,* in *The Times Educational Supplement,* No. 3959, May 15, 1992, p. 23.

Just what have we here? A fierce bad rabbit rides his motor bike through the forest, scooping up defenceless creatures in his butterfly net and bashing them over the head with a mallet. Repeated warnings from the Good Fairy fail to deflect him and he is turned, as threatened, into a goonie, a nonspecific green creature. But even retribution does not reform him. The goonie is, unchastened, casting a beady eye on the mallet . . . Do we really want little children exposed to such immoral anarchy? Definitely.

THE DEADMAN TAPES (1991)

Robert Protherough

SOURCE: A review of *The Deadman Tapes,* in *The*

School Librarian, Vol. 38, No. 1, February, 1990, p. 31.

This lively, readable volume is a version of Browning for our times, a set of eight dramatic monologues for adolescents. The 'tapes' of the title are recordings supposed to have been discovered in an attic by Paul Deadman; recordings that nobody else seems to want, but that fascinate him. The monologues, set as verse, are apparently spoken by young people reflecting on highly emotional occasions in their lives: the death through employers' negligence of a father who is an illegal immigrant, girls discovering unpleasant truths about important men in their lives, the feelings of a boy from a broken home, a girl's only half-intended arson that ends in the death of a friend. There are snatches of love and of hatred across racial divisions.

The 'tapes' demand that young readers should construct the meaning and make moral judgements from the hints in the transcripts, and this may be for teachers the chief merit of the collection. It is perhaps a pity that, despite Deadman's guess that 'they are part of some investigation or other', there is not interrelation (except of a thematic kind) between the tapes. All eight speakers seemed to me to use the same sort of voice, but this may be missing the point. Michael Rosen's popularity with young readers, the potential for 'using' the book in schools, and the reasonable price should combine to ensure a welcome for this book.

David Bennett

SOURCE: A review of *The Deadman Tapes,* in *Books for Keeps,* No. 72, January, 1993, p. 10-11.

Forget the jokey Rosen you know and love. This collection of monologues, supposedly taped by teenagers, are bitter in tone and content, and hard to get the mind around in one reading. A puzzling tension builds as stories of grief, infatuation, desertion, prejudice, etc. unfold in the 'memorable speech' style for which this author is regarded. It deserves to be stocked for its sheer, intriguing otherness.

CLEVER CAKES (1991)

S. M. Ashburner

SOURCE: A review of *Clever Cakes,* in *The Junior Bookshelf,* Vol. 55, No. 5, October, 1991, p. 218.

The seven stories in the book have the feel of traditional fairy stories. They tell of the triumph of good over bad, the small over the giant, and feature demons, wolves, goats and so on.

It is an easy to read book, too obviously 'make believe' to frighten most children. The language is generally straight-

forward but varied and effective, and there is good evocation of atmosphere.

The black and white illustrations have a smudged and stark appearance, as if partly drawn with charcoal, although the people and creatures depicted are clearly delineated and caricature-like. They add to the book's overall atmosphere.

Clever Cakes is most appropriate for reading aloud to the infant level child, or for the able upper infant or lower junior reader to read independently.

Jill Bennett

SOURCE: A review of *Clever Cakes,* in *Books for Keeps,* No. 73, March, 1993, p. 8.

Seven stories with appropriately amusing line drawings by Caroline Holden. Each story features a child character who has to use his or her wits to get out of trouble with such adversaries as the Devil-dog and Gobbleguts the giant. As well as being perfect for reading aloud, Rosen's lively, direct style is highly accessible to confident solo readers who will no doubt want to relish these gems for themselves.

A WORLD OF POETRY (compiled by Michael Rosen, 1991)

Jan Mark

SOURCE: A review of *A World of Poetry,* in *The Times Educational Supplement,* No. 3915, July 12, 1991, p. 25.

In his introduction Michael Rosen has a stab at explaining what poetry is, and how you identify it . . . and gives up, like the rest of us. At the other end of the book is a rather arbitrary attempt to catalogue "forms, styles and technical devices" which may confuse more than it elucidates. But sensible children, feeling peckish and given a substantial sandwich, peel off the bread and gobble the contents; and the contents here are rich indeed.

This is another box of delights, beautifully and generously produced by Kingfisher, and true to its name assembles poetry and verse from all over the world. The earliest is from the 4th century BC, the most recent written as it were yesterday, by children. Thus eight-year-old Moagi from South Africa rubs shoulders with Shakespeare, Nancy from London with Walt Whitman, Kit Wright with Jacob Nibenegenesabe, a 19th-century Swampy Cree Indian, Geoffrey Chaucer with Jim Wong-Chu. No one gets preferential treatment. A cursory flip through the pages may land you with Shelley or Dryden or, as likely, with a limerick, a riddle, or a helping of doggeral from no one in particular. From time to time you do pause and wonder, Is this a poem? Ought it to be here? only to find that you have paused long enough to justify its inclusion. There are very few out-and-out bummers, the kind of trifle that provokes the response, Why bother? That is, why bother to write it? But many do provoke the thought that, however arresting at first sight, however admirable at second reading, much modern poetry is unmemorable and, by extension, unmemorizeable. Which came first, the decline in the practice of learning poems by heart, or the decline of the poem that *can* be learned by heart?

Whether or not learning poetry by heart is desirable is beside the point. No matter how cryptic or arcane a Shakespearean sonnet may seem, it is still easier to remember than verses beginning, "Dad! When will I be able to shave? / When will I have whiskers like you? / DAD!!!" or, "I like wrestling with Herbie because / he's my best friend. / We poke each other . . ." What is missing is not rhyme or metre but the abiding image, the hook on the line that embeds itself in the mind and plays it like a fish, for ever. When Samuel Foote composed "The Great Panjandrum" he set out to write a poem that could not be committed instantly to memory, and immediately defeated himself by compiling such resounding *non sequiturs* that it is almost impossible to forget. Could the recent astronomical proliferation of children's poetry books be down to the fact that without the printed page the poems will cease to exist? When *Fahrenheit 451* becomes fact, who will save them?

Any road up, Rosen's collection is full of cunningly baited hooks. You come away tingling from such opening lines as "The night was coming very fast; / it reached the gate as I ran past". or John Agard's "I want to give up being a bullet / I've been a bullet too long," and the awful inevitability of "'Butch' Weldy" by Edgar Lee Masters:

> After I got religion and steadied down
> They gave me a job in the canning works,
> And every morning I had to fill
> The tank in the yard with gasoline . . .

I begin to suspect that Poetry, like History, "*is what you can remember*."

Sue Rogers

SOURCE: A review of *A World of Poetry,* in *The School Librarian,* Vol. 39, No. 3, August, 1991, p. 112.

Michael Rosen is a 'lover of words' and in this, his second poetry anthology for Kingfisher, he has again managed to produce a wide variety of verse representing both the different forms that poetry can take and the diversity of verse from many countries. Chaucer and Milton shake hands with Bob Dylan and Lennon and McCartney. Over 250 poems are included in all, with the main selection presented in alphabetical order of poet. Ballads, Limericks, Riddles in Rhyme, and Nonsense Verse have sections to themselves.

The production is outstanding. Clear well-spaced text is interspersed with complementary line drawings and beautiful full-colour plates by artists such as Errol Lloyd, Colin

West and Inga Moore. The attention to detail is a dream, with an Index of Titles and First Lines, a List of the Poets giving their dates and nationality, a Subject Index, and a list of Examples of Forms, Styles and Technical Devices. For example, the poem 'Deep-piled snow' represents a weather poem and is also an epitaph!

Through this collection poetry becomes accessible to all; and its format will help both pupils and teachers to match a poem to a topic. It also represents excellent value for money.

Judith Nicholls

SOURCE: A review of *A World of Poetry,* in *Books for Your Children,* Vol. 26, No. 3, Autumn-Winter, 1991, p. 24.

Don't sit down with this exciting collection unless you have time to spare: there are 256 pages, and it's difficult to leave! Michael Rosen has drawn together a huge variety of appealing poems spanning thousands of years of writing from all corners of the world: Nicaragua, Norway, ancient Greece, Japan, Czechoslovakia, a nineteenth century Swampy Cree Indian poem. . . . ! Many of the poems will be unfamiliar; they are all sufficiently arresting to demand attention and re-reading. Subject matter is wide: as the compiler says in his brief introduction, the book covers 'a world of thoughts and feelings, images and ideas'. On a more practical level, apart from the usual indexes of poets (with dates and nationalities), titles and first lines, there is also a useful subject index and page reference to examples of forms, styles and technical devices. Difficult to put a starting age on this book; it would make a wonderful gift for a child around 11 or 12 upwards. I wouldn't want to put a top age limit on it—I really enjoyed it!

WHO DREW ON THE BABY'S HEAD? (1991)

Marcus Crouch

SOURCE: A review of *Who Drew on the Baby's Head?,* in *The School Librarian,* Vol. 40, No. 1, February, 1992, p. 17.

Until now, Michael Rosen's happiest partnerships have been with Quentin Blake. Here is the beginning of one quite as successful. Riana Duncan has the same good-humoured and sardonic view of the modern world, the same gift for conveying a universal truth with the simplest of means. Her swift, unsentimental, unambiguous designs entwine the page, supplementing the verses and adding their personal gloss. I have put the artist first because she gives this book of Rosen's verses its particular distinction. The poet is at his most characteristic here, whether playing with words, twisting tongues, finding innocent double meanings, or recording common dilemmas (the loose tooth down the plughole without benefit of the tooth fairy, playing with baby brother, a camping holiday and 'a frying pan without a handle'). Then there is the articulate foetus—'I'm in my mum'—and the stuck zip. The subtle rhythms may be overlooked with all this fun and good sense.

The Junior Bookshelf

SOURCE: A review of *Who Drew on the Baby's Head?*, in *The Junior Bookshelf,* Vol. 56, No. 2, April, 1992, p. 66.

The prolific poet Michael Rosen (a prime mover in the 'new-poetry-for-children' world) brings out yet another slim collection of zany, nutty free verse for youngsters up to the age of around 8/9 years. The poems are untitled, and could well confuse readers by the way in which they sweep effortlessly from one page to the next. The poems look at contemporary family experiences—climbing all over dad, being born, going on a camping holiday, pets, dreaming. Humour, child-centred and often off-beat, are the fuel for these poems. Riana Duncan's 'dotty family' illustrations appear colourfully on every page. The poems themselves have plenty of white space within which to breathe.

This is verse as a 'narrative read'. It is a million miles away from the poetic structures of an A. A. Milne but Rosen manages a thoroughly up-to-date tone and gives readers stacks of stuff they can identify with and hoot over. Lively, funny, energetic, madcap; energy to spare. And a book that can be a through-read, or for dipping into.

📖 MINI BEASTIES (edited by Michael Rosen, 1991)

Richard Brown

SOURCE: A review of *Mini Beasties,* in *The School Librarian,* Vol. 40, No. 1, February, 1992, p. 27.

Michael Rosen's anthology *Mini beasties* is full of suitably short poems and rhymes about insects, the kind which will enrich any infant project on the subject. Almost every poem has a picture to itself and these are lovingly detailed, accurate and colourful. We need more poetry books like this for the very young. I hope this one will not only lead the way but help set the standard.

M. Crouch

SOURCE: A review of *Mini Beasties,* in *The Junior Bookshelf,* Vol. 56, No. 2, April, 1992, p. 65.

Michael Rosen looks to a rather older audience with a lively collection of verses, mostly by his contemporaries, about bees, bugs and other 'mini-beasties'. Here is an anthologist who knows just what he wants and where to find it. A joyous, funny and serious collection enhanced

greatly by Alan Baker's accurate and attractive pictures. These would be equally at home in a field-guide, except for the sausage-and-chips and other domestic settings.

Liz Waterland

SOURCE: A review of *Mini Beasties,* in *Books for Keeps,* No. 83, November, 1993, p. 10.

An attractive anthology of poems and verse about insects and spiders. Despite the unfortunate publisher's blurb which seems to assume that children will only be interested in poetry if it's described as 'funny rhymes', the selection ranges widely; some of it is, indeed, funny but much is thoughtful and beautiful as well. A good mix, well served by attractively decorated and colourful pages, which will interest most primary children.

📖 HOW THE ANIMALS GOT THEIR COLOURS: ANIMAL MYTHS FROM AROUND THE WORLD (retold by Michael Rosen, 1991)

Publishers Weekly

SOURCE: A review of *How the Animals Got Their Colors: Animal Myths from Around the World,* in *Publishers Weekly,* Vol. 239, No. 10, February 17, 1992, p. 61.

Nine folklore samples—from sources as diverse as the Zuni Indians, India's Khasi people and the ancient Greeks—explain how various creatures received their colorations. The first eight selections focus on particular animals but the final piece, adapted from an Ayoreo Indian legend, offers an alternate view, praising the sun god who supposedly painted all the creatures. Though the book deals with an intriguing topic, its arrangement seems somewhat pedantic and may prove confusing. Also, perhaps because of the variety of sources, the narrators' attitude toward the subjects is inconsistent. In general Rosen's (*We're Going on a Bear Hunt*) writing is skillful, but does not dazzle in the manner of Kipling's *Just So Stories.* [John] Clementson's flashy, tropically colored illustrations *do* dazzle, however; their primitive designs reflect elements from the legends and their roots. For instance, the magical tree in **"Flying Fish"** resembles vegetation one might find in New Guinea, where the tale originated. In the book's dynamic design the text, in blocks of stark white, contrasts dramatically with the surrounding luxuriance.

Kirkus Reviews

SOURCE: A review of *How the Animals Got Their Colors: Animal Myths from Around the World,* in *Kirkus Reviews,* Vol. LX, No. 6, March 15, 1992, p. 404.

Nine *pourquoi* stories drawn from named sources such as Bulfinch, *The Journal of American Folklore,* and the work of various anthropologists. Rosen's retellings are spare but fairly lively; Clementson's illustrations, vibrant with sharp-edged areas of joyfully intense color that appear to have been cut with scissors, dramatically frame the stark white areas of text. Concluding notes about cultural sources and the animals themselves are addressed to young readers; it's too bad that the credited sources are not also mentioned. An outstandingly handsome, eye-catching book—one that's likely to be especially useful to storytellers and teachers.

Carolyn Phelan

SOURCE: A review of *How the Animals Got Their Colors: Animal Myths from Around the World,* in *Booklist,* Vol. 88, No. 20, June 15, 1992, p. 1843.

Rosen retells nine animal tales from around the world, including an African story explaining how the leopard got its spots, a native American *pourquoi* tale of how the coyote got its yellow eyes, and a Greek myth explaining why frogs are green on their backs and white on their bellies. Vibrant paper-cut collages fill the pages with diverse patterns and contrasting colors. Despite their cluttered appearance, many of the illustrations have a vitality of line and a rhythmic repetition of form that make them effective. Appended notes on the tales include information about the people who told them and the animals themselves. In a pleasing decorative touch, each description in the notes is accompanied by a striking depiction of the animal, drawn from the illustrations but isolated on the blue-bordered, white pages. First published in England, this is a possible source for storytelling or reading aloud.

C. H. Jones

SOURCE: A review of *How the Animals Got Their Colours: Animal Myths from Around the World,* in *Books for Your Children,* Vol. 27, No. 2, Summer, 1992, p. 20.

Stories about animals have an endearing quality. Michael Rosen has chosen a selection of nine from around the world in countries as far apart as Papua, New Guinea and Liberia. These retellings are accompanied by fascinating cut paper collages in bold bright colours which have an immediate warmth and friendliness. Coyote, flying fish, frog and leopard, dance across the page acquiring spots, stripes; turning into iridescent frogs or having a golden crest to match the sunlight.

Each story is matchless and easy on the eye and ear and could be memorised and recounted aloud on future occasions. The origins of each story are explained with details of size, habitat and feeding habits of each creature.

Betsy Hearne

SOURCE: A review of *How the Animals Got Their Colors: Animal Myths from Around the World,* in *Bulletin of the Center for Children's Books,* Vol. 45, No. 11, July-August, 1992, p. 304.

From the Zuni, New Guineans, Greeks, Chinese, aborigines, Loma of Liberia, Khasi of India, Ugandans, and Ayoreo Indians of South America, these nine myths explain animal characteristics from the time of creation. Rosen's sources are listed at the book's beginning, but the bibliography of respectable folklore journals gives no hint of how freshly the pourquoi tales are told here in present tense, with wit and neat compression. Leaving the archetypal integrity undisturbed, Rosen nevertheless manages to characterize the animals with funny refrains ("I know, I know, I know," says Tiger over and over), to preserve chanting rhythms (*"See our paddles dive into the water, / See our paddles fly out of the water, / See our paddles shoot through the air"*), and to keep vivid sound effects ("*Foop, foop, foop,* go Leopard's paws. *Shoo, shoo, shoo* go Nyomo's feet"). Short and sweet, these will fit neatly into brief bedtime sessions or story hour niches between longer tales. The angular, collage-effect art leans on designer patterns that leap off the page in technicolor.

MIND THE GAP (1992)

A. R. Williams

SOURCE: A review of *Mind the Gap,* in *The Junior Bookshelf,* Vol. 56, No. 4, August, 1992, p. 167.

Of the sixty four poems/verses in **Mind the Gap** some two of three might be considered to be bordering on the bone and could lead to sniggers at worst; racy rather than risqué, pungent if both. On the other hand, the writing takes a wide view of the current social scene and some broadness of mind goes with the scope of the subject matter. Offerings vary from the humorous to the nostalgic often wrapped in satire rather than spleen. Michael Rosen rather specialises in unexpected associations: cricket is associated with a dying mother; the school caretaker, Mr. Tyrell belongs with the demise of William Rufus; a dirty book relates to Oxfam. Nothing is ruled out. There are tours de force such as the phonetic transcription of a train announcement at Victoria (could Three Ditches possibly be Three Bridges?). Mood extends even to ironic comments on racial attitudes as in **"Arsenal"**. We are funny people: there is the boy taken to Switzerland who insists it doesn't compare with South Harrow Gasworks; the boy who irrationally throws an apple at a Sikh; and the boys who fire a Pakistani shop.

Mind the Gap emphasises our oddness without passing judgment, making us laugh at the same time. This is not to say the author is not serious-minded; to give him credit he looks at sadness and misery as well. The withering send-up of statistical surveys in **"Liars"** suggests he is not daft either. For those who are not happy with mention of condoms, farting and easy sex, reading will need to be restricted or the book mutilated. We are no longer in a world where the ultimate grace is *A Child's Garden of Verses.* The format has its own part to play, depending largely on a variety of type faces superimposed on slogans, headlines or advertisements, often giving an extra bite to the pith of the verses. The illustrations [by Caroline Holden] show both ingenuity and wit.

Adrian Jackson

SOURCE: A review of *Mind the Gap,* in *Books for Keeps,* No. 76, September, 1992, p. 13.

Lots of anecdotes as poems with the usual bright and very funny voice of the poet clowning for attention. But there are other voices here too, sometimes harsh and even bitter, as Rosen edges his humour into areas of race and political injustice. Teenagers will love it—some of it immediately. Worth buying as many as you can afford. It's a fine collection, both in the poems themselves and the orchestration of the easy and uneasy laughter.

Sue Rogers

SOURCE: A review of *Mind the Gap,* in *The School Librarian,* Vol. 40, No. 4, November, 1992, p. 156.

A brilliant new collection of poetry by Michael Rosen which contains a wonderful mixture of comic, sad, controversial and thought-provoking verse ranging from the touching memories of his dying mother in **'Test match cricket'** and **'Then'** to his hilarious experience on television in **'Telly star'**. The poems are based on both Rosen's own experiences and his thoughts on modern society. They are immediate and hard-hitting.

The design of the book is excellent with black and white drawings and images accompanying the verse. My only concern is that Rosen is appreciated by all age groups and this collection is deliberately aimed at the teenage market, with the hilarious **'Flight problem'** and **'Condom'** very much for the older age group.

Otherwise the collection represents good value for money and is great to dip into or for inspiring budding poets.

SONSENSE NONGS (compiled by Michael Rosen, 1992)

Frances Ball

SOURCE: A review of *Sonsense Nongs,* in *The Junior Bookshelf,* Vol. 56, No. 5, October, 1992, p. 200.

Michael Rosen's popular **Sonsense Nongs** is now available in this paperback edition. The book came into being when Michael Rosen approached A. & C. Black with the idea of a competition which would ask children to write silly songs and devise a book title. **Sonsense Nongs** was the winning title, and 'The King of Gunerania's Wedding Cake' was the winning song. Other contributions from children are mixed with old and new favourites, and for

each song the music is shown or stated. For some, alternative words are provided for established songs. In these cases, there are directions such as: 'Tune: While shepherds watched their flocks' or 'Tune: Clementine'. For others, the music is given. The tone throughout the book is light and amusing but use of the material would be likely to encourage a deeper understanding of language as well as much fun and laughter. Shoo Rayner was a good choice as illustrator, capturing the mood of the book with ease.

ITSY-BITSY BEASTIES: POEMS FROM AROUND THE WORLD (edited by Michael Rosen, 1992)

Karey Wehner

SOURCE: A review of *Itsy-Bitsy Beasties: Poems from Around the World,* in *School Library Journal,* Vol. 38, No. 12, December, 1992, p. 129.

Despite its cloying title, this collection of 31 short poems about invertebrates is light and lively. Most of the verses on insects, spiders, snails, etc., originated in the U. S. or England, but there are also entries from Australia, Scotland, Canada, the Caribbean, and Japan. The majority have been published before; about two-thirds are available in other anthologies, some widely (eight are included in Prelutsky's *Random House Book of Poetry for Children.*) The selections, in rhyme and free verse, are a nice mix of the silly, mildly humorous, and sublimely lyrical. Appealing, brightly colored pen-and-ink drawings [by Alan Baker] appear on every page. Some that illustrate the more humorous offerings are anthropomorphized (a few of these show worms and spiders with anatomically incorrect antennae—an interesting anomaly since the dust jacket states that the artist originally wanted to become a zoologist) but most are realistic depictions of the animals. While this collection is not as saucy as Prelutsky's *Poems of a Nonny Mouse,* it is an entertaining read-aloud for the younger set.

ACTION REPLAY (edited by Michael Rosen, 1993)

David Bennett

SOURCE: A review of *Action Replay,* in *Books for Keeps,* No. 80, May, 1993, p. 15.

This ought to attract a very wide audience. Each poem or piece of 'memorable speech' tells a story or anecdote, sometimes a familiar one, which is generally very accessible and often amusing.

A wide range of styles is presented with contributions from India, China, Japan, Poland and Czechoslovakia.

In my experience these are just the sorts of writing to switch kids on to the possibilities of poetry.

Dennis Hamley

SOURCE: A review of *Action Replay,* in *The School Librarian,* Vol. 41, No. 3, May, 1993, p. 71.

Michael Rosen has culled from myriad sources poems, epigrams, accidental statements which are anecdotal: they tell stories, define particular significant moments, present sharp little vignettes. This is both the raw material of poetry and its apogee (the book closes with 'A letter was returned to the Post Office with the following inscription: "Dead. Address unknown"—Gunter Grass's brilliantly-worked, savagely epigrammatic paradox "Family matters" is different in degree, not kind').

The collection is a delight. 'Found' poetry like the quotation above; many well-known and some less-known writers; a broad sweep of foreign poets—all share the pithiness of acute observation. . . .

This is a first-rate resource for both library and classroom at Key Stages 3 and 4. If literature in schools is to be forced into a prescriptive heritage model, it becomes more important than ever that books like these are available to provide the true link between art and life. Besides which, there is plenty here for pupils to emulate in their own writing—to see there is a way forward for their own paradox and epigram based on everyday observation. Buy it: it's a gem.

📖 *NUTS ABOUT NUTS* (1993)

Frances Ball

SOURCE: A review of *Nuts about Nuts,* in *The Junior Bookshelf,* Vol. 57, No. 3, June, 1993, p. 101.

Michael Rosen takes a look at eight popular foods: ice cream, honey, nuts, cake bread, eggs, rice and apples. For each one, the same pattern is followed. The food is described, celebrated and examined—all in lighthearted, fast-moving verse. Sam Sweeten has worked with Michael Rosen before, and her illustrations extend his ideas in various directions. Mostly, she shows what would happen if an idea were taken towards its conclusion: the bride and groom hidden beneath the rice, a giant bowl of scrambled eggs that runs the length of the table, a bath full of honey, and so on. Together, author and illustrator provide images of food that could make an ordinary meal the start of wild imaginings or amusement. Children of infant school age, and younger juniors, will find much to enjoy, with a range of word play likely to encourage their own writing.

📖 *HOW GIRAFFE GOT SUCH A LONG NECK . . . AND WHY RHINO IS SO GRUMPY: A TALE FROM EAST AFRICA* (retold by Michael Rosen, 1993)

Publishers Weekly

SOURCE: A review of *How Giraffe Got Such a Long Neck . . . and Why Rhino Is So Grumpy,* in *Publishers Weekly,* Vol. 240, No. 30, July 26, 1993, p. 71.

This gorgeous book may not lead to a movie deal for its author, but might well bring a great wallpaper deal for its illustrator. [John] Clementson's vibrantly hued, densely patterned cut-paper compositions have soared in wit and personableness since his last collaboration with Rosen, *How Animals Got Their Colors.* Happily, this tale is neatly told verbally as well as visually. "In the beginning of the beginning Giraffe wasn't as tall as the trees. She was more like a deer, lean and quick and no taller than a bush." But drought comes, drying up all but the highest leaves in the trees. When Giraffe and Rhino ask Man to help them reach the trees, he gives them a magic herb. Rhino forgets to eat his, and so Giraffe imbibes both portions, resulting in a doubly long neck and a cranky Rhino. Although this is a traditional tale in East Africa, it is tendered here with markedly unconventional style.

Elizabeth Bush

SOURCE: A review of *How Giraffe Got Such a Long Neck . . . and Why Rhino Is So Grumpy: A Tale from East Africa,* in *Booklist,* Vol. 90, No. 7, December 1, 1993, p. 695.

In the beginning, Giraffe's neck was short. Because he and laconic Rhino are unable to reach juicy tree leaves during a drought, they seek the help of Man and his magic herbs. The next day, Rhino arrives too late to collect his share. Giraffe has already consumed both portions, grown an enormously long neck, and is happily chomping away on the highest leaves. Rhino, to this day, remains cross with Man, Giraffe, and himself for missing out on the magic. Rosen's narration moves with a smooth cadence, and the ample dialogue, punctuated by Rhino's frequent "Oomphs," is rhythmic and lighthearted. The combination of simple plot, nicely differentiated animal characters, and arrestingly bold and colorful graphics inspired by Maasai design makes this a good choice for both independent and classroom reading.

📖 *SONGBIRD STORY* (1993)

Irene Babsky

SOURCE: A review of *Songbird Story,* in *The School Librarian,* Vol. 41, No. 3, August, 1993, pp. 104, 106.

This is an original story that reads like a traditional one; it has echoes within it of the Willow Pattern story, the Magic Flute, and many other bird/freedom/love stories. It is very competently written by a (rightly) well respected author who adopts a rather prosaic, sinewy style to tell a story which might have become maudlin in the hands of a less sure writer. Two birds go through the various vicissitudes of forming a friendship through their wonderful singing ability, then of being captured and separated; eventually together finding friendship and freedom again.

The illustrations [by Jill Dow] are beautifully conceptualised and executed; they combine with the text to give a very tangible sense of 'once upon a time . . . it was here . . . it was there . . . it was some-other where . . .'. The visual style is realistic with lots of supportive details that tempt and reward the eyes; yet it is the evocative use of colour for mood setting that makes this book outstanding. A thoughtful story that will appeal most to children under nine.

MOVING (1993)

Chris Powling

SOURCE: A review of *Moving,* in *Books for Keeps,* No. 82, September, 1993, p. 40.

After death and divorce, we're told moving house is the next most stressful of human predicaments. This may account for the downbeat, sepia tints of *Moving* which comes complete with a poster 'to frame and keep'. Sophy Williams' painterly illustrations have a haunting and addictive charm, though, that will outlast many a flashier foray into the subject. The colour variations she achieves with her restricted palette catch perfectly the mood of Michael Rosen's text.

Take the spread, for instance, that shows the boy alone in his new, bare bedroom with his parents fully occupied off-page:

> Now they will worry,
> now they will be sorry,
> now they will want me
> to come from nowhere,
> but I won't.

Does this refer to the child or the tabbycat telling the story? The answer is both, of course. The counterpoint of kid's-eye view and cat's-eye view, in matching word and image, is one of the delights of this rich, subtle picture book.

M. Crouch

SOURCE: A review of *Moving,* in *The Junior Bookshelf,* Vol. 59, No. 3, June, 1995, pp. 93-4.

In an exquisite paperback Michael Rosen and Sophy Williams tell a story which is just as true and even more beautiful and moving. *Moving* is told by the cat, a wise, sensitive animal who knows all about comfort and independence and how to reconcile them. As much as any human this sturdy tabby values home. When the family move house he, more than anyone, realises that in a new home he is lost. Only patience can win him to acceptance of the new life, and even then he will at times be 'nowhere and everywhere'. The cat's words, rhythmic and repetitive, make a poem, and Sophie Williams matches them with a sequence of lovely cat studies, full of truth and mystery.

POEMS FOR THE VERY YOUNG (edited by Michael Rosen, 1993)

Books for Your Children

SOURCE: A review of *Poems for the Very Young* and *Moving,* in *Books for Your Children,* Vol. 28, No. 3, Autumn-Winter, 1993, p. 2.

For a slightly older audience, Michael Rosen has come up with a splendid anthology of *Poems for the Very Young,* illustrated by Bob Graham. Like all good collections this contains some rhymes mum and dad will remember, and others that are absolutely new—

> Man fat
> Top hat
> Fell flat
> Squashed hat.

The layout of the book is exemplary and there's plenty of space for young eyes to wander about the pages and to absorb the images. Bob Graham has never been funnier and this collection proves once again how readily he sees the world through a child's eyes.

In a quieter mood, Michael Rosen has also written *Moving,* with illustrations by Sophy Williams. Rosen shows the arduous business of moving house through the eyes of the family cat and this oblique approach gives great scope for sympathy to the young reader. Rosen's sure feel for the rhythm and atmosphere of a text are quite stunning. The other half of the book belongs to Sophy Williams who makes the whole process of moving look as disturbing as it is to an uncertain child and yet manages in the end to bring comfort.

Kathleen Whalin

SOURCE: A review of *Poems for the Very Young,* in *School Library Journal,* Vol. 40, No. 1, January, 1994, p. 110.

Rosen shows his mastery of the sound of good poetry in this anthology. It is a mix of traditional rhymes, verse by poets, and pieces written by children that ranges over time and cultures, united by a sure sense of the richness of well-chosen words. The obvious care behind each poem's selection is matched by [Bob] Graham's humorous watercolor cartoons that extend, interpret, and celebrate their subjects. Like the compilations of Lee Bennett Hopkins, X. J. Kennedy, Myra Cohn Livingston, and Jack Prelutsky, this title demonstrates that a strong poetry collection, like a good recipe, relies on the quality and subtle blending of the various ingredients.

Carolyn Phelan

SOURCE: A review of *Poems for the Very Young,* in *Booklist,* Vol. 90, No. 9, January 1, 1994, p. 821.

Yes, it's another illustrated anthology of poems for young children, but from the promising jacket through the lively introduction to the "don't stop now" quality of the verse itself this is more than just another poetry book. Keenly aware of the playful, physical aspects of poetry for children, Rosen has chosen poems for "their tone of revelation and discovery." He includes anonymous nursery verse ("Wakey, wakey, rise and shine, / Make your bed, / And then make mine") as well as rhymes written primarily by British, American, and Canadian children's poets, and does not rule out poems by Japanese, Australian, and African writers. The inclusion of a few rhymes written by children is unusual, but the collection is so eclectic in origin and boisterous in tone that they fit right in. [Bob] Graham's appealing, cartoonlike drawings with bright, watercolor washes give the pages a look of constant motion and irreverent humor. An irresistible collection for reading aloud, just for the fun of it.

Chris Brown

SOURCE: A review of *Poems for the Very Young,* in *The School Librarian,* Vol. 42, No. 2, May, 1994, p. 57.

This anthology is larger and has more in it than most other collections of poetry for the very young. There is a pleasing variety of sources: traditional, current and 'anon' poets; and there is a satisfying mixture of thoughts, rhymes, rhythms, nonsense and fun. In spite of the large number of items, the appearance of clarity and space has been maintained and the book can safely be recommended for any library—and especially for parents and others wishing to share poetry pleasure with children.

ARABIAN FRIGHTS AND OTHER STORIES (adapted by Michael Rosen, 1994)

Elizabeth Baynton-Clarke

SOURCE: A review of *Arabian Frights and Other Stories,* in *The School Librarian,* Vol. 43, No. 1, February, 1995, p. 66.

In this outrageous new adaptation of *The Arabian nights,* Michael Rosen uses intensive word play to transform well-known stories and verses into bizarre alternatives. Hence we meet such characters as 'Old King Goal' and 'Abaddin', and are treated to the delights of 'Hot Cross Bums', all wildly illustrated in brilliant colour by Chris Fisher. Not only confined to titles, the word play is sustained throughout the entire text. The result is a towering surrealism in both language and plot, the absurdity of which is likely to appeal tremendously to some word-happy 8 to 12-year-olds, but pass others by completely. Similarly, while the collection is little short of a gift to teachers exploring word play, it is likely to be the object of much eyebrow-raising among less broadminded colleagues and parents.

The unmistakable genius of Michael Rosen is ever present throughout this book, which will be treasured especially by those who relish his delight in the unconventional. Rather than a 'safe' option, however, *Arabian frights* is liable to be loved by some, dismissed as unadulterated nonsense by others. A brave new book!

CROW AND HAWK: A TRADITIONAL PUEBLO INDIAN STORY (adapted by Michael Rosen, 1995)

Publishers Weekly

SOURCE: A review of *Crow and Hawk,* in *Publishers Weekly,* Vol. 242, No. 9, February 27, 1995, pp. 102-03.

Abandoned babies, birth mothers vying with adoptive mothers for custody, a tearful judgment—this Pueblo story has all the ingredients of a bad made-for-TV movie. When Crow abandons her nest, Hawk moves in to care for the eggs, then stays to tend the hatchlings. When Crow finally returns to claim her youngsters, Hawk responds that she is their true mother because she has raised them. Eagle, King of the Birds, sides with Hawk and bluntly tells a crying Crow that "this is the way it must be. You left the nest; you have lost the children." Just as distressing as the cheerless story, though, is the overstimulating chaos of pattern, color and scenes-within-scenes in [John] Clementson's cut-paper collages. In contrast to the restraint he showed in the vibrant illustrations for *How Giraffe Got Such a Long Neck,* there is neither visual hierarchy in these pictures nor an easy point of entry for the young audience.

Karen Hutt

SOURCE: A review of *Crow and Hawk,* in *Booklist,* Vol. 91, No. 16, April 15, 1995, pp. 1503-04.

Crow is tired of sitting on the eggs in her nest and abandons them, so Hawk takes over and continues to care for the baby crows after they hatch. When Crow returns and tries to take the babies back, Hawk refuses to relinquish them. The birds appeal to Eagle, king of the birds, who, after listening to what the little crows have to say, tells Crow she has lost her children because she deserted them. Vivid cut-paper collages with colorful borders fill the pages and reflect the directness, simplicity, and clarity of the text. The story is an especially pertinent traditional tale because it mirrors contemporary society's increasing struggle with a complex family issue. Told to Ruth Benedict by an elderly storyteller of the Cochiti Pueblo, it appeared in Benedict's 1931 *Tales of the Cochiti Indians.* Rosen and [John] Clementson's new interpretation is just right for picture-book and folktale collections.

Joanne Schott

SOURCE: A review of *Crow and Hawk,* in *Quill and Quire,* Vol. 61, No. 6, June, 1995, p. 60.

Crow grew tired of sitting on her nest so she flew away.

Hawk saw the nest and took pity on the poor eggs. She sat on them and when they hatched, she cared for the little crows. One day Crow remembered her nest and found that Hawk was mothering her children. She demanded them back. Hawk refused, so the two mothers took the matter to Eagle, king of the birds, for judgment.

Michael Rosen presents here a story collected by Ruth Benedict from a noted Pueblo storyteller and first published in 1931. His own wide experience in selecting, editing, and retelling folktales is evident in his sure touch with this one. Using great economy of language, simplicity of structure, and repetition, he recreates a story once "learned by the fireside . . . as a normal part of growing up."

The illustrations, in cut-paper collage, use warm desert colours and simple angular shapes with accents of stylized feathers and decorative borders. The images repeat the narrative with the same kind of simple elegance found in the text and give central place to the drama of the conflict and the justice of the solution. Starkly beautiful, this is one of the season's best examples of integrity in book-making for children.

Lisa Dennis

SOURCE: A review of *Crow and Hawk: A Traditional Pueblo Indian Story,* in *School Library Journal,* Vol. 41, No. 7, July, 1995, p. 74.

Striking, stylized cut-paper collage illustrations elegantly decorate this deceptively simple adaptation of a Pueblo Indian tale. Crow, tired of sitting on her nest of eggs, abandons it. Hawk comes along, hatches the eggs, and cares for the young birds. When Crow eventually remembers her nest and returns, the two squabble over which of them should keep the children. They take their quarrel to Eagle, King of the Birds, who decides in Hawk's favor. Rosen's spare text, perfectly cadenced for effective storytelling, is drawn from a collection of tales compiled by Ruth Benedict. [John] Clementson's imaginative pictures combine decorative borders, small vignettes, and larger compositions on each double-page spread. Bold geometric designs and the predominance of turquoise, brown, black, gold, and coral further enhance the story's Southwestern flair. The sophistication of the art indicates clearly that despite the brevity of the text, this is a story best appreciated by primary-grade students. Eagle's decisive decree could be disconcerting to young children whose families are struggling with divorce and custody issues. This is not a criticism of the original story, or of Rosen and Clementson's excellent interpretation, but merely a point that those using the story may wish to consider.

📖 *EVEN STEVENS F.C.* (with John Rogan, 1995)

Wendy Cooling

SOURCE: A review of *Even Stevens F.C.,* in *Books for Keeps,* No. 93, July, 1995, p. 25.

Wayne is mad about football and because of injuries he gets to play for Even Stevens, the Shakespeare Street team—they all live in houses or flats with even numbers. Miracle follows miracle as the team make it to the first round of the FA Cup—and in fact all the way to Wembley. A strong story with the sort of imaginative leap that will delight young football fans. The mix of text, speech bubbles and illustration follows the very successful 'Jets' formula that works so well.

Robert Hull

SOURCE: "Game, Set . . . and Literature," in *Books for Keeps,* No. 97, March, 1996, pp. 24-5.

Since sport tends towards solemnity, there's a good deal of pleasure to be had from books that are subversive—of gravitas not games themselves. Michael Rosen and the illustrator John Rogan have executed some neat one-twos in *Even Stevens F.C.,* assisted by Eddie Rosen—technical advice? I don't normally read the team notes before a game, but here I'd make an exception: *'Rodney Travis: 38, Wayne's dad. Bad back, bad right knee, bad shoulder. Part-time postman.'* The dialogue is tough and realistic: *'That fractured eye-lash was a set-up.'* A wikkid book.

📖 *PILLY SOEMS* (compiled by Michael Rosen, 1995)

Janette Perkins

SOURCE: A review of *Pilly Soems,* in *The School Librarian,* Vol. 43, No. 3, August, 1995, p. 116.

Pilly soems is a *very* silly collection of poems from Michael Rosen, conveniently categorised into sections such as Festering Food; Clothes for Clots; Personal Peculiarities: Amazing Animals; Big Boasts; Mega Monstrosities; Riotous Relatives, and many more. Some we are already familiar with, some originate from the Music Hall and the playground, others are rap and folk based. It is a masterpiece of fun for the 10-plus age group, a little book for 'dipping into' rather than a serious text. Whenever someone detects a bit of gloom and doom advancing in the classroom, a dose of *Pilly soems* is called for. Teachers will need a copy to read aloud on a rainy Friday afternoon; pupils will need one at home to read out the Verbal Bubbles; we all need one to chant poems on a long car journey. Indeed, the songs we adults chanted in our own childhood are gathered up in this semi-serious book.

This pocket-sized little gem is arranged in a very readable style, with some witty diagrams by Shoo Rayner.

📖 *THE BEST OF MICHAEL ROSEN* (1995)

Publishers Weekly

SOURCE: A review of *The Best of Michael Rosen,* in

Publishers Weekly, Vol. 242, No. 51, December 18, 1995, pp. 54-5.

Although both author and illustrator [Quentin Blake] have been honored in Britain for their work for children, this all-new collection is a long way from the best work of either. Rosen's (*We're Going on a Bear Hunt*) free-verse poems range from nonsense rhymes ("Tiffy taffy toffee / on the flee flo floor . . . Kiffy kaffy coffee / in a mig mag mug") to prosy, four- or five-page monologues with nary an image. In **"The Field Trip,"** for example, the narrator/ teacher scolds, "All right / as you know / it was our plan to go out today— / to the Science Museum . . . I saw that, Mark, / I saw it. / Any more and you'll be out. / No trip, nothing." The so-called illustrations consist of a single monochrome drawing that is used as a border on every page; while the border design is detailed, the cumulative effect is numbing, as if the poems had been printed on a stack of stationery. All ages.

Carolyn Phelan

SOURCE: A review of *The Best of Michael Rosen,* in *Booklist,* Vol. 92, No. 11, February 1, 1996, pp. 929, 931.

This collection features 65 poems by Michael Rosen, an English writer whose light verse is colloquial and child-like. Children who enjoy [Jack] Prelutsky's work will find much to like in Rosen's poems: excellent descriptions of childhood experiences, sharp insights into people, and quite a bit of humor. Framing every two-page spread is a border: dozens of appealing characters from the poems lean in toward the page, acting out their roles, interacting a bit, and hamming it up for the reader. Rosen may need some introduction to American children, but they'll return to this volume for the pleasure of rereading his entertaining verse.

📖 *MICHAEL ROSEN'S ABC* (1995)

Margaret Mallett

SOURCE: A review of *Michael Rosen's ABC,* in *The School Librarian,* Vol. 44, No. 1, February, 1996, p. 16.

This exciting ABC for 4-year-olds and above features a new poem for each letter of the alphabet. The very first poem is a wonderful invitation to all that follows:

> Come into a magic wood
> Where you might meet anything . . .

The language play is great fun becoming a little contrived only occasionally. At its best it is full of the sort of humour young children love. For example:

> Jack and Jill went up the hill
> Juggling a jug of jelly
> A passing bug jumped in the jug
> Which made the jelly smelly.

Part of the fun of the poems is the liberty taken with many mythical and nursery characters including Goldilocks, Humpty Dumpty and Red Riding Hood. The poems are full of surprises, for example, a meeting between Mother Goose and Miss Muffet and, in this delightfully topsy turvey would, a mouse jumping over the moon. The repetition, rhyme and ingenious use of the alphabet will encourage a genuine love of words and word play.

Elaine Williams

SOURCE: "It's Not Always as Easy as ABC," in *The Times Educational Supplement,* No. 4153, February 2, 1996, p. 12.

English is a very visual language. Words become recognisable as much for the pattern made by letters as for their sounds. Children learn to read as the words take on visual resonance and the sounds become familiar shapes.

Michael Rosen's ABC takes all this on board masterfully. We are led through the alphabet with rich alliteration and musical rhythms, Rosen's witty, pithy and jubilant rhymes combining with the Chagall-like illustrations of Bee Willey to build up a sense of the exciting possibilities of the written word.

Alphabet books are tricky. Many lack clarity, illustrations and letters failing singularly to inspire or instruct. Though Bee Willey's pictures are arty, they also relate directly to the text as well as providing limitless possibilities for exploration.

Alphabet letters are written in various styles of lower case and upper case, providing a structure for the composition of pictures and text. Rosen combines his own versions of familiar verse, including archetypal characters such as King Arthur and Humpty Dumpty, with wholly original passages, weaving them together with a sharp, cheeky humour. In the case of the E words, for example:

> That elm tree is really an elk in disguise.
> Everything else that you see is enchanted.
> Even the trees were magically planted.
> Electric? Wow!
> That eagle! The beak!
> Elastic? Incredible!
> Those eels! Eeeek!

Willey's pictures combine the weird, the wonderful and the wicked, very much in the spirit of nursery rhyme. This is a truly wonderful book that children of different ages would enjoy together.

Jill Bennett

SOURCE: A review of *Michael Rosen's ABC,* in *Books for Keeps,* No. 97, March, 1996, p. 28.

Charlie Chaplin, Goldilocks, the Gingerbread Man, Humpty Dumpty (who had a headache), Ivan the Terrible, King Kong, the Lady of the Lake, Miss Muffett, Mother Goose, Red Riding Hood and even Rudolph the Red-nosed Reindeer—an unlikely mix if ever there was one—are gathered together in this glorious glut of alliterative nonsense. There are tongue-twisting, vervy variations on original verses such as Yankee Doodle and Jack and Jill. Few will find fault with this fun-packed phantasmagoria which fixes phonology firmly in the forefront of the mind.

Every page is peppered with wondrous words and exciting images whose inspiration is the initial letter featured on each double spread.

Peter Sís

1949-

Czech author and illustrator of picture books for children.

(Name is pronounced "cease.") Major works include *Rainbow Rhino* (1987), *Beach Ball* (1990), *Follow the Dream: The Story of Christopher Columbus* (1991), *Komodo!* (1993), *The Three Golden Keys* (1994).

INTRODUCTION

Peter Sís is internationally known for his beautifully illustrated children's books. A talented artist, Sís's artwork complements and enhances the mood the author is trying to relay in the text. He has also written several of his own books for children, which he subsequently illustrated, including books that teach colors and counting to primary grade readers and impart historical information to middle grade readers. His illustrations balance his straightforward text. Often surrealistic, his oil paintings use color, sweeping skies, and expansive landscapes to create a definite mood or feeling. Sís enjoys experimenting with different styles and illustrative techniques. He has used oil paints on a plasterlike background to create the old-world look of fifteenth-century paintings in *Follow the Dream: The Story of Christopher Columbus,* and maps, scripted text, and stamps to convey a Renaissance tone in *Starry Messenger: Galileo Galilei* (1996). Allen Raymond described Sís's work as "beautiful pictures that startle, surprise, amuse, enthrall and captivate all who are exposed to his remarkable talent."

Biographical Information

Sís was born in Prague, Czechoslovakia, in 1949. His father was an explorer and filmmaker who traveled to exotic places such as Tibet and Borneo. His mother was an artist. Sís loved drawing from an early age and was encouraged by his parents to pursue art as a career. Sís attended various art schools in Europe and studied with Quentin Blake at London's Royal College of Art, before starting his career as a maker of animated films. Sís also worked as an illustrator for television programs and films throughout Europe, but he really wanted to illustrate his own stories and adapt them into animated films.

Sís came to the United States in 1982 to work on an animated film about the winter Olympics. He decided to stay in Los Angeles since that city is the heart of the filmmaking world, but Sís was discouraged by the lack of serious work for an illustrator. At the suggestion of a friend, Sís wrote to renowned author and illustrator Maurice Sendak, sending along samples of his work. Sendak

called Sís and suggested that he move to New York to be closer to major book publishers. Despite the advice, Sís remained in Los Angeles. In 1984, Sendak called again. He was in Los Angeles for the American Library Association's annual convention and thought he could introduce Sís to some publishing contacts. The introductions resulted in a contract for Sís to illustrate a title for Greenwillow Books.

Major Works

Sid Fleischman's *The Whipping Boy* (1985) was one of the early titles Sís illustrated for Greenwillow. A retelling of the *Prince and the Pauper, Whipping Boy* is the story of an orphan, Jemmy, who becomes the commoner scapegoat that endures the punishment for all the mischief that the spoiled and lazy Prince Brat causes. According to a *Booklist* reviewer, Sís's rustic illustrations gave the work a Dickensian flavor. George Gleason, writing in *School Library Journal,* noted that Sís's illustrations not only complemented but added to Fleischman's story, and Ethel L. Heinz wrote in *Horn Book* that the pictures had "an appropriate air of droll exaggeration."

The artwork Sís created for his own books has been equally impressive. In *Rainbow Rhino* he created a magical wilderness for a rhinoceros and his three rainbow bird friends. The foursome leads a happy, peaceful existence until the birds leave for more colorful—but also more dangerous—surroundings. Each bird moves to a locale of its own hue: blue bird to a blue lake; yellow bird to a yellow banana tree; red bird to a red poppy field. But each new place has a color-coordinated danger—hyena, snake, and crocodile—from which rhino saves his feathered friends. The result, according to Pamela Miller's *School Library Journal* review, is a story "to treasure as a beautifully illustrated, timeless tale."

The cleverness and intricacies of Sís's illustrations are always noticed. The watercolors of *Waving* (1988) are not just beautiful. They artfully reinforce the book's counting theme: A woman with ten suitcases counts ten joggers. Building names and addresses like the Seven Dwarfs Restaurant continue the number motif. The Twins Shop is on page two. Sís even hid Roman numerals in the pictures, as well as number jokes and puzzles. The detail and invention in the illustrations for *Beach Ball* also are remarkable. In the book, Mary's beach ball bounces along the shoreline. Each spread of pages invites the reader to enjoy a new theme. On one two-page spread, a flock of flying seagulls spells out "name the animals." Other themes explore the alphabet, colors, and numbers with equal ingenuity. Similarly, according to the *Bulletin of the Center for Children's Books*, "graphic ironies abound" in *An Ocean World* (1992). This story of a whale that is set free after being raised in captivity has numerous illustrations mimicking the whale's form, such as a whale-shaped island with a palm tree spout. The ink drawings in the picture-book fantasy *Komodo!* also include captivating details for observant readers to ponder. *Komodo!* is a dragon-crazy child's adventure, and the pictures are awash with dragons: in the wallpaper, in terrariums, in toy trains, and in the jungle foliage. The story involves a child's clandestine trip to a jungle to view a real Komodo dragon when the tourists' dragon-show one never materializes, so the stippled drawings and antique end papers combine with the plot to create an atmosphere of exploration and mystery.

The artwork in *Follow the Dream: The Story of Christopher Columbus* has been called extraordinary for its Age of Exploration ambience as recalled by Sís's portrayal of the maps and charts of Columbus's era. Detailed images and decorative use of sea motifs like monsters of the deep, ships, and nautical instruments abound. Walls also appear frequently in the illustrations to represent the barriers of fear and ignorance that Columbus broke, and, in the book's introduction, Sís draws a parallel between Columbus's walls and explorations and Sis's own lack of personal freedom in a country behind the Iron Curtain and his emigration to the United States. (Sís was naturalized in 1989.)

Sís recounts memories of his childhood in Prague for his daughter Madeleine through the beautiful and symbolic illustrations in *The Three Golden Keys*. In the book, a man is blown off course in his hot-air balloon, landing somewhere in Prague. He finds the door of his childhood home bolted by three padlocks. He follows a cat to a library, the Emperor's garden, and the town's clock. He collects keys at each of the three stops from legendary Czechs and returns to unlock the house. Only then does he gain access to his old home, a place he had once thought he had said good-bye to forever.

Awards

Sid Fleischman's *The Whipping Boy,* a book illustrated by Sís, won the Newbery Medal in 1987. Both *Rainbow Rhino* and *Beach Ball* were named "one of the best illustrated books of the year" by the *New York Times* for 1987 and 1990. In addition to his book awards, Sís has been honored throughout the world for his films. In 1980, *Heads* won the Golden Berlin Bear at the Berlin International Film Festival. *Players* received the Grand Prix Toronto in 1981, and *You Gotta Serve Somebody* won the Council on International Non-Theatrical Events's Eagle Award in 1983.

AUTHOR'S COMMENTARY

Peter Sís

SOURCE: "The Artist at Work," in *The Horn Book Magazine,* Vol. LXVIII, No. 6, November-December, 1992, pp. 681-87.

I don't actually remember when I first knew I wanted to be an artist, but I began to draw at a very young age. My father, who worked in Czechoslovakia as a film director, was always giving me concepts. He'd tell me to think about something—like the concept of father and son—and then we'd talk about it in three weeks. He was already setting deadlines for me as a child—which helped when it was time for me to meet publishers' deadlines! My father traveled a lot, and he would tell me stories about the places he had been. I would sit in the kitchen, and he would describe things that I would never otherwise have been able to comprehend. Someday I would like to do a book where the father has a very exact picture of what he has seen, and the son is trying to re-create that picture for himself.

As a child I also had an obsession with American books. My grandfather was in the United States in the 1930s, when my mother was a little girl. He was a railway engineer, and he designed railway stations in Cleveland and Chicago. However, he promised the Czech Immigration and Naturalization Service that when his mission was over, he would go back to Europe. All sorts of people said, after Hitler got to power, that maybe it wasn't such a good idea to return, but he said, "I promised to do it." Life was never again as nice as it had been for him in the United States, but, luckily for me, he brought back many fine American children's books. Because my grandfather didn't want children with dirty fingers to look through these books, they were locked in a bookcase. On special occasions, my grandfather would show them to us. They looked different—even smelled different—but I wasn't allowed to touch them. But I used to pore over a huge book he had made that contained all the American Sunday comic strips of the era. That book I fell in love with—Little Orphan Annie and the Katzenjammer Kids—all those comics which were absolutely wonderful. But the other books I was never able to touch. I remember some of the pictures, but the books themselves—one was a Mother Goose—are gone.

At fifteen I went to art school for four years, and then for six years attended the Academy of Applied Arts. My friends and I had fun doing some independent magazines, which were completely influenced by what was happening in the United States in the 1960s. Just after school, in 1975, I did my first book for the Czech state publishing house, a little booklet of fairy tales. These booklets were quite popular because they cost very little and were nicely illustrated; however, the quality of paper was poor. There was just one publishing house, which was the monopoly, so the people at art school would have a chance to do a book just once in two or three years. I spent most of my time working on my own animation, including a film called "**Island for Six Thousand Alarm Clocks**." It was a fairy tale about alarm clocks that get upset because they get hit by people every morning, and so they decide to go far away and ring as they please. It sounded simple and naive, but unfortunately it also had political intonations, so in the end I had to change the ending and the narration. It was my first experience trying to create art and making instead a political statement.

A famous Swiss author for children, Eveline Hasler, happened to come to a show of some of my paintings in Prague and said I would be the perfect illustrator for her book about Little Witch Licorice. Because of that chance meeting, I was connected with Little Witch Licorice for about ten years. It's a very popular series of books in German-speaking countries, and it was great for me because I was paid money in Switzerland—much more than what I could have made behind the Iron Curtain. But I had to keep my work secret.

The Czech government did let me out to work on a Swiss television series, but the situation was getting more and more difficult. All the money I would earn would go to the film company or the government in Prague, and I would only get a small percentage of it. I stayed in Switzerland for a year, but I wasn't able to receive money there. Most of all, I was never sure, each time I returned home, that they would ever let me out again. Someone would ask me if we could, say, meet in Stockholm and see a certain exhibit, and I would have to say that I didn't know if I could get a permit to go. Also, I started to feel strange, because there were people who couldn't travel at all, and they would say to me, "Obviously you must be serving the government if they let you go out." I would reply, "I'm doing my art," and they said, "Yes, but you are still supporting the system." So I thought if there would be any opportunity, I would like to be somewhere else.

When I first came to the United States, I was working on an animation project in Los Angeles. All of a sudden the Russians pulled out of the Olympics, and the Czech passport office said that I should return home. But I had just had enough. I just simply didn't go back. And about a year after I became an American citizen, democratic changes in Prague began to take place.

I'm glad that children's books are so apolitical in the United States. Politics has no place in children's books—but I think it's wonderful when you can convey a sincere message. In Czechoslovakia we were a generation of people who had a great deal of disillusionment in our lives, so it's wonderful for me to believe in something and be able to get that message across. In *Follow the Dream* I wanted to tell a story of a man believing in something for many, many years and finally achieving his dream. But I would never want a book's content to be too pretentious or didactic.

I studied with Quentin Blake in the late seventies in the department of illustration at the Royal College of Art in London. Quentin was a tutor, and later he became [a] professor of illustration. I think he was responsible for helping lots of people who didn't have any direction, and I know that he helped me enormously. It's a pleasure to see his books over and over again.

Also at that time I made my first rounds with my portfolio around English publishing houses. They weren't at all interested in my work, but the experience was good for me, for the future. Showing my work in England helped me, because I learned how to get together a portfolio and take it to publishers. It would have been overwhelming for me to approach publishers in New York if I hadn't had this previous experience.

My first book in this country was *Bean Boy*. Maurice Sendak had introduced me to Ava Weiss at Greenwillow, and she had this story by George Shannon that Greenwillow wanted me to illustrate. I had just done a book, for a Swiss publisher, called *Little Singer*—a very idealistic story about a little dwarf who sings to his friends and collects berries and water and nuts. When he exchanges his songs for gold, he loses his songs. The book had an abstract, idealistic, European concept. Immediately after that I started to work on *Bean Boy,* which was about somebody who becomes a very successful entrepreneur selling beans. The plot was much more materialistic—and much more American!

I used the pointillist style—hundreds and thousands of dots—for that book and others because I am a perfectionist. My professor in Prague would always say, "Go back to drawing; this is more construction than drawing." But I liked the idea of creating shades and spaces. I developed the technique as an art student, and I still like it very much. If I have a good drawing, I can do all kinds of things with the technique. I create the background first in my drawings and then evolve the details. The only problem with pointillism is how time-consuming it is, especially if I have to cover a big space. For *Follow the*

Dream, for instance, I did the drawings three times the size of the actual book, because I was trying to achieve certain effects with the background. Perfectionism again, probably. Now, if I look at the book, I still like it, but the originals were so different.

I used Strathmore drawing paper and a nonwaterproof ink, and at first I wasn't used to the humidity on the East Coast. So there were a few disastrous times when I would try to erase something, and the drawing would smudge completely, and the paper would buckle. It took a while to figure out what was the best medium for me.

Then I came up with a completely different approach—very simple concept books such as *Going Up!, Beach Ball,* and *Waving,* which are in watercolor. I went through three or four versions, getting more and more colorful, until the pages were really bright. Sometimes it's even surprising for me when I see the books. But I really played with the color, and it was very satisfactory to try new things.

For someone who never wanted to do a single counting book, I'm amazed that I've done three. It shows just how much of an influence my editor at Greenwillow, Susan Hirschman, has been on me. I wanted to do something about the streets of New York; I wanted to do something about elevators; I wanted to something about beaches—but not necessarily to do them as counting books. But I am glad that Greenwillow gave me these, and other, intellectual puzzles and that I was able to solve them. I felt I made a real contribution as an illustrator, and those books led me to think of my own ideas for stories, like *Rainbow Rhino.* Almost everybody turned that book down. But Frances Foster worked for about a year getting it in shape, and it is still one of my favorite books.

For *Follow the Dream,* I had this very strong vision of the children I wanted to reach. I thought it was an important book for today's children, many of whom feel, "Oh, we can't change this," or "We were born in this place, so we're stuck with it." If you are from a country behind the Iron Curtain, if they let you go out at all, you're happy. Once you are in a free society, all of a sudden there are many more choices. If you're assigned an airline seat and it's not near a window, you complain. Immediately one starts to be picky and to take things for granted. I thought Columbus was the ideal example of persistence, of somebody who held on for many years to a dream and finally accomplished something important.

The book evolved very slowly. I was particularly interested in explorers and in the idea of somebody going to another country, coming back home, and trying to describe what he has seen; he doesn't make sense, and people think he is a little bit crazy. I realized that the reaction of people at home to Cook and all the English biological expeditions would be disbelief—they couldn't begin to imagine or believe in hippopotamuses or elephants. I came up with a line of explorers who were pretty amazing people, especially Marco Polo. He was so close to having two societies find some sort of understanding about each other, yet it never happened. And then, somehow, I be-

came more and more impressed with Columbus. He was not an appealing person, but he was amazingly stubborn and tenacious. Frances Foster and I worked together for a long time, and I had some pictures done from the beginning. I wanted the book to resemble a medieval family book of photographs and miniatures. I knew I would want to have a ship full of the provisions that they would have to take with them; I knew I would want to have pictures of the sea monsters. But I never thought very much about a text. I thought that the pictures were so rich that the text should be really minimal. My wife helped me with the story a great deal.

I have a few favorite parts when I create a book. The most enjoyable part is doing the initial sketches, putting the book together—the thinking part. Then, of course, through the painting process, there are moments that become unbearable. It seems short when you start; then you find out it's agonizingly long, and you can never finish the book on time. But when you are done, you say, "Oh, this was nothing, I did it in no time." I like receiving the first proofs, but after I see more and more proofs, I get confused about which ones are better than others. My reactions to my own work are changing all the time. I used to look at a drawing and say, "This is absolutely terrible; I hate it!" Now I can see the same drawing after seven years and say, "It's not that bad." And in fifteen years I hope I can say, "This is quite interesting." Time is yet another dimension in an artist's work. Even ten years can make a great deal of difference in how you look at design.

I've always admired medieval artists like Bosch and Brueghel, and the whole German Gothic school. At one time my hero was David Hockney, especially his drawings and books. I am really impressed with Quentin Blake, because before I did my own books, I thought it would be very easy to create one. Now I realize what he was going through—lots and lots of drafts!

GENERAL COMMENTARY

Allen Raymond

SOURCE: "Peter Sís: A Creative Journey," in *Teaching Pre K-8,* Vol. 18, No. 7, April, 1988, pp. 44-6.

We're going on a journey, you and I. It will, I hope, take us inside the head of an illustrator named Peter Sís.

Impossible, you say?

Not so. In fact, the man whose head we want to investigate has already performed the feat himself, not once, but often. Among his many talents, including those of an artist and illustrator, Peter Sís apparently has the ability to get inside the heads of others and discover what makes them tick.

When he comes out of those heads he is able to draw

illustrations of what he found inside. Sometimes those illustrations are on paper, sometimes he'll draw them on the surfaces of little three-dimensional papier-mâché heads he's created.

If *he* can do it, so can we. Get inside someone's head, that is. But we can't draw, we're not artists.

We can *write* about it, however, and we shall. In this case, we're going to write about what goes on inside the head of Peter Sís. Are we only guessing? You decide.

In order to go on this journey, however, we first had to find Peter Sís. We did. He lives alone in a small walk-up apartment in New York's Greenwich Village, an apartment which also serves as his studio.

We spent the morning with him, made him late for his appointment at *Time* magazine, learned a lot and wished we'd had time to learn more.

In one corner of his head we found the Czechoslovakian native who loves his country, remembers fondly the people with whom he grew up, and is sad he cannot return to visit his mother, father, brother and sister.

"If I returned, the Czechoslovakian government would probably pick up my passport," he says matter-of-factly.

We learned, however, that he would become an American citizen in a month or two.

Our next stop in the exploration of Peter Sís' head brought us to his "historic district," if there is indeed such an area in anyone's head (and we think there is).

We'd learned Peter Sís was famous in Europe as both an illustrator and a serious, creative and very talented film animator.

We'd also learned that because of this talent he had been sent to Los Angeles about five years ago to create an animated film dealing with the Winter Olympics.

When East-Bloc nations boycotted the 1984 Summer Olympics, the film on which Peter had been working was also cancelled.

"I decided to stay in Los Angeles," he said. "I'd always heard it was the film capital of the world."

Unfortunately, his fame in Europe had not followed him to America. People were not beating a path to his door, either for films or illustrations.

"I got a few illustration jobs," he said, "but not enough. And I didn't want to do animation for Saturday morning cartoons. That's commercial animation, not art. I was discouraged, very discouraged."

A friend suggested he write to Maurice Sendak, well-known children's author. He did, enclosing samples of his work and a copy of a children's book he'd illustrated in Europe (where he has illustrated many books).

Sendak called and suggested that if he were serious about wanting to illustrate books he should consider moving to New York City.

Almost all major book publishers are in New York, not Los Angeles, Sendak told him.

Several months later he had another phone call from Sendak. Peter picked up the phone and said, "It's nice of you to call all the way from Connecticut."

"I'm not in Connecticut," Sendak replied, "I'm in Los Angeles. Come down to the Biltmore Hotel, I'd like to see you."

As they talked in the hotel that day—this was 1984—Peter told him he had decided to move. "I'm not getting anywhere here in Los Angeles," he said. "I remember that in our first phone conversation you told me all major publishers were in New York."

Sendak interrupted him to say, "No, all publishers are not in New York, all publishers are here in this hotel!"

As luck would have it, The American Library Association was holding its annual convention in Los Angeles and Maurice Sendak felt he could open a few doors for this young and talented artist from Czechoslovakia.

So, after spending less than five minutes talking to Peter and looking at his portfolio, Sendak arranged to have him meet several book publishers.

One of those he met was Ava Weiss of Greenwillow Books, who, as it turned out, was born in Prague, Czechoslovakia, although she left while still an infant.

"She is," he said in a voice filled with emotion, "like a really good angel to me. She and Susan Hirschman asked if I'd like to illustrate **Bean Boy** for Greenwillow.

"They gave me my chance in America," he said. "In just two hours my whole future was changed."

Of the 15 books he has illustrated since that day in 1984, one is dedicated to Ava Weiss, another to Susan Hirschman.

The discouraging efforts to find sufficient work to make ends meet were not over, however, even in New York. Illustrating one book for Greenwillow would not pay the rent.

So, Peter Sís took his portfolio and went door-to-door, visiting almost every publisher of magazines, newspapers and/or books in New York City. When someone seemed interested he would say, "Don't tell me you'll call; give me some work to do *now!*"

The *New York Times Book Review* editor liked his work,

and gave him an assignment. Soon he was doing illustrations for *The Times* almost every week, and he still does.

In 1987, *Time* magazine, after seeing his illustrations in *The New York Times,* phoned and asked him to talk with them. He now illustrates for *Time* on a regular basis.

In 1987, a book he illustrated, Sid Fleischman's *The Whipping Boy* won the John Newbery Medal. In 1987 *The New York Times* honored his new book, *Rainbow Rhino,* as "One of the Year's Best Illustrated Children's Books." All this in only five years from the day he first landed in Los Angeles!

He is both the author and illustrator of *Rainbow Rhino,* but gives full credit to Frances Foster, his editor at Knopf, for being willing to work with him on the book, which he dedicated to her. It is a book he had wanted to have someone publish for many years, but with little success.

"Without Frances the book wouldn't exist," he said. "It's a wonderful feeling to do an entire book."

He's just authored and illustrated another entire book, *Waving,* to be published in March 1988.

Which brings us, finally, to the largest area inside the head of Peter Sís, the part where we find the creativity.

How can his creativity be described? Is he a surrealist? No? Then, how to explain some of his surrealistic, off-beat illustrations?

Is he a humorist, using illustrations to give voice to his wacky thoughts? No? Then how to explain his fanciful, often hilarious drawings?

Is he a perfectionist? No? Then how to explain his stipple-like style, wherein thousands of meticulously positioned dots create an illustration that conveys mystical emotions we can almost feel?

Is he a combination of many artistic talents, one who marches to several different drummers? It would appear he is, or how else to explain his ability to create so many moods, using so many styles.

He is, without doubt, a workaholic, or how else to explain his ability to illustrate 15 books in three or four years, while simultaneously working for *The New York Times, Time* magazine and a host of other publishers? As he says, "I work night and day. I'm eager to prove myself after what I like to call My California Experience."

Above all, however, it seems that the head of this 38-year-old artist contains strange connections which, when activated, set off little sparks and explosions.

And, like one of those toy kaleidoscopes we looked through as children, the sparks and explosions in the head of Peter Sís continue to produce beautiful pictures that startle, surprise, amuse, enthrall and captivate all who are exposed to his remarkable talent.

It is easy to imagine, today, that there are people all through this land who are saying to themselves, "Thank you, Czechoslovakia, for Peter Sís."

TITLE COMMENTARY

STORIES TO SOLVE: FOLKTALES FROM AROUND THE WORLD (written by George Shannon, 1984)

Barbara Elleman

SOURCE: A review of *Stories to Solve: Folktales from Around the World,* in *Booklist,* Vol. 82, No. 7, December 1, 1985, pp. 574-75.

Shannon aptly combines folklore and puzzles in this short collection of 14 stories from around the world. The tales, not more than a page or two long, present situations in which someone figures out a problem or solves a mystery. Readers are then asked to suggest how it was done. For those who can't—and many of the stories are abstract—solutions are provided. Though children aren't likely to pick this up by themselves, librarians and teachers may find this effective as an introduction to folklore or other library units, and it should provide good brainteasers in work with the gifted. Black-and-white speckled drawings add decoration, and some are cleverly used in illustrating the answers. Short source notes are appended.

R. Baines

SOURCE: A review of *Stories to Solve,* in *The Junior Bookshelf,* Vol. 50, No. 1, February, 1986, p. 29.

George Shannon has had a good idea for an intriguing book. From world-wide sources he has collected fifteen very short stories, each of which poses a problem.

How can two fathers and two sons go fishing and there be only three people on the river bank? How would you ferry a wolf, a goat and a cabbage across a river in a tiny boat so that none of them suffered harm? King Solomon sees his famous decision about the nature of mother-love attributed to a Tibetan sage, but gets credit for discovering which is the one real flower in a room full of artificial blossoms. However short it may be each story is printed on a double page spread, enabling the solution to be hidden overleaf.

The unusual black and white illustrations by Peter Sís, which are composed from innumerable tiny dots, complement the originality of this anthology admirably.

THE WHIPPING BOY (written by Sid Fleischman, 1985)

George Gleason

SOURCE: A review of *The Whipping Boy,* in *School Library Journal,* Vol. 32, No. 9, May, 1986, p. 90.

Roles are changed when young Prince Brat, as everyone calls him (he is so altogether rotten that "Not even black cats would cross his path"), runs away with Jemmy, his whipping boy (the commoner who takes the Prince's punishments). Because Brat has never learned to write and Jemmy can, a couple of prince-nappers decide that Jemmy is the real prince. Chiefly through Jemmy's cleverness, the two escape and return to court. Brat has learned much and changed for the better during his adventures. He winds up calling Jemmy "friend," and he is certain to be a better prince hereafter. This whimsical, readable story delights in the manner of Bill Brittain's books *The Wish Giver* and *The Devil's Donkey.* Full-page black-and-white illustrations—somewhat grotesque but always complementary—add attractiveness to the story. The mistaken identity plot is always a good one: children, even fairly old ones, like disguises and this kind of mix-up. Supplementary characters are well-drawn both by Fleischman and by Sís, so the whole hangs together in basic appeal. Readers could well move from *The Whipping Boy* to its much longer cousin, Mark Twain's *The Prince and the Pauper.*

Publishers Weekly

SOURCE: A review of *The Whipping Boy,* in *Publishers Weekly,* Vol. 229, No. 26, June 27, 1986, p. 90.

With his flair for persuading readers to believe in the ridiculous, Fleischman scores a hit with his new creation. Sís's skillful pictures emphasize events in the adventures of the orphan Jemmy, kept in his king's palace to be thrashed for the offenses committed by the royal heir, known as Prince Brat. It is forbidden to punish Brat, whose tricks multiply until Jemmy is tempted to escape the daily round of flogging. But the prince himself takes off and forces the whipping boy to go with him. As they get into and out of trouble on the outside, Jemmy hears that he has been accused of abducting Brat. When the prince arranges for their return to the palace, poor Jemmy fears the worst, but things turn out for the best at the story's satisfying close. Colorful types like a thief called Hold-Your-Nose Billy, Betsy and her dancing bear Petunia, et al., increase the fun.

RAINBOW RHINO (1987)

Kirkus Reviews

SOURCE: A review of *Rainbow Rhino,* in *Kirkus Reviews,* Vol. VI, No. 21, November 1, 1987, p. 1580.

In this first book authored by a talented Czech-born illustrator, a rhinoceros is kept company by three birds until each elects a life in a landscape that matches his color: blue lake, yellow banana tree, red poppy field. Rhino wanders lonely and gray—then pursuit by bees takes him back just in time to rescue each of his three friends from a fierce predator: hyena, snake, crocodile.

The story is slight, but the illustrations have the serenity and interest invoked by Sís's unique style, and would make an unusually attractive vehicle for learning the primary colors.

Janwillem van de Wetering

SOURCE: "Float and Slither," in *The New York Times Book Review,* November 8, 1987, p. 42.

Rainbow Rhino is a tale of friendship and togetherness by the Czechoslovak-born film maker and painter Peter Sís, who also lives in New York. A mystic rhino, almost the sole survivor of a long-ago dream time, has all he desires, including three feathered companions. But no one, not even this animal, an emblem of joyful quest who is further inspired by a triad of sensuous and colorful muses, can content himself with mere bliss that is too easily available. Curiosity may kill even the rhino, but first it leads him on a journey of splendid adventures, nearly continuous highs and, of course, pain and grim discomfort, as the birds leave him.

In a panic-stricken and ponderous manner, he retraces his blundering, much-mistaken steps. His misery is first neutralized, then, as the rainbow birds rejoin him, all the components of his childlike imagination return and reinforce his strength. The rhino symbolically confirms that there is no place like home.

The text is neat: just a few lines sketch out each panel adequately and eloquently. Pictures are calmly spacious in order to accommodate unlimited imaginations. Yakky, and powerfully colored, denizens of nastiness (the horrendous popeyed hyena, the slithering banana snake and the crunchifying crocodile) supply fierce challenges to be overcome by shared and friendly energy. Helpful morals weigh on our willing shoulders lightly in such children's books until we heed them, voluntarily yielding to the wide stretches of subtly blending colors—glorious vistas that allow the eye to rove restfully, while taking in beauty. All this elaborate work looks simple enough, for this is pretty sophisticated art, getting close to true innocence through a variety of skillful techniques.

Uncluttered and exact, yet dreamily pleasing, *Rainbow Rhino* is an invitation to a quiet spell of selfish parental enjoyment, before we take it upstairs to a young reader.

Pamela Miller Ness

SOURCE: A review of *Rainbow Rhino,* in *School Library Journal,* Vol. 34, No. 5, January, 1988, p. 70.

A delightfully original fairy tale, **Rainbow Rhino** recounts the adventures of a rainbow rhinoceros and his three colorful avian companions who live in a tropical valley. They lead a peaceful, contented existence until they wander out of their familiar territory, where new sights lure each bird away from his friends, until Rhino finds himself alone. Each friend finds that his own exotic paradise contains hidden dangers, and he ultimately returns to the comfortable friendship of the group. The moral implications are simple and sincere: the grass really isn't greener on the other side of the fence, and that true friendship is to be valued. Sís' stylized but sophisticated full-page drawings in muted tones with splashes of primary color, resembling old master stipple engravings, perfectly balance the spare prose and the quiet universality of the tale. Through its gentle humor, simple wisdom, and subtle sophistication, **Rainbow Rhino** is a satisfying contemporary fable. This is a special book for parents and librarians to share aloud with preschoolers, for first and second graders to enjoy independently, and for adults to treasure as a beautifully illustrated, timeless tale.

Elizabeth S. Watson

SOURCE: A review of *Rainbow Rhino*, in *The Horn Book Magazine,* Vol. LXIV, No. 2, March-April, 1988, p. 196.

In the first book Peter Sís has both written and illustrated, he has developed a simple adventure story of a rhinoceros whose three bird friends choose to leave him for more colorful surroundings, only to find their new homes are more dangerous than anticipated. The rhino rescues each bird in turn, and they all go back to their former peaceful existence. The illustrations work well with the text but clearly outshine the story. Sís's style offers freshness in composition, color, and texture. The pictures vary from lush tropical scenes to spare grassland vistas. Danger, fear, curiosity, and satisfaction are all portrayed with the slightest variation in line. Each of the double-page spreads exudes vitality, appealing to the young viewer, who will be reassured by the cozy conclusion.

M. Crouch

SOURCE: A review of *Rainbow Rhino*, in *The Junior Bookshelf,* Vol. 53, No. 6, December, 1989, p. 271.

The moral of **Rainbow Rhino,** unstated, is You are best off where you belong. Rhino lives contentedly in his valley with his friends, the red, yellow and blue rainbow birds. When they explore beyond their home ground Rhino loses, one by one, his companions to more colour-compatible environments. Left to himself Rhino has a fright and heads for home. On the way he collects his friends, each of whom has also had an unfortunate experience. Back home they settle down contentedly. A very thin story provides the excuse for a series of finely detailed drawings, notable equally for draughtsmanship, colour and design. They will appeal I suspect, more to adults than children, and the latter may find Rhino sadly lacking in personality.

📖 ***WAVING: A COUNTING BOOK* (1988)**

Beth Ames Herbert

SOURCE: A review of *Waving: A Counting Book,* in *Booklist,* Vol. 84, No. 13, March 15, 1988, p. 1268.

In this amusing book, Sís combines waving and counting in a delightful story chain that grows in size and humor. The pictures begin by showing little Mary's mother waving for a taxi and two bicyclists waving back. Then three boys wave at the cyclists and four girls return their greeting. Soon mail carriers, police officers, waiters, joggers, musicians, and finally taxi drivers are all waving, as Mary and her mother go home. Sís' striking visuals cleverly blend bright watercolors that center the counting action with gray-toned pen-and-ink backgrounds that, on close observation, reveal their own reinforcement of the book's counting motif. Youngsters will not only relish the silliness of all the people waving at each other, but they will also be intrigued by the many ways supplied for them to count from 1 to 15.

Kirkus Reviews

SOURCE: A review of *Waving: A Counting Book,* in *Kirkus Reviews,* Vol. LVI, No. 6, March 15, 1988, p. 459.

A mildly interesting notion for a counting book: when Mary's mother waves for a taxi, two bicyclists wave back, then three boys wave at the cyclists, and so on. This rather limited idea is distinguished by Sís's carefully designed illustrations. Sequentially numbered doors on a city street are rendered in grisaille to form a background for details that make playful use of the numbers: e.g., each of six policemen has a horse, and there [is] a "Seven Dwarfs Restaurant" and a lady with ten suitcases watching the ten joggers. The numbers are also hidden in the pictures in Roman numerals, spelled out, and (in one case) in French. After 15 taxi drivers wave back at everyone, Mary and her mother walk home. Although not exceptional, **Waving** serves its purpose.

Anna Biagioni Hart

SOURCE: A review of *Waving: A Counting Book,* in *School Library Journal,* Vol. 34, No. 8, April, 1988, pp. 90-1.

This inventive counting book will delight not only city folk, but many other grownups and children as well. Mary's mother waves for a taxi, and two bicyclists wave back. Soon, in this cumulative nonsense tale, mounted police, girl scouts, and many others are waving, including 15 taxicab drivers waving at everybody waving at them! Mother and daughter resign themselves to walking home. This book has the economy, originality, and humor of Pat Hutchins' *Rosie's Walk* and will make even the younger children smile. A frieze of city buildings in gray and black decorates the background on each page. Many number details, jokes, and puzzles are penciled in for sophisticated readers to enjoy. Against this unobtrusive background moves a jolly cast of characters painted in bright watercolors. Taxicab yellow accents escort readers from page to page. The ethnic diversity and individuality of a large city has been captured for young readers in a book to which they will surely return. An unusually attractive, humorous working of one of our oldest picture book genres.

Karla Kuskin

SOURCE: "Smiling as They Go By," in *The New York Times Book Review,* May 8, 1988, p. 24.

There are 117 words in this cheerful counting book, but who's counting? When discussing a picture book for the very young the point is not the word count but the underlying idea. Is it fresh and strong enough to act as an armature for the illustrations, and are they, in turn, doing an effective job of illuminating and augmenting both what is written and what is between the lines?

Peter Sís' well-matched text and pictures explore the art of waving, as practiced by some typical city dwellers. It is a good, playful idea, familiar enough to interest 4- and more-year-olds. Who, at that age, has not been thrilled when a passing bus driver waved back?

On the first page Mary's mother waves for "1 taxi." It drives on by, but "2 bicyclists waved back at her." Then "3 boys walking dogs waved at the bicyclists" and you've got the picture. The plot never thickens, but everenlarging groups keep waving at each other.

All of this very friendly action takes place against a background of city blocks drawn in light pen line with an overlay of blue-gray wash. In the foreground the wavers, delicately outlined in black, pass by like a brightly colored, "hi"-spirited parade. The city is a generic one. The neighborhood could be Manhattan's Chelsea, the mailmen wear United States Postal Service uniforms, the taxis are Checkers, the tour bus looks English and the police seem to be from São Paulo or Rhode Island or some place like that. While a nice ethnic mix is maintained throughout, there may be more than a few parents who wish they could find some women among the mail carriers, musicians, waiters, police officers and taxi drivers.

Traditionally, counting books are stocked with details waiting to be counted. Often, as in, say, "The 12 Days of Christmas," the characters from one verse stay on stage to join the next group until the pages are bursting with actors and actions. Mr. Sís prefers a wipe-the-slate-clean approach. In his pages each group bows out as its successor enters. The results are attractively composed, uncluttered and suitable for a very young audience.

And the artist, a Czechoslovak émigré who in the few years he has lived in New York has illustrated many books, has made sure that there are still special rewards for a

nonreader's sharp, searching eye. Building numbers change from page to page to match the number of wavers present. Roman numerals appear here and there, although they might have been more fun to hunt for if they were used consistently. Store names and background objects have numerical significance, too. For instance, 14 tiny ducklings waddle across the 14 page, and there is a "Seven Dwarfs Restaurant," a "Five Little Pigs" store (could we have a pig recount?) and so forth.

The very last spread features a fleet of 15 lovely Checker cabs. Not only is every smiling driver waving, but every cab is empty. Of course, by the time they go by, Mary and her mother have reached home. Isn't that the way it always is? When you don't need a taxi they're *everywhere*—smiling and waving.

Ethel R. Twichell

SOURCE: A review of *Waving: A Counting Book,* in *The Horn Book Magazine,* Vol. LXIV, No. 3, May-June, 1988, p. 345.

As one taxi drives by, a little girl's mother waves for it. Two bicyclists wave back at her, and in turn three boys with dogs wave at the bicyclists. A simple counting book evolves using a city street as background and a lively collection of joggers, firemen, and Little Leaguers, who stream across the pages in congregates of the appropriate numbers. The colorful groupings are full of small, interesting details of clothing and belongings and include a broad ethnic representation. Each clutch of people and an assortment of their horses, taxis, and musical instruments are paraded against a dimly limned gray frieze of barbershops, bakeries, houses, bookstores, and restaurants. A closer glance at the background reveals some little visual jokes. A dozen fish are displayed behind the bus carrying twelve tourists, and a shop called Twins appears on the page featuring the number 2. Even the addresses and numbers carry out the matching numerical theme. While unpretentious in size and format, the book with its bright colors and variety of people and activities should be attractive to the very young and, as each component is identified, teach a bit more about the busyness and diversity of urban life.

THE SCAREBIRD (written by Sid Fleischman, 1988)

Marilyn Iarusso

SOURCE: A review of *The Scarebird,* in *School Library Journal,* Vol. 35, No. 1, September, 1988, p. 158.

Spacious pictures executed in paint and drawing portray the broad horizons and big skies of a farm so far out "that crows pack a lunch before setting out." Lonesome John, a farmer whose family is gone and whose old dog is buried in the pasture, builds a headless scarecrow for his cornfield. Soon his need for companionship causes him to add

From Beach Ball, *written and illustrated by Peter Sís.*

a head, to talk to his "Scarebird," and share harmonica music in the evenings. By the time Sam, a weary-looking orphan, arrives, looking for work, John has begun to play checkers with his creation. Although he resents having his game interrupted, he offers hospitality and some short-term work so the youth can repay him. As the touchingly hopeful-looking boy begins to work, John retrieves for Sam, piece by piece, the protective clothing that he had given to the scarecrow. By the end of the book, John is ready to accept a real-life companion in place of an imaginary one. The civility with which he treats the scarecrow as he takes back his clothing makes readers know that the new relationship will prosper and enrich both the old man and the boy. Sís'[s] art captures the human need for connection in a gentle way. An appealing picture book about loneliness and friendship, told in Fleischman's typical colorful language, that will work well as a read aloud or for independent reading.

Hanna B. Zeiger

SOURCE: A review of *The Scarebird,* in *The Horn Book Magazine,* Vol. 64, No. 5, September-October, 1988, pp. 614-15.

Called Lonesome John by the townspeople because he lives so far out of town that "crows pack a lunch before setting out," John Humbuckle works his land by himself. To keep crows out of his corn, he stuffs straw into some old clothes and sets up a headless scarecrow. Deciding after a while that the scarecrow really needs a head, he creates one with big yellow eyes that make it look "like sunshine on stilts." With his family gone and his old dog buried, John has been in the habit of talking to himself. Now, he greets his scarebird morning and evening and

brings it gloves and shoes to keep its straw from blowing away. A hat for the hot sun and a slicker for the rain are added, and John feels less lonely with the scarebird to keep him company. One day, as he is sitting by the scarecrow playing checkers, a young boy, "barefooted and bareheaded," appears asking for work. A little reluctant to have his routine and privacy interrupted, John gives the lad work only a day or so at a time. As the man comes to know a little about the boy and watches him work hard, John takes gloves, hat, shoes, and slicker away from the scarecrow and gives them to the boy who needs them. When the boy joins John on the porch one evening to swap tunes on the harmonica, he offers him a job; and when he asks, "Do you play checkers?," we know he is no longer Lonesome John. The oil paintings by Peter Sís are wonderfully evocative. They capture the quiet dignity of the sturdy old farmer and of the farm set in a vast expanse of field and sky. Together, words and pictures create a memorable portrait of a loving human being.

📖 *GOING UP!: A COLOR COUNTING BOOK*
  (1989)

Zena Sutherland

SOURCE: A review of *Going Up!: A Color Counting Book,* in *Bulletin of the Center for Children's Books,* Vol. 42, No. 8, April, 1989, p. 205.

A slight narrative framework is used for an inoffensive but ineffective concept book. Mary buys some flowers, gets on a building elevator at the first floor, and is followed by a witch with a black violin case (2nd floor), a chef in a white hat (3rd floor), and a color-marked addition on each succeeding floor. By the time the elevator gets to the 12th floor, it is crowded with costumed characters (blue space suit, regal purple robes, gray wetsuit, etc.). All shout "Surprise" and "Happy Birthday" to Mary's mother. Odd to see a counting book with no numbers spelled out, no digits pictured except in the tiny elevator dial. The art work is clean and bright, but pedestrian in conception.

Kirkus Reviews

SOURCE: A review of *Going Up!: A Color Counting Book*, in *Kirkus Reviews*, Vol. LVII, No. 7, April 1, 1989, p. 554.

With subtlety and imagination, an illustrator of notable talent embellishes his two themes. Walking along a street—rendered in grisaille with points of interest (like vehicles) in bright color—Mary buys flowers and then returns to her building. There she takes the elevator, with a stop for an additional, gaily costumed passenger at each floor. By the time the elevator reaches the 12th floor, both cardinal and ordinal numbers have been rehearsed, the elevator contains people dressed in ten basic colors, and there is a mystery—where is everyone going?—happily solved when it turns out that this is a surprise party for Mary's mother's birthday. The delicately drawn backgrounds contain dozens of clever details to discover. Delightful.

Beth Herbert

SOURCE: A review of *Going Up!: A Color Counting Book*, in *Booklist*, Vol. 85, No. 17, May 1, 1989, p. 1554.

Young Mary gets into the elevator of her apartment building and, at each floor, she is joined by a neighbor. They are quite a collection: a witch dressed in black, a chef clad in white, even a man dressed as a banana. The residents' colorful costumes enable the floors to be associated with numbers and colors as the group ascends upward to surprise Mary's mother with a birthday party. Illustrated in a similar style to Sís'[s] *Waving,* this features candy-colored scenes inside the elevator framed by gray, ink-decorated walls. This latest volume may not be quite as clever as the first, but it ably extends Sís'[s] counting theme.

Patricia Dooley

SOURCE: A review of *Going Up!: A Color Counting Book*, in *School Library Journal*, Vol. 38, No. 12, August, 1989, p. 132.

As Mary's roomy elevator takes her from 1 to 12, it stops on each floor to collect a costumed passenger: a chef in white, a yellow banana, an orange clown, etc. Their strict eyes-front elevator reserve lasts until they all emerge on 12 with a shout of "Surprise!" to celebrate Mary's mother's birthday. While Sís'[s] drawings are cheerful, the or-

dinal numbers in the text are abbreviated, and the cardinal numbers on the "clock" above the elevator are barely legible. The colored windows of each floor, shown on the first page, don't always correspond to the color worn by that floor's occupant. As far as one can tell, the male guests are a king, an astronaut, a chef and a surgeon; the females are a witch, Little Red Riding Hood, a honeybear, and a girl in a wet suit. Better to wait for the next car.

THE MIDNIGHT HORSE (written by Sid Fleischman, 1990)

Kirkus Reviews

SOURCE: A review of *The Midnight Horse*, in *Kirkus Reviews*, Vol. LVIII, No. 14, July 15, 1990, p. 1003.

With the help of a dead magician, a quick-witted young orphan foils a dastardly plot—in this breathless new adventure from the author of *The Whipping Boy* (1986, Newbery Award).

When Touch pays a call on his great-uncle and sole surviving relative, Judge Henry Wigglesforth, he finds himself under pressure to sign over a previously unknown inheritance from his roving father. Wigglesforth is also leaning on pretty Miss Sally Hoskins to sell her Red Raven Inn for a pittance—rumor has it that a gold-toothed guest was murdered there, and business has fallen off. Meanwhile, Wigglesforth's sinister confederate Otis Cratt (why does he keep his face muffled?) is lurking about, intent on a certain bag of Pacific Island pearls. Touch is never one to let injustice go unchallenged; enlisting the aid of the ghost of The Great Chaffalo, a local magician, he tricks Cratt, stymies Wigglesforth, and saves the pearls as well as the Red Raven.

Once again, Fleischman's storytelling is grandly melodramatic; a clear line separates good from evil, scenes are set with brisk economy, and characters speak their lines with grace and emphasis. Sís'[s] dark, posed, slightly distorted figures add to these theatrics an undercurrent of mystery and a "Touch" of wit. Outstanding.

Denise Wilms

SOURCE: A review of *The Midnight Horse*, in *Booklist*, Vol. 86, No. 22, August, 1990, p. 2171.

An orphan boy named Touch is at the heart of Fleischman's latest tale, a neatly crafted gem set in some vague, nineteenth-century past. Touch has come to the tiny burg of Crinklewood to meet his only living relative, Judge Henry Wigglesforth. The meeting goes badly, with the Judge intent on committing Touch to an orphanage after the boy catches on to some shady behavior surrounding his inheritance. Wigglesforth turns out to be the mastermind behind another swindle that Touch manages to foil, this one involving a kind innkeeper whose business the Judge is plotting to steal. The special twist to all of this is Touch's luck in having a friendly ghost on his side. The spectre of a magician called The Great Chuffalo rises to help Touch at several critical junctures, a contrivance that Fleischman pulls off without undermining his tale's credibility in the least. This good, old-fashioned piece of storytelling by the author of *The Whipping Boy* will easily please independent readers; it's also a first-rate read-aloud. Sís'[s] distinctive black-and-white drawings enhance the book's design. A fine bit of entertainment.

Michael Cart

SOURCE: A review of *The Midnight Horse*, in *School Library Journal*, Vol. 36, No. 9, September, 1990, p. 226.

It's "raining bullfrogs" when readers first meet the skinny and bareheaded orphan boy Touch with his hair "as curly as wood shavings." Touch is en route—by horse-drawn coach—to Cricklewood, New Hampshire, where he will meet his great-uncle and only surviving relative, Judge Henry Wigglesforth. The boy's traveling companions are an honest blacksmith, a mysterious thief, and a shadowy figure on the coach's roof. "Merciful powers!" the blacksmith exclaims, "It's The Great Chaffalo!" It seems that since the magician became a ghost, he has developed the disconcerting habit of turning up in odd and unexpected places. How he becomes Touch's ally against the conniving Judge Wigglesforth readers will delight in discovering for themselves. The process is pure pleasure. Fleischman—who has always had a fondness for magicians—has himself become a master magician with words, producing dazzling and seemingly effortless rhetorical effects from his writer's sleeve. How he does it is his secret, but it surely has something to do with inspired plotting, masterful timing, and a wonderful ear for comic language, lively dialogue, and the best similes and metaphors this side of Leon Garfield. The illustrations by the talented Sís perfectly capture the spirit of the text while complementing its substance. The book is part ghost story, part tall tale, part picaresque, and totally enjoyable, for it is that old enchanter Sid Fleischman at his magical best.

BEACH BALL (1990)

Publishers Weekly

SOURCE: A review of *Beach Ball*, in *Publishers Weekly*, Vol. 237, No. 32, August 10, 1990, p. 443.

A stiff breeze blows Mary's beach ball along the water's edge for miles and miles. People, objects and animals appear and disappear as Mary gallops from page to page, chasing the ball that remains just a bit ahead of her. Her mostly wordless quest is augmented with a different concept worked into each spread. The reader is made aware of various things to look for by clever signals in each left-hand corner. A spread devoted to different kinds of animals is indicated by a flock of birds flying in formation spelling out the words " . . . name the animals." This added bit of fun makes combing the beach for different things a game of infinite variety. Sís's inimitably cheerful illustrations fuse a riot of unsullied color with deft details and endless invention.

Trev Jones

SOURCE: A review of *Beach Ball*, in *School Library Journal*, Vol. 36, No. 11, November, 1990, pp. 98-9.

A great choice for beach-chair travelers. The wind has taken little Mary's ball, causing her to chase it through double-page spreads of color identification, numbers, shapes, opposites, and more, oblivious to the wild assortment of oddly dressed people basking in the sun. This backdrop of leisure activity is the essence of the book, as young beachcombers are encouraged to sift through the chaos to find objects from A-Z, count fish or sunglasses, or identify animals on an ark. Surprises abound as new objects are spotted—a little elf in green sitting under a mushroom umbrella, a shark and an alligator lurking in shallow water, a boy blowing up an elephant balloon larger than himself. Sís'[s] quirky illustrations have the grainy, gritty texture of sand, causing the book itself to appear as though it had been at the beach—the perfect place to take it for an afternoon of fun.

Carolyn Phelan

SOURCE: A review of *Beach Ball*, in *Booklist*, Vol. 87, No. 7, December 1, 1990, p. 753.

Mary and her mother set up their beach paraphernalia for a day of seaside fun, but the wind blows Mary's beach ball away. As she chases it down the shoreline, scene after scene appears, each showing a new section of the beach. This essentially wordless picture book offers an opportunity for a new game in nearly every scene: find objects for every letter of the alphabet; help Mary find her way through the maze; count the objects; identify the shapes, animals, opposites, and colors; and find Mary. While the multitude of tiny figures and objects may be visually confusing to preschoolers, slightly older children will find the games diverting. Bits of visual humor add to the fun. Separated by the wide horizontal stretch of sandy beach, azure bands of sky and sea border each double-page spread; everything turns peach-colored in the sunset of the last scene. A playful romp.

MORE STORIES TO SOLVE: FIFTEEN FOLKTALES FROM AROUND THE WORLD (written by George Shannon, 1991)

Julie Corsaro

SOURCE: A review of *More Stories to Solve: Fifteen Folktales from Around the World*, in *Booklist*, Vol. 87, No. 14, March 15, 1991, p. 468.

As he did in *Stories to Solve* Shannon combines the

folktale and the riddle in a brief collection that brings together 15 international stories that are varied in content but are unified by the single theme of the weak prevailing over the strong. Readers are challenged to explain how a jungle firefly defeats 100 haughty apes, how a playful frog escapes from a bucket of cream, and how a clever lawyer helps his father give the devil the slip. Again, Sís'[s] black-and-white drawings are impressive, inventively adding layers to the simple, direct text. Answers are provided, as are notes on the sources and additional variants of each tale (i.e., "A Last Request" is a Chilean folktale retold by Frances Carpenter in *South American Wonder Tales,* Carpenter worked from the Soustelles' *Folklore Chilien*).

Dorothy Houlihan

SOURCE: A review of *More Stories to Solve: Fifteen Folktales from Around the World,* in *School Library Journal,* Vol. 37, No. 4, April, 1991, p. 114.

Shannon and Sís again bring together a collection of folkloric riddles, replicating the previous format and success of their *Stories to Solve.* Each of the 15 selections comes from a different culture, with the source usually identified in the text of the riddle or discernible from visual clues in the accompanying illustrations. Further information is provided at the end of the book. The tales vary in difficulty, although the answers are generally contained within the text. The weakest one involves a banker who cheats a Brahman; unlike the others, the solution lies in moral, rather than logical, reasoning. Sís's stylized pen-and-ink drawings support the stories and entertain. Overall, a satisfying gathering of brain teasers, sure to please riddle lovers and especially useful for teachers introducing the global village concept through world folklore.

Betsy Hearne

SOURCE: A review of *More Stories to Solve: Fifteen Folktales from Around the World,* in *Bulletin of the Center for Children's Books,* Vol. 44, No. 9, May, 1991, p. 226.

Like its predecessor, *Stories to Solve,* this collection combines the appeal of short, easy-to-read folktales with a riddling quality that turns the stories into solve-it-yourself mysteries. Shannon has been careful not only to select from widely varied cultural traditions, but also to cite his sources more carefully than most children's book authors. From peoples of Southeast Asia, South and North America, Africa, and Europe, these include unusual motifs as well as familiar ones with a new twist. Not surprisingly, most are trickster tales. The governing characteristic is enigma, and there's enough of it to keep kids guessing, either independently or in interactive story-hour sessions. Answers are given after each selection to keep young readers' frustration levels to a minimum, while capacious pen-and-ink hatch drawings—well designed to frame and vary the text—serve the same end.

Ethel L. Heins

SOURCE: A review of *More Stories to Solve: Fifteen Folktales from Around the World,* in *The Horn Book Magazine,* Vol. LXVII, No. 3, May-June, 1991, pp. 342-43.

Illustrated by Peter Sís. Riddles and verbal puzzles rank with myths, fables, folk tales, and proverbs as the earliest universal types of formulated thought. With their appealing combination of mystery and logic and their compact expression, they are easily absorbed into the oral tradition and insure their own preservation. As in Shannon's *Stories to Solve,* the new collection of brief tales features animal or human heroes—usually small, humble, and powerless—who shrewdly meet the challenges of problems and enigmas. Adults will find many of the stories thematically well known with familiar motifs and situations; children should find the narratives stimulating and amusing. Answers to the puzzling queries that close each story are clearly given, but the final tale poses an age-old philosophical conundrum for which "the wisest answer may be that there is no answer." Hatched and cross-hatched black-and-white drawings are an integral part of the ingenious page designs and greatly extend the drollery of the tales. Notes give sources for the fifteen stories and also indicate where variants are found.

FOLLOW THE DREAM: THE STORY OF CHRISTOPHER COLUMBUS (1991)

Peter Sís

SOURCE: "Following the Dream of Columbus," in *The Five Owls,* Vol. VI, No. 1, September-October, 1991, pp. 1-3.

I am trying to remember when, as a baby barely able to walk, I first discovered the unknown of the dark corner in my grandmother's garden, only to panic at the first strange sound and dash back to safety.

I am trying to recall the adventures of Jules Verne's brave heroes facing and overcoming *any* danger—and always coming home safely.

The same is true more or less about the stories of Columbus, Robinson Crusoe, Amundsen, Tenzing, Dr. Livingstone (I presume). I could almost always be sure of happy endings in all the books I read, since I had already previewed the illustrations.

My father, too. He left in my childhood for Tibet ("I'll be back for Christmas," he told my mother—little did he know that it would be three Christmases later) and other exotic territories, and he came back every time with unusual presents, tales, and fragrances. Once, he had been shooting a film in Indonesia—this time with my mother—and they returned with a baby, my brother David.

Reading and thinking about explorers, I was therefore

conditioned to expect triumphant returns to the place of departure. The place of departure: this was the main obstacle for me. By the time I reached traveling age, I realized that while my literary explorers seemed to leave at their will, I was being kept firmly behind something called the Iron Curtain. So the hardest part was not the actual exploring but getting the permission to leave to explore. ("How long will you be gone? Report what you have seen. If you do not return, your family might be persecuted.")

In Columbus's time, the Golden Age of Discovery, there were no travel documents, work permits, political asylums, or green cards. But Columbus waited years to get his ships, just as I waited to get my passport, permit to leave, and visa to arrive.

Early in this century, Czech explorer "Eskymo" Welzl also traveled without documents. He left Austria-Hungary via Russia-Siberia with just a horse and cart and ended up as an Eskimo chief in the islands of the Arctic. He prospered through the fur trade. When his ship full of furs capsized outside of San Francisco in the twenties, he was questioned by the U.S. Coast Guard. Since burly Eskymo Welzl did not know anything about the First World War, he did not realize that there was a new country called Czechoslovakia. The authorities on the other hand took him for an imposter, since it was common knowledge then that no one was able to survive winters up in the extreme north. To complicate matters even more, the good old chief was using his own geographical terms, which nobody else recognized, and of course he had no papers. He was deported to Hamburg, where everyone took him for Baron Münchhausen. It took him years to collect enough money to get back to his golden North.

Explorers have always been challenged by nature, changing times, and politics equally. Portuguese chased Spaniards, who were attacked by English warring with the French. Dutch and Scandinavians were doing business as quietly as possible, while Russians took what was left. Germans went for Africa, as did the Italians.

How petty is all this when you hear Eugene Cernan, another explorer/astronaut of Czechoslovakian descent. One of three men in Gemini 9, the spacecraft used to produce the first color photographic survey of the earth, Cernan described how "without blinking an eye, I could see the high Andes, the Pacific Ocean, the jewel-like Lake Titicaca, the rainforest of the Amazon Basin and the Chaco plains on down our orbital path. The broad western bulge of Africa was the most interesting area of the world to see from space. Its dry desolate terrain was nearly always free of clouds, and it was a delight to photograph because there was so little haze to dim its beauty. The tiny Indian subcontinent was especially fascinating, representing the lives of 500 million people whose lives were dependent upon the scattered pre-monsoon cloud cover so clearly visible. Also conspicuous were individual houses in haze-free Nepal, the wake of the Brahmaputra, an old refinery near Perth, Australia, and numerous other phenomena such as the Four Corners power plant in New Mexico, whose smoke emission was detectable from 1,000 kilometers out in space, submarines, individual city streets, blast furnaces, and a wealth of hurricanes, storms, cyclones, as well as the launch facilities at Cape Kennedy. Isn't it amazing that in a matter of seconds lands were traversed that took the fourteenth-century Arab explorer Ibn Battuta thirty years of his life? Battuta is estimated to have covered 95,000 miles, without taking into account detours."

I am sure the account of someone arriving in one hundred years will be yet completely different. Still there were, are, and will be explorers, since, as Sir Vivian Fuchs has said, "every child is an 'explorer' at birth, but as the years pass we are all conditioned by our environment to an appropriate way of life. Gradually the early urge 'to discover' is channeled and to some extent repressed. Yet despite their circumstances and sometimes because of them, a few people retain their initial sense of curiosity, which drives them on to a search for satisfaction. Throughout history mankind has benefited from those restless urges of the few, who step by step have revealed to us the unknown."

When I set out at last to "discover" America, I felt close to Columbus and other explorers. I suddenly understood the challenge and fear of the exploration enterprise. The unknown. The dark corner of the garden. The black hole. There was no way I could run back to mother, nursery, house, or country.

You might think the great ones left for the unknown while I *knew* where I was going. Well, don't let the advances in mapmaking mislead you. It takes more than a dream to reach into the darkness. Explorers need a goal, a destination, a point of arrival. Call it the moon, the North Pole, Cipango—or America. Without it, one might leave for California and land in Ireland (as a notorious aviator did in this century). Giovanni da Verrazano on April 17, 1529, while searching out a passage in the north to the land of Cathay, landed almost on the same spot I did at the entrance of New York Harbor, "a very pleasant place, situated amongst certain steep little hills," and here at the mouth of the Hudson River, the Indians appeared "dressed out in the feathers of birds of various colors" like in the East Village today.

People in the Middle Ages knew that silk, treasures, and spices came from the Orient, and Columbus expected to find these treasures where he landed. He thought the islands he had come to must surely be part of the Orient; the Indians certainly *looked* Chinese to him. And from the mysterious words they spoke, he thought he recognized sounds like *Kublai Khan* and *Xanadu*—words that evoked images of gold and silk. He had believed his dream too long to change it now.

My ideas about America were made up of pictures of the first team of astronauts, the winning cars in the Indianapolis 500, postcards of New York, and covers of old issues of *Saturday Evening Post*. So it is no wonder that after I got over my joy of landing, I was seeing astronauts, cowboys, Santa Claus, and Mickey Mouse. I had to begin a new expedition to separate the real America from the

America of my dreams—and then another, and another. It has been a nine-year expedition now, and it is far from finished.

According to all the books I read (maybe with the exception of *The Mutiny on the Bounty*), the explorer was supposed to return to his ruler or benefactor, bringing gold and parrots. But my triumphant return and tales of eight-foot-tall basketball players, five-story-high hamburgers, and a giant lady holding a torch and a book never materialized. I did not go back. Columbus did.

I hope the reader understands that the parallel of my journey and that of Columbus is purely a mockery. There are explorers landing somewhere around the world virtually every second. And every day thousands of immigrants and refugees leave their homelands and arrive in countries that are strange to them.

Maybe Columbus was in charge of too many people and ships. Maybe there were too many people watching him. Or it could be that the state of affairs in Spain was not all that disturbing to him. But if he had had more time to sit down with the native people he met—learn a little of their language, get to like their songs, food, sports, traditions, dances, and weather—then maybe the harsh order to return to Spain right away with gold, parrots, and natives would have made him think twice. And more. He might have decided to give up the titles of Admiral of the Sea and Viceroy of the Indies, and give up Isabel and Ferdinand, and stay in the "New World."

That would have given him the chance for yet another exploration, the exploration of his soul. He would have found out that he could never become fully like the people he lived with, but that he would never be completely European again, either. He would have been that much sadder to think of himself as a marginal person, but he would have been that much prouder and richer to be able to call himself a citizen of the New World.

Jean H. Zimmerman

SOURCE: A review of *Follow the Dream: The Story of Christopher Columbus*, in *School Library Journal*, Vol. 37, No. 9, September, 1991, p. 249.

A fascinating artistic representation of the discovery of the New World. In a preface, Sís makes reference to Columbus escaping the walls of fear and ignorance that encompassed 15th-century Europe and uses that motif freely throughout—as a curtain framing a view of Genoa, a background for pictures of Columbus's early life, and in an endpaper map of Europe surrounded by a wall. The illustrations, executed in a variety of media—oil, ink, watercolor, and gouache—show scenes from the explorer's life as well as some of the many imaginary creatures that populated the Europeans' picture of the outside world at that time. Sís uses colors ranging from drab browns and grays, to a rose-colored sky that is a background for the king and queen of Spain, and deep blues and greens for the ocean. A double-page medieval-style map is bordered with important dates and small pictures representing those dates, while another double page shows many postage-stamp-size representations of the sea as described in Columbus's log. The many details on each page invite individual readers to pay close attention, but the brief, clear text and framed illustrations lend themselves equally well to group sharing. Make room on your crowded Columbus shelf for this one.

Carolyn Phelan

SOURCE: "First Sighting of Christopher Columbus," in *Booklist*, Vol. 88, No. 1, September 1, 1991, p. 48.

This unusual picture book briefly describes the life of Columbus and illuminates it with stunning artwork. Reminiscent of Renaissance paintings, engravings, and (especially) maps, the illustrations combine the naive and the surreal in a very individual, sometimes haunting, way. The medium is "oil, ink and watercolor, and gouache . . . following a technique similar to fresco painting." Though misleading readers somewhat by implying that only Columbus believed the Indies could be reached by sailing west, Sís gives a fair summary of Columbus'[s] life. The story begins with his childhood dreams of adventure and ends with his landing in what he believed to be the Orient. The book's abrupt ending sentence, "Columbus, however, never really knew that he had reached 'America,'" raises more questions than it answers. Still, this is a good book to share on Columbus Day, primarily for the beauty and originality of Sís'[s] artwork.

Ellen Fader

SOURCE: A review of *Follow the Dream: The Story of Christopher Columbus*, in *The Horn Book Magazine*, Vol. LXVII, No. 5, September-October, 1991, pp. 614-15.

A small boom in publishing is underway in anticipation of the 1992 observance of the five hundredth anniversary of Christopher Columbus's voyage. Sís's noteworthy addition to the genre, a brief examination of the explorer's life, employs as its unifying element the title's theme: that Columbus's life was spent trying to fulfill his "dreams of adventure and discovery." The text is smoothly written and informative. Yet it is Sís's illustrations that make *Follow the Dream* so distinctive; his pictures, executed in oil, ink and watercolor, and gouache, complement and extend the narrative, adding additional facts and capturing young readers' interest by humanizing Columbus and vividly rendering his vision of a new world. Although the pages are large, the important elements in the pictures are often very small, so the book may find its best audience with an individual child or small group. Close attention to the minutely detailed illustrations will bring many rewards: a cutaway view of the provisions stacked below deck on the Santa Maria; a six-section storyboard picturing Columbus's joyous reaction to Queen Isabella's acceptance of his plan; and an imaginative double-page spread, resembling a fifteenth-century map, marking some major events in Columbus's life. Sís's survey ends as the explorer sets foot in the Americas and does not broach any of the more complicated issues, such as his crew's brutality to the original inhabitants . . . . Sís has expertly distilled the essence of Columbus's achievements for young readers; this volume will be welcomed for its simplicity, energy, and idealism.

Betsy Hearne

SOURCE: "Sail On: A Convoy of Columbus Books," in *Bulletin of the Center for Children's Books,* Vol. 45, No. 2, October, 1991, pp. 27-8.

It doesn't take much critical acumen to observe that a poet laureate's greatest lifetime work is generally not inspired by a coronation or royal birthday. The five hundredth anniversary of Columbus'[s] "discovery" of America has generated a whole raft of juvenile books about the subject, many of which will be suitable for the occasion and not much else. Young readers may even wonder just how many children went on those voyages, given the range of historical fiction narrated by ships' boys. Since Columbus Day is a social studies event in school, however, it pays to examine the material with which it will be celebrated. . . .

Follow the Dream, by Peter Sís, is a . . . sober, subtly illustrated account for an older picture book audience or even for primary-grade readers. The highly stylized art, blending archaic map conventions with modern surrealism, plays on a motif of Columbus'[s] breaking through the walls that were sometimes depicted as surrounding fifteenth-century Europe. The primary color is antique brownstone until an intense aquamarine takes over to alternate with an optimistic rosy hue. Kids who might be distanced by the formalism will be engaged by illustrations that diagram a ship's cross-section or that log daily weather changes in miniature picture strips. The writing is spare and carefully crafted. Instead of Columbus'[s] growing up "to be a weaver, like his father . . . he kept weaving dreams of adventure and discovery." The ending is abrupt, which is unfortunate in light of a rather graceful introduction, where Sís explains the personal relation he feels to the Columbus story because of his immigration from "a country surrounded by a 'wall,' known as the Iron Curtain."

J. Richard Gorham

SOURCE: A review of *Follow the Dream: The Story of Christopher Columbus,* in *Science Books & Films,* Vol. 27, No. 7, October, 1991, p. 214.

Since I am well beyond the age group for which this book is best suited, I thought it prudent to let Kerrie, my favorite second grader, have a look at it. She read the book and gave it a very favorable report; I concur with that evaluation. The story line is simple, straightforward, and brief. It follows the life of Columbus from birth to discovery and

does not overlook the troubles that lay along that path. First-grade teachers will want to read the story to their students, but most second and third graders will sail through the text, encountering only a few troublesome words. Kerrie was enthusiastic about the pictures, and so am I. The paintings, all in spectacular color, are truly wonderful, both in design and message. Run-of-the-mill kid's book pictures they are not. Rather, they are pleasing reproductions of the fresco-like originals. The illustrations invite long, careful, repeated looks by readers of all ages. One of them, for example, conveys the aura of gloomy apprehension surrounding the sailors during the long and lonely voyage. The misguided notion that Columbus was somehow to blame for bringing undesirable European influences to our shores has no place in this book. Rather, the story is one of an ordinary man who displayed extraordinary courage in the persistent pursuit of his dream.

AN OCEAN WORLD (1992)

Linda Greengrass

SOURCE: A review of *An Ocean World,* in *School Library Journal,* Vol. 38, No. 10, October, 1992, p. 96.

A young whale, raised alone in the aquarium, has at last outgrown his confines and is ready to be released into the ocean. But, having never seen another whale, Sís wonders "what it will be like for her!" In an amusing series of illustrations, he speculates just that as he depicts her encounters with leviathan-shaped entities—a blimp, a cloud, a school of fish, a barge—until finally another whale appears. The two swim off into the sunset as love conquers all. From the dedication page to the postcard home from Ocean World, which sets up the premise, to the gently gibing drawings of an aquarium, this nearly wordless book features fine, sophisticated watercolor illustrations and sly humor. Full-page and numerous smaller frames reflect the vastness of the whale's new home, and ecological implications are raised when a barge dumps its load of trash right into her face. The pictures are appropriately muted, and the color of the sea and sky vary with the changing light. Very young children may see this as a quick glance-through picture book, but possibilities of usage abound for clever teachers and older students who can appreciate its subtleties.

Kirkus Reviews

SOURCE: A review of *An Ocean World,* in *Kirkus Reviews,* Vol. LX, No. 19, October 1, 1992, p. 1261.

Virtually the only text in this book dedicated "To all who care about our world" is a postcard from Sís to his family, explaining that a whale raised at "Ocean World" is soon to be set free. The illustrations that follow show the whale outgrowing her pool, traveling (by sling) out to sea, and then—in a lovely, serene series of frames and full-page paintings—experiencing her new world at different times of day, on the surface and deep beneath it. This is a fascinating tour de force: with many illustrations composed simply of the whale, tiny in the immensity of the sea, the interest here (aside from some delightfully playful pictures where another form mimics the whale's—a blimp, a submerged galleon, an island whose single palm tree resembles her spout) is derived from interpreting quite subtle changes of color and texture. At the end, romance blooms with a pair of tails diving beneath a glowing valentine of a sunset. Exquisitely designed; charmingly offbeat.

Betsy Hearne

SOURCE: A review of *An Ocean World,* in *Bulletin of the Center for Children's Books,* Vol. 46, No. 3, November, 1992, pp. 88-9.

Sís has applied the practise he got painting vast expanses of water as background for Columbus'[s] voyage in *Follow the Dream* to an imaginative, nearly wordless pictorial narrative about a whale released from captivity into the sea. The irony of contrast between the artificial "Ocean World" tourist attraction, where the baby whale grows up to crowd his tank, and the real ocean world, where he's free to roam and find a mate, becomes visually clear through a deliberated variation of space. Other graphic ironies abound: an endpaper New York City so befogged that it appears to be underwater (with a ghostly whale shape floating above the buildings); a reference to Leo Lionni's *Swimmy* in the shape of a school of white fish with a dark one for an eye; a number of ocean objects shaped like the whale, including an island, a cloud, a submarine that exchanges sonar signals with the whale, a shipwreck, a garbage boat, and finally . . . another whale. Of course, it's love at first sight. In spite of the controlled simplicity of composition, there's plenty of textural variation to hold the eye, and kids will enjoy hearing the pictures storytold, "reading" the pictures alone or writing a story to accompany them, and playing that world-famous game of find the whale shapes in every picture. The game, really, contains the environmental message: it's more fun to look for whales swimming free in the sea than overfilling a pool.

Joanne Schott

SOURCE: A review of *An Ocean World,* in *Quill and Quire,* Vol. 58, No. 12, December, 1992, p. 29.

In another virtually wordless picture book, almost the only text is provided by a postcard from the artist to his family in which he describes a whale, captive in Ocean World since her infancy and now ready to be released to the real ocean world. Will she recognize others of her kind, having known only humans? The pictures explore her search and her frequently amusing encounters with objects that echo her own shape but are not whales. One of these encounters is a delightful visual quotation from Leo Lionni's *Swimmy* as she meets a whale-shaped school of white fish with a black fish as its eye. The simple story has a

happy ending, and the illustrations are exceptional. Sís exploits the qualities of watercolour, ink, and textured paper to create luminous skies, changing weather, and an ocean of many moods and depths that is almost palpably wet. A beautiful book that will be a pleasure to look at again and again.

📖 *KOMODO!* (1993)

Kirkus Reviews

SOURCE: A review of *Komodo!,* in *Kirkus Reviews,* Vol. LXI, No. 10, May 15, 1993, p. 668.

As in Martin/Gammell's *Will's Mammoth,* reality turns to fantasy when a child is so fascinated by dragons that her parents take her to the Indonesian island of Komodo, where, escaping crowds of tourists, she wanders into the jungle and encounters a ten-foot monitor lizard—the Komodo dragon of her dreams. Sís's visual realization of this slight storyline is splendidly imaginative. On the opening spreads, the young enthusiast is already creating dragons from a rich variety of materials: sand, topiary, her own shadow. After a Waldo-style mob scene where she's identified by her dragon T-shirt, Sís depicts her sumptuous apartment, in tones of brown, as virtually a museum, crammed with dragon artifacts and images in contemporary media: fax, computer screen, etc. Bali's crowded tourist traps are drawn with satirical wit; the lush blue-green jungle, burgeoning with plants that all mimic benign lizards and dragons, is fascinating. A note adds a bit more about this rare "survivor of the carnivorous dinosaurs." Lucid, elegantly rendered art with a wealth of intriguing details; wonderfully appealing subject.

Stephen Fraser

SOURCE: A review of *Komodo!,* in *The Five Owls,* Vol. VII, No. 5, May-June, 1993, pp. 113-14.

Peter Sís remains one of the truly distinctive picture-book creators today—quirky, sophisticated, and imaginative. Since his debut in children's books several years ago, each new book has been an elegant surprise. His familiar black-and-white miniature drawings have graced the pages of *The New York Times Book Review,* yet his pictures also have a childlike sense of playfulness that is instantly appealing to children.

His latest book, a lushly illustrated paean to the monitor lizard better known as the Komodo dragon, is sure to delight all lizard-loving children and adults. An oversized, full-color picture book, which combines high interest nonfiction and *Where's Waldo*-like hidden details, *Komodo!* is one boy's dream come true, a face-to-face encounter with a real Komodo dragon.

The story is simple: a dragon-loving boy and his affluent parents take a trip to Indonesia to visit the island of Komodo. They wait in long lines of tourists and when he disappears on his own through the trees, the boy sees a Komodo dragon and thereby returns home happy. The text is short: simple and straightforward, just as a young boy would narrate it.

While this is a probable, albeit farfetched, story, focusing on the boy's rich inner world transforms this into pure fantasy. Sís has created an elaborate counter-narrative with his illustrations. From the small protagonist's wind-up dragon toys, dragon posters, and dragon T-shirt to the dragon-comforter on his bed, dragon magic is in the air. His parents, it seems, are just as dragon-silly: their posh living room features dragon-patterned wallcovering, drapes, rugs, and even two fierce, fire-breathing dragons spread luxuriously full-length on their doors. Looking carefully at the illustrations, page by page, readers will find innumerable dragons of all kinds. Even the Indonesian fauna in later scenes has startling dragon-like eyes, shapes, and shadows. The ever-so-fine line between fantasy and reality is illustrated in an ingenious spread: the boy imagines what it is like to see the Komodo dragon face-to-face, and several pages later, when this fantasy is borne out, the exact same spread is repeated.

Readers will actually learn facts about this marvelous and strange creature. One two-page spread contains factual information about the Komodo dragon, details that fact-seekers will eat up. (An author's note at the end of the book presents additional facts.) The ever-present fantasy element, however, comes with the last sentence of the entry: "People have been known to disappear on [the Indonesian island of] Komodo." What child would not be wildly curious to pursue this adventure, or at least, to turn the page? This is a book children will spend time poring over. Whether dragon or dinosaur, legendary creatures are necessary to childhood, and Peter Sís has brought one whimsically alive for young readers.

Maeve Visser Knoth

SOURCE: A review of *Komodo!*, in *The Horn Book Magazine,* Vol. LXIX, No. 3, May-June, 1993, p. 325.

The young hero of Sís's imaginative adventure tells the reader that he has always loved dragons. This is an understatement. The boy's bedroom is filled with dragons, from a drawing of Saint George slaying one to a dragon on his computer screen. In deference to his obsession, the boy's parents take him on a family vacation to Indonesia to view a live Komodo dragon. The trip threatens to be a disappointment until the boy takes matters into his own hands and leaves the other tourists, walking through the jungle alone. There he encounters a Komodo dragon amidst a lush-green jungle and plants that all begin to resemble dragons. The boy states that it is "the best place I'd ever been." Sís has created a perfect fantasy, in which the hero leaves his parents just long enough to fulfill his desire. The text itself is brief and direct, and Sís complements it with large, full-page illustrations that give the reader details of the story. The family is eminently modern—the boy's parents receive information about their trip on a fax

machine. Dinosaur lovers and anyone who has ever had a passionate interest will recognize themselves in the young boy and will want to read of his journey again and again.

Deborah Stevenson

SOURCE: A review of *Komodo!*, in *Bulletin of the Center for Children's Books,* Vol. 46, No. 10, June, 1993, pp. 330-31.

The androgynous young narrator of this book is fascinated by dragons of all kinds, so s/he is thrilled when Mom and Dad decide they'll all take a trip to Komodo in Indonesia to see the Komodo Dragon. After a long trip, the narrator and family arrive at the island only to find it disappointingly crowded (litter-flinging tourists huddle around in a ring waiting to see the "Dragon Show"), but the young dragon-lover wanders away and has a brief private encounter with a wild Komodo. The story, assisted by the art in its moodily surreal tone, is simply written but implies worlds, and not just about Komodo Dragons (information about which is discreetly inserted in an illustration and an endnote, both relevant but neither mandatory to the story's enjoyment). Sís'[s] illustrations are what really bring allure to the story; his delicate stipple and hatch faux-engraving pairs with the dappled verdancy of the watercolors to create a lushly precise view of the world. Visual treats await the patient observer, including a couple of *Where's Waldo*-like pages in which the narrator is subsumed into a crowd, and the constant repetition of dragon figures in places both realistic (the narrator's wallpaper and curtains) and fantastic (the foliage on Komodo suggests dragons in no uncertain terms). The subject's a little off the beaten path, and that's part of what the story's about—young readers will be lured by this tale of obsession, adventure, and the magic of private experience.

Joy Fleishhacker

SOURCE: A review of *Komodo!*, in *School Library Journal,* Vol. 39, No. 7, July, 1993, p. 72.

A young boy's lifelong fascination with dragons takes him on a mystical journey to Indonesia. From cover to endpapers, there are dragons everywhere. On the title page, mysterious eyes peek out of the foliage-filled letters that spell *Komodo!* The boy's bedroom is bursting with dragon paraphernalia: live lizards lurk in leafy tanks, dragon toys hide in nooks and crannies, colorful dinosaur posters grace the walls—there's even a graphic of a dragon on the computer screen. In a living room decorated with dragon-bedecked wallpaper and rugs, the child's parents announce their plans for a trip to see a "real dragon." After sailing to the island of Komodo, the family is disappointed to find a large throng of tourists. When the boy wanders off alone into the lush jungle, where cleverly drawn dragon shapes and features hide in vines and leaves, he finally comes face to face with a majestic Komodo dragon. By combining simple, straightforward sentences with carefully detailed, imaginatively designed drawings, Sís extends and enhances the text through a visual feast of images. His pen-and-ink and watercolor paintings have the texture of aged parchment and the charm of an antique map, adding to the adventurous mood of a safari. With its subtle environmental message and interesting facts about the largest monitor lizard, this picture-book fantasy successfully combines information with imagination.

A SMALL TALL TALE FROM THE FAR FAR NORTH (1993)

Deborah Stevenson

SOURCE: A review of *A Small Tall Tale from the Far Far North,* in *Bulletin of the Center for Children's Books,* Vol. 47, No. 1, September, 1993, p. 24.

A Czech legend named Jan Welzl, possibly a real person, possibly not, possibly a liar, possibly not, reportedly left Central Europe at the end of the nineteenth century and became a denizen of the far north (Alaska, Siberia, northern Canada). Sís depicts Welzl's cross-continental journey to the Bering Sea, his near-disastrous encounter with a strange magnetic mountain, and his rescue by friendly Eskimos, with whom Welzl forms a bond. The art here is mystical and haunting, with Sís'[s] usual densely-layered stipple and line work illuminated by blinding, bestial snow in the tundra or dim firelight in the Eskimo's whale-shaped, folktale-bounded home. The story echoes the art's dreaminess with its gentle pace and wry humor (in the final resolution, Welzl decides he will lead intruders to their doom on the magnetic mountain so as to prevent them interfering with his beloved Eskimos). A few of the spreads are a bit confusing (should one read right to left or up and down in the cave-building sequence?), but the language of the text remains simple while the pictures stretch the perceptual skills of young readers. It's an evocative picture of northern adventure for youngsters with a taste for gentler tall tales.

Kate McClelland

SOURCE: A review of *A Small Tall Tale from the Far Far North,* in *School Library Journal,* Vol. 39, No. 9, September, 1993, pp. 226-27.

A fascinating fragment of an adventure story, this book tells of the intrepid Czech folk hero Jan Welzl, who traveled to the Arctic regions in 1893. When "Eskimos" save him from freezing to death, he resides among them and learns respect for their capacity to live in harmony with their harsh environment. It is when Welzl foresees the trouble gold hunters will bring with their guns, whiskey, and greed, that he devises an ironic solution. Sís's recognizable style of magical realism is well suited to a tale that is one part fact and three parts fantasy. The format is varied. Many double-page spreads resemble the actual, meticulously illustrated journal entries made by explorers. They reveal careful details of Inuit life that, although

they may in fact be a mixture of both Alaskan Eskimo *and* Canadian Inuit traditions, are authentic in the main. There is even a pictograph of an Inuit tale encircling the shape of a whale. The fantasy is mixed with the illustrator's distinctive blend of irony and humor. One painting depicts the vast emptiness of an Arctic snowstorm. "I am very much alone," says the stalwart explorer, while close scrutiny reveals puffs of blowing snow—all with cats' faces and eyes. Full of action, good humor, idealism, and cryptic detail, this book will invite repeated readings. If it has a flaw, it is that the extremely small script in some captions will be too difficult for some early graders. Nor will it be appropriate for group sharing, because the pleasure is in the minutiae. Still, Sís has succeeded masterfully in translating his own childhood fascination with Welzl into a highly original, irresistible adventure that children will pore over with relish.

David Small

SOURCE: "Gentle Giants," in *The New York Times Book Review,* November 14, 1993, p. 46.

In *A Small Tall Tale from the Far Far North,* Peter Sís tells of a similar journey and deals with similar themes [as François Place's *The Last Giants*], but in a form that even the youngest readers will appreciate. Here is his account of a fanciful journey to the north undertaken by the real Czech folk hero Jan Welzl (1868–1951), as Mr. Sís imagines it. Out on the ice flats, Welzl comes across what appears to be a glowing mountain of gold but is really a big magnetic stone. With all his metal equipment, the adventurer becomes stuck to the stone and fears he will freeze. He is rescued by Eskimos. Gentle, loving, they live in harmony with their surroundings. Welzl stays with them and learns from them, but also pities them for the hardships they must endure. He dreams of bringing them the benefits of civilization. Then, up from the horizon, bringing whisky, guns and vicious dogs, come the gold diggers. Welzl realizes the Eskimos are as trusting as children and will be easy prey. In an inspiration, he leads the gold diggers off to "the glowing golden mountain."

As an artist, the Czechoslovak-born Mr. Sís is a sorcerer. He communicates through the medium of dreams, which he paints. His pictures, at once intricate and lucid, are filled with surprises that occur beneath the skin of what we think we are seeing. Often he will border a series of storytelling panels with rubic images, the meanings of which hover just on the edge of consciousness. As in dreams, the theme of transformation runs through this book—sometimes humorously, at other times with quiet solemnity. On one spread the artist creates a blizzard in which the pelting bits of snow are transformed into the fierce faces of cats. Elsewhere, as we rotate the book to read a coiled, snakelike script narrating a dream (a dream about transformation for the sake of survival), the slow spinning of the book at the pace at which we read draws us farther into the artist's trancelike vision.

The art of Peter Sís—which has an undeniably mad quality—would be creepy if it were not immediately evident that it is all informed, even haunted, by a huge, benevolent heart. This book, the latest in a succession of works both uncannily lovely and astonishing, is a shaman's dream that, in a wish for a better world for us all, clears troubles away with an exquisite sleight of hand.

Joanne Schott

SOURCE: A review of *A Small Tall Tale from the Far Far North,* in *Quill and Quire,* Vol. 59, No. 12, December, 1993, p. 36.

Tall tale, legend, or real account? In both prologue and epilogue, Peter Sís outlines what is known of Jan Welzl, the Czech folk hero whose adventures he read as a boy. These have grown in his imagination, he says, to produce this tale of a man who leaves his troubled country. The Arctic beckons the man, and with resourcefulness he begins his solitary existence. But he soon finds himself irresistibly attracted by the glow of a golden mountain. Its magnetism holds him fast until Eskimo hunters save him. He remains with them, learning their way of life and developing great respect for them. When gold hunters come, he fears for his friends' future and lures the prospectors away, to the golden mountain.

Sís writes the story as a journal, with some of the text appearing as though handwritten. The account, in a few simple sentences, is direct and personal. The illustrations, complex and varied, are a joy to ponder. The map of the journey from Welzl's town to the Arctic is full of detail that makes a story in itself. The picture of him recovering from the mountain's magnetism, as dreams and Eskimo songs and stories weave in and out of his consciousness, is full of insight and narrative power. Using coloured inks, Sís incorporates fine lines into his illustrations. In combination with watercolours and rubber stamps, they produce drawings that bear the unique signature of an original artist.

Ellen Fader

SOURCE: A review of *A Small Tall Tale from the Far Far North,* in *The Horn Book Magazine,* Vol. LXX, No. 1, January-February, 1994, pp. 66-7.

Sís relates a brief story about Jan Welzl, a folk hero in the author-illustrator's native Czechoslovakia. In the prologue and epilogue, Sís explains that no unanimity of opinion exists as to whether Welzl ever lived, even though a Yukon tombstone records his birth and death dates as 1868 and 1951; or if he did exist, whether his writings contain any truth. In spite of this uncertainty, Sís uses his considerable imagination to enlarge upon the stories he remembers from his own childhood to create a lively, modern tall tale. In 1893, as the book begins, the restless twenty-five-year-old central European locksmith sets off to seek his fortune elsewhere. After obtaining the proper provisions, including reindeer and a sled, he finds the freedom he seeks in the vast frozen spaces of the Arctic. His fantastic adventures include a rescue by Eskimo hunters after being stuck fast to a fabled magnetic meteorite. The Eskimos, whom he considers to be the kindest people he has ever met, teach him winter survival skills, and he, in turn, shares with them his knowledge of modern scientific phenomena. But gold seekers, with their destructive guns and whiskey, begin to impinge upon the Eskimos' harmonious lives, and, in an ironic conclusion, Welzl protects his Eskimo friends by leading the intruders to the glowing mountain, the magnetic meteorite from which he was originally rescued. The story's voice is straightforward and deliberate, a style that contrasts effectively with the wildness of Welzl's adventures and the detailed intricacy of Sís's illustrations. As in *Follow the Dream,* Sís's picture-book biography of Christopher Columbus, he draws upon a variety of techniques, including pictographs, maps, borders, and storyboards, to recount Welzl's story. The myriad, meticulously recorded details in the illustrations will be best appreciated upon close inspection. While the story's conclusion is a bit abrupt, readers will be captivated by this glimpse into a different time and place. Another inventive and often humorous effort from an author-illustrator who continues to explore the visual boundaries of storytelling.

📖 THE THREE GOLDEN KEYS (1994)

Patricia Hampl

SOURCE: "Once upon a Time in Prague," in *The New York Times Book Review,* November 13, 1994, p. 34.

Prague, more than any other European city, reproduces the fantastic landscape of the Western imagination. Its only serious competition in the magical business of unreal estate is Venice, that other improbable city. But in Venice, we enter a dream. In Prague, we step into a fairy tale.

The fairy-tale capital has found its artist in Peter Sís. His brilliant homage to his hometown is at once charming and grave, filled with the countless nuances and details that only a loving eye will notice.

The Three Golden Keys is presented as a keepsake for Mr. Sís' little daughter, Madeleine, who, he notes in an opening letter to her, was born "in the New World," in New York. "Surely," he writes her, "you will be wondering one day where your father came from. This book is to explain just that."

In fact, it does much more. Its subject may be Prague, but the book really demonstrates how to love the place you know to be your own, even if you are separated from it forever. And in learning that first love of home, we learn how to love and be at home in the wider, harder world.

Mr. Sís tells his fairy tale memoir-style. "Madeleine," he begins companionably on the first page of the story, as if she were on his knee, "a wild and turbulent storm took control of my hot-air balloon and sent me far off course." He lands in the deserted square of a great city (discernibly Prague) where, he soon realizes, he is in the land of his childhood.

The family's old black cat claims him, and leads him toward the keys to his family home. The place looms at a scary slant from the little figure gazing up at it. All the buildings in Peter Sís'[s] Prague are just slightly human—doors with debonair mustaches, gates sporting decorative nose rings. But for all this seeming fellow-feeling, he can't get into the house. Three great padlocks close him out, and he lacks the three golden keys to open his home, his past, his deepest world. The facelike windows of the house have a ghostly vacancy that suggests they won't help him with his problem, either.

But the black cat, his Virgil, leads him through the labyrinthine city to the grand Strahov Library by the Hradcany district. There the librarian magically emerges from an animate wall of books, bearing a scroll with a golden key attached to it.

A poster-size picture of this cunning librarian, whose body is composed of books and open pages in a thrilling fantasy portrait, belongs on the wall of every public-library children's room in the land. If any image suggests the magic world of books, it must be this wonderful papery man with his patrician leather-bound book-spine nose, his open encyclopedia of hair and his tidy goatee of trimmed pages, the tomes of his hands holding—what else?—books and maps and open pages. Come to think of it, maybe he belongs in the grown-up reference room of every library too.

The librarian hands Mr. Sís the first of the three golden keys he will need to enter truly into his past. And with the key, as with those that follow, comes a legend of the city. These legends are civic fairy tales inside the private fairy-tale search for home. To find his own past, Mr. Sís manages to say without saying, in the artless and compelling way of a true storyteller, he must first find the communal past—of mythic Prince Bruncvik, whose sword is embedded in the Charles Bridge; of the Golem who ran amok in the Jewish community; of Hanus the artist-craftsman who made Prague's astronomical clock and was blinded by jealous townsmen.

The narrow streets of Mr. Sís'[s] Old Town and Mala Strana (Prague's Left Bank) don't simply twist; they twine as they rise up to the castle above the Vitava River. There is something almost sentient about his riverine streets with their wily turns and cul-de-sacs, lamplight pooling in lost corners.

Like all the best children's picture books, this is one an adult will keep reaching for. For Peter Sís has succeeded in creating a book not only for his child, but for the adult she will one day be. He has made a book even his magical Strahov librarian would clasp to his heart—or maybe *make* his heart.

Sally Lodge

SOURCE: "Peter Sís Goes Home Again," in *Publishers Weekly,* Vol. 241, No. 45, November 14, 1994, p. 26.

"It's a time of great anxiety. I'm trying to stay calm, but it is so hard to be calm at this point, when I don't yet have any reaction from anybody," remarks Peter Sís on the eve of the November publication of *The Three Golden Keys,* in which the Czech-born artist weaves three legends of Prague into a haunting reminiscence of his childhood in that city. Why should Sís, who has written and illustrated eight previous children's books and provided the art for more than two dozen others, feel such trepidation about the release of yet another title? Clearly, this book means something special to him. "It is, simply, a dream come true," he states. "Always, always, I have wanted to do a book on Prague. I finally had the opportunity to do it."

Sís credits the late Jacqueline Onassis, who was a senior editor at Doubleday, for giving him the long-awaited chance to create what became *The Three Golden Keys.* Her support of the project came after some frustrating experiences, Sís recalls. "When I came to New York to become a children's book illustrator, I proposed a book on Prague a number of times, but no publisher was interested in doing it. And then I said, 'All right, I'll do a book on New York.' But I was told I couldn't do *that,* since I hadn't grown up in New York. I became so jaded, wanting to be part of the New York publishing scene, but knowing that no one cared about the book I really wanted to do."

Sís nevertheless had no shortage of book projects—nor accolades. His *Rainbow Rhino* was cited by *Time* as one of the outstanding children's books of the year, and five books he has illustrated have made *The New York Times*'s annual list of best illustrated books of the year.

But a 1990 phone call from Mrs. Onassis set him in a new direction. She had seen photographs of eggs the artist had painted to supplement his income, and was taken by his talent. "It was hard work painting the eggs," Sís remembers, "but as it turned out, those eggs were good to me. After Mrs. Onassis phoned me, we met and she was so gracious. She said, 'We have to do something together,' and for a while we pitched ideas to each other. But I never dared to bring up Prague. And then she happened to go on a five-day visit to that city, and she came back incredibly knowledgeable about it. She said to me, 'You have to do something on Prague.' I was flabbergasted. This was the chance of my lifetime."

A Difficult Trip Home

Yet the process of writing and illustrating *The Three Golden Keys* was "very arduous," according to Sís. He revisited the city several times, and found it much altered from the city of his childhood. "When Communist rule of Prague ended in 1989, everything changed," he explains. "I went back to try to remember everything as it was: what

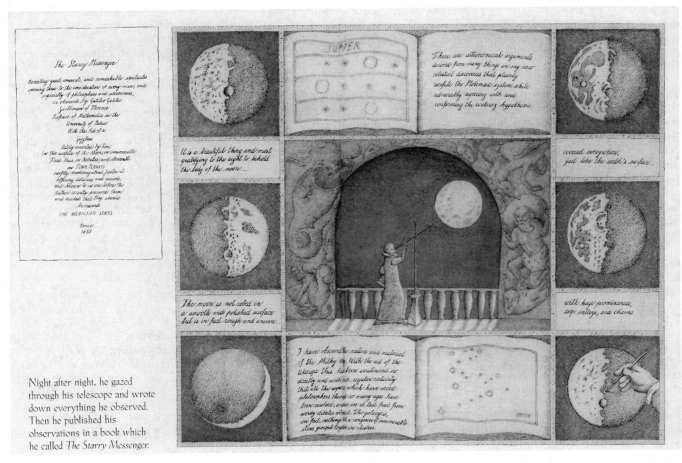

From Starry Messenger: Galileo Galilei, *written and illustrated by Peter Sís.*

a knob on a door looked like, how many cobblestones there were from my door to the other side of the street. I wanted to make everything as it was, but the city was so different. In my childhood under the Communists, I'd cross Charles Bridge and there, standing in the fog on the other side, was a single person. Now that the city is opened up, there are thousands of tourists, and I can't even get across Charles Bridge. The city is not part of my life anymore, and that made the book difficult. I had to go back to my memories, which was overwhelming to me."

Creating the intricate paintings and narrative for **The Three Golden Keys** took Sís more than a year—longer than most of his previous books, he notes. And there were some discouraging moments. "Dealing with my past life within the walls of my studio became heavier and heavier," he recalls. "I had moments of despair, and at those times Mrs. Onassis became my encouragement. She was like a muse. And when I showed her the sketches, at which point most editors would say, 'Okay, let's decide which ones we'll use,' she said, 'Great—let's use them all.' This is when I realized that she was letting me do what I had always wanted to do. For the first time, I felt I had complete freedom."

Last Christmas Eve, Sís brought the book's final art and text—which opens with a note to his two-year-old daugh-ter, Madeleine—into his editor's office. "She loved it, and sent me a beautiful note and flowers for my daughter," he says, and adds wistfully: "Right after Christmas I noticed she wasn't looking that well, and then I heard that she was ill. Now I'm worried that she never saw the final book. When one of my books comes out and I am still so full of it that it is hard to be objective, I usually rely on my editor to say, 'It is very good.' Right now I would like to call her and say, 'What do you think?' But for the first time I cannot do that. It is very strange and very sad."

And Sís will have to wait several years before he can similarly query Madeleine—and her infant brother Matej, born in September. "I want this book to help explain to my children where their father came from," he says. "I am so curious what their reaction will be, but I know I have to postpone asking, since they are so small. But I really can't wait to find out what they think."

Julie Cummins

SOURCE: A review of *The Three Golden Keys,* in *School Library Journal,* Vol. 40, No. 12, December, 1994, p. 87.

When a storm blows a man's hot-air balloon off-course, he lands in a city where everything recalls his childhood in

Prague. He finds the family house but it is locked with three rusty padlocks. He follows the family cat through the empty streets to the library, the Emperor's garden, and the famous town-square clock. In each place, figures from the past emerge from the walls and unroll a scroll that holds a key and relates the traditional Czech legends of Prince Bruncvik and his magic sword, the Golem, and Hanus the clockmaker. With the three keys in hand, he returns home where he recollects voices, sounds, and pictures. From the foreword to his daughter to the first-person voice, Sís has created a personal journey that is multilayered with images, memories, and symbols. The art itself is layered with felines, faces, and ghostly figures imposed over backgrounds, camouflaged in streets and structures, and emerging from misty reflections. With tiny, delicate lines and meshlike textures, the artist's distinctive style is evocative. The scroll stories are handscripted in numbered sequences with a pictogram bordering the two-page spreads. The tiny handwriting is so intricate it requires close focus. Overall the book is intriguing, with visual and textual subtleties interconnecting with cultural and historical ties. Older picture book readers should appreciate the beauty of the illustrations and the symbolism.

Deborah Stevenson

SOURCE: A review of *The Three Golden Keys,* in *Bulletin of the Center for Children's Books,* Vol. 48, No. 5, January, 1995, p. 177.

In an introduction addressed to his young daughter, Madeleine, Peter Sís writes that this book is to explain to her where her father came from, to give her the keys to the mystery of Prague. In the book's text, the narrator's hot-air balloon is blown off course and lands in Prague, where he finds his old house but is unable to unlock the three padlocks on the front door. He roams, and a librarian made of books, an emperor made of foliage, and a robotic baron each give him a scroll containing a folktale from Sís'[s] childhood and a golden key; when he returns to the house, the keys admit him and Madeleine to the house of his youth. Sís'[s] illustrations are framed in textured yellow borders on a rough-looking cream surface; his precise and delicate linework, in subdued and occasionally monochromatic tones, is frequently overlaid with images of cats, fanciful spirits, and zodiacal personages in a way that won't show in the far back of a classroom but is eerie and absorbing at closer distances. The length of the book, especially with the interpolated folktales, makes it rather tedious and too protracted for most of the usual picture-book audience; the dense penmanship of the tales (and the quotes from Camus and, untranslated, Gide) renders the book above the level of unsophisticated readers; few youngsters of any age will identify with an adult's search for the key to return to his childhood. What Sís does best here, in fact, is to create his fantasy vision of the city—the most successful use for the book might be with middle-school and older kids who have an interest in art and fantasy and who don't mind the too-young-for-them plot; the picture-book crowd may enjoy peeking over their

parents' shoulders at an illustration or two as the adults page through a book more for them than for their children.

Michael Cart

SOURCE: "Carte Blanche: How Memory Looks," in *Booklist,* Vol. 91, No. 10, January 15, 1995, p. 907.

Designed, Sís tells us in a prefatory note, to show his New York-born daughter, Madeline, "where her father came from," *The Three Golden Keys* tells the richly imagined and dreamlike story of a man—Sís himself, presumably—whose hot-air balloon is blown off course and lands in the Prague of his long-ago childhood. Leaving his balloon behind, the man rushes through the empty, serpentine streets of the city and arrives, finally, at his boyhood home, only to find the door secured by three rusty padlocks. A black cat—his childhood pet, perhaps—appears and, with magical, shining eyes, guides him to three local landmarks, all favorite places from his childhood. In each, he meets a strange person: first, a librarian made, in homage to the style of the sixteenth-century artist Arcimboldo, of books, charts, and papers; then, it's an emperor composed of plants; and lastly, a mechanical baron and his entourage of "strange, mythical robots." Each gives him a golden key and a scroll containing an important local legend. Armed with these literal and symbolic keys, the man returns to his house, unlocks the door, and finds the shadowy figures of his parents waiting—a boy again, he has come home.

Each of Sís'[s] elaborate pen-and-ink drawings, executed on paper stained to resemble parchment washed in memory-muted colors, is contained in a gold frame, a device that suggests that reading a book is like strolling through a wonderful museum of memory. As Sís continues his quest, seasons and scenes change, but in each, the artist plays with perspective and fills his pictures with the kinds of symbolic images that haunt our dreams: an aerial view of the city shows the streets forming the shape of a cat; the Zodiac fills the sky like a sun that circles the seasons round; faces appear in the windows of deserted-looking buildings—they look like ghosts or like memories of the day when Sís said "good-bye to this forever."

Mary Burns

SOURCE: A review of *The Three Golden Keys,* in *The Horn Book Magazine,* Vol. LXXI, No. 2, March-April, 1995, pp. 189-90.

Dazzling design, opulent production, meticulous execution, and an aura of mystery transform memories into a magical tour of the ancient city of Prague, Peter Sís's childhood home. The story recounts the experiences of a man whose hot-air balloon, blown off-course in a storm, lands in a seemingly deserted city. But it is inhabited by recollections which are made tangible in elegantly crafted, breathtaking fine line illustrations, marvelous to behold, where the visages of ghostly apparitions are superimposed on architectural details. Searching for the three keys necessary to open the doors to his former home, the man traverses the wintry streets to the great library, where the librarian, a figure made of books in the tradition of seventeenth-century tradesman's cards, presents him with the first key; it is rolled in a scroll that recounts the legend of Prince Bruncvik and the Prague Bridge. Subsequent encounters bring him two more keys and additional legends—a version of the Golem story and the tale of Master Hanus, builder of the famous astronomical clock. As the man's journey comes to its conclusion, the palette lightens as spring—or is it joy?—permeates his being. Certainly, there is no more enticing remembrance of things past than this enigmatic, haunting evocation of childhood. But, less a picture book than an illustrated memoir, is it a book for children or one which adults think is for children? Certainly, quotes such as those from André Gide and Albert Camus which are incorporated into the text suggest an evolution of form and function far removed from Caldecott's day. Yet as an objet d'art, the book will find an audience, for its images resonate and fascinate.

STARRY MESSENGER: GALILEO GALILEI (1996)

Wendy Lukehart

SOURCE: A review of *Starry Messenger: Galileo Galilei,* in *School Library Journal,* Vol. 42, No. 10, October, 1996, p. 118.

In *Follow the Dream* Sís depicted both the humanity and heroism of Christopher Columbus. In *Starry Messenger,* Sís turns his considerable talents to another infamous Italian—Galileo Galilei. He layers his telling so that young children or groups may focus on the short version printed in large type at the bottom of each page. Older readers will glean more from the quotes pulled from the astronomer's treatise (the work that inspired this title) and other primary sources, such as Inquisition documents. This second layer is printed in script and presented in a variety of decorative patterns (suggesting ideograms) to distinguish it. The sophisticated details of Sís's watercolor, pen, and rubber-stamp illustrations provide yet another dimension as well as ambiance. A master of symbol, the artist creates scenes that focus on the subject—"a boy born with stars in his eyes"—and shows how he shines against the darker aspects of his time. The aging scientist stands alone in a circle of yellow light, suggesting his identification with the heliocentrism for which he was being condemned, surrounded by a sea of red-clad Cardinals. The text is no less powerful: "He was tried in the Pope's court, and everyone could see that the stars had left his eyes." The pathos, the painstaking copies of Galileo's famous sketches of the heavens, and the attention to current scholarship make this book a fascinating find.

Deborah Stevenson

SOURCE: A review of *Starry Messenger: A Book Depict-* ing the Life of a Famous Scientist, Mathematician, Astronomer, Philosopher, Physicist Galileo Galilei, in *Bulletin of the Center for Children's Books,* Vol. 50, No. 3, November, 1996, p. 115.

Galileo is, of course, the most famous adherent of the Copernican theory of astronomy, known not only for his genius but for his persecution by the Roman Catholic church. Printed text and cursive notes join in briefly tracing Galileo's life from birth, through schooling and scholarship to inventions, writing, great fame, and eventual downfall; quotes from Galileo's own writings and contemporaneous writings about him add context to the account. This isn't the most factually useful biography of the great astronomer: included maps show few of the mentioned cities, the text leaves inconsistencies unexplained (Galileo proudly affirms his correctness based on what he saw with his own eyes, but the Ptolemaic theory has essentially the same basis), and the marginal information doesn't always blend with the mainstream of the chronicle. Art and design are the real draws here: Sís'[s] images combine delicate textural hatching with precise drawing and dreamlike imagery to give the maps and global views the feel of Renaissance geography and the life scenes the air of a landscape of the mind. Whether Galileo himself would approve of his story being brushed with the magic it's tinged with here is an interesting question, but it makes for an elegant, if not entirely informative, book.

Publishers Weekly

SOURCE: A review of *Starry Messenger: Galileo Galilei,* in *Publishers Weekly,* Vol. 243, No. 45, November 4, 1996, p. 76.

Extraordinary pictures light up this tribute to Galileo, telling the story of his discoveries, rise to prominence and excoriation by the Church. Sís (*Follow the Dream*), an experienced and sophisticated chronicler of history's visionaries, outdoes himself with his illustrations. Detailed and delicate, ingeniously conceived, his paintings convey abstractions with an immediate impact. The artist expresses the simultaneous wonder and prevision of Galileo's celestial observations, for example, in a luminous multipaneled composition: in the center, Galileo trains his telescope on the moon; surrounding panels replicate Galileo's notes about and sketches of the lunar surface. Other paintings take inspiration from contemporaneous maps and treatises; still others borrow historical imagery to convey the loneliness of the censored scientist. Handwritten passages from Galileo's own works embellish the pages and supply information missing from the text. Even with the powerful art, however, this volume does not open up Galileo's story to the uninitiated: the brief text oversimplifies the issues, even for a picture book, and seems to presume the reader's awareness of the historical significance of Galileo's struggles. While the book's usefulness may be limited, its strengths are not: it is a book with deep if not broad appeal.

Roger Sutton

SOURCE: A review of *Starry Messenger: Galileo Galilei*, in *The Horn Book Magazine*, Vol. LXXIII, No. 1, January-February, 1997, pp. 79-80.

Less a picture-book biography than is Leonard Everett Fisher's *Galileo*, this book instead takes the essentials of Galileo's life and discoveries to frame a rich galaxy of paintings that recall both the scientist's times and the persistence of wonder. Captions ("Night after night, he gazed through his telescope and wrote down everything he observed") and quotes from Galileo's writing ("The moon is not robed in a smooth and polished surface but is in fact rough and uneven") border and embellish the large pages, while the paintings enliven a Renaissance tone with Sís's own peculiar style of iconography: inset portraits and vignettes, stamps and medallions, intricate borders. Much of the text is printed in script and, when the lines whimsically spiral and swoop, is not always easy to read. The best pictures are both sweet and surreal, like the one showing baby Galileo, "born with stars in his eyes," tucked in amidst a host of babies less blessed; or a phantasmagorical map of Europe. Endpapers take the story from the past to the present, the opening spread showing a cityscape of Galileo searching the Florentine skies, the closing one revealing a contemporary skygazer looking at the New York City night. Like Galileo, you should look and look carefully, for there is much to see.

Additional coverage of Sís's life and career is contained in the following sources published by Gale Research: *Contemporary Authors*, Vol. 128, and *Something about the Author*, Vol. 67.

Paul Zindel

1936-

American author.

Major works include *Confessions of a Teenage Baboon* (1977), *The Pigman's Legacy* (1980), *Harry and Hortense at Hormone High* (1984), *A Begonia for Miss Applebaum* (1989), *The Pigman and Me* (1991).

For information on Zindel's career prior to 1978, see *CLR*, Vol. 3.

INTRODUCTION

Zindel is primarily known for his novels describing the trials and tribulations of adolescent life. Sometimes criticized for presenting a rather bleak, even pessimistic view of life, Zindel has also charmed many readers who find the Zindelesque world compelling, moving, and true to life. His works feature a zany, surreal, and sometimes sinister collection of inane teachers, alcoholic parents, impossibly dysfunctional families, and confused but courageous adolescents facing a universe of adult imbecility. Zindel, critics agree, shows an uncanny ability to compose the kind of realistic dialogue, reflecting a character's mood and state of mind, that fully engages the reader, involving him or her directly in the lives of his protagonists. His plots, even those deemed too breathless and incredible by some critics, do not obscure the fundamental issues addressed in his stories, issues which are all, it seems, variations of the theme of an adolescent's survival in an adult world gone mad. As commentators have noted, Zindel also possesses the ability to recreate the mental universe of adolescence: the voices of his characters, in all their anguish, confusion, rebellion, and exasperation, always ring true. In the chaotic, topsy-turvy stories of adolescent sadness, loneliness, and confusion, two dominant themes emerge: the gift of friendship and the miracle of human wisdom. In sharp contrast to the "official" adults of everyday life (parents, teachers, etc.), Zindel introduces a mysterious figure—a friendly, somewhat eccentric, old man who appreciates young people. Although representing an archetype that is therefore timeless, the Old Man figure, who may also be interpreted as the figure of Death, shares his wisdom with his young friends. As Zindel emphasizes, the encounter with the "Pigman" is a life-altering experience. Zindel's novels, in addition to their captivating dialogue and often spellbinding plots, thus present the world from a young person's point of view, suggesting that youth, despite its apparent helplessness in a world that seems alien, can benefit from timeless sources of wisdom which their contemporaries lack. By exploring the world of adolescence from a point of view which places everyday paradoxes and absurdities within the context of timeless truths, Zindel has, as critics have asserted, significantly contributed to society's understanding of and empathy

toward young people who are crossing the threshold separating childhood from adulthood.

Biographical Information

Zindel was born and raised on Staten Island, New York. His parents divorced when he was a young child, and his childhood was unhappy: poverty-stricken and chaotic. As an adolescent, Zindel experienced the kind of isolation and alienation that he describes in his novels. After completing his studies, Zindel worked as a chemistry teacher for ten years. As a high-school teacher, Zindel became intimately acquainted with the world of adolescence. His experience as a teacher, critics have remarked, influenced his work as a novelist, enabling him to knowingly address the important issues of adolescence. While working as a teacher, Zindel also wrote plays. One of his plays, *The Effect of Gamma Rays on Man-in-the Moon Marigolds* (1965), a family drama praised for its emotional power, was such a sensational success that it eventually established him as a leading playwright. Produced on Broadway, the play won the 1971 Pulitzer Prize for Drama. Among the admirers of Zindel's play was the eminent children's writer and editor Charlotte Zolotow, who, having seen a local, pre-Broadway production of *The Effect of Gamma Rays on Man-in-the Moon Marigolds,* recognized Zindel's ability to capture the intense drama of human relationships, and talked him into writing a novel for adolescents. Zindel agreed, and his first novel, *The Pigman* (1968), was so successful that critics have regarded it as a watershed event in the history of young adult literature. In his subsequent novels, some of which develop the main theme of *The Pigman*—the friendship between adolescents and an old man—Zindel has created a fascinating panorama of adolescence, addressing many crucial issues, such as death, love, and the meaning of life, which had traditionally been reserved for older readers.

Major Works

Confessions of a Teenage Baboon is the story of a fifteen-year-old boy, Chris, whose efforts to find a place in the world are frustrated by a domineering mother. Chris finds a mentor in thirty-year-old Lloyd Dipardi, a troubled, depraved man who, despite his immoral behavior, encourages Chris to be true to himself. While some reviewers have criticized the novel as excessively pessimistic, others have found it a poignant and moving story. Praised as a worthy sequel to *The Pigman, The Pigman's Legacy* develops the same motif: two teenagers befriend an old man. But not everything is the same: John and Lorraine, the protagonists of *The Pigman,* are a year older (sixteen), and their involvement with their new friend, while providing new opportunities for zany escapades and incredible events, shows that they have matured. And as John and Lorraine mature, Paxton Davis notes in the *New York Times Book Review,* "their tale takes on broader implications; it is a surprising, beautiful and even profound story." *Harry and Hortense at Hormone High,* despite its humorous title, describes the efforts of two teenagers to penetrate the tragic and frightening world of a schizophrenic boy. Writing in the *Times Literary Supplement,* Sarah Hayes defined Zindel's book as "a dark novel with a weight of cruelty, intolerance and despair." Other critics concurred, remarking that Zindel's wit and humor are obscured by the profoundly pessimistic tone of the narrative. In *A Begonia for Miss Applebaum,* Zindel has two teenagers, Zelda and Henry, deal with mortality as a real-life situation. Their favorite science teacher, the eccentric Miss Applebaum, is terminally ill but involves the adolescents in her efforts to live the rest of her life to the fullest. In a *Junior Bookshelf* review, M. Hobbs remarked that the "story raises quite a number of uncomfortable questions, which is no bad thing in the hands of such an accomplished writer." *The Pigman and Me,* Zindel's memoir of his childhood, in addition to providing a rich context for the themes and motifs of his novels, presents a fascinating tapestry of unforgettable events and characters, including the real-life "Pigman." As Hobbs stated in a *Junior Bookshelf* review, all "the narrative verve and vividness of characterisation that have made Paul Zindel's books so popular are here applied to an autobiographical account of a significant period of his childhood."

Critical Reception

While *The Pigman* received undivided critical acclaim, Zindel's later novels, particularly the books written in the 1970s, elicited mixed reactions. Critics appreciated his verve and ability to combine witty dialogue with impossible situations, but seemed alienated by the tone of despair. John A. Davis defined Zindel's "middle" phase, exemplified by such books as *Confessions of a Teenage Baboon,* as "possessed of a Dostoevskian mood of gloom and despair." In addition, critics felt that the general atmosphere of hopelessness and absurdity in Zindel's 1970s novels reflected a total rejection of contemporary society, which was a dangerous, perhaps noxious, world view to share with young people. For example, discussing *Confessions of a Teenage Baboon,* Janet P. Benestad wrote that it "is sad, and . . . an exaggeration on Zindel's part, to suggest that this culture is so destitute that help for a boy like Chris can come only from a derelict." However, while critics such as Davis defined the 1970s Zindel as a "hybrid Zindel," rejoicing over his "return," in the novels written in the 1980s, to his original voice, other critics, rejecting this critical "authentic versus hybrid Zindel" dichotomy, praised Zindel's "dark" novels for their stunningly convincing pessimism. For example, Stanley Hoffman declared that *Confessions of a Teenage Baboon* "may be, in fact, Zindel's best novel precisely because it breaks with the formulas of his past books." Essentially, according to Hoffman, Zindel is the type of writer that drives critics to despair because he is not easily defined. In this critic's view, "Zindel may be the Jekyll and Hyde of modern adult fiction; his books get better, worse, better, worse, and one never knows what will come next." Hoffman concludes: Zindel's work "is an adventure, each separate path as unpredictable as the one before it and to follow."

Awards

The Pigman and *Pardon Me, You're Stepping on My Eyeball!* were listed as *New York Times* Outstanding Books, while *The Pigman's Legacy, Pardon Me, You're Stepping on My Eyeball!, A Begonia for Miss Applebaum,* and *The Pigman and Me* were listed as ALA Best Books for Young Adults. In addition, *The Pigman* and *The Pigman and Me* were listed as ALA Notable Children's Books. Zindel also won the Pulitzer Prize for drama in 1971 for his play *The Effect of Gamma Rays on Man-in-the-Moon Marigolds.*

AUTHOR'S COMMENTARY

Paul Zindel with Judith James

SOURCE: In an interview in *Reading Time,* Vol. 36, No. 1, 1992, pp. 8-10.

[The following excerpt is from a telephone interview between Paul Zindel and Judith James.]

Paul Zindel discussed *The Pigman & Me: A Memoir,* his latest book, in which he gives an insight into his childhood development as a writer and the motifs in his books. Paul's memoirs reveal a great attention to detail and a photographic memory. How does he manage that?

Paul: I was amazed that things came back to me—it was as much as a surprise to me that I was able to recreate it as well. Fortunately the camera had already been invented, I can't imagine how people imagine their childhood before the invention of a camera.

Judy: Did you research these newspaper headlines from your early life?

Paul: Actually I always liked newspaper headlines and I had always collected them, and even used them and found myself using them before people were even writing them in strange supermarket newspapers. There was only one newspaper, when I was a kid, that used to print them, the *National Enquirer.* I used to save them, and I found them useful when I began to teach chemistry—I found kids always liked strange facts. I was introducing, for instance, a section on nutrition and I brought in a picture on a 900 lb man. For some reason I was always interested in the shock of the new and new kids like unusual things. I don't know where it came from—it's like the water baby (in *The Pigman & Me*)—these mysteries lie around us and kids have a great interest in them.

Judy: Many of your books follow the same pattern—the boy/girl friendship being a big part of that, and this has been a part of your experience, as we see in your friendship with Jennifer. Do you recreate the pattern intentionally?

Paul: Yes, I say what I genuinely feel. If you write enough, you begin to find out what some of those things are. I have a brother-in-law who doesn't always compliment me much, and he'll read one of my books and say, "Oh, you killed another animal in that one." I did hear a remark the other day which I thought was very good, and that was when you sit down each time you think you are going to write something completely different, or you're going to be some completely different person, and after you start writing a piece, you realise, "Oh, it's me again!" I think it's something that is built into a part of me, I guess I like looking at things through both the boy's and the girl's point of view, and I think also, it gave me more dimension—it let me say more than if I had only one view.

Judy: The boy is always a compassionate person and has the courage to be different—even if some adults think that the boy is 'off the rails'. The readers know that he is all right. Although the boy is a rascal, he is a good role model because he cares about people.

Paul: But he doesn't like going around bragging about it.

Judy: We (adults reading your books) feel good about those male characters; but adults in their middle years don't get a very good press in your work, certain teachers excepted. It's either the young and the old, or the teachers—have you noticed that?

Paul: Yes, I did. I noticed something changing now, I guess when I first began to write, it was when I was a school teacher, so I was surrounded by all the kids, and I would meet a lot of parents on the PTA nights and parent/teacher conference nights, and I guess the one thing I learned early on, was that kids like to solve their own problems—they don't like parents who know all the answers—I guess that's the way new worlds are discovered—by kids setting out on their own adventures. I didn't set out to give parents bad press—I knew that the kids didn't want parents who knew everything—if they knew everything, there would be no story; no adventures for them to go out on. So, even if the parents are wise, they don't want to admit it until they get much older. Also, the big change that occurred in my writing, that you may have noticed in *A Begonia for Miss Applebaum*—what's now apparent in my teenagers, a girl that's 14 and a boy that's 16, is that I'm beginning to understand now why—as a result, I now have much more compassion for parents. And I'll find a way to put it in, so it doesn't kill off the necessity of the kids to go forth, like Luke Skywalker, and battle the universes. I do find that some kids, when I go out to talk to them, tell me, "Hey, listen, I have lovely parents—they're really wonderful." So there are some kids that can really appreciate their parents and look to them for advice. But in our family, for instance, my daughter really wants to do everything herself, and my son is nicer to us, but he likes his independence and his secrets too. I think there was a bit of wisdom I read somewhere, that it's better for the parents to speak the truth than to be content to whisper. I think that may be the choice my parents are going to make in all of my future books; I don't think they have to be bad parents. There are parents who have problems of their own because we don't have easy answers at any age. But I think most parents that I know, really love their children; they want the very best for them, and sometimes don't know the way to go about that—but I know that the kids are the ones who lead us to the brave new world. I think the parents aren't going to dominate this story.

Judy: The advice that Pigman, (Nonno Frankie in real life) gave to you, *io sono differente*—I am different, and then he takes you on to show that being different isn't enough; is that still true? He took you out and played the 'mind' game—the secret of life, showed you a picture of you in a coffin—it echoes the game of life in *The Pigman's Legacy*.

Paul: I always keep my eye open, for little stories that are really verbal *Rorschach* tests. They have been around for many years, if not centuries, and they are very hard to come by, but those that are good tend to emerge every 20-30 years and are rediscovered, and I was very impressed by one I heard when I was 15, and that was the one I used in *The Pigman's Legacy,* about the wall and finding the objects along the wall/path. That was a very interesting thing, because it gave you a chance to articulate your own feelings about the classic emotions of life, and the great path of life. I remember in one Italian town, it is the custom for the boy, I guess it is part of the rite of adolescence, to be transported in a coffin, so that one experiences one's own funeral while alive. They say that in growing up, the rites of passage, that an injury must be inflicted upon the adolescent, which I think is the metaphor for what Pigman has meant on some more mythical levels for myself. I think in order for most people to learn something, something dies, they lose something. One kid sent me a cartoon one time which I think was very significant of what the Pigman meant—he drew two teenagers standing on the edge of a piece of land, and out at sea was a sailboat with an old man in it, labelled the Pigman, the sail on the boat was labelled innocence, and I felt that he had tapped into something. This is what Nonno Frankie led me to discover.

Judy: As adults, we think about archetypal and mythical patterns in books. What do you think?

Paul: Oh yes, I really did get very interested in that, long before Joseph Campbell came to popular fame here in the States. I was quite interested as a kid, and I found them interesting when I read them in college. But I didn't really feel the need so much as I guess in my adult years when life becomes more troublesome, when it felt that God was dead, and we were all looking for how do we find goals, what do we believe in, how do we find strength to go from one day to the next. Somewhere around that time (this will freak you out a little bit), I met a schizophrenic, and I didn't really know what a schizophrenic was clinically, it just seemed like some funny term that was bandied about. This was a person who thought he really was Alexander the Great, and one that I based the book *Harry and Hortense at Hormone High* and this person was in his own madness so filled and educated in myth and the need to stay in touch with myth, that I began to explore it, and to read in that area. So by the time Joseph Campbell became popular here, I had already been through, and done all that reading, and I had been going to philosophical societies where people were giving lectures on these sorts of things. So the need to get in touch with the universal and the mythical was something that obviously, I think, our society needed. We have all jumped on the bandwagon, but it is not the band-aid that we thought it might be. But one of the things that I do as a writer is consider at some point, preferably after the story has been written and I'm going to do a final draft, I think what mythical elements are there, what is the universal connection. So it serves me well as a writer, to be aware of myth, its functions, its universal inheritance, and to make sure I don't use them in a gut fashion; I use them in an honest fashion. It comes out of me first in inspiration, and then I can tune them when I attend to mythic viewpoint during rewrite. . . .

Judy: Have you had objections to any of your books being read by young people?

Paul: In my case the censoring has just been about the right amount. I want to give you my glib answer first.

Mine caused just the right amount of controversy—they'd only be banned in one or two tiny towns where you really had silly people—really harmless, and it actually gave me good publicity. It would put me on a little list so that people could take notice of, but it never damaged me. Since then however, I have had more occasions to be enlightened about the censoring process and some of the dangers that it has. So I don't take it as lightly now, and I think I am concerned also for my fellow writers who may run into deeper problems. It's not a big problem for me, because one, I don't use curse words. There was one book I used curse words in but I had new printings to take those out because they weren't necessary, and two, I tend to use classical themes lying underneath the adolescent excitement, and three, I don't use slang—I give an illusion of slang using colloquial approaches, using hyperboles, so that there is not much they can come after me for. What are they going to say?

GENERAL COMMENTARY

Stanley Hoffman

SOURCE: "Winning, Losing, But Above All Taking Risks: A Look at the Novels of Paul Zindel," in *The Lion and the Unicorn,* Vol. 2, No. 2, Fall, 1978, pp. 78-88.

My first contact with Paul Zindel was *The Pigman*. John, Lorraine, lonely old Mr. Pignati.

I cried.

I actually cried.

I loved it.

Next came *My Darling, My Hamburger*. I didn't love it nearly as much but certain parts moved me deeply. Maggie growing up, Liz disillusioned, Sean and Dennis going where? Not much plot, really, but plenty of feeling. Kind of nice.

I Never Loved Your Mind followed. Something was changing which I think a lot of readers didn't like. Unlike *Pigman* and *Hamburger,* novels which, like nearly all of Zindel's works, revolved around the actions of couples—boy meets girl and they team up to move the plot along—the "couple" in *I Never Loved Your Mind* rarely team up and one of them doesn't even live with her family. This last fact is a major departure for Zindel and the atmosphere of the novel, in part because of this, weaves a spell of potential hopelessness. Dewey, the male of the couple, may move forward at novel's end but the commune-living, free-loving Yvette might not turn out as fortunate. As with all of Zindel's couples, along the way of the story a certain innocence is lost, but the innocence is often heavy baggage without which the real world can be seen more clearly—and the clearer one can see, the better one might be able to cope. Indeed, if there is any one "message" that runs through Zindel's works, it has to be this: if reality is ugly, in facing it we can prepare ourselves to see beyond the ugliness to something hopeful. Thus, Dewey, after all his tribulations at Yvette's hands, closes out the novel on an up note.

> I don't really know what I'm going to do. It's not going to be that Love Land crap. And I'm not going to give civilization a kick in the behind, because I might need an appendectomy sometime.
>
> But I'm going to do something, and I have a strange feeling it's going to be phantasmagorically different.

The detractors of Zindel—a growing number, I suspect, though it's a safe bet his admirers are also on the increase—point to his seeming inevitable pessimism and its potential infectiousness on the young reader. Representative of this view is Myles McDowell, who writes [in *Children's Literature in Education* (March 1973)]:

> I think that the newer sub-Salinger writers, such as Zindel, despite their virtues of freshness and an authentic teenage voice are on the whole unsuitable for children. There is such an overall cynical depressive quality about Zindel's books, which seems to me to be destructive of values before values have properly had time to form. It is the depression I would want to protect emergent minds from.

McDowell is, I think, both right and wrong. Cynical depression is assuredly a large part of Zindel's teenage universe, yet to "protect emergent minds" from it recalls John Milton's warning in *Areopagitica* to the effect that "A cloistered virtue is no virtue at all." The question is whether Zindel's world is a real one and, if it is, should it be kept hidden from impressionable young minds. To this, Beverly A. Haley and Kenneth L. Donelson have some suggestive thoughts on the matter [*Elementary English* (October 1974)]:

> Paul Zindel is one writer who speaks to young people about man's cruelty. . . . In these amusing, provocative, and very-much-of-our-time works, Zindel presents questions to his readers, and if they care (and they do), they will search for answers. Their own answers.

In short, if Zindel is dangerous then we are all in trouble. More to the point seems to be not whether Zindel is dangerous as a philosopher, but rather whether his approach to the realities of life is vastly oversimplified. By that I mean are his novels constructed along formulated, predictable lines which ultimately render them shallow—the worst sin of a novelist, short of being boring, being that of emptiness. And, if so, why is he so popular? Is it because he does have something vital to offer or simply that he has fooled so many? I think the answer lies somewhere in between and is best discovered in his two latest books, *Confessions of a Teenage Baboon* and *The Undertaker's Gone Bananas.*

Next to *Pigman,* I think that *Baboon* is Zindel's most haunting novel in the best sense of that word. It stays with you long after it's been read and presents the most curious—and believable—adult character in any of his works. Indeed, the pathetic, lonely booze-hound, Lloyd, whose mother is days away from death in the room next to his, is even more poignant than Mr. Pignati in Zindel's first book. Similarly, the fifteen-year-old narrator of the novel, Chris, is Zindel's most moving—and believable—teenager. We get hints of this right off when Chris implores us at the end of chapter one:

> The only thing that's going on in my mind is that I hope when you finish reading this you won't hate me. Please don't despise me for being the one to tell you that the days of being Huckleberry Finn are gone forever.

Baboon may be, in fact, Zindel's best novel precisely because it breaks with the formulas of his past books. In a like manner, *Undertaker* may well be his worst because in it he reverts back to the formulas of old. Where *Baboon* is fresh, direct, a tiny sparkling gem of a story, *Undertaker* is stale, contrived, at times—God, I hate to say this—an embarrassment to read. Amazing that these two books are only a year apart; what that might say about the development of one writer's craft is, at the least, puzzling. Zindel may be the Jekyll and Hyde of modern young adult fiction; his books get better, worse, better, worse, and one never knows what will come next. Yes, it is an adventure, each separate path as unpredictable as the one before it and to follow.

In *Baboon,* Chris treks along with his insensitive domineering mother—even at fifteen, he is still forced by her to urinate in his own special milk bottle so as not to disturb those around him by having to use the bathroom!—who is a live-in nurse about town. Theirs is a semi-vagabond existence, their lives, to put it mildly, in a state of constant uncertainty and chaos. The mother is a high-strung neurotic who thrives on hysteria and yelling; Chris is a mellower neurotic whose major fetish centers around his dead father's gigantic Chesterfield coat which he takes with him from household to household. The present household, bizarre in the extreme, finds Chris's mother tending one Carmelita Diparti, an old woman stricken with terminal cancer coming home to die, a fact which permeates the novel's atmosphere. Her family consists of Lloyd Diparti, a strange, bitter, brooding man in his late 30s who throws nightly parties in the house. His constant companion is Harold, a fifteen-year-old who is Lloyd's cook and maid, and the house is always filled with boisterous teenagers. Apparently, Lloyd has no adult friends whatsoever.

The relationship formed between Lloyd and Chris—formed like a slow, masterful ballet, inching forward, quickly retreating, going back and forth in disarrayed but growing harmony—is the path to the latter's enlightenment, an enlightenment both profound and very possibly permanent. Lloyd is that pathetic, though all-too-real adult who has true wisdom to impart to everyone save himself. He knows the Truth that can potentially set everyone but him free. Near the end—the night, in face, of the man's suicide—Lloyd tells Chris:

the reason I was so mean to you was because you remind me of *me*. . . . What I'm saying is that maybe the reason I'm so demanding of you is because you remind me of *me* when I was your age. Half developed. Half conscious. And half a man. . . . And that means you only have half your work done. Take a look at me. I'm twice your age and where has it gotten me? My life is no better than it was when I was fifteen. And kid, I don't want to see you make the same mistakes I did. . . . I know what it's like to have a witch for a mother. And just because my father was around physically doesn't mean I had a father any more than you do. I really feel for you, kid, and I don't want to see you grow up twisted. . . . One of these days your dead father will let go of you, and you'll be free. No more a slave to a dream which can never come true. Then, kid, it's up to you. You can cut the power line your mother has plugged into you, and stop blaming her for your failures. Start accepting the responsibility for your own life and then you can be a man.

A few pages later, Lloyd has shot himself, the scene fully witnessed by Chris. Hours later, he is walking with his new friend, Rosemary, beneath the moonlit sky when all that Lloyd has tried to impart to him finally rings true.

The moon was playing tricks, casting only half a shadow. I suddenly realized that what seemed like an illusion was really true. I was only half a shadow and only half of what I could be. And it was at this instant something momentous happened to me. I remembered I had left my father's coat behind but this time it didn't matter. I felt as though I was unfolding under the moonlight. I was opening up like a seed that had been thrust painfully and deeply—even ruthlessly—into the ground and given a merciless warning and command to grow. The cloud that had been hanging over me for so many years of my life on earth was suddenly lifting thanks to an anguished, tormented man who now lay lifeless on a bed not far away. And when the moon moved again from behind the cloud it seemed I felt an understanding and a compassion for the entire human race. Especially for Lloyd, for Rosemary, for Helen [Chris's mother], for my father who had run away. . . . Even for a full moon there is always its dark side which can never be seen, which can never be fully known, and which will always be the mystery that is called Life. And I was ready to accept that, and yet for some reason I was most interested in the things in my life I *could* change. The things I could see if I tried hard enough. The things I *deserved,* as Lloyd had told me.

This from a boy who at book's beginning had to ask not to be despised for telling us "that the days of being Huckleberry Finn are gone forever." It is Zindel's most moving tribute to the possibilities of boys growing into men. Certainly *not* the product of cynicism and despair.

One would expect—would naturally *want* to expect—that the follow-up novel to this would be, if not superior, then at least brimming with a somewhat similar profundity—writers, like others, hopefully growing as they get older and a little wiser. Unfortunately, neither is the case here. *The Undertaker's Gone Bananas* is a shamelessly con-

trived story, disappointing in the extreme. It circles—as in *The Pigman*—around the adventures of two lonely teenagers, Bobby and Laurie, who live in a new luxury highrise in New Jersey, so new and so luxurious that—conveniently for the story about to unfold—most of the apartments are unoccupied. To add to the artificial eeriness of this, neighbors soon move in next door to Bobby, one Mr. and Mrs. Hulka, a boozing, arguing couple approaching the ennui of middle-age and stable affluence. Mr. Hulka is an undertaker, his wife—well, she is apparently just his wife. They make small talk when Bobby and Laurie come to welcome them to the building and they quickly show the teenagers how well they have turned superficial conversation into an art.

The Hulka family presence in the book seems pointless until one day Bobby hears screaming coming from their apartment and, looking into their terrace window (conveniently adjoining his own), the boy sees what he thinks is Mr. Hulka pummelling his wife to death. The police are called, but what Bobby thought is obviously not the case (Mrs. Hulka enters alive and well) and the cops leave with angry warnings on their tongues.

It is here where the plot strains our credulity to the breaking point. Strange noises come from the Hulka apartment—chains rattle, machines roar, finally the trash compactor is employed. Bobby is convinced that Hulka has indeed now killed his wife for sure, cut her up as only a veteran undertaker can and is about to take her out as literal garbage. He tells Laurie—whose skepticism at Bobby's imaginings is only surpassed by the reader's—who indulges him just for the sake of playing the game. Things follow swiftly now as Bobby closes in on the Hulkas' mystery. Without elaborating further—not for fear of spoiling the story but simply because there's little point—the truth is finally revealed when, snooping in the Hulka apartment, Laurie comes across Mrs. Hulka's dismembered head in the interior of the TV set, warm dripping blood and all. Wild chases ensue, including, even before the discovered head, Bobby swiping Mr. Hulka's hearse and driving it into the neighborhood McDonald's where not even his "peers" (though, except for Laurie, Bobby rather understandably has no peers) believe him. At the end, Hulka is nabbed, Bobby believed and—who knows, one guesses that's a "happy" ending of sorts.

What makes these outrageous contrivances even more embarrassing is Zindel's attempts to include them in a story where the two main characters are potentially so memorable and even charming. What happens, though, is that this potentiality gets buried under the spotty movements of the plot. Laurie is a girl obsessed with death. Indeed, her major preoccupation is ruminating on the scores of ways she can be killed. As for Bobby, he is afraid of something else, not made quite clear, afraid perhaps of being accepted by others so he makes sure they reject him before either he or his schoolmates has a chance. He has no friends aside from Laurie (conveniently, she hasn't any either), and the two of them team up as they weave their respective neuroses around each other. If I'm not being too clear here it's because the novel isn't either. All one can sense is the idea of brilliant characterization which has somehow failed in the execution, sacrificed to a plot that shouldn't be. Never has the possibility for brilliance been so hinted at without being realized. It is a shame.

Perhaps Zindel, at least in this genre, has few places left to go. If so, one would hope he comes to realize this and goes on to expand his evident talent elsewhere. At best, the erratic quality of his novels is disappointing; at worst, upsetting in the extreme. To modernize that famous old saying, "When he's good he's damn incredibly good; when he's bad, we wish we hadn't known him."

But lest this be the final thought, I think a word of appreciation is due. For even when Zindel is downright bad, it is so evident that we can learn from it. He is hardly ever mediocre and that, I think, is a virtue. And if he isn't always successful with his "young adults" he almost always hits the mark with older people, especially parents. Lloyd, though not a parent, is the next closest thing and his character may be Zindel's best. Chris's mother is also memorable and unique—a singularly unlikeable woman— and Zindel spares us nothing when dealing with these supposed adults. In his second work, ***My Darling, My Hamburger,*** we see this in most vivid fashion. Here is a brief scene presented in its entirety to show Zindel's portrait of a parent at its best. In it, Sean, boyfriend to Liz whom he really loves—his first love, be it noted—is introduced by his father to business friends. Sean is upset because Liz won't go "all the way"—though he views her in the purest way—and would love to ask his old man for advice. Also, Sean is an excellent writer, sensitive and generally interested in the arts. His father evidently has very different notions of his son. Sean has trouble just talking with the man.

"Dad!"

"We're in the den," Mr. Collins called back as he stirred a batch of martinis.

Sean came to the doorway. When he saw that his father had company, he decided he'd say hello and leave.

"Come on in," Mr. Collins boomed heartily. "You know Mr. Wilson and Mr. Stanley?"

"I don't want to interrupt."

"Hell, no. You come on in here. We're just talking about some of the good old college days—with a little straight business between halves." He slapped Mr. Stanley on the back, and the three laughed heartily.

"Hello," Sean said.

"Looks like you're going to have another football player in the family," Mr. Stanley beamed.

"Long as he applies himself, right, son?" Mr. Collins said. He put his arm around Sean for a moment. Then he refilled the glasses sitting in front of his guests. "Got a sixty-eight in physics, didn't you?"

"Yes, Dad."

"You're not going to play football anywhere with a sixty-eight in physics. Is he, boys?"

"I got a ninety-six in English."

"You're *supposed* to know English. It's physics. Physics. That's where the money is. Anybody'll tell you that. Right, Dan? Or chemistry. Mr. Wilson's in chemistry, you know."

"Dad . . ."

"Something the matter?" Mr. Collins asked.

"No."

"Need a little extra for your date?"

"I'm not seeing Liz tonight."

"What?" Mr. Collins let out one of his raucous laughs. He put his arm around Sean again and practically marched him closer to the smiling faces of Mr. Wilson and Mr. Stanley. "Saturday night and my boy's not going out. What happened with that little blond wildcat?"

"Dad . . ."

"She's giving you a hard time?"

Sean couldn't answer.

Mr. Collins turned to the others. "He's going hot and heavy with that Carstensen girl. Did you ever see her?"

Sean resented his father's tone and turned to get his arm off his shoulder. "She's a nice girl."

"You can say that again." Mr. Collins sat down, with an insinuating laugh. Mr. Wilson and Mr. Stanley joined in.

Sean looked at the three of them sitting in their deep plush chairs, and they reminded him of squatting Buddhas.

Then Mr. Collins spoke seriously. "Then what's the problem?"

Sean looked directly into his father's eyes. He wished that one day he could manage to talk to him—just talk, without all the put-on.

"Nothing," he said.

With this scene freshly in mind, one can remember Zindel at his best. He is absurdly uneven, but so what? Better to have him risk terrible books—trial and error is often the writer's lot; if we sometimes become subject to it, that is the risk of the reader—because somewhere he's bound to come up with another winner. To repeat, anything is better than the smooth, content consistency of mediocrity. And Paul Zindel can certainly never be accused of that.

John A. Davis

SOURCE: "Welcome Back, Zindel," in *The ALAN Review,* Vol. 9, No. 1, Fall, 1981, pp. 2-4, 10.

I have most recently been reminded of the show ["Welcome Back, Kotter"] as I read the two adolescent novels published by Paul Zindel in 1980: *The Pigman's Legacy* and *A Star for the Latecomer,* the latter written in collaboration with his wife, Bonnie. What called to mind the Kotter show, and particularly the show's theme song which welcomes Kotter back to where his talents are truly needed, is that in these two novels Zindel seems to have also come back where he is needed after something of a departure in *Pardon Me, You're Stepping on My Eyeball* and *Confessions of a Teenage Baboon*. This is not to say that these novels were not written for an adolescent audience, or that they were not read by the thousands of Zindel admirers, or that they failed to show an acute understanding of the adolescent experience. It is to say that Zindel's 1980 novels seem more akin to the vintage Zindel of *The Pigman, My Darling, My Hamburger* and *I Never Loved Your Mind,* an avuncular Zindel always nearby, always compassionate, always understanding, and above all, always reassuring his charges that although adolescence was a time of turmoil and stress they could meet it.

Pardon Me, You're Stepping on My Eyeball and *Confessions of a Teenage Baboon* seem hybrid Zindel. Marsh Mellow and Edna Shinglebox of *Pardon Me* and Chris Boyd of *Confessions* appear to be condemned to a legion of the damned with Zindel standing at the gates of Hell watching his progeny enter with no reassuring word or quip to alleviate their misery. The hybrid Zindel of these two books is a grafting of a Zindel who could balance the trials of his adolescents with humor, irony, and optimism—as he did in his other novels—to a Zindel who seems possessed of a Dostoevskian mood of gloom and despair.

Before attempting to demonstrate what I have suggested above, let me remove *The Undertaker's Gone Bananas* from the discussion. This book was advertised as Zindel's first murder-mystery and so it was. It is fast paced and roundly humorous but reveals only tangentially the character and persona of the adolescent. The usual concerns of Zindel's adolescents are subordinate to a Hardy Boys concern to unmask a killer. I read it as a deliberate departure by the author from his earlier novels where the adolescents were victims of their own frustrations; here Zindel used the macabre figure of a murderous undertaker to hound his adolescents. Perhaps the book was an exercise in restorative therapy, a kind of literary purgative for the agony of his two previous novels.

Certainly *Confessions* and *Pardon Me* show marked kinship to all of Zindel's novels. A survey of his twelve-year migration over the adolescent landscape will reveal the unique Zindel features found in all his novels. He unfailingly has pursued similar themes throughout. He has cast his dramas with like characters: the lost, lonely, becalmed, frightened, and frustrated adolescents. He peoples his books with dishonest parents or authority figures whom few of his adolescent characters hope to emulate. He accentuates the natural loneliness of the adolescent by the cruelty and indifference of ruthless parents and peers. He breaks the family bonds by death, divorce, or desertion. And in all, humor and irony intrude.

Zindel has a favorite storehouse of themes which he fictionally depicts from a Pandora's Box of adolescent anxieties, fears, dreams, and failures. One of the more persistent themes was elaborated initially in *The Pigman* where John Conlan and Lorraine Jensen recoil in horror at the prospect of reaching adulthood and acquiring its inevitable accretion of hypocrisy, deceit, and self-delusion as palliatives. John muses, "Maybe I would rather be dead than to turn into the kind of grown-up people I know." Maggie Tobin in *My Darling, My Hamburger* sees the penalties as well as the inevitability of having to accept an adult role in a somewhat philosophical vein at the book's end and accepts the necessity of change, not necessarily as desirable but as a factor in achieving one's adult integrity. In *I Never Loved Your Mind,* a kind of tongue-in-cheek Baedeker for the adolescent lured by the Hippie life, Dewey Daniels refuses to follow Yvette Goethals to her Taos commune and its promise of eternal adolescence, but only because he sees some peripheral good in the adult world where one might sometime need an appendectomy.

In *Confessions of a Teenage Baboon* and *Pardon Me, You're Stepping on My Eyeball* Chris Boyd and Marsh Mellow respectively hold tenaciously to their childhood by pursuing the spectral figure of a dead father as an anchor to a non-existent, dream-created childhood. Chris carries with him in his peregrinations with his nurse-mother the one solid, romantic relic left by his father, a Chesterfield coat. Marsh, in his wish-fulfillment fantasies, creates a romantic life-script worthy of Harlequin Romances in which he and his father are loved by all the exotic beauties of the world.

In *A Star for the Latecomer* Brooke Hillary passively views an adult life planned for her by a mother determined to make a star. Brooke herself prefers a love and marriage scenario, but for the most part is willing to accept her mother's equally romantic notion of a life of first nights and public admiration. The John and Lorraine of *The Pigman's Legacy,* although still students of Franklin High, are less inclined to view maturation with the horror shown in *The Pigman,* but they still cling to the child's romantic notion that life can be a mysterious and exciting adventure when they seclude Colonel Glenville from the talons of the IRS and arrange his deathbed marriage to Dolly Racinski.

Another premier theme in the Zindel canon is the adolescents' burden of accumulated guilt and its destructive aftermath. John and Lorraine appropriate the guilt for Mr. Pignati's death at the end of *The Pigman* and recognize that their part in his death has exacted a death of a part of their being, their innocence; it is, they feel, a terrible price to pay. In *The Pigman's Legacy* John and Lorraine assume responsibility for the Pigman's reincarnation, Colonel Glenville, because of a desire to atone for Mr. Pignati's death. But once again the two are partners in an act potentially as destructive as the wild party they threw at Mr. Pignati's home when John gambles away the modest nest egg Colonel Glenville entrusted to him. Once again the two adolescents have acquired a burden of guilt for their immature behavior.

In none of the other Zindel novels does the burden of guilt assume the proportions and generate the psychotic effects it has on Marsh Mellow. When his drunken father is run over by a bus, Marsh feels himself responsible, a crime of omission for not stopping his father's reckless drinking. This feeling of his culpability in his father's death has preyed on Marsh until he finally constructs a delusion in which his father is not dead but a prisoner of nebulous officials who are trying to silence his effort to reveal their collective perfidy. All of this Marsh fleshes out in his daily intercourse with Edna Shinglebox, in forged letters and in ambitious plans for his father's rescue, even though the urn containing his father's ashes rests all the while under Marsh's bed. The potential for a similar overwhelming accumulation of guilt is present in *A Star for the Latecomer* where Brooke watches her mother die of cancer without Brooke having made that one triumphant step toward stardom that her mother so longed for. However, the anguish Brooke feels for having failed her mother vanishes in the girl's realization that her mother's dreams for her were the somewhat selfish dreams of a frustrated woman and were not her own dreams.

As identical themes reappear in Zindel's novels so too do characters who might very well be the consequence of incestuous inbreeding in the writer's ink. Aside from the tormented adolescents burdened by feelings of guilt, inadequacy, and rejection, the most familiar figure in his works is the anguished parent, generally the mother, who is incapable of showing love or affection for the child because some real or imagined inadequacy or rejection has warped her life. The mothers of Lorraine and Chris have been deserted by their husbands and vent their life-hatred on their defenseless children. Marsh's mother in those rare moments of sobriety demeans and humiliates Marsh with charges that he is either a sex fiend or a drug addict or both, implying that this acorn did not fall far from the tree. That Zindel has not abandoned the lament of the deleterious effect of the possessive, frustrated mother is noticed in *A Star for the Latecomer*. Here Brooke's mother, whose life as a wife and mother was ultimately unsatisfactory, drives her daughter, with a callous obsession, to be a star, to be famous.

I mentioned earlier that irony is a prevalent feature in all of Zindel's novels, but nowhere is it more apparent than in a kind of archetypal scene of physical or psychical destruction that climaxes each novel. The incident, begun in adolescent innocence, ends as a kind of Gotterdammerung of adolescence where the fragile fabric clothing the adolescents' lives is shredded. It is as though Zindel feels the need to dramatize his compassion for the adolescents by some symbolic representation of the death of

adolescence and innocence, with flamboyant and theatrical proportions.

In *The Pigman* this scene is the roisterous party thrown by John and Lorraine. The destruction of Mr. Pignati's treasured collection of pigs and his wife's wedding dress also demolishes the sanctuary John and Lorraine had built against life. In *My Darling, My Hamburger* Liz undergoes her abortion on the night of the senior prom, a grim contrast, and among the other casualties are Maggie's romantic naivete and the adolescent quietude of Liz, Sean, Dennis, and Maggie. Zindel chooses a hippie commune, "Love Land," in *I Never Loved Your Mind* for a violent free-for-all among the "flower people" to inform Dewey of the fakery of the life Yvette has chosen and his ineptitude for such a farcical existence.

In *Pardon Me, You're Stepping on My Eyeball* Zindel produced a classic model for an adolescent Armageddon. A teenage party degenerates into an orgy of sex, drinking, drugs, and vandalism where the guests are rewarded for their folly by the awesome destruction of the hostess' beautiful home by fire. In this fire Marsh's pet raccoon, which has served him as a kind of lifeline to his humanity, burns to death. Another party, again unreal in its cast and consequences, serves as the catalyst to shatter Chris's fragile equilibrium in the world in *Confessions of a Teenage Baboon*. Lloyd Dipardi's drunken brawl with his adolescent faithful occurs as his mother dies in an adjoining room and terminates when Lloyd commits suicide, forcing Chris to a realization that there is and always will be a dark side to life.

The climactic scenes in Zindel's last two novels follow the Zindel guidelines but have more of the optimistic overtones underlying the conclusions to *The Pigman, My Darling, My Hamburger,* and *I Never Loved Your Mind.* In *A Star for the Latecomer* Brooke has her mother's coffin opened at the funeral home so she can place her dancing shoes in the coffin and whisper to her mother, "I may not be what you want me to be, but I do hope, whatever I choose, that you'll be proud of me." Only after the painful, agonizing death of her mother is Brooke free. Zindel's flair for the dramatic setting in which his adolescents apprehend the death of their innocence is apparent in *The Pigman's Legacy.* Here in a gaudy Atlantic City casino, amid all the pathetic dreams of miraculous wealth, John compulsively gambles away Colonel Glenville's money, to realize once again that he had trespassed into the adult world of lies, deceit, and delusion.

What is it then that caused *Confessions of a Teenage Baboon* and *Pardon Me, You're Stepping on My Eyeball* to stand out so starkly and ominously from the rest of Zindel's novels. It was not an alteration in the thematic insistence that adolescence is hell, no matter how it is viewed nostalgically over a distance of years. Nor was it the appearance of a new cast, for Chris, Marsh, and Edna, although more somber, less resilient, and quicker to despair, are the same troubled adolescents as John and Lorraine and Dewey and Brooke. It was not a different structural design since the two novels build to the same moment of truth, a disastrous and dramatic incident, which signals the end of childhood innocence and the acceptance, hereafter, of the responsibility for one's behavior. Nor were compassion and sympathy for the ineffectual and harassed adolescents absent in these novels; Zindel seems to love his various literary offspring equally.

The answer, I believe, can come only from the author himself. In the biographical data that has surfaced about Zindel since the success of *The Pigman* and his Pulitzer Prize play, *The Effects of Gamma Rays on Man-in-the Moon Marigolds,* there is evidence of a troubled and unhappy childhood, of agony and anger over the separation of his parents. One can only speculate that the Zindel who wrote *Confessions* and *Pardon Me* was deliberately purging some personal demons, demons that forbade even a modest relief to the miseries of Marsh or Edna or Chris. He allowed them no momentary interlude of adolescent happiness or rapture such as John and Lorraine enjoyed in Mr. Pignati's home, or as Brooke enjoyed with Brandon on their picnic, or as Dewey experienced as the lovely Yvette vacuumed the living room in the nude. Instead March, Edna, and Chris suffer a continuous anxiety, endure misfortune and humiliation without hope of relief, even with a sometimes psychotic acceptance of the inevitability of despair. In only one other adolescent novelist have I noticed this propensity for making the adolescent the *total* victim, Robert Cormier in *The Chocolate War* and *I Am the Cheese.*

Marsh, Edna, and Chris are victimized relentlessly throughout by an unrelieved anxiety; Marsh is unable to free himself of the guilt of his father's death; Edna is constantly reminded at home and at school that she is the "Super-Loser"; Chris suffers the endless indignity of squatting in the homes of strangers who are sick or dying. The chances for relief from these pressures are defeated constantly by the characters themselves or those around them, or merely by an unlucky throw of fate's dice. Marsh, who has lied to himself to keep his father alive, perpetuates the lies to maintain the one contact with reality he has found, his tenuous friendship with Edna. Edna, who has come to accept her mother's appraisal of her as "a sad sack," "in the forest of romance a desert," is unwilling to jeopardize the relative safety of anonymity and views high school as "just one more place (she) won't have to face the world." Chris' reclusive and hapless life of passively following his mother from case to case is mocked by the scorn and derision of the cruel, but well-intentioned Lloyd Dipardi and the innocent promiscuity of Rosemary. These anxieties mercilessly hound the three to the novels' conclusions.

The unrelieved tensions weighing on each character are compounded by the squalid, sterile, or hostile environments in which the three characters forever move. Marsh's home is a pigsty; his high school life includes daily attendance in a group-therapy-experience class peopled by the school's misfits, including Edna; his mother drinks herself senseless each night; he frequents the "kooky" bars his father has raised him in. Edna's home life is palled by her parents' loveless marriage; her natural sexual anxi-

eties are magnified by her mother's intention to make her into a likely candidate for a conventional middle class marriage with no concern as to how the transformation is achieved—she suggests Edna engage in a little "hanky-panky" on her dates and do a little research to learn where the erogenous zones are located; her despair in dealing with Marsh takes her to the foul-smelling, roach-infested shack of a charlatan palmist named Miss Aimee. Chris passes his adolescent years living in an attic or cubicle in the homes where his mother is nursing; his school life is equally lonely and he is derided by his classmates as a mother's boy; he is in constant contact with the sick and dying; his meager childhood possessions, which fit into one small, cheap cardboard suitcase, contain only one treasure, his dead father's Chesterfield coat. The succession of scenes depicting Marsh's, Edna's, and Chris' trails remind me of nothing so much as Hogarth's pen and ink sketches of the miseries of London life.

Even the redoubtable Zindel humor has taken on a black cast in these two novels. Although there is always an undercurrent of pathos in Zindel's humor, the humorous episodes in *Confessions* and *Pardon Me* do nothing so much as reinforce the misery of the moment. Witness the scene in the office of the guidance counselor where Edna's mother is tripping over herself in her haste to catalogue Edna's failures as Edna listens in total despair; or friendless Marsh's frantic recital of all the friends he has made among the freaks of the circus and of the women who just can not resist him—an exotic dancer in a topless bar, a curvaceous daughter of a congressman, hookers; or Chris's mother's wholesale thievery from the Dipardi's while she refuses to allow Chris to use Lloyd Dipardi's toilet and instead presents him with an empty milk carton.

But with *The Pigman's Legacy* and *A Star for the Latecomer* the Zindel of the earliest novels is back, back where he is needed. The latter-day Lorraine and John leave the dead Colonel's room where Dolly now performs the mourning rites to walk past the hospital's nursery where the promise of life is most obvious, a promise which prompts a declaration of love for Lorraine by John. Brooke survives her mother's agonizing death with a regret that she was unable to fulfill her mother's dreams but with no sense of personal guilt. The reassurance Zindel offered his earlier adolescents is back, and though adolescent readers of Zindel will never be led to the false notion that the quality of adolescence is unbounded joy, with the rerouted Zindel they will not see in it only the blackness suggested by *Confessions of a Teenage Baboon* and *Pardon Me, You're Stepping on My Eyeball.*

And this, I believe, is good. Adolescence is not a time to demolish thoroughly those faint lingering childhood myths of the world's perfection; it is a time to call the adolescents' attention to some of the fraying edges of the myth, to some of the imperfections of the warp and woof of the fabric, but not a time to destroy the myth's whole cloth. If adolescents are permitted to let the myths dissolve slowly, I feel there is far more likelihood they will attempt to reweave the myth as best they can throughout their lives. Welcome back, Zindel.

Glenn Edward Sadler

SOURCE: "The Unspoken Power of Humor in Paul Zindel's *Pigman* Trilogy," in *Teaching and Learning Literature,* Vol. 6, No. 3, January-February, 1997, pp. 30-5.

Paul Zindel's novel, *The Pigman,* which was published in 1968, about two lonely high school teens who find themselves caught up in the process of growing up is still one of the most impressive and widely read YA novels ever written. As a playwright, screenwriter, and novelist, Zindel has won numerous awards including the Pulitzer Prize for drama in 1971 for his play *The Effect of Gamma Rays on Man-in-the-Moon Marigolds.* A former high school chemistry teacher, Zindel draws on his scientific background in his recent YA novel, for reluctant readers, *Loch.* Zindel continues to write novels which have a special appeal for both teens and adults who find something extraordinary and captivating in each of his novels. His novels have been described as being "wacky, zany" and written in a "contemporary idiom" that provokes laughter and genuine delight.

The major praise of Zindel's work is that he demonstrates an unusual ability to empathize with his young adult audience. Explaining his commitment to YA fiction, Zindel wrote: "Young adult books should be used to improve the lives of our youth. A book is created by a writer who observes life and then freezes it into words. I think here's where we really need the school experience and the inspired teacher and librarian. . . . What I'm trying to say is that a YA book in particular is a grand opportunity to take full advantage of word and phrase configuration as a take-off point from which a boy and girl can enter into *performance* of life. Jung knew a single alien letter from an unknown alphabet was enough to trigger endless thoughts in the human mind. Imagine the power of a whole book in the hands of a teacher and class. Right now in America we are just beginning to dream of turning away from fact bombardment and opening up our ears to listen to the kids."

Although Zindel wrote these words in 1980, they still reflect his theory of the power of books to change the lives of young adults. "Listen to the kids" is a phrase that Zindel repeatedly uses to insist that teachers and parents stop and take time to listen to what their teens are saying to them. Zindel continues: "So many children in schools are denied expressing their experiences, and hearing of the experiences of others. So many never had a chance to think of goals, success paths, or, simply opportunities to practice showing their emotions."

"Our schools have been for open books and closed mouths. To hell with that. Let's let our kids lift their books *and* their voices. Maybe, just maybe, the young will no longer hate reading, school, and the world as much. Words should at every age mean a better life for the reader."

Helping YA readers to reach maturity, and learn to speak, think, and act for themselves has been Zindel's major concern throughout his lengthy literary career. In his classic trio—*The Pigman, The Pigman's Legacy,* and *The Pigman and Me*—Zindel is at his best as a YA author. Considered individually or as a trilogy, the "Pigman" books prove that teens can establish meaningful relationships with adults and that they can learn much about life in the process. Noted for their humorous approach to life, wacky situations, and unconventional characters, which are surprisingly developed without much detail, the "Pigman" books represent for some critics the best of YA novels. Other readers, less enthusiastic about Zindel's work, say his books are overly simplistic, morally confusing, and offensive to parents, who generally are portrayed in a rather negative manner.

Taking a Journey to Meet the Pigman

Since the publication of *The Pigman's Legacy* in 1980 readers have been interested in the origin of the story and the characters. In answer to numerous requests for more information about how he wrote the book, Zindel published in 1991 *The Pigman and Me,* in which he describes his own early life as a teen.

Starting with the family's move to Staten Island, New York, the book recounts the major events and influences on Zindel. One such influence was his mother, who proudly announced to her son and daughter after their sudden move: "Yes, kids! We'll have a home of our own, with nobody to tell us what to do! Nobody! It'll be *Heaven!*" Although not "heaven" the family's new home did provide the individual freedom and creative way of life that seems to have been characteristic of the Zindel family.

It is perhaps best to begin Zindel's "Pigman" trilogy by reading *The Pigman* first before his fictionalized biography, *The Pigman and Me.* It is helpful for students to know that *The Pigman and Me* contains sketches of Zindel's life as a teenager as well as relating how he came to write *The Pigman* and its sequel, *The Pigman's Legacy.* In 1993, at an ALAN (Assembly on Literature for Adolescents, National Council of Teachers of English) breakfast, Zindel retold the story of his meeting with The Pigman and how he wrote the book. This amusing and informative piece is an ideal introduction to reading the "Pigman" books. Zindel tells us that the Pigman, Angelo Pignati, John Conlan, and Lorraine Jensen had their origin in real people whom he met when he housesat at The Horrman Castle, which had previously been a convent. "By the time I moved in," Zindel says, "the castle was an ex-convent, and I had to sleep in a bed that nine nuns had died in, not all at the same time."

Like the characters in *The Pigman,* Zindel's own teenage years were somewhat troublesome. His reactions to life at school were more of a sporting game than a pursuit of serious study. Often playing pranks on others (students and faculty) became his only creative escape from an academic environment that provided him with little that he valued or seemed to need. Lorraine's meeting with John, at the beginning of *The Pigman,* is typical of Zindel's own carefree, sometimes irritating behavior as a teen:

Then one day John had to sit next to me on the bus because all the other seats were taken. He wasn't sitting there for more than two minutes before he started laughing. Laughing right out loud, but not to anyone. I was so embarrassed I wanted to cry because I thought for sure he was laughing at me . . .

Making Teens Laugh at Right and Wrong

One of the major problems facing the young adult writer today is how to treat moral justice in a YA novel. Most YA novelists believe it is crucial for the teen reader to comprehend the consequences of their characters' actions particularly when their behavior brings harm upon themselves and others. This is especially important when the characters violate a moral law of human behavior that may have serious negative results. I recall hearing Paul Zindel say, when he and his wife Bonnie were guest lecturers for my YA class of 300 at UCLA, that laughter is one of the YA author's greatest weapons for moral justice. Teens, claimed Zindel, can be influenced far better by laughter than by sermons and direct confrontation. Because teens are trying to find their way as adults, they are keenly aware of the moral attitudes and actions of others. But they resent being pressured into making moral decisions suggested by adults.

What appeals most to YA readers about the "Pigman" books is that its main characters, John and Lorraine, learn without pressure from adults to make decisions for themselves. Through their association with the lonely Mr. Pignati, John and Lorraine find the comfort of true parental guidance normally missing in their lives. As they start taking care of the Pigman, they also begin to learn some of life's most meaningful lessons.

It is interesting to trace the steps in John and Lorraine's guarded acceptance of the Pigman in contrast to his open acceptance of them from the beginning. Gradually, as the Pigman shares his home and interests with John and Lorraine, they not only are drawn into his isolated world but become participants in it as well.

Finding Surrogate Parents and Children

Because many adolescents today have to cope with the complexities of a changing moral structure and face the challenge of finding themselves a sensible place within that structure as well, a major theme that appears in many of today's YA novels is that of personal exploration. In most instances, the responses teenagers get to their questions and concerns about relating to the often confusing circuitry of daily life depend upon the quality of involvement of adults in their lives. Parents are frequently considered to be nothing more than—as John calls his—"the Old Lady and the Bore." Nicknames which are not actually disrespectful or as derogatory as they may seem from the teen's point of view. By using these descriptions of parents, Zindel is attempting only to see them through the eyes of their own teens, not criticizing all parents. Adults frequently forget how they sometimes felt about their own parents when they were teens. Because John's and Lor-

raine's parents are unwilling (or unable?) to give their children the time and affection that they require, their children must look elsewhere for the parenting they so desperately need.

An underlining motif throughout the "Pigman" books is the fact we learn at the beginning of *The Pigman,* that neither John nor Lorraine like school or find it meaningful. John exclaims: "I don't like school, which you might say is one of the factors that got us involved with this old guy we nicknamed the Pigman." And Lorraine confesses: "I was in a severe state of depression the first few weeks because no one spoke to me." Both John and Lorraine are looking, as so many teens are today, for experiences of life together outside the classroom. They are looking for a life-adventure and they find it with the Pigman. The acceptance they experience with Mr. Pignati, is in sharp contrast to what they experience at home: "Eat your peas, John," the Old Lady said, dabbing her mouth with a napkin. "Don't roll them around." John, describing Mr. Pignati's acceptance comments: "It was great how happy he was to see us. I can't remember Bore, or my mother either for that matter, ever looking happy to see me, let alone when I came into the house with a friend."

One of the most striking features of the "Pigman" books is Zindel's personal narrative style. With a rapid succession of alternating chapters and direct dialogue, he allows the reader to hear how John and Lorraine feel and react to situations. It is almost as if one were watching a play, listening to the characters reveal their inner feelings. The reader experiences the story from two points of view.

As the narrative develops the reader follows John's and Lorraine's comments about each other, and on life in general. The friendship that develops between John and Lorraine is one many teenagers will come to admire—and to some extent wish that they, too, will someday be able to enjoy a similar relationship. Along with filling the parental roles missing in John and Lorraine's life, the Pigman also becomes their friend, confidante, and teacher.

Central to Zindel's "Pigman" books is the idea that teenagers need the companionship of an adult with whom they can share life's anxieties. Finding one's Pigman is like discovering one's true self in advance. After a visit with the Pigman, Lorraine reflects:

> When I got home that night, I thought of them [the Pigman and his wife] again, but another thought struck me. I realized how many things the Pigman and his wife must have shared—even the fun of preparing food. Good food is supposed to produce good conversation, I've heard. I guess it's no wonder my mother and I never had an interesting conversation when all we eat is canned soup, chop suey, and instant coffee.

Throughout the story of *The Pigman* John and Lorraine repeatedly make comparisons between their life at home and life with their newfound friend. In contrast to the "don'ts" John hears constantly at home, the Pigman invites him to: " . . . please do whatever you like. Make yourself comfortable. If you want something out of the refrigerator, help yourself. I want you to feel at home." This sense of being "at home," or spirit of place is a recurring experience for John and Lorraine throughout their adventures with the Pigman.

Establishing a Meaningful Relationship

What John and Lorraine learn most from their involvement with Mr. Pignati is that relationships of any kind are built on trust and mutual acceptance. That honesty is essential if the relationship is to survive. Following the pattern of the traditional fairy tale, Zindel cleverly builds a strong relationship between the teens and the Pigman, then introduces trials which test the permanence of the relationship.

Even the best relationships may not last forever. And so it is with John, Lorraine, and their Pigman. It is at the beginning of chapter 11 that John and Lorraine, placed in the context of confirming reality learn that good times also run their course. Roles become reversed as John and Lorraine enter "parenthood" and attend as best as they can, to the needs of the hospitalized Pigman, who is now the child. One of the most moving scenes in the novel takes place as the teens, laden with flowers, come to visit Pignati. They find him with a "great big grin on his face" and enjoying his stay in hospital like a guest in a hotel. With the keys to his house, John and Lorraine now must try out their new roles of man and wife—but are they ready for these roles?

Teens Face Developmental Tasks

An interesting approach to many young adult novels is to consider the relationship of adolescent needs and expectations with those of the characters in the novel. [In *Identity and the Life Cycle* (1959), Erik] Erikson suggests the major task of teens is to formulate or reformulate a sense of personal identity. The question of "Who am I? is being asked by most teens. . . .

It is interesting to note that throughout **The Pigman** Zindel seems to be aware of the developmental tasks facing most teens and progressively allows John and Lorraine to experience several of these with a surprising degree of success: new and more mature relations with each other; a more highly defined sense of masculine and feminine roles; emotional independence from parents; preparation toward marriage and family; and a sense of social responsibility.

In the last four chapters of **The Pigman** both John and Lorraine experience the joys, frustrations, and sorrows of parenthood—without actually becoming parents themselves. In words charged with emotion, John, who up to this point has been unable to experience life with little more than a shrug or a flippant comment, realizes that life does have its serious side and that there is actually no one to blame for life's losses:

'Let's go, Lorraine,' I [John] said softly, standing beside her. I lowered the sunglasses, and she took them

again trying to get them, almost dropping them again trying to get them on. Her hand lingered near mine, and I took it gently. She seemed funny peering up at me over the thin metal rims. We looked at each other. There was no need to smile or tell a joke or run for roller skates. Without a word, I think we both understood.

In language that teen readers will perhaps understand better than adults, Zindel concludes his novel with simplicity and few words, suggesting that the unspoken word is for teens more powerful, in the end, then all the lectures in the world.

TITLE COMMENTARY

CONFESSIONS OF A TEENAGE BABOON (1977)

Kirkus Reviews

SOURCE: A review of *Confessions of a Teenage Baboon,* in *Kirkus Reviews,* Vol. XLV, No. 18, September 15, 1977, pp. 996-97.

A misfit like most of Zindel's teenagers, Chris is more than usually dislocated, living in a sleazy hotel with his dominating mother between her assignments as a live-in practical nurse. Her latest case takes them to the home of an old lady who has been discharged from the hospital to die in the company of her senile, reclusive husband, her 30-year-old son Lloyd, and Lloyd's teenage friend Harold, about sixteen, who does the cooking and all but lives in the house. Mom clashes at once with boorish, drunken Lloyd, who fills the house with partying teenagers in seeming disregard for his suffering mother. Chris too is disturbed by Lloyd's rude badgering, but then it does appear that Lloyd is only trying to shape him up. It seems they have something in common (their mothers—Lloyd's being almost literally castrating, having come after him with scissors when he was a "naughty" child). By that last wild night—when Mom gets the police after Lloyd for unspecified offenses against Harold, the old lady quietly dies, and Lloyd shoots himself in the head—Chris has taken his lesson to heart. Though more organic than Marsh Mallow's cure in . . . *Eyeball,* Chris' sudden emancipation is a bit more than the theatrical characterization will bear. But it's hard to fault in the presence of Zindel's caustic comic touch (witness the old lady, who bites Chris and speaks her crazy mind) and his talent for spotlighting bizarre and dramatic scenes. You won't be moved by Lloyd's suicide (since **Pigman,** it's been hard to feel for Zindel's characters), but you will be fascinated by his smashing performance.

Janet P. Benestad

SOURCE: A review of *Confessions of a Teenage Ba-*

boon, in *Best Sellers,* Vol. 37, No. 11, February, 1978, p. 368.

Dominated by his overbearing mother, Chris is a fifteen-year-old misfit. It is to this that he confesses, and the story he tells in *Confessions of a Teenage Baboon* is about his redemption from the hell brought on by such a sin.

Chris' redeemer is Lloyd Dipardi. At thirty years old, Lloyd is friendless, except for sixteen-year-old Harold, and drunk most of the time. His favorite entertainment is giving wild, lewd parties for the neighborhood teenagers. He is kind to no one and seems to take pleasure in humiliating everyone around him, especially Chris, in whom Lloyd sees the image of himself fifteen years ago. Not until the last, bizarre night of Lloyd's life does Chris realize what Lloyd is trying to tell him—to accept responsibility for himself and let no one, even his mother, degrade or emasculate him.

Through Chris' *Confessions,* Zindel explores a most delicate and serious problem—the acute suffering of a teenager whose mother's domination and insensitivity prevent him from becoming a man. Zindel's treatment is sympathetic, realistic, and appropriately written for a young adult audience. It portrays vividly the moral bankruptcy of modern man in the character of Lloyd, who sees his problems clearly yet is incapable of coping with them in any way other than to sink deeper into immorality. It is sad, and I think an exaggeration on Zindel's part, to suggest that this culture is so destitute that help for a boy like Chris can come only from a derelict.

Isabel Quigly

SOURCE: "Banking on Lloyd," in *The Times Literary Supplement,* No. 3966, April 7, 1978, p. 383.

The articulate American teenager is always a credible narrator for a teenage novel and Chris Boyd, hero of *Confessions of a Teenage Baboon,* is no exception. Like the other heroes of Paul Zindel's books he can explain, in language that comes convincingly from a sixteen year old, what the bizarre circumstances of his life have brought him to. His mother is a kleptomaniac nurse who takes him round to her patients' houses when she's hired. In between jobs they live out of two suitcases and three shopping bags in a rundown rooming house called the Ritz Hotel. So, no home, no stability, and—since he ran off when Chris was five and then died—no father. Chris's baboonery strikes no one till he and his mother land up looking after an apparently sweet old lady with an apparently alcoholic, violent son of thirty called Lloyd. The sweet old lady turns out to have some old habits (such as biting people) and her son some socially suspect attitudes and ways of behaving. But he does seem to care that Chris is being crushed by his mother and is lonely, dissatisfied, hopeless, and a loser; a degree of psychic disorder that calls for tough treatment, which, in his way, Lloyd seems to try and give him. The result: the police, blackmail, violence, death.

Is Lloyd a corrupter of local youth, as seems clear to most outsiders, certainly to anyone who accepts today's sexual and psychological cliches? Or a Socratic figure who gives youngsters self-knowledge and self-respect, and, out of his own failures, tries to teach them to overcome theirs?

Paul Zindel makes his points about compassion and the unlikely forms of human goodness with tender eccentricity of expression. His action is fast, noisy, explosive; people's behaviour in it makes one uneasily aware of one's own snap judgments and cowardice in the face of the ambiguous or the half-understood: the Lloyds around us, so easily labelled and then comfortably dismissed.

Needless to say, it is not the stuff that teenage novels used to deal with; but then the stuff of teenage life is not what it used to be, either, and what counts is the way Paul Zindel handles it, with a delicacy at once funny and heart-felt, outspoken and sensitive. He comments on the mess that adults have made of the world their children inherit by showing, with candour but a certain gentleness as well, a young-eyed view of it. His children are never type-cast, nor are the situations he puts them in. They show the variety as well as the weirdness of behaviour and of life itself; thus stretching teenage experience and, more importantly, imagination.

M. Crouch

SOURCE: A review of *Confessions of a Teenage Baboon,* in *The Junior Bookshelf,* Vol. 42, No. 4, August, 1978, pp. 214-15.

The famous Zindel shock-tactics are not quite so much in evidence here. Can he really be moving into a mellow middle-age? Or is it that his readers have become tougher and more resistant? "I'm afraid it's going to shock a few people", he warns on the first page, but he scarcely sustains the threat—or promise.

Chris is a bit of a mother's boy. It is not really his fault. He had a perfectly good father, but he went out one day to buy an evening paper and finished up in Mexico. So Chris grows up under mother's powerful thumb, sustained only by the sight of his father's treasured overcoat. It is a handsome garment, but—symbolically—it is a great deal too big for the boy.

Mother—he calls her Helen—carts him around with her on her jobs as a resident nurse. When she is assigned to a dear old lady named Carmelita Dipardi, Chris comes under the devastating influence of the patient's son Lloyd. Lloyd and Helen detest one another at sight, and Chris becomes an involuntary ball to be kicked about between them. It is a dreadful household, and scarcely the right setting for a terminal illness. Carmelita dies to the sound of rowdy parties and noisier fights. Lloyd, who has made a mess of his own life, tells Chris how to put his affairs to rights, and, in a sense, he does so. At least he detaches himself from his father's coat and his mother's apron-strings, and learns instead how to hold a nice girl's hand.

Mr. Zindel is of course a master of colloquial adolescent (American) speech. He is perhaps overfond of wisecracks, especially similes, and he keeps the verbal tension at full stress all the time. He tells the English teenager, in this book, all he needs to know, and possibly more, about his American counterpart. One admires his shrewdness and his breadth of sympathies, without wishing to apply the former or emulate the latter. He lacks, I feel, one important attribute of the really good novelist, the ability to involve the reader. It is never difficult to retain one's detachment and independence of judgment.

THE UNDERTAKER'S GONE BANANAS (1978)

Karen M. Klockner

SOURCE: A review of *The Undertaker's Gone Bananas,* in *The Horn Book Magazine,* Vol. LV, No. 1, February, 1979, p. 73.

The author's books can be identified by an ironic blend of tongue-in-cheek humor and a sympathetic treatment of character. Bobby Perkins is constantly being punished in school for his rebellious, independent attitude; Lauri Geddes suffers from a fear that everyone is trying to kill her. The two become friends—"as close as if they had signed a pact in blood"—on the night Lauri stands up to the police on Bobby's behalf. Lauri's feelings for Bobby are romantic, and though he never expresses such inclinations, the friendship remains unshakable. The plot centers around Bobby's suspicions that Mr. Hulka—the undertaker who has moved into the apartment next door—is attempting to murder his wife. Lauri is the only one who takes Bobby seriously, and in this case even she is doubtful. In pursuit of evidence, the two find themselves inside such unlikely places as a shiny metal coffin in Mr. Hulka's funeral parlor and a locked apartment which Mr. Hulka is trying to break into. Bobby is not nearly as hysterical a character as Marsh in *Pardon Me, You're Stepping on My Eyeball!,* but he has some of the same tendencies. Although there are a few grisly scenes, the narrative is thoroughly entertaining and filled with genuine humor; it has all the ingredients of a suspenseful murder mystery, complete with the hero and heroine riding off together at the end.

Bernard Weinstein

SOURCE: A review of *The Undertaker's Gone Bananas,* in *Best Sellers,* Vol. 38, No. 12, March, 1979, p. 411.

The central character is Bobby Perkins, a precocious, cynical, Salingerian fifteen-year-old, who plays at being an outcast among his peers, living in the illusion of his own temperamental and moral superiority. "The kids all react to me in the worst ways," he says. "The boys particularly. They think I'm an idiot and a professional jerk because I hold poetry, goodness and beauty above other qualities." Equally isolated is Lauri Geddes, another teen-

ager who falls into love and friendship with Bobby. Having witnessed the tragic deaths by fire of a neighborhood, she has become morbidly obsessed with the imminence of her own death.

These two adolescent fugitives from normalcy meet and form a warm and nutritive friendship, the fulcrum of which is their obsession with a sinister neighbor who may or may not have murdered his wife. Most of the book is taken up with their stalking of the mysterious undertaker, Mr. Hulka, and their frustration at the hands of various authority figures.

The murder mystery is sometimes labored and unconvincing (imagine a real-life villain named Hulka, who is also an undertaker; or consider the facile way Lauri recovers from her trauma at the end). The novel sometimes seems like an amalgam of *Catcher in the Rye* and Hitchcock's *Rear Window,* but the scenes between Bobby and Lauri hold a good deal of warmth and conviction and a sensitivity to the way contemporary teenagers talk and act.

A. R. Williams

SOURCE: A review of *The Undertaker's Gone Bananas,* in *The Junior Bookshelf,* Vol. 43, No. 4, August, 1979, p. 231.

Possibly less zany and better constructed than one or two of Paul Zindel's previous novels, **The Undertaker's Gone Bananas** has a riveting situation at its centre—the possibility of a murder in the undertaker's flat adjacent to that of Bobby Perkins—but no one will believe Bobby, and Lauri Geddes, although Lauri is not entirely convinced a large part of the time. It is a long haul to the solution of this mystery but Zindel does not allow adults—except for the police and the Hulkas—to intrude on the boy and girl partnership in investigation to any extent. The dialogue seems sharper and more relevant in the absence of anyone to impress, but there is still plenty of fun.

A STAR FOR THE LATECOMER (with wife, Bonnie Zindel, 1980)

Jack Forman

SOURCE: A review of *A Star for the Latecomer,* in *School Library Journal,* Vol. 26, No. 8, April, 1980, pp. 129-30.

Whatever one expects of a novel by Paul Zindel, this is not it. (It is co-authored by his wife.) There are no drunk mothers, wayward fathers, and "off the wall" kids trying to find one another. There is not even the ambiguous mixture of cynicism and hope which has become the Zindel trademark. What there is is a sugarcoated though surprisingly moving family story and teen romance about a 16-year-old, Long Island girl named Brooke Hillary, who attends a Manhattan high school for potential stars in the performing arts. (Brooke's mother has convinced her that she will be a great dancer someday.) With an appealing, sometimes hard-to-believe naivete, Brooke narrates the past year of her life—a time when she learns of her mother's terminal illness, experiences "first love" and "disappointment" (in the tradition of soda shops and good night kisses), and discovers that her real aspirations have nothing to do with her mother's dream for her. What makes this story so unusual is the warm, close relationship Brooke has with her mother—and the involving, heartrending scenes of Brooke seeing her mother waste away physically while fighting valiantly against pain to maintain her dignity and strong support for Brooke. The rest of the characters are one-dimensional and almost incidental to the story—an older brother who can't face his mother's death; a father who maintains a constant and monotonously loving support; a boy friend whose rising stardom takes away from any feeling he had for Brooke; and just to show the insensitivity of the world, an agent who offers Brooke a job if she will sleep with him.

Kirkus Reviews

SOURCE: A review of *A Star for the Latecomer*, in *Kirkus Reviews,* Vol. XLVIII, No. 7, April 1, 1980, p. 444.

Unpromising at first glance, but then an agreeable surprise on several counts. First, this is about a 16-year-old girl whose mother is dying of cancer, and the two are overly attached to one another and express those feelings; but if some of the lines are maudlin the tone of the story isn't, because the authors know the difference between the girl's viewpoint and their own and don't force readers to identify with her. Second, the mother is one of those who wants her daughter to fulfill her own longings: she's had Brooke dancing since age three, sends her to auditions and a special school, and Brooke tries desperately for her mother's sake to get that one break that will start her to stardom before her mother dies. Yet, though the mother is grossly wrong (when she does die, Brooke feels freed from a career she never wanted), she is also warm and attractive, not one of those monster middle-class mothers who inhabit the suburbs of much juvenile fiction. A third surprise is that though Paul Zindel is co-author (with his wife Bonnie), this is played straight, without his usual bizarre social-satiric enlargements. Still, this being Zindel, the performing-child scenes are just a little sharper, Brooke's typical teenage fantasies just a little more convincingly hers, and her relationship with her mother just a little less black-or-white than in other stories of child-star trials or bereavement.

Margery Fisher

SOURCE: A review of *A Star for the Latecomer*, in *Growing Point,* Vol. 19, No. 3, September, 1980, p. 3760.

Brooke Hillary was given dancing lessons at the age of three to correct a disability in her leg but the lessons continued mainly because of her mother's passionate ambitions for her and by the age of sixteen Brooke has

accepted her narrowly specialised life as a sacred duty, for her mother is dying of cancer and she must achieve success quickly, putting aside her attachment to handsome Brandon and her envy of her older brother's sturdy independence, and putting aside too the feeling that she is denying her true self in submitting to this exclusive life. It is not until a year after her mother's death that the girl admits she has followed the wrong path. The long-drawn-out personal confession, and the gruesomely sentimental conversations with her mother, make this a story almost ludicrously over-written, the story of a situation rather than of a person.

THE PIGMAN'S LEGACY (1980)

Mary M. Burns

SOURCE: A review of *The Pigman's Legacy,* in *The Horn Book Magazine,* Vol. LVI, No. 5, October, 1980, pp. 531-32.

Published in 1968, **The Pigman** was instrumental in establishing the current realistic teenage novel as a distinct genre; and after more than a decade the author has produced a sequel to this frequently discussed work of fiction for adolescents. He continues to use the framework of the first story; and, as before, the milieu is Staten Island. John Conlan and Lorraine Jensen again alternate in supplying an account of their adventures; and the narrators continue in their original, often brash style, even to the use of symbols in place of profanity. Guilt-ridden because of the Pigman's death, they cannot avoid visiting the old man's derelict house, where they find—coincidentally—another elderly tenant, Colonel Glenville, a former builder of subways, who is ill and hiding from the Internal Revenue Service. They help and humor him but soon realize that his end is near. In this second round of zany experiences with an old man, John and Lorraine discover that they are in love and feel that they have received a legacy of life, not of death, from the Pigman. Although the two teenagers are still at loggerheads with their parents, they have developed a sense of maturity and responsibility. For example, Lorraine writes, "Sometimes I wish schools could just teach sex ignorance courses so I could spend more time being myself and less time worrying about what everybody else is doing." As in his most effective writings—adult as well as juvenile—the author has made use of contemporary jargon, quirky characters, and bizarre situations to uncover a fundamentally human meaning lurking beneath the madness.

Sally Holmes Holtze

SOURCE: A review of *The Pigman's Legacy,* in *School Library Journal,* Vol. 27, No. 2, October, 1980, p. 160.

Four months after the end of **The Pigman,** John and Lorraine discover Gus, a sick, lonely old man, living inside Mr Pignati's house and force themselves on him in friendship. They tell the story in the same alternating first-person chapters; similarities from the plot (Gus dies at the novel's climax) to small incidents (Gus initiates a psycho-analyzing parlor game as Mr. Pignati did), to vocabulary and jokes ("five-fingered discount" for shoplifting) parrot *The Pigman,* but the strong characterization, credibility, and skilled story development is missing. Gus is stereotypically "feisty"; John and Lorraine seem pallid versions of their former selves, and their narratives are almost interchangeable. The boy who once set off bombs in the school bathrooms suddenly gets along with his parents, defends a janitorial worker from the harassment of fellow schoolmates, and sets out boy scoutlike to save a stranger from loneliness. The plot loosely chronicles the wild adventures of John and Lorraine: they gamble in Atlantic City (never mind that they are minors); they provide a priest who performs a marriage ceremony for Gus in an intensive care ward (forget that blood tests or marriage licenses are required); they even manage to bring Gus' dog into the ward. A romance between John and Lorraine, too timid for 16 year olds, is chronicled in clumsily injected sections; and out of nowhere, John professes a lifelong commitment, stretching credibility even further.

Paxton Davis

SOURCE: A review of *The Pigman's Legacy,* in *The New York Times Book Review,* January 25, 1981, p. 27.

John Conlan and Lorraine Jensen are 16, high-school sophomores and inseparable companions. John is adventuresome, street-smart and a fast fellow with a wisecrack. Lorraine is cooler, deep into pop-psych lingo and analysis, and keener about John than either of them knows. And they are the busiest buttinskis since Florence Nightingale went to glory.

A few years back they went out, did their bit to help an old man they called "The Pigman," and came a cropper for their troubles when he died. That adventure, which won Mr. Zindel awards, attention and an avid audience for his prize-winning books and plays, left them feeling guilty—but still on the lookout for others to uplift.

Now it all comes round again when they discover the Pigman's Staten Island house inhabited again—this time by a derelict old man, mysterious and at first hostile, whose appearance on the scene echoes strangely the death of the Pigman. Because they can't help but involve themselves in other people's troubles, once again they're off and running.

It's a mystery of sorts and also a tale of second chances for both John and Lorraine, not to mention the puzzled beneficiary of their ministrations and an elderly cleaning woman whom they bring into their derring-do. But—though the details should not be told here—it's a rousing adventure yarn too. Mr. Zindel is an old hand at plunging from one episode to the next in such whirlwind fashion that a few implausibilities are concealed along the way. Here he deepens his narrative by alternating narrators chapter-by-chapter between John and Lorraine, which gives

us not only John's headlong zest for action and Lorraine's perspective on what's happening but a fine change-of-pace that keeps the tale turning.

Sequels are risky, of course, as they too often merely try to imitate a previously successful formula. But Mr. Zindel is on to something bolder here: Instead of merely tacking it on, he's wrapped his sequel around its precursor, returning to old themes but enlarging and deepening them. The result is a story in which we become involved with recognizable youths who grow and mature. And as they mature, their tale takes on broader implications; it is a surprising, beautiful and even profound story.

Joyce Wyatt

SOURCE: A review of *The Pigman's Legacy,* in *Books for Your Children,* Vol. 16, No. 1, Spring, 1981, p. 19.

The Colonel is a vividly drawn eccentric old man who, unable to resist the friendship so persistently offered by John and Lorraine involves them in hair-raising escapades both humorous and exciting. These end inevitably, in his death, but not before his life has been transformed. The teenagers discover more about themselves and their relationship, extended their understanding of other people, and begin to realise the significance of the "Pigman's Legacy". A profound book, written in language which is rich, authentic and accessible to the reader. One of the few genuine teenage books of quality, a distinguished sequel to *The Pigman.*

THE GIRL WHO WANTED A BOY (1981)

Zena Sutherland

SOURCE: A review of *The Girl Who Wanted a Boy,* in *Bulletin of the Center for Children's Books,* Vol. 35, No. 1, September, 1981, p. 20.

Sibella is fifteen. She can fix anything, and has earned quite a bit doing so. She's good at anything scientific and technical, and she's never had a date. In fact, she's avidly reading *How to Pick Up Boys,* dreaming of the perfect male, jealous of her popular older sister. Yet she's resistant when her Mother nags. "You're getting old enough to have a little action for yourself," Mom says when Sibella complains about the men she brings home, "I'm not going to let a bellyaching physics major of a daughter cramp my style." Sister Maureen takes Sibella to a club where men do a strip act, having decided "Oh my God, my poor sister is fifteen years old and she hasn't gone all the way yet." Starved for love, Sibella tracks down a young man whose picture she's seen in the paper, dogs his footsteps, professes her love even when he makes it clear that she's a nuisance, finally withdraws her savings so that she can buy a van and give her adored Dan his dream: a way to leave town. He rejects her, comes back to accept the van, which then serves as a place for them to make love. This is carefully elided: "As his lips touched hers, she knew why she had been born. The last picture in her mind before she fell so totally into his body was that of a great proud lion, a shouting ringmaster. And then came the prancing white horses as the circus came to town." That's the end, save for Sibella's musings about the strength and beauty of love. There are sexist overtones throughout the book, which has an unconvincing plot, adequate if uneven style, and characters that seem just exaggerated enough to be not quite credible.

Judith N. Mitchell

SOURCE: A review of *The Girl Who Wanted a Boy,* in *Voice of Youth Advocates,* Vol. 4, No. 4, October, 1981, p. 40.

This is the story of how Sibella Cametta, 15 year old clod and scientific whiz, learns that it is better to have loved and lost than not to have loved at all. Zindel's adolescent novels are not everyone's cup of tea, but I love them. This one, too, is a fun house ride where one careens from heartache to hilarity without time to adjust to the author's antic zaniness. Sibella's mother and sister are faintly likeable horrors, the object of her affections is a poor girl's Brando, and Sibella herself has a juggernaut methodology that invests her quest for a boyfriend with genuine black comedy. Perhaps it's this term black comedy, hastily borrowed from stage parlance, that is the key to Zindel's adolescent novels: he is to the teen novel what Albee is to drama. It's a mistake to chide him for fantastic plot shifts, or a gallery of grotesqueries masquerading as normal people. His exaggerations pin point the absurdities of normalcy, and his novels carry the theme of loving and being loved like contraband with a homing device.

That is not to say that there are no flaws in *The Girl who Wanted a Boy;* Sibella's father is a bloodless oracle, and her mother's insightfulness comes a little too late in the story. Readers of Salinger, who remember Zooey's phone call to Franny, where he spills out the meaning of life over several pages of the hortatory subjunctive will find Zindel's concerns familiar. What is new and compelling is the force with which Sibella's pain is delineated—she knows what she wants, and she is utterly without the proper resources to procure it. Her misery and her refusal to be done in by that misery will communicate to kids and haunt adults.

Dorothy Nimmo

SOURCE: A review of *The Girl Who Wanted a Boy,* in *The School Librarian,* Vol. 30, No. 1, March, 1982, p. 62.

Feminists will get worked up about this one, right from the title and the opening scene in which Sibella longs for a yearbook full of the signatures of sensational boys. Then they will be jolted by Sibella's toolbox, her auto-repair manual and her bank balance.

Sibella is determined to get a boy (her mother and her

awful sister are even more determined to get her one) and she goes after the boy who operates the mini race track. When he rejects her, even though she spends her savings on buying him a Surfer van, she thinks she will kill herself; but thinks again because she is only fifteen and can wait for love. Paul Zindel, as always, has an infinitely tender sensitivity to the nuances of adolescent feeling and behaviour but there does seem to be a split in this book between what is true of Sibella and what one is convinced she would know about herself.

A. Thatcher

SOURCE: A review of *The Girl Who Wanted a Boy,* in *The Junior Bookshelf,* Vol. 46, No. 1, February, 1992, p. 40.

By British standards, the fifteen year old American girl, Sibella Carmetta is very mature. She has achieved a substantial bank balance by working efficiently for neighbours. She is able to build and fit bookcases, or install fluorescent lights, and she knows more about car engines than most garage mechanics.

Her father, a brilliant scientist, had encouraged her talents, but he and her fun-loving mother had divorced. Sibella lives with her mother, and a succession of boy friends, and from time to time, with her dim but attractive sister Maureen.

This eighth novel by an author who certainly understands American teenagers is a brilliantly and sensitively written story of Sibella's search for her ideal of love. She rejects offers of help and advice from her mother and sister, and turns instead to a book called "How to Pick Up Boys."

She "falls in love" with a newspaper photograph of a nineteen year old boy called Dan, and hunts him down. He is as unsure and unstable as she is, but Sibella is unable to accept this. She loves him, so he must be something special, and her love and belief in him must be able to work miracles. The story moves inexorably towards the inevitable rejection and heartache. At least, she does learn a great deal about herself and her emotions from this traumatic experience.

I found the book very disturbing and I cannot believe that this kind of probing and analysis can do any good for those emotionally so immature. I found very distasteful the emphasis placed on sex experience for those too young to appreciate it as anything more than an appetite to be satisfied. The casual acceptance as "normal" for parents to write-off their teenage children when they get difficult I found very hard to swallow.

HARRY AND HORTENSE AT HORMONE HIGH (1984)

Stephanie Zvirin

SOURCE: A review of *Harry and Hortense at Hormone*

High, in *Booklist,* Vol. 81, No. 1, September 1, 1984, p. 60.

A black comedy of sorts in which two friends—Harry Hickey and Hortense McCoy—discover a modern-day hero who is convinced he is Icarus of Greek mythology and destined to save the world. When Jason Rohr first approaches Harry and Hortense with the crazy idea of rescuing students at Hormone High (so called by narrator/ protagonist Harry) from their own apathy and abominable behavior (Harry comments at length on this), the pair understandably balk. But heroes real or imagined being few and far between and Jason's tragic background arousing their compassion, Harry and Hortense agree to overlook the young man's obvious insanity in favor of his selfless goals. What happens is thoroughly in keeping with Zindel's penchant for the outrageous. Unfortunately it takes a long time for him to get his plot moving, and padding meant to build humor grows tiresome. But there's a surprising, affecting poignancy about Jason's weird behavior, and the preposterous nature of the story in general is bound to attract teenagers who love Zindel's offbeat characters and feel comfortable with his zany style and humor.

Zena Sutherland

SOURCE: A review of *Harry and Hortense at Hormone High,* in *Bulletin of the Center for Children's Books,* Vol. 38, No. 4, December, 1984, pp. 76-7.

Harry is the narrator who describes the triangular friendship he and Hortense reach with remarkable speed when they meet Jason Rohr. They know Jason is a borderline psychotic (he's convinced he's Icarus and puts up letters on the school bulletin board that are signed, "Icarus, a god.") but they also are aware that Jason is in need of their friendship and that he burns with an idealism that has only altruistic motives. Jason wants to save and improve the world and he proposes to start with Hormone High. As a story of friendship, this is moving; as the story of a disturbed adolescent it has conviction. What weakens the book is the exaggeration (for humorous effect) in describing people, particularly adults, and events, so that the impact of the real and tragic story is lessened.

Sarah Hayes

SOURCE: "Maintaining a Balance," in *The Times Literary Supplement,* No. 4273, February 22, 1985, p. 214.

Paul Zindel's first and most successful novel was modestly titled *The Pigman.* It dealt with two crazy teenagers who came to know and love an odd old man called Mr Pignati who collected pigs. In the book the teenagers hastened his death, though they also enhanced his life, as the old man did theirs. This view of life—in evil there is good, in death there is life, in guilt there is self-knowledge—is part of the Zindel philosophy. All his subsequent novels have, despite increasingly bizarre titles and preoccupations, a degree of balance and decorum. To counterbalance the eccentric behaviour, the wild flights of

language, and the intimate confessional stance, there is always the Zindel honesty and humour.

In the new novel, the counterbalancing elements seem to be missing. The gaps between hope and despair and between sanity and madness have become too great. The Laingian message underlying the novel—that only in madness is there truth and reality—has worn very thin by the end. Harry and Hortense are not at the endocrinological zenith indicated by the title; not in love, but merely attending a school styled for the purposes of fiction "Hormone High". The lives of the teenagers are changed for ever by the arrival at the school of Jason, a schizophrenic boy obsessed with the heroic ideals of the Greeks, and with the image of Icarus. As the novel progresses, Harry and Hortense's interest in Jason turns from curiosity into a mixture of horror and compassion. Though warned off by the unpleasant Dean of the school, they go along with Jason's crazy ideas without admitting to themselves that he is ill. They discover that Jason's mother was murdered by his father when he was six, and that he has been in and out of psychiatric hospitals ever since.

Loyalty blinds the friends to the truth until they find that Jason is living rough on a building site, perched like a great bird on a nest of hay in a watchman's hut. A letter from Hortense explaining that she and Harry can no longer accept Jason's fantasies and that he must seek help, tips Jason over the edge. After blowing up the school record office he flies off on a home-made powered hang-glider. The whole school watches as the great white wings are blown off course and Jason/Icarus crashes to his death. For Harry and Hortense it is a hero's death which leaves them with the hope of a bright future.

Harry's optimism seems inappropriate in the context. Nearly all Zindel's novels have a background of death and anarchy. Here they predominate. The teenagers' changing reactions to the schizophrenic boy are handled with subtlety. Jason is a sad and sensitive portrait and despite elements of self-parody, the novel is as compelling as those which have preceded it: the characteristic energy, the punch-you-in-the-eye style and the ability to recreate the tragi-comic chaos of the teenage mind are here in force. The Zindel formula—boy and girl meet crazy person with tragic consequences—has gone as far as it can go, however. This is a dark novel with a weight of cruelty, intolerance and despair, and the hope remains that Paul Zindel will turn towards the light with his next book.

Mike Angelotti

SOURCE: A review of *Harry and Hortense at Hormone High,* in *The ALAN Review,* Vol. 13, No. 3, Spring, 1986, p. 45.

The lives of Harry Hickey and Hortense McCoy change dramatically after they meet Jason Rohr, an intriguing new student who looks like a Greek god and who confides in them his belief that he is the reincarnation of the demigod Icarus returned to earth "to lead everyone out of the dark labyrinth." Ultimately, Harry (the writer) and Hortense (the psychiatrist) discover that although Jason's cloak of godliness attracts, it is his unique human quality that intrigues them and touches their lives. The story is told as Harry's account of the final weeks of Jason's quest. Through Jason, Zindel addresses the question "Where have all the heroes gone?" and leads us to discover that the answer has become so elusive because we may be asking, after all, the wrong question. The more appropriate one may be "Where has the hero in each of us gone?" That is Jason's mission—to reveal to a groping society the way to find again the hero within. Don't be deceived by the lightweight title. *Harry and Hortense* is rich in content and theme. It provides opportunities for exploring folktale, myth and the heroic quest in a contemporary setting, as well as schizophrenia and reincarnation. It entertains, it teaches and it very well may be Paul Zindel's best novel for young adults.

THE AMAZING AND DEATH-DEFYING DIARY OF EUGENE DINGMAN (1987)

Sherry Blakely

SOURCE: A review of *The Amazing and Death-Defying Diary of Eugene Dingman*, in *Voice of Youth Advocates*, Vol. 10, No. 4, October, 1987, p. 210.

Zindel has presented us with another clever title to an equally clever story. Eugene is "sent away" on his 15th birthday to be a waiter at a very ritzy resort hotel in the Adirondack Mountains, at which time he begins a diary of his daily trials and tribulations. Eugene is somewhat of a nerd, but very smart, with eclectic tastes in literature which run from the classics to supermarket tabloids. His social skills are a bit lacking, probably stemming from the fact that he is from what we call today a "dysfunctional family." In other words, his divorced parents are a little bit nuts.

Basically a good and entertaining coming-of-age tale, my one criticism of the book is of the stereotypical characters which people Eugene's existence. There is beautiful, but loose Della with whom he is in love and puts all his hope for happiness. There is Bunker, the despicable bully who tries to make life for Eugene as miserable as possible on a daily basis. But most of all there is Mahatma (believe it or not) an enigmatic, high-voiced Indian mystic who shows Eugene what really matters in life. Zindel himself was a waiter at a similar large summer hotel when he was a young man which lends authentic atmosphere to the backdrop for the story.

Stephanie Zvirin

SOURCE: A review of *The Amazing and Death-Defying Diary of Eugene Dingman*, in *Booklist*, Vol. 84, No. 4, October 15, 1987, p. 385.

Humor leavens but doesn't mask the desperation and sadness in Zindel's newest novel, which . . . concerns an unhappy teenager who focuses his life on a pretty, unat-

tainable girl. A bookish, serious outsider, unable to adjust to his parents' divorce, 15-year-old Eugene Dingman finds himself abandoned once more, this time by his flaky mother who shuttles him off to a job in a resort hotel, where he once again becomes odd man out. Easily pegged as a victim by Bunker, a disgusting bully on the hotel kitchen staff, and by the unpleasant assortment of customers for whom he waits tables, Eugene's only pleasures come from reading his hometown paper and observing pretty Della, serving meals across the room. Unfortunately Bunker dates Della—and so, Eugene eventually learns, does everyone else but he. Why? he wonders. It takes his discovery that Della is using him to fool her mother to make him finally rise up in his own defense, and he records his anguish and debasement, as well as his eventual besting of Bunker, in classic confessional form. Zindel demonstrates ample evidence of his continuing bent for the zany in the character of old Mahatma, Eugene's only friend, who pontificates about the mysteries of life. The author's equally clever tailoring of newspaper headlines to the plot adds a further bizarre quality to Eugene's already negative view of the world and of himself.

The Junior Bookshelf

SOURCE: A review of *The Amazing and Death-Defying Diary of Eugene Dingman*, in *The Junior Bookshelf*, Vol. 52, No. 2, April 1, 1988, p. 111.

Eugene Dingman is a sad, introspective adolescent who relies on his diary, in much the same way as Adrian Mole, to help him through his troubled and lonely times. Zindel is a master of fly-on-the-wall writing. He appears to be able to write as if he were a teenager again himself and that is his great strength and appeal for his readers.

Eugene comes from a separated home. His mother is as insecure as he is and his father whom we never meet though hear about, seems a pathetic cowardly figure. Eugene, on the other hand, although naive and immature, stands up to a great deal of bullying and ribaldry at the hotel in which he works as a waiter during the summer vacation. He shows his sensitivity with a girl who strings him along terribly. He is upset, of course, but not cruel or bitter, merely hurt.

The novel does lack the tickling humour of "Adrian Mole" and that is its main weakness. It is a very American novel and will not have as instant an appeal to British readers as some of this author's other work. It was an easy read in some ways, though Eugene's imaginings and pseudonyms for the hotel guests began to pall a little after a while.

Altogether a somewhat disappointing novel.

A BEGONIA FOR MISS APPLEBAUM (1989)

Gerry Larson

SOURCE: A review of *A Begonia for Miss Applebaum*,

in *School Library Journal,* Vol. 35, No. 8, April, 1989, p. 122.

Zindel skillfully weaves humor and suspense into his message that caring often means taking risks. In a dual-narrator format, high-school friends Henry and Zelda become Saturday companions to their beloved retired science teacher, Miss Applebaum. Despite her losing battle with cancer, Miss Applebaum exudes a contagious zest for learning, life, fun, and helping the homeless in New York City's Central Park. After encounters with Miss Applebaum's eccentric doctor and hostile niece, Henry and Zelda assume the role of protectors, attempting to get her better treatment and eventually carrying out her last request to be buried in Central Park. (This scene may be totally unbelievable to many readers.) By example, Miss Applebaum teaches Henry and Zelda that beauty and mystery are everywhere and that everyone has a responsibility to treasure and preserve the world around them. Henry and Zelda are a balanced pair of likable, forthright characters: Henry is impulsive and direct, while Zelda is cautious and emotional. The two are believably absorbed by their close encounter with dying and death. A thought-provoking, well-paced, fresh addition to the Zindel collection.

Linda Halpern

SOURCE: A review of *A Begonia for Miss Applebaum,* in *Voice of Youth Advocates,* Vol. 12, No. 2, June, 1989, p. 109.

Zindel's latest offering is another smashing success. Many of its elements impart a sense of deja vu in their similarity to his previous titles. But no matter; YAs who pick up the book will devour it from beginning to end. The themes are those of death, and the quality of life for the terminally ill. Lest you be put off by such heavy-duty themes, be assured that the vivacity and good humor of the characters make this a delight to read.

The narrators are Henry and Zelda, 15 year old New York City classmates. They "write" the story on the school's Apple during computer class, in alternating voices. Henry and Zelda bring a begonia to the apartment of their favorite science teacher, Miss Applebaum, who has retired due to ill health. Their affection and reverence for her is based on her ability to excite students about science with her sometimes bizarre, always enlightening methods. Now the trio forms a new, close relationship during Miss Applebaum's last months of life. Taking them to Central Park, to Museums, and around the City, she teaches them to view the world in a new, vibrant way. She teaches them to care for people in need. Dying of cancer, she teaches Henry and Zelda important lessons about living life to the fullest, and about dying with dignity.

The novel isn't perfect. Henry and Zelda are each fresh and charming in unique ways, but a little *too* precocious. Their mode of alternating voices by interrupting each other makes it unclear, frequently, who is speaking.

Still, the characters and the zany episodes are irresistible.

Zindel speaks to YAs sincerely in their own language. He illuminates matters that many teens may find puzzling or troubling, but can't articulate. He accomplishes this with a light touch. A good story.

M. Hobbs

SOURCE: A review of *A Begonia for Miss Applebaum,* in *The Junior Bookshelf,* Vol. 53, No. 4, August, 1989, p. 198.

Paul Zindel has lost none of his persuasiveness and vigour in *A Begonia for Miss Applebaum.* (He allows himself a private joke or two in the surnames!) This is a serious and disturbing theme, however, for Miss Applebaum, Zelda and Henry's favourite teacher, whom they used to stay behind and help in the biology lab, has terminal cancer, with which they have to come to terms. She is a rare and surprising woman, who wants to live life to the full for her last three months. She involves the children in this—they learn to take time to look fully at things, the strange scientific articles and plants around her home, the wonders of Central Park, where they help feed the homeless and once more enjoy childish pastimes. They come into conflict with Miss Applebaum's niece, though they learn the hard way they have misjudged her concern for her aunt, and not only for her money. We are made, too, to see they may not have been right to interfere by asking for a second opinion, since in the end, nothing can be done and the treatment is painful and unpleasant. There is an element of (perhaps excusable) selfishness in Miss Applebaum's involving the children in her dismissing herself from hospital to die at home, and in the final and questionable deception of her burial, which Paul Zindel not surprisingly skates over rather gingerly. The story raises quite a number of uncomfortable questions, which is no bad thing in the hands of such an accomplished writer.

Linda Newbery

SOURCE: A review of *A Begonia for Miss Applebaum,* in *Books for Keeps,* No. 72, January, 1993, p. 10.

Alternate chapters by teenagers Henry and Zelda tell the story of the last few months in the life of an eccentric science teacher. The gift of a begonia leads to a closer acquaintance, as a result of which the two friends decide that Miss Applebaum should be treated in hospital—a decision they later regret. The lasting impression of Miss Applebaum is of her energy, enthusiasm and enormous general knowledge, but Paul Zindel's larger-than-life characterisation eclipses his two narrators and distances the reader from the events he portrays.

THE PIGMAN AND ME (1991)

Geoff Brown

SOURCE: A review of *The Pigman and Me,* in *Books for Keeps,* No. 71, November, 1991, p. 21.

Many people would include Paul Zindel's *The Pigman* on their list of significant teenage novels. Now, more than twenty years after it was published, Zindel has written an 'autobiography' of the time in his teens when he met his own Pigman, Nonno Frankie, who made him laugh, cry and think and taught him 'the greatest secret of life'.

It's a story with which teenagers will identify as Zindel recollects moments of embarrassment, guilt, and fear (the terrors of a new school and encountering the local hoodlums). But perhaps most memorable is the sheer zaniness of Zindel's home life shared with the wonderful Vivona family and twenty odd Lassie lookalikes, bought to restore the family fortune!

Biographies for teenagers tend to be worthy but uninspiring. *The Pigman and Me* is a powerful, funny and touching read; it will be enjoyed by a wide age range of existing Zindel fans and will make some new ones. A very good addition to the biography shelves.

M. Hobbs

SOURCE: A review of *The Pigman and Me,* in *The Junior Bookshelf,* Vol. 55, No. 6, December, 1991, p. 270.

All the narrative verve and vividness of characterisation that have made Paul Zindel's books so popular are here applied to an autobiographical account of a significant period of his childhood. We feel with him the agonies of embarrassment caused by his moody, deserted, feckless and unscrupulous mother. His mother cons a voluptuous Italian divorcee into buying and sharing a ramshackle house in the downtown area of Travis, an almost entirely Polish town on Staten Island, and Zindel meets the most memorable character of his childhood, his own personal 'pigman' or mentor, Connie Vivona's old Italian father, with execrable jokes one can't help laughing at because he is so happy. The family's vigorous arrival with the hyperactive young twins, and their generous loving warmth, their dream cooking, and Nonno's transformation of a squalid barren 'lot' into an Italian smallholding, change Paul's and his sister's life. Nonno Frankie takes the place of the father Paul needs at times of crisis like school fights and exams, and gives him a philosophy to carry him through; Connie becomes Betty's confidante in place of her inadequate mother. When their mother resents this, and with Connie's imminent remarriage takes her family off once more for an insecure gipsy existence, Paul has acquired inner reserves for this future. The characters are keenly observed, the school bullies, the black families, one with an encephalitic baby which fascinates local children, above all Paul's friend Jennifer, who dreads the inevitable fate of the town's Polish girls: to marry and become drudges to unimaginative husbands. In a moving backward look later, we learn that despite meeting Nonno and dreaming of escape, Jennifer became entrapped by the town. The endpapers are covered with old photographs which make the reader feel part of the family's life.

Susan R. Farber

SOURCE: A review of *The Pigman and Me,* in *School Library Journal,* Vol. 38, No. 9, September, 1992, p. 288.

Thousands of YAs have read and loved Zindel's *The Pigman*. In this tragicomic memoir, he describes one of his own teen years spent with his mother and sister on Staten Island. He is in rare form here. While he's not the first to turn teenage angst into humor, he is certainly among the best. His neurotic, wheeler-dealer mother talks her way into purchasing a house with Connie, another single mother, who has a set of out-of-control, identical twins. Travis is a very insular town, consisting largely of Polish families, and Zindel's one friend, Jennifer Wolupopski, warns him of the less-than-cordial reception he's bound to receive in September. His fears are somewhat soothed when he meets Connie's father, who is destined to become his pigman. He is the first male adult who listens to the boy, laughs with him, and really loves him. Always telling silly jokes and working in Connie's garden, he is never too busy to talk to and advise Zindel on the important things in life, such as how to get fried killies and how to win his first fistfight. The old man changes his life, making it more bearable when his spirit could have been crushed by his family situation. *The Pigman & Me* allows readers a glimpse of Zindel's youth, gives them insight into some of his fictional characters, and provides many examples of universal experiences that will make them laugh and cry.

Betsy Hearne

SOURCE: A review of *The Pigman and Me,* in *Bulletin of the Center for Children's Books,* Vol. 46, No. 4, December, 1992, p. 129.

Those who consider *The Pigman* a touchstone of young adult literature but who find some of Zindel's later works glib may approach this memoir with trepidation. Don't worry; it's the freshest writing he's done for a long time. In fact, the Pigman here—and the relationship between him and the author as adolescent—is developed with a depth not always accorded their fictional counterparts. Zindel's mother is a neurotic peripatetic wanderer who moves with her two children into a cockroach-infested house with a divorcee named Connie Vivona, Connie's young twins, and, on weekends, Connie's visiting old-country parents, who cook fabulous Italian dishes for the whole household. Nonno Frankie is the prototype of the Pigman, and this account of Paul and Nonno Frankie's relationship, which includes a neighborhood girl like Lorraine in *The Pigman,* has a less dramatic ending than betrayal but a more authentically sad one—the common tragedy of separation. Zindel fans will find motifs from many of Zindel's stories, along with his characteristically bizarre perspective, but here we see that they come from a specific personal situation rather than a generic teenage condition. From food to feelings, this is a vividly detailed account that will tap into its audience with accessible humor via Nonno Frankie, a font of wisdom and recipes:

"In every fat book, there's a little thin book trying to get out!" he counsels Paul, who is struggling with school work, and later, "a closed mouth gathers no feet!" That kind of advice could sustain a kid through anything, and the kid here had reason to need it.

ATTACK OF THE KILLER FISHSTICKS (1993)

Molly Godley

SOURCE: A review of *Attack of the Killer Fishsticks*, in *School Library Journal*, Vol. 39, No. 10, October, 1993, pp. 136-37.

A funny, realistic story about the adventures of five fifth-grade friends. Dave, Liz, Johnny, and Jennifer, who call themselves the WACKY FACTS LUNCH BUNCH because they eat lunch together and share trivia and jokes, nominate their new friend Max to be Student Council Rep. The plot develops quickly as the group gets behind "the new kid" and supports him in the race against the other candidates, particularly Nat, who is a Nasty Blob bully. Max has also been dealing with the recent death of his mother, so the understanding and support of his peers is essential. The age-appropriate vocabulary and style make this book an excellent choice for most collections.

Janice Del Negro

SOURCE: A review of *Attack of the Killer Fishsticks*, in *Booklist*, Vol. 90, No. 3, October 1, 1993, p. 347.

The opening title of **"The Wacky Facts Lunch Bunch"** series introduces four fifth-grade classmates: Dave, Johnny, Jennifer, and Liz. When the four friends team up to help the new kid Max, they take on the Nasty Blobs, two bullies with more problems than brains. Max is recovering from his mother's death when the Lunch Bunch talk him into running for fifth-grade class representative. After a short campaign and an aborted attempted by the Nasty Blobs to discredit him, Max wins the day (surprise!), and all ends happily. The plot is based on stock character quirks instead of character development; however, this is an undemanding, easy chapter book with a cover that sells itself.

Publishers Weekly

SOURCE: A review of *Attack of the Killer Fishsticks*, in *Publishers Weekly*, Vol. 240, No. 43, October 25, 1993, p. 64.

The Wacky Facts Lunch Bunch series kicks off with a rather bland offering. Four friends—two girls, two boys—solemnly pledge to make their year in fifth grade "cram full of laughs, good times, and mind-boggling adventures." To this end they gather in the cafeteria, keep a file of facts that are "shocking, amazing or gross," and trade jokes.

When they see that Max, a new kid, has been targeted by the class bullies ("the Nasty Blobs"), they decide to protect him, then ask him to join their group. Soon they nominate Max to run for class representative against one of the Nasty Blobs, in the process helping Max to heal his grief at his mother's recent death. The serious subplot about mourning feels tacked on, a vain effort to give this story some purpose. But, like most of the Lunch Bunch's storehouse of trivia, the characters and their concerns lack vitality. Zindel . . . can do better.

DAVID AND DELLA (1993)

Alice Casey Smith

SOURCE: A review of *David and Della*, in *School Library Journal*, Vol. 39, No. 12, December, 1993, pp. 138, 140.

This novel develops like a stand-up comedy routine and reads like the headlines in the *National Enquirer*. David Mahooley, 16, is home alone is his New York City apartment, suffering from depression and writer's block after his girlfriend's suicide attempt. His parents, unsympathetic toward her and unconcerned about their son's mental state, take off for Budapest. David finds Della through a bulletin-board ad; she is an acting/directing/writing coach who vows that, for a fee, she can cure his block. A flaky, alcoholic actress, also 16, she captures his imagination. He pursues her in frenetic chases through the city, loves her (habitual lies and all), and regains his creative energy. Della's friend Ed, a cross-dressing teen with his own TV show, is solicited to produce David's play, which will star Della. The plot is advanced with strings of one-liners, silly quotes, and lists of products and place names, bombarding readers with trivia. While YAs will appreciate the slapstick humor and the alienation of the misfit characters, the story will lead them to no great insights. Zindel, who quotes William Hazlitt ("One truth discovered is better than all the fluency and flippancy in the world") should take that advice.

Ruth E. Dishnow

SOURCE: A review of *David and Della*, in *Voice of Youth Advocates*, Vol. 16, No. 6, February, 1994, pp. 375-76.

David, the main character, contacts Della, a teenage actress who is selling her services as an acting coach. He wants her to help him break the writer's block he developed when his girlfriend tried to commit suicide. He wants to write a play. Della explodes into his life like a cartoon Tasmanian Devil and sucks him into a chaotic whirlwind.

The reader is treated to strange encounters between these two teenage New Yorkers, David and Della, beginning with her arrival at his apartment for their first lesson. She pretends to be blind and robs the liquor cabinet. Their next meeting is at the zoo. Della arrives in a floor length black sequined gown, having come directly from the funeral of her psychiatrist. She proceeds to rub his feet and massage mousse into his hair, under the watchful eyes of Japanese snow monkeys. She then leaves David standing in the street with a half frozen turkey in his arms, madly in love with her.

The whirlwind doesn't slow down long enough for the relationship between David and Della to become as close as David would like. Not just physically close, though the references to "making out" like animals are quite interesting. Della tells David that her prior boyfriend "Al was Love jumping at my throat like a jaguar." Al also had gravity boots and he and Della "hung upside down in a closet and made out like African fox bats." David cannot match or beat Al's animated techniques. Into this whirlwind relationship, Zindel throws a myriad of adolescent issues and concerns. Della had a baby. Della is an alcoholic. Della was admitted to a psychiatric ward. David is depressed because his girlfriend tried to kill herself by jumping out of the third story window at school. David is an adolescent latch key kid who resents getting his journalist parents' faxed messages from around the world. Della's friends Ed and Gabriella cross dress as a social-political experiment. But, none are covered in depth. The pain and anger Della suffers after giving up her baby for Al, whom she realizes, too late, that she does not love, deserves more coverage. The reader flies through, or by, so many issues and concerns that there is no time to internalize or put them into a framework of importance in the story.

If Zindel is trying to make the point that adolescence can be a period in time when one blindly hangs onto the side of life's roller coaster, screaming all the way through the ride, he does that exceedingly well with the pace of *David and Della*. Lambasted by weird encounters, offbeat neighbors, strange friends, and social issues thrown in helter-skelter a reader may, however, come off of Zindel's roller coaster read feeling like he/she just ate too much cotton candy. Though bits of this story are as intensely sweet as the spun sugar that melts in your mouth, as a whole, it is not satisfying.

Elizabeth S. Watson

SOURCE: A review of *David and Della*, in *The Horn Book Magazine*, Vol. LXX, No. 2, March-April, 1994, p. 209.

Funky, at times outrageous, this character study of two creative Manhattan teens who just might be in love if Della can stay out of detox and David gets over his writer's block reads like greased lightning. Sixteen-year-old David is a fledgling playwright who has a pretty good life, but would really like a good friend; enter Della, an eccentric teen with definite ideas. With David's parents in Europe, the coast is clear for him to devote time and resources to his new relationship without pesky adult intervention. David's first-person narrative is interspersed with dialogue; each chapter ends with quotations that are sometimes obviously applicable and sometimes inscrutable. Neither David nor the reader can be certain about the truth in anything Della says or does, but somehow a

relationship does progress that is believable and, at the book's end, still promising.

LOCH (1994)

Deborah Stevenson

SOURCE: A review of *Loch,* in *Bulletin of the Center for Children's Books,* Vol. 48, No. 3, November, 1994, p. 110.

Young Luke Perkins is nicknamed "Loch" after he sees the famed monster in Scotland; ten years later, fifteen-year-old Loch is saddened by the recent death of his mother and the subsequent decline of his scientist father. Dr. Sam seems to be completely cowed by his employer, Mr. Cavenger, a tabloid publisher who sends Loch's father on quests for proof about mythological beings such as Sasquatch and Nessie, and who has decided to investigate a small Vermont lake for eerie underwater inhabitants. It turns out to have them in droves—primeval yet evolved marine creatures (the book labels them plesiosaurs) who fight back savagely and gorily against the heartless humans who seek to destroy and exploit them. Loch and his sister, Zaidee, discover a softer side to the creatures, however, when they befriend a stranded young one whom they call "Wee Beastie"; with the help of Cavenger's daughter, Sarah, they protect Wee Beastie from the money-grubbing publisher and his henchmen until the not-so-wee beasties slay their foes and make it back to their original, bigger habitat. This is sort of a cross between *ET* and *Jaws*—the kids desperately attempt to protect the misunderstood against the arrogant, but the bad guys bite the dust with great drama ("Erdon's last conscious thought was the realization that he was being chewed in half"), leaving grisly bits of people floating about the lake. The characters are pretty stock, the sentimental undertones rather unsubtle ("We're a family again, aren't we?" asks Zaidee as she gazes up at her re-empowered father after the great boss-killing denouement), and nobody seems much worried about what will happen to the residents of the bigger lake to which the creatures flee. Still, it's a good, rip-roaring, kids-know-best adventure that would make a terrific beach paperback and has "reluctant reader" written all over it.

Connie Tyrrell Burns

SOURCE: A review of *Loch,* in *School Library Journal,* Vol. 41, No. 1, January, 1995, p. 138.

Zindel draws on his scientific background in this story of Luke Perkins, 15, nicknamed "Loch" after claiming to see a lake monster as a little boy. He and his younger sister, Zaidee, join their oceanographer father on an expedition searching for enormous prehistoric creatures sighted in Lake Alban in Vermont. Their leader, Cavenger, is a ruthless despot who would just as soon annihilate as preserve the Plesiosaurs, water beasts thought to be extinct for over 10 million years. The siblings and Cavenger's daughter befriend Wee Beastie and help it and its family escape to safety; Dr. Perkins, who has been diminished in his own and his children's eyes by selling out his ideals in his need for money, redeems himself. The book is really about what makes a family, whether human or creature, as Loch and Zaidee adjust to their mother's death and help their father regain his self-respect. The gruesome attacks by Pleisosaurs on some humans are gory and grisly enough to satisfy even the blood-thirstiest of middle schoolers. Zindel's style capably blends descriptive, figurative language with YA dialogue.

Anne C. Sparanese

SOURCE: A review of *Loch,* in *Voice of Youth Advocates,* Vol. 18, No. 1, April, 1995, p. 30.

Fifteen-year-old Loch got his nickname from an incident that happened when he was five. Sitting alone one dark evening on the shore of Loch Ness, he saw an extraordinary sight: a monster emerged from the shallows and devoured two unfortunate drinking sheep. Now, ten years later, Loch and his sister Zaidee are at a remote lake in Vermont searching for reported lake monsters with their father, who works for a company that seeks reputed beasts and publishes sensationalist magazines about their "finds." Unfortunately, this delicious beginning is not supported by the rest of the novel.

Loch contains elements which assail the believability of the story, even when the basic premise is accepted. While the early scene of the creature bursting out of the water and killing the photographer is graphic and exciting, the whole family of long-necked monsters is found too easily, even though they have presumably been hiding from humankind successfully for thousands of years. The further development of the plot then depends on an unlikely total secrecy by expedition members, as well as their lack of common sense.

The adult monsters are volatile, aggressive, and dangerous, but Loch and Zaidee easily befriend the babies, who are highly intelligent, lovable, and empathetic. The ruthless expedition owner and their father's boss, Cavenger, clearly wants these beasts trapped and/or killed for photos and trophies rather than conserved for science and study. Loch's father, who remains weak-willed and Cavenger's pawn until the last pages, is of no help. It seems logical that if an ecologically aware teenager like Loch, who despises Cavenger, really wanted to save the animals, he would have tried to make contact with outsiders, the EPA—someone! But instead, he enlists the help of Sarah, Cavenger's teenage daughter and Loch's romantic interest, to help save the beasts. The ending is predictable with the meanest monster and the meanest human meeting nasty ends.

Perhaps for the younger, more gullible reader, this story can work as an adventure. But for avid suspense aficionados, it will be disappointing in both plot and character development.

THE DOOM STONE (1995)

Steven Engelfried

SOURCE: A review of *The Doom Stone,* in *School Library Journal,* Vol. 41, No. 12, December, 1995, p. 132.

While driving past Stonehenge on his way to visit his anthropologist aunt, Jackson, 15, sees a creature mauling a young man. It turns out that Aunt Sarah is leading a team of scientists and military personnel who are investigating a series of mutilations in the area. Jackson tags along as the monster is sighted and manages several narrow escapes. The creature, actually an intelligent and bloodthirsty hominid living beneath Salisbury Plain, kills several people, and Zindel describes the deaths in gruesome detail. The action and thrills are nonstop, but the hunt for the beast poses moral dilemmas, too. Jackson and his friend Alma discover a similar but harmless new species as well, and Jackson wants to keep them a secret. At times the plot is contrived. It seems unlikely that Jackson would really be asked to take part in the search, or that he and Alma could travel so freely about in a conveniently available dune buggy without being spotted. But the intriguing premise and suspenseful, fast-paced action will surely please readers who like horror stories with a bit more substance than the latest Pike or Stine.

Publishers Weekly

SOURCE: A review of *The Doom Stone,* in *Publishers Weekly,* Vol. 242, No. 49, December 4, 1995, p. 63.

Zindel . . . wastes no time on subtleties or philosophizing in this all-action supernatural/SF thriller. Even before Jackson, a 15-year-old New Yorker, arrives at his anthropologist aunt's lodgings near Stonehenge, he gets a nasty glimpse of the murderous beast that the British Army has engaged his aunt to track down. As Jackson and his aunt, Dr. Cawley, determine, the monster, "Ramid," is an ancient mutant hominid that, in tune with the 19-year cycle of the moon, comes out of its home in abandoned flint mines to feed. When a bite from Ramid gradually puts Dr. Cawley in its thrall, it's up to Jackson and a comely local girl to hunt the monster. Zindel makes plentiful use of local scenery and Stonehenge lore and, for YA thrill-seekers, there's plenty of gore and creepy-crawly slimy stuff. The final showdown on the roof of Salisbury Cathedral is a spine-tingler.

Deborah Stevenson

SOURCE: A review of *The Doom Stone,* in *Bulletin of the Center for Children's Books,* Vol. 49, No. 6, February, 1996, pp. 210-11.

There are, alas, no crop circles in this book, but it includes just about all the other supernatural motifs: cattle mutilations, Stonehenge, telepathy, phases of the moon, and an ancient species whose survival depends on remaining hidden from humankind. Fifteen-year-old Jackson Cawley encounters all these when he visits his anthropologist aunt in England and discovers that a vicious missing-link-type hominid has been killing and eating people. After the creature bites Aunt Sarah, thereby causing her to begin changing into such a creature herself, Jackson hunts through the countryside and history to find a way to destroy the evil menace without destroying himself in the process. This has the same brisk pacing and old-fashioned, satisfyingly kid-driven adventure as *Loch*. Zindel's excesses here, however, are often more histrionic than dramatic, which makes the book seem self-parodic at times (as when the transforming Aunt Sarah begins to howl "BEEF! GIVE ME BEEF!"). There are also several questionable plot points: it's not clear how Jackson knows that the den of hominids he and his friend Alma stumble into are, unlike the man-eater, friendly; the creature's telepathic capabilities aren't well-explained; and Jackson's repeated and successful use of pig Latin as a secret code isn't particularly believable. Still, the creature is scary enough and the action lively enough that horror fans (who will appreciate the snarling skeletal face on the cover) probably won't mind.

Additional coverage of Zindel's life and career is contained in the following sources published by Gale Research: *Authors and Artists for Young Adults,* **Vol. 2;** *Contemporary Authors New Revision Series,* **Vol. 31;** *Contemporary Literary Criticism,* **Vols. 6, 26;** *DISCovering Authors: Modules* **(CD-ROM);** *Drama Criticism,* **Vol. 5;** *Dictionary of Literary Biography,* **Vols. 7, 52;** *Junior DISCovering Authors* **(CD-ROM);** *Major Twentieth-Century Writers; Major Authors and Illustrators for Children and Young Adults;* **and** *Something about the Author,* **Vols. 16, 58.**

CUMULATIVE INDEXES

How to Use This Index

The main reference

Baum, L(yman) Frank
1856-1919 .... **15**

lists all author entries in this and previous volumes of *Children's Literature Review*.

The cross-references

See also CA 103; 108; DLB 22; JRDA;
MAICYA; MTCW; SATA 18; TCLC 7

list all author entries in the following Gale biographical and literary sources:

AAYA = *Authors & Artists for Young Adults*
AITN = *Authors in the News*
BLC = *Black Literature Criticism*
BW = *Black Writers*
CA = *Contemporary Authors*
CAAS = *Contemporary Authors Autobiography Series*
CABS = *Contemporary Authors Bibliographical Series*
CANR = *Contemporary Authors New Revision Series*
CAP = *Contemporary Authors Permanent Series*
CDALB = *Concise Dictionary of American Literary Biography*
CLC = *Contemporary Literary Criticism*
CLR = *Children's Literature Review*
CMLC = *Classical and Medieval Literature Criticism*
DAB = *DISCovering Authors: British*
DAC = *DISCovering Authors: Canadian*
DAM = *DISCovering Authors Modules*
   DRAM: dramatists module
   MST: most-studied authors module
   MULT: multicultural authors module
   NOV: novelists module
   POET: poets module
   POP: popular/genre writers module

DC = *Drama Criticism*
DLB = *Dictionary of Literary Biography*
DLBD = *Dictionary of Literary Biography Documentary Series*
DLBY = *Dictionary of Literary Biography Yearbook*
HW = *Hispanic Writers*
JRDA = *Junior DISCovering Authors*
LC = *Literature Criticism from 1400 to 1800*
MAICYA = *Major Authors and Illustrators for Children and Young Adults*
MTCW = *Major 20th-Century Writers*
NCLC = *Nineteenth-Century Literature Criticism*
PC = *Poetry Criticism*
SAAS = *Something about the Author Autobiography Series*
SATA = *Something about the Author*
SSC = *Short Story Criticism*
TCLC = *Twentieth-Century Literary Criticism*
WLC = *World Literature Criticism, 1500 to the Present*
YABC = *Yesterday's Authors of Books for Children*

CUMULATIVE INDEX TO AUTHORS

CUMULATIVE INDEX TO NATIONALITIES

AMERICAN

Aardema, Verna 17
Adkins, Jan 7
Adler, Irving 27
Adoff, Arnold 7
Alcott, Louisa May 1, 38
Alexander, Lloyd (Chudley) 1, 5
Aliki 9
Anglund, Joan Walsh 1
Armstrong, William H(oward) 1
Arnosky, James Edward 15
Aruego, Jose (Espiritu) 5
Ashabranner, Brent (Kenneth) 28
Asimov, Isaac 12
Atwater, Florence (Hasseltine Carroll) 19
Atwater, Richard (Tupper) 19
Avi 24
Aylesworth, Thomas G(ibbons) 6
Babbitt, Natalie (Zane Moore) 2
Bacon, Martha Sherman 3
Bang, Molly Garrett 8
Baum, L(yman) Frank 15
Baylor, Byrd 3
Bellairs, John (A.) 37
Bemelmans, Ludwig 6
Benary-Isbert, Margot 12
Bendick, Jeanne 5
Berenstain, Jan(ice) 19
Berenstain, Stan(ley) 19
Berger, Melvin H. 32
Bess, Clayton 39
Bethancourt, T. Ernesto 3
Block, Francesca (Lia) 33
Blos, Joan W(insor) 18
Blumberg, Rhoda 21
Blume, Judy (Sussman) 2, 15
Bond, Nancy (Barbara) 11
Bontemps, Arna(ud Wendell) 6
Bova, Ben(jamin William) 3

Brancato, Robin F(idler) 32
Branley, Franklyn M(ansfield) 13
Brett, Jan (Churchill) 27
Bridgers, Sue Ellen 18
Brink, Carol Ryrie 30
Brooks, Bruce 25
Brooks, Gwendolyn 27
Brown, Marcia 12
Brown, Marc (Tolon) 29
Brown, Margaret Wise 10
Bryan, Ashley F. 18
Bunting, Eve 28
Burnett, Frances (Eliza) Hodgson 24
Burton, Virginia Lee 11
Byars, Betsy (Cromer) 1, 16
Caines, Jeannette (Franklin) 24
Calhoun, Mary 42
Cameron, Eleanor (Frances) 1
Carle, Eric 10
Carter, Alden R(ichardson) 22
Cassedy, Sylvia 26
Charlip, Remy 8
Childress, Alice 14
Christopher, Matt(hew F.) 33
Ciardi, John (Anthony) 19
Clark, Ann Nolan 16
Cleary, Beverly (Atlee Bunn) 2, 8
Cleaver, Bill 6
Cleaver, Vera 6
Clifton, (Thelma) Lucille 5
Coatsworth, Elizabeth (Jane) 2
Cobb, Vicki 2
Cohen, Daniel (E.) 3, 43
Cole, Brock 18
Cole, Joanna 5, 40
Collier, James L(incoln) 3
Colum, Padraic 36
Conford, Ellen 10
Conrad, Pam 18

Cooney, Barbara 23
Corbett, Scott 1
Cormier, Robert (Edmund) 12
Cox, Palmer 24
Creech, Sharon 42
Crews, Donald 7
Crutcher, Chris(topher C.) 28
Curry, Jane L(ouise) 31
Danziger, Paula 20
d'Aulaire, Edgar Parin 21
d'Aulaire, Ingri (Mortenson Parin) 21
Day, Alexandra 22
de Angeli, Marguerite (Lofft) 1
DeClements, Barthe 23
DeJong, Meindert 1
Denslow, W(illiam) W(allace) 15
dePaola, Tomie 4, 24
Dillon, Diane 44
Dillon, Leo 44
Disch, Thomas M(ichael) 18
Domanska, Janina 40
Donovan, John 3
Dorros, Arthur (M.) 42
Dr. Seuss 1, 9
Duncan, Lois 29
Duvoisin, Roger Antoine 23
Eager, Edward McMaken 43
Ehlert, Lois (Jane) 28
Emberley, Barbara A(nne) 5
Emberley, Ed(ward Randolph) 5
Engdahl, Sylvia Louise 2
Enright, Elizabeth 4
Epstein, Beryl (M. Williams) 26
Epstein, Samuel 26
Estes, Eleanor 2
Ets, Marie Hall 33
Feelings, Muriel (Grey) 5
Feelings, Tom 5
Ferry, Charles 34

221

Nationality Index

WELSH
Arundel, Honor (Morfydd)   **35**
Dahl, Roald   **1, 7, 41**

CUMULATIVE INDEX TO TITLES

Title Index

Title Index

283

Title Index

ISBN 0-7876-1139-5

90000

9 780787 611392